Mika Rottenberg: The Production of Luck

Gregory R. Miller & Co. in association with the Rose Art Museum

The Production of Luck

Christopher Bedford

In the very first frame of her video *Bowls Balls Souls Holes* (2014), Mika Rottenberg captures the principle terms of a dialectic that structures this characteristically intricate riddle. Though this frame can hardly be said to gloss all that unfolds in the video—nothing could be further from the truth—one could call it an establishing shot which, if revisited as Rottenberg's plot thickens, unravels, and re-tangles, can ground the fantastical 30-minute experience. The blazing glow of a full moon shining through a thin layer of cloud cover marks a relationship to the rhythms of the earth that play throughout the video. The moon is wholly present as image and as energy, yet this celestial icon remains distant and unknowable, its light everywhere but its matter out of reach. The moon casts its glow over a rundown hotel, its neon signage barely illuminated, its facade dull and decrepit, the windows onto the dark interior betraying no signs of human activity. Here the celestial and the terrestrial meet, beginning a play of unlikely connectedness that deepens from minute to minute. At stake in this worldly/otherworldly back and forth, as the title of this short essay suggests, is the production of the phenomenon we refer to as luck, a concept that is as commonly invoked—"how lucky!," "you're so lucky!," "lucky break!"—as it is utterly beyond our rational grasp. Accordingly, since luck as a property is more myth than science, Rottenberg feels free to explore a line of reasoning that is self-consciously outlandish, yet, absent any more convincing data, effectively unchallenged. If not this version, then whose?

Although the narrative structure of her work is invariably intricate, and her conceptual concerns gaseous and elusive, Rottenberg, more than the vast majority of her contemporaries, acknowledges and accounts for the demands placed on the visitor when they are asked to experience a work of video in a museum setting. Unlike movie theatres—those cultural emporiums of the moving image, replete with stadium seating, popcorn, and an ever-growing panoply of comfort amenities—video art in museums asks a great deal of the viewer, while offering comparatively little in return.

Small dark spaces commonly known as black boxes are the containers for this still-young medium. Quite often absent seating, and always absent food and beverage, these uninviting caves ask the viewer to invest in a moving image experience that could already be half over and very likely does not abide by the easy narrative conventions that structure Hollywood film, typically designed to sweep the viewer up and confiscate their attention immediately. In fact, most video art withholds or inverts the conventions that make popular movies so simple to enjoy, crafting instead a different mode of address entirely that makes casual consumption next to impossible. Not only does video art have to contend with the easy seduction of popular film, it also must justify itself relative to all manner of personal electronic devices, most of which offer users access to high quality moving images in an instant and from wherever they might be. Naturally then, these related questions of viewer attention and expectation are absolutely fundamental to the medium condition of video in museums, and to the degree of effect video can hope to have on the viewer. The question artists working with the moving image pose—or should pose—to themselves might be stated as follows: to what extent does the video in question consider the conditions of viewer consumption, and does its content, mode of address, and means of presentation confiscate attention adequately such that the effect it aspires to have on the viewer is a plausible expectation?

Like some of her most ambitious peers, including Paul Pfeiffer, Sharon Lockhart, Matthew Barney, Pipilotti Rist, Christian Marclay, and Ragnar Kjartansson, these questions have always been pertinent to Rottenberg's work, but in *Bowls Balls Ṣouls Holes* she is both more demanding in what she expects of her viewers and more effective in meeting that demand halfway. The sculptural dimension of the installation does a great deal of this work. A diminutive yellow curtain set into a soaring white wall is the entrance into Rottenberg's installation. One passes through this thin curtain into a musty wooden chamber featuring an assortment of objects—some readily identifiable, some not—including a black air mattress, a buzzing, window-mounted air conditioner, a lock of blonde hair attached to a rotating stainless steel gizmo, a filthy ashtray, an array of empty glass jars, a raggedy rug, a wall-mounted sculpture made of tinfoil and gum, and a small, illuminated bubbling contraption of indistinct application.

The room is beguiling and makes very little sense until one proceeds through a concealed revolving door into a screening room with rows of old-fashioned wooden cinema seating where Rottenberg's video plays. Within the first two minutes of the video, viewers encounter in the form of a moving image the very same room they passed through to arrive at the video, those projected images made real by their concurrent status as physical sculpture, and the room activated as more than sculpture by its prior life as a set used to record the video that is playing. Before a viewer even experiences Rottenberg's video, then, this finely tuned preamble makes the eventual encounter with the moving image feel strikingly real and unusual, justifying in a sense the demand for attention made by the video that, by virtue of its presentation, is positioned *a priori* as exceptional.

And all of this is just as well since the video in fact necessitates an excess of attention. Rottenberg's thematic preoccupation in *Bowls Balls Souls Holes* is, as I've said, the production of luck and the task she sets for herself is as simple as it is impossible: to imagine the mechanism by which this phenomenon is produced. Like many of her videos, the experience of *Bowls Balls Souls Holes* is comparable to watching the progress of a production line, and, like her other videos, here the emphasis is not placed on a determined outcome, but rather upon process, and specifically the cause and effect scenarios that drive the action and connect the various characters and places. A synopsis of this action could take a variety of forms, such is the density of Rottenberg's content, but the narrative, if one can refer to it as such, unfolds roughly as follows. After the opening shot of the hotel's facade, we are taken inside one of the rooms, a strikingly shrunken space where we meet a woman who has spent the evening accruing energy (maybe electricity), which she seems to attract and channel through her feet, which are wrapped in tinfoil and held in place by multicolored clothespins. The space she occupies, including its assorted detritus and contraptions, is the same diminutive space the viewer walks through to access the video.

This woman, who in Rottenberg's videographic cosmology represents The Sun, then makes her way to an underground bingo hall by way of an electric blue three-wheeled scooter, which she rides on the sidewalk. Once inside the bingo hall, she marches to the front of the room and assumes her place as the game's announcer, quickly and adroitly manipulating the mechanisms at her fingertips while the players already assembled in the room ready themselves for her first announcement. As the game begins, she calls out numbers into a microphone and the players mark their cards. These players—The Stars in Rottenberg's cosmology—are together a motley bunch, a varied collage of humanity bound by their unifying focus on bingo. As the game proceeds, we are introduced to another figure, a black woman sitting in the bingo hall leaning against a wall and apparently asleep. This figure—The Moon per the narrative construct—remains inert until an accumulation of water from an overhead air conditioner causes water to drip onto her exposed shoulder. Suddenly, The Moon comes to life, her possibly telekinetic influence combining with the power exerted by The Sun to determine which bingo ball drops. So the action proceeds and, after a while, The Sun begins dropping colored clothespins through a trapdoor in the floor that leads, via a series of Technicolor mechanical contraptions, into the hands of a man sitting alone in a very compressed space. This character, The Conductor, solemnly attaches the clothespins to his face. Breaking up this primary narrative periodically, we are shown images of melting glaciers, implying a distant cause and effect relationship between the increasing temperature of the earth, the glaciers' slow melting, and the buildup of condensation on the overburdened air conditioner whose dripping activates The Moon, influencing the production of luck.

This transcontinental production line, connecting environmental conditions across the globe to the phenomenon of luck in a bingo hall, proceeds as such until The Conductor, his face a field of primary colors, begins to rotate on his stool, gaining speed until he evaporates into nothing, the pegs on his face falling onto a pebble beach on a sea of quietly melting glaciers. With luck presumably determined for the day, The Moon settles down to sleep once again and darkness descends over the facade of the hotel, returning the narrative to its point of origin. This is the lifecycle of luck. Where the video ends, it begins again.

The cinematic logic Rottenberg employs in *Bowls Balls Souls Holes* achieves a number of objectives simultaneously. First, her use of a set featured in the video as the sculptural gateway to the viewing space creates a playful back-and-forth between the real and the virtual that compels immediate interest. Second, the cause and effect structure of the 30-minute narrative operates a little like a Rube Goldberg machine, generating a "what comes next?" tension, which more than meets the confiscation of attention quotient for a video of this length. Lastly, this cause and effect structure is used to interweave chain reactions that are deliberate follies with others that are based on real world causal relationships, most obviously in this case, global warming. Whether or not luck is in fact produced as Rottenberg suggests is ultimately immaterial. Rather, the substance of Rottenberg's work lies in her ability to use media in combination to advance a proposal that demands prolonged attention, not because it purports to be true, but because her rhetoric is irresistible.

Installation view detail: The Rose Art Museum, “Mika Rottenberg: Bowls Balls Souls Holes,” 2014

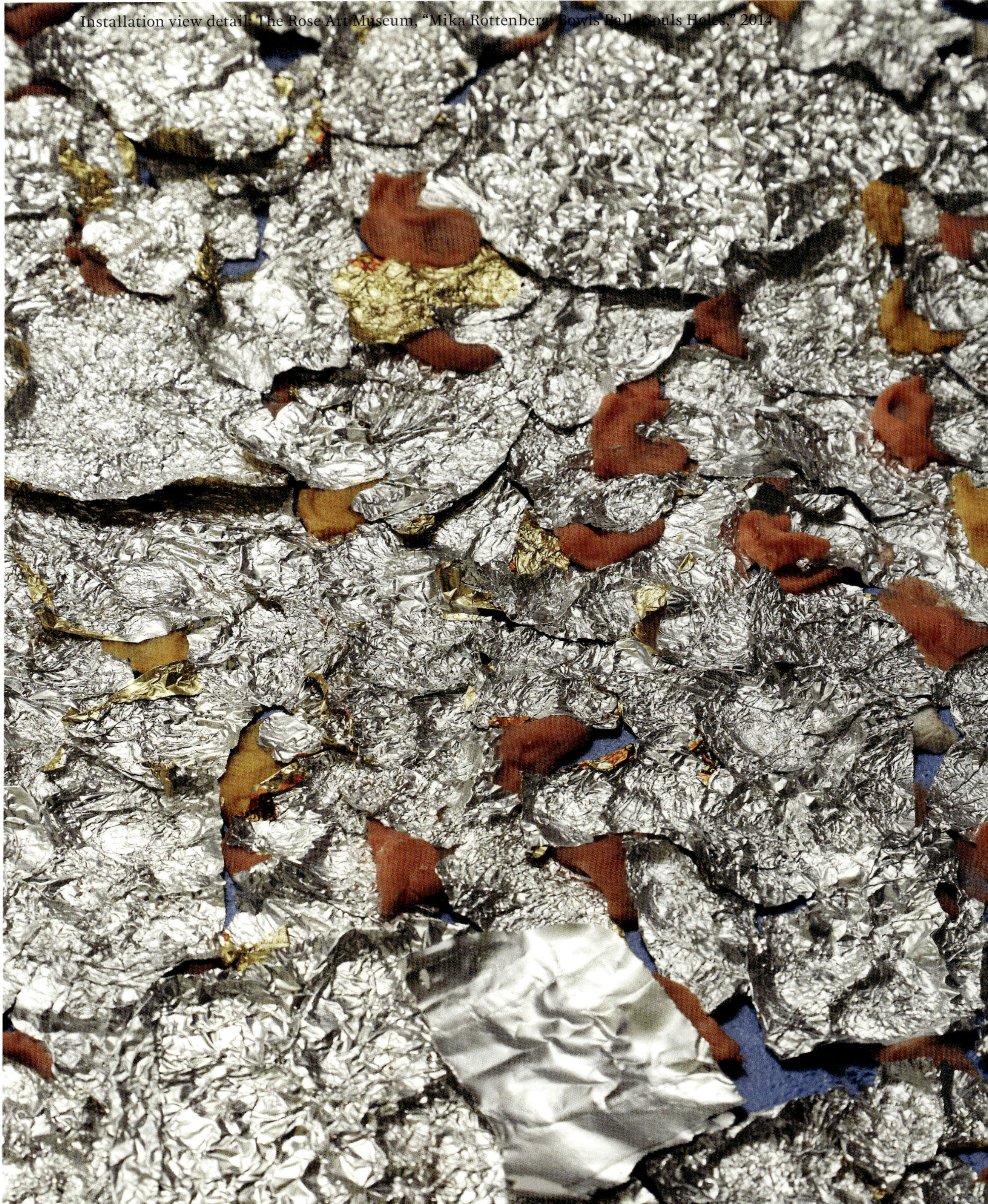

bowls balls souls holes

CRISTOPHER BEDFORD: Your latest major project, *Bowls Balls Souls Holes* (2014), was recently installed at the Rose Art Museum. What are your thematic interests in this ambitious new work?

MIKA ROTTENBERG: This piece spins around relationships between the physical and metaphysical. Rooms become characters, the bingo balls become electrons bouncing, the clothespin guy is the conductor, the sleeping moon lady is a vessel, and the announcer is the gatekeeper. They all affect temperature and move architecture. Internal psychological space extends beyond the body's border, shaping the exterior by using parapsychology.

Cause and effect, as a basic mode of progression, has been a main interest for me from a psychological, sculptural, and social perspective. In this new piece, I address this idea less in a physical direction and more in an abstract direction, extending it to the metaphysical and to processes that are not necessarily visible, like the production of luck or the loaded phenomenon of global warming. You can't really see how these things work—both are cause and effect relationships that are abstract. Weirdly, I find that it's easier to

 Still from *Bowls Balls Souls Holes*, 2014

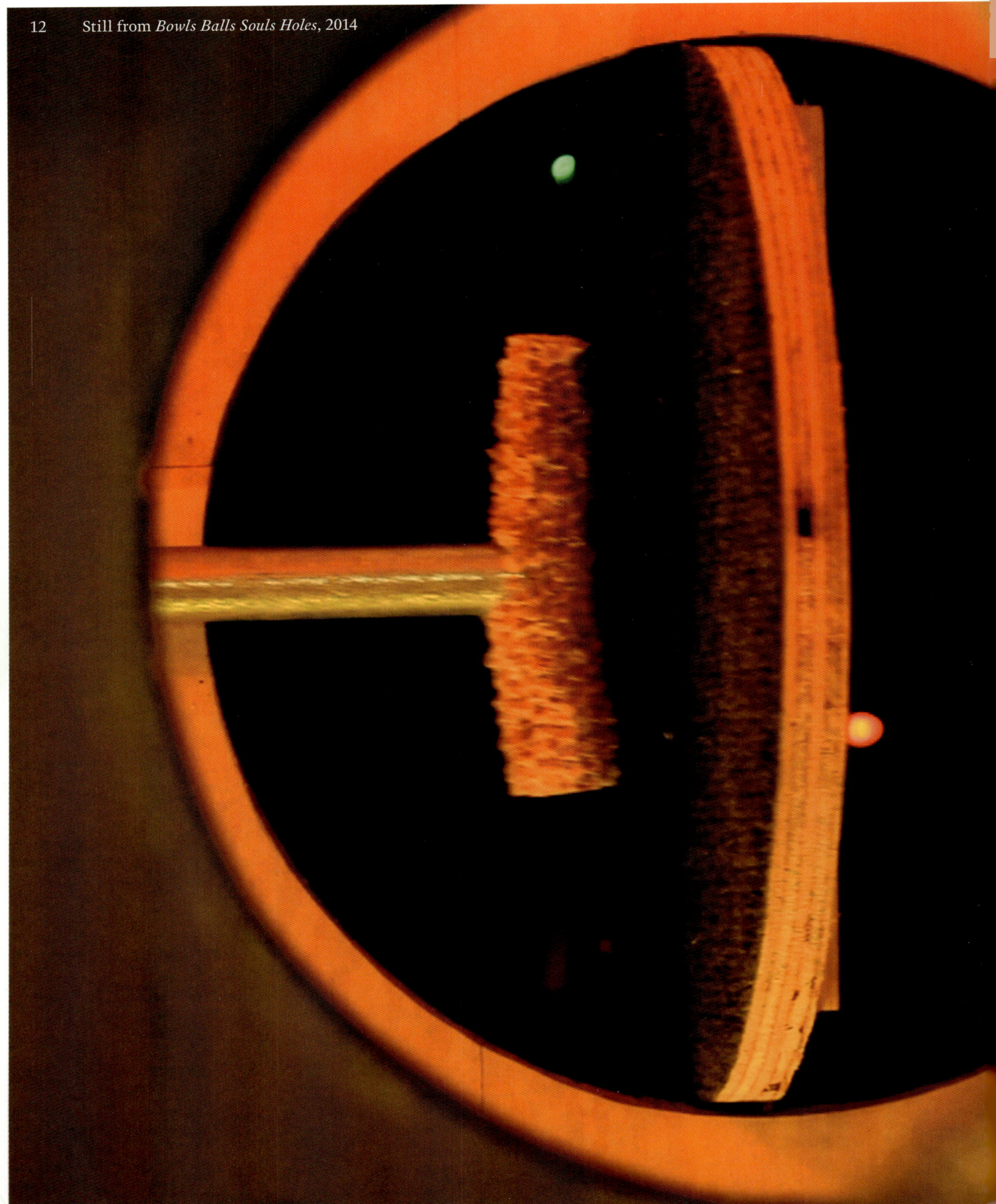

believe in your ability to influence luck than to see how you play your part in climate change. I use cinema as a tool to make viewers believe in an immaterial chain of cause and effect. Cinema allows that type of deception, so the production of luck becomes real and glaciers melting into a bingo hall become real. I also use cinematic structures to manipulate space from a sculptural perspective. When making *Bowls Balls Souls Holes*, I was drawn to a bingo hall in Harlem that seems to me like it is its own little universe. You hardly notice the sign when you walk on 125th Street, but once you enter you discover all these people playing for hours. They seem to function in a different time and according to the rhythm of the random numbers being called: I-20, O-72, B-12, etc. What if these numbers are some kind of code and the people are not playing bingo? What if the numbers actually write a sequence that opens a wormhole into another dimension, where cause and effect rely on laws different from the laws of physics?

14 Installation view: The Rose Art Museum, “Mika Rottenberg: Bowls Balls Souls Holes,” 2014

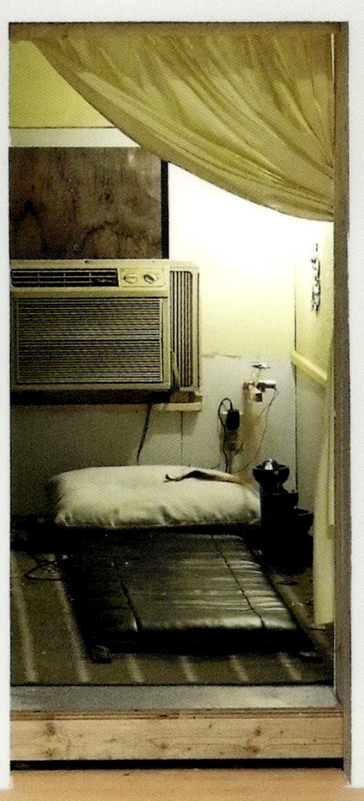

Installation view: The Rose Art Museum, "Mika Rottenberg: Bowls Balls Souls Holes," 2014

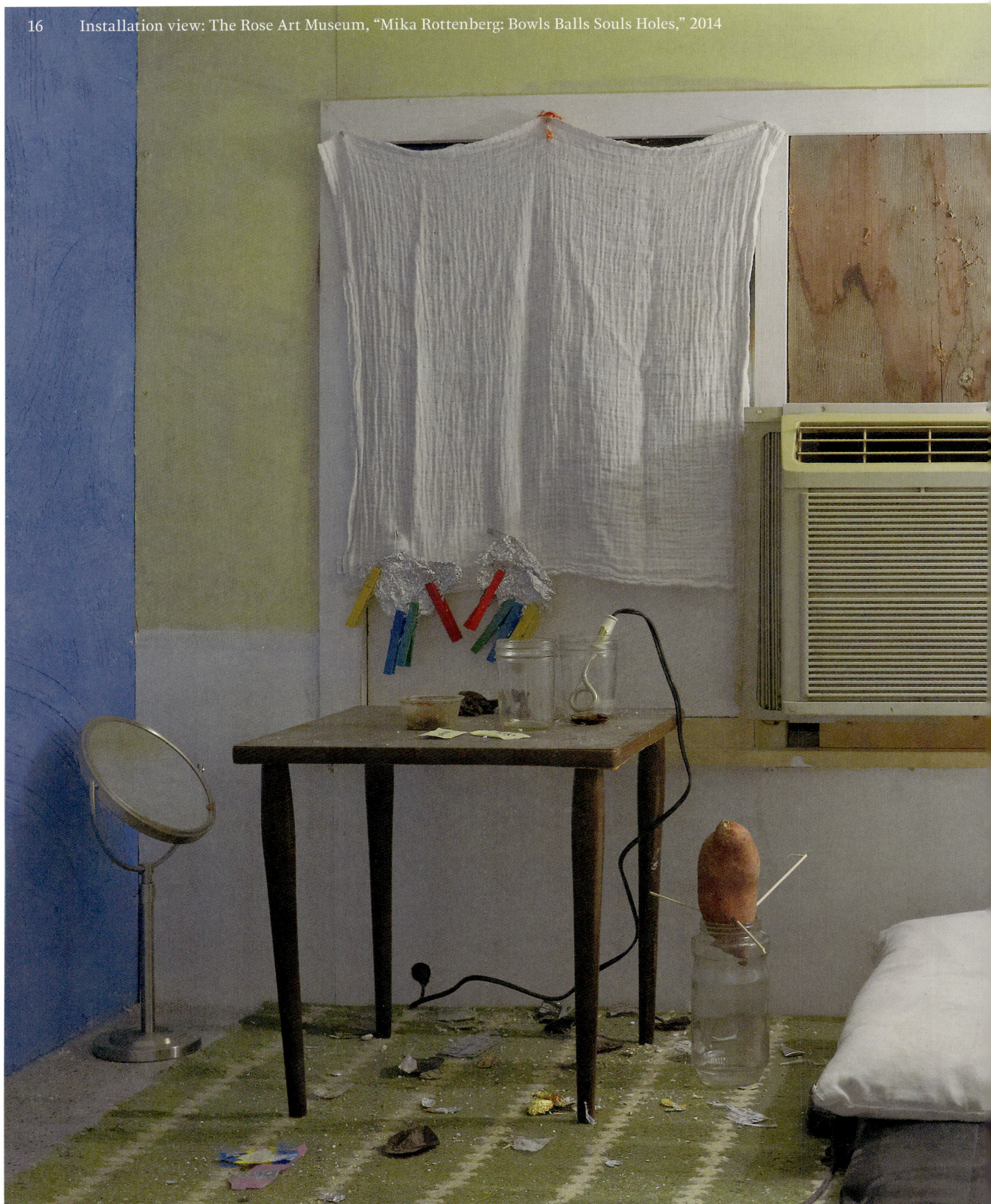

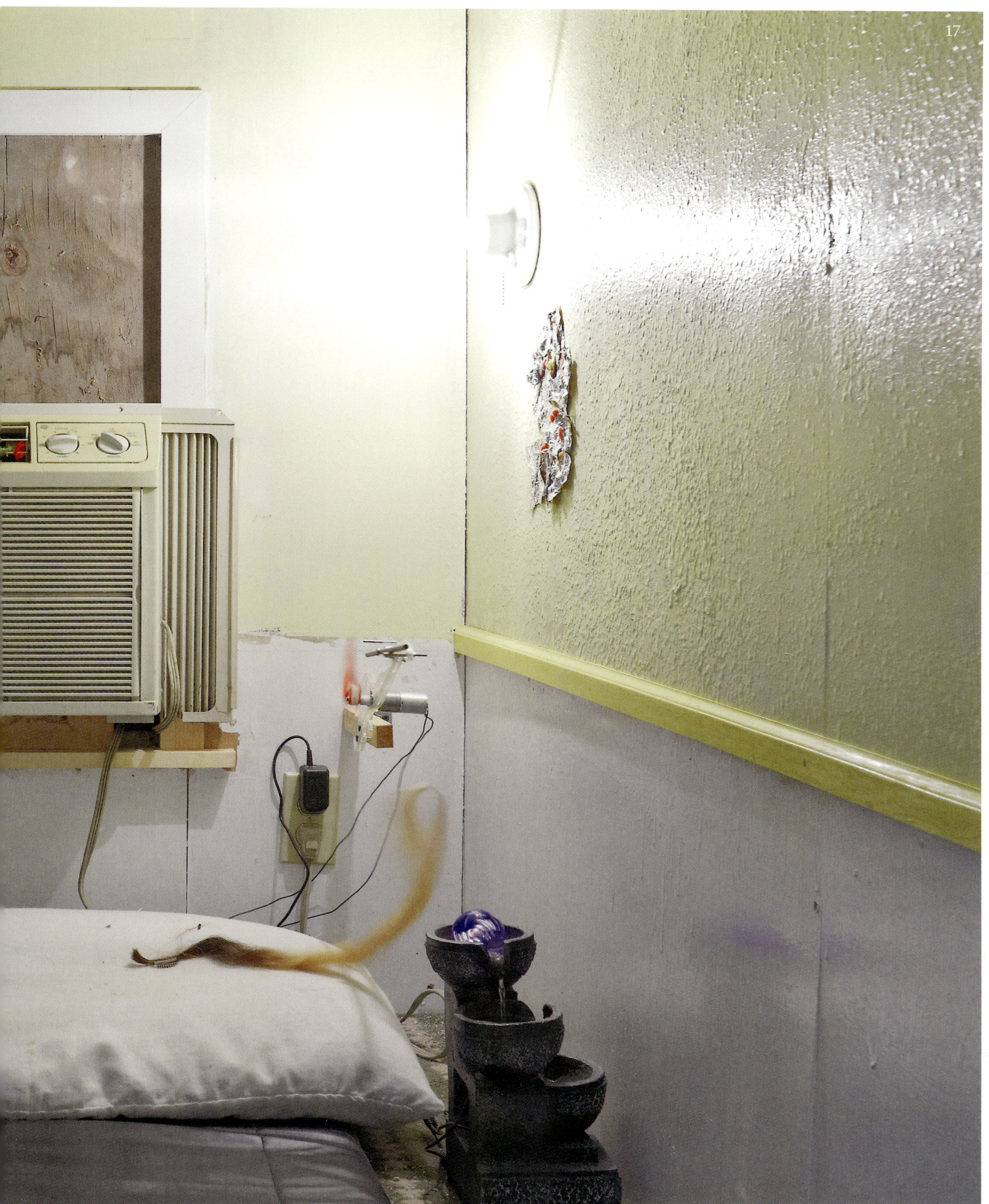

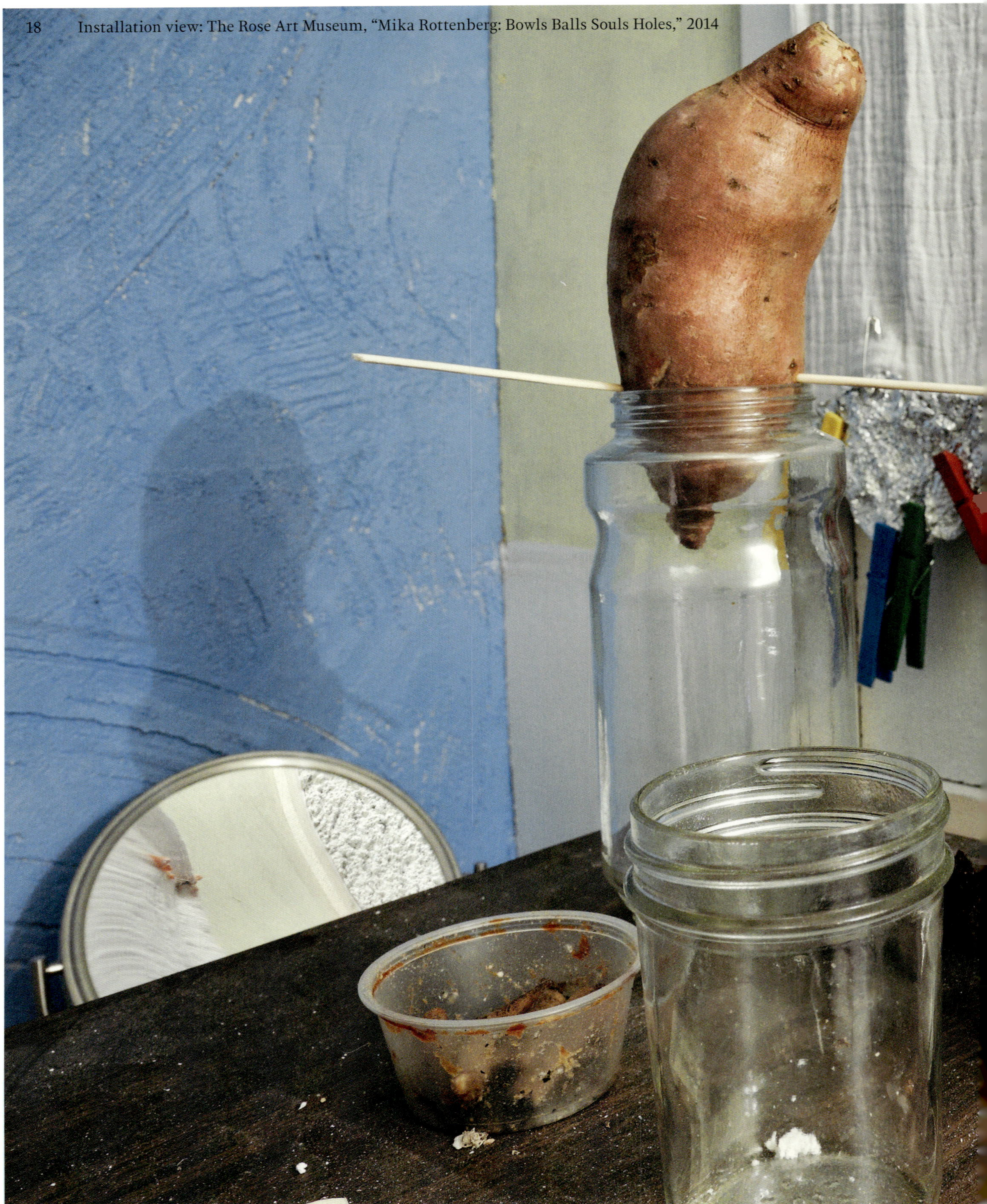

Installation view: The Rose Art Museum, “Mika Rottenberg: Bowls Balls Souls Holes,” 2014

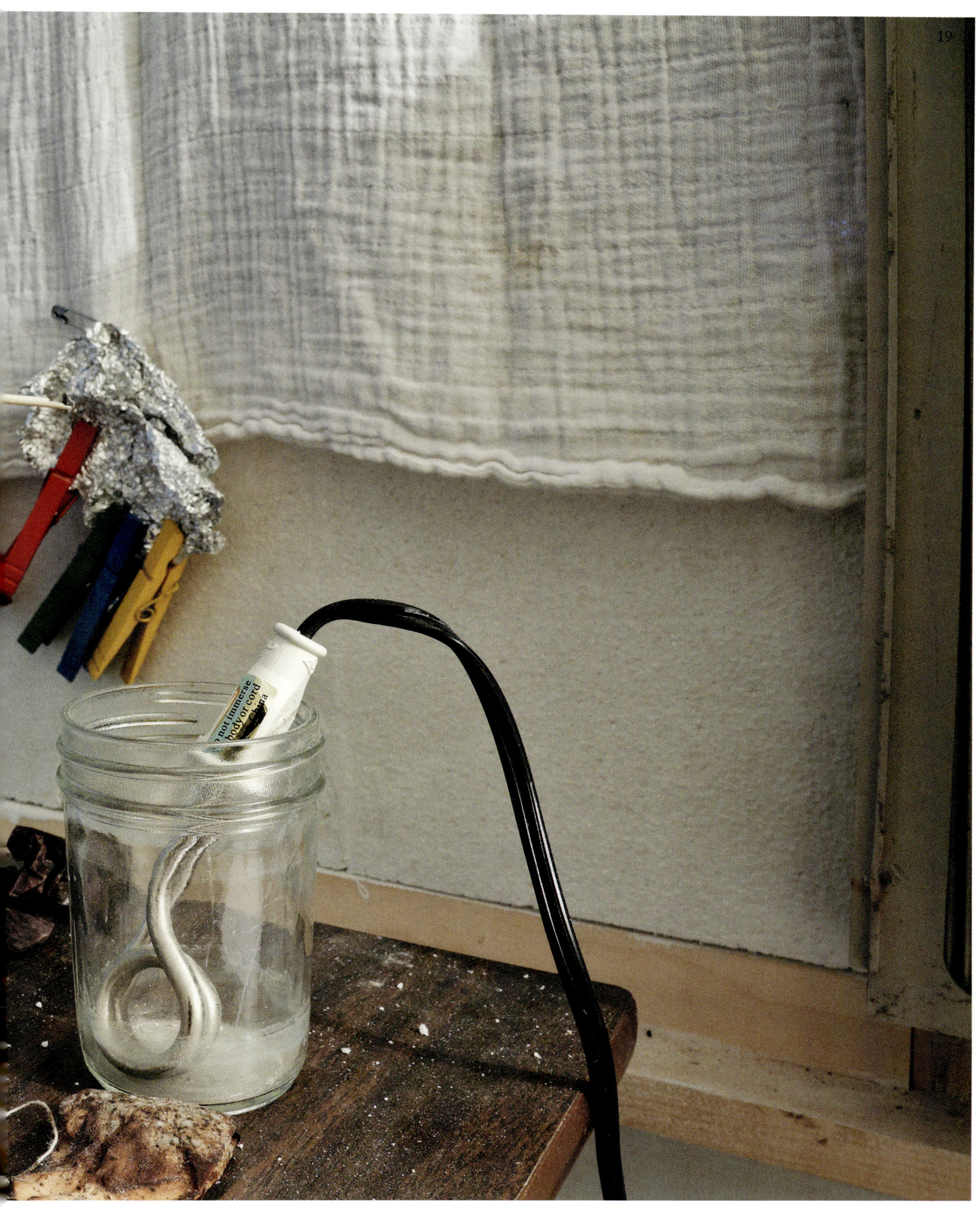
not immerse
body or cord

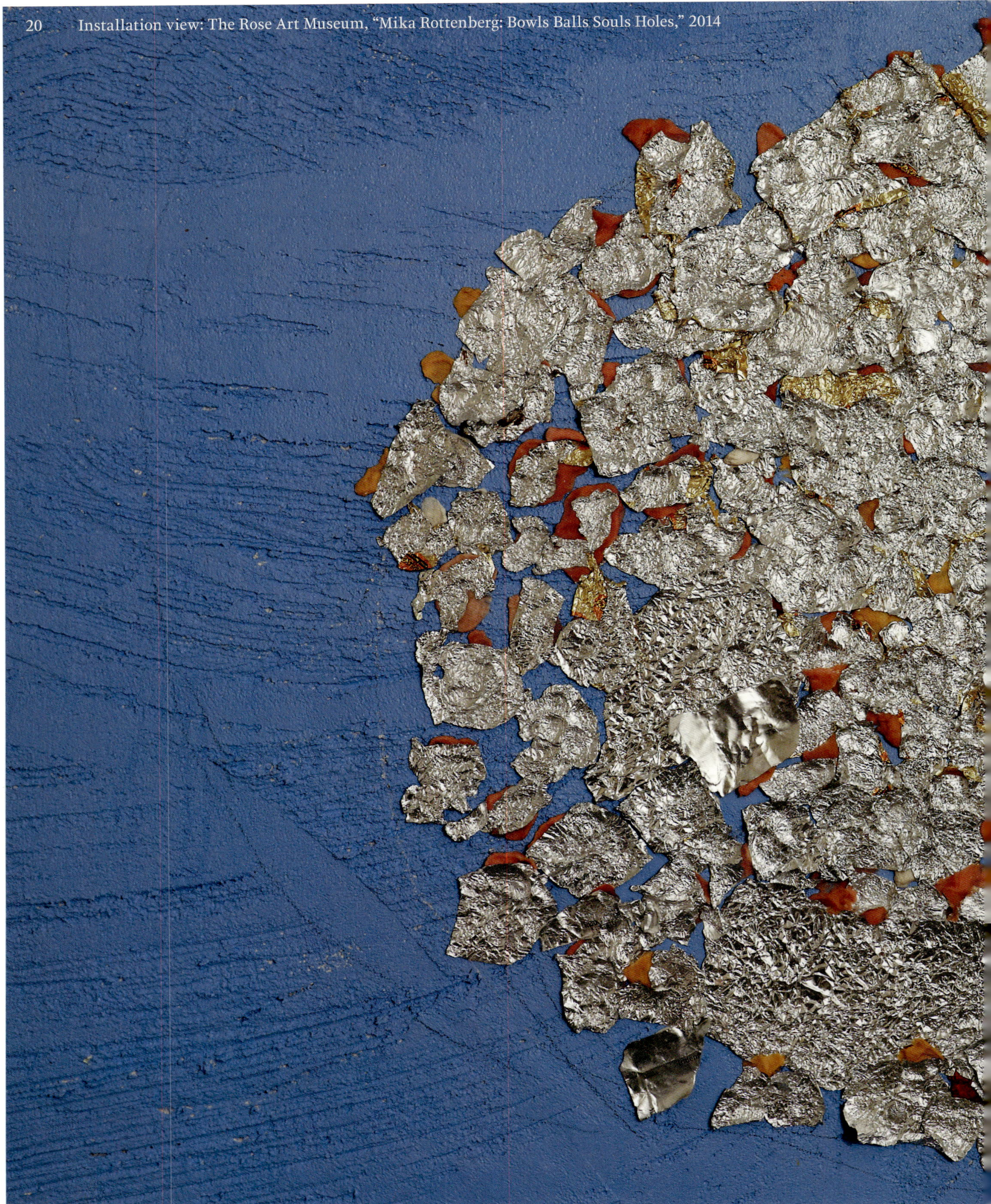

Installation view: The Rose Art Museum, “Mika Rottenberg: Bowls Balls Souls Holes,” 2014

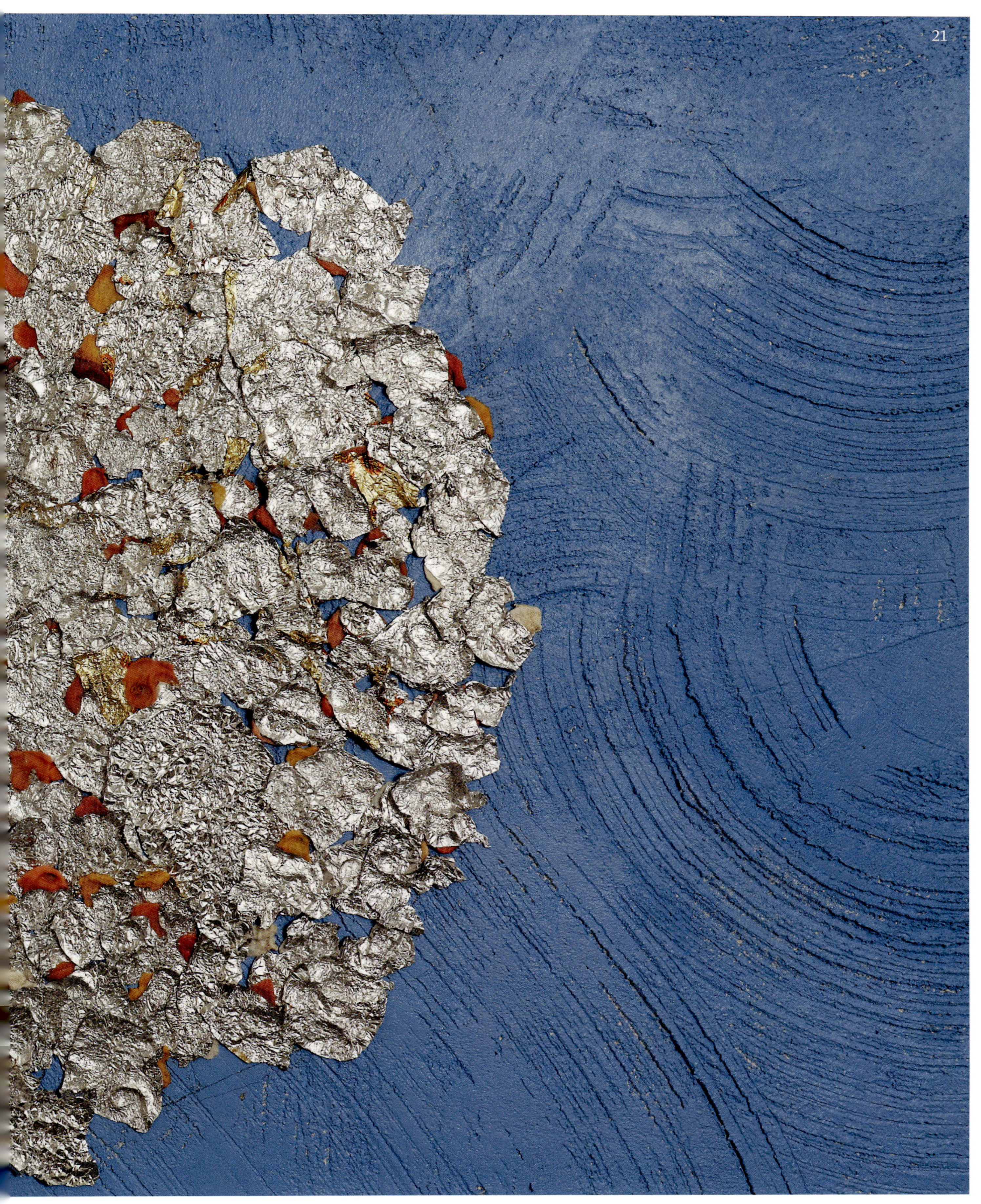

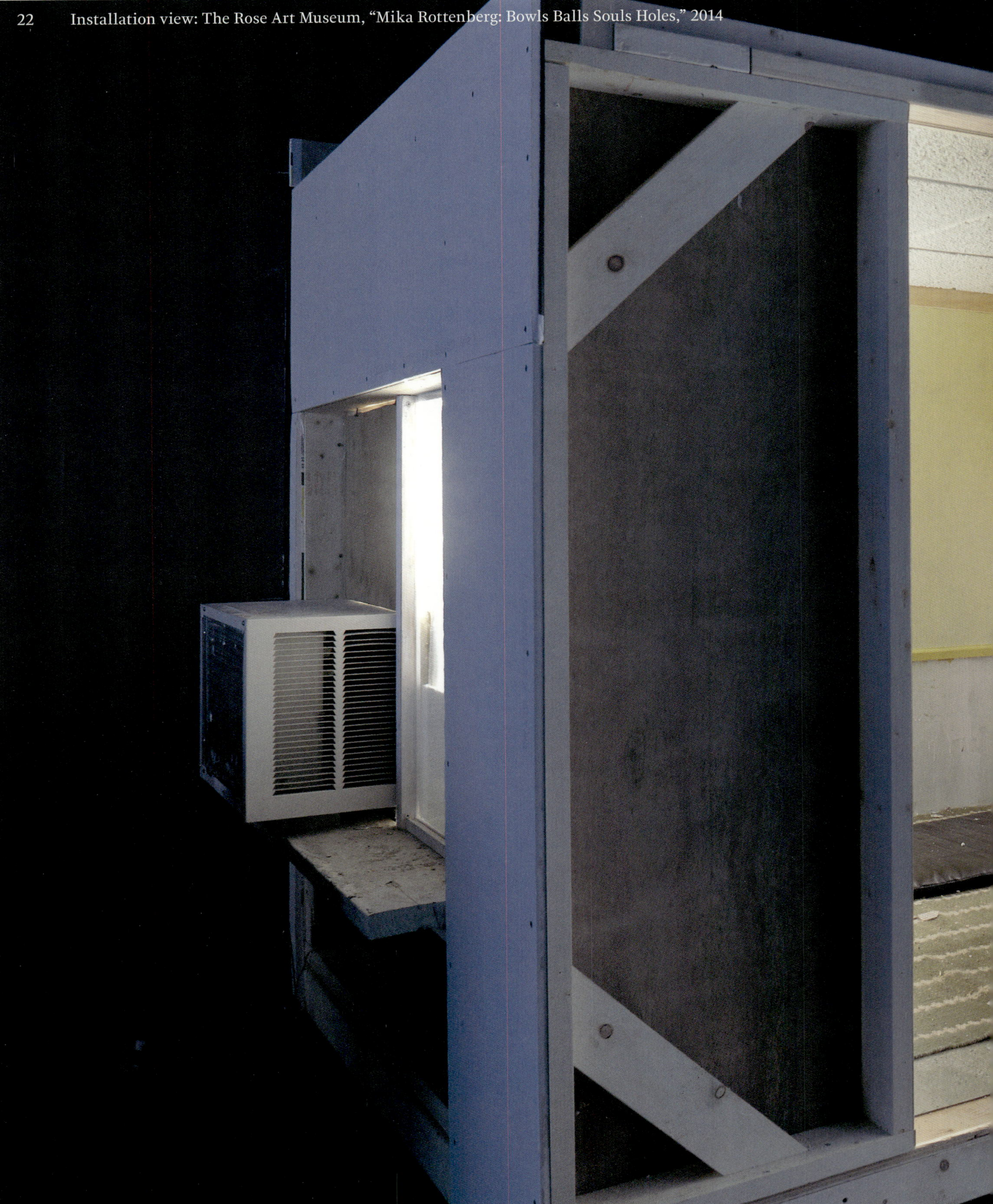

Installation view: The Rose Art Museum, "Mika Rottenberg: Bowls Balls Souls Holes," 2014

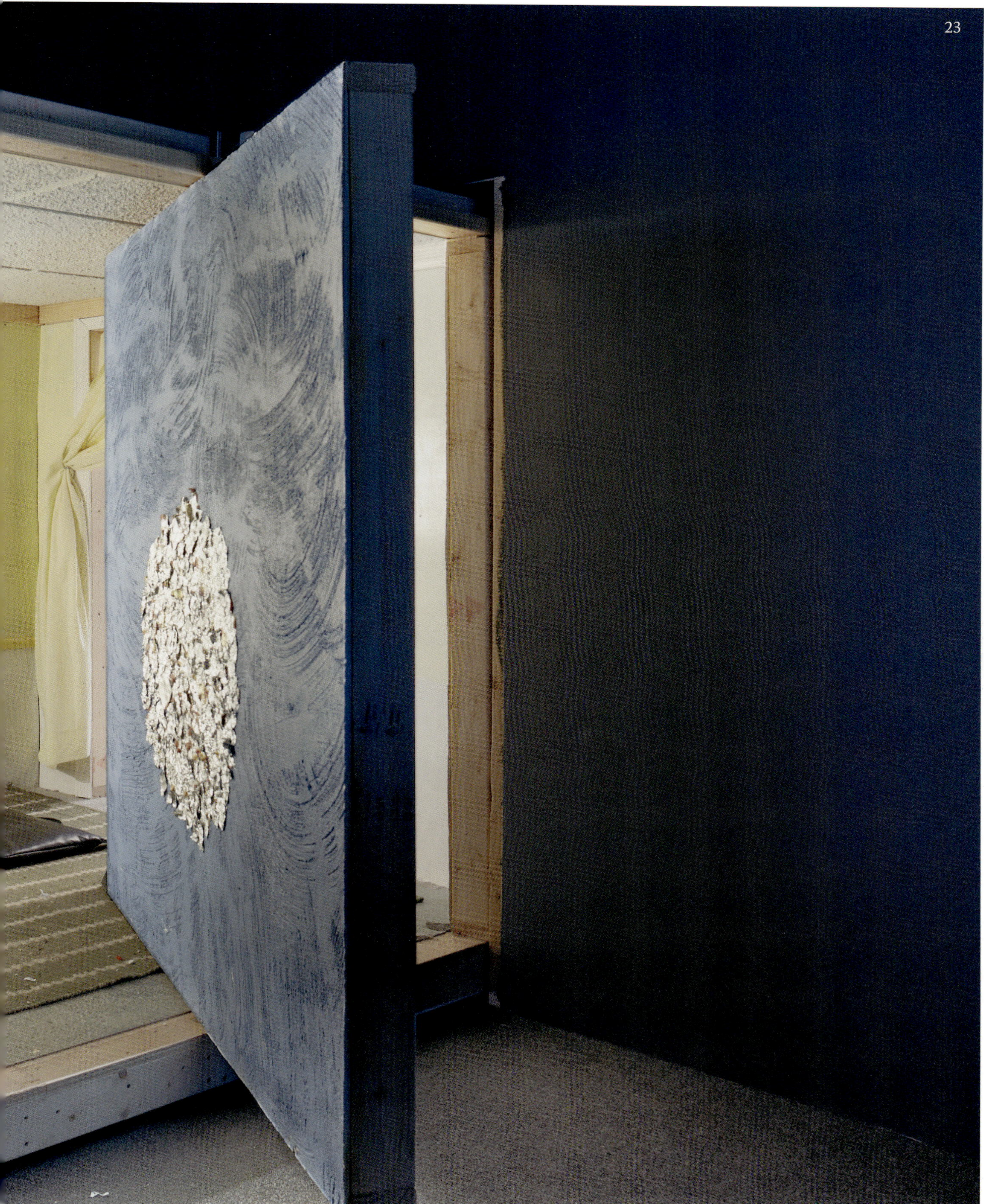

Installation view: The Rose Art Museum, "Mika Rottenberg: Bowls Balls Souls Holes," 2014

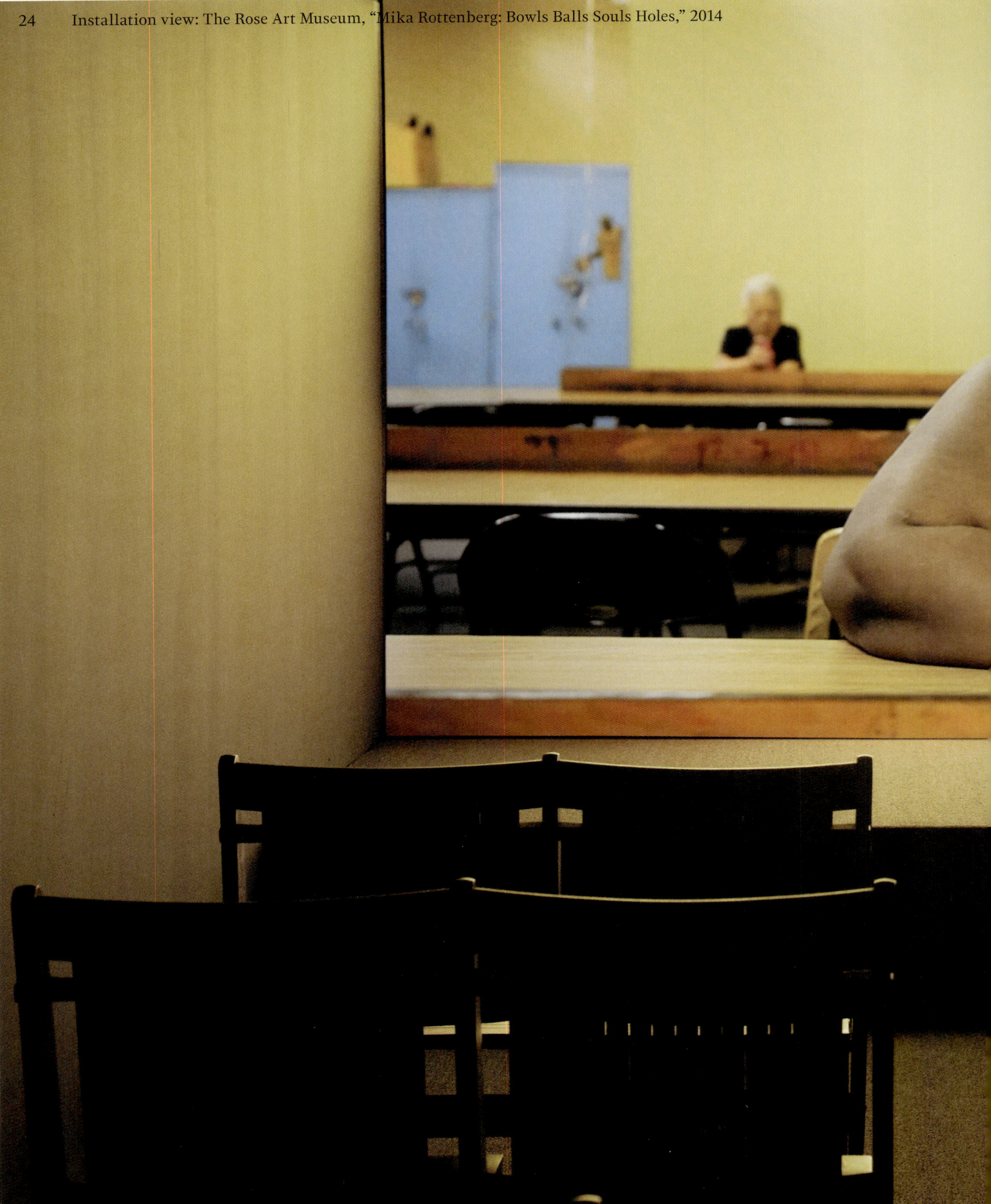

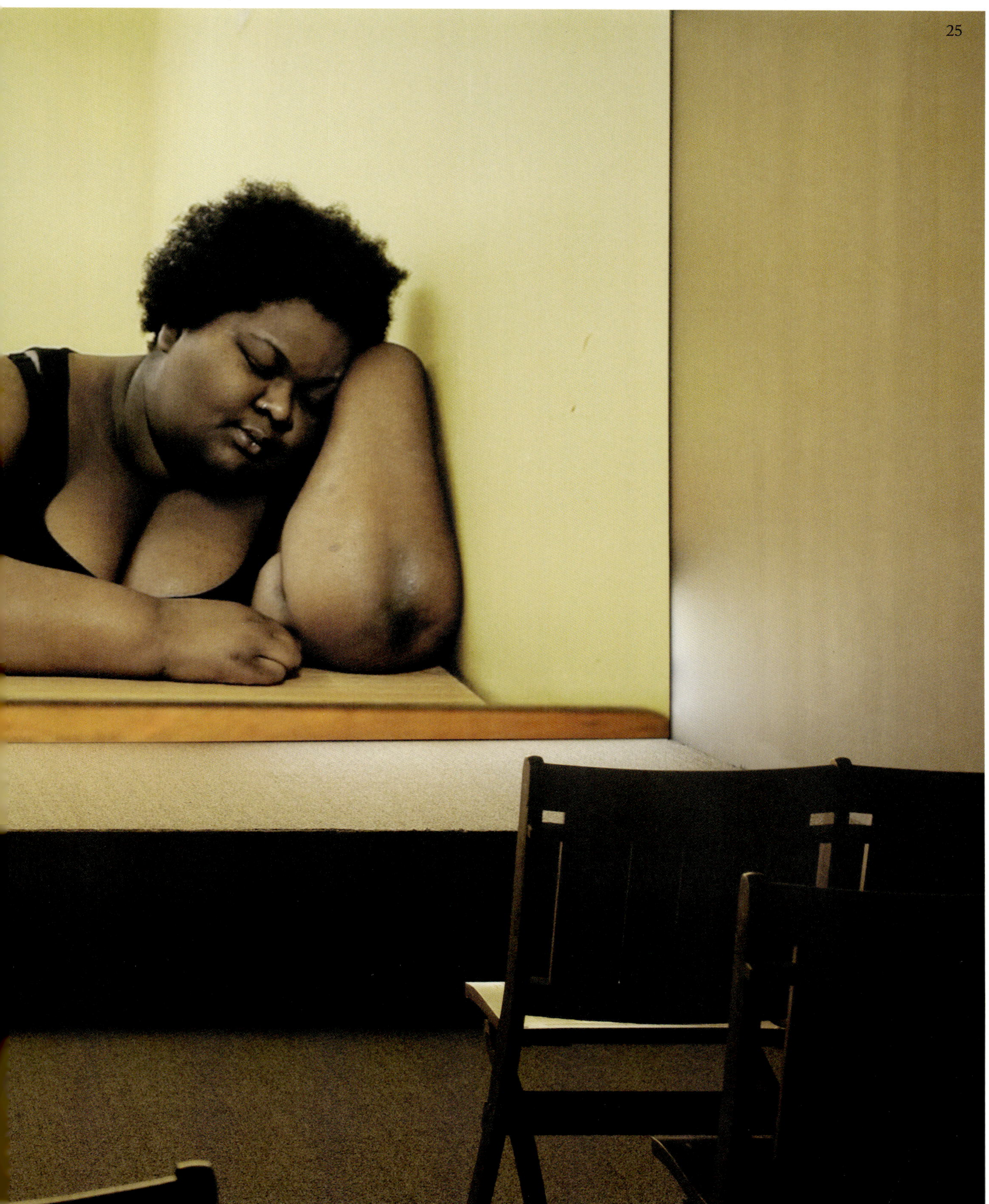

Still from *Bowls Balls Souls Holes*, 2014

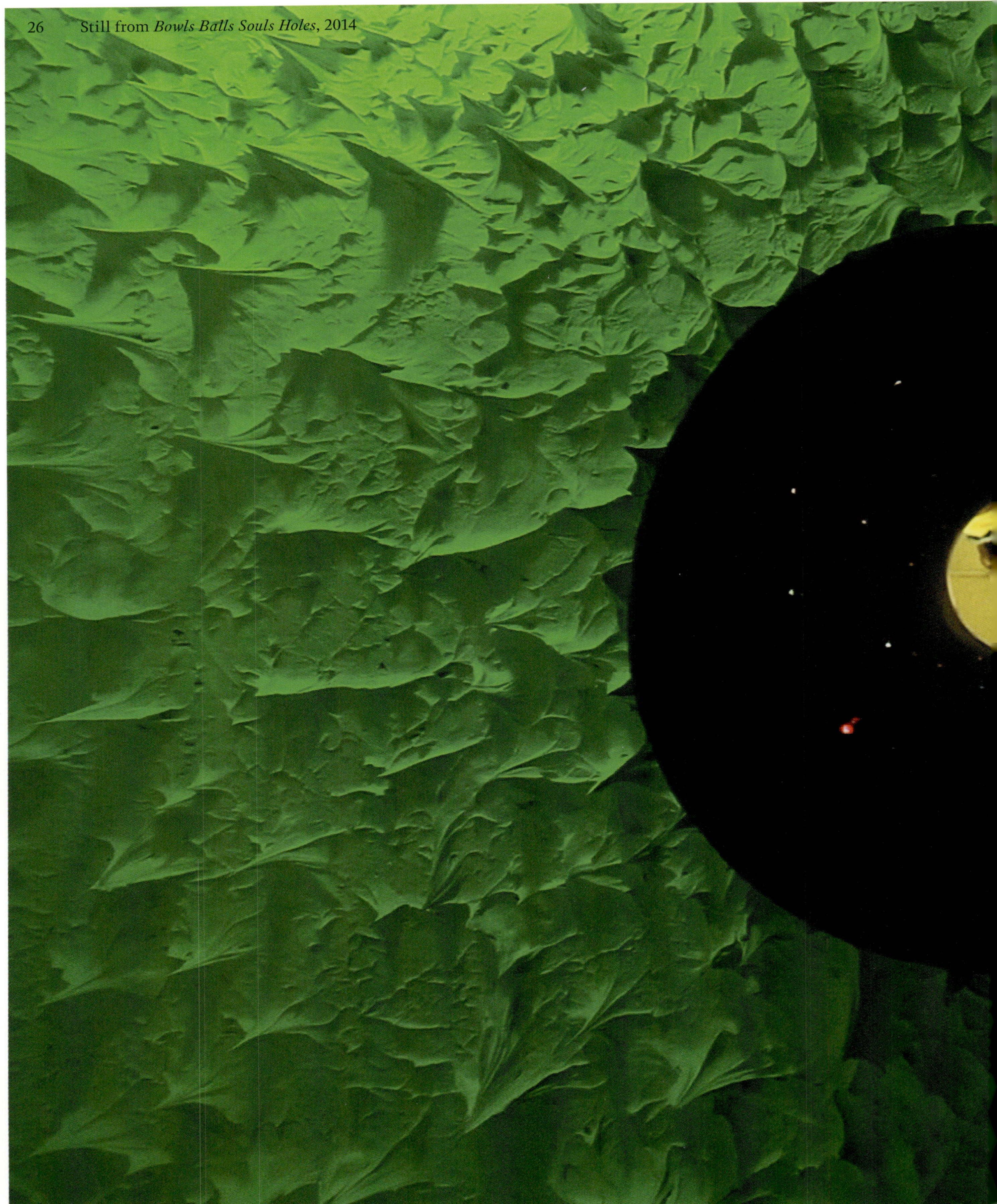

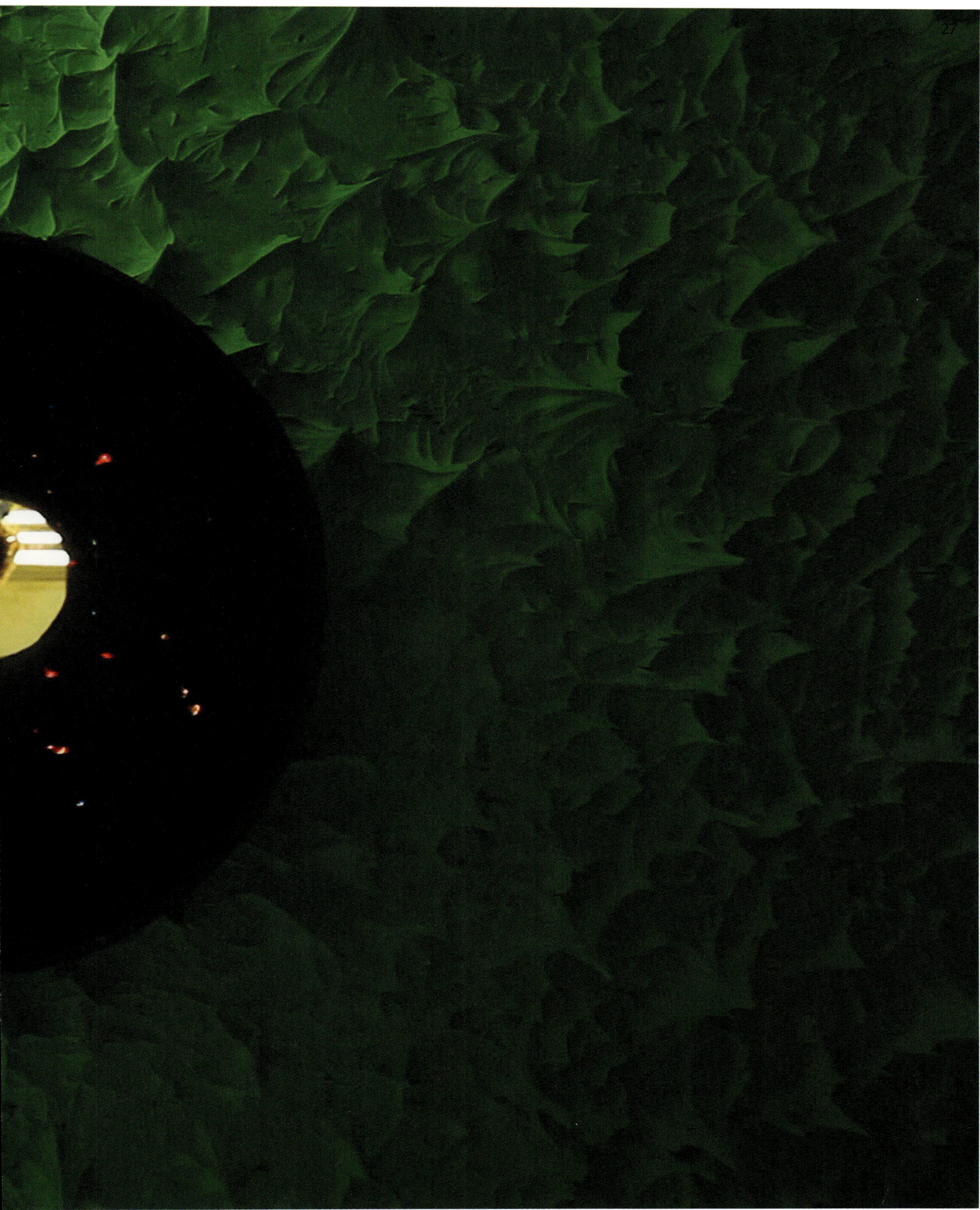

 Installation view: The Rose Art Museum, “Mika Rottenberg: Bowls Balls Souls Holes,” 2014

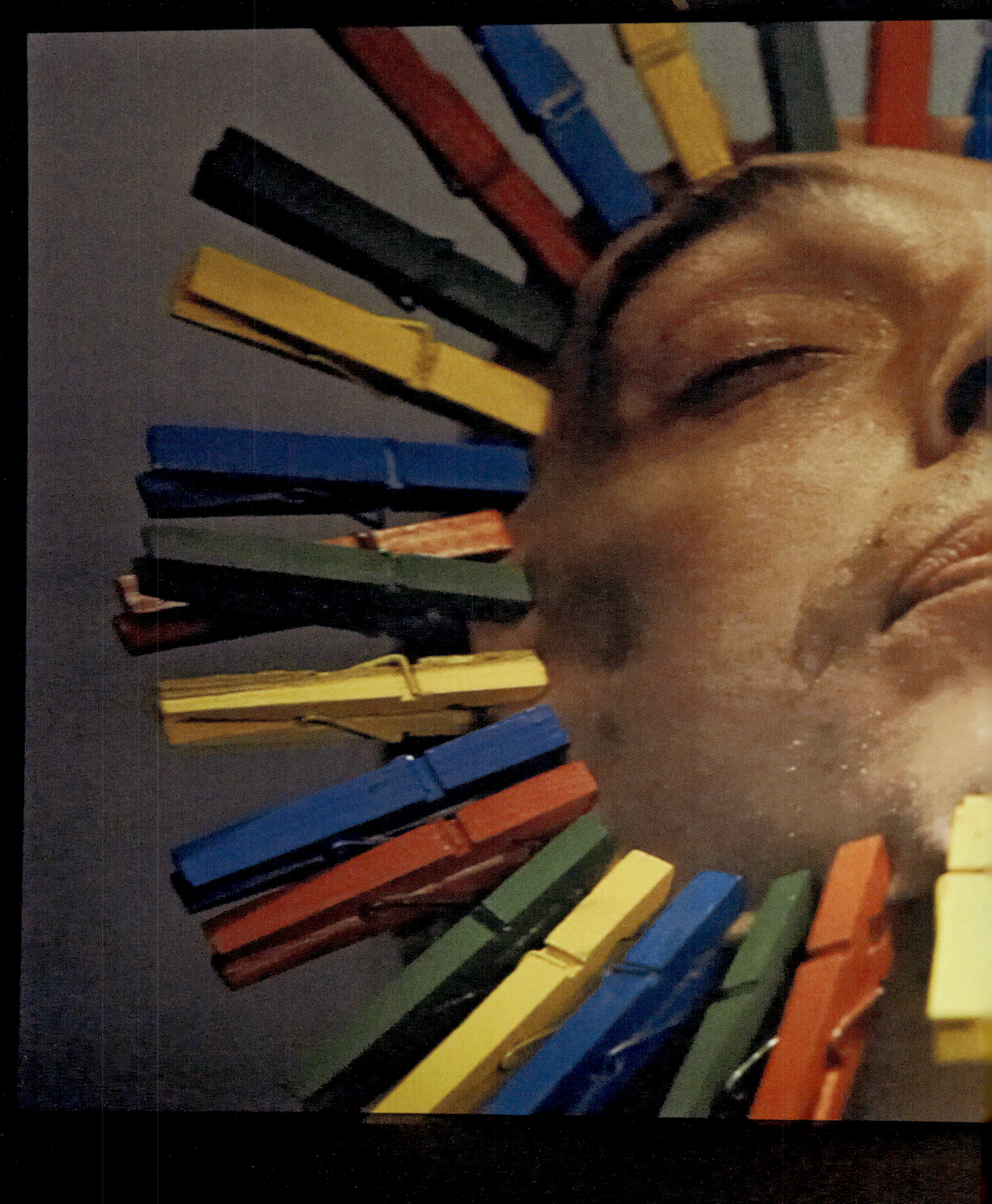

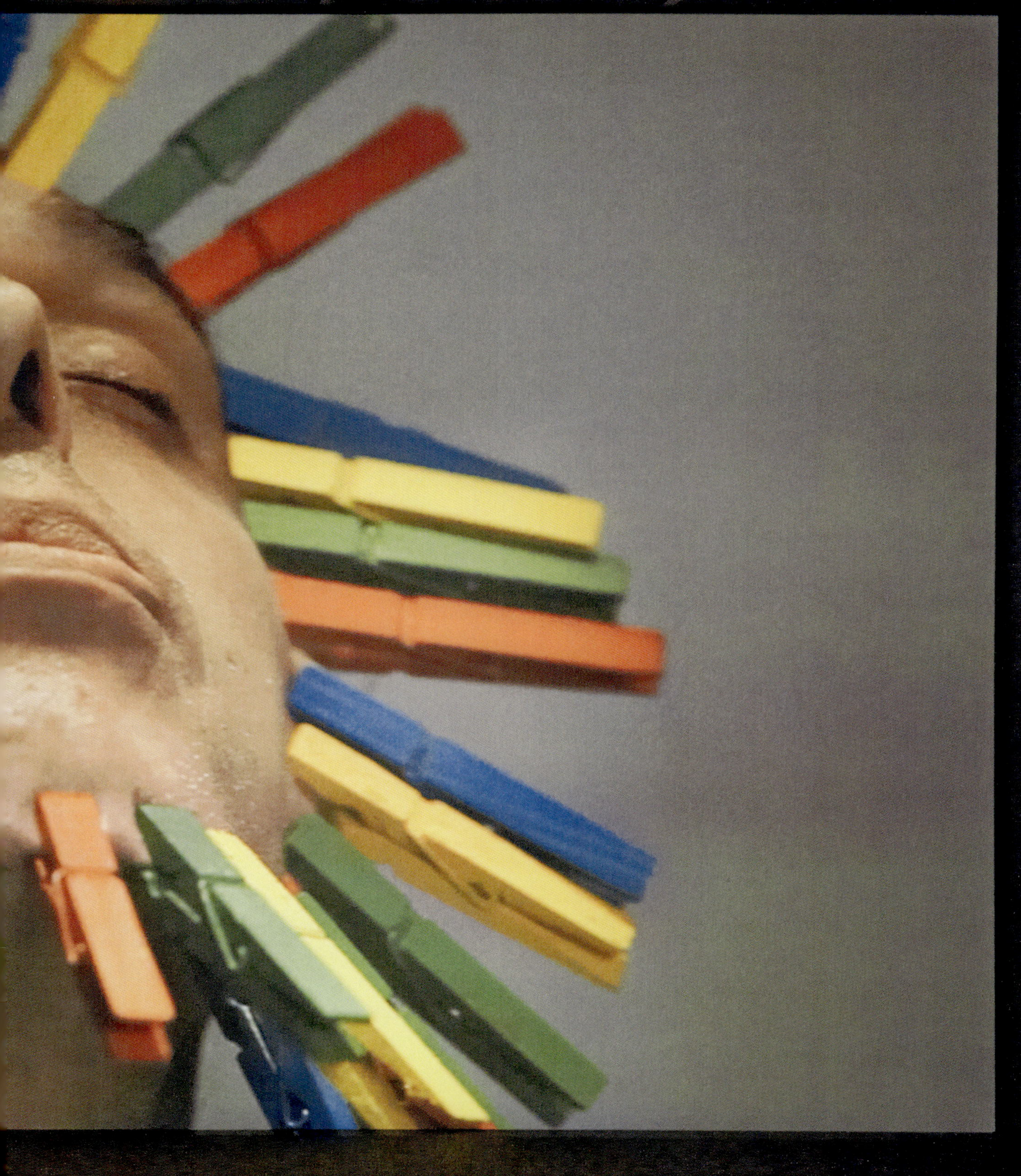

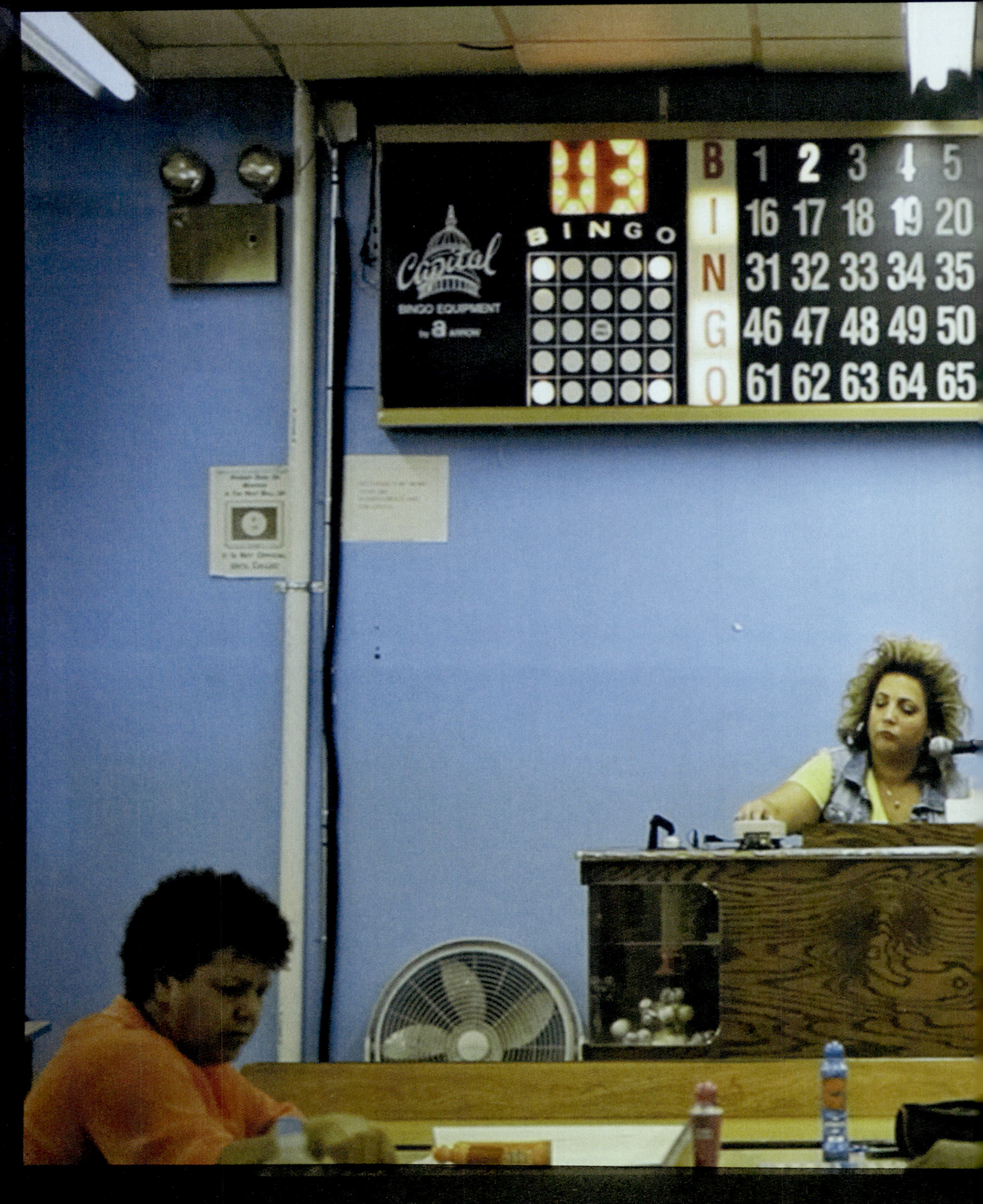

Installation view: The Rose Art Museum, "Mika Rottenberg: Bowls Balls Souls Holes," 2014

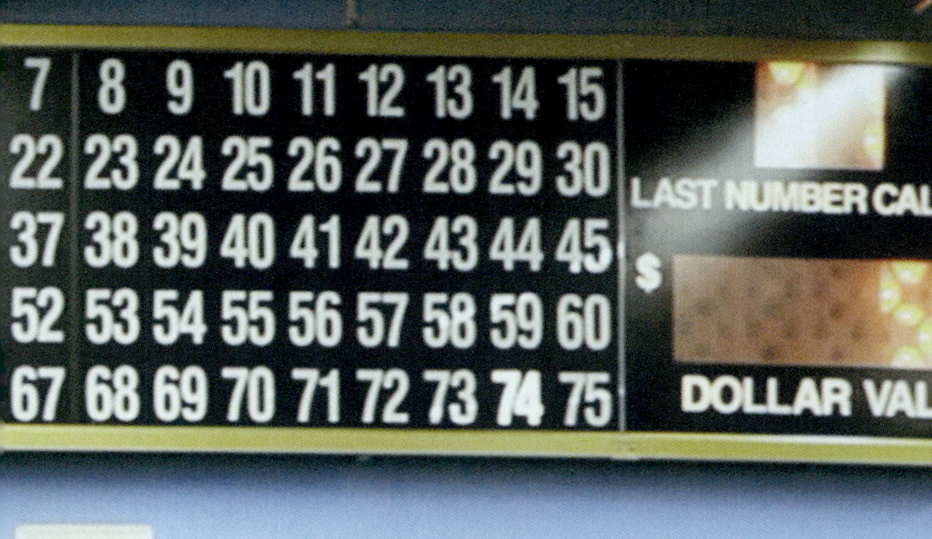
7 8 9 10 11 12 13 14 15
22 23 24 25 26 27 28 29 30
37 38 39 40 41 42 43 44 45
52 53 54 55 56 57 58 59 60
67 68 69 70 71 72 73 74 75
LAST NUMBER CALLED
$
DOLLAR VALUE
NO SMOKING
IN THIS
AREA

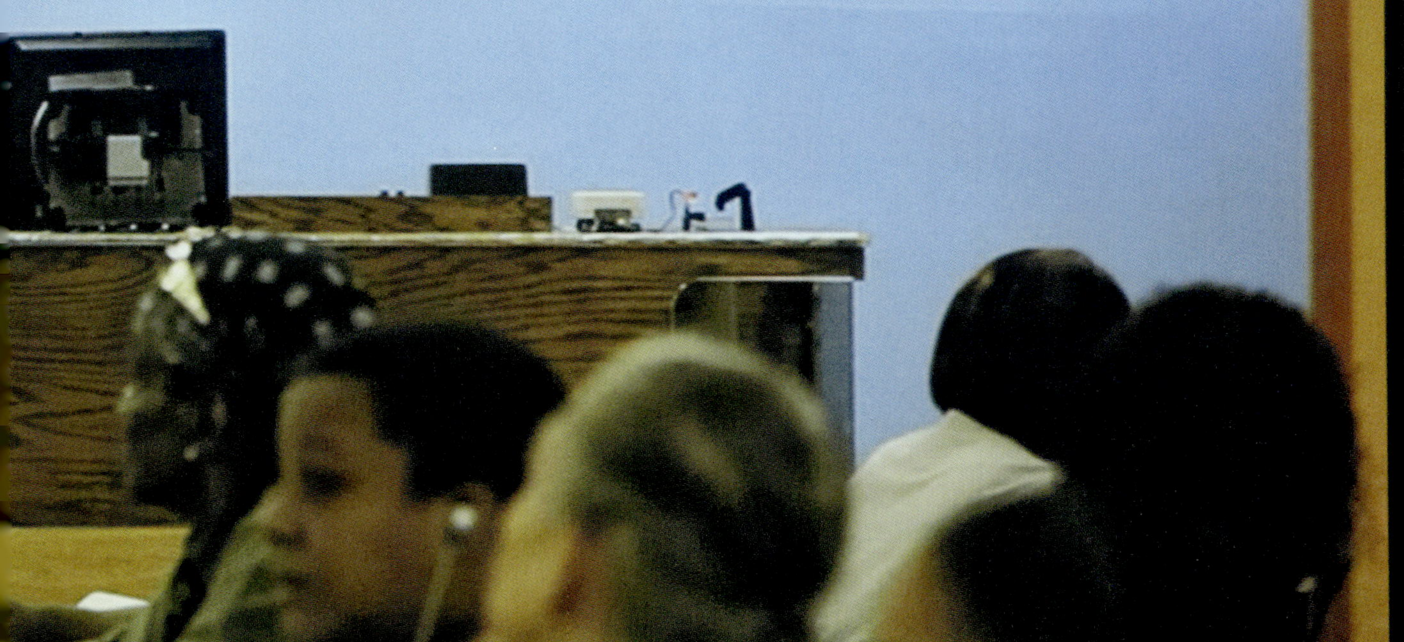

 Stills from *Bowls Balls Souls Holes*, 2014

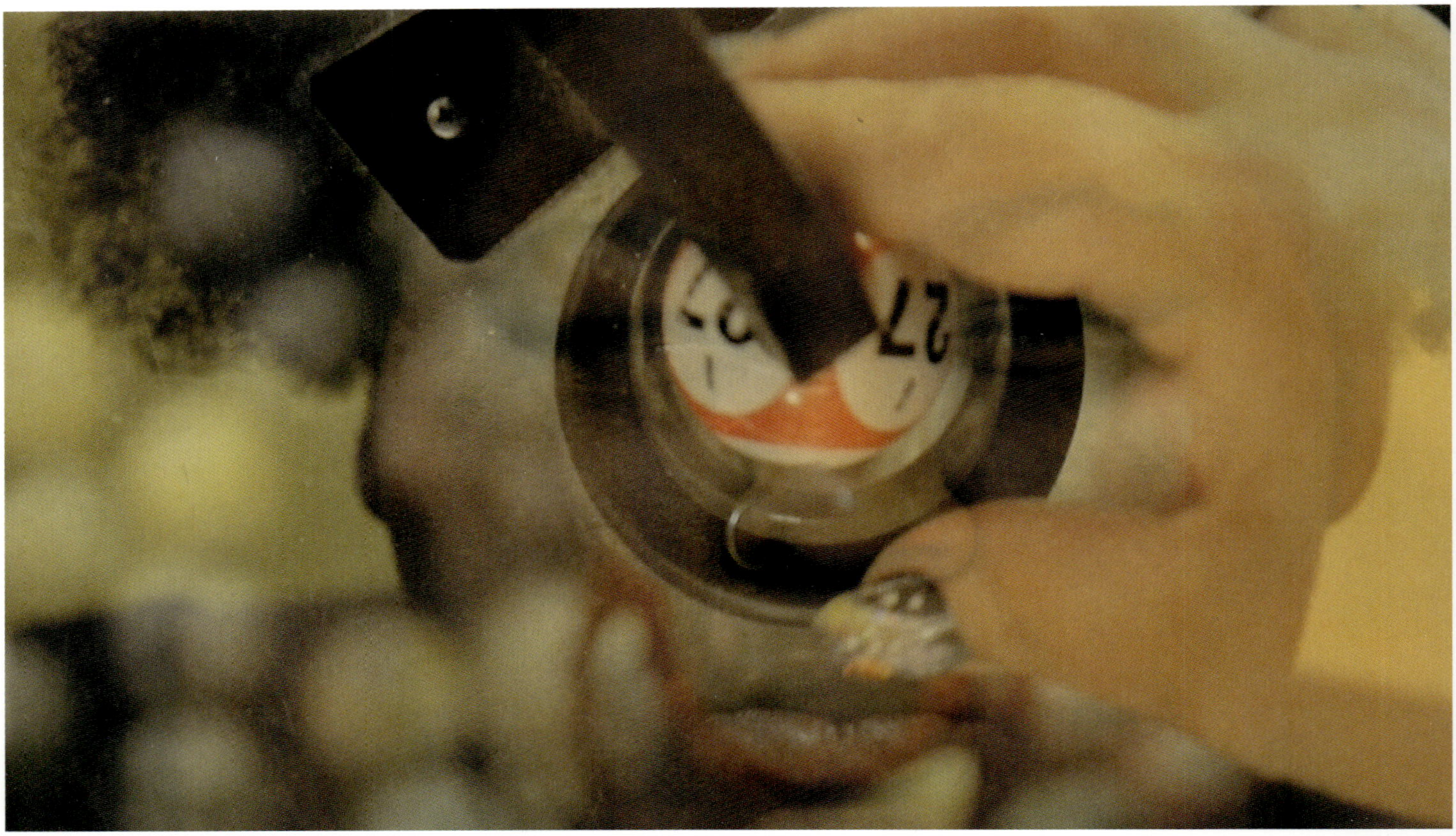

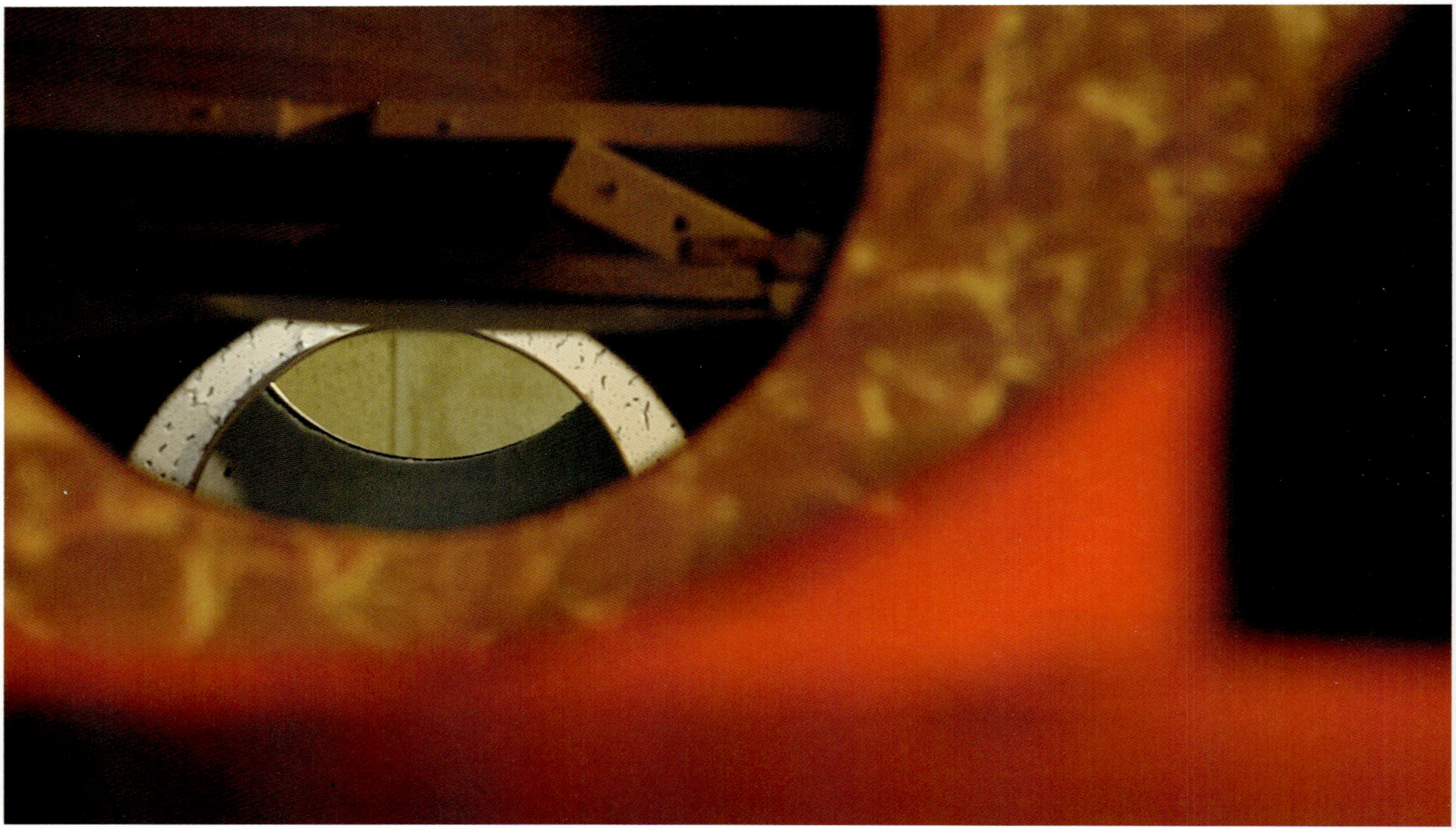

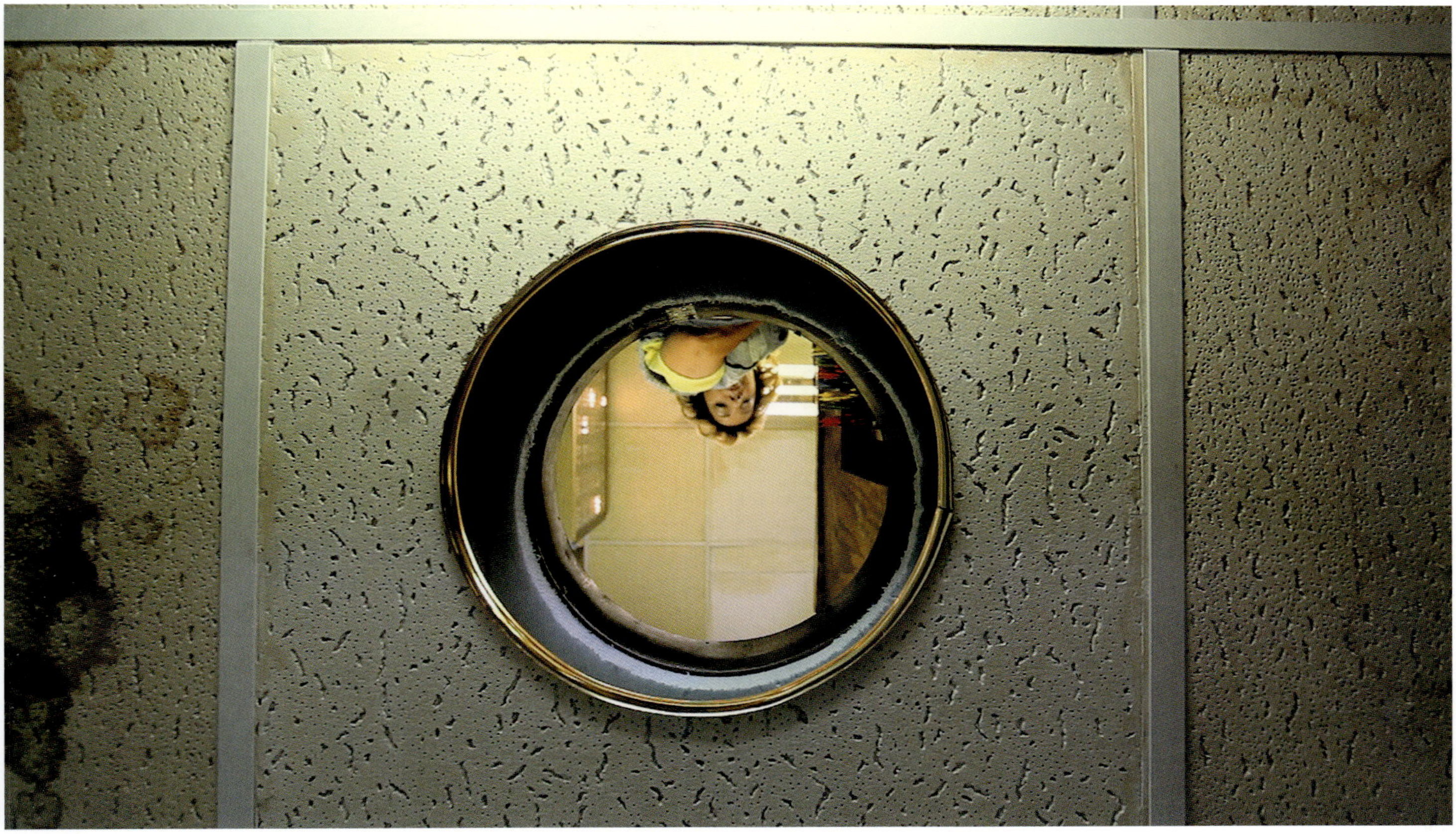

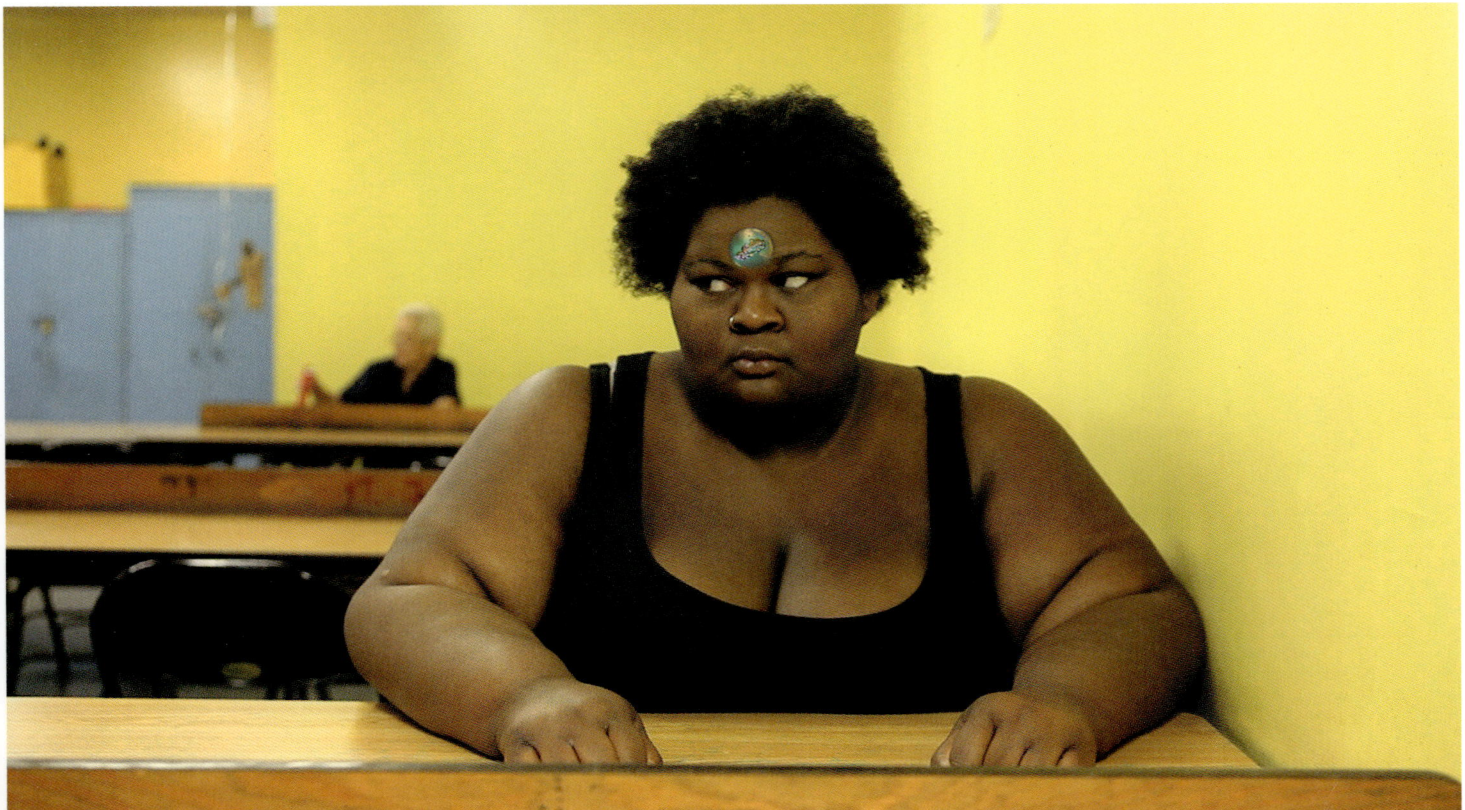

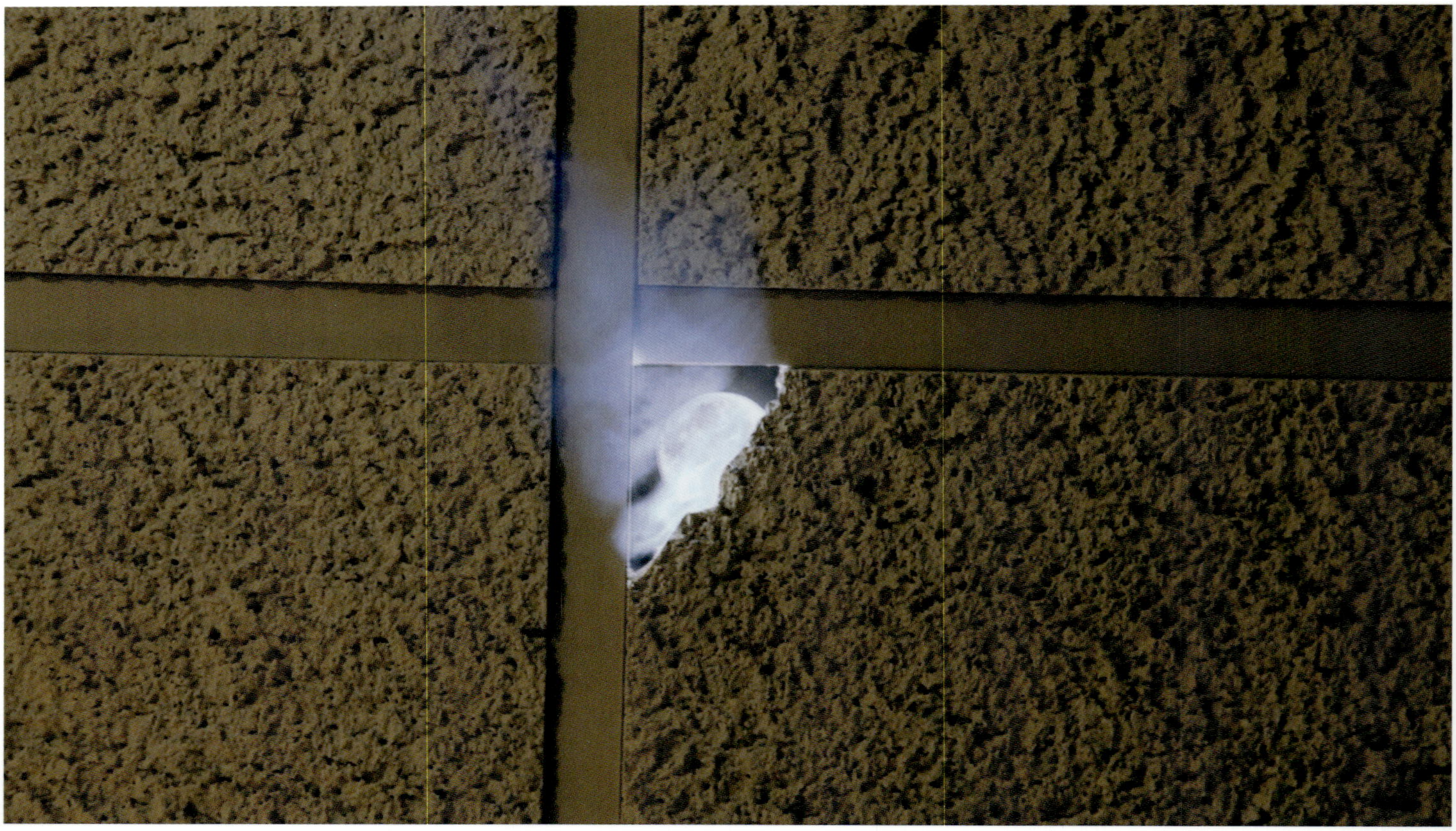

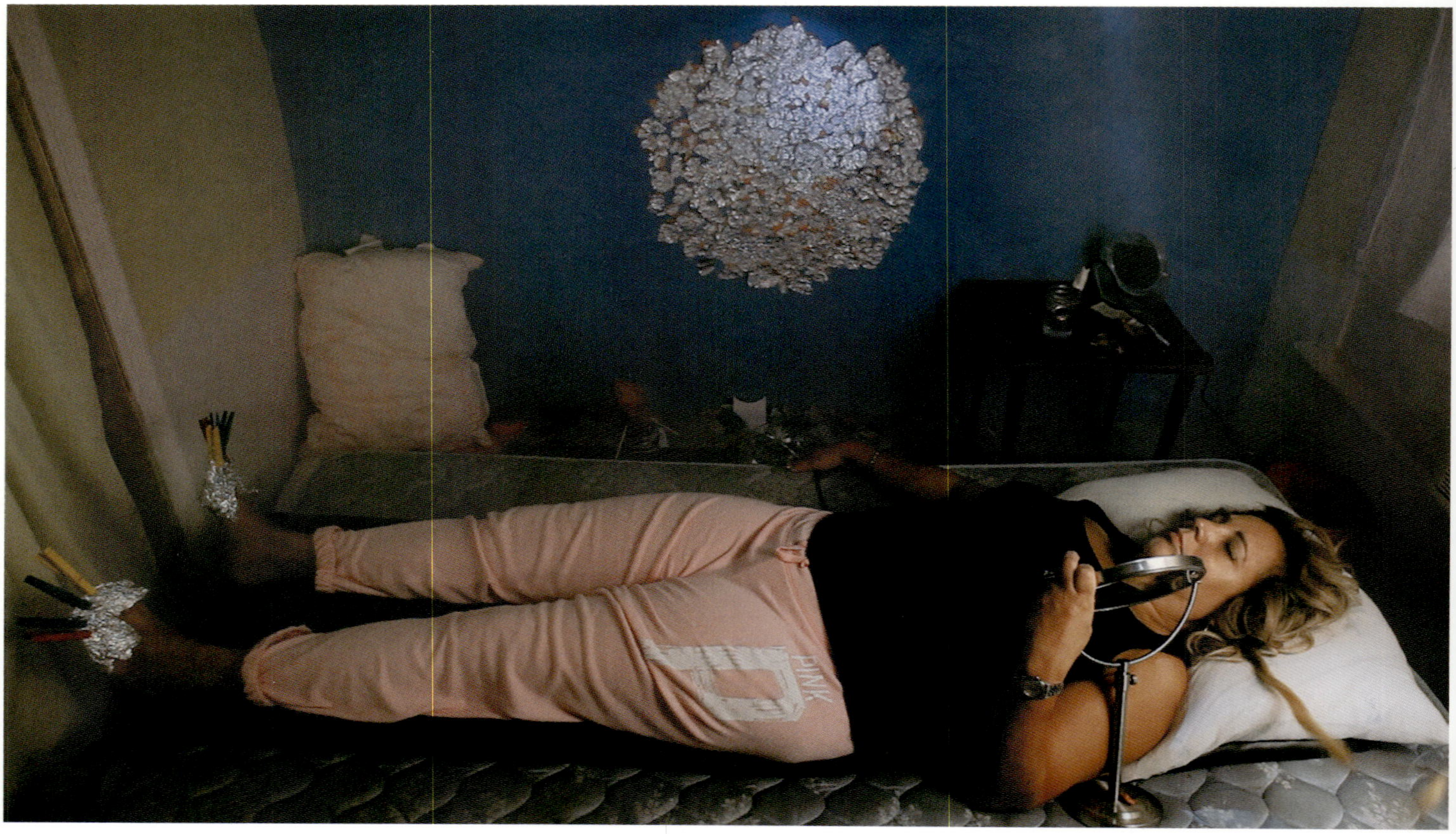

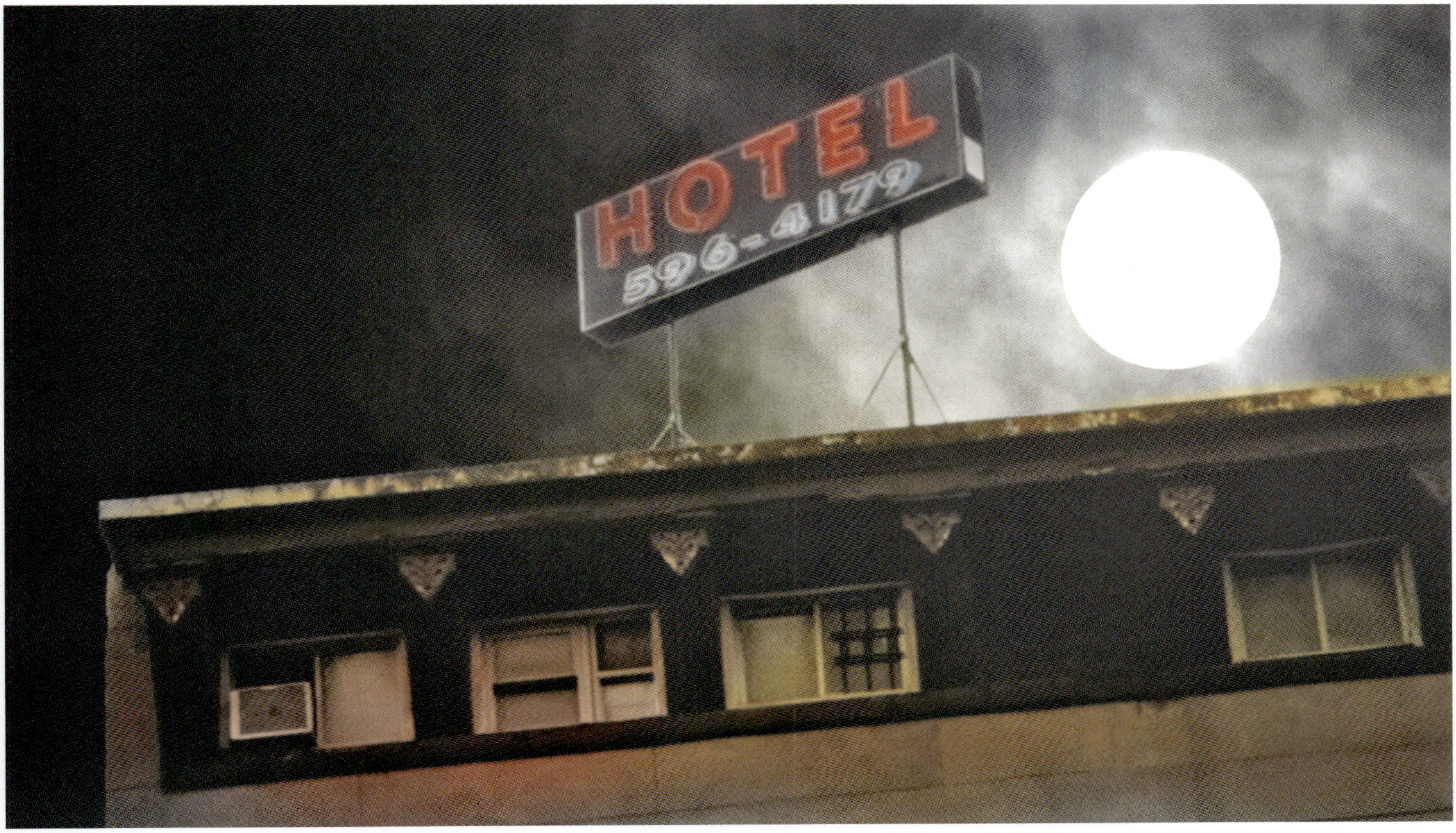

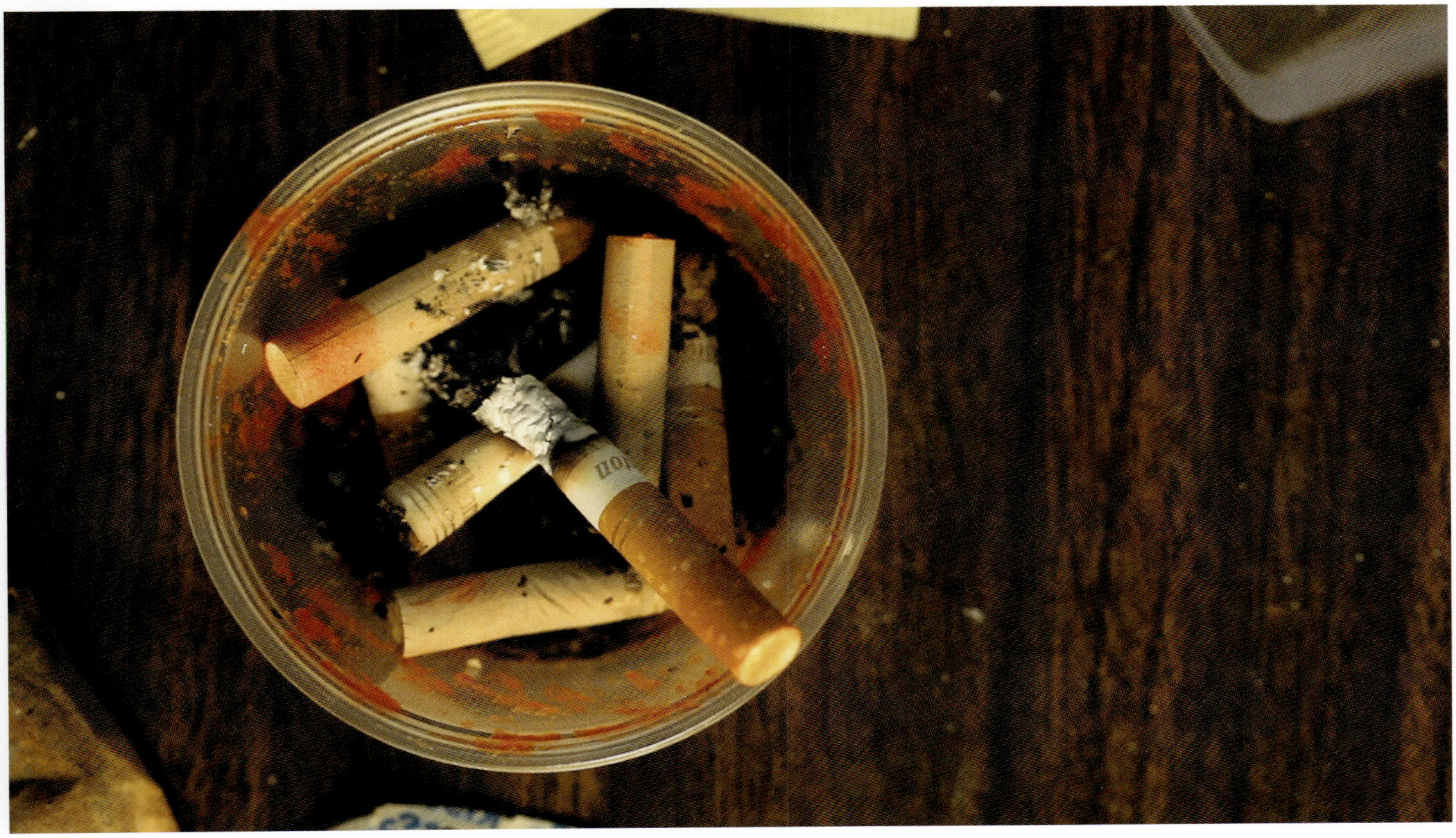

 Still from *Bowls Balls Souls Holes*, 2014

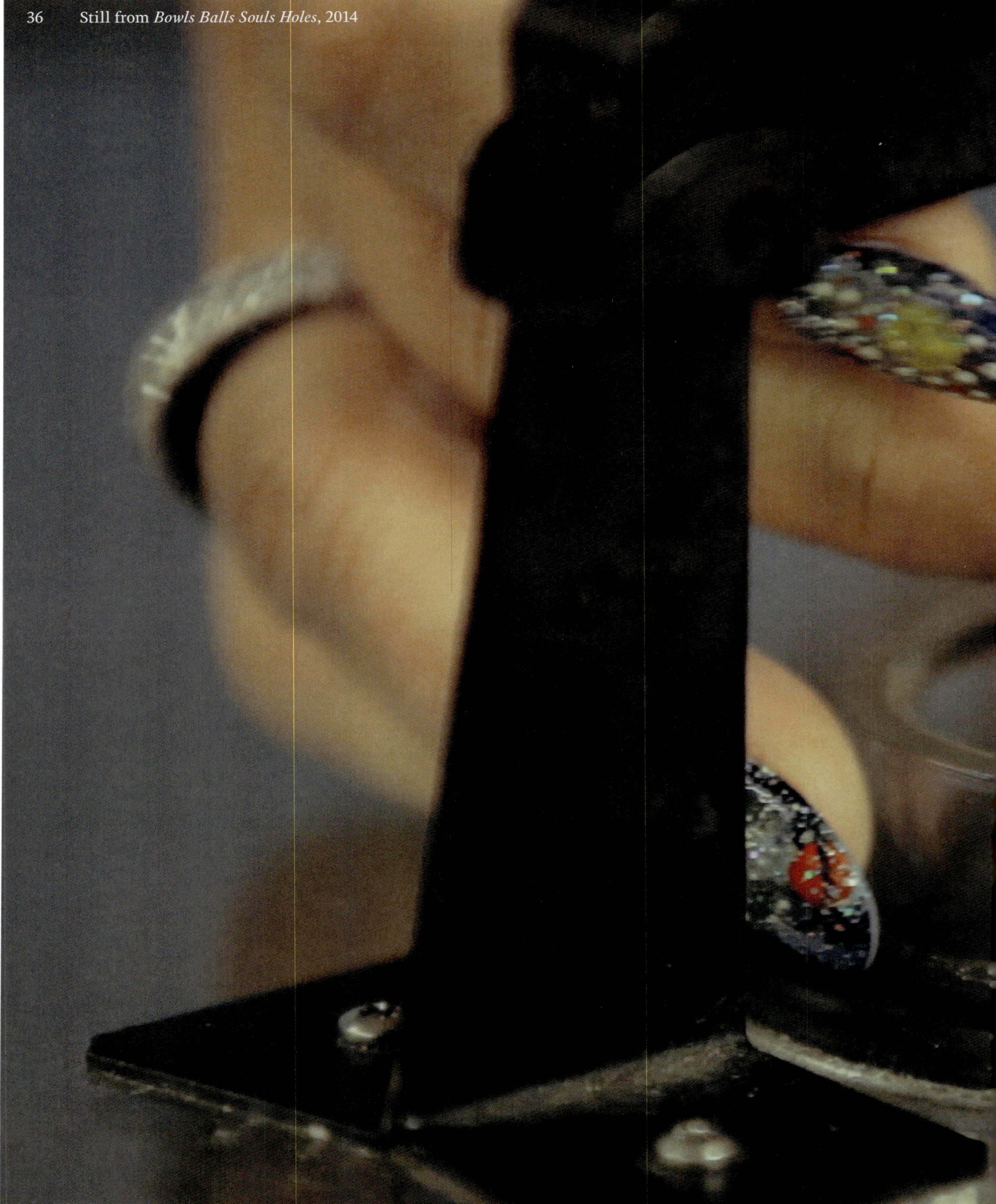

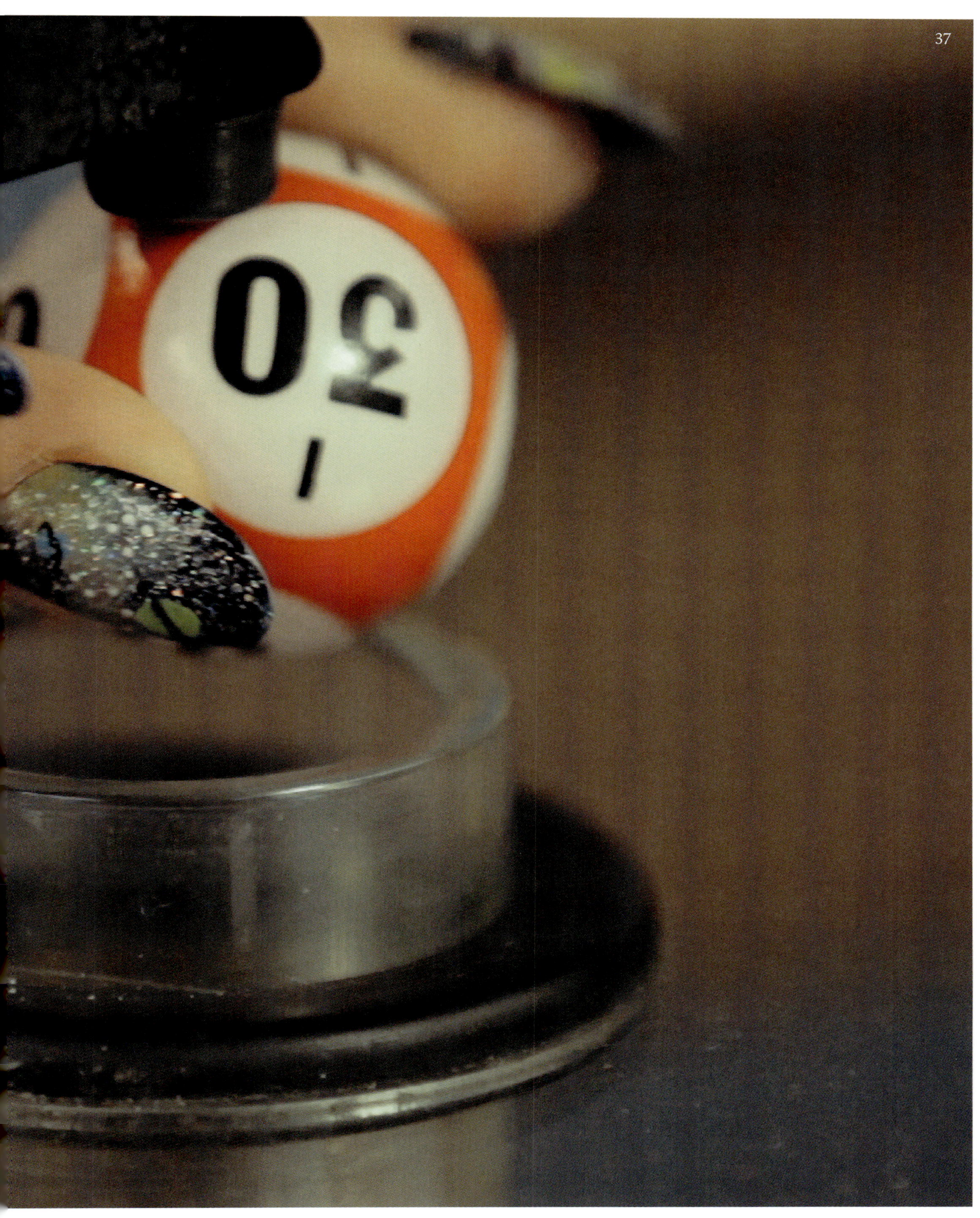

Stills from *Bowls Balls Souls Holes*, 2014

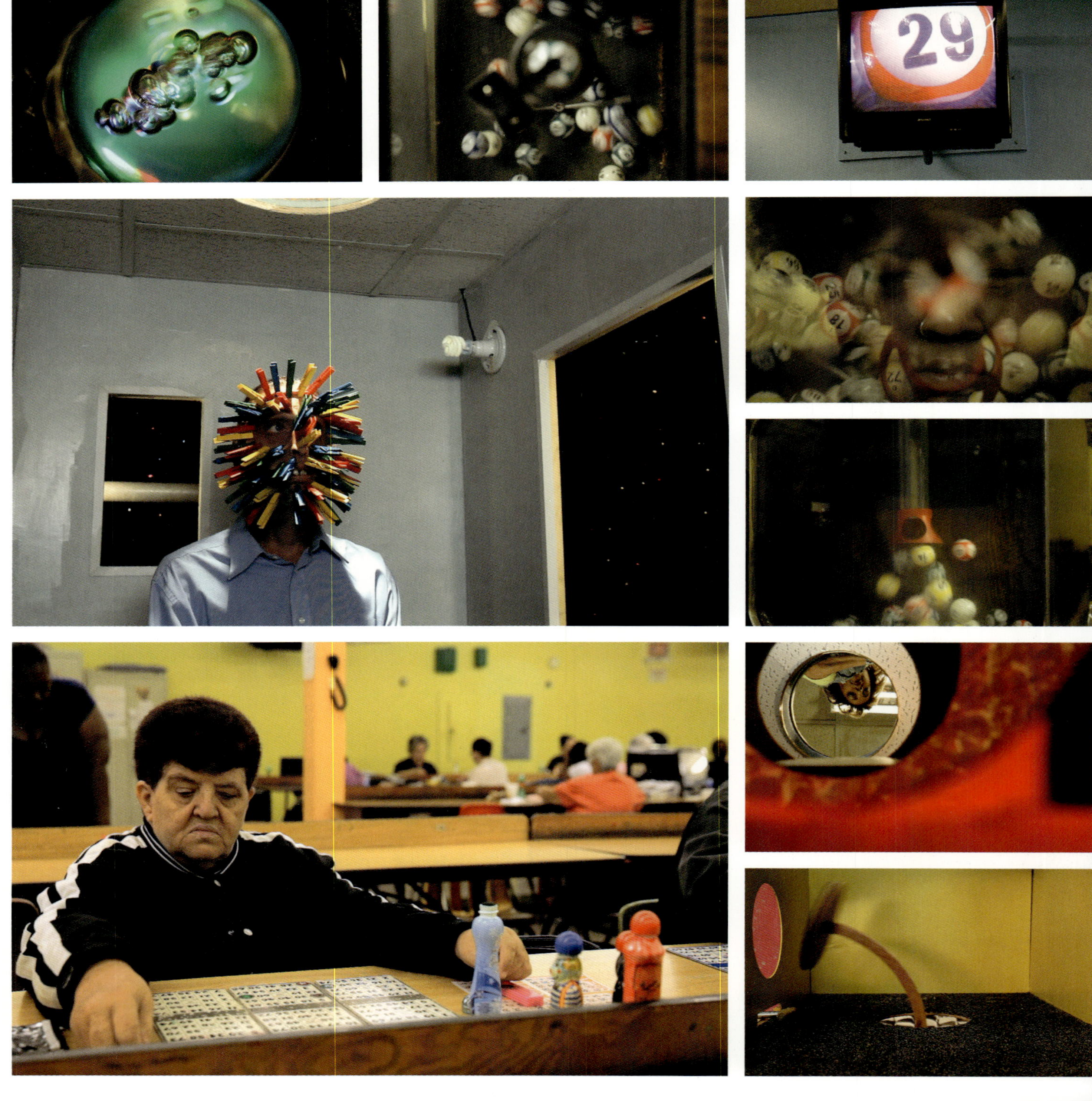

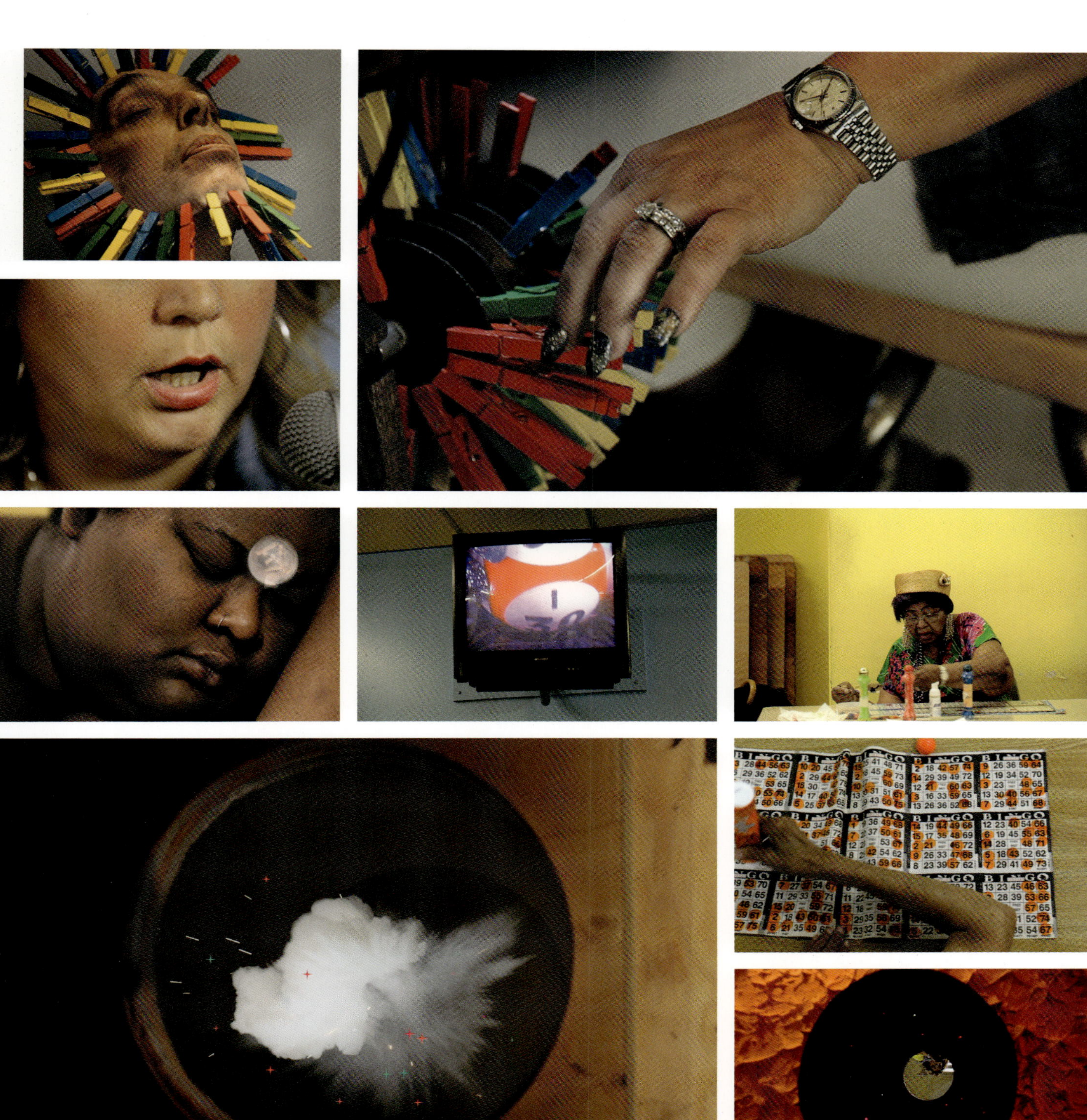

 Stills from *Bowls Balls Souls Holes*, 2014

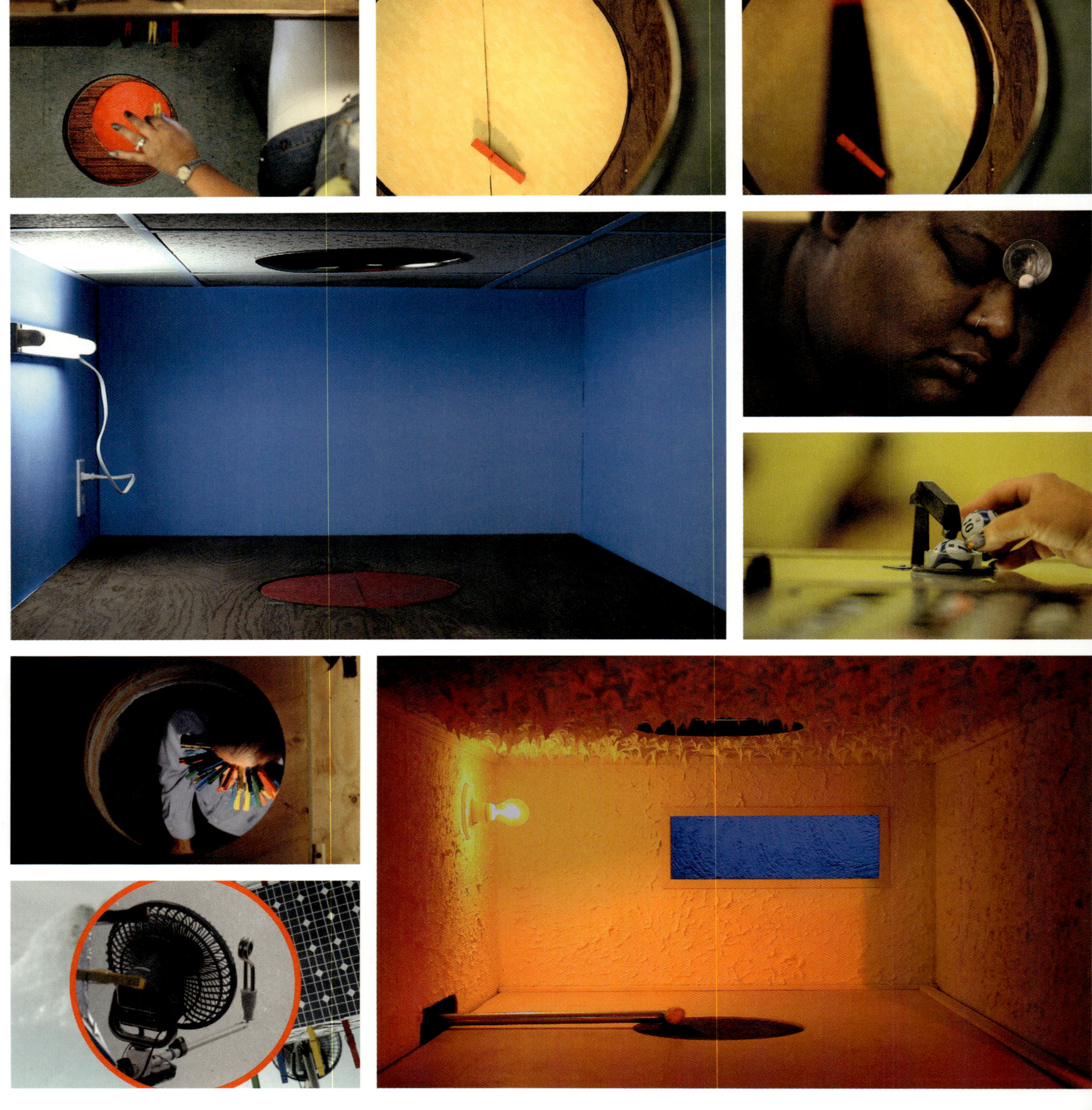

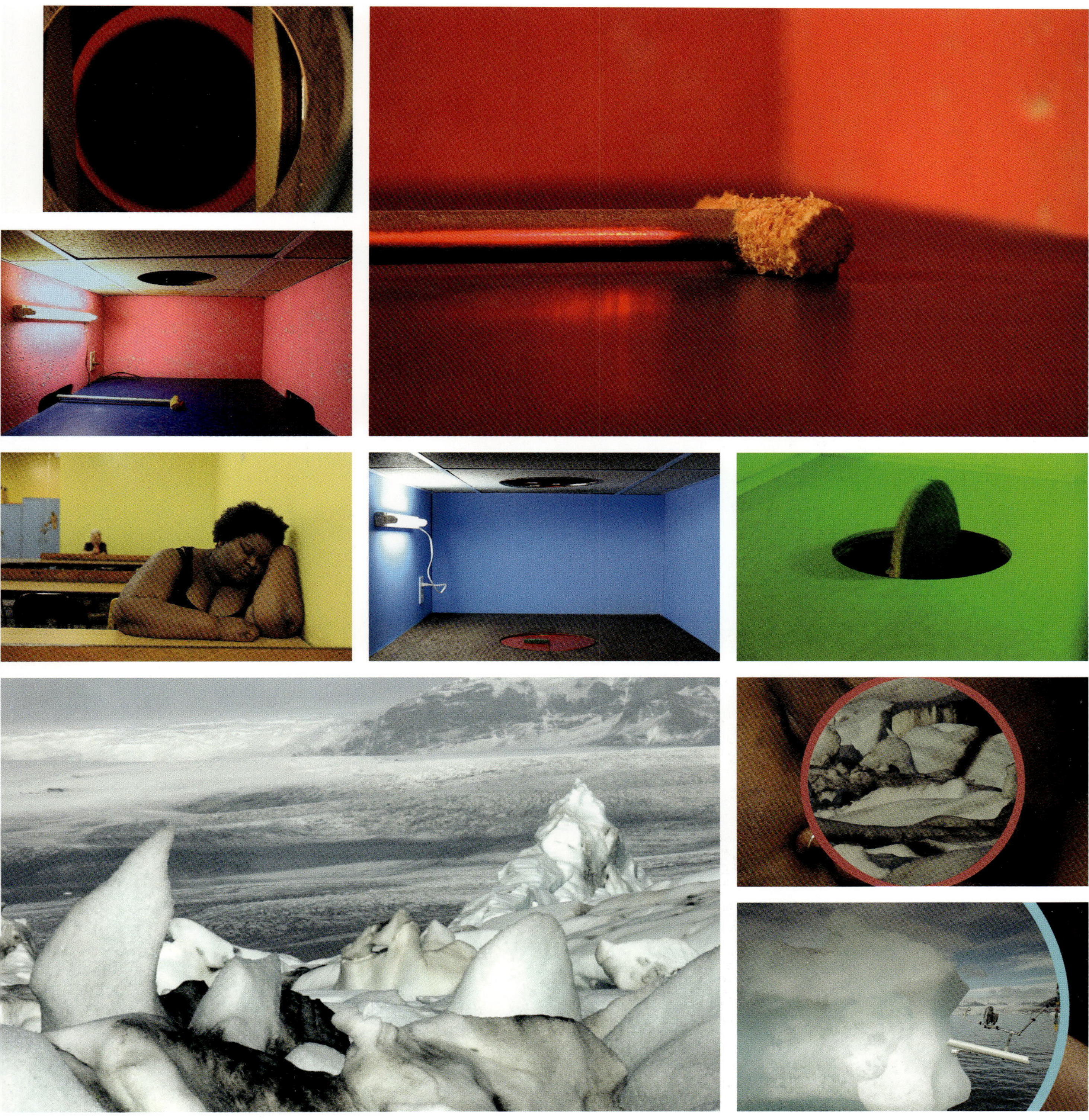

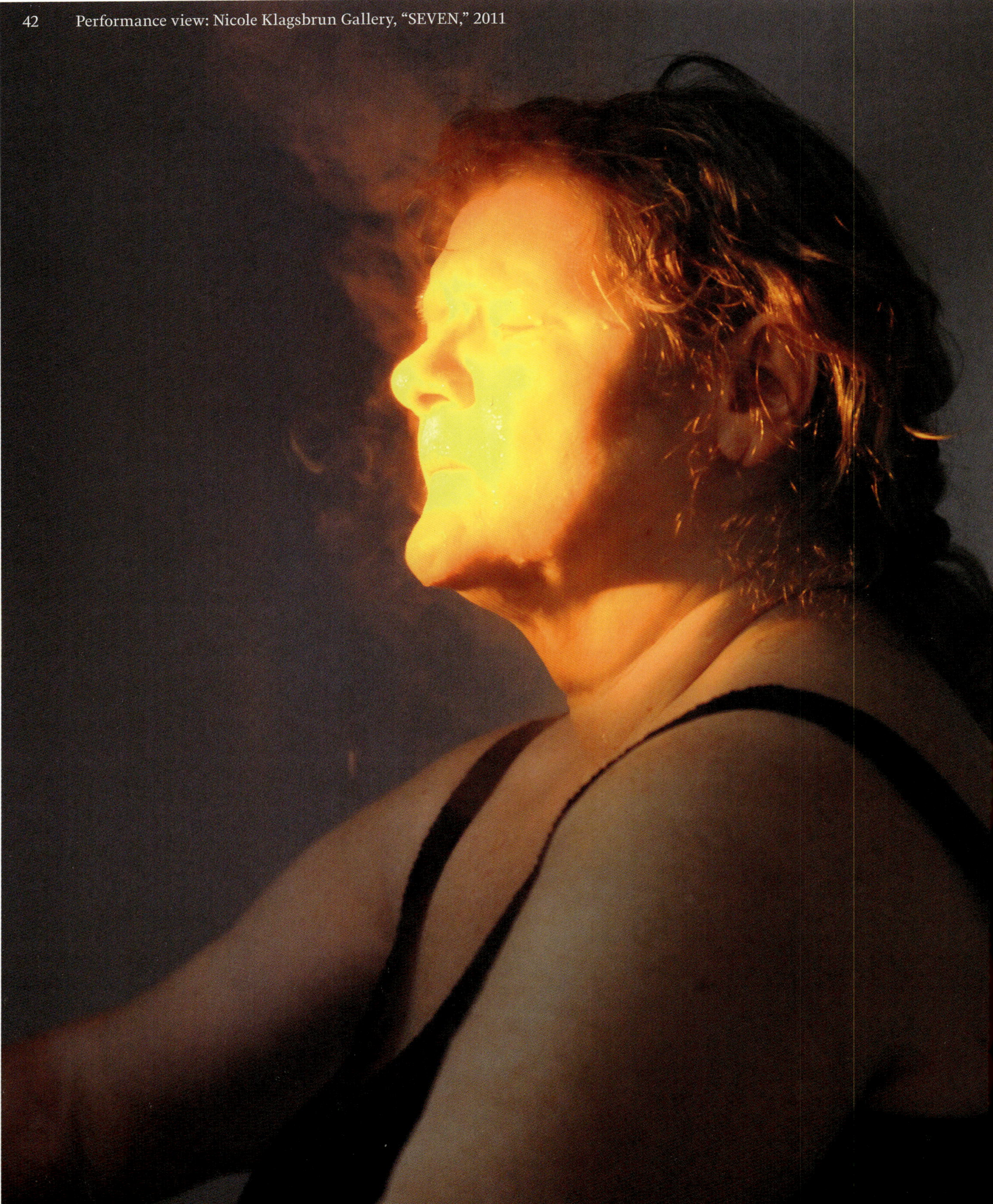

Performance view: Nicole Klagsbrun Gallery, "SEVEN," 2011

seven

A collaboration with Jon Kessler

CB: Your work in all media—video, sculpture, drawing—has a determinedly hand-crafted quality. Why is this important to you?

MR: *SEVEN* is a collaboration with Jon Kessler. When you see his crazy makeshift contraptions, it's clear why the hand-crafted quality is important. My contraptions have a homemade quality, too, and our collaboration made sense around this shared aesthetic and attitude. For me, the homemade quality is important because it brings back the human touch to objects. Industry wants to remove the hand from the product because you don't want to be reminded of how many people touched, either mentally or physically, the product you are using. You also want to think of yourself as the owner of it. Too much "hand" by others will make you question your ownership.

Left to right, details of Mika Rottenberg and Jon Kessler, *SEVEN (Sunita)*, *SEVEN (Jason)*, *SEVEN (Alex)*, *SEVEN (Juan)*, *SEVEN (Cecil)*, *SEVEN (Marshall)*, *SEVEN (Chris)*, 2012

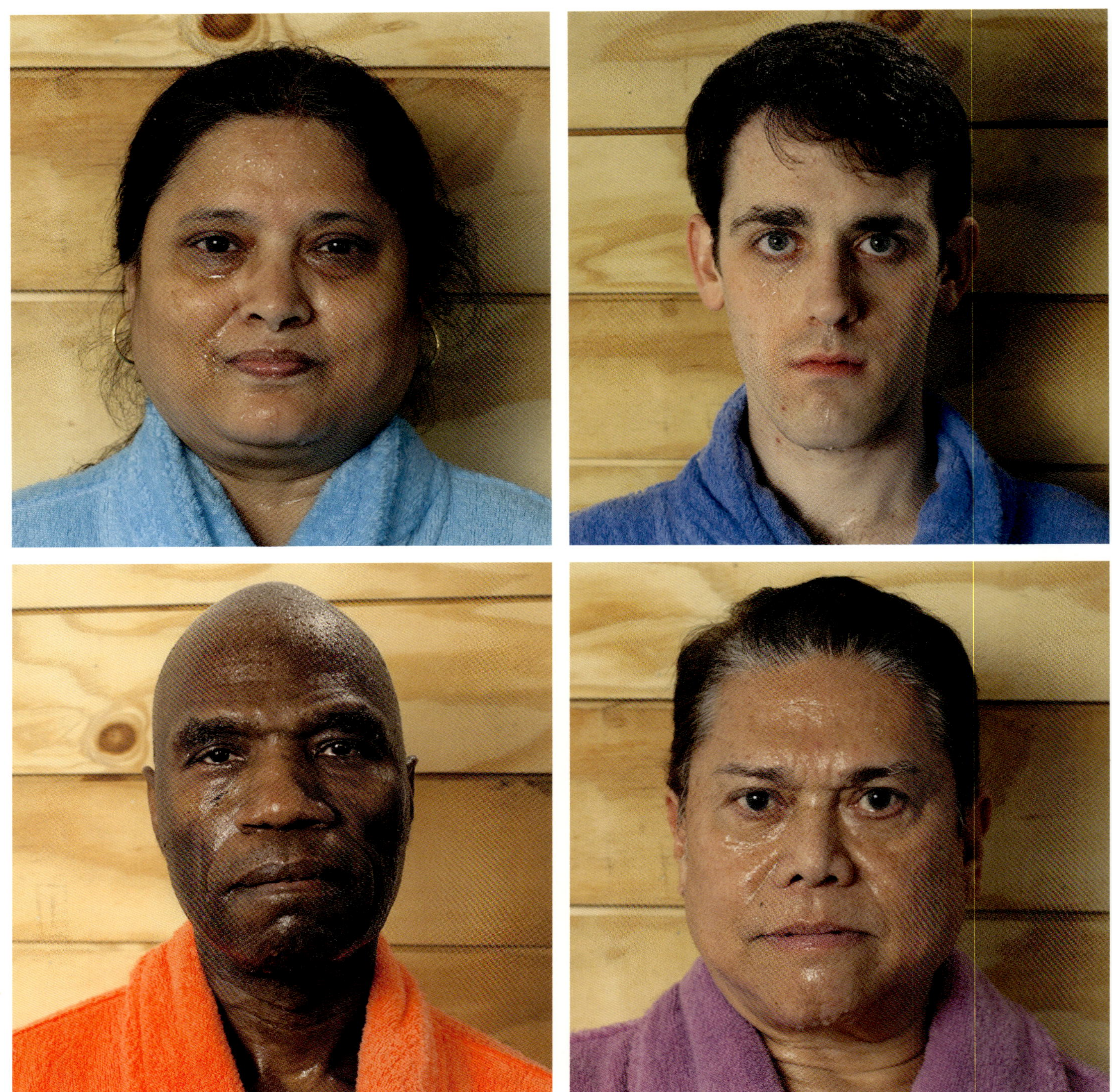

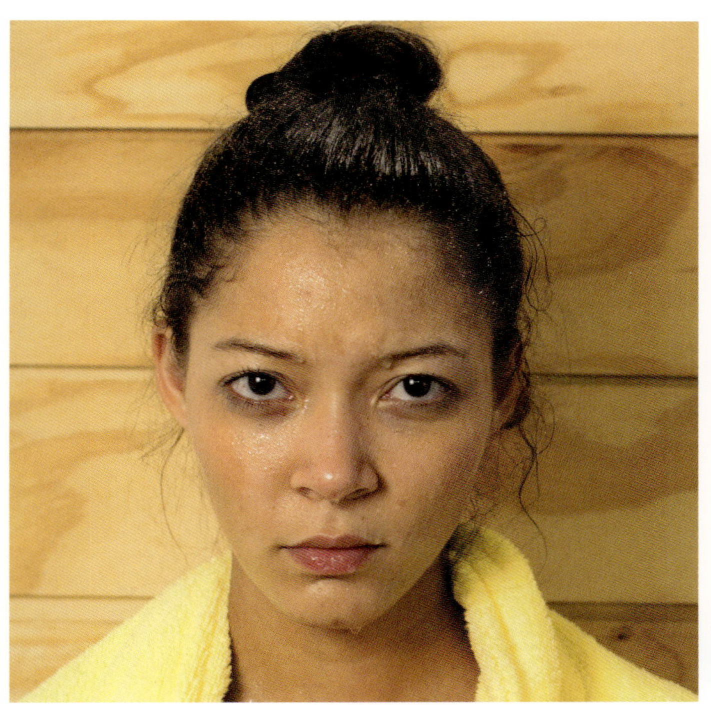

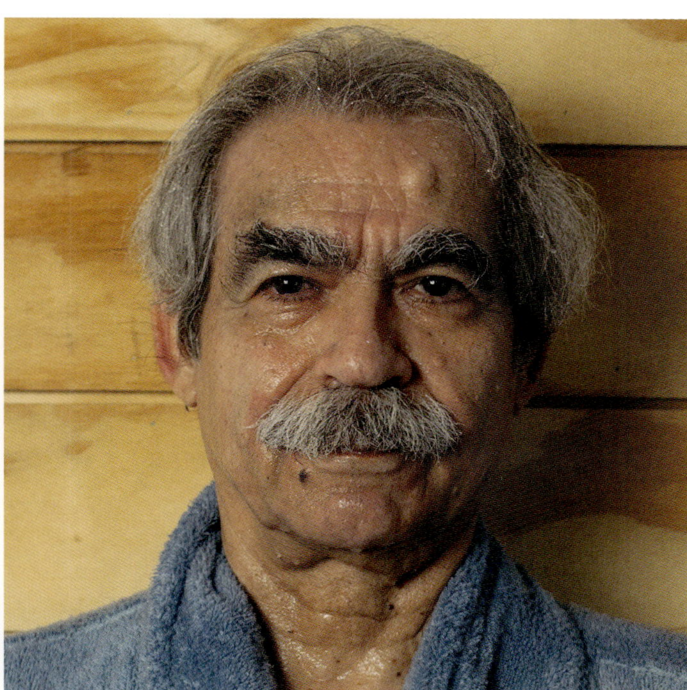

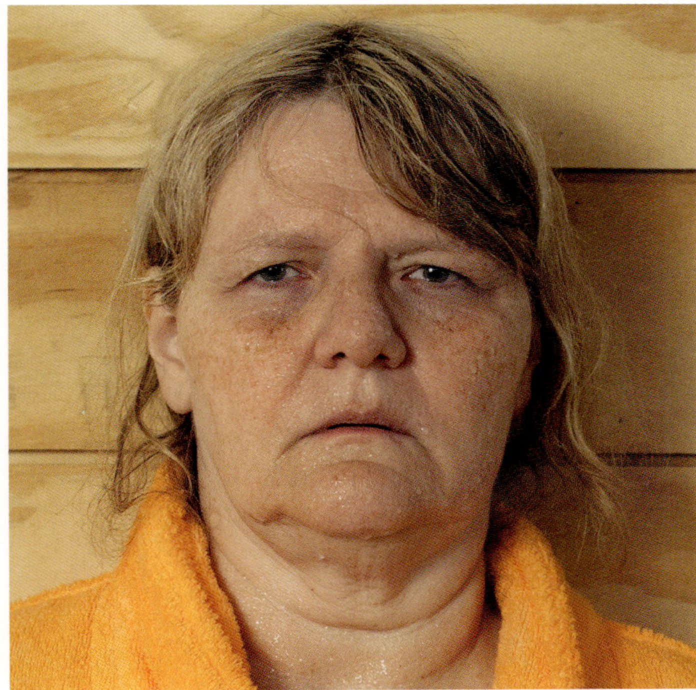

 Performance view: Nicole Klagsbrun Gallery, "SEVEN," 2011

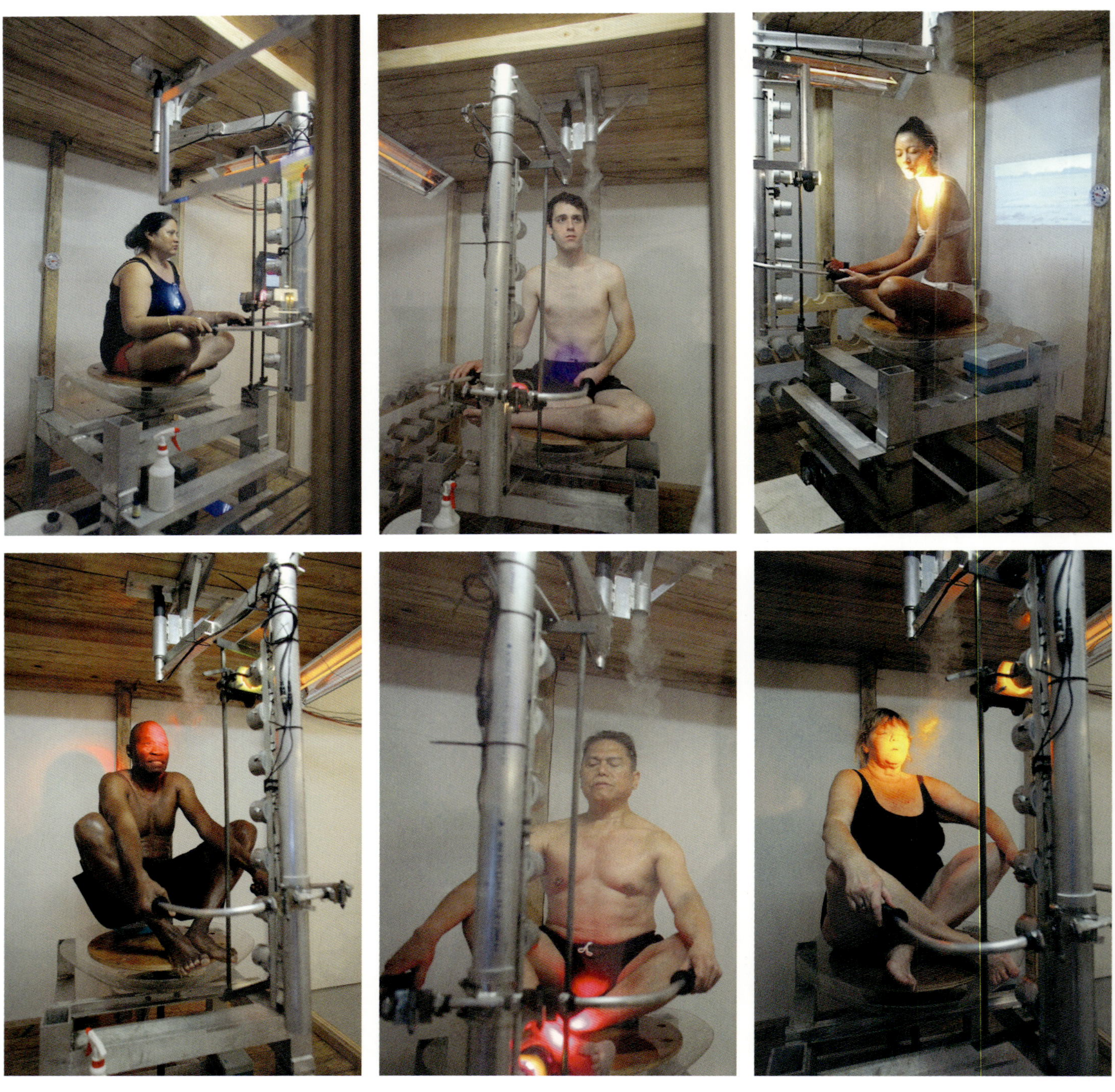

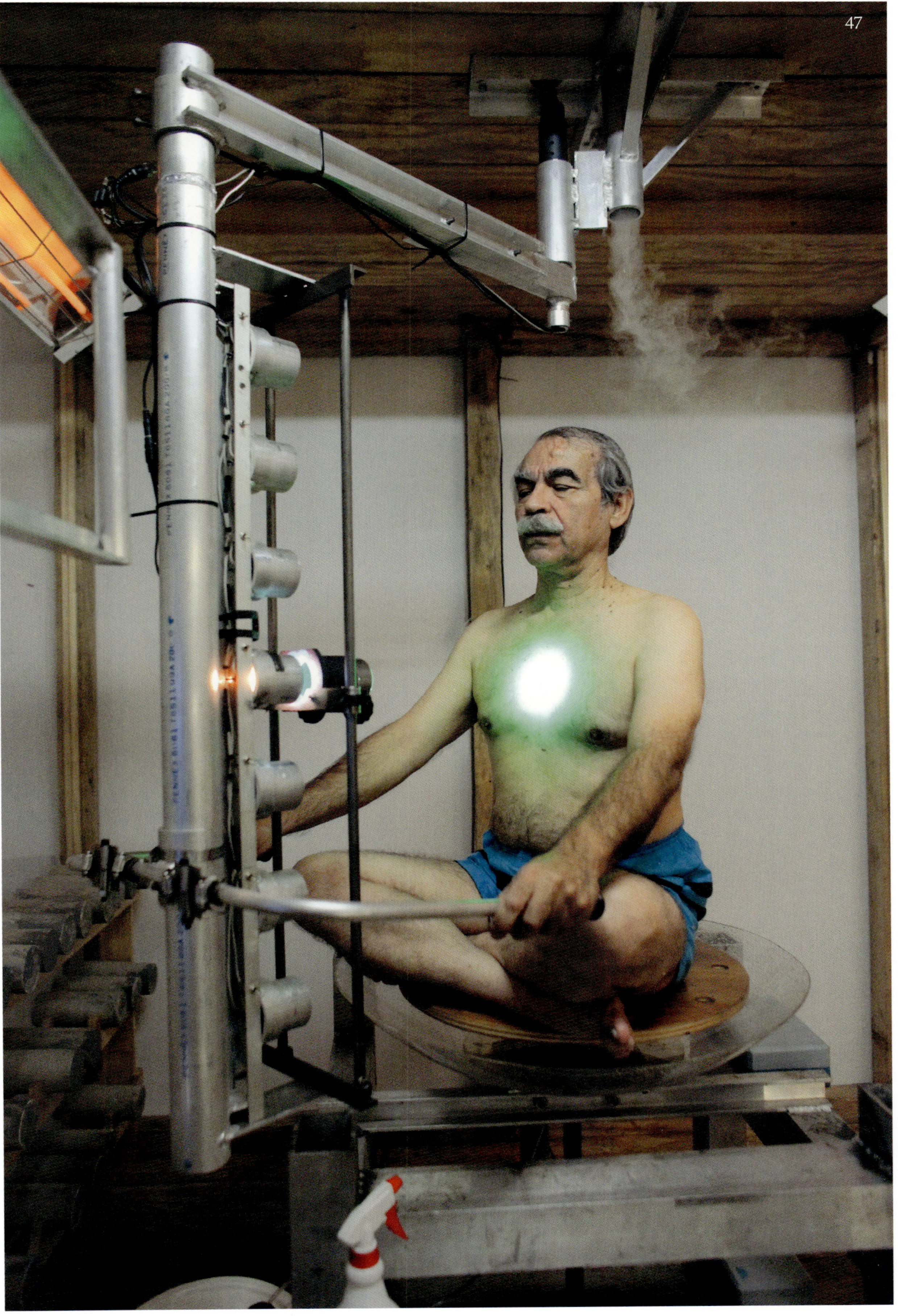

 Performance view: Nicole Klagsbrun Gallery, “SEVEN,” 2011

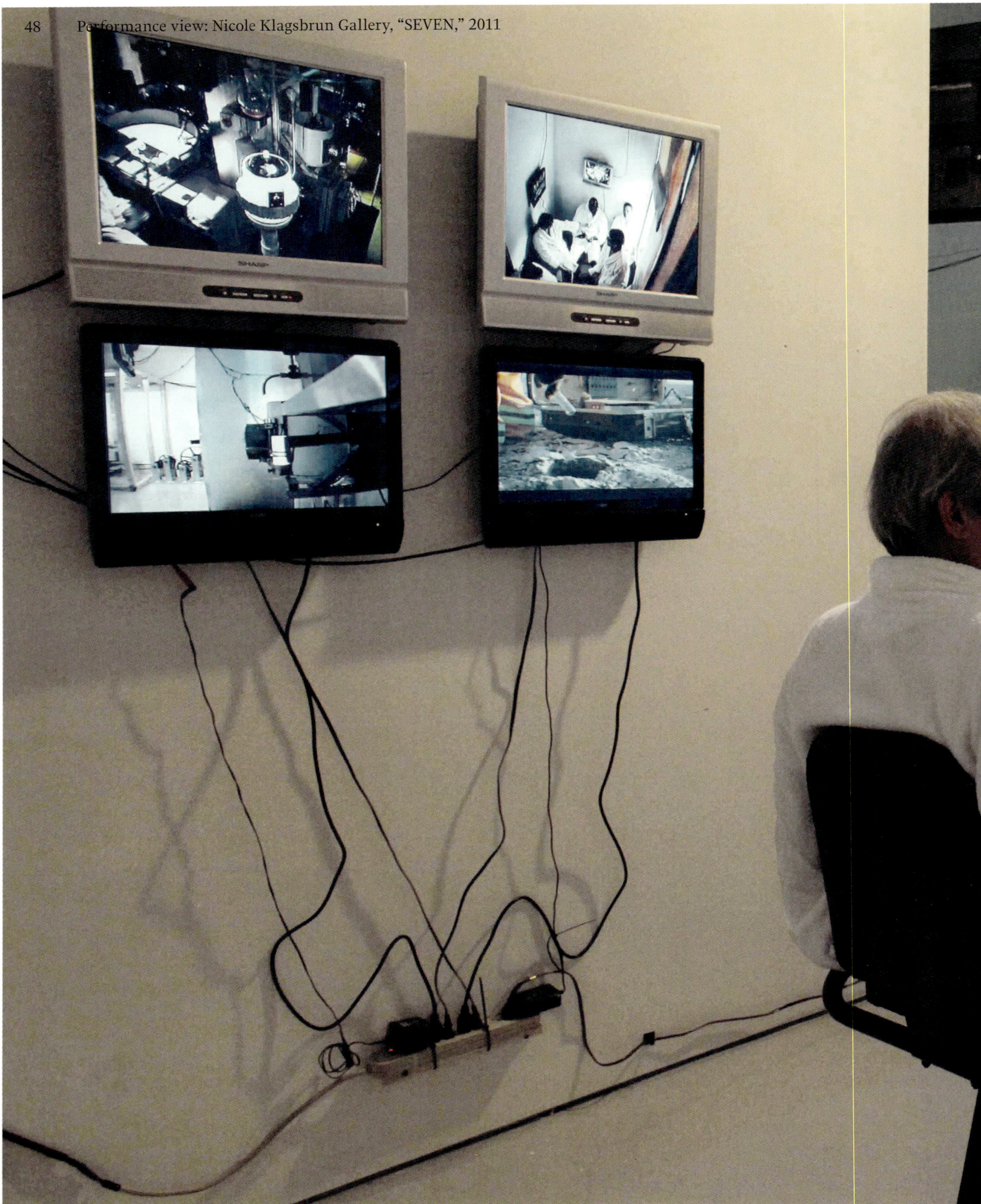

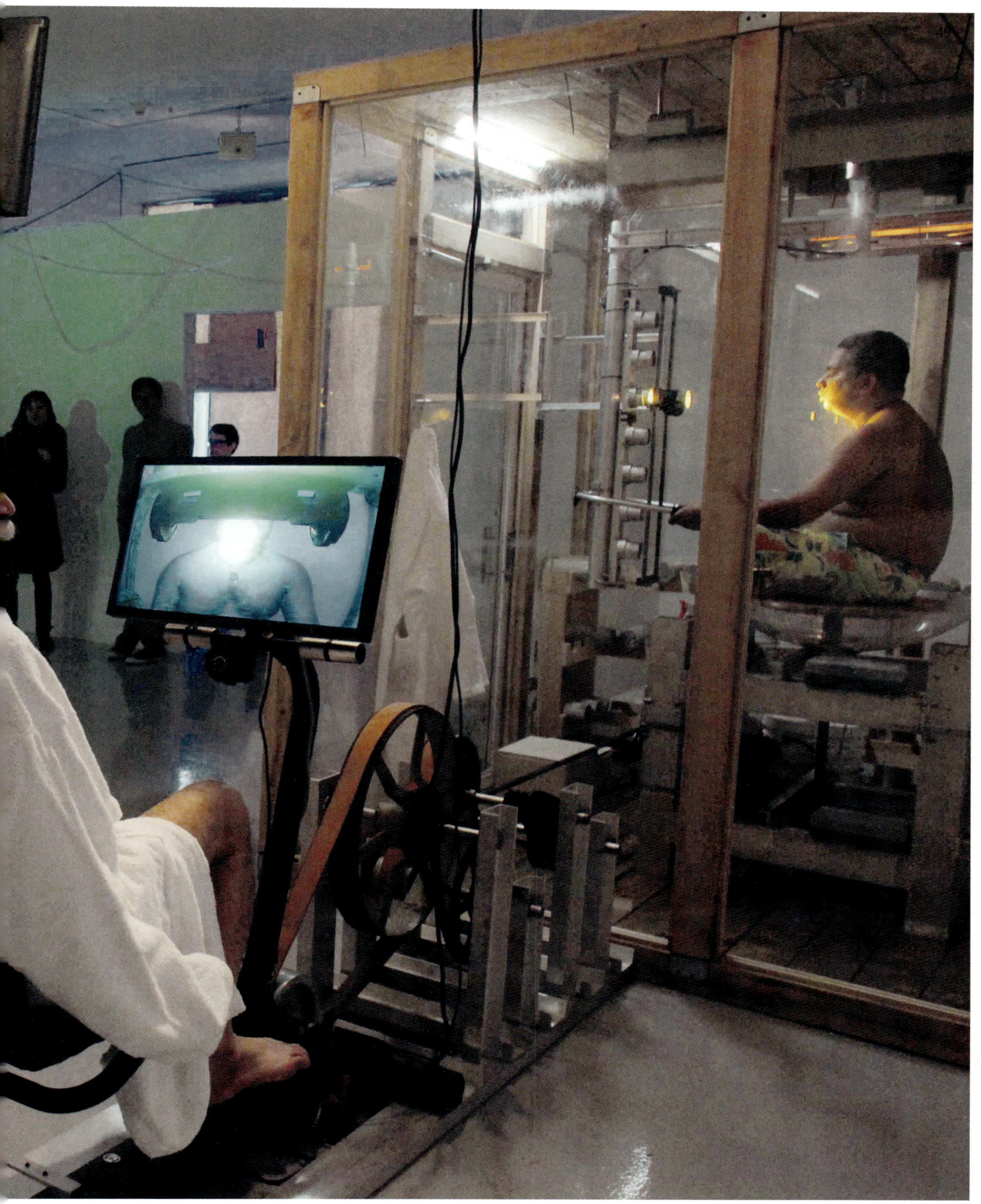

 Performance view: Nicole Klagsbrun Gallery, "SEVEN," 2011

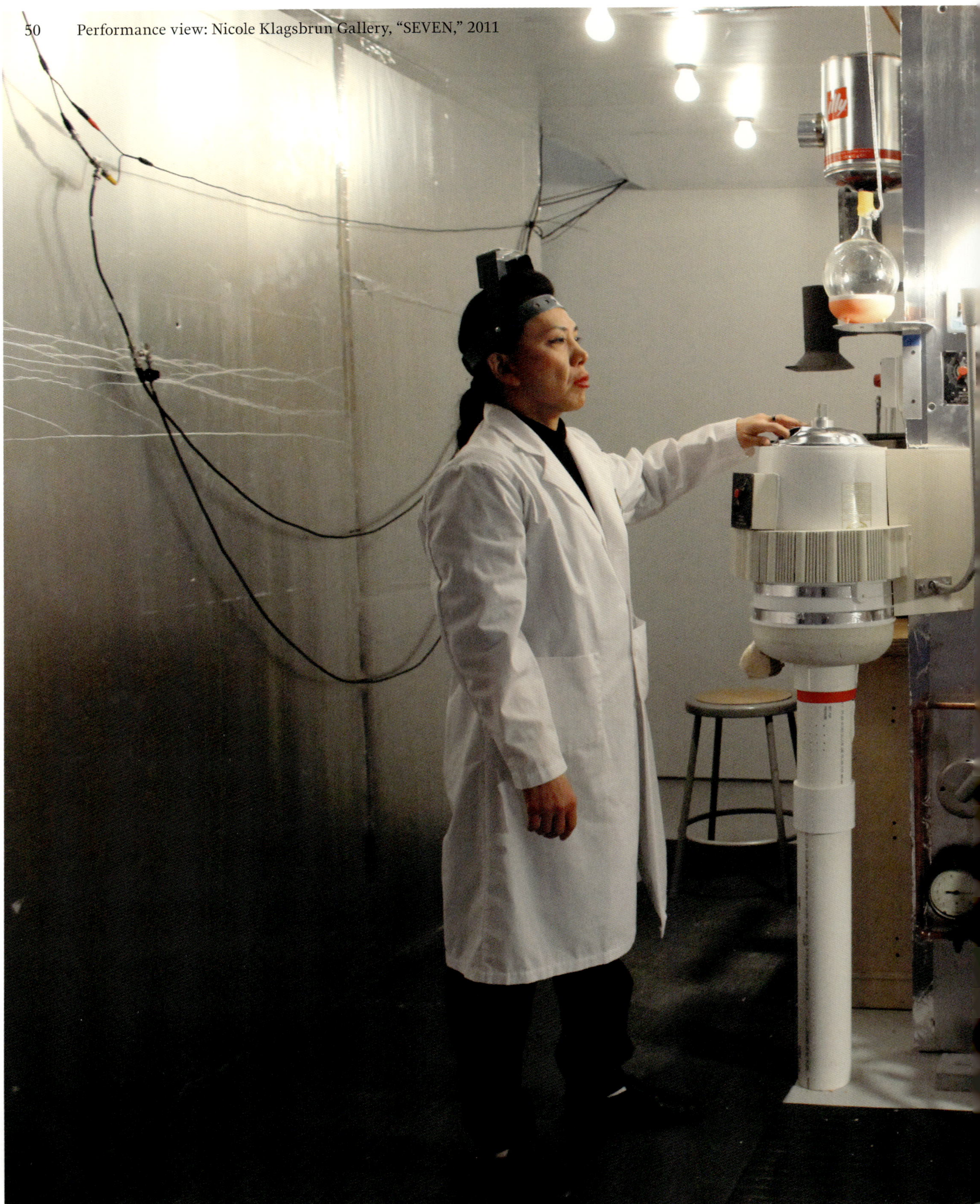

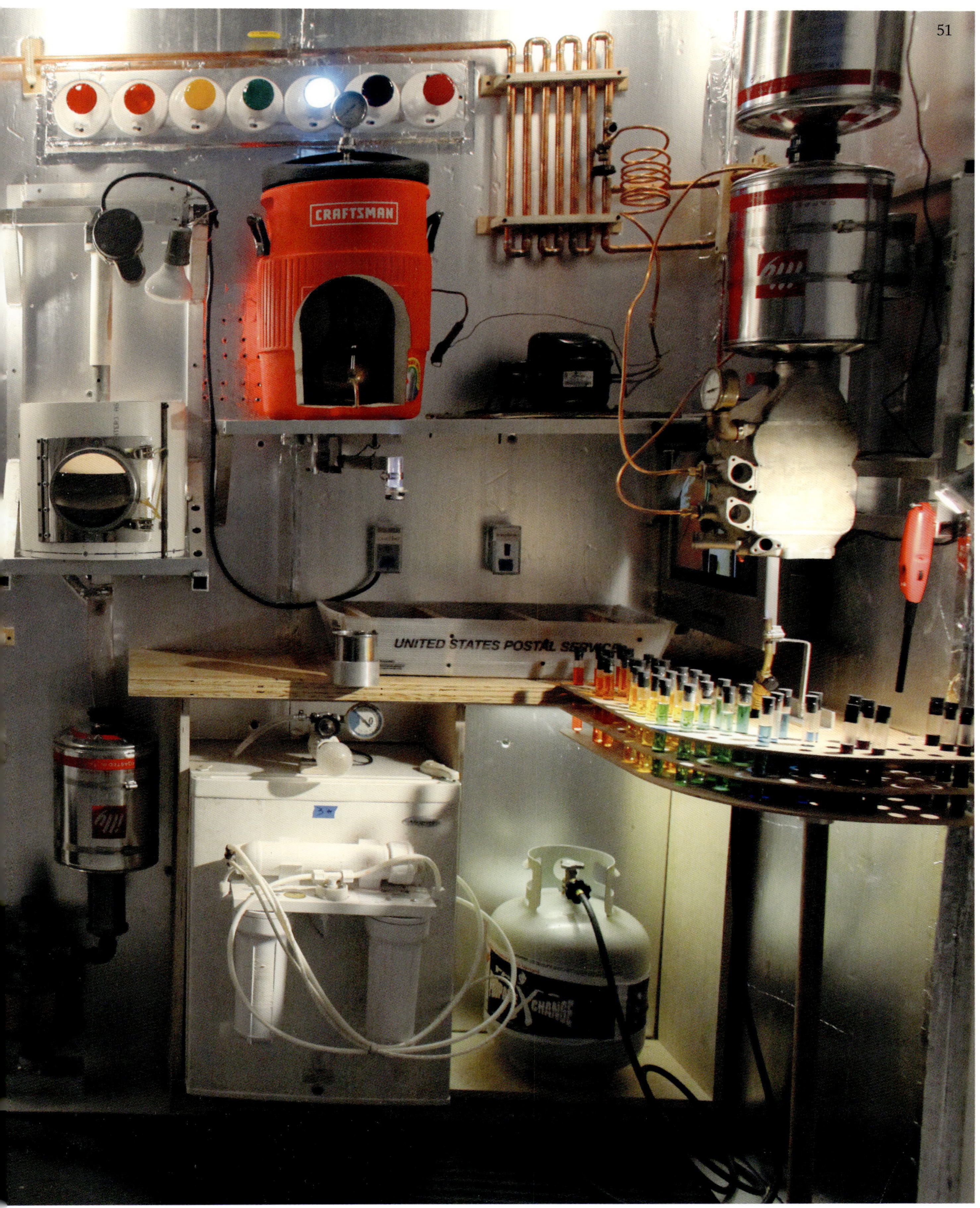
CRAFTSMAN
UNITED STATES POSTAL SERVICE
illy
EXCHANGE

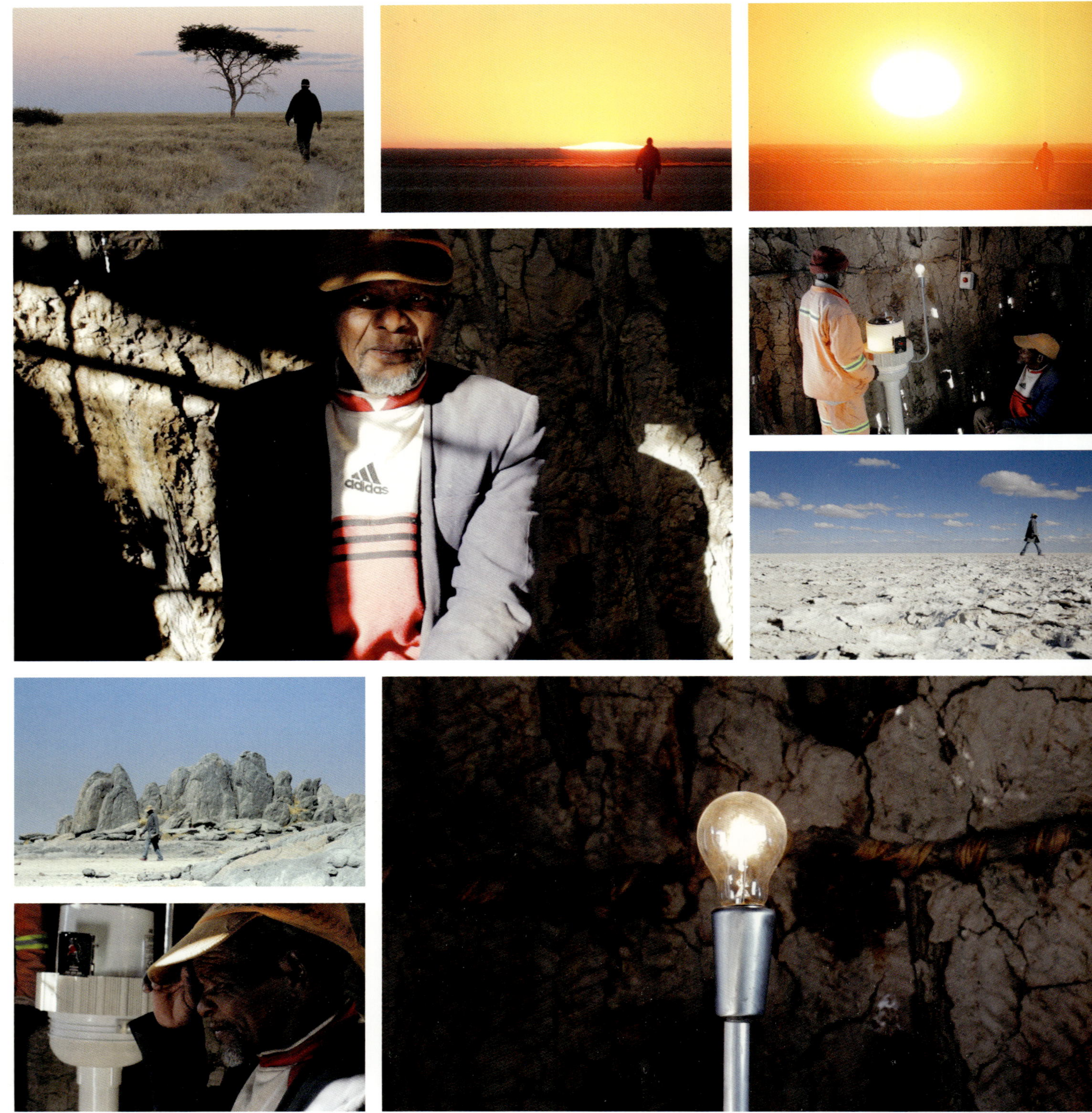
adidas

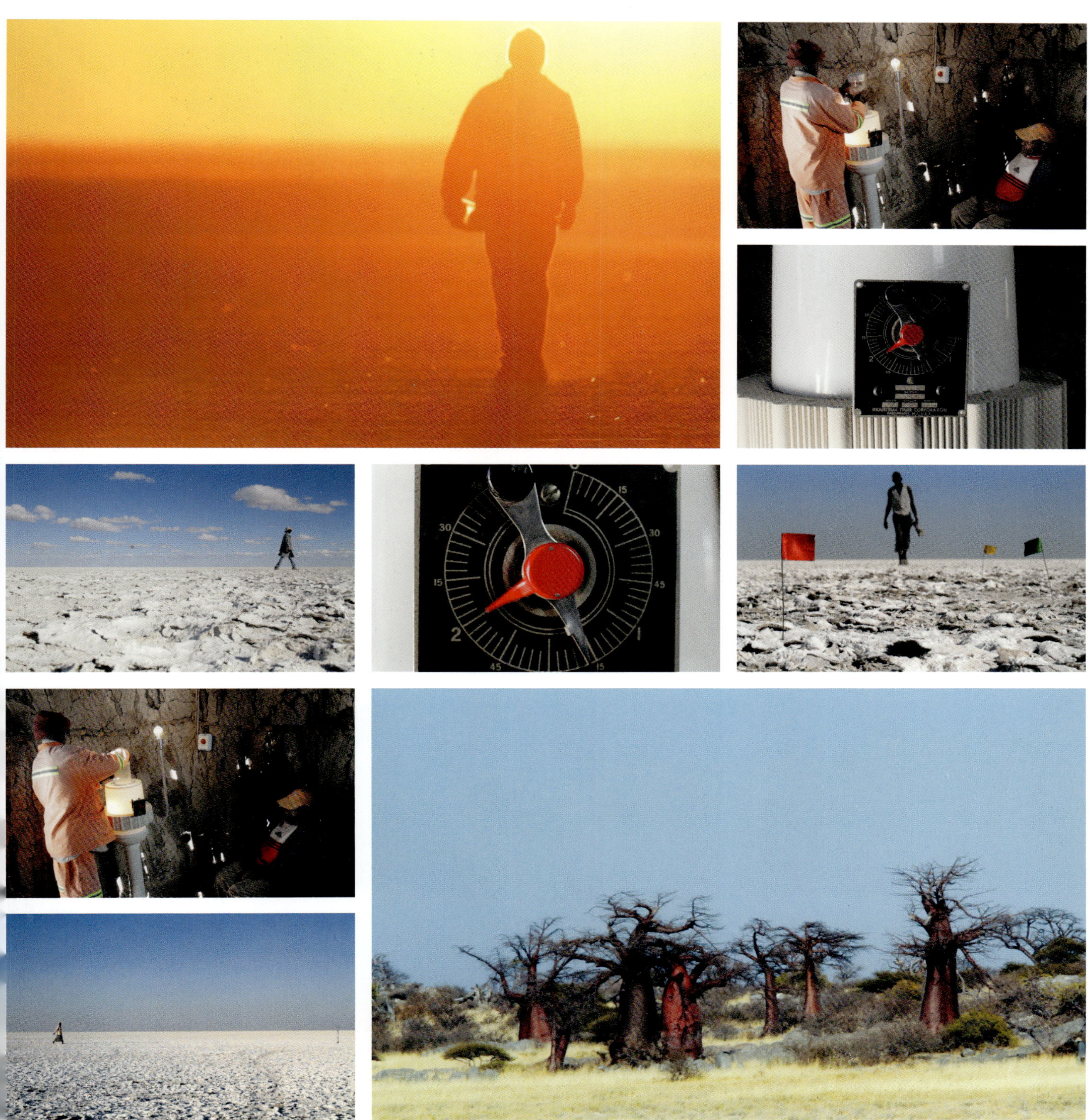
INDUSTRIAL TIMER CORPORATION
15
30
30
15
45
2
1
45
15

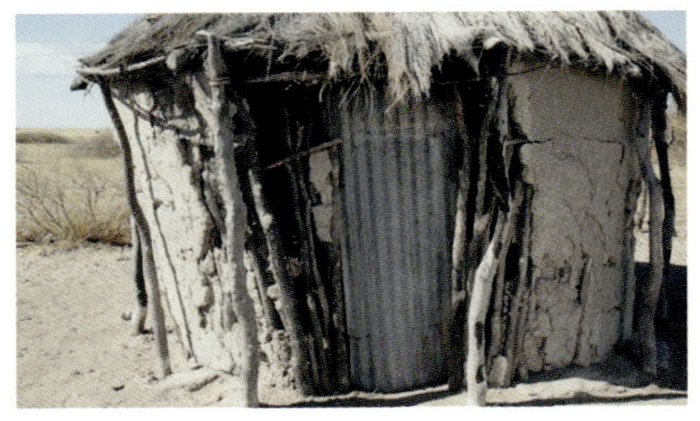

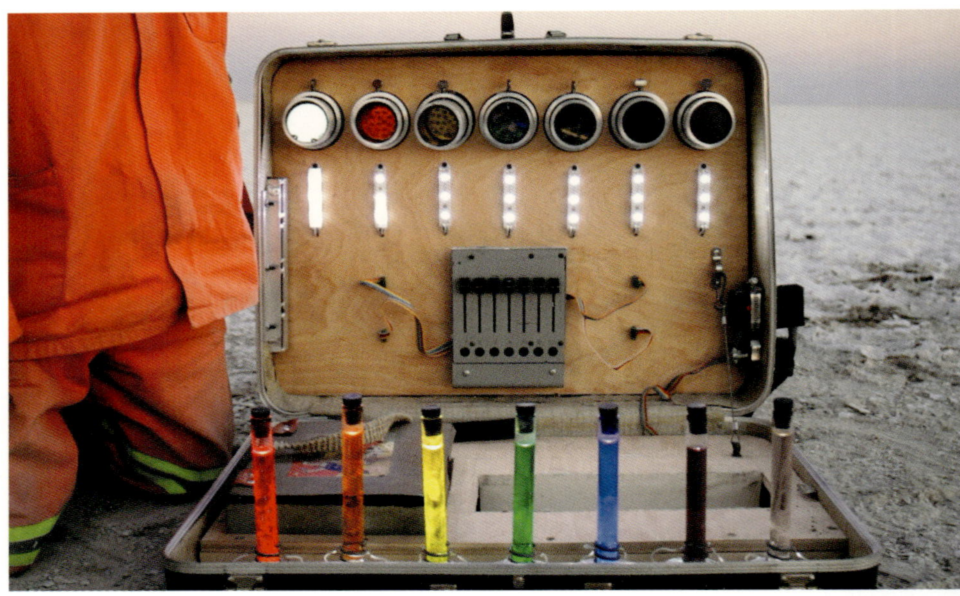

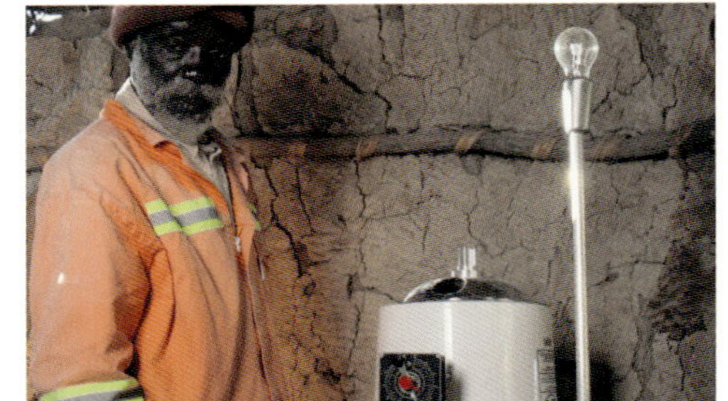

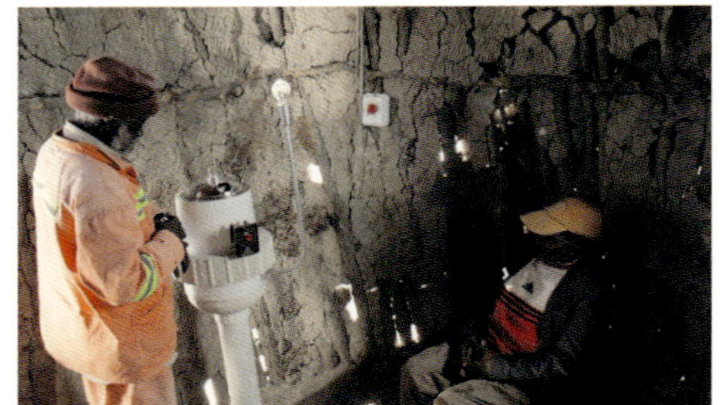

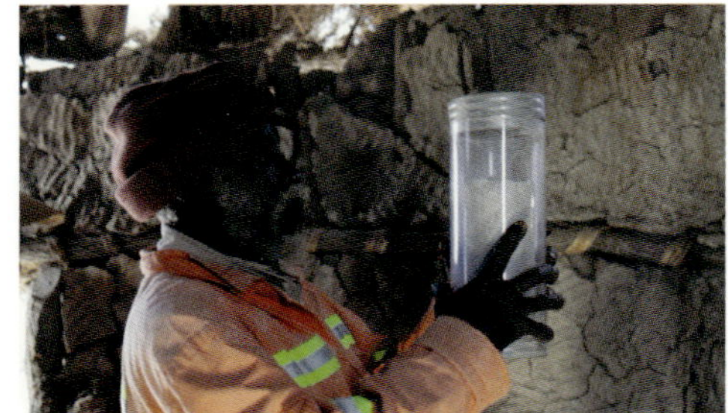

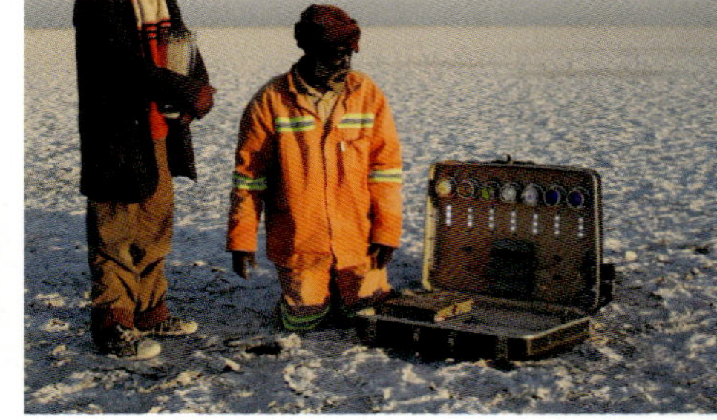

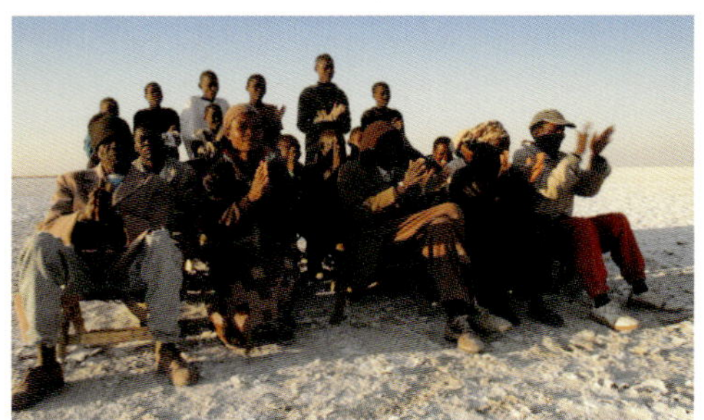

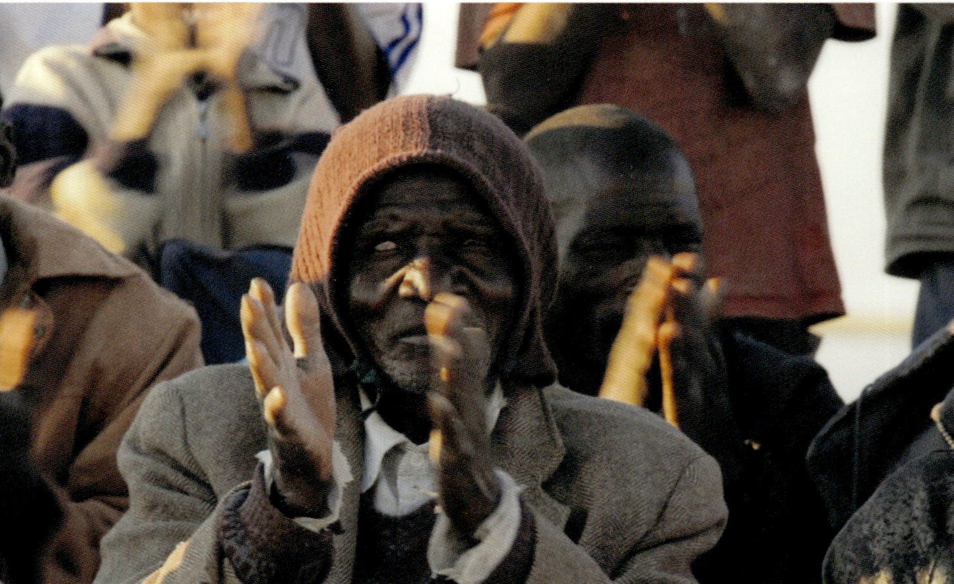

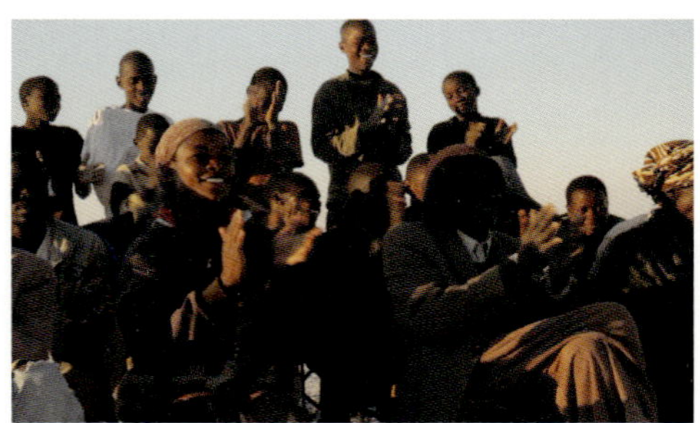

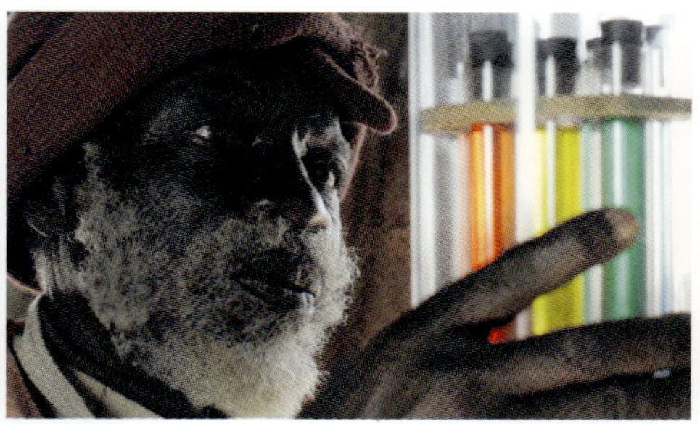

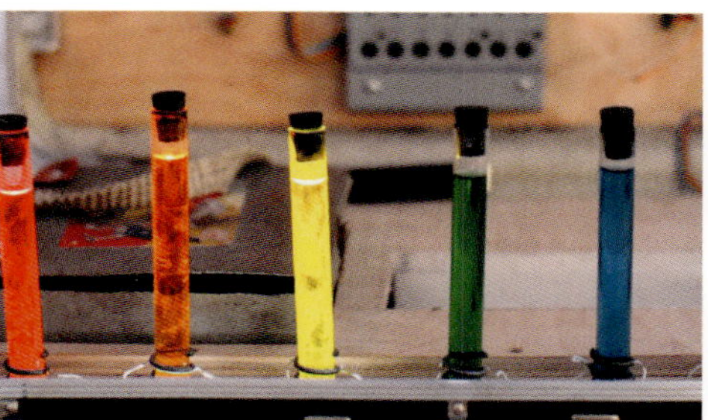

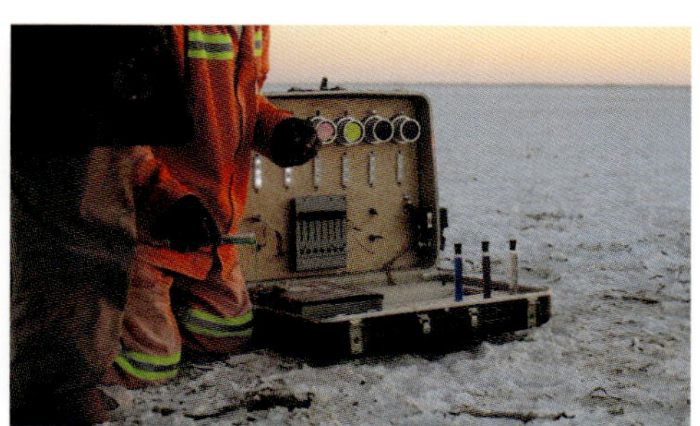

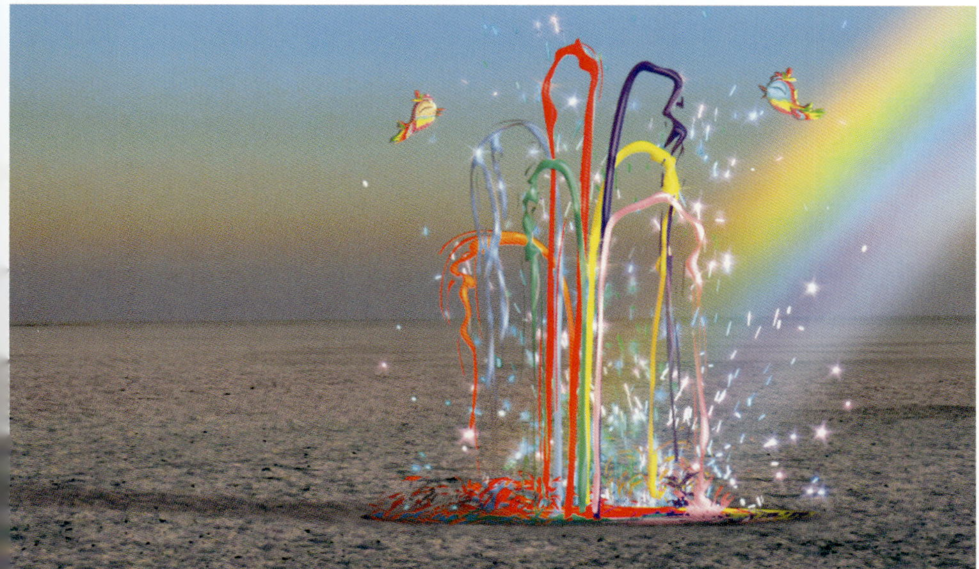

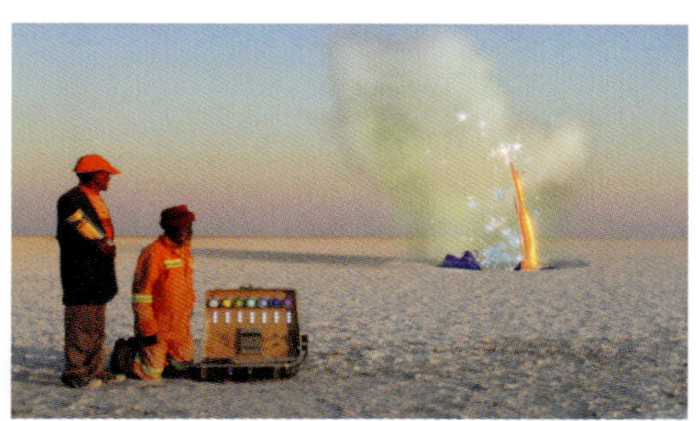

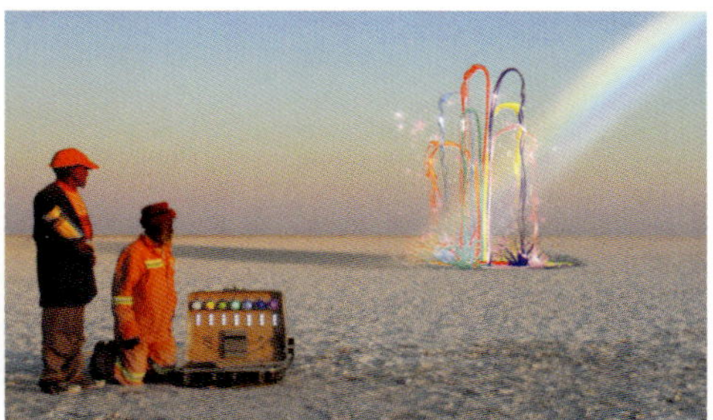

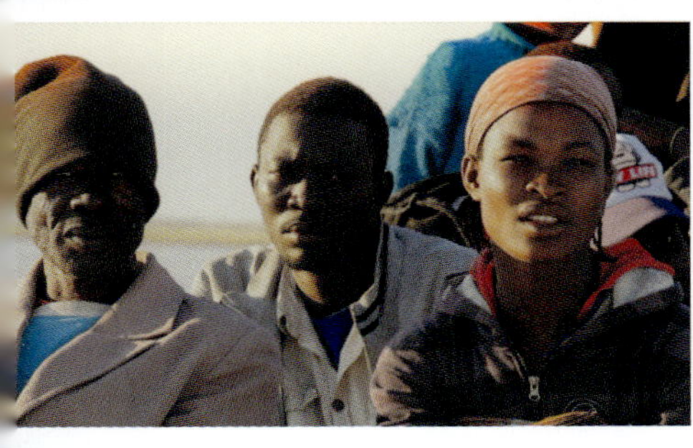

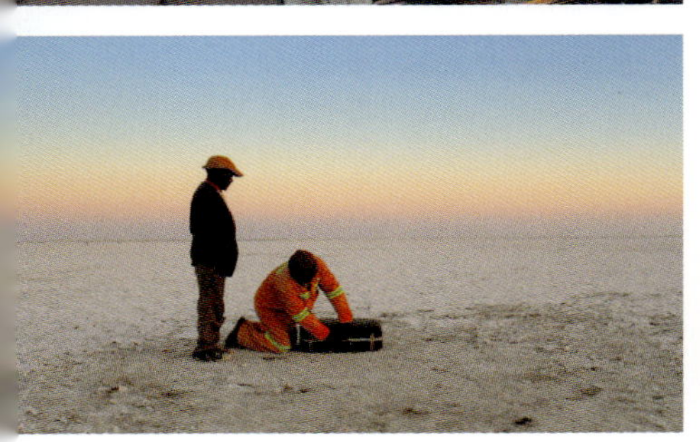

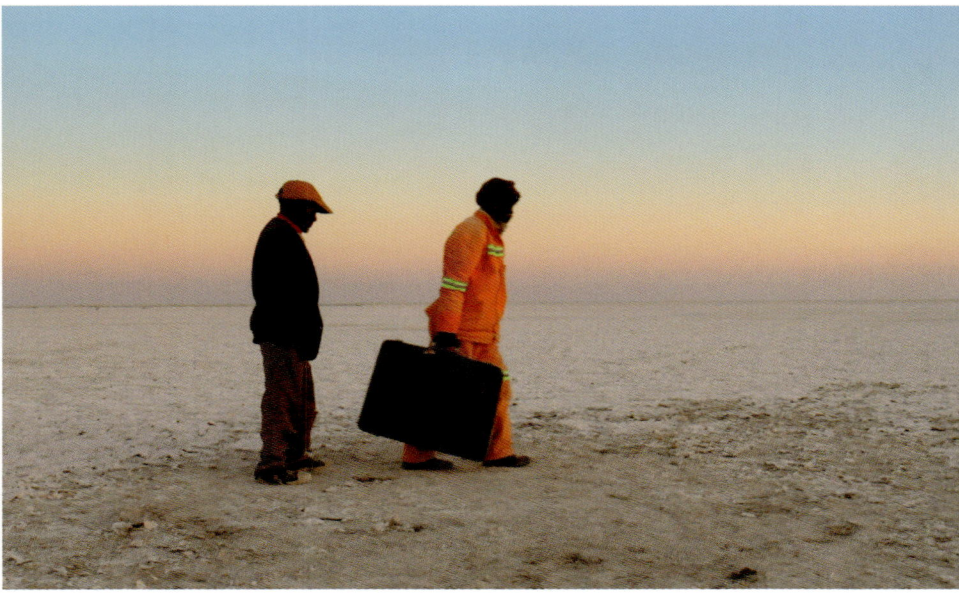

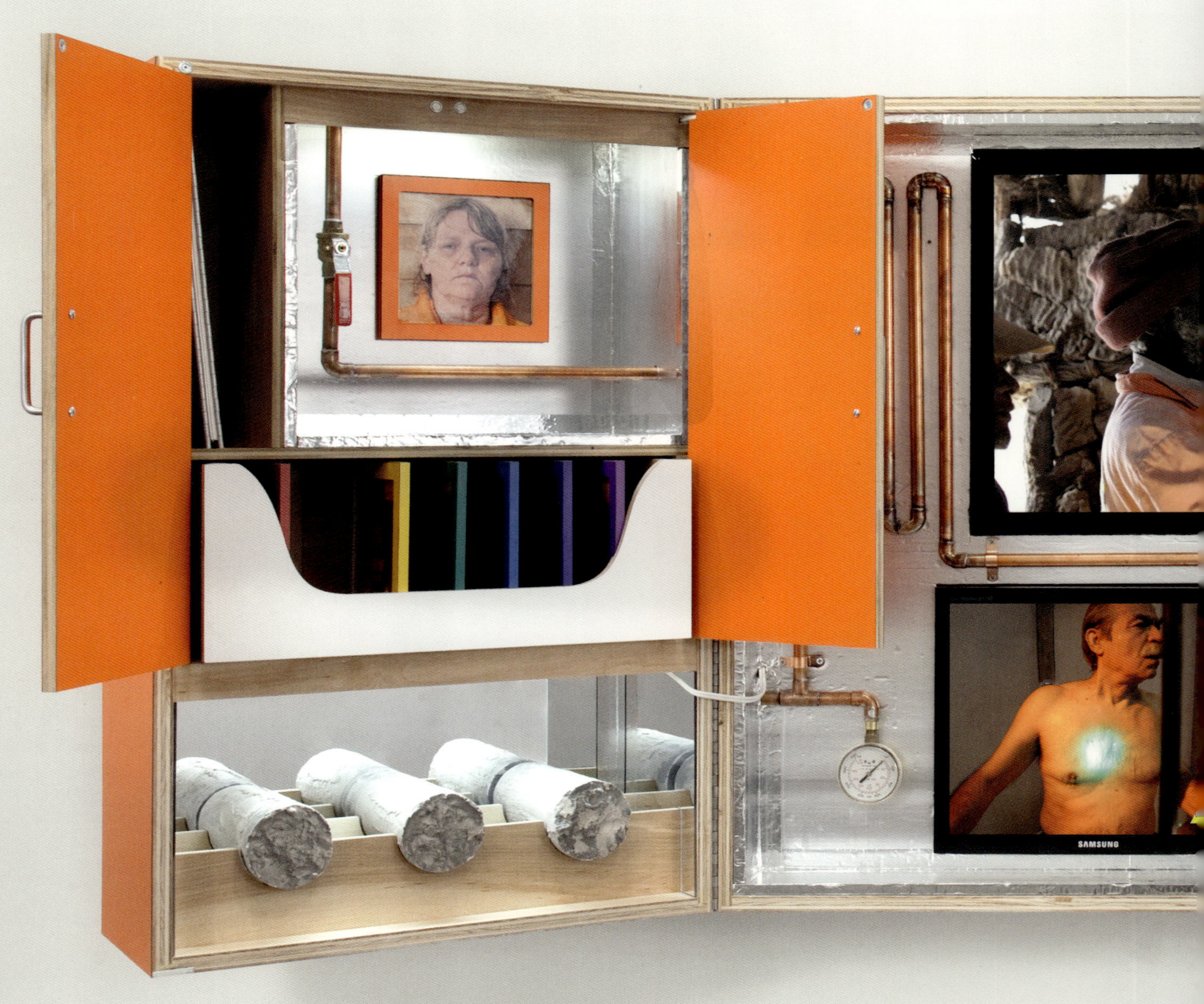
SAMSUNG

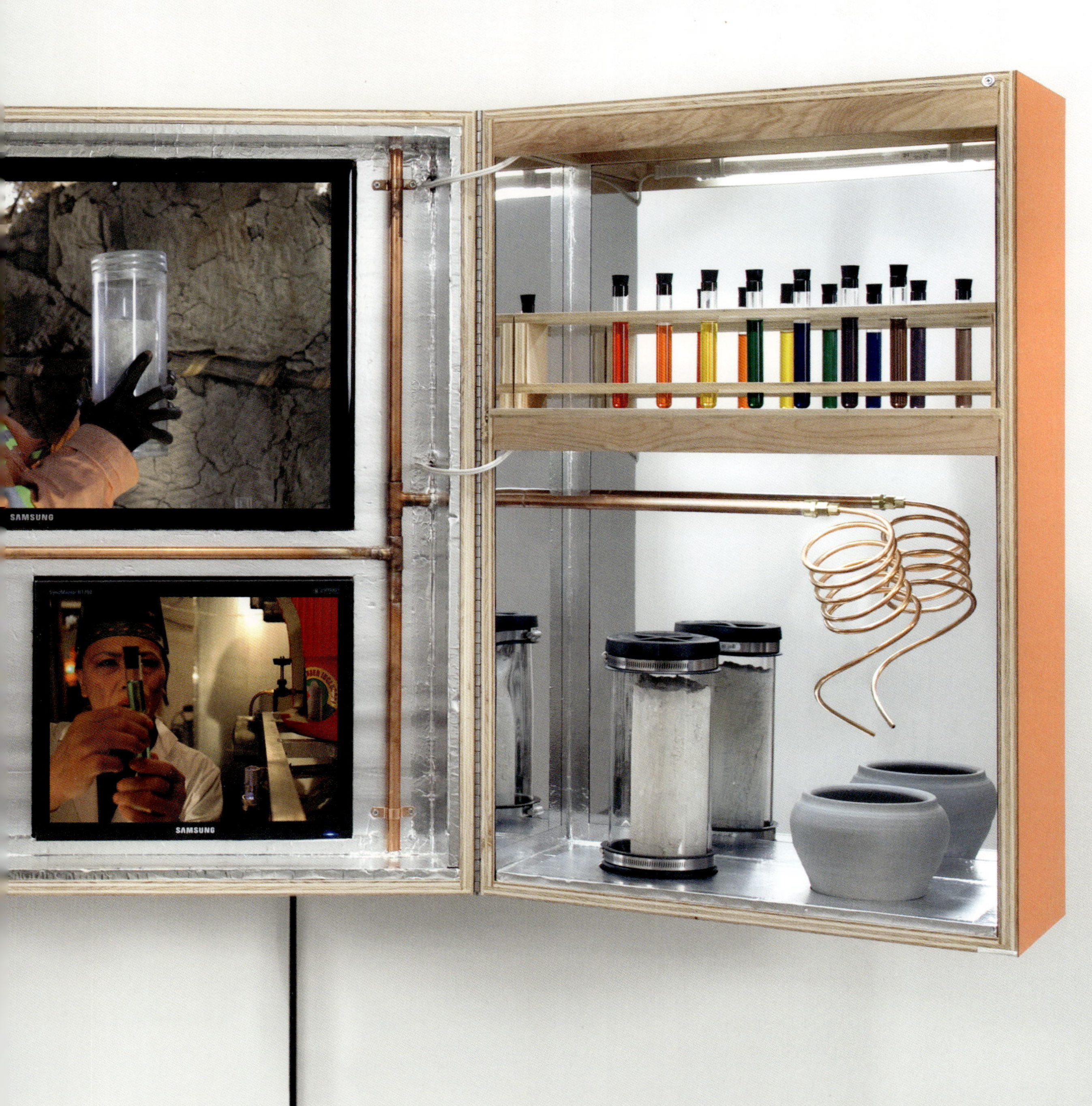
SAMSUNG
SAMSUNG

Closed view: *SEVEN (Chris)*, 2011

Preparatory drawing for *Squeeze*, 2010

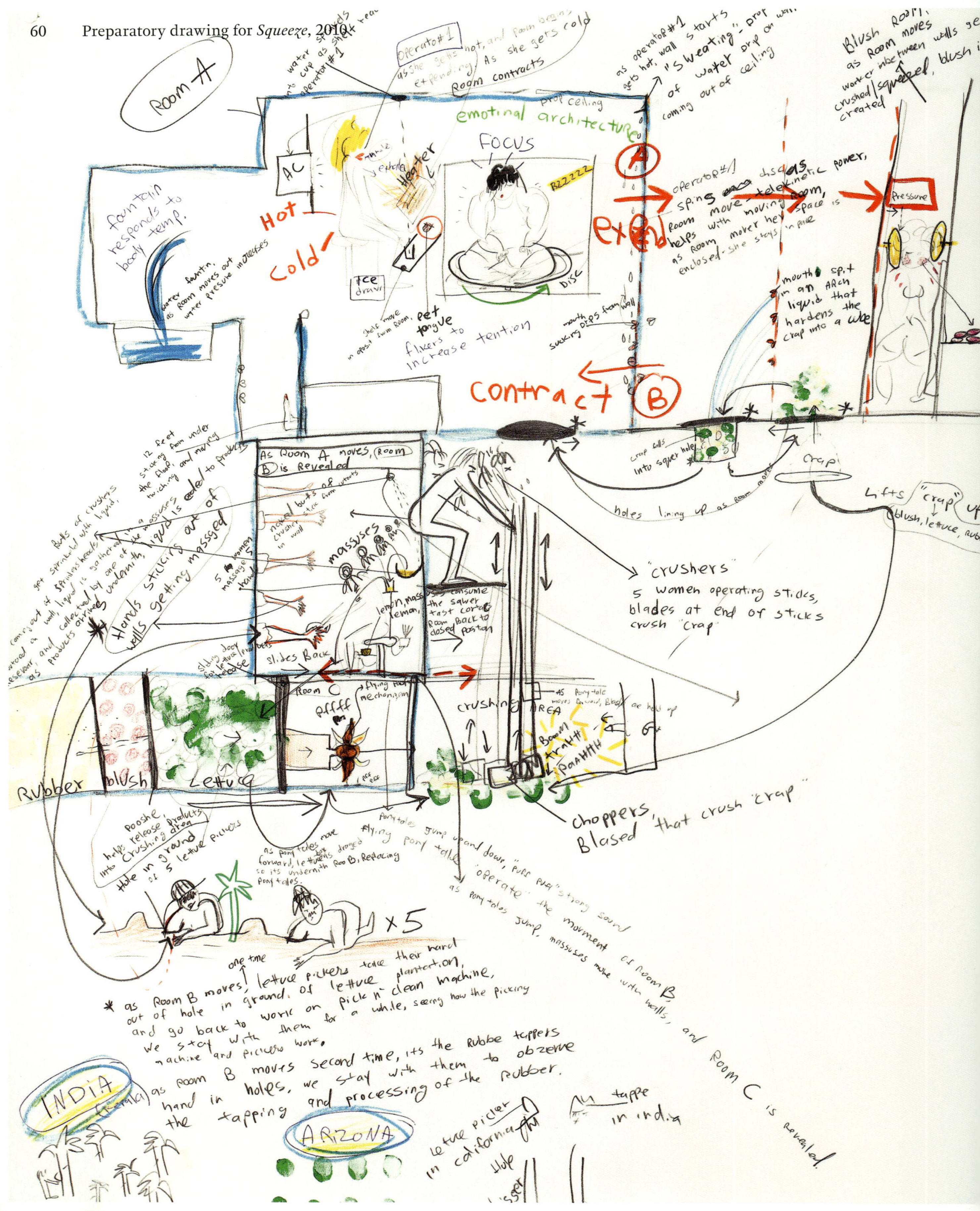

squeeze

CB: Watching *Squeeze* evokes the experience of observing a production line in action. People and things are modified by one mechanism before being passed on to the next. What is being produced in *Squeeze*?

MR: Value is being produced in *Squeeze*. Physical reactions are being produced. Energy is being produced. All these formless things materialize and take the shape of a small sculpture: a one square-foot cube that you never completely see. I removed the final objects and focused on the process alone. The video itself describes an architectural structure that connects locations around the world and collapses real spaces into psychological spaces. I use cinema to create a space that can only exist in a time-based medium, and I use a time-based medium to create a physical structure which you move through in space rather than time.

 Installation view: Mary Boone Gallery, "Squeeze," 2010

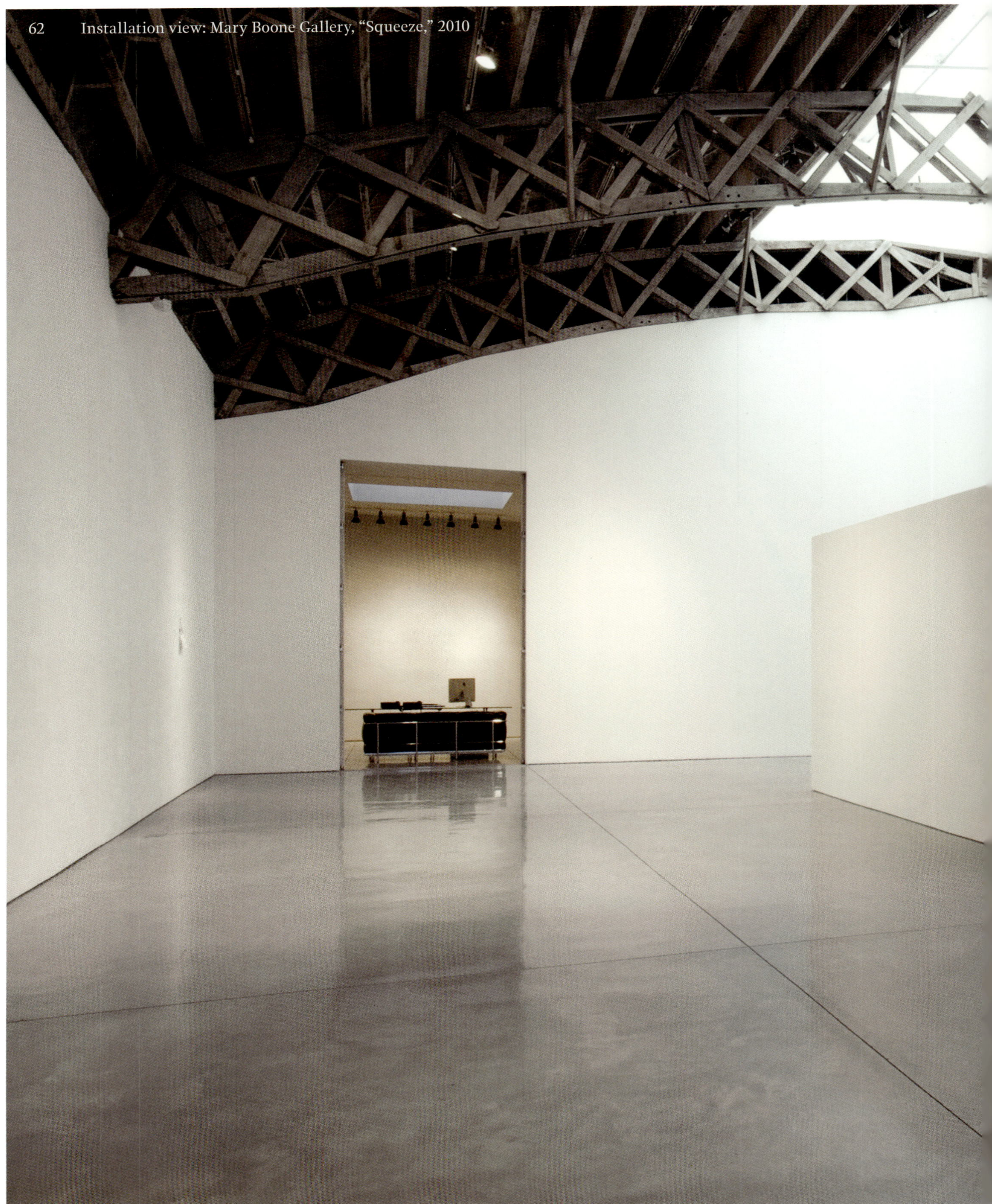

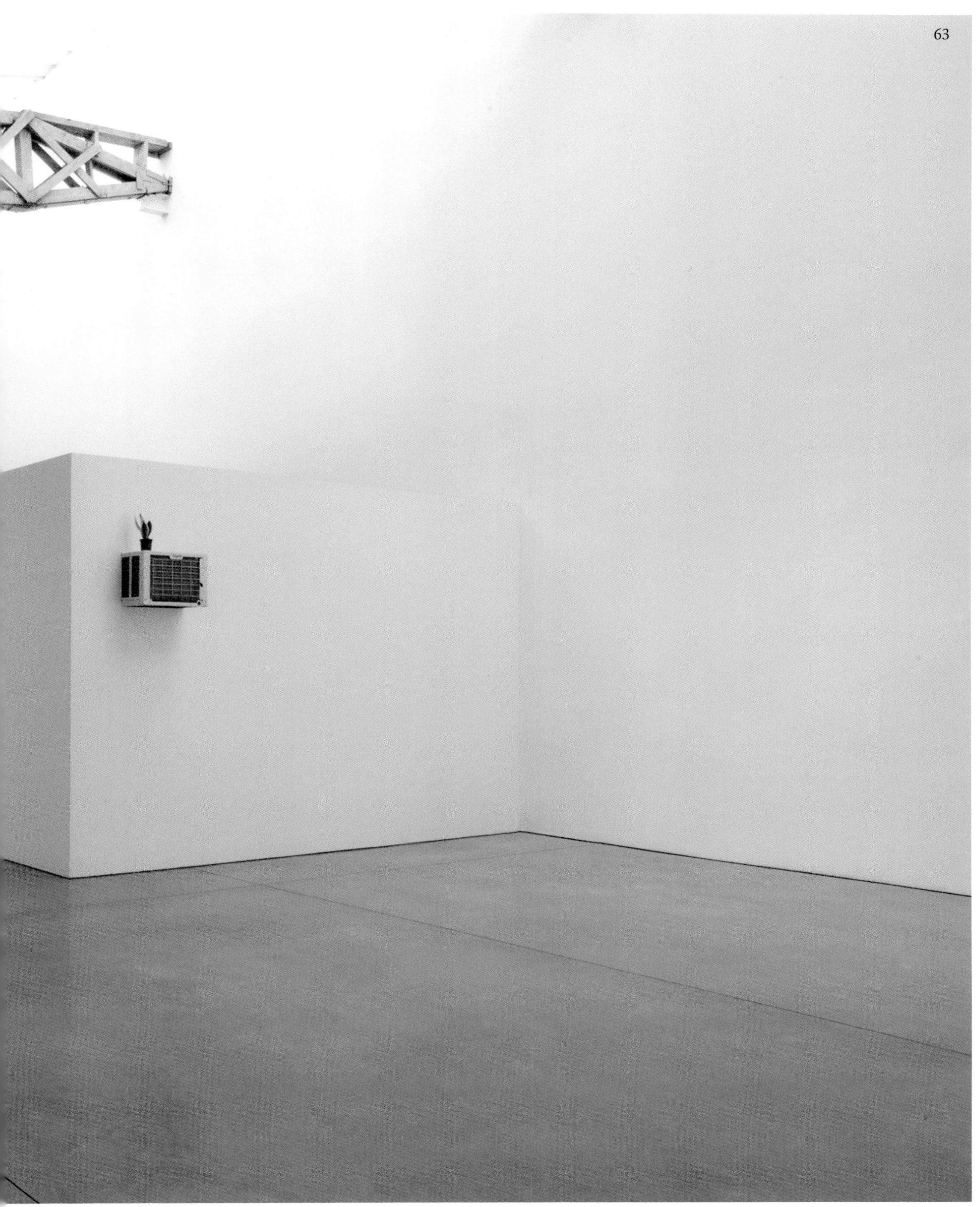

 Installation view: Mary Boone Gallery, "Squeeze," 2010

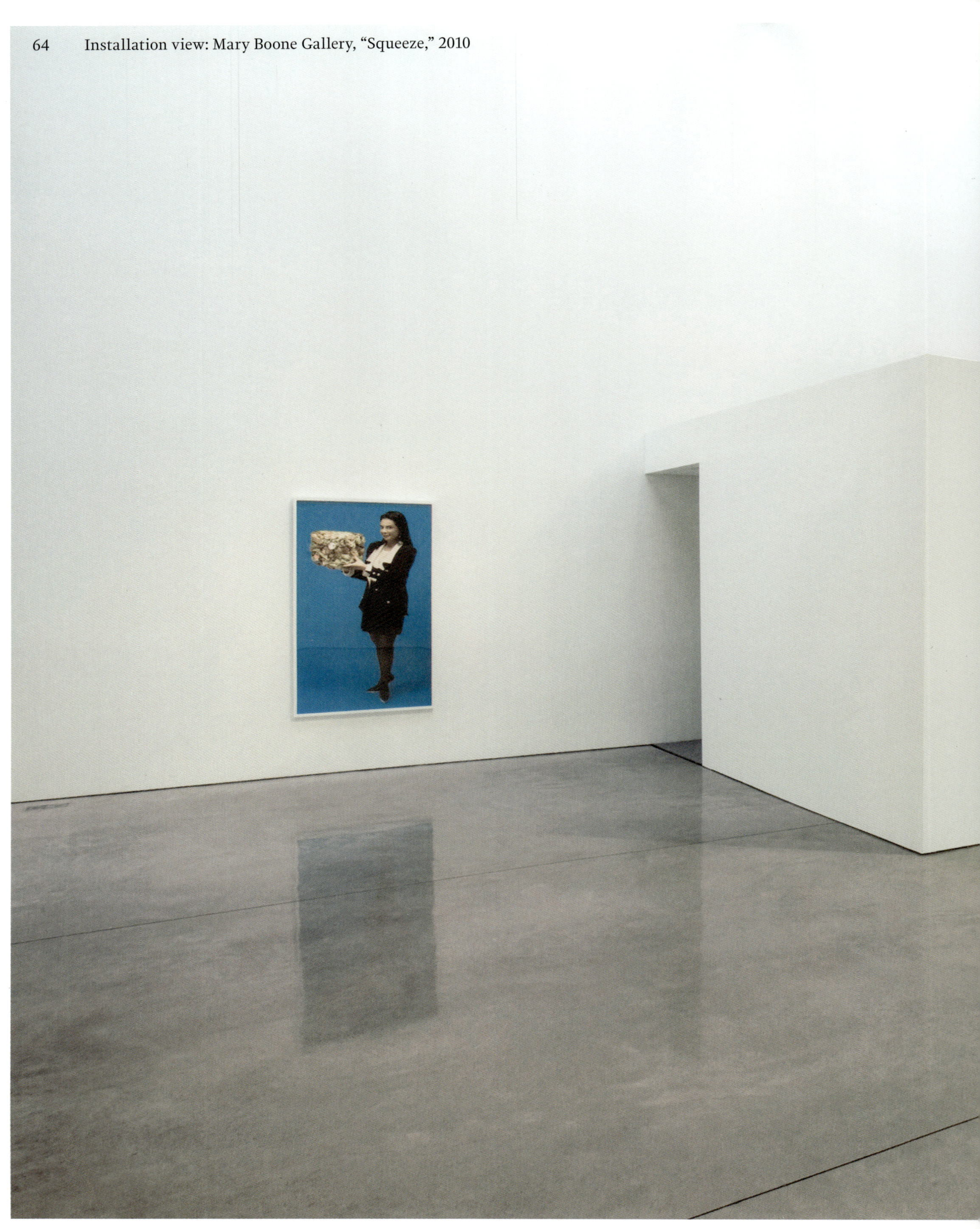

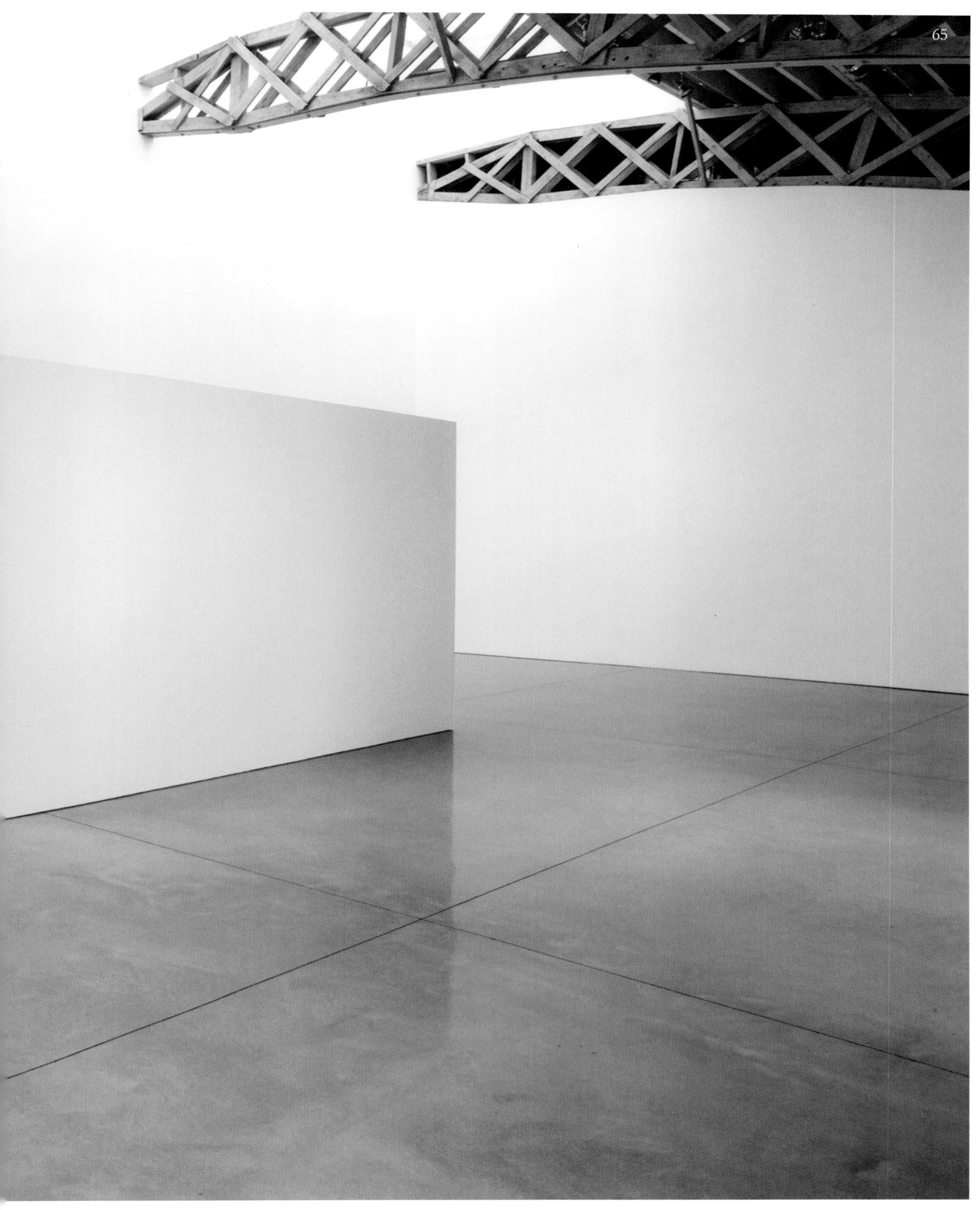

Installation view: *Tsss*, 2013 (Exhibition Version), The Israel Museum, "Squeeze: Video Works by Mika Rottenberg," 2013

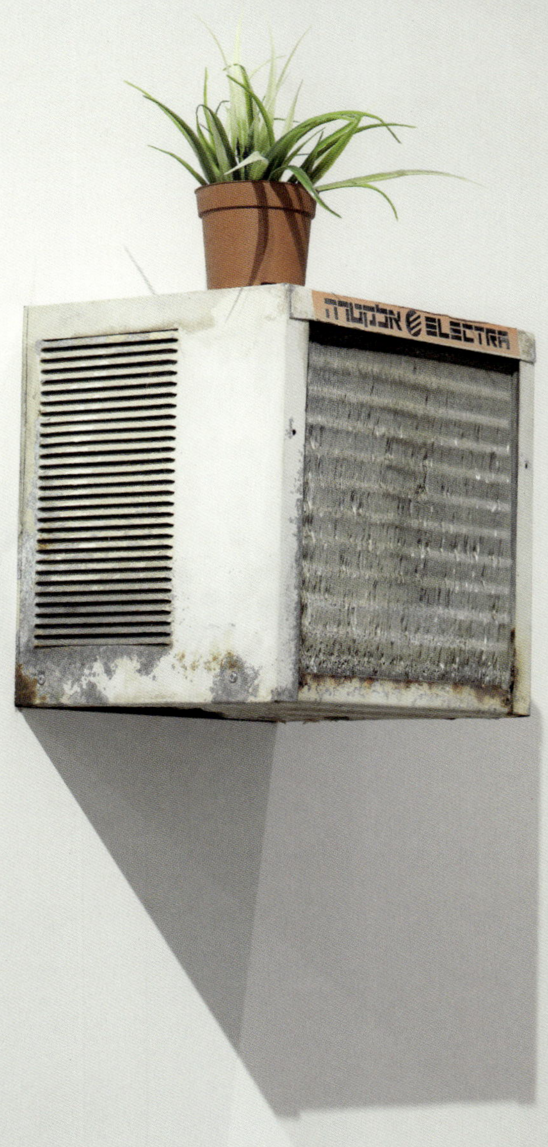

Installation view: M–Museum Leuven, “Cheese, Squeeze, and Tropical Breeze: Video Works 2003–2010,” 2011

 Installation view: San Francisco Museum of Modern Art, “New Work: Mika Rottenberg,” 2010

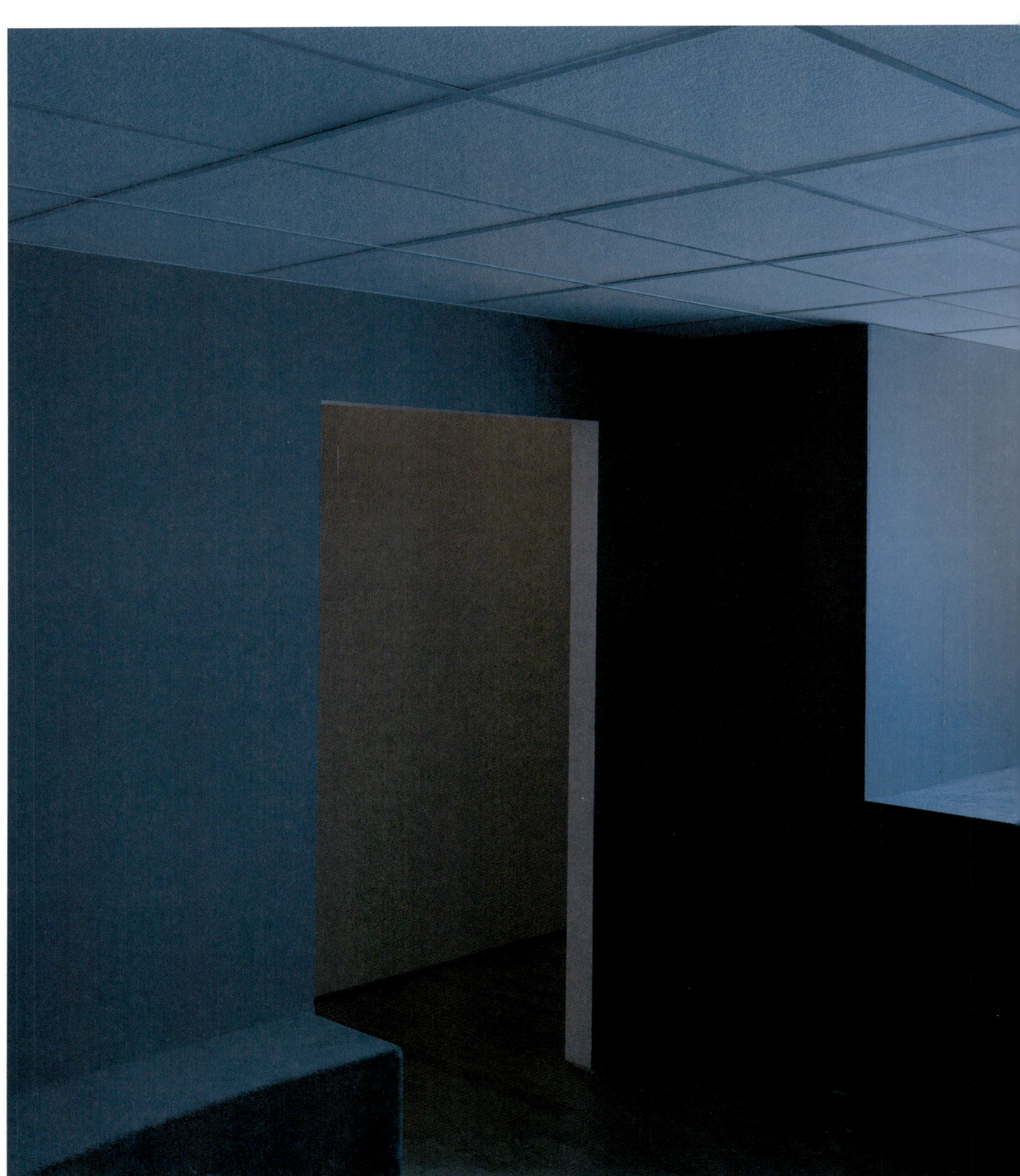

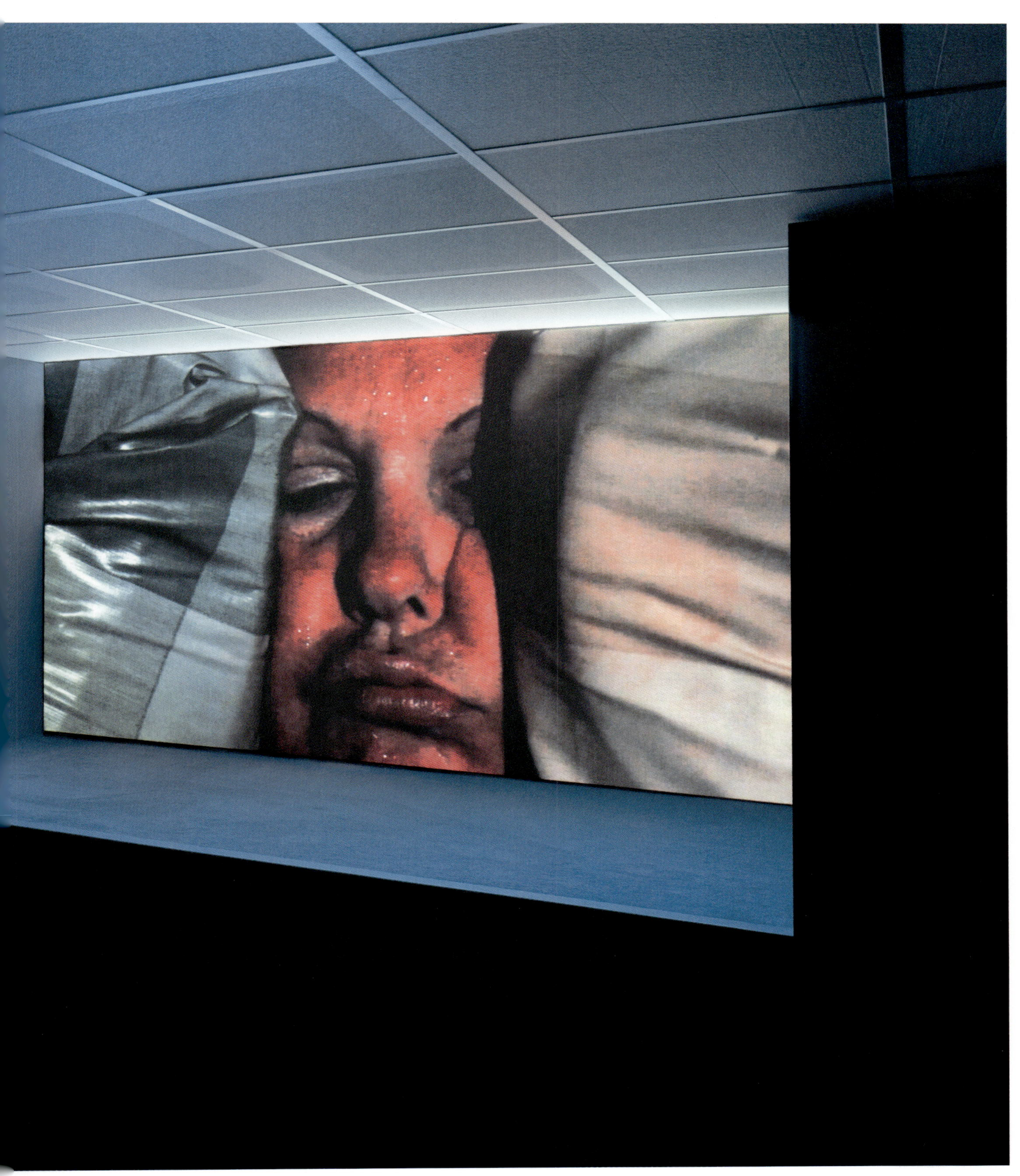

 Interior installation views: Coreana Museum of Art, Space*C, “Tell Me Her Story,” 2013

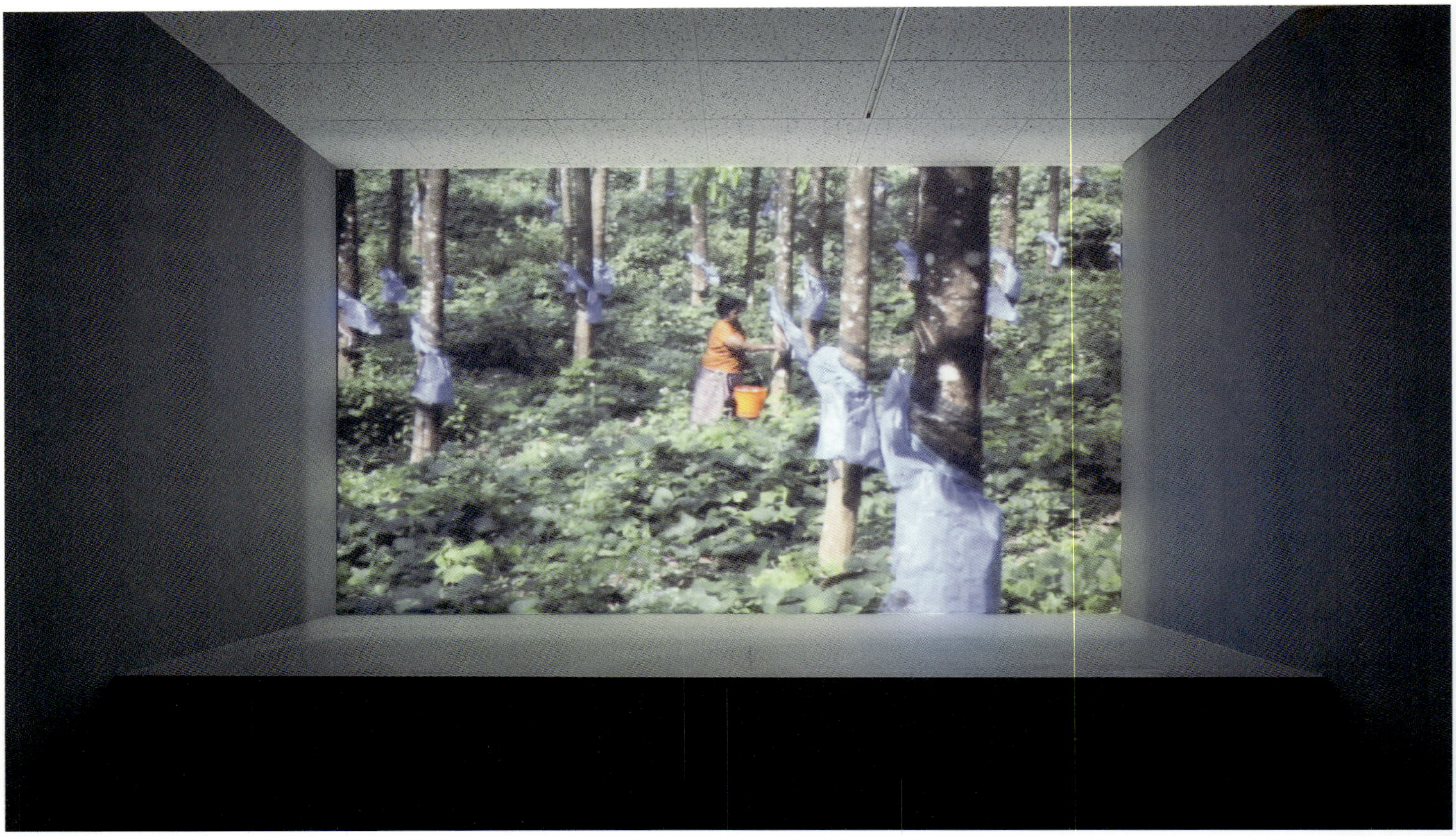

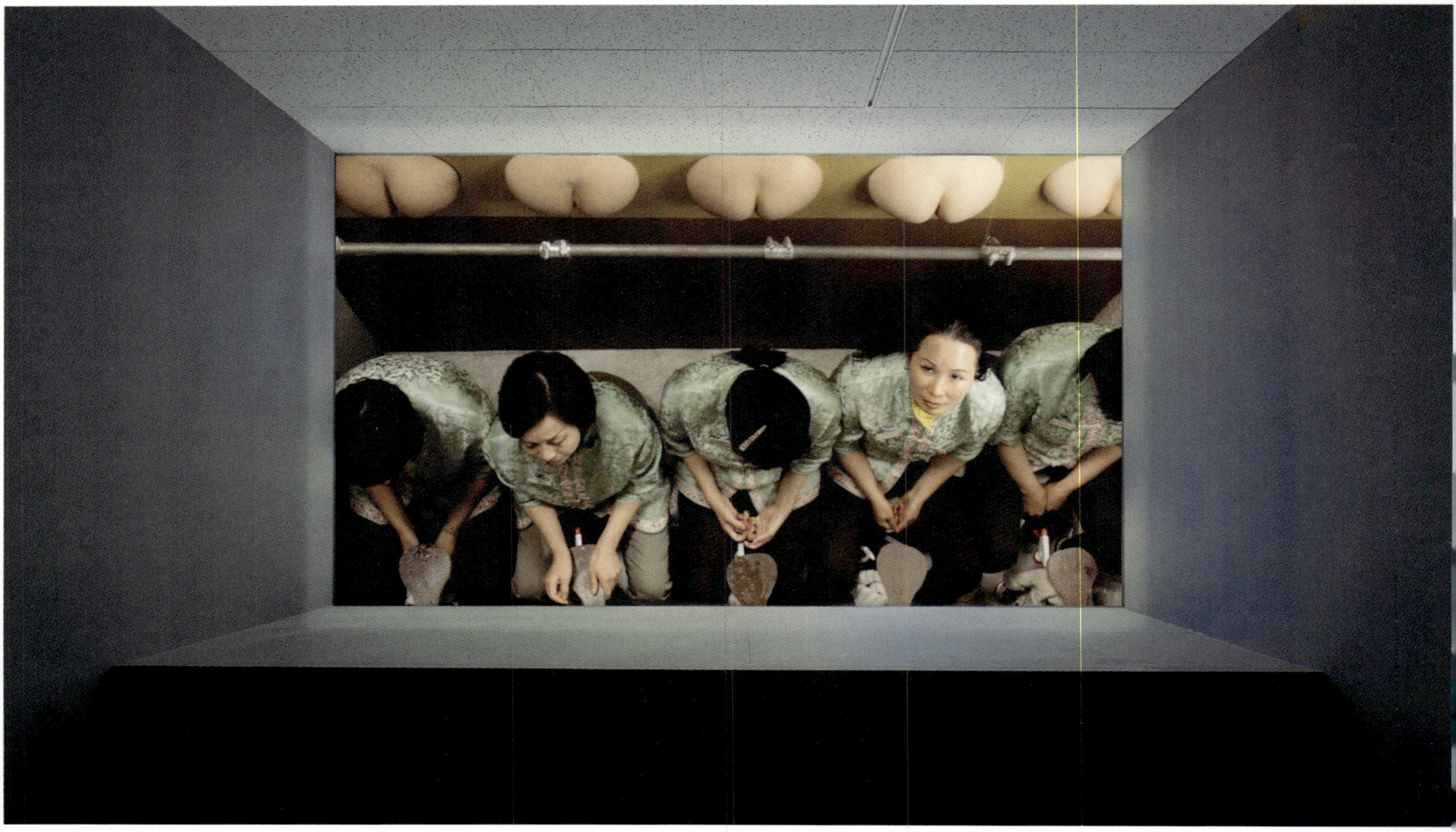

Interior installation views: M–Museum Leuven, "Cheese, Squeeze, and Tropical Breeze: Video Works 2003–2010," 2011

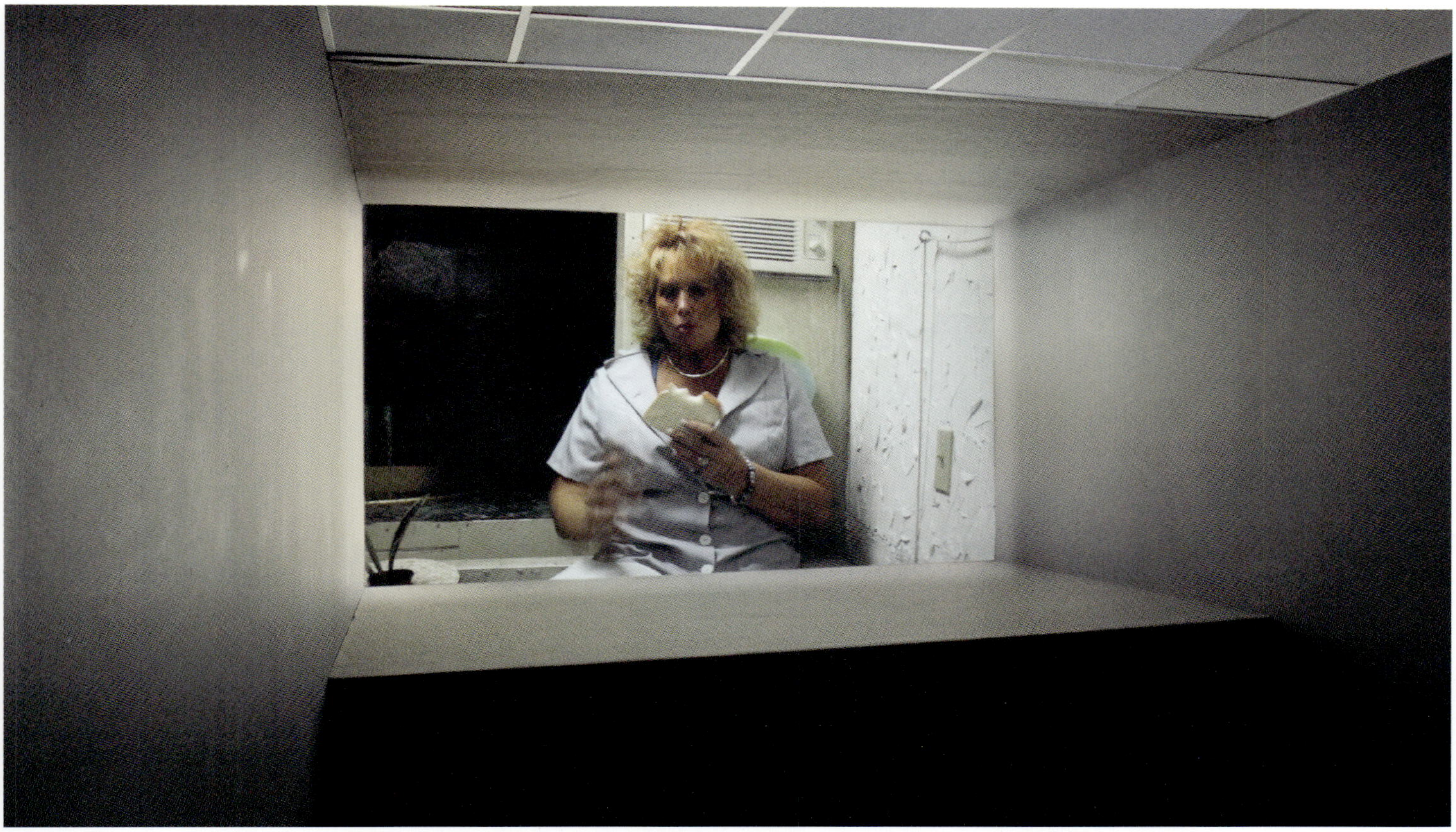

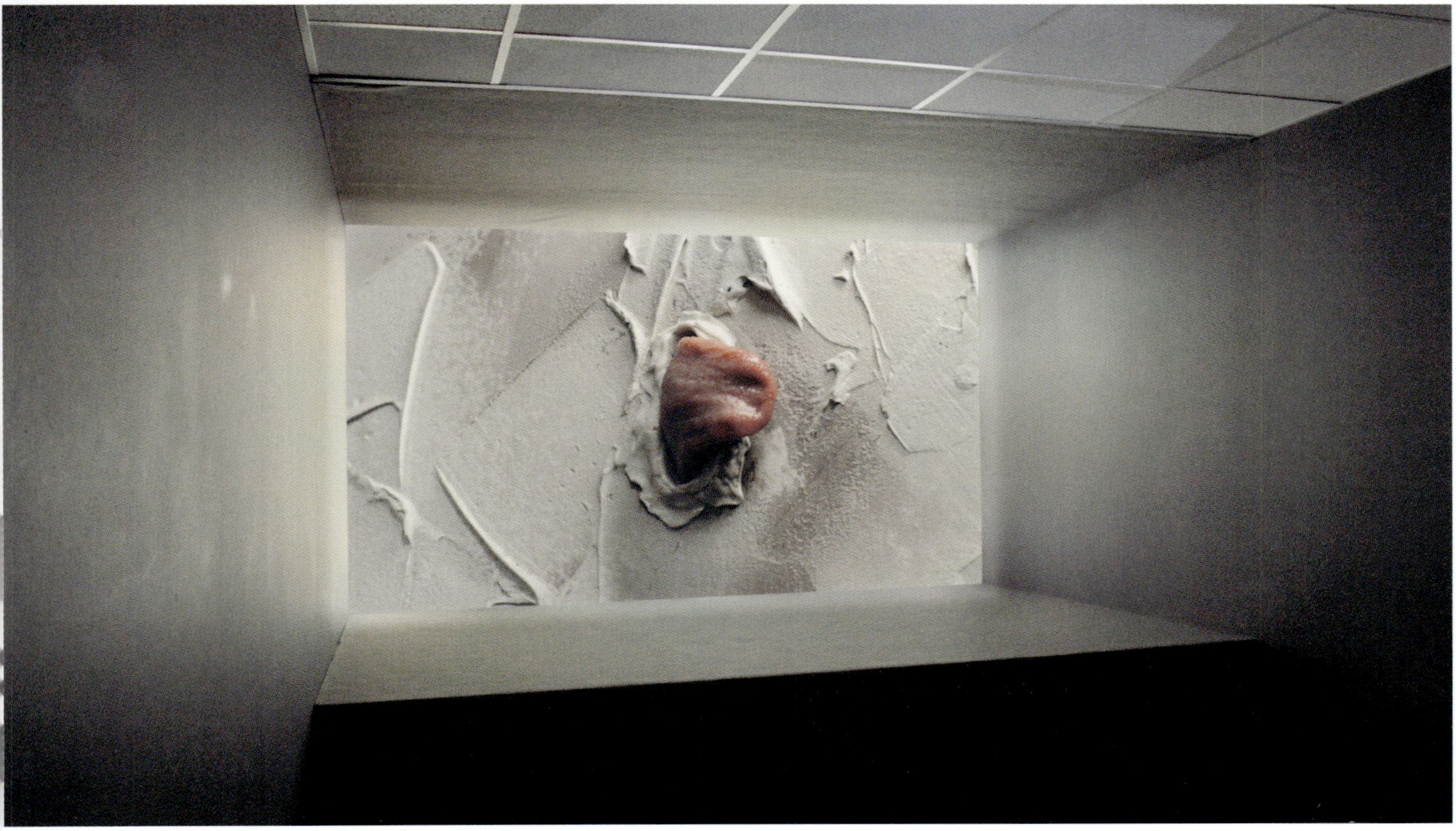

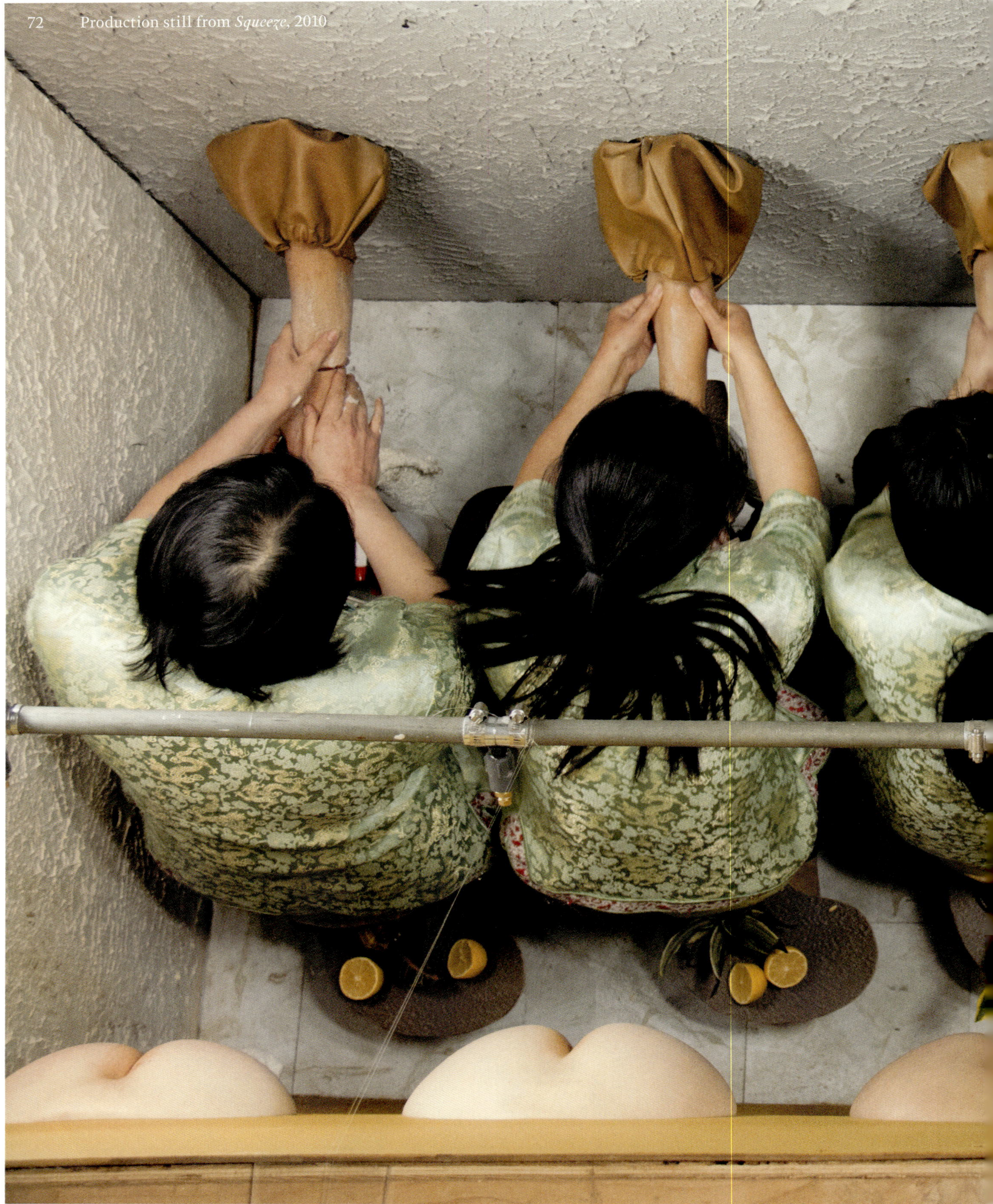

Production still from *Squeeze*, 2010

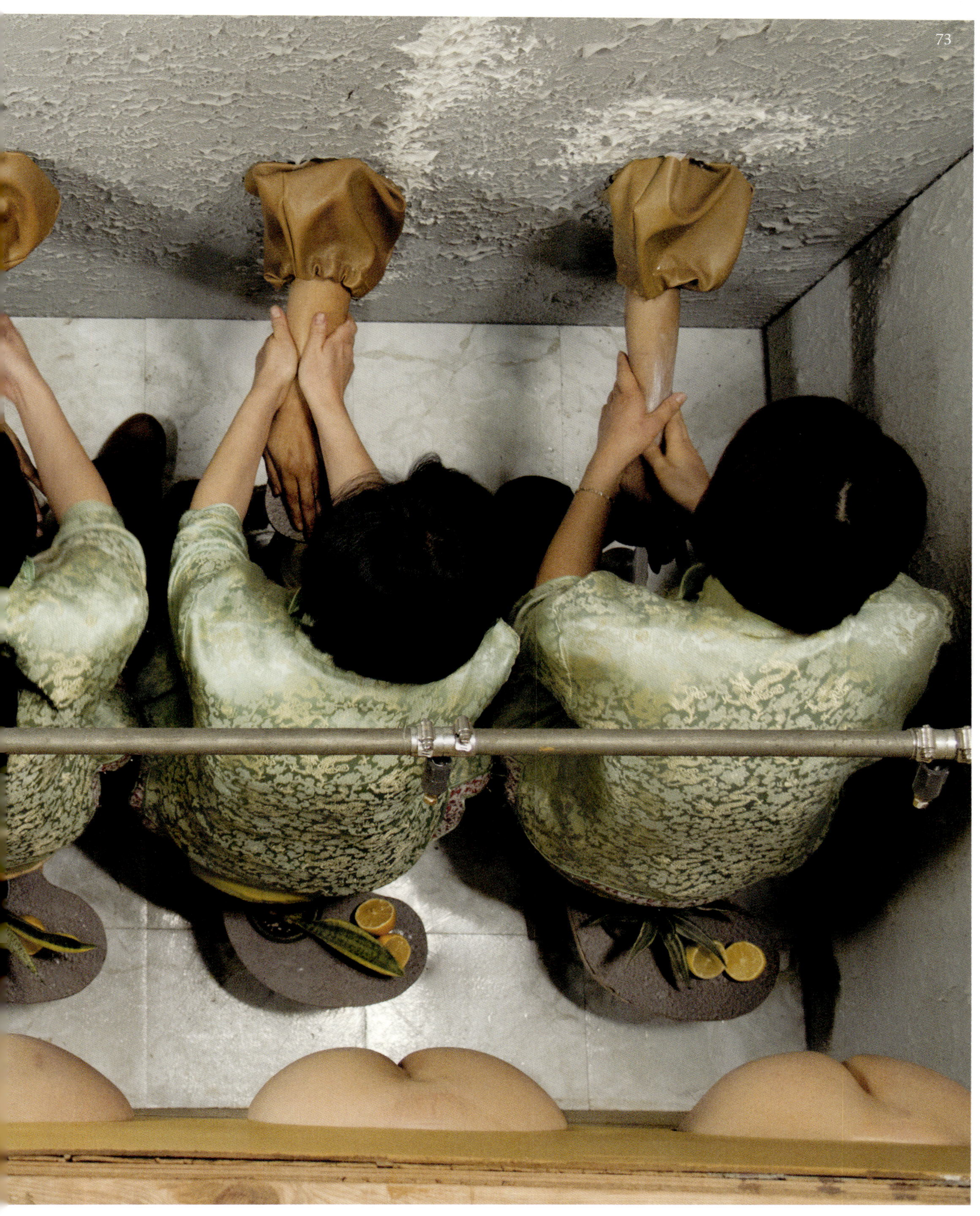

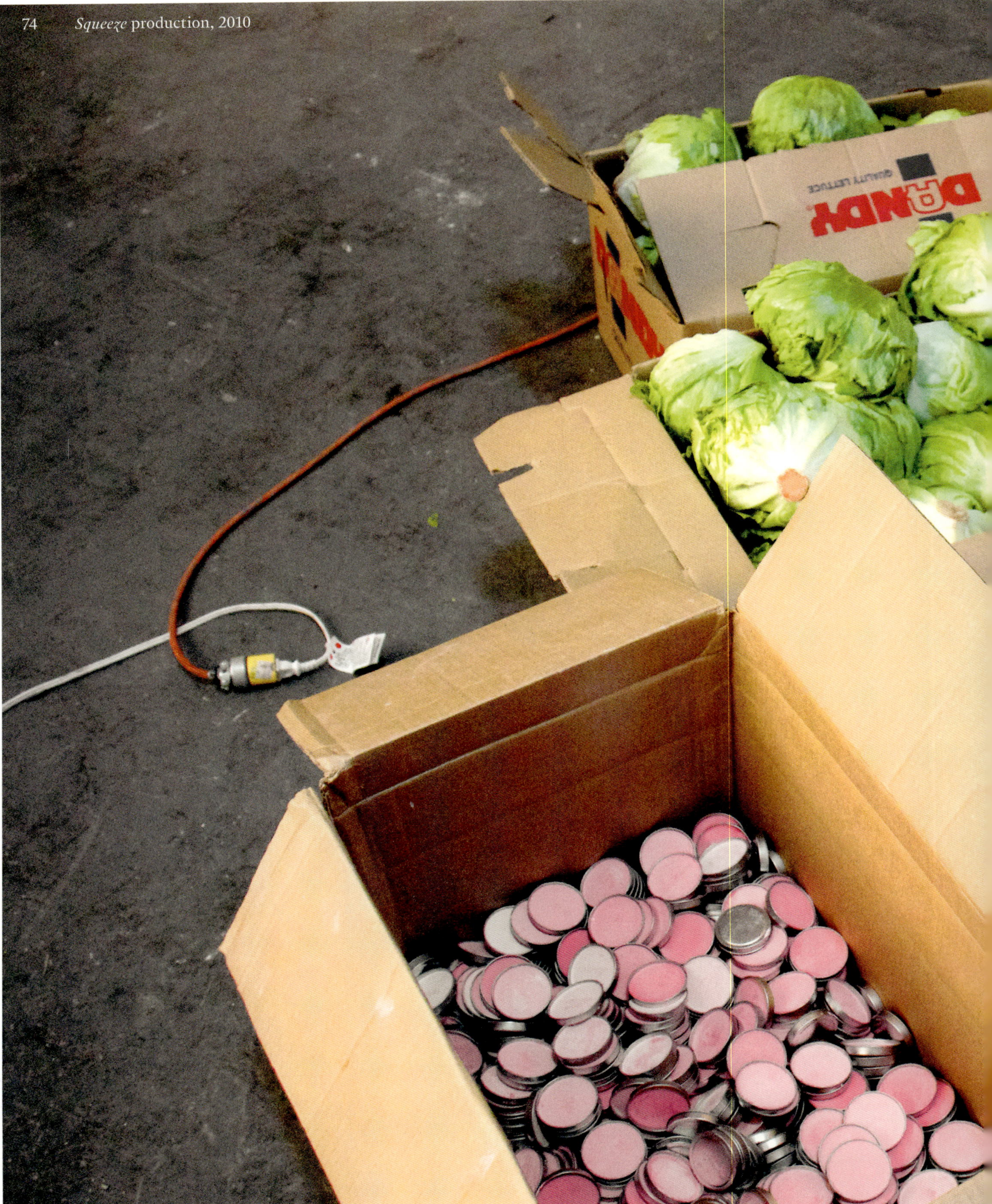

Squeeze production, 2010

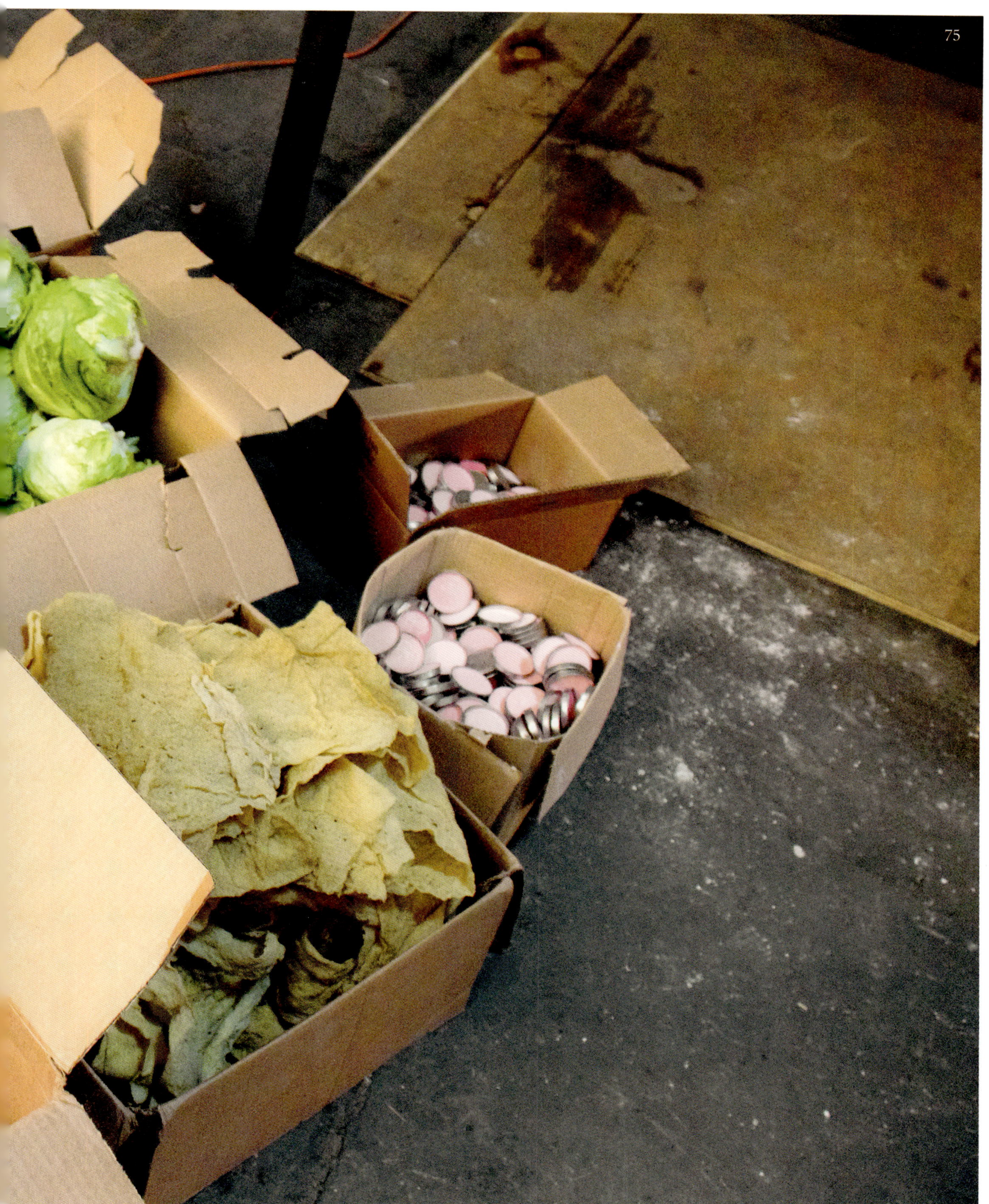

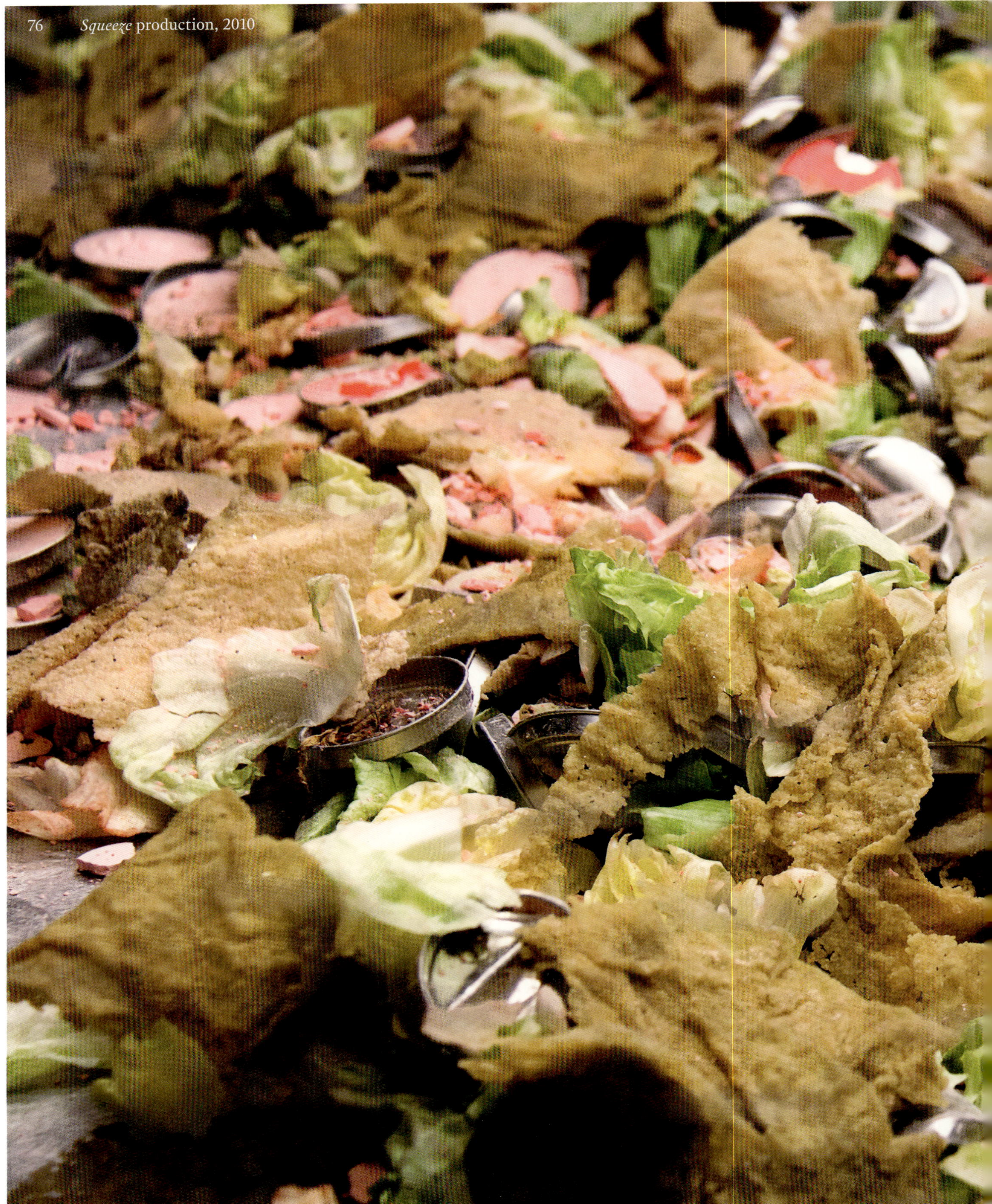

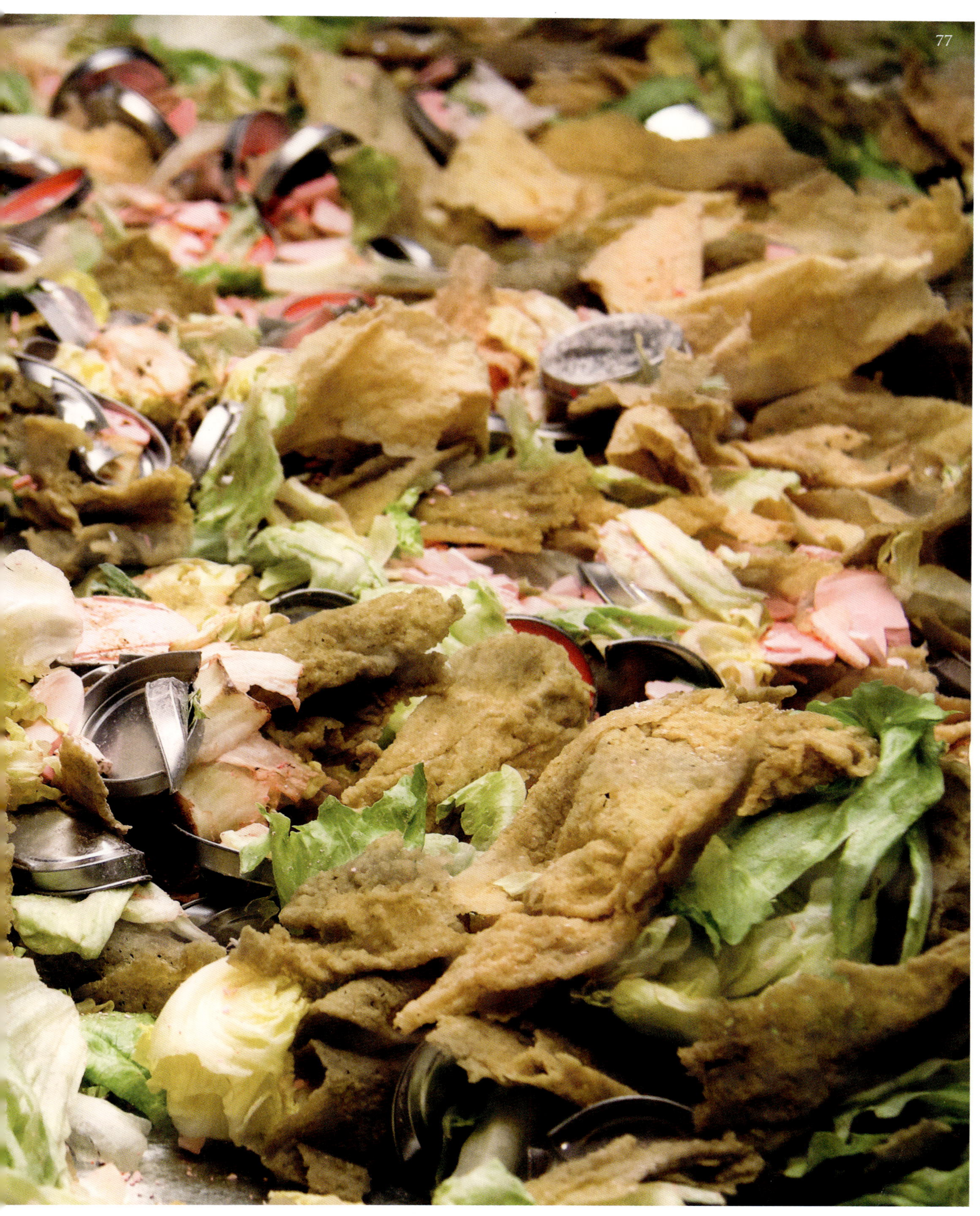

 Detail of *Squeeze*, 2010: *Mary Boone with Cube*, 2010; digital c-print

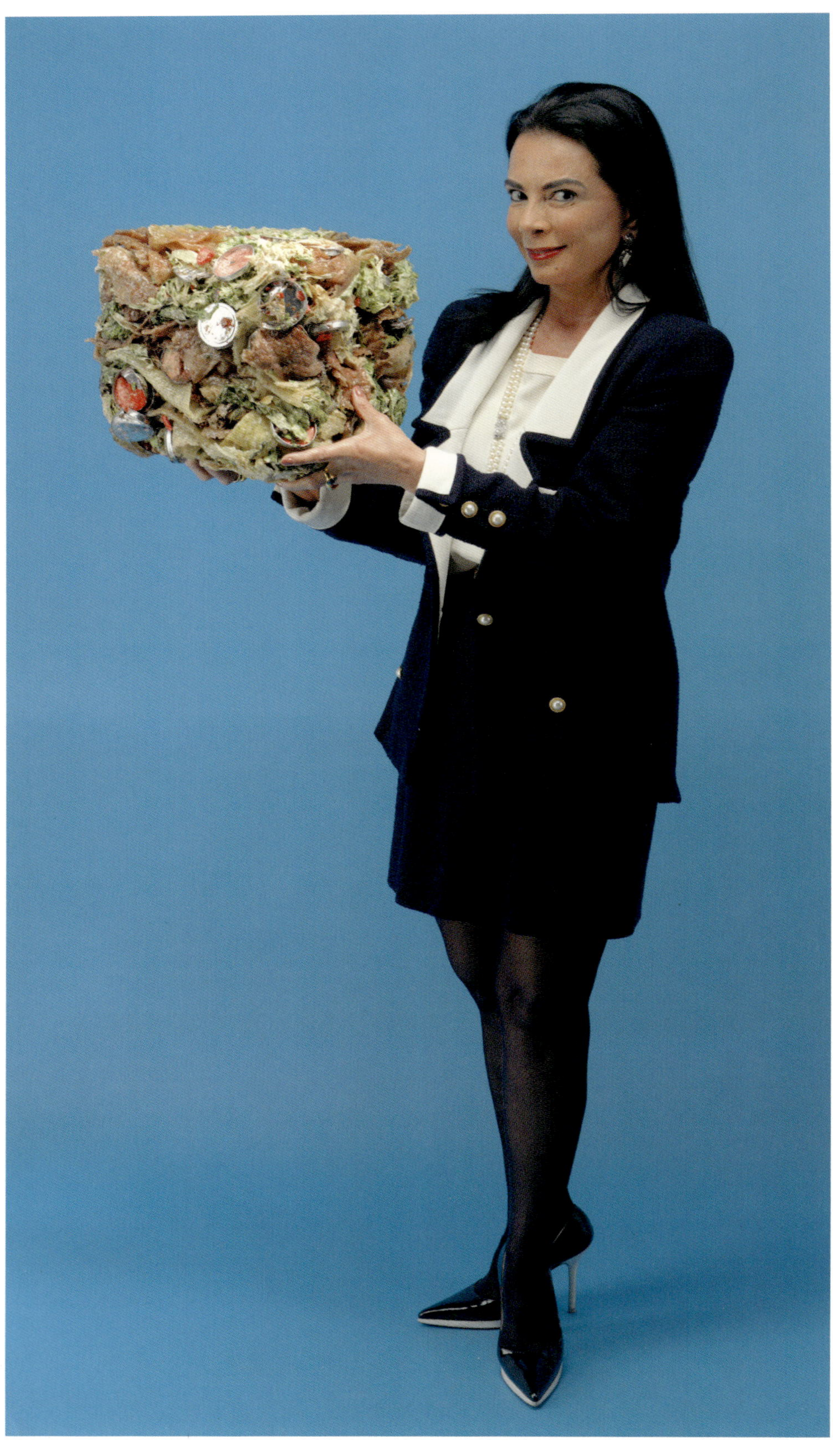

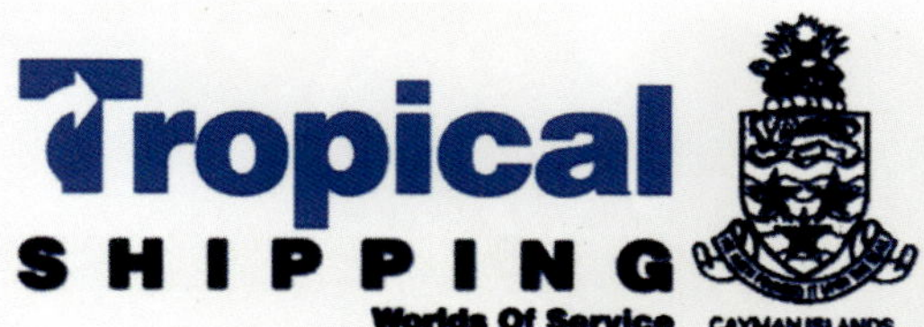

INCOMING CONDITION REPORT

Consignor: Mika Rottenberg	Consignee: Tropical Shipping & Storage Ltd.
Port of Origin: New York, NY USA	Port of Arrival: Grand Cayman

Fine Art; 30.5 x 30.5 x 30.5 cm (1 cubic foot); vegetable matter, Pure Latex Cream (PLC); cosmetics

Type of package and number: 1 crate	**Insurance value:**

For official use only

Date of presentation of entry

Entry examined by

Passed for collection of duty

AMOUNT RECEIVED CI$

Paid by cash/cheque No.

Receipt No. 37886349

Signature of cashier

ENTRY NUMBER

OFFICIAL STAMP AND DATE

GRAND CAYMA[N]

CAYMAN ISLANDS

Ship Date: 15 October 2010	**Log Date:** 17 October 2010
Country of Origin: USA	**Country of Receipt:** Grand Cayman, Cayman Islands
Statistical Code: 4781	**Quantity in appropriate units:** 1

CONDITION
Object as described; object shows signs of natural decay; surface appears intact; uneven coloration

TERMS OF STORAGE
Per contract with consignee, object to be stored in perpetuity*
Class A climate control safe; access to object limited according to terms described*
* Refer to contract

Special handling instructions provided	**Yes** ☒ **No** ☐	**Details:** See contract
Installation instructions followed	**Yes** ☐ **No** ☒	**Details:**

PACKING

Gross weight: 2 kg External dimensions (HxWxD): 304 x 304 x 304 mm

(tick and comment) bin ☐ crate ☒ pallet ☐ flight case ☐ other ☐

Details (pre-wrap tissue, etc.)

CHECKED

Venue	Date	Condition	Examiner
C.I. Customs Clearance	10/17/10	As above	Mr. Alfred Ebanks

LIST OF DOCUMENTS ATTACHED Contract

It is a condition of storage agreement that no changes are to be made without the written permission of the lender

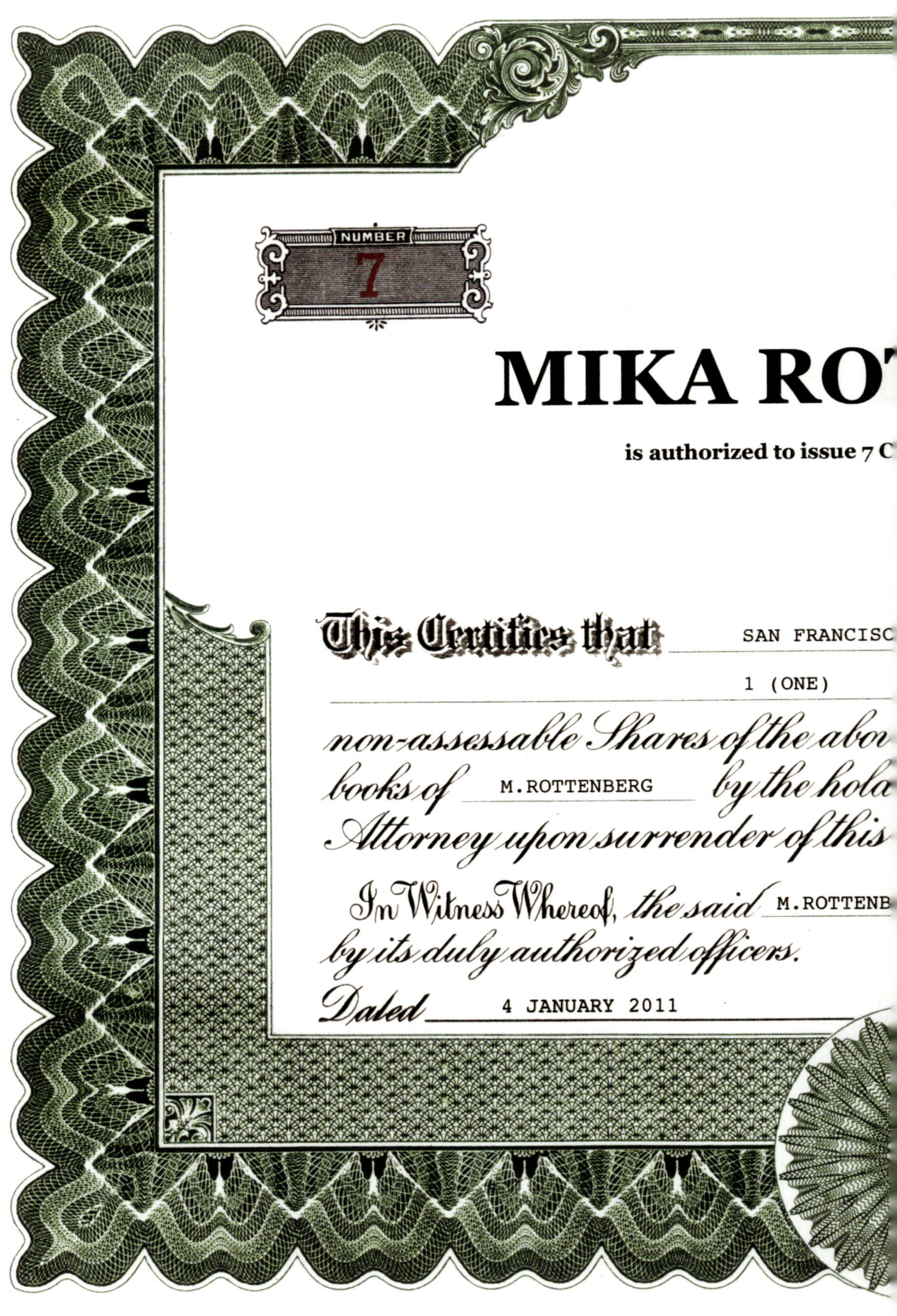
NUMBER
7
MIKA RO
is authorized to issue 7 C
This Certifies that
SAN FRANCISC
1 (ONE)
non-assessable Shares of the abo
books of
M.ROTTENBERG
by the hol
Attorney upon surrender of this
In Witness Whereof, the said
M.ROTTENB
by its duly authorized officers.
Dated
4 JANUARY 2011

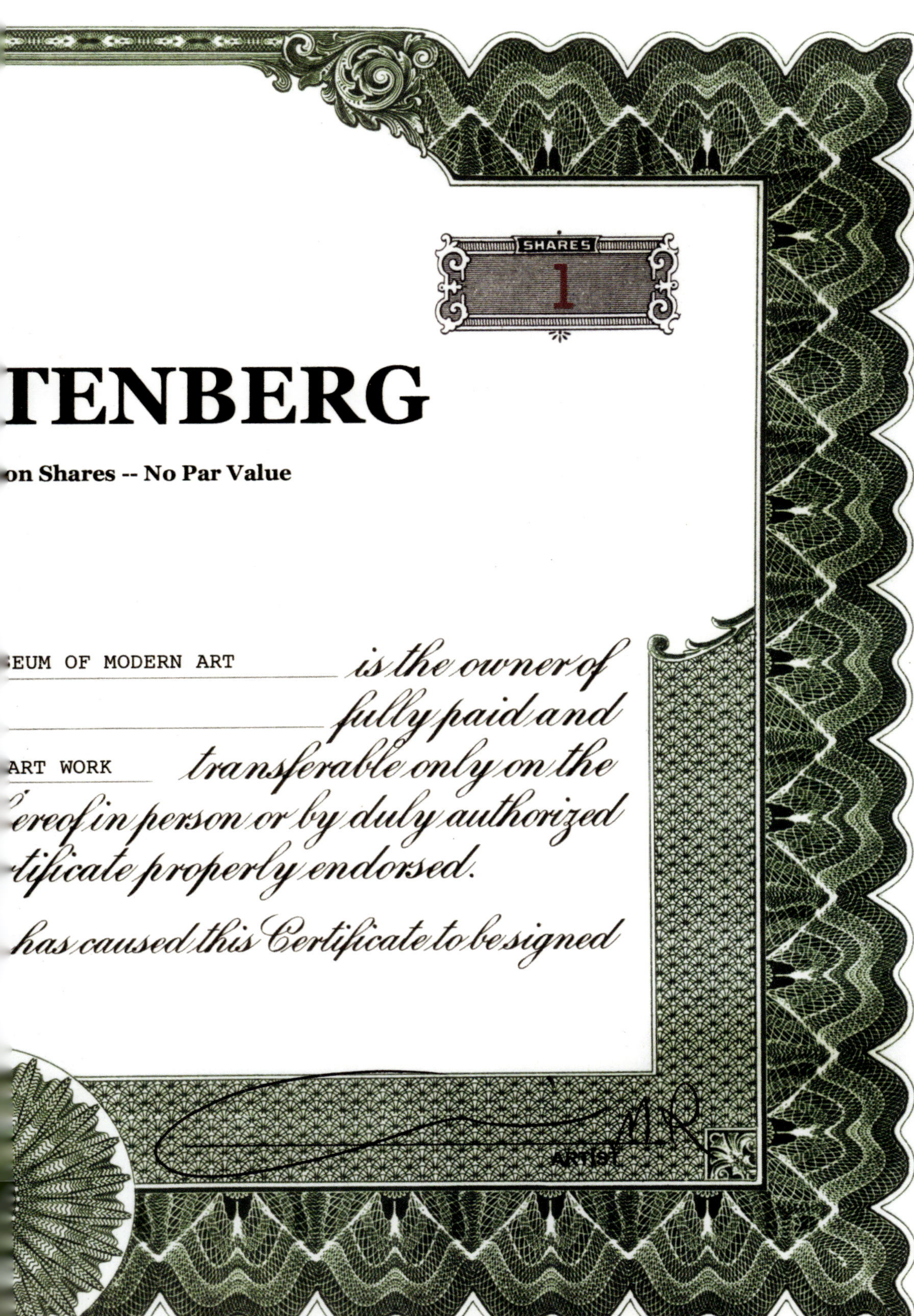
SHARES
1
TENBERG
on Shares -- No Par Value
EUM OF MODERN ART
is the owner of
fully paid and
ART WORK
transferable only on the
ereof in person or by duly authorized
tificate properly endorsed.
has caused this Certificate to be signed
ARTIST

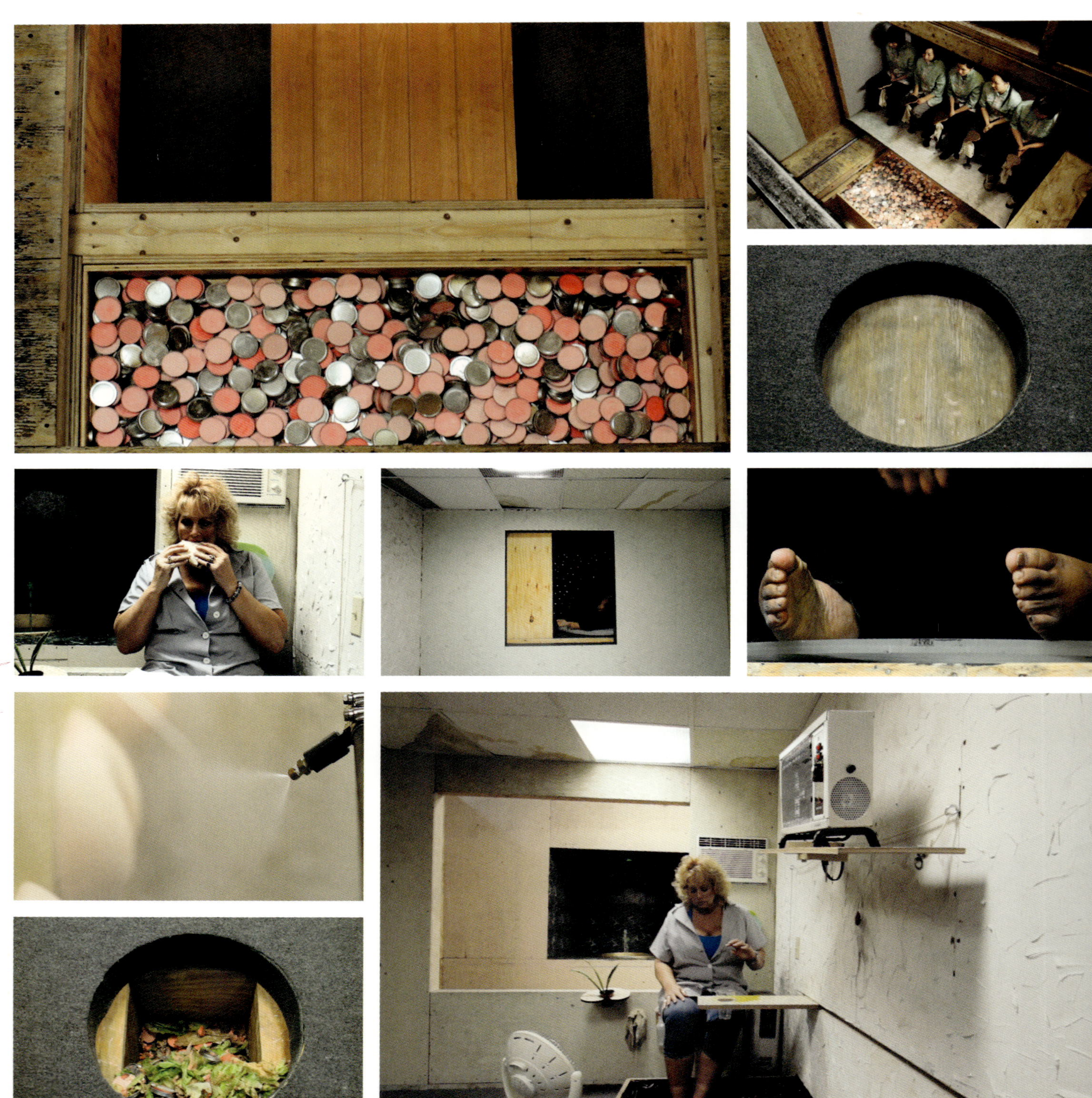

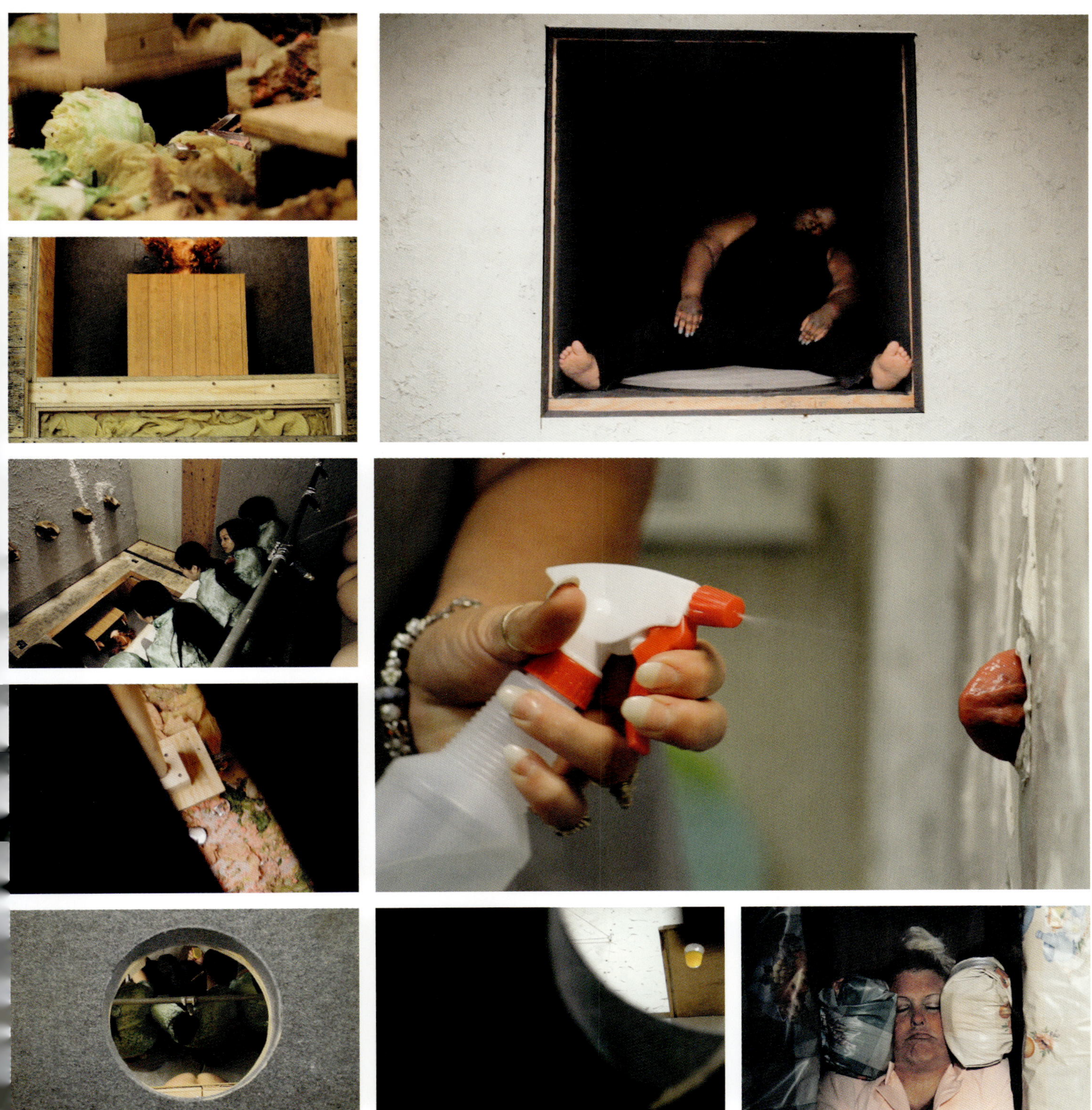

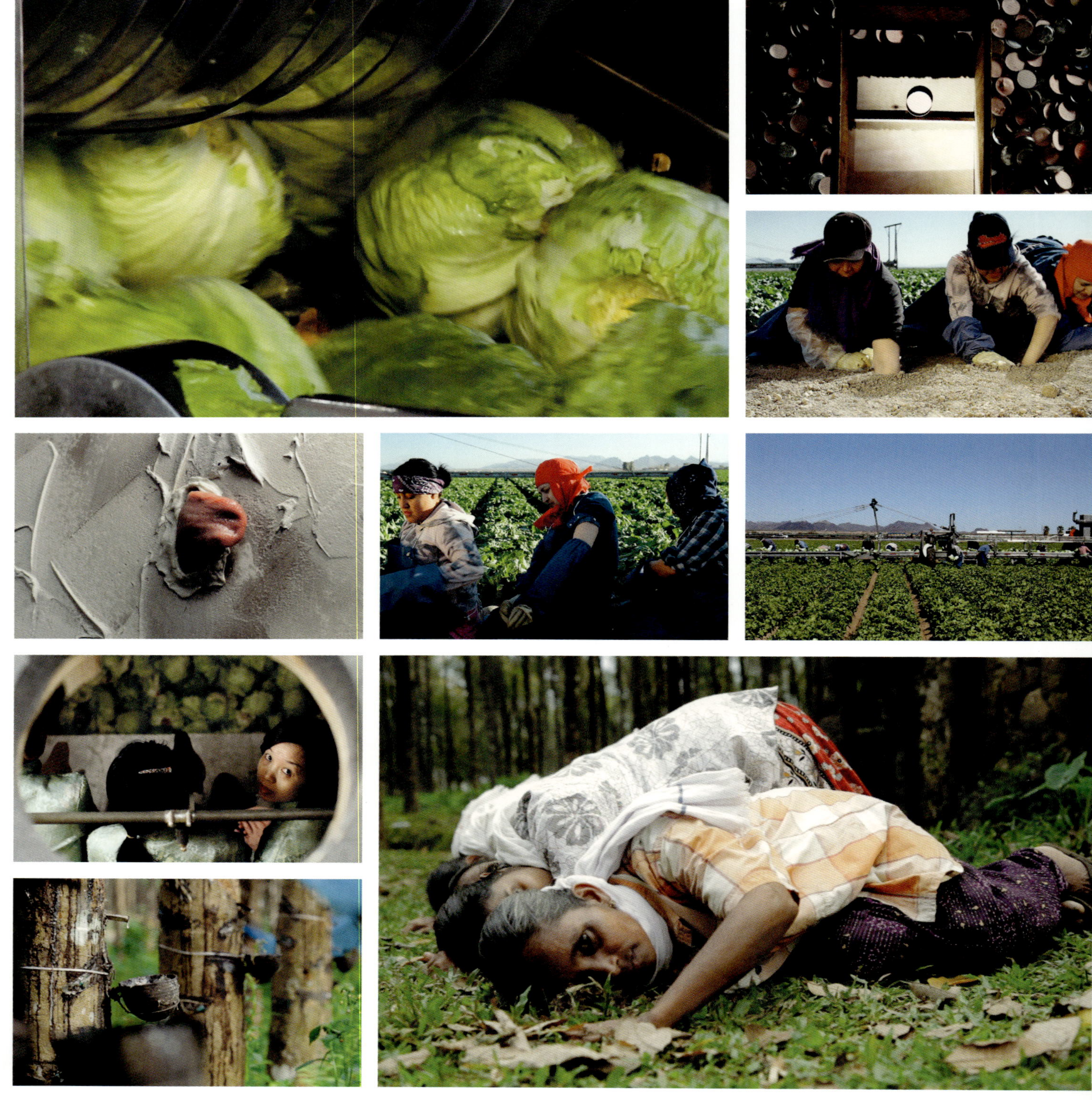

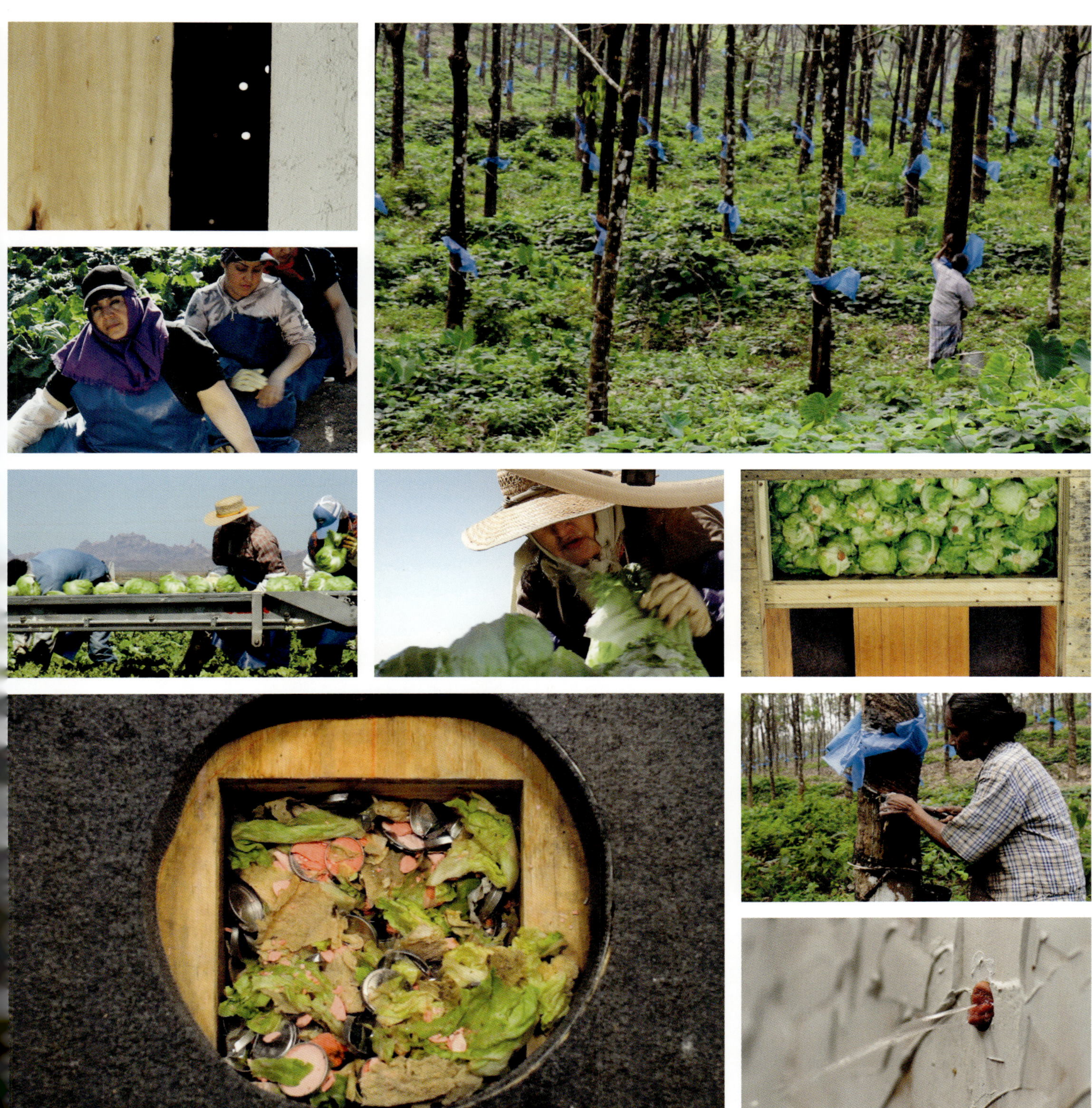

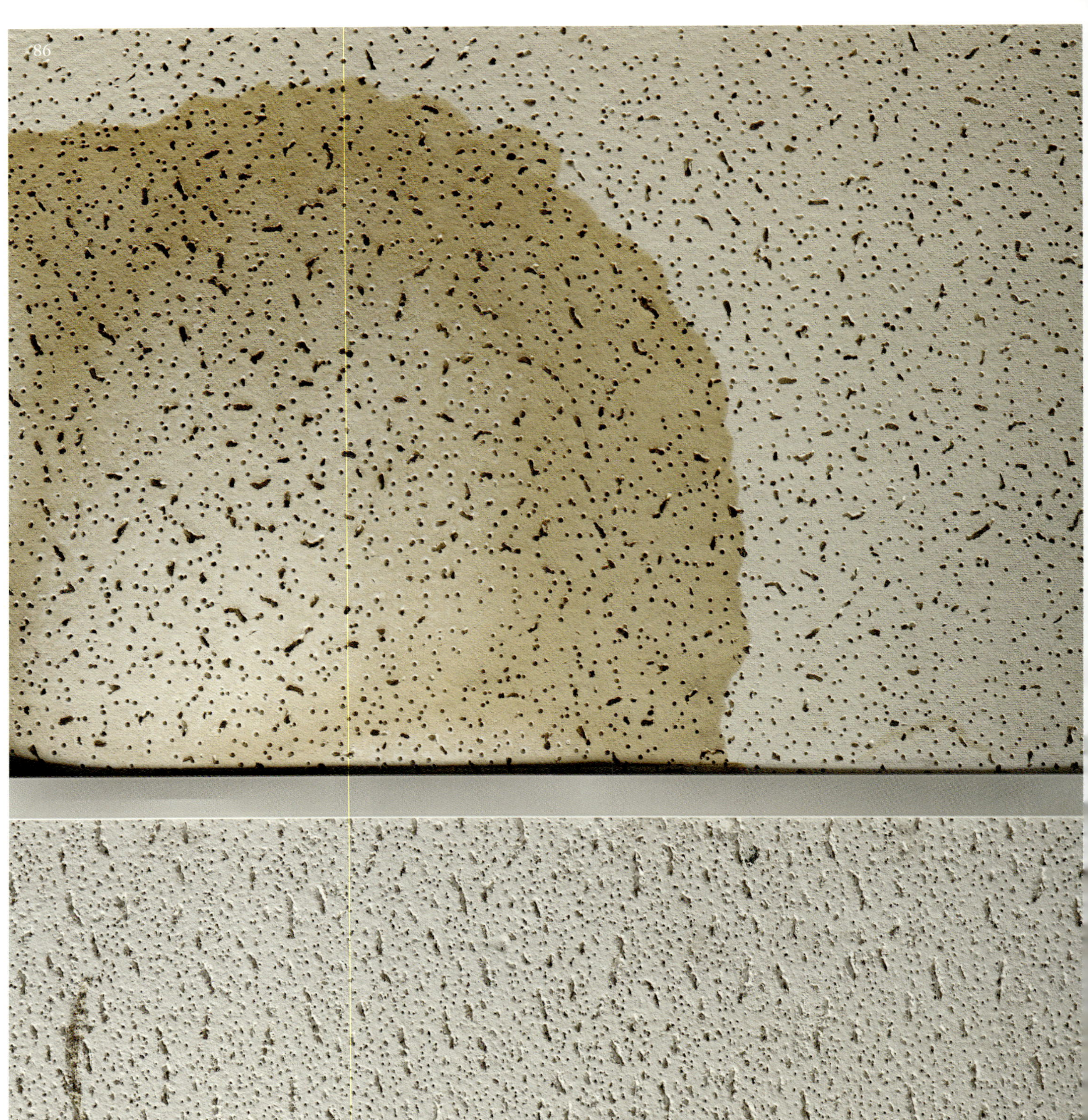

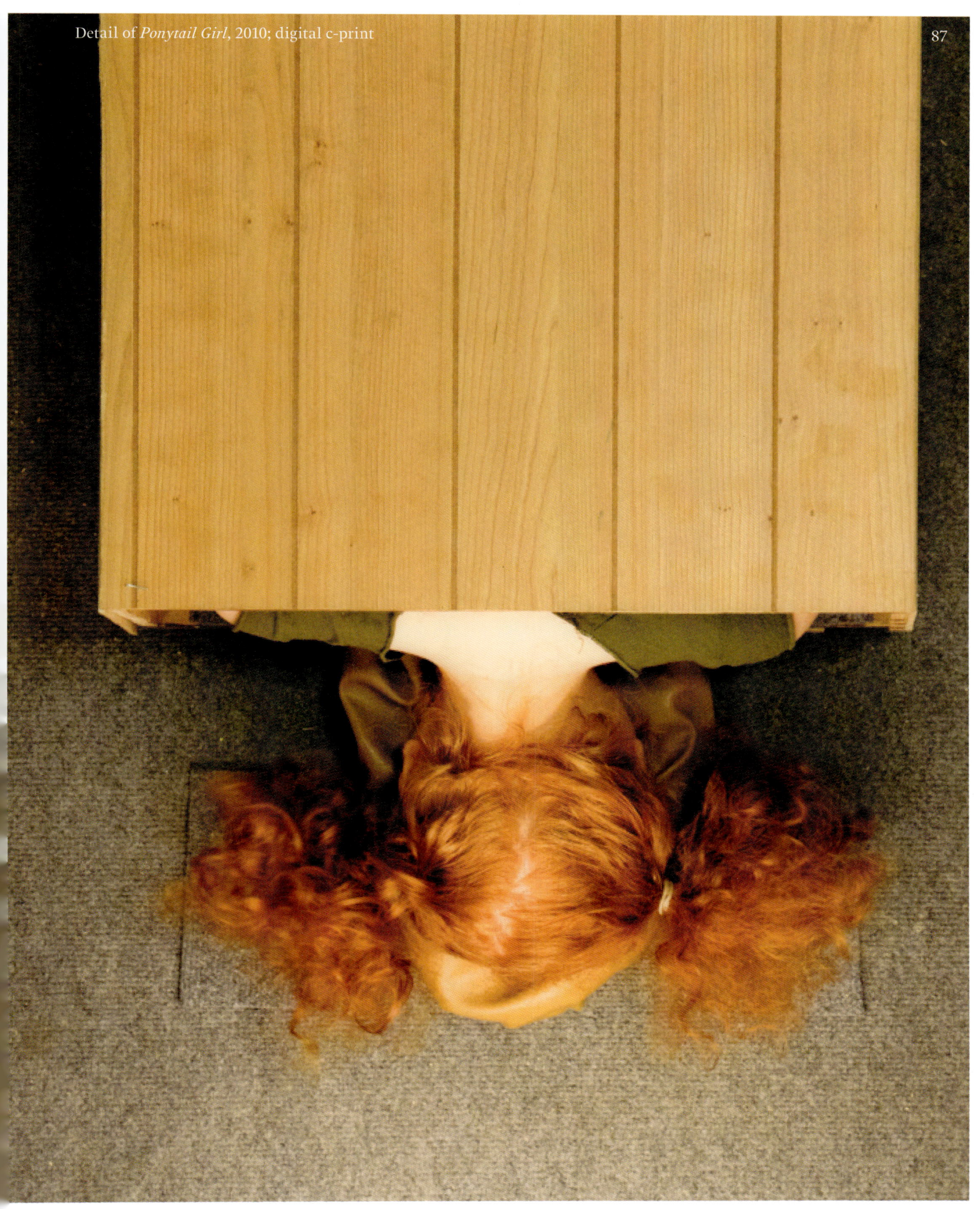

Detail of *Ponytail Girl*, 2010; digital c-print

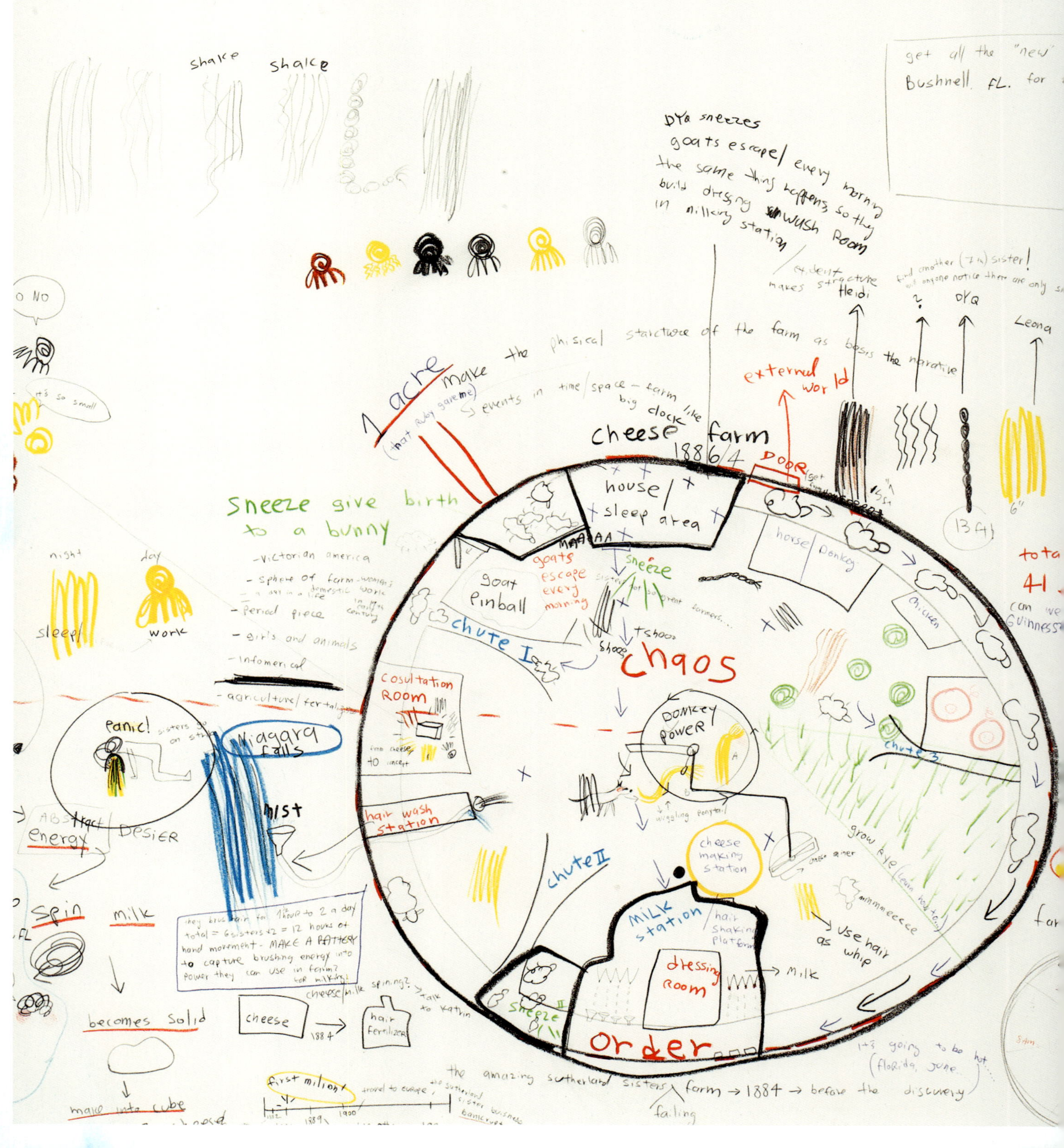

Preparatory drawing for *Cheese*, 2008

cheese

CB: Long hair, variously manipulated, recurs as a motif in your work. Can you explain why and what this motif means to you?

MR: Hair is one of the prettiest things that the body produces. On a basic level, I have a pure attraction to it and maybe it is a fetish of mine. On a more conceptual level, hair exists halfway between function and uselessness. It marks some kind of border between the self and the world because it's a part of you that you can cut away. It's also something that your body grows which can have monetary value. I find that interesting.

Cheese began when I discovered, one night while searching the internet for long hair, a group of sisters called the Seven Sutherland Sisters from upstate New York who in the mid-1880s became millionaires overnight for developing a hair tonic—"Seven Sutherland Sisters' Hair Grower"—that they claimed was a magical cure for baldness. *Cheese* was inspired by them.

 Installation view: *Cheese #3*, 2008; Herzliya Museum of Contemporary Art, “Theatrical Gestures,” 2013

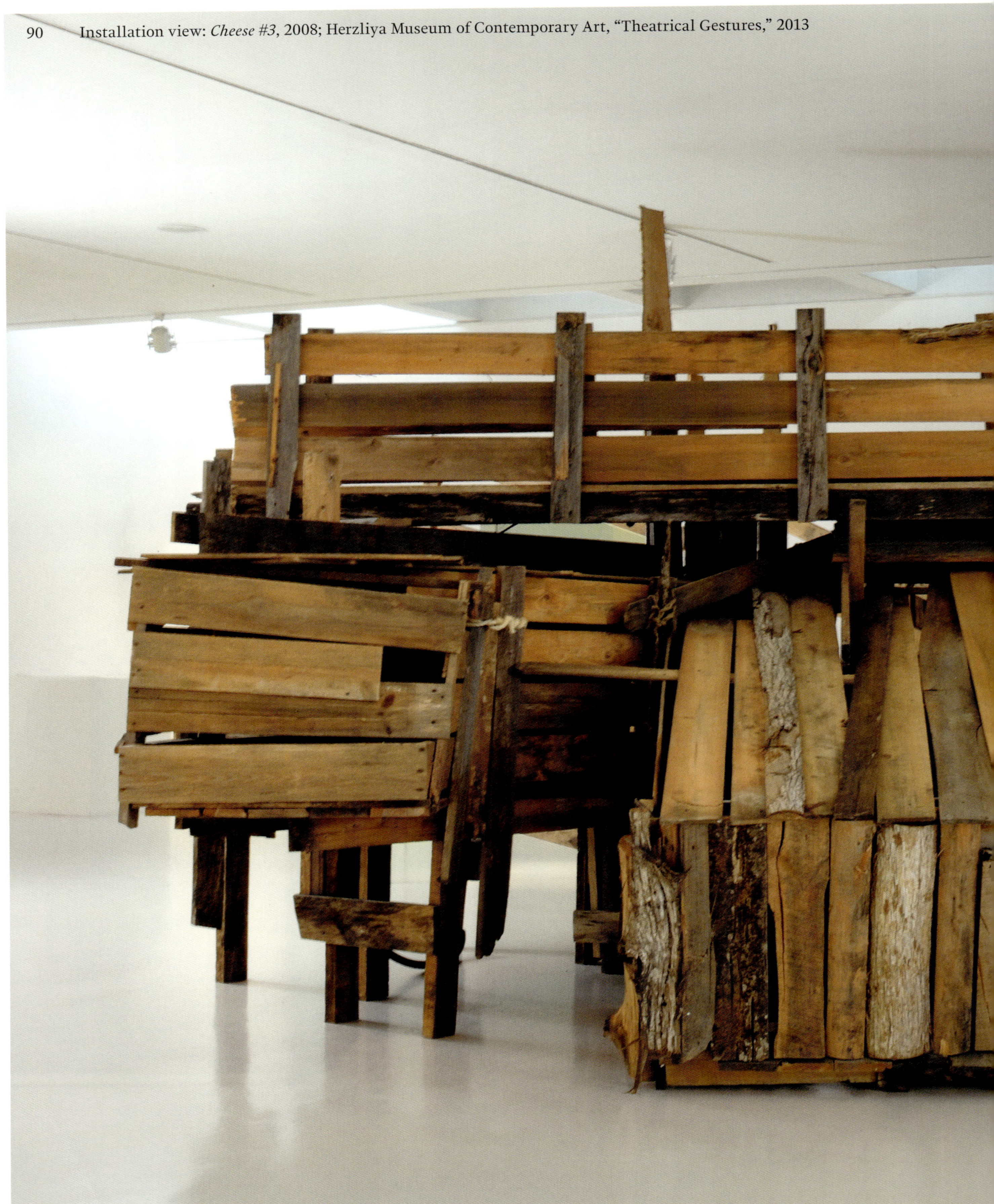

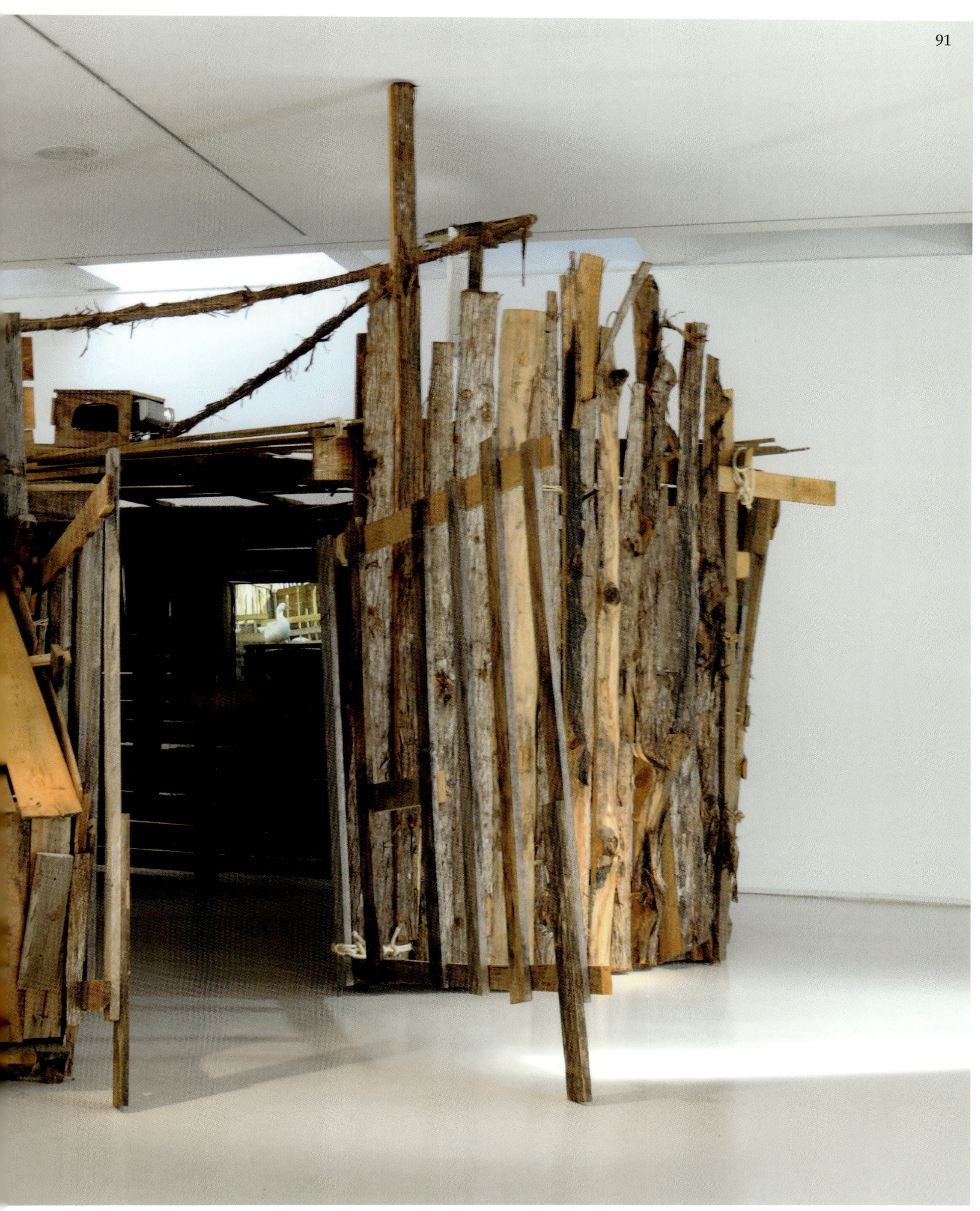

 Installation views: *Cheese #3*, 2008; Herzliya Museum of Contemporary Art, "Theatrical Gestures," 2013

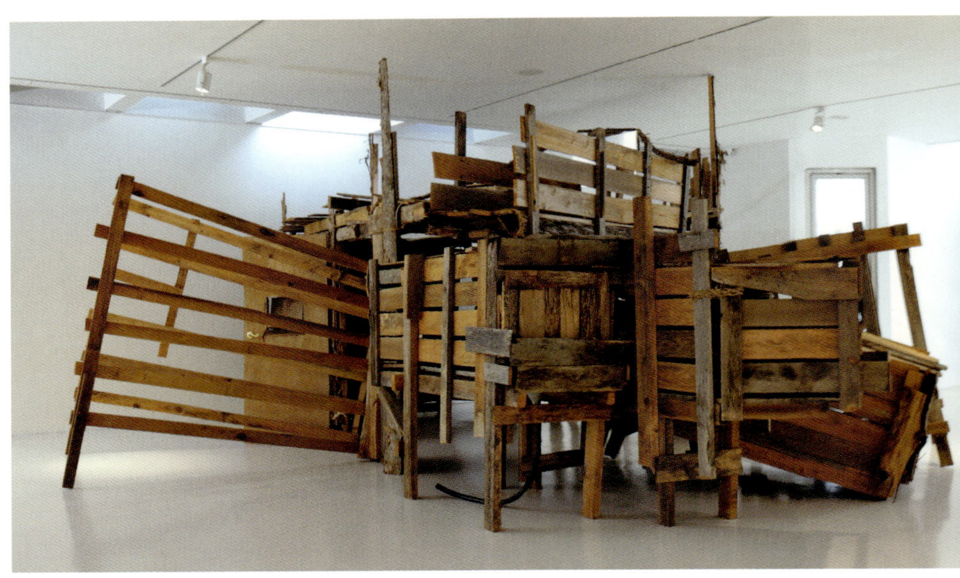

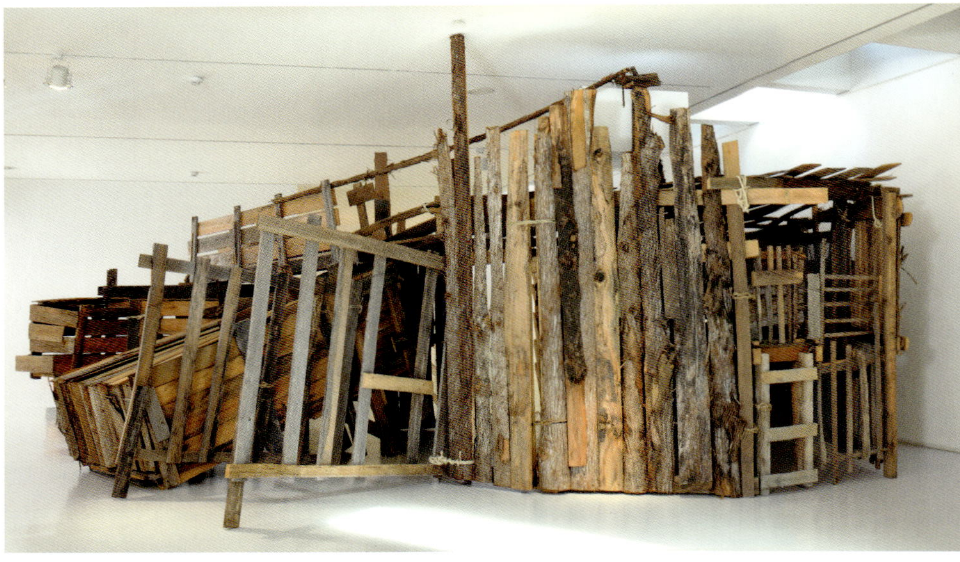

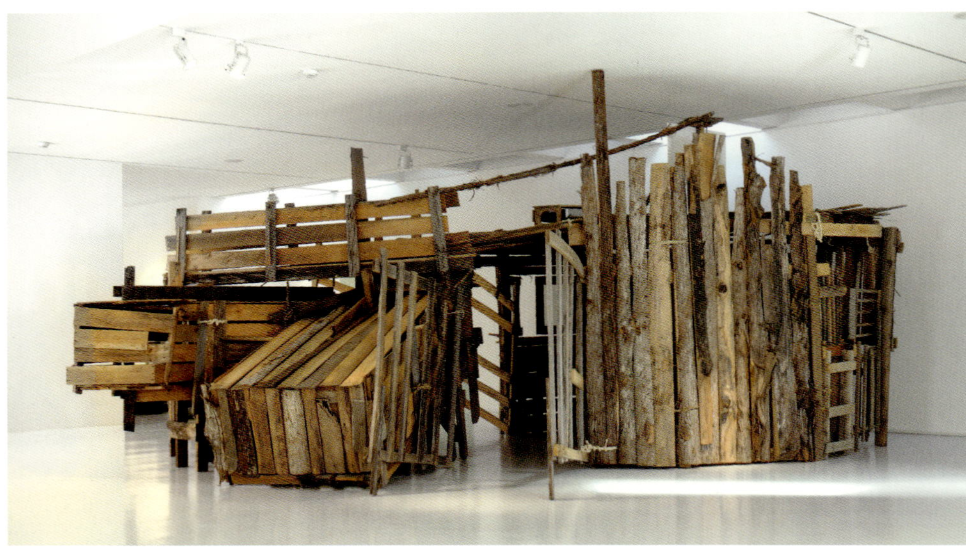

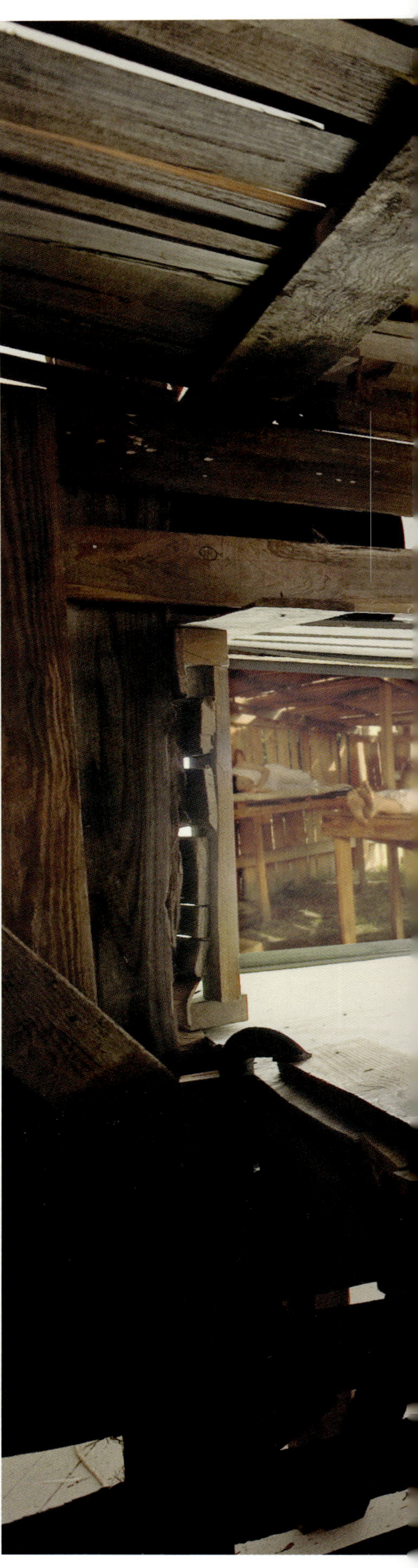

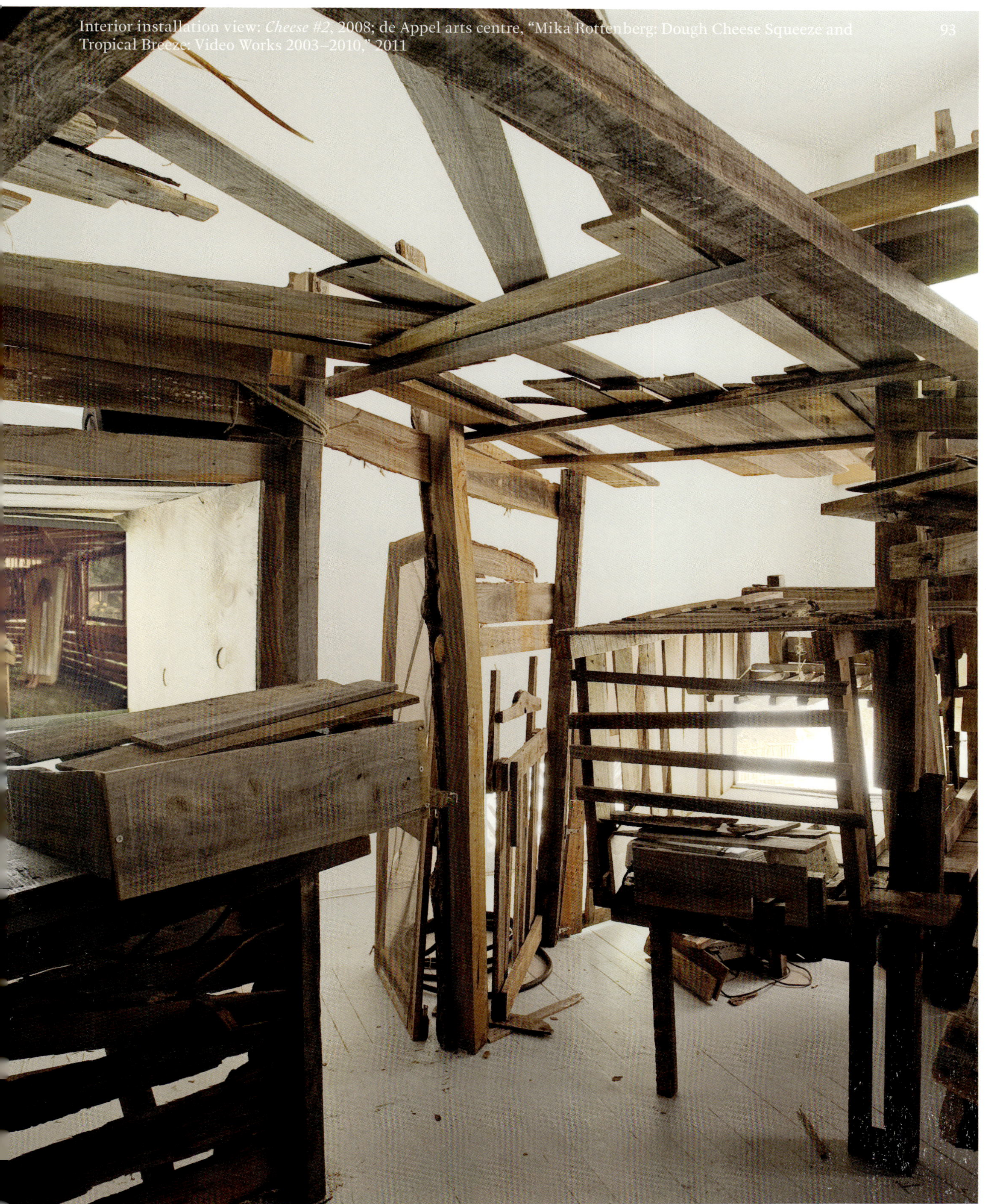
Interior installation view: *Cheese #2*, 2008; de Appel arts centre, "Mika Rottenberg: Dough Cheese Squeeze and Tropical Breeze: Video Works 2003–2010," 2011

Interior installation view: *Cheese #3*, 2008; Herzliya Museum of Contemporary Art, "Theatrical Gestures," 2013

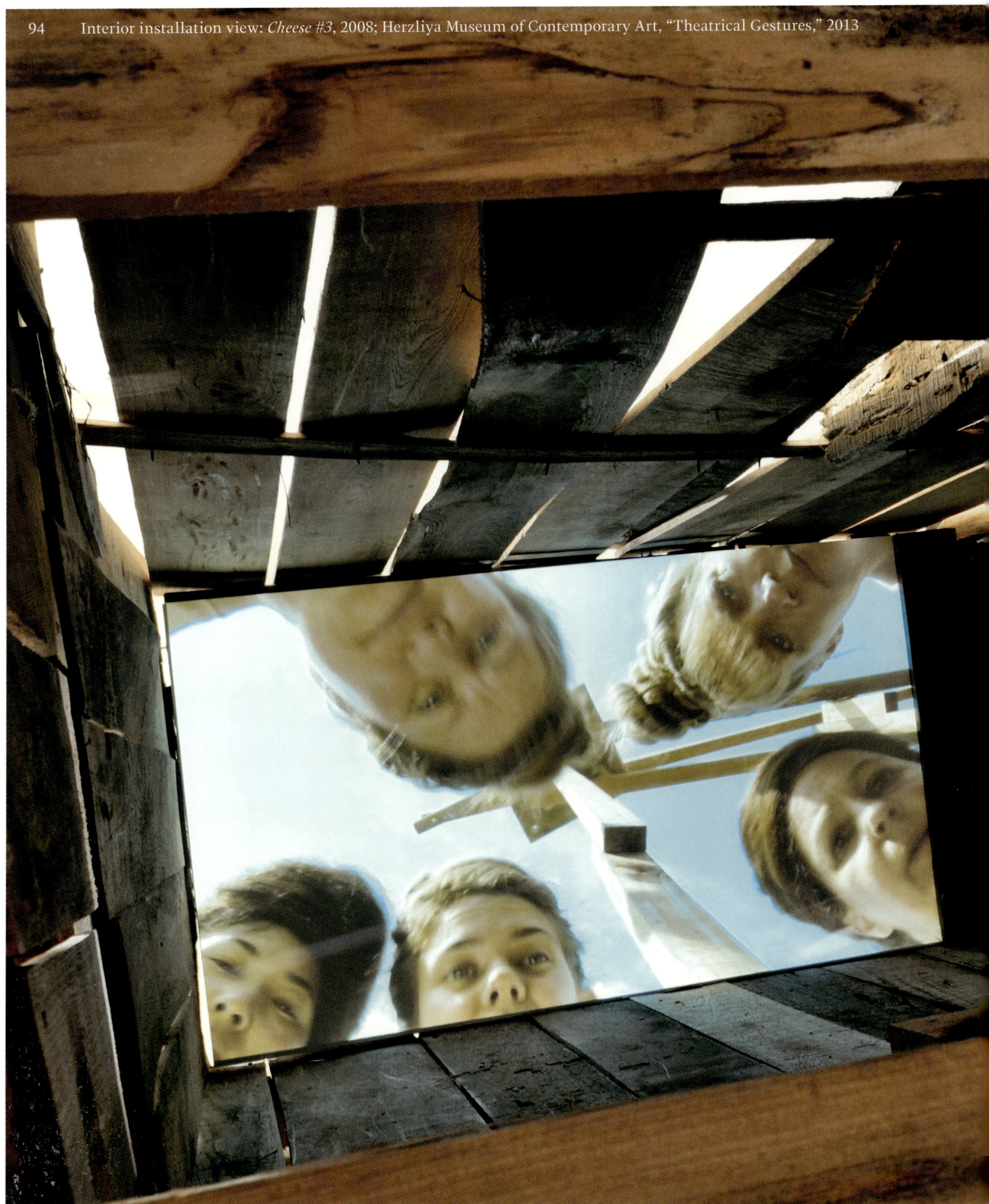

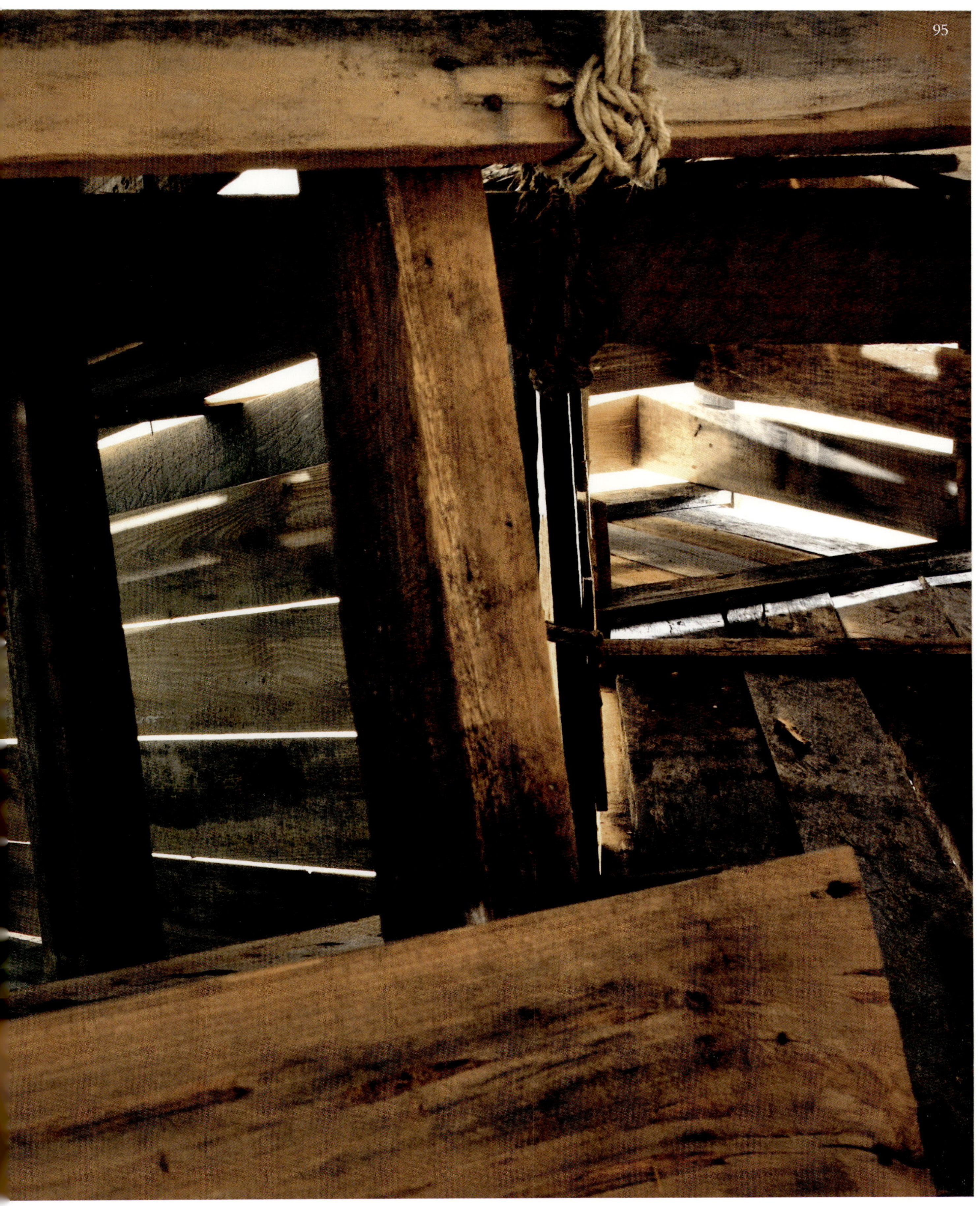

Interior installation view: *Cheese #3*, 2008; Herzliya Museum of Contemporary Art, “Theatrical Gestures,” 2013

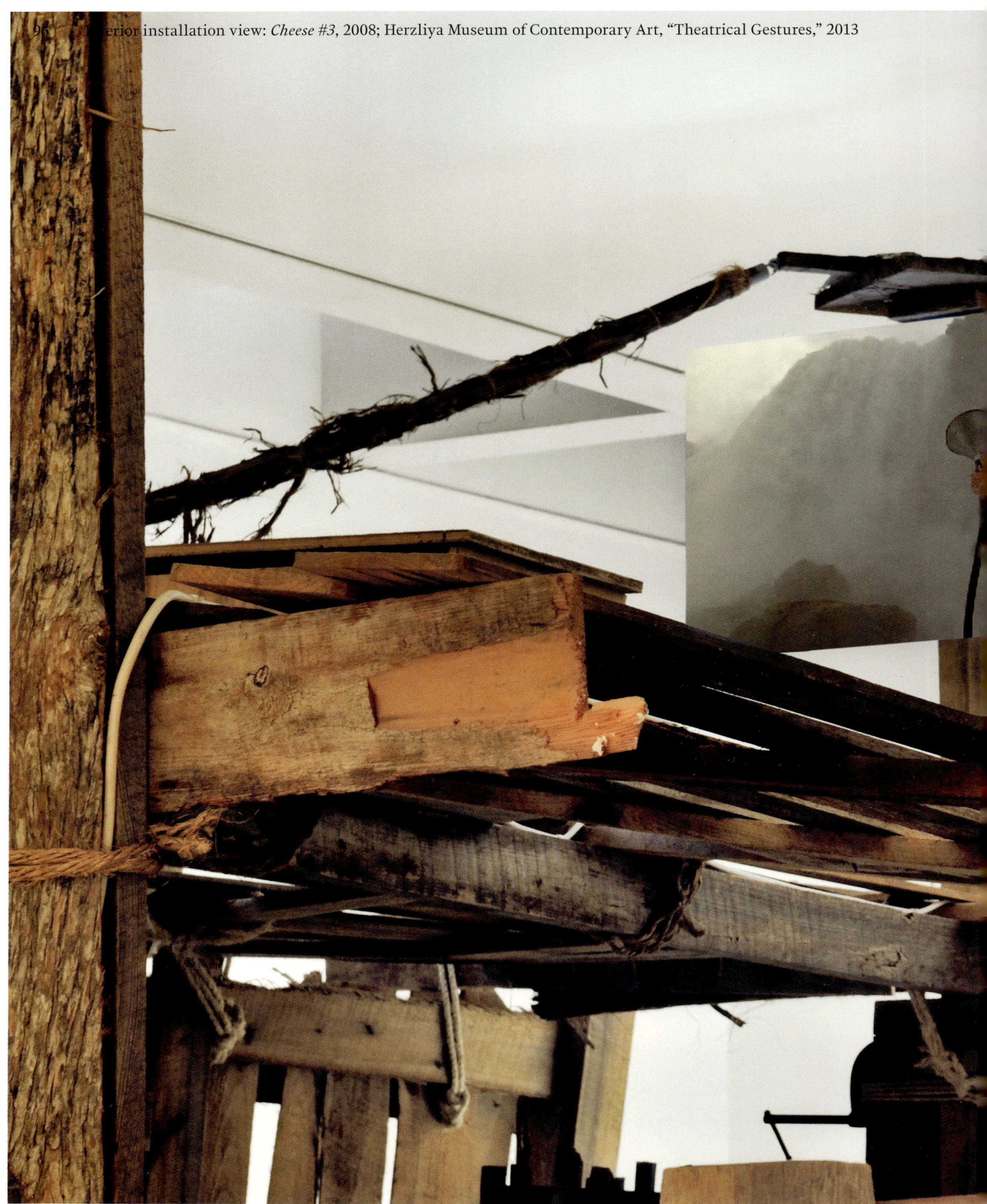

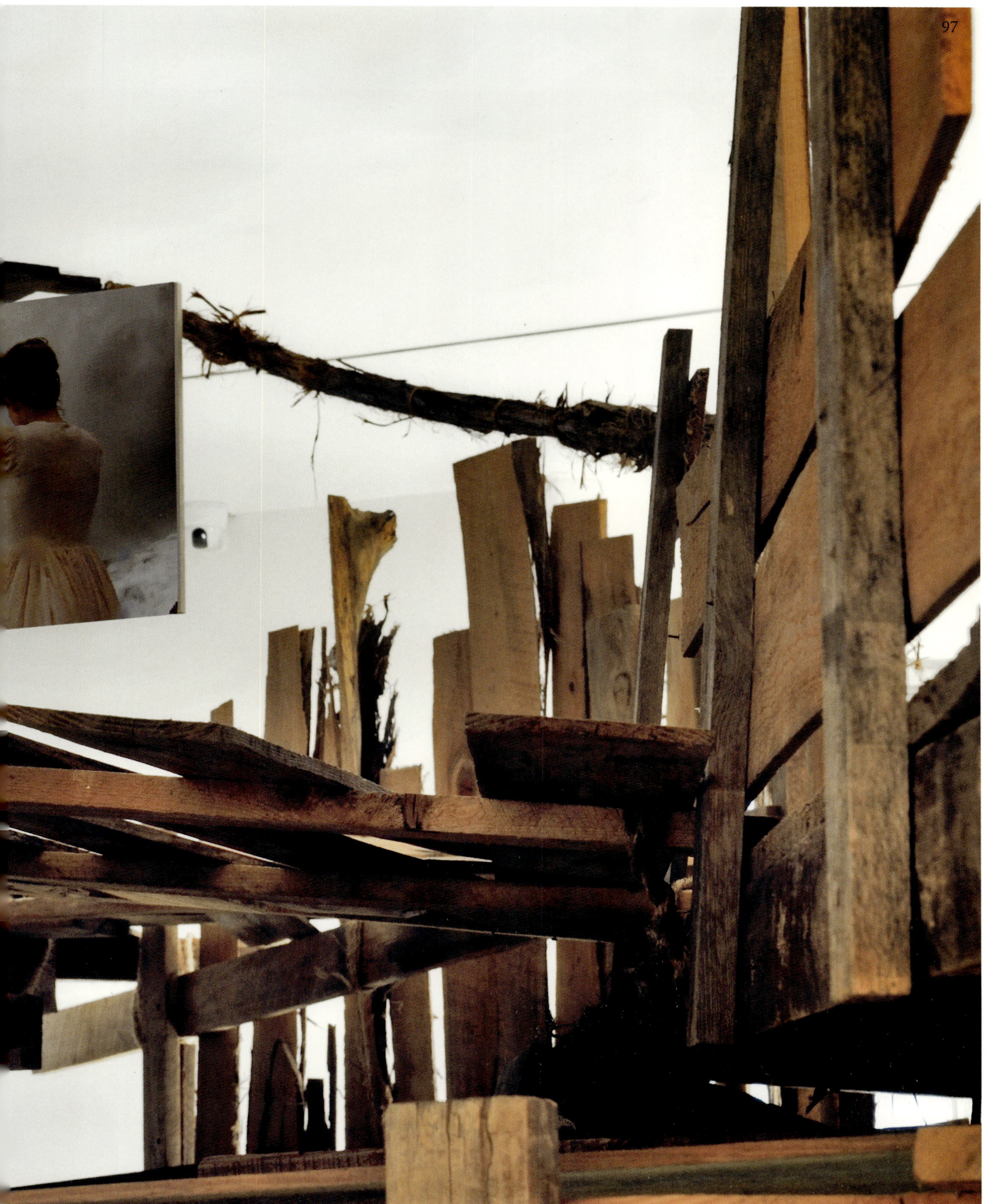

Installation views: *Cheese*, 2008 (La Maison Rouge Exhibition Version); La Maison Rouge, "Mika Rottenberg," 2013

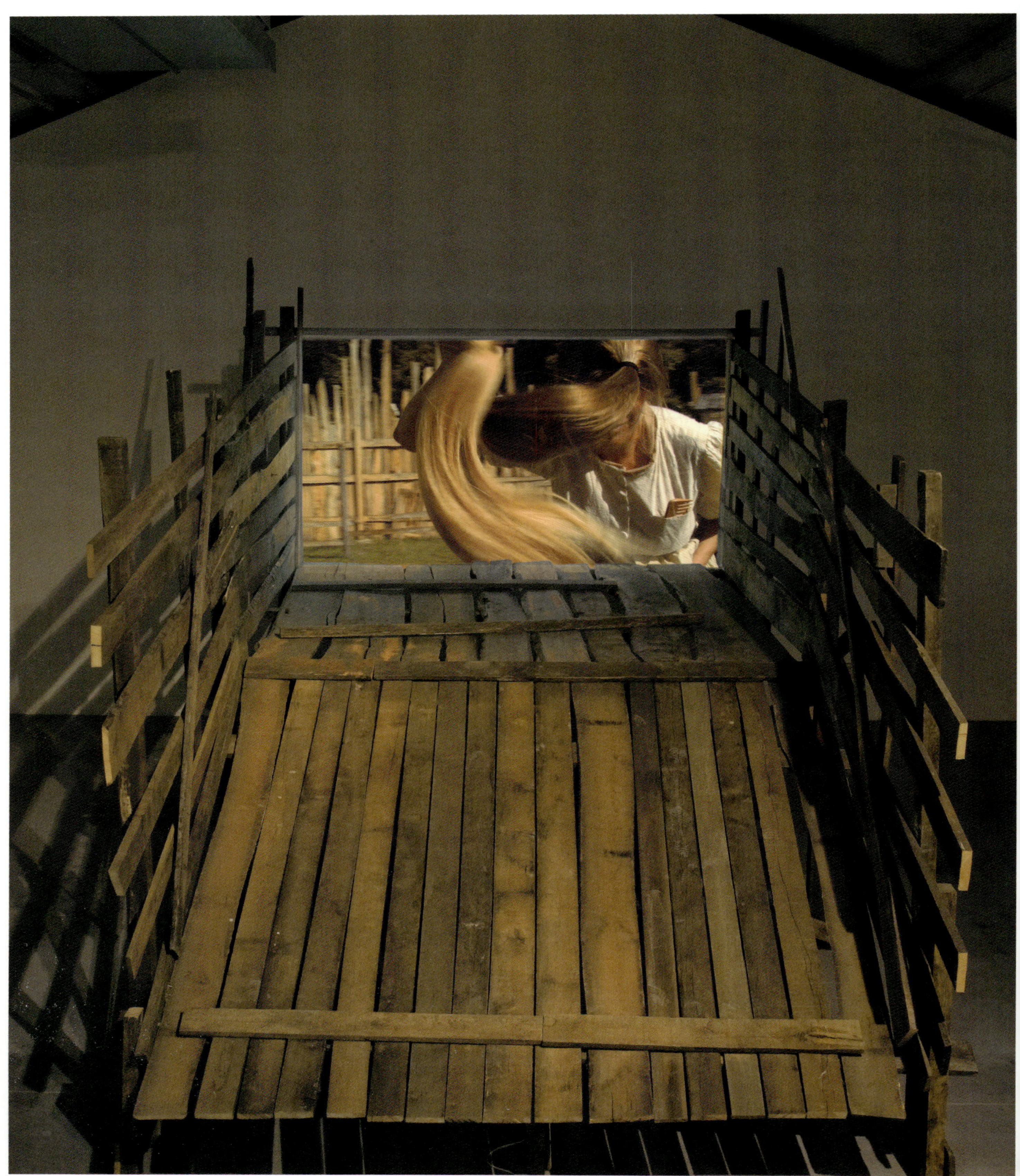

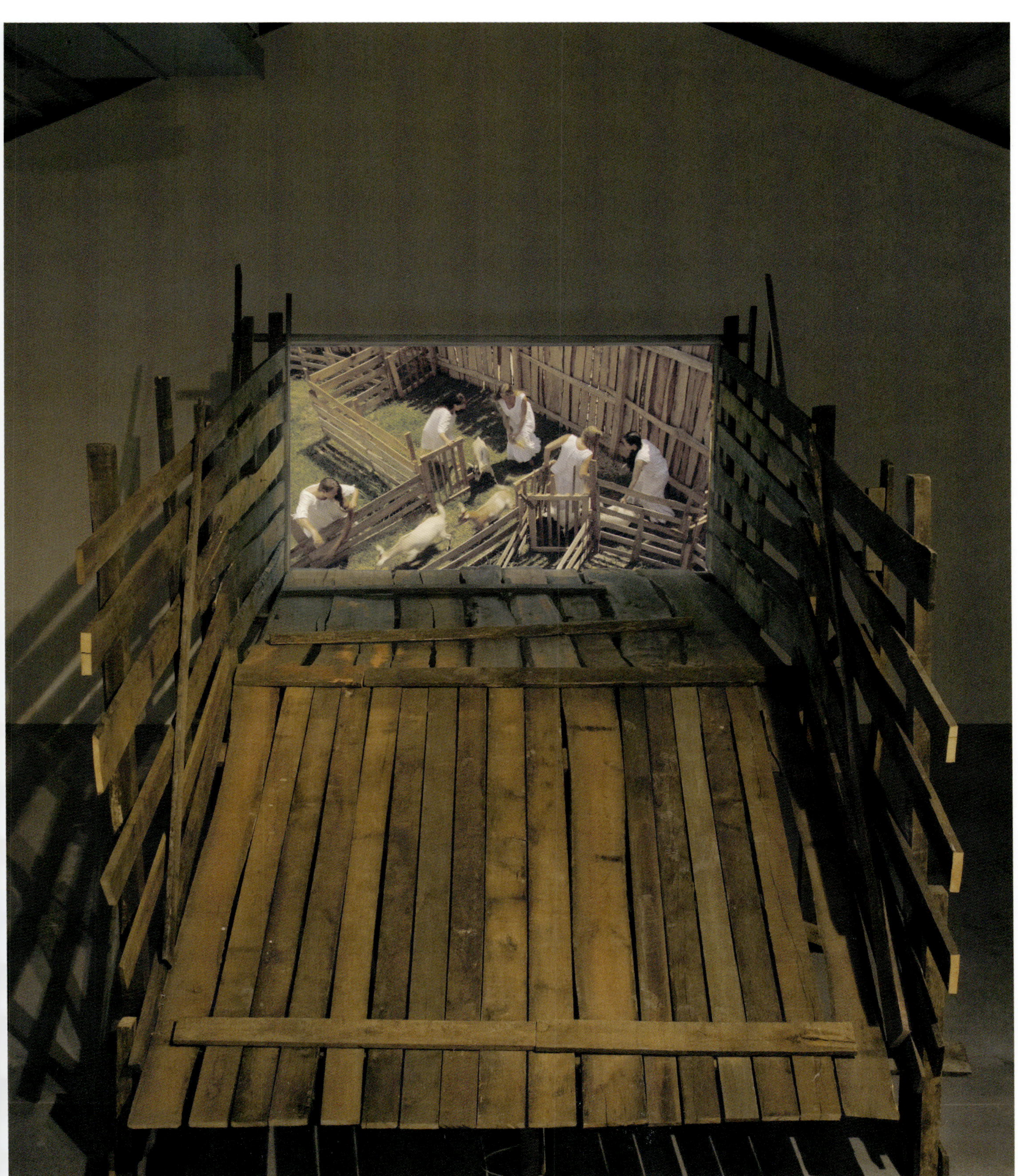

 Still from Cheese, 2007; digital c-print

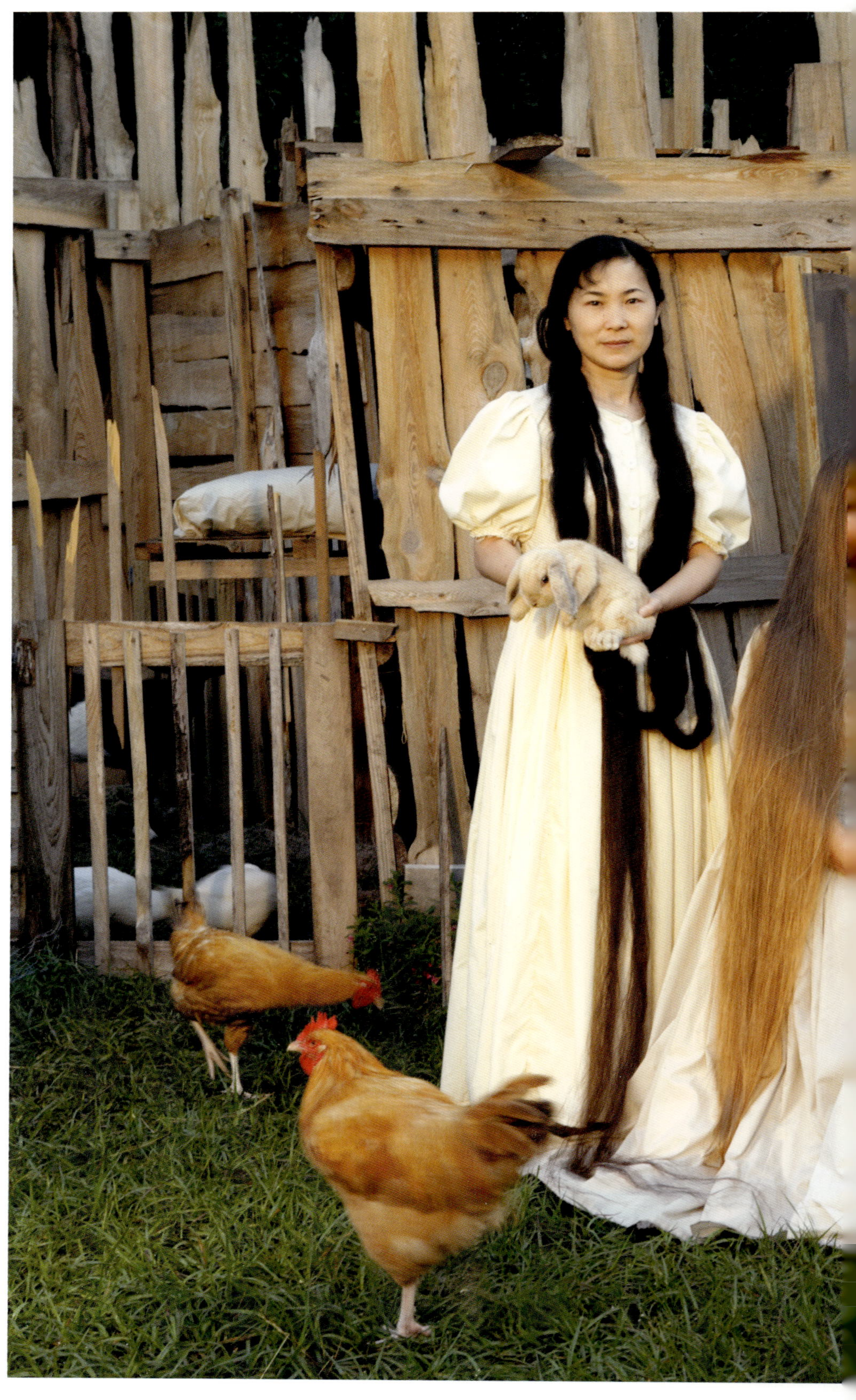

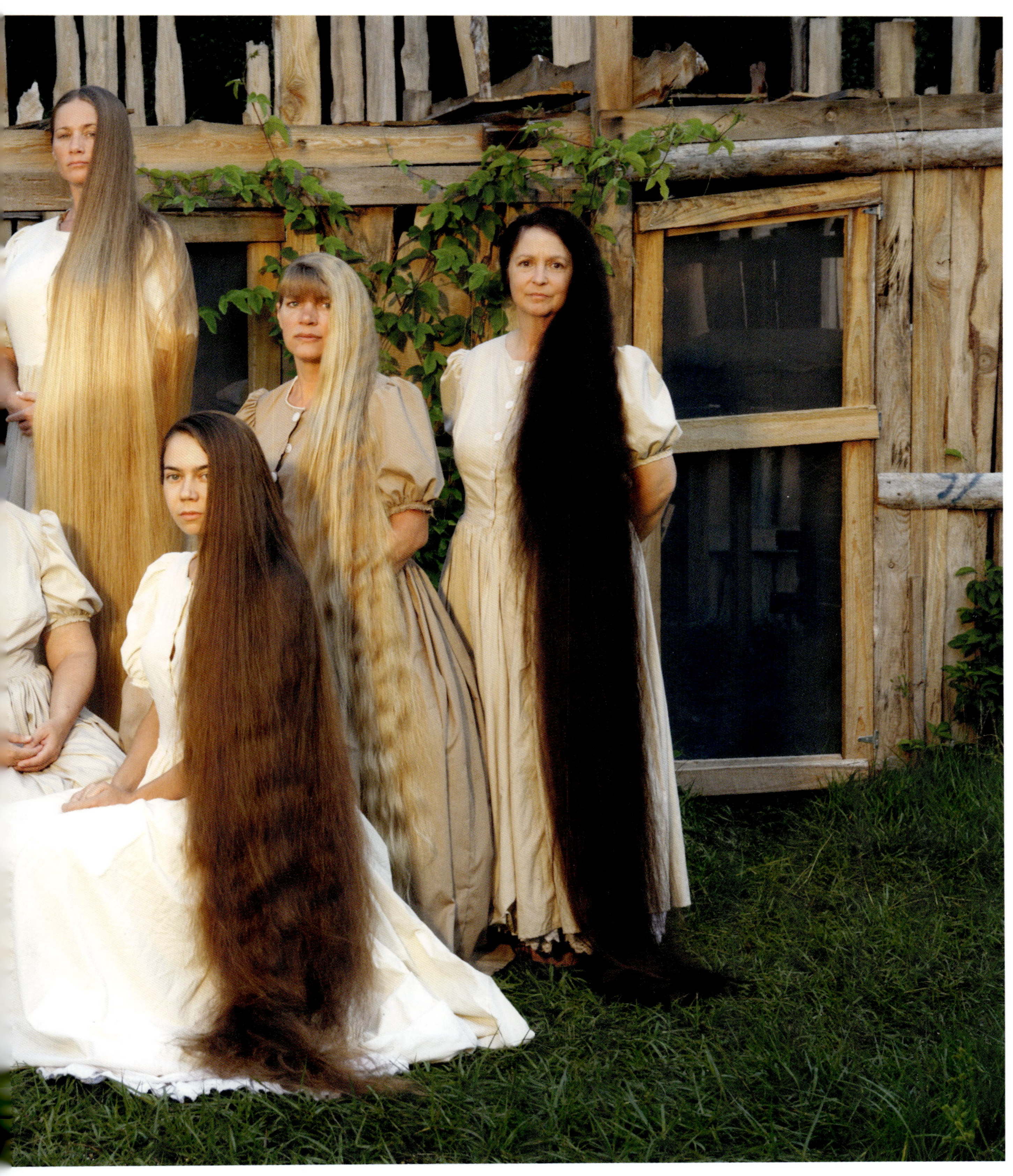

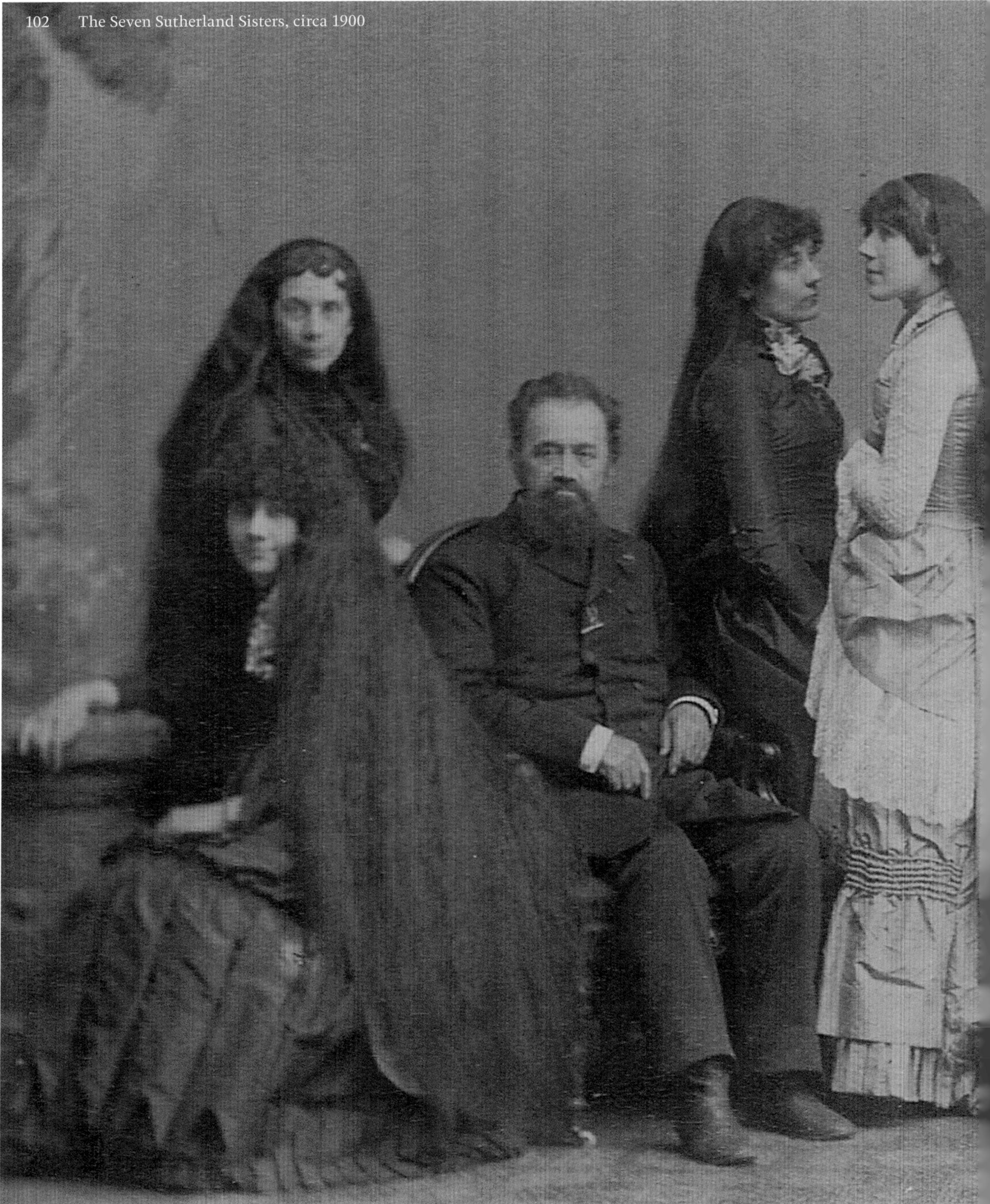

The Seven Sutherland Sisters, circa 1900

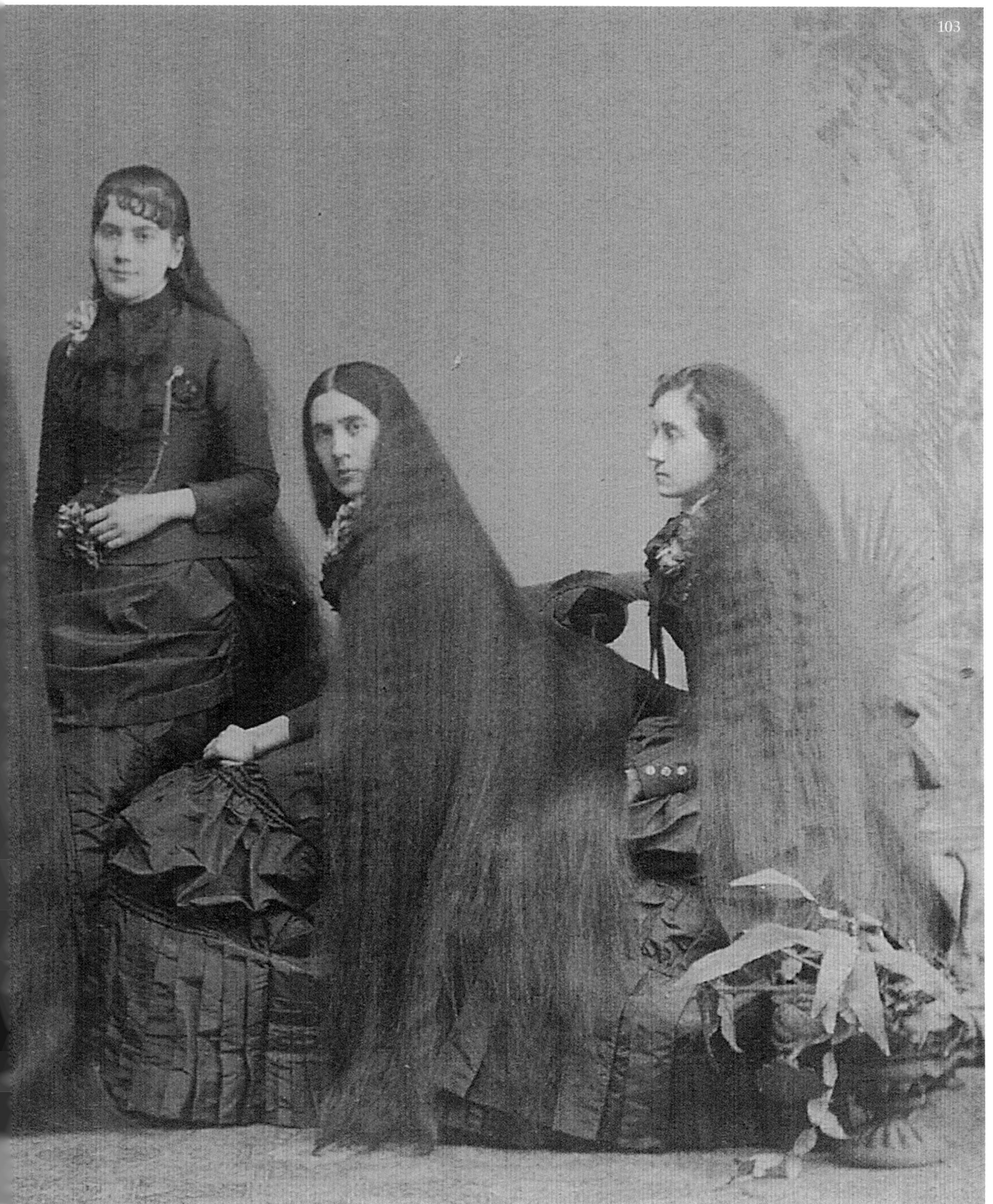

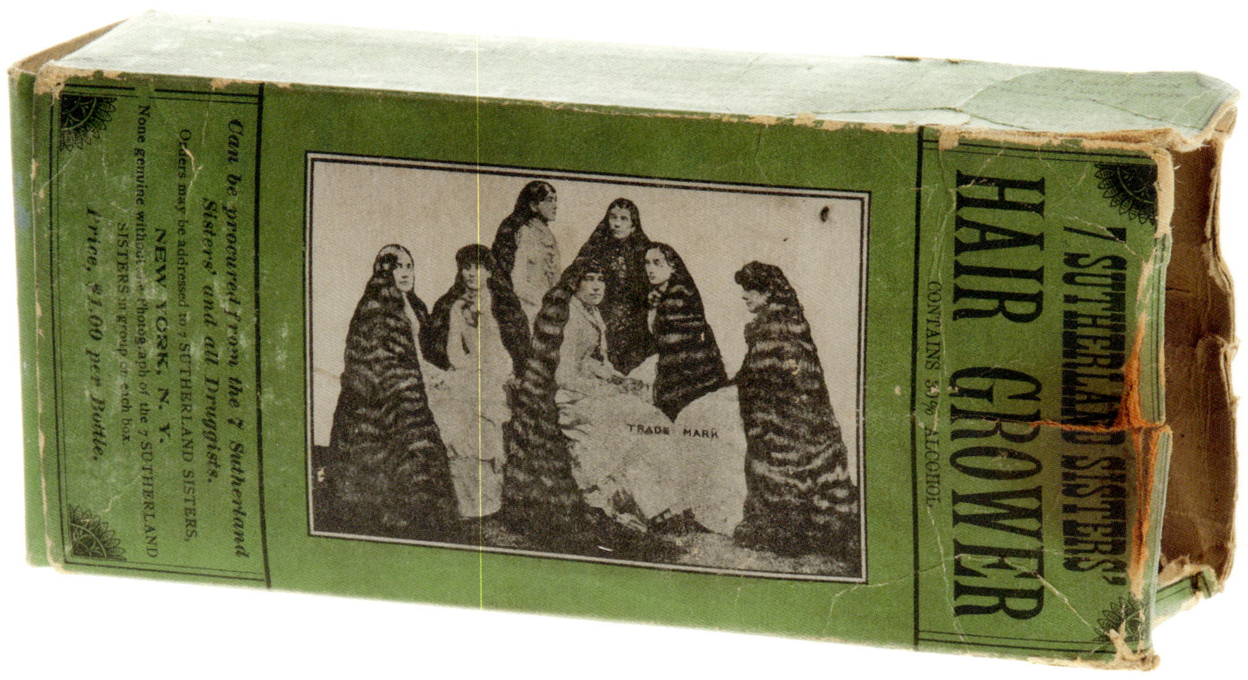
7 SUTHERLAND SISTERS'
HAIR GROWER
TRADE MARK
Can be procured from the 7 Sutherland Sisters' and all Druggists.
NEW YORK, N. Y.
Price, $1.00 per Bottle.

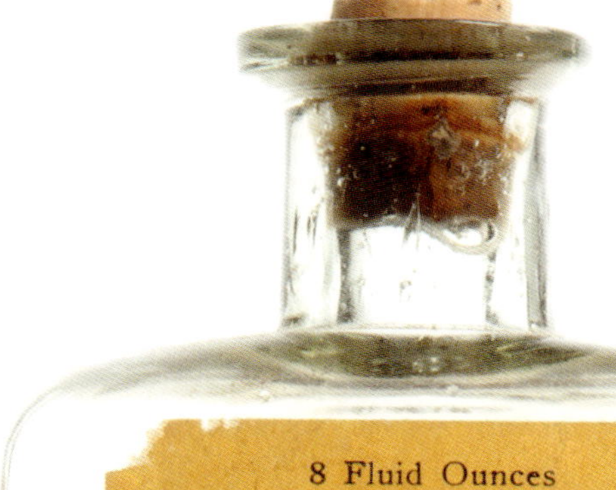
8 Fluid Ounces
THE LUCKY NUMBER
7
SEVEN SUTHERLAND SISTERS'
HAIR GROWER
CONTAINS 15% ALCOHOL
An Elegant Hair Dressing.
Will Stop Hair from Falling Out.
A Preparation Free from Irritating Matter.
For preserving and beautifying the Hair and rendering it soft and glossy, it is one of the best.
This preparation possesses the peculiar properties which so exactly suit the various conditions of the human hair.
NOT A DYE.
DIRECTIONS.— Apply every day before retiring, if convenient, saturating thoroughly the roots and hair. Be sure to wash the hair and scalp every week with the 7 Sutherland Sisters' Hair and Scalp Cleaner. Dry with sun, fan or artificial heat.
MANUFACTURED ONLY BY THE
7 SUTHERLAND SISTERS' Corp.
NEW YORK
The Genuine bears the Seven Sutherland Sisters' Photograph in group.

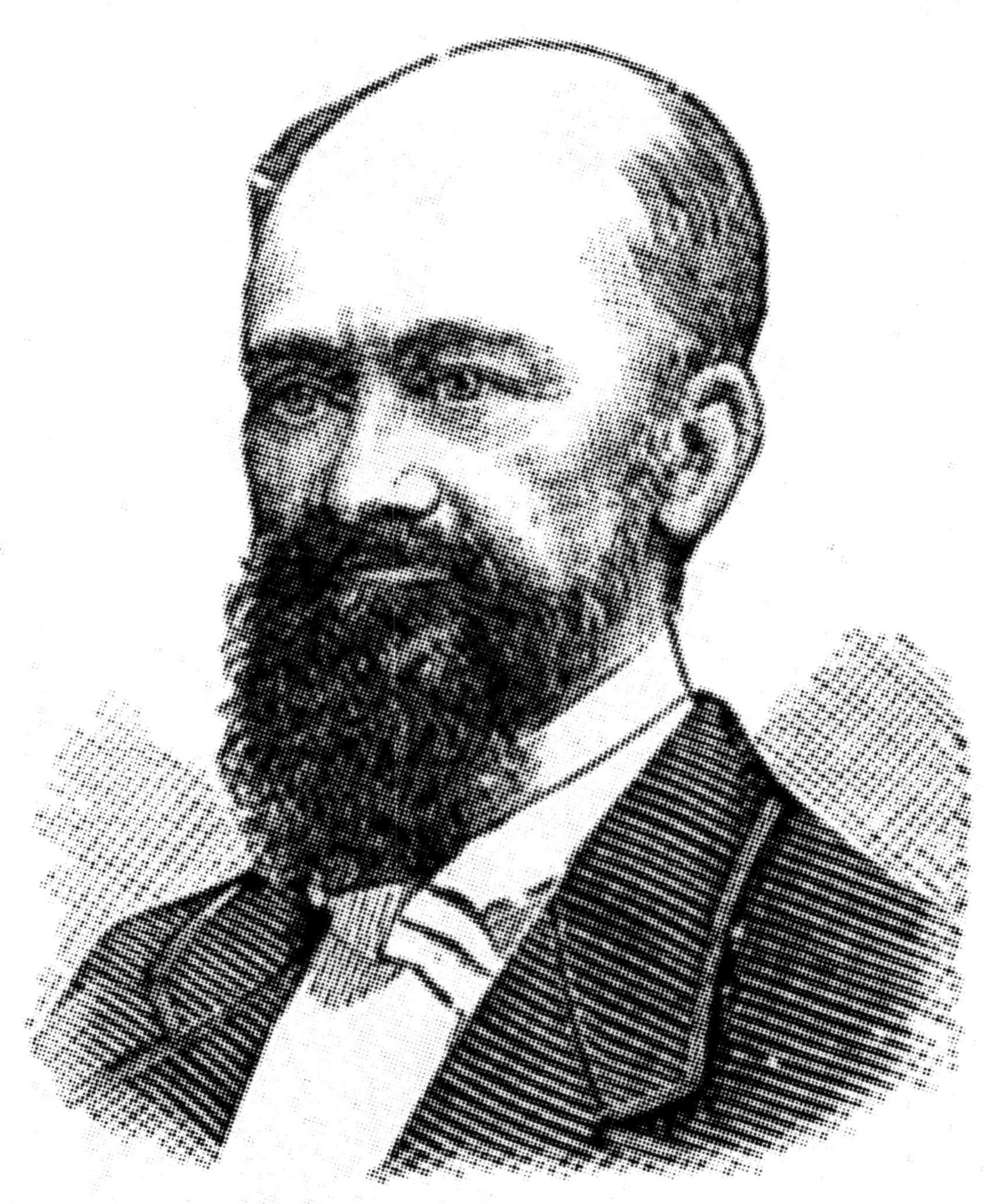
BEFORE USING.

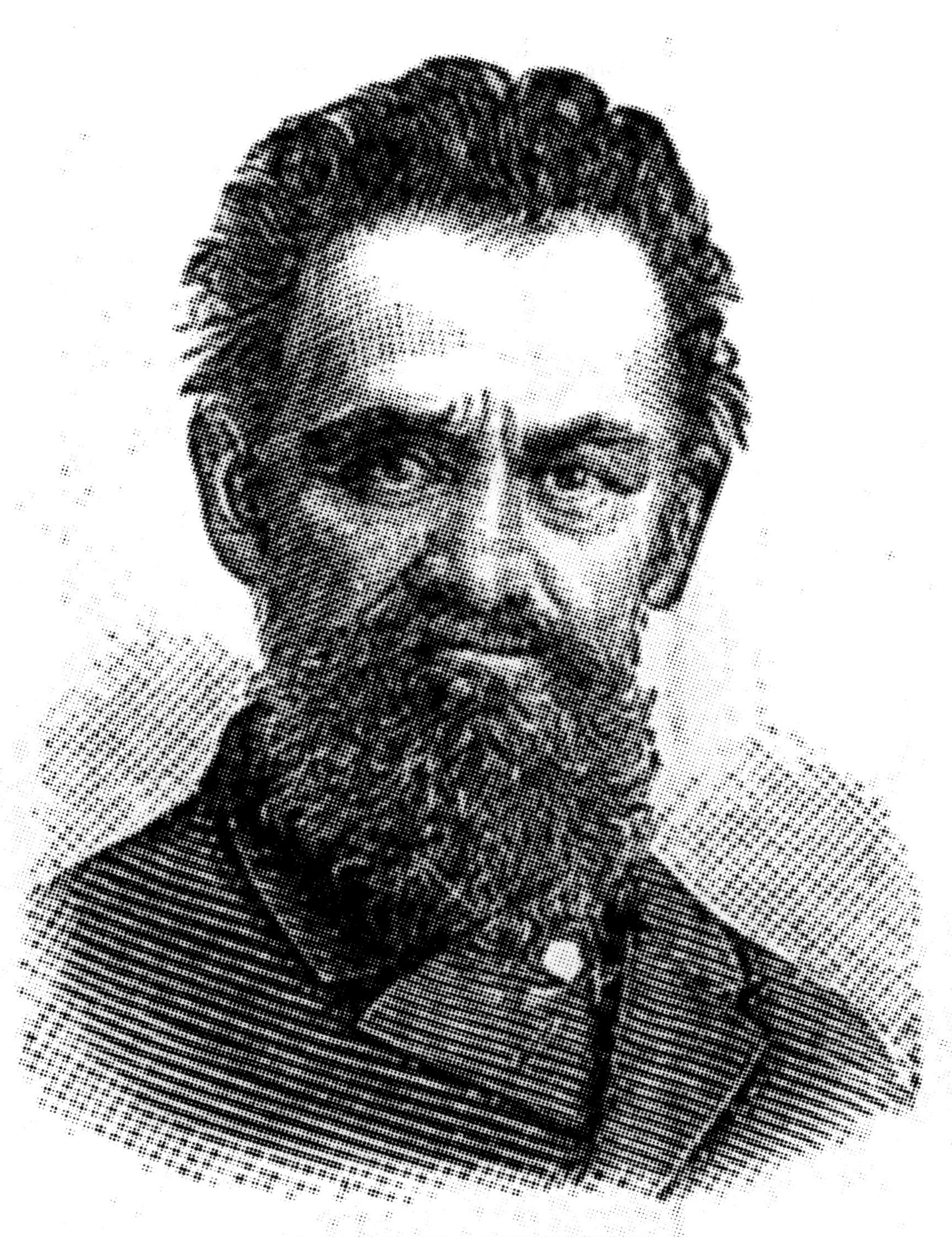

AFTER USING.

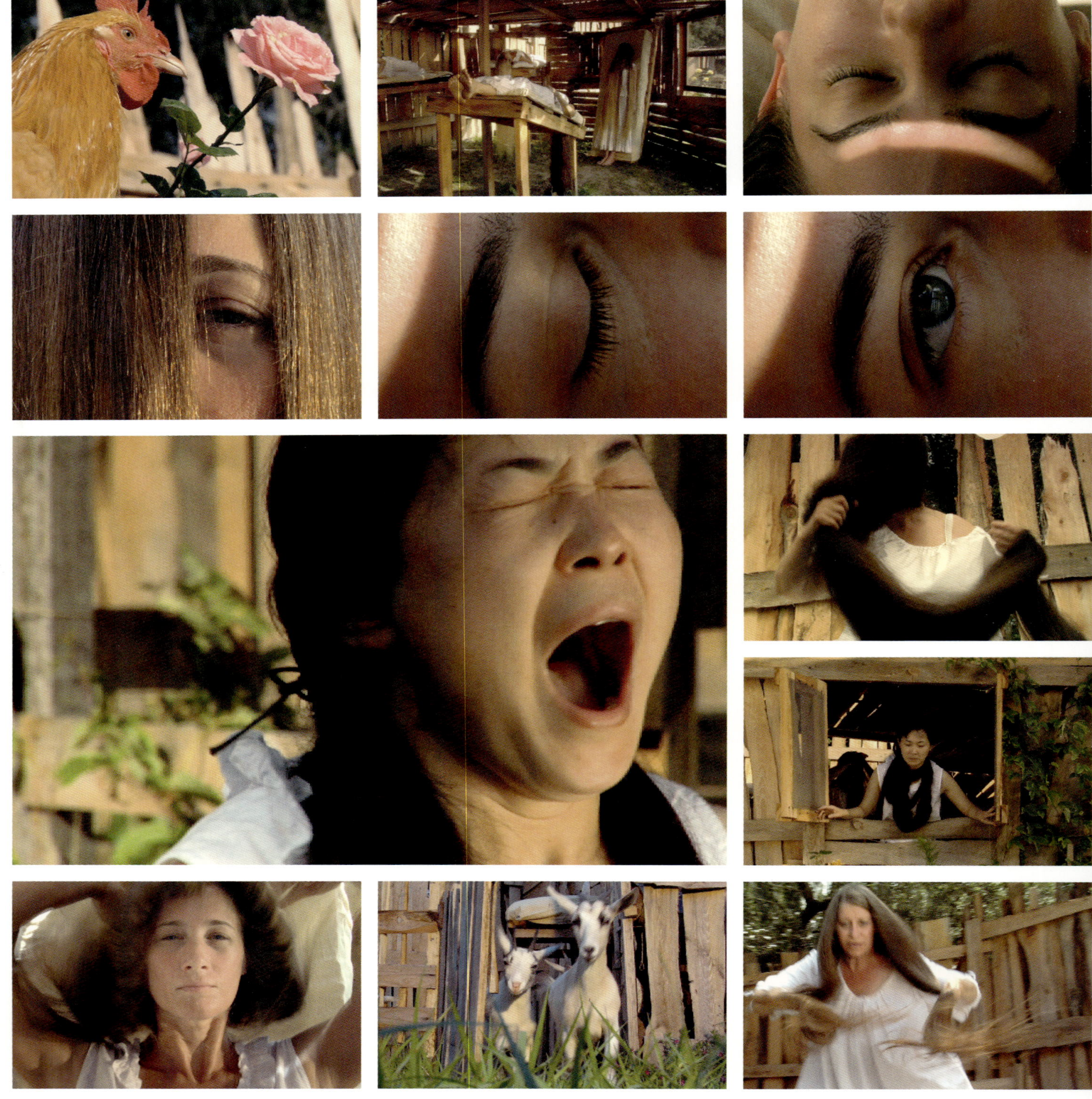

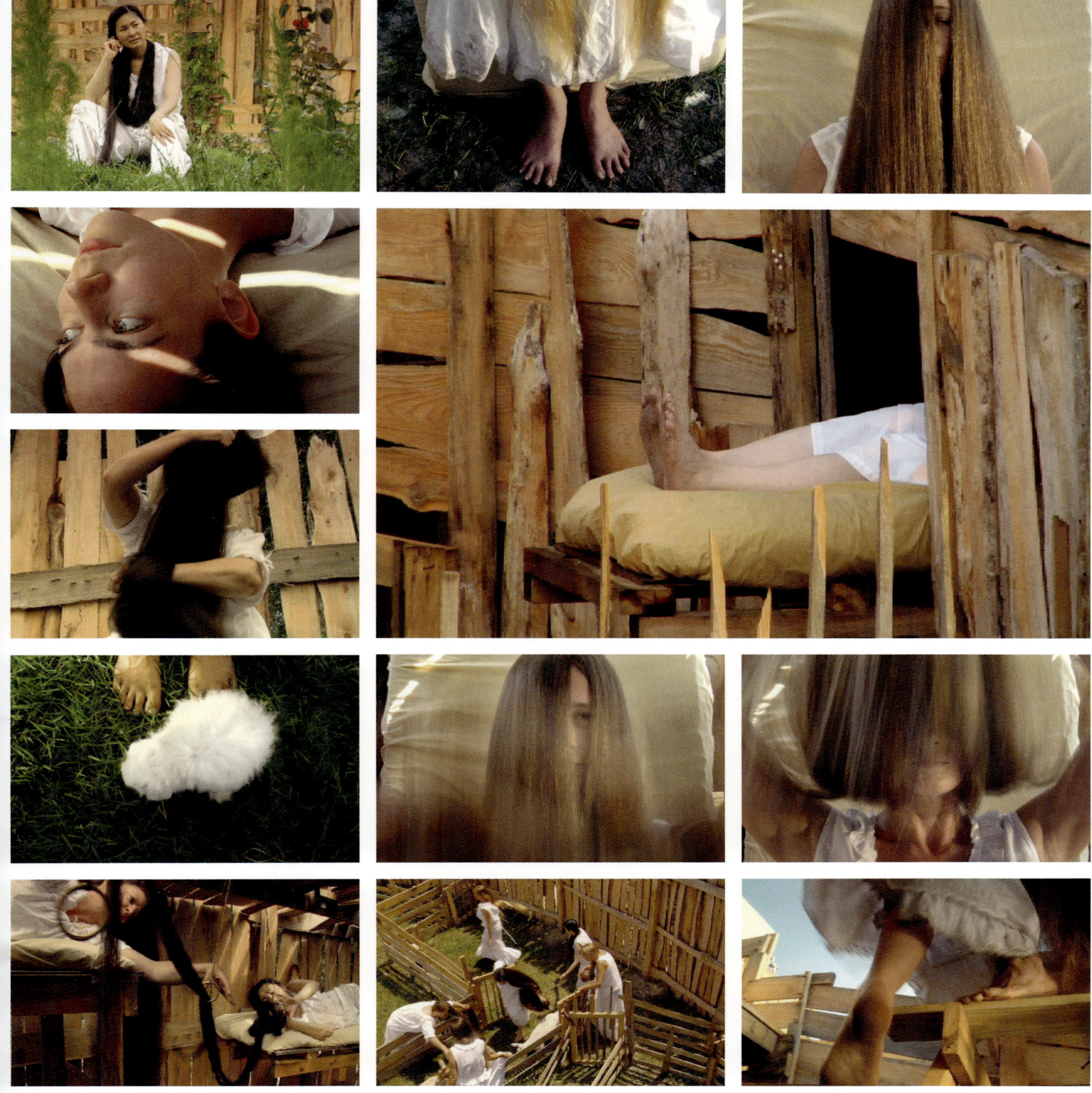

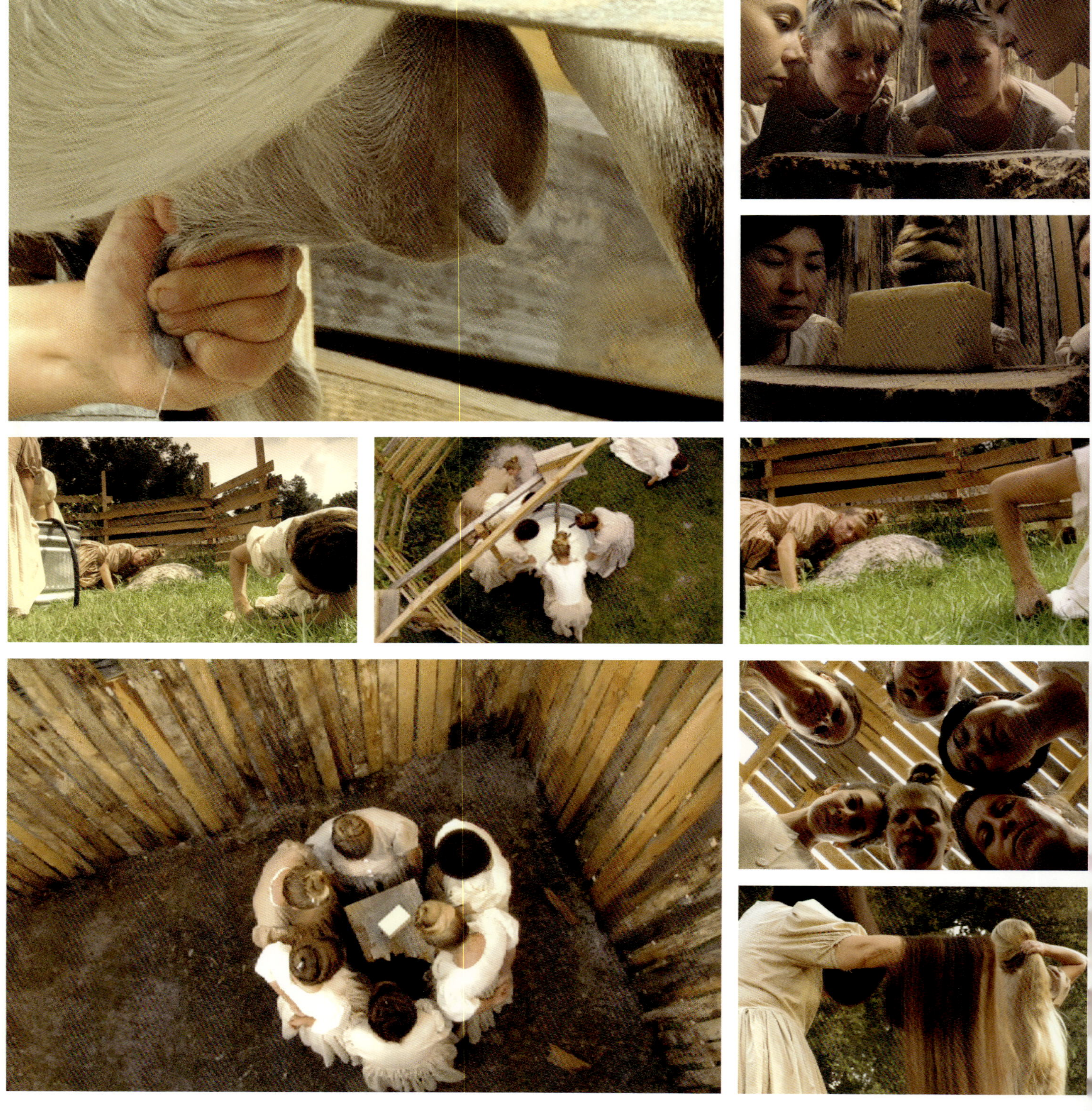

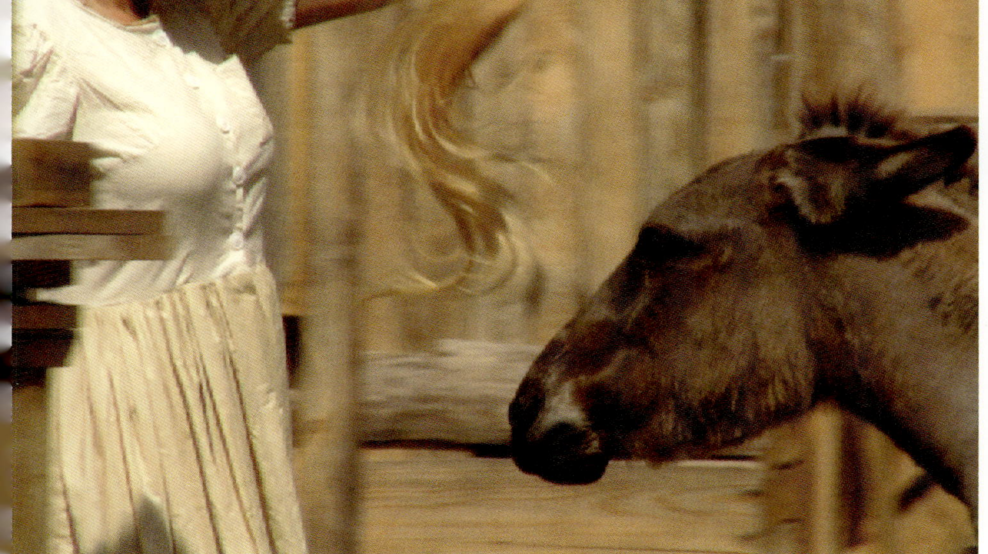

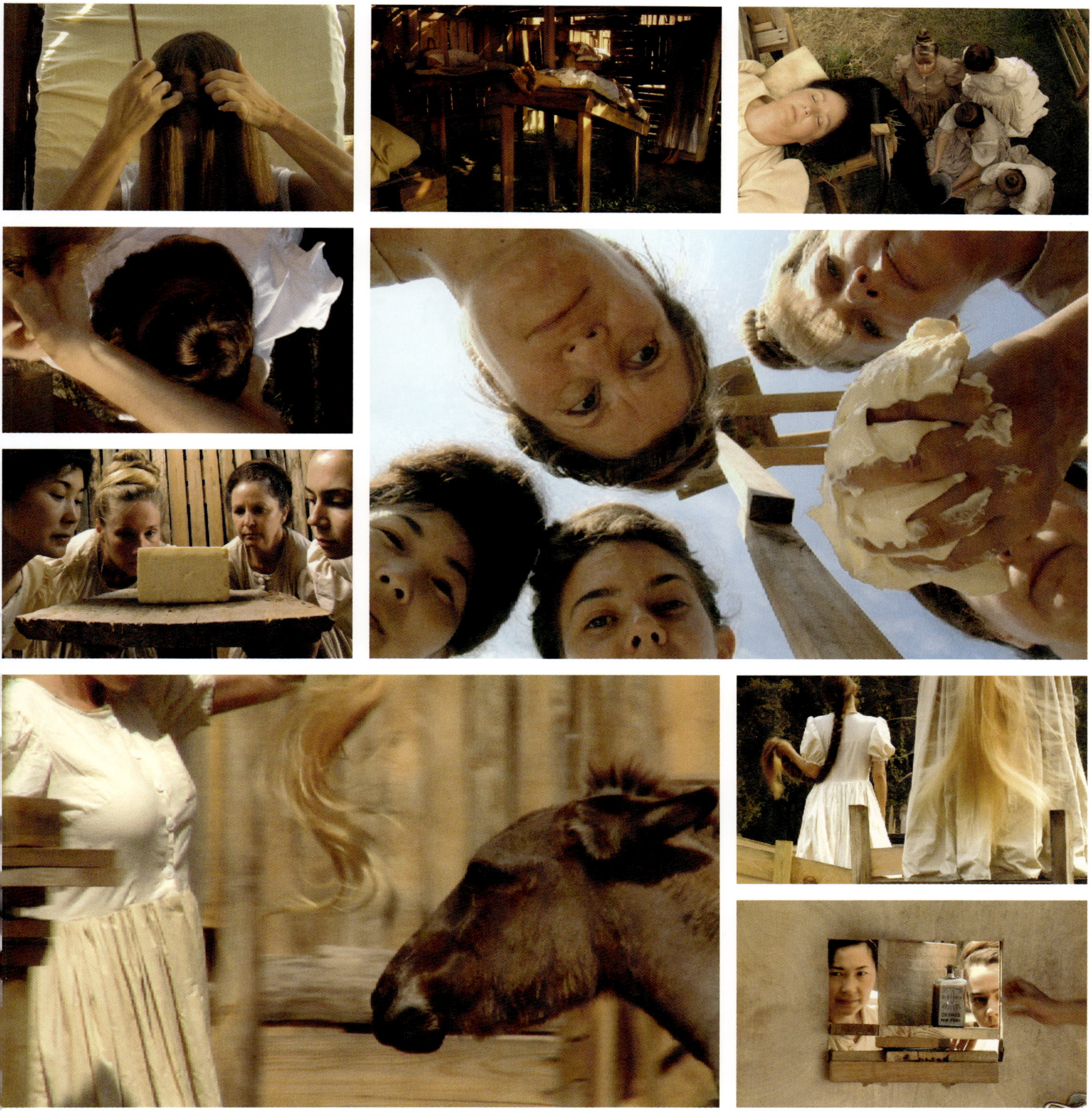

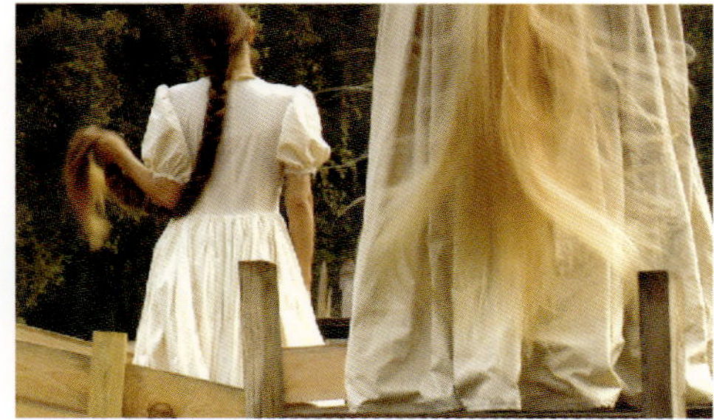

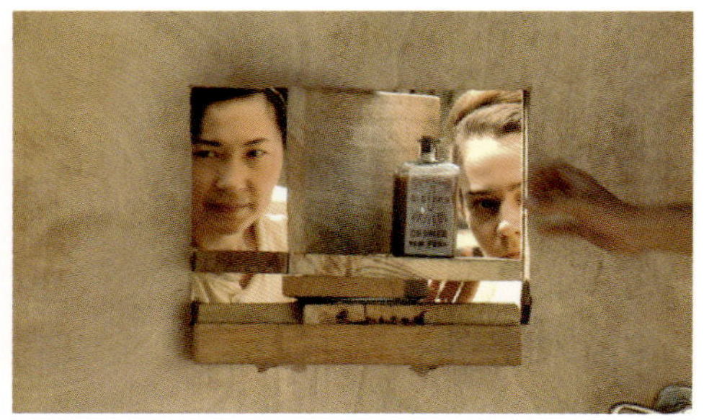

Mika Rottenberg's Video Spaces

Julia Bryan-Wilson

"Space is a practiced place."
— Michel de Certeau

"Geography matters to gender."
— Doreen Massey

ceilings

In *Dough*, Mika Rottenberg's seven-minute video installation from 2005-6, long tubes of stretchy dough pass between hands through vertically stacked architectural spaces, as women at various "work stations" feed the stuff through orifices in the floor and coax it down from crude holes cut in ceiling tiles [Fig. 1]. *Mary's Cherries*, from 2004, likewise features the transport of substances through small round passageways in floors and ceilings, as female workers wearing yellow visors transform fingernails into maraschino cherries through a series of manipulations and physical techniques [Fig. 2]. And in *Squeeze* (2010), a woman produces bright liquid that streams to the room beneath her as she is compressed on both sides by a creaking device, one of many moments in which the "above" and the "below" are connected units. Throughout her practice, Rottenberg provokes us to look up and imagine the ceiling not as a limit or a boundary, but as a porous membrane through which objects are delivered and scatological bodily emissions are conducted [Fig. 3].

This is true, too, of her walls, as they become permeable skins where a wagging tongue might protrude to await its periodic misting, or

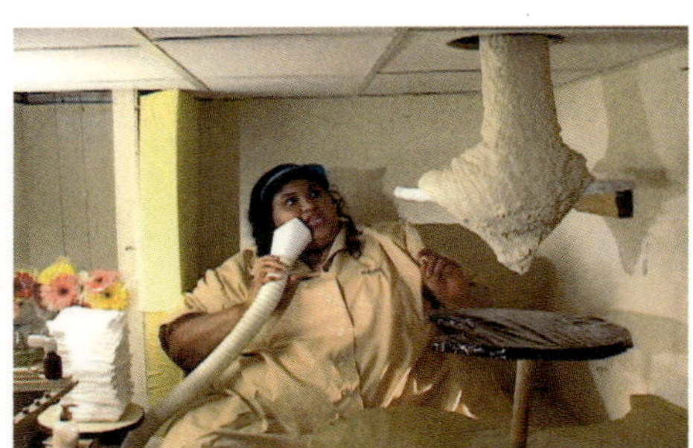

1. Still from *Dough*, 2005-2006

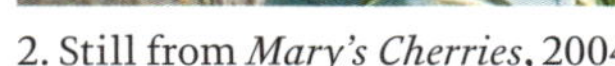

2. Still from *Mary's Cherries*, 2004

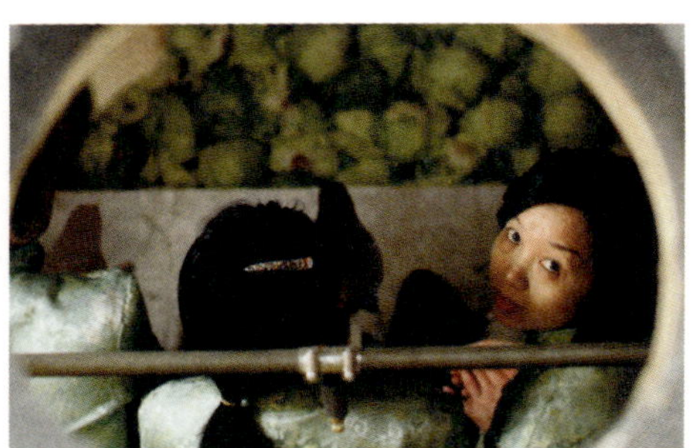

3. Still from *Squeeze*, 2010

where arms from another region of the world might abruptly appear, eager to be massaged [Fig. 4]. Rottenberg's architectures do not merely organize local spaces, but move beyond their self-contained coherence to become portals by which seemingly remote places are suddenly understood as adjacent, linked by the procedures of global capitalism. In her videos, Rottenberg creates specific environments in which her characters and their actions are sited, often building elaborate sets that include carefully designed components such as textured walls and patterned carpets, movable compartments and connected chambers. Within these scenes, figures proceed with their proscribed activities, duties, and labors according to temporal cues that remain somewhat opaque, but seem to be triggered by shifts in the built environment: work is frequently redirected as partitions slide open and shut.

In this regard, Rottenberg activates Michel de Certeau's sense of space as produced by "vectors of direction, velocities, and time variables. Thus space is composed of intersections of mobile elements. It is in a sense actuated by the ensemble of movements deployed within it."[1] Approaching space with a feminist lens, she proposes that these vectors, velocities, and movements primarily congeal around the efforting female body and its byproducts. As feminist geographer Doreen Massey proposes, "gender relations vary over space."[2] She writes, "From the symbolic meaning of spaces/places and the clearly gendered messages which they transmit, to straightforward exclusion by violence, spaces and places are not only themselves gendered but, in their being so, they both reflect and affect the ways in which gender is constructed and understood."[3]

To augment her gendered spatializing, Rottenberg constructs site-specific assemblages to contain, display, and frame her videos, ones that extend recognizable features from her somewhat otherworldly scenarios out into the literal gallery space to be encountered by the viewer. Though the criticism on Rottenberg's work has tended to account mainly for the content of her videos, not least their feminist and Marxist overtones and their Taylorist fabulations, the artist also critically foregrounds the *form* of video installation as a special situation of spectating. By highlighting the spatial conditions in which she both produces and circulates her work, she critiques the universalizing

1 Michel de Certeau, *The Practice of Everyday Life* (Berkeley: University of California Press, 1984), p. 117.

2 Doreen Massey, *Space, Place, and Gender* (Cambridge: Polity Press, 1994), p. 178.

3 Massey, p. 179.

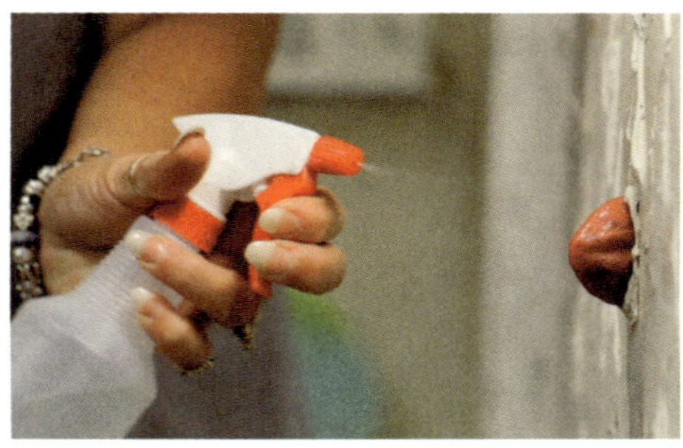

4. Still from *Squeeze*, 2010

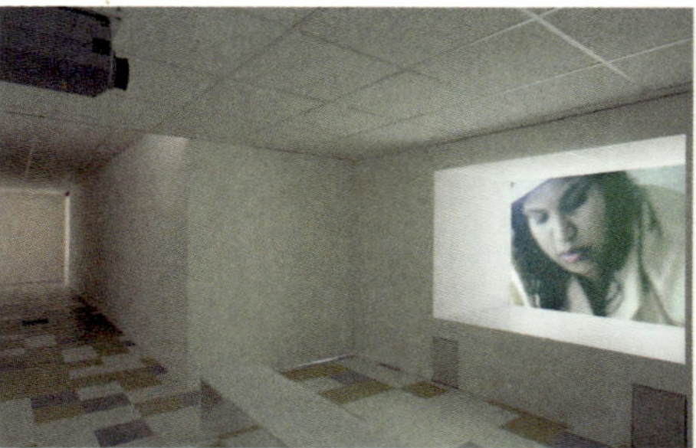

5. *(Big) Dough*, 2005–2006

conventions of what de Certeau calls the continual rehearsal and practice of space, accounting for the unevenness and dislocations wrought by gender, race, nation, and class. Viewers watching *Dough*, for instance, at the KW Institute for Contemporary Art in Berlin, would find themselves under drop ceiling tiles that visually rhyme with those in the video [Fig. 5]. Rottenberg invites us to consider every surface within the space of reception. She has installed linoleum floors and walls with thick raised lick-marks, cobbled together rustic wooden forts (*Cheese*, 2008), gouged out peepholes (*Fried Sweat*, 2008), and stacked boxes within a modified shipping crate (*Tropical Breeze*, 2004) [Fig. 6, Fig. 7]. Rather than being projected in darkened rooms or played on monitors that are placed unobtrusively within an undifferentiated viewing area of the gallery, in many instances her videos enfold you, inviting you to peer through, to duck under, to crouch down and go inside.

With these material continuities, Rottenberg intimately situates her spectating subjects in proximity to the filmed bodies and their efforts on screen. "Are we being put in the position of managers scrutinizing [the characters] for lapses of attention?" queried one art critic, noting how Rottenberg's videos make us "uncomfortably aware of our own privileged status."[4] We are made alert of our bodies as they are sometimes forced into less-than-comfortable viewing positions, even as the images captivate the eye and ear; as Efrat Mishori asserts, "To watch Rottenberg's works is to stumble into them; we are carried away by an oscillating force field and begin to move with it."[5] To watch her videos is not only to enter into her intricate and absorbing narratives, but also to be made aware of the floor you are standing on, the walls that surround you, and the ceiling that looms overhead. In contrast to Brian O'Doherty's assertion that the ceiling is often effaced within modern art, in Rottenberg's videos, ceilings (as tangible barriers and as metaphors for the limits of women's upward mobility, as in the so-called "glass ceiling") are particular places of concern. As O'Doherty wrote in his well-known argument against the apparent neutrality of the "white cube" gallery:

> We don't look at the ceiling much now. In the history of indoor looking up, we rank low. Other ages put plenty up there to look at. Pompeii proposed, among other things, that more women than men looked

4 Claire Barliant, "Mika Rottenberg," *Artforum* (April 2006): 247.

5 Efrat Mishori, "Welcome to Mika Rottenberg's Video-Actopus Factory," in *Mika Rottenberg* (New York: Gregory R. Miller & Co., 2011), p. 86.

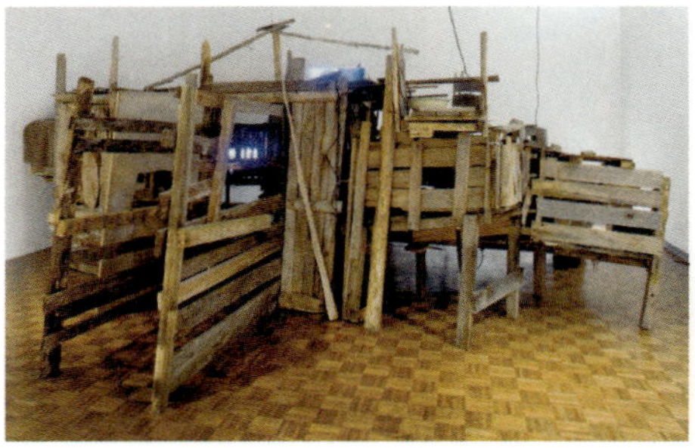

6. *Cheese #1*, 2008

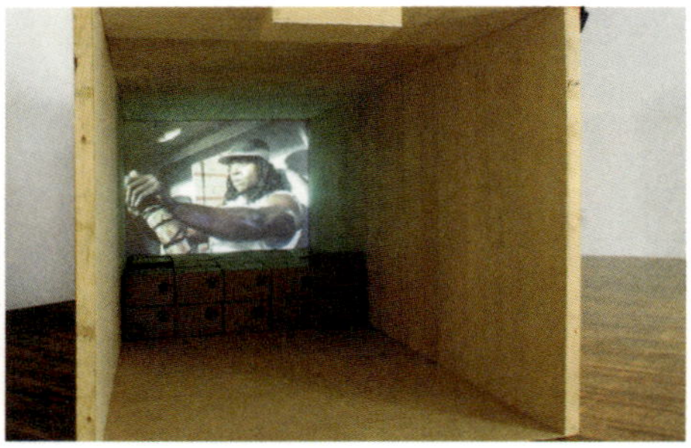

7. *Tropical Breeze*, 2004

> at the ceiling. The Renaissance ceiling locked its painted figures into geometric cells. ... With electric light, the ceiling became an intensely cultivated garden of fixtures, and modernism simply ignored it. The ceiling lost its role in the ensemble of the total room.[6]

6 Brian O'Doherty, "Context as Content," *Inside the White Cube: The Ideology of the Gallery Space* (Berkeley: University of California Press, 1986), p. 66.

Both within the internal logic of her tightly paced video-spaces, and within the built environments in which we view them, Rottenberg pays attention to all facets of the practice of seeing art within the "ensemble of the total room."

rooms

From its earliest days, video installation has had a long history of incorporating viewers within various settings, providing a range of aesthetic and ideological contexts for reception. Nam June Paik embedded screens within unconventional or atmospheric surroundings, as in his *TV Garden* from 1974. Dan Graham's pieces in the 1970s with multiple screens and dividers implicated the viewing subject within larger networks of surveillance and feedback, as well as reflected upon "the social order of public/private space and the psychological sense of self."[7] Mona Hatoum's exploration of the visceral boundaries between inside/outside in her endoscopic-technology piece, *Corps étranger* (1994), stands the viewer inside an enclosed cylinder evocative of a medical imaging device looking down at a projected image as the camera moves inside the artist's body, producing a relay between what is seen and how it is seen [Fig. 8].

7 Dan Graham, "Video in Relation to Architecture," in *Illuminating Video: An Essential Guide to Video Art*, Doug Hall and Sally Jo Fifer, eds. (New York: Aperture, 1990), p. 168.

These concerns with the spatial, dimensional, corporeal aspects of video display—video's *sculptural* effects—locate it as a medium at a remove from both the televisual and the cinematic models to which it is often compared. Thus, while Rottenberg's work has clear resonances with the animation of Czech filmmaker Jan Švankmajer, with his distortions of scale and merging of the organic and inorganic, her emphasis on unexpected architectural openings can also be fruitfully compared to New York Post-Minimal artist Gordon Matta-Clark. Matta-Clark orchestrated architectural interventions such as *Conical Intersect* (1975), a spiraling cut through two derelict buildings in Paris which re-oriented exterior and

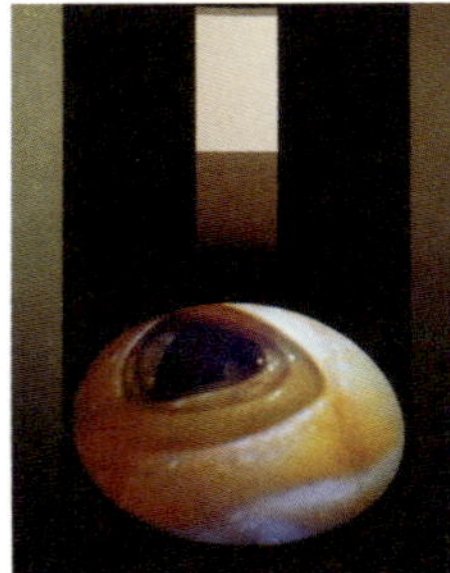

8. Mona Hatoum, *Corps étranger*, 1994

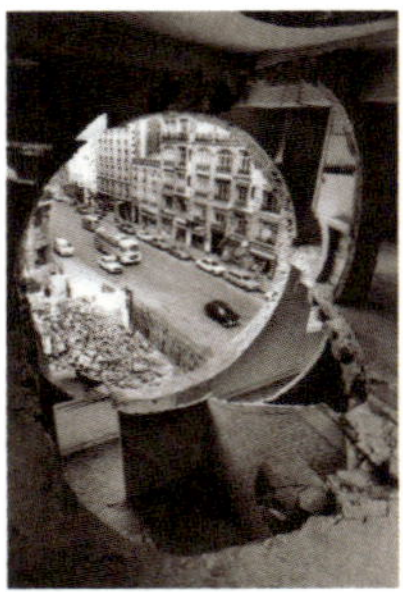

9. Gordon Matta-Clark, documentation of *Conical Intersect*, 1975

interior [Fig. 9]. And in *Splitting* (1974), he sliced a suburban house down the middle. Both Rottenberg and Matta-Clark reconsider how architecture demarcates spaces, and they seek to scramble the lines between public and private, exposed and enclosed. In Rottenberg's spliced-together edifices, the public/private divide is further freighted with gendered notions about the domain of the domestic as "a woman's place."

Rottenberg's rooms appear crowded, but they are efficient; by this I mean that every element within them serves a purpose. A crudely customized wooden holder might contain a spray bottle, conveniently at the ready to spritz waiting appendages. Small potted plants operate as signifiers of bare-bones "decoration" while also referring to personalized touches in office cubicles. Seemingly superfluous actions are productive, as when sparkling dust rubbed off a woman's face solidifies into the compact circles of blush. Rottenberg is keenly attuned to how furniture and interior design—as well as dress and ornamentation like artificial fingernails—can powerfully signify gender and class, how quickly and effectively they can visually register economic status [Fig. 10]. Stained tiles, popcorn-style interior textures, pink and sea-foam green uniforms: these are trappings of the feminized working classes who perform services (i.e., rituals of grooming, bodily upkeep, and maintenance) as well as manufacture goods. Rottenberg has exhibited fragments of walls—entitled "Textures"—as freestanding sculptures [Fig. 11]; their coarsely speckled surfaces bear a resemblance to Piero Manzoni's achromes, the obsessive accretions of Yayoi Kusama, and the prickly wax-and-resin pieces of Lynda Benglis [Fig. 12].

In Rottenberg's universe, production consists of low-tech but strenuous manual labor such as rolling, kneading, clipping, chopping, or excreting (i.e., crying and sweating). The bodies that undertake these tasks demand periodic care, as when workers from disparate places on the globe harvesting lettuce and rubber in *Squeeze* stop and plunge their hands through the ground to receive applications of lotion by women who, widening the circuit of bodily ministrations, have their own asses occasionally misted. (Those asses are seated in cavities in the wall and protrude comically into a separate room.) The mingling and mutual constitution of her

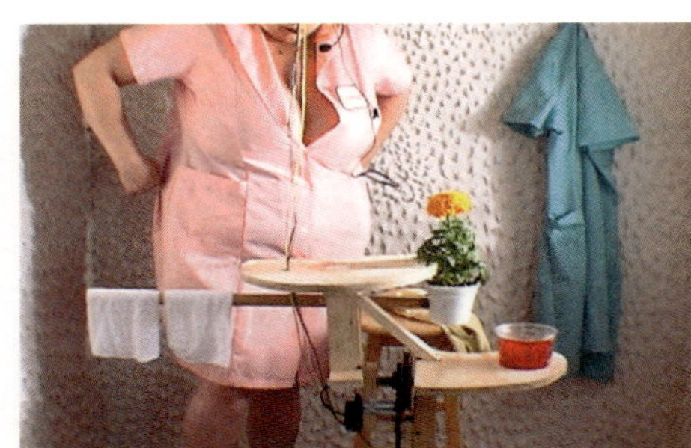

10. Still from *Mary's Cherries*, 2004

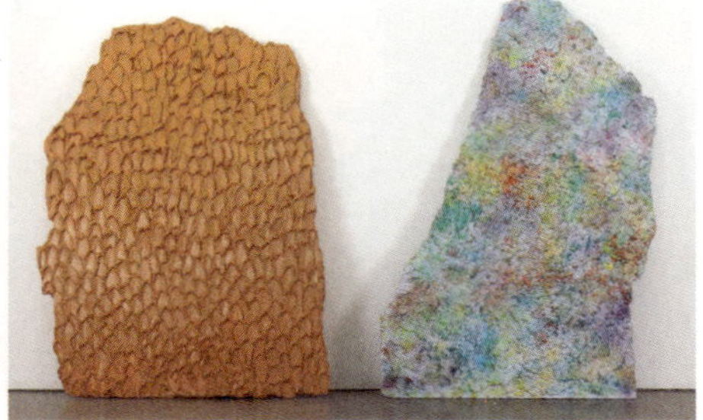

11. *Texture 1 & 3*, 2013

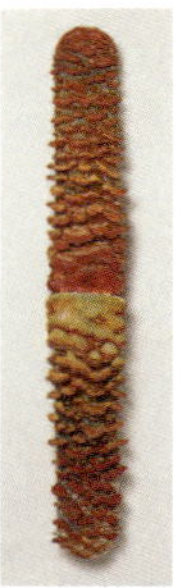

12. Lynda Benglis, *For Bob*, 1971

spheres of service and production—however absurd the act of care or useless the final product—render them relational and interdependent.

Like the organs of a body, Rottenberg's spaces are dynamic and interconnected as they circulate matter to be processed. They form a system, and it is a system in which the viewer is understood to play a role, even if that role is primarily that of a voyeur who stands outside the action beyond the threshold of the "fourth wall." Her constructed little ersatz factories, with bodies and furniture and equipment that are fitted neatly, just so, inside of them, are filled to near-bursting [Fig. 13]. Every detail is plotted, with objects and actors and rooms niftily nested together to suggest a dollhouse or diorama. As with the sculptures of Joseph Cornell that imbue everyday, found objects with fascination by virtue of being carefully selected, arranged, and framed, Rottenberg's spaces are minor miracles of curation and compression. Like Cornell, too, she exhibits whimsy at the same time that she gestures to much darker registers, including alienation, isolation, and ceaseless toil; the sense of endlessness is especially strong given the looping nature of her moving-image work.

boxes

Rottenberg's spaces are forged not through actual construction but through editing; our sense of how the rooms flow together is structured by the seamless flow of the video, as cuts between discrete areas are sutured within the viewer's mind to create a credible, if incongruous, architectural whole [Fig. 14]. Though her fabricated sets do not operate the way they appear to, her meticulous sense of spatial continuity generates what feels intuitively to be a complete order. Yet it is an uncanny and unsettling order, one that is continually ruptured and reconstituted, by turns familiar and incomprehensible. Echoing a Surrealist ethos as well as the disjunctions that attend to late capitalism, Rottenberg presses together the peculiar and the mundane. Take the scenario for *Tropical Breeze*: a bodybuilder creates wet wipes by swabbing her sweat on tissues. She herself is fueled by an energy drink that helps create the tissues' "lemon scent." An assistant whisks the tissues from a pile on the floor with her extraordinarily agile

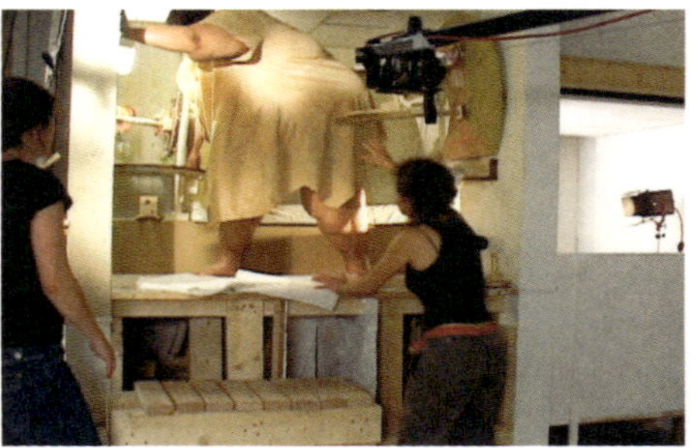

13. *Dough* production, 2005

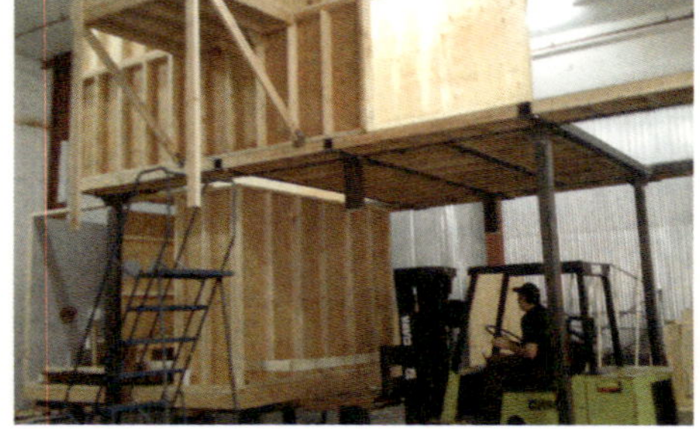

14. *Squeeze* production, 2010

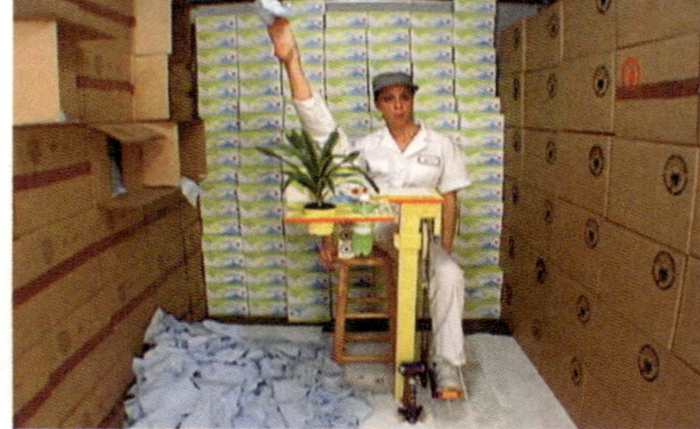

15. Still from *Tropical Breeze*, 2004

feet [Fig. 15]. The brisk tempo and florid colors of the video, mimicking that of an advertisement, establish this scenario as a paradigm of good-natured organization, in which no efforts, not even sweat, are wasted, but rather packaged to be bought and consumed. (In fact, Rottenberg tried to sell boxes of these completed wet wipes on eBay, expanding out from art world economies into other circuits of exchange, but she did not find any takers.)

Rottenberg has been compared to David Cronenberg, Jean Cocteau, and (most insistently) Matthew Barney,[8] but she is also in dialogue with feminist precedents such as the work of British conceptual artist Helen Chadwick. Chadwick created "architectural sound sculptures" like *Model Institution* (1982), a piece that reproduced governmental booths such as those found in postal, social security, and public housing offices and played audio about the nature of bureaucracy, control, and helplessness. A cohort of kindred contemporary video artists might include Los Angeles duo Harry Dodge and Stanya Kahn, who in their collaboration together explored performance-based video fictions, and Chicago-based Amie Siegel, who in her 2013 video *Provenance* traced Le Corbusier furniture on a backwards journey from a well-appointed townhouse in West London to its original site in Chandigarh, India [Fig. 16].

Siegel then sold her 40-minute video at auction and documented its sale in a separate film, *Lot 248*, acknowledging her own place within markets of art and design. This self-reflexive move recalls Rottenberg: a major component of *Squeeze*—one that conceptually frames how the piece is witnessed—is a large photograph of art dealer Mary Boone holding a condensed, quasi-minimal cube of broken-up blush, lettuce, and rubber, which is the output of the machinations portrayed within the video [Fig. 17]. The cube, which resembles ground-up car parts mixed with digested flesh, was shipped to Grand Cayman to be held in perpetuity; the certificate of shipping accompanies the piece as part of its documentation. Linda Williams, in an excellent text, describes *Squeeze* as "a critique of commodification that is also a surreal imitation of commodification," adding that "it is the brilliant culmination of Rottenberg's ongoing exploration of female labor on grotesquely eloquent assembly lines."[9]

8 For comparisons with Barney, see David Frankel, "Mika Rottenberg," *Artforum* (January 2011): 216; and Roberta Smith, "Art Review/Summertime at PS1," *The New York Times* (July 16, 2004).

9 Linda Williams, "On Squeeze," in *Mika Rottenberg*, p. 183.

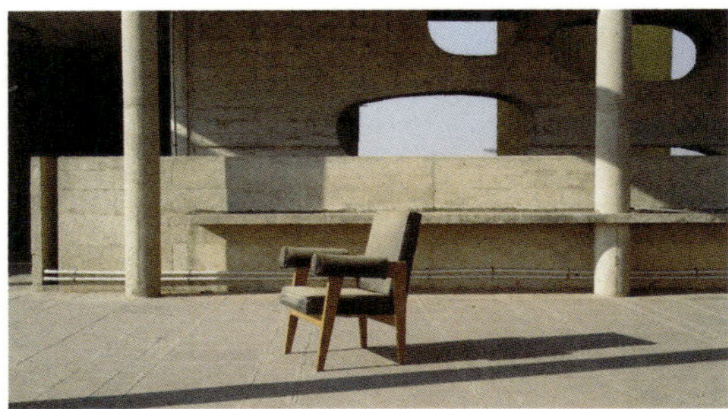

16. Amie Siegel, still from *Provenance*, 2013

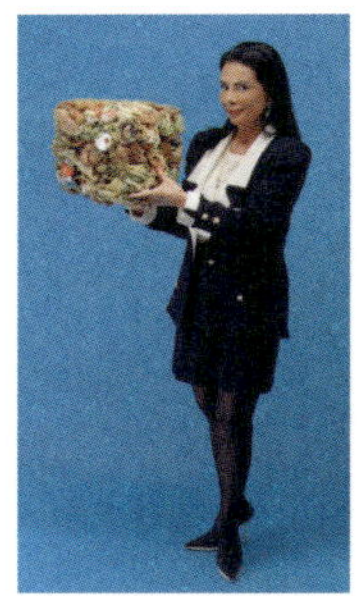

17. Detail of *Squeeze*, 2010: *Mary Boone with Cube*

In *Cheese*, Rottenberg has also produced a version of a pastoral landscape that gestures to life somewhat distant from this consumer world, though it, too, has its routines, its repairs, its end-product. Long-haired, white-gowned maidens awaken from their sleep, unwinding their hair from hanging loops that keep it out of the way during the night. Their life on the farm commences when one of the women sneezes out a bunny. She and her companions spend their day shepherding animals and tending to their tresses, only to have the cycle begin again with the sneeze and its resultant discharged bunny. (Sneezed-out rabbits are also at the center of Rottenberg's video *Sneeze*, 2008.) Conventionally private moments of self-care are collectivized and made public and, in this instance, productive, as hair is milked and used to make large blocks of cheese [Fig. 18]. As this brief description indicates, Rottenberg wields humor strategically, as a defamiliarizing device, injecting funny moments to interrupt bleak or banal moments.

Rottenberg's largely but not exclusively female cast, one that is racially diverse, has been widely commented upon (she has pointed out that if her cast were all male, it would likely not be considered remarkable).[10] Her concern with gendered work, with the commodification of bodies, and with the global feminization of labor that brings into meaningful juxtaposition lettuce farming in Arizona and latex extraction in India, dovetails with feminist theories of space like those articulated by Massey and Gillian Rose.[11] As with Rottenberg's fractured locations that are nonetheless envisioned as part of a wider system, Massey calls for a sense of globalization that is "aspatial," that is, one that does not conform to conventional contiguities of geography.[12]

10 Ann Demeester, "Simply Fantastic (Realism): Mika Rottenberg Responds to FAQs and FPPs," in *Mika Rottenberg*, p. 17.

11 Gillian Rose, *Feminism and Geography: The Limits of Geographical Knowledge* (Minneapolis: University of Minnesota Press, 1986).

12 Doreen Massey, *For Space* (London: Sage, 2005).

factories

Though Rottenberg's videos lend themselves to explication using theoretical rubrics of space, labor, and gender, they are always, importantly, *in excess* of those theories, unable to be easily or simply boxed-in by totalizing interpretations. Rottenberg is an artist who develops, builds upon, and works through her theoretical and political interest by producing art—art that is fictional and allegorical rather than academic. Her videos generate their

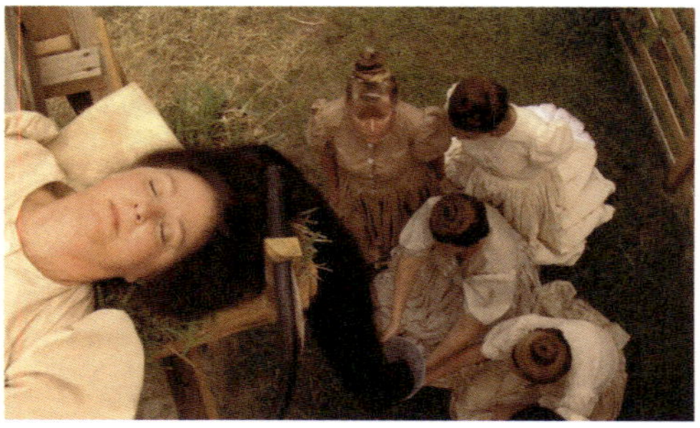

18. Still from *Cheese*, 2008

own surpluses, including the pleasure of her elegantly choreographed camera motions, the satisfactions derived from her precise use of sound, and the embodied comfort with their skins that many of her characters exhibit. The architectures of confinement that she presents exist in tension with her expansive sense of invention—her videos speak to the confining aspects of the workplace, as well as to its eccentricities, its intimacies, its small gratifications. In this, though her women might go through "typically Rottenbergian exertions,"[13] they also have relationships with each other that remain unknown and unknowable to the viewer. If they purport to be surrogate factories, they are alternative factories of imagination, producing new thoughts about uneven development, work conditions, and habitus. And for all their formal structure, at the heart of her videos lies the *informe*—fungible, goopy blobs like creeping dough that has been salted by tears or rubber in quivering sheets.

13 Roberta Smith, "Art in Review/Mika Rottenberg and Jon Kessler: 'Seven,'" *The New York Times* (November 10, 2011).

With her groaning gears and rasping wooden mechanisms—all those pre-industrial sliding drawers and cubbyholes—Rottenberg's sets resemble a tinkerer's workshop or an old-fashioned laboratory for bodily science experiments, where saliva, allergies, muscle power, and breath become part of her equations. By creating intentionally naïve (if complicated) back-stories for common materials, she taps into the childlike desire to spin fantastic "what if" scenarios. Where does vacuum-packed, uncooked dough come from? How do maraschino cherries get made, anyway? Part of the perennial appeal of educational and how-to videos that take us through, step-by-step, the process of making things is watching how things are assembled before they appear, as if by magic, on store shelves. Rottenberg's videos slow things down by embellishing, and making strange, the process of manufacturing, spinning narratives and open-ended stories within these fictional spaces.

The ability of video to decelerate—especially in contrast to rapidly streaming televisual time—has been utilized by feminist artists such as Dara Birnbaum, who commented about her own work and its "attempts to slow down the 'technological speed' attributed to this medium; thus 'arresting' moments of tv-time for the viewer. For it is the speed at which issues are absorbed and consumed by the medium of video/television, without examination and without self-questioning, which at present still remains astonishing."[14] When Rottenberg, in *Squeeze*, captures the "real" world of latex and lettuce with long sequences in near-documentary fashion, she asks us to measure the distance between this sort of work and that of her own artistic labor, which so differently gathers, cuts, and selects [Fig. 19; Fig. 20].

The actors in Rottenberg's videos are what she calls "talents," people who are paid, usually by advertising on the Internet, for their physical attributes such as their heft, their flexibility, their long hair, or their strength. Hsuan L. Hsu remarks, "If some of these conspicuously abnormal bodies appear to allegorize the ways that physical labor distorts the worker's physique, they more literally inhabit a sector of immaterial labor far removed from the assembly line."[15] These bodybuilders and size-fetish activists should not be conflated with the characters they portray in Rottenberg's videos; she casts them in part because they self-consciously understand themselves to be embedded in a social field of relations in which their physical oddities are spectacularized, sexualized, and valued. "I've been a product for some time now!" affirms the bodybuilder from *Tropical Breeze* in an interview with the artist.[16] Yet Rottenberg's economies are not entirely transparent; her camera lens presses up close to faces and hands to capture her characters' vexing emotional gestures, psychologically charged interactions, and expressions that hint at internal worlds we do not have access to. In *Squeeze*, a large woman seated on a rotating platform appears to be the central energy source of the entire operation, her clenched hands and focused face wordlessly generating power [Fig. 21]. In an interview with Raqui, who plays this pivotal role in *Squeeze* and is also featured in *Dough*, Rottenberg asks, "Did you trust me?"[17] (Raqui's answer: yes, trust was built over time.) Trust is a vital, and tricky, terrain for both Rottenberg and her viewers to navigate, given that her videos circulate in a particular sphere of visual consumption—the art industry—that remains somewhat distinct from the multiple worlds inhabited by her paid "talents."

In her most recent work, *Bowls Balls Souls Holes* (2014), Rottenberg departs from her previous concerns with production to focus on temporality,

14 Dara Birnbaum, "Talking Back to the Media," in *Resolution: A Critique of Video Art*, ed. Patti Podesta (Los Angeles: Los Angeles Contemporary Exhibitions, 1986), p. 52.

15 Hsuan L. Hsu, "Mika Rottenberg's Productive Bodies," *Camera Obscura* no. 75 (September 2010): 41-73; reprinted in *Mika Rottenberg*, p. 101. Hsu's article is a comprehensive look at Rottenberg's oeuvre that compellingly thinks through her work in terms of biopolitics and immaterial labor.

16 "Heather Foster Interviewed by Mika Rottenberg," in *Mika Rottenberg*, p. 39.

17 "Raqui interviewed by Mika Rottenberg," in *Mika Rottenberg*, p. 81.

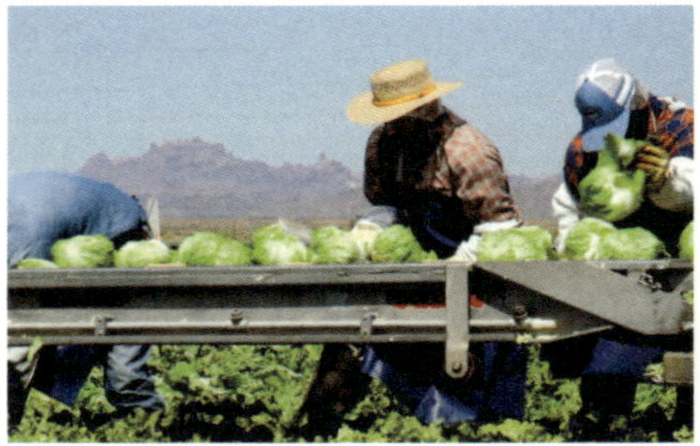

19. Still from *Squeeze*, 2010

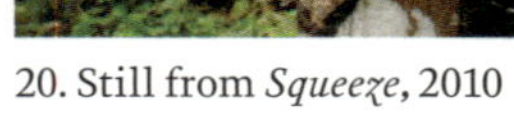

20. Still from *Squeeze*, 2010

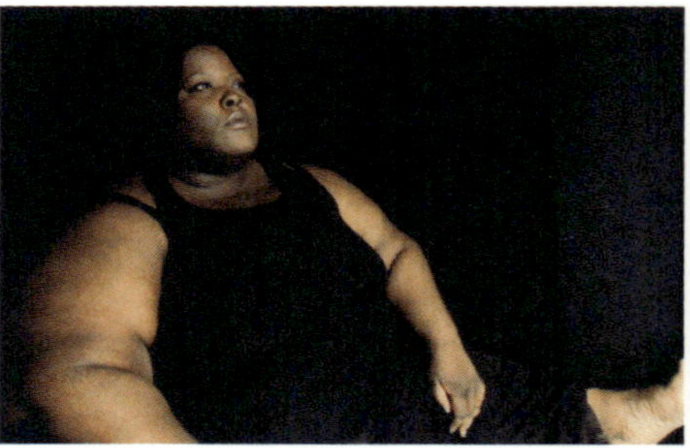

21. Still from *Squeeze*, 2010

waiting, the indeterminate zone between waking and sleeping, and the possibilities of fantasy. A bingo caller transitions from her home in a shabby hotel to her workplace, traveling by motorized scooter and descending down many steps to oversee a vast hall where the game clatters endlessly, as if being perpetually played [Fig. 22]. As with all of her video work, Rottenberg's exquisite sound design creates the connective tissue between disjunctive spaces; in this piece, she marshals the noises of late capitalist leisure. Fluorescent lights sputter and buzz. Air conditioners drip and whine. Fans whir. Letters and numbers are called. Balls clack and roil as the camera slowly pans over women marking their gridded bingo cards: nobody ever wins. A woman with no card in front of her dozes in her seat, dreaming of distant, icy vistas. When she is awakened by a leak of water, she balls her hands up, reminiscent of the gathering-of-energies fist-clenching in *Squeeze*.

Within this space of chance and gaming, Rottenberg inserts an incongruous vignette: the bingo caller occasionally drops brightly colored clothespins through a trapdoor at her feet, where they are shunted via a series of mechanical arms through other holes, ready to be received by a man who methodically fastens them to his face. (The bingo caller also uses clothespins on her feet as she rests, perhaps as part of a beauty or medical regimen, forging an affinity between the two characters.) In *Bowls Balls Souls Holes* Rottenberg returns to one of her most frequently used motifs, the crossing of objects between rooms via holes in ceilings and floors [Fig. 23]. Look up—what is secreted there? The ordinary ceiling tiles, so grimly restricting in other videos, here crack open to reveal a shining full moon [Fig. 24].

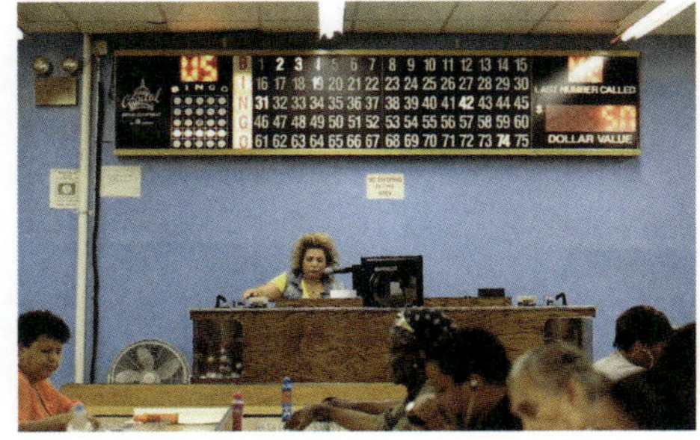

22. Still from *Bowls Balls Souls Holes*, 2014

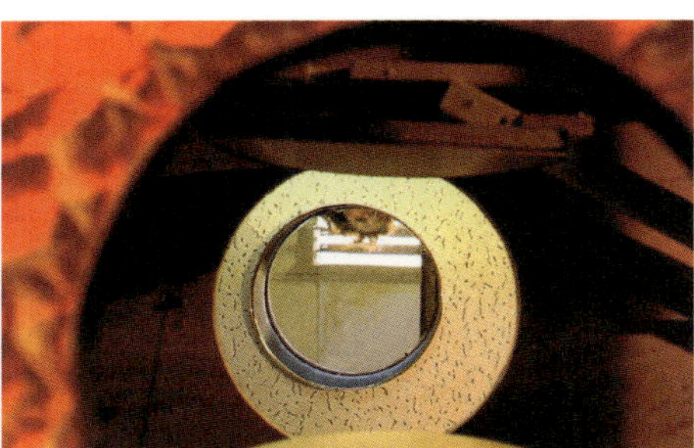
23. Still from *Bowls Balls Souls Holes*, 2014

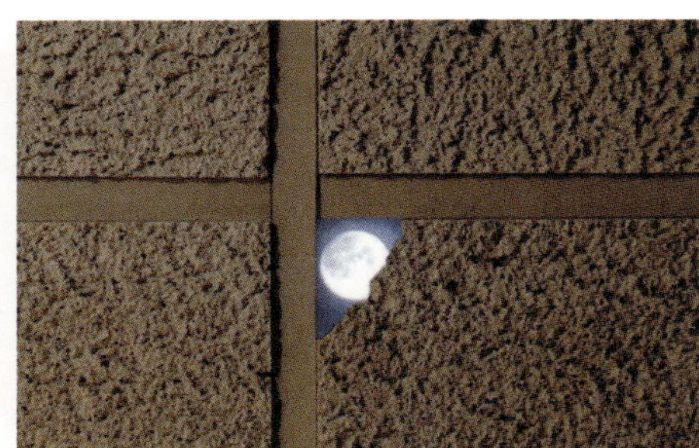
24. Still from *Bowls Balls Souls Holes*, 2014

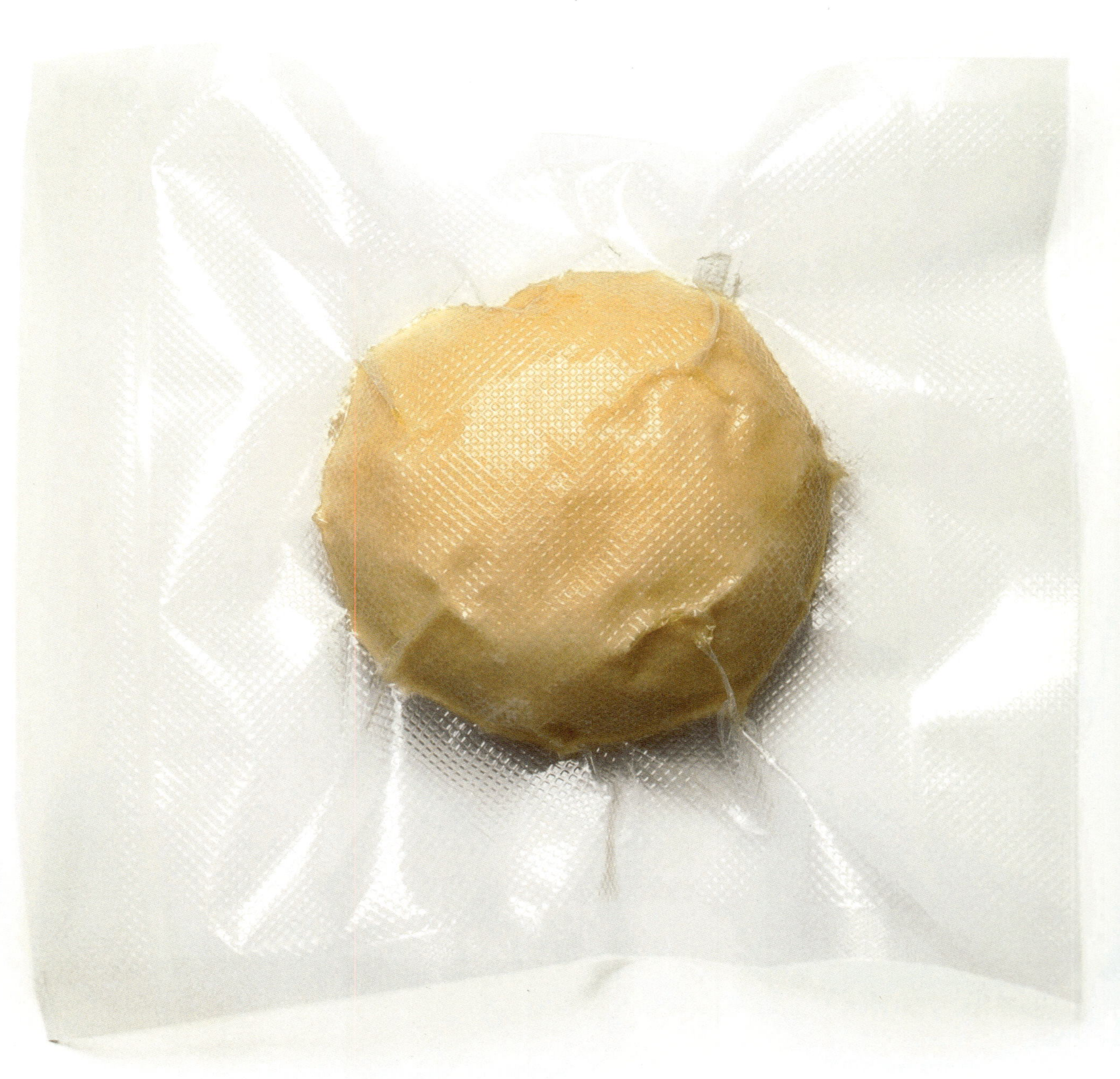

dough

CB: You often build sets to film your videos, and those sets are frequently repurposed as sculptures that contain the eventual video work, meaning that the viewer sees an image of a space and literally inhabits that space at the same time. Why is this approach important to you?

MR: I prefer to work with non-actors. I choose people because of who they are and how they carry themselves; I make the work around them. I will probably never ask someone to fit into my work or to act for me. Instead, I make the work fit them, in many cases literally. In *Dough*, I tailored the rooms around Raqui and Kat's unusual bodies. In earlier works, including *Dough*, I found my performers online. For me, it was very important that they already advertised themselves and presented themselves in their ads in the way they wanted to be looked at.

In *Dough* specifically, I hired performers who "rent out" part of their body. For example, 6-foot, 9-inch Tall Kat rents out her tallness. 600-pound Queen Raqui makes a living from squashing people. I am inspired by the alchemy that happens when they transform something that can be considered a handicap into an income and spirit generating quality. I like how they also open up a dialogue about work, alienation, and empowerment.

Preparatory drawing for *Dough*, 2005–2006

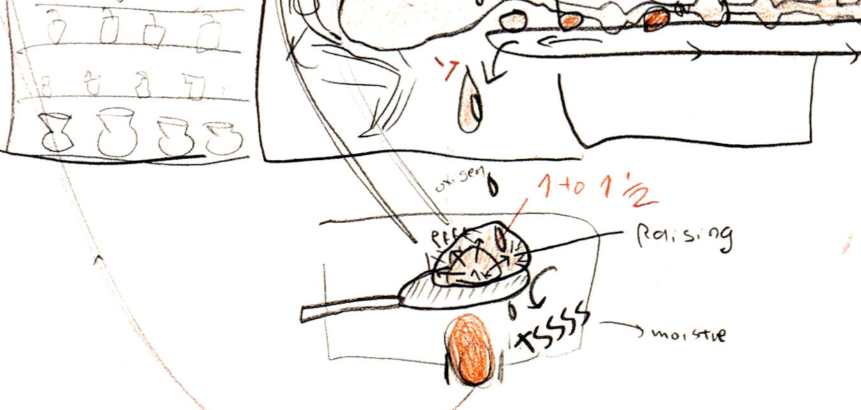

MAKE A UNit

invent my own unit of measurement.....

creat surplus

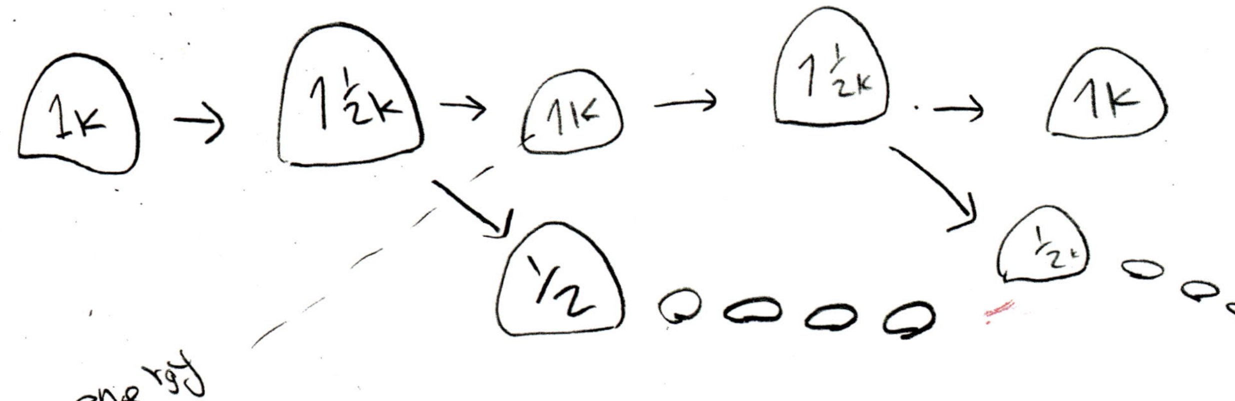

energy
yeast

make more - - - -

Invent machine to measure labor, Packede surplus

unit

tool

Natural Resource

Installation view: *Dough*, 2005–2006; Julia Stoschek Collection, "Number Two: Fragile," 2009

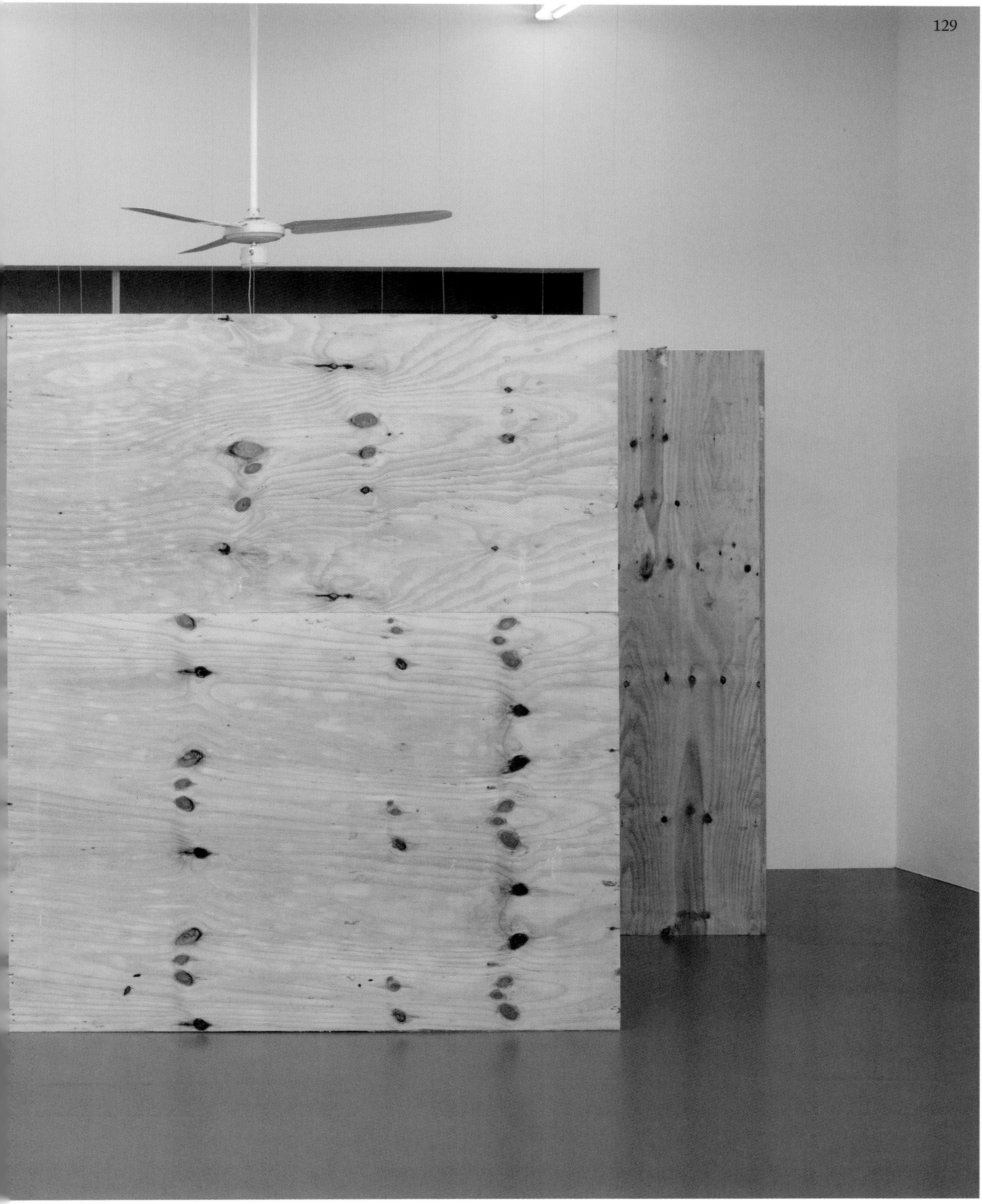

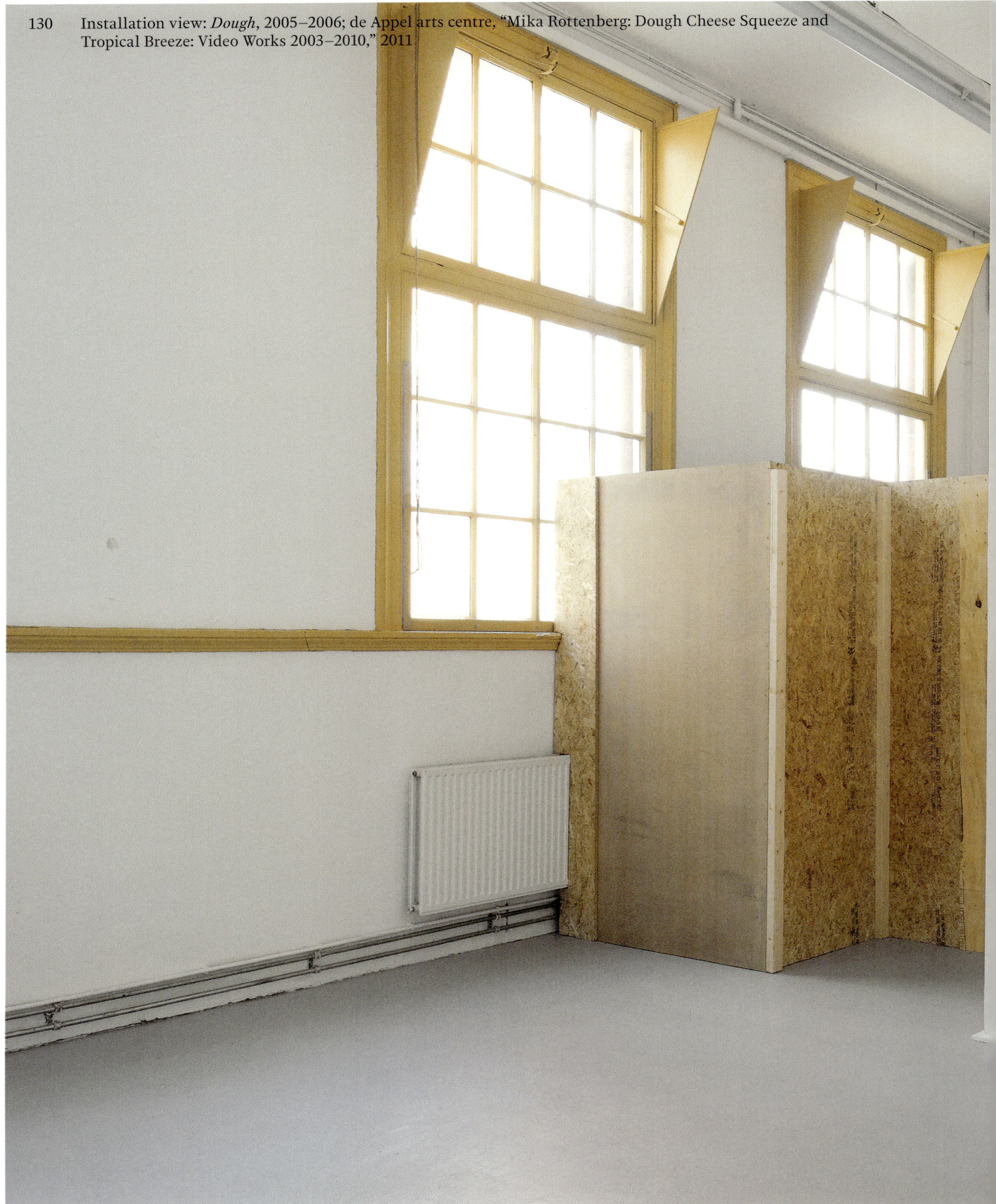

130 Installation view: *Dough*, 2005–2006; de Appel arts centre, "Mika Rottenberg: Dough Cheese Squeeze and Tropical Breeze: Video Works 2003–2010," 2011

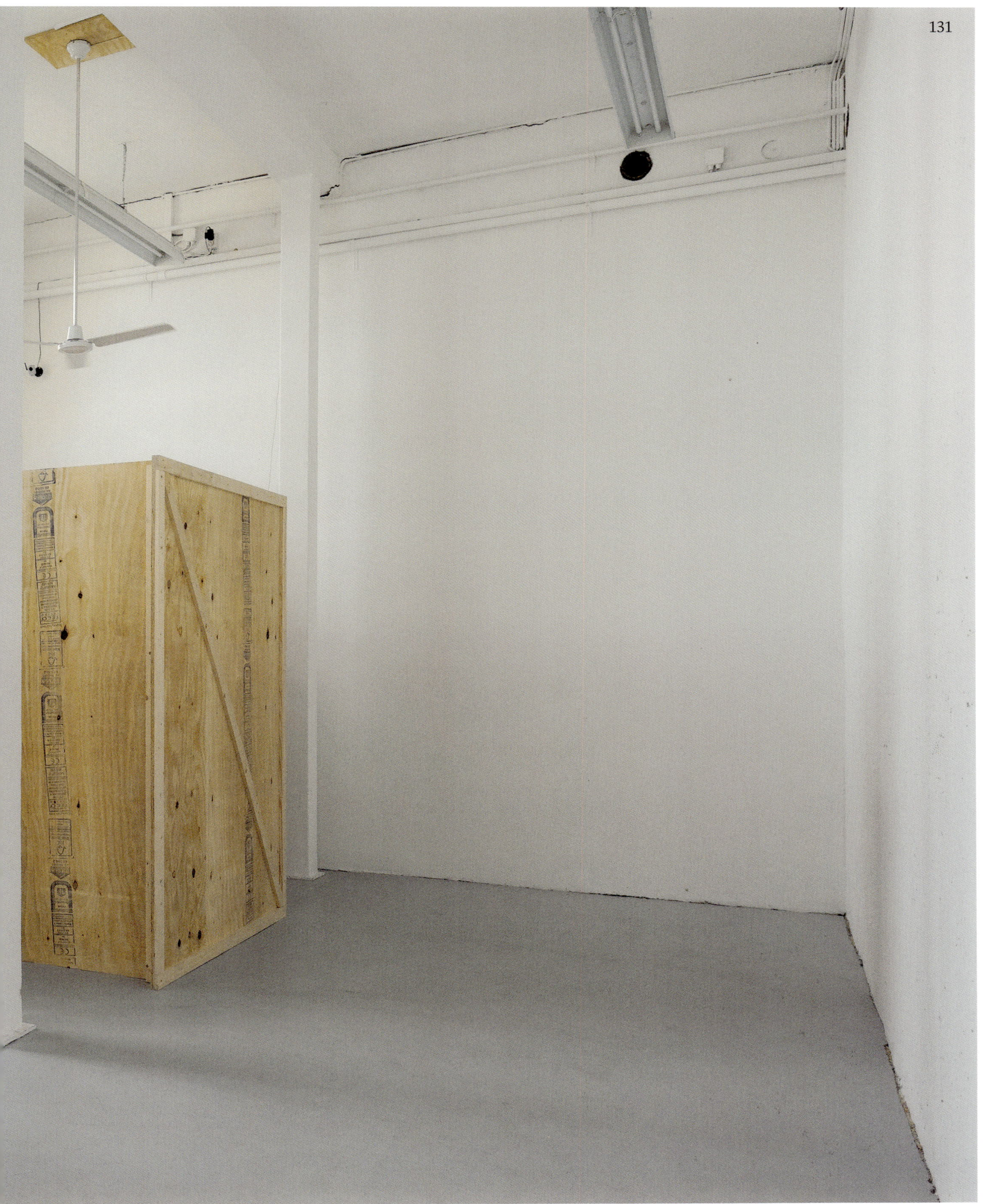

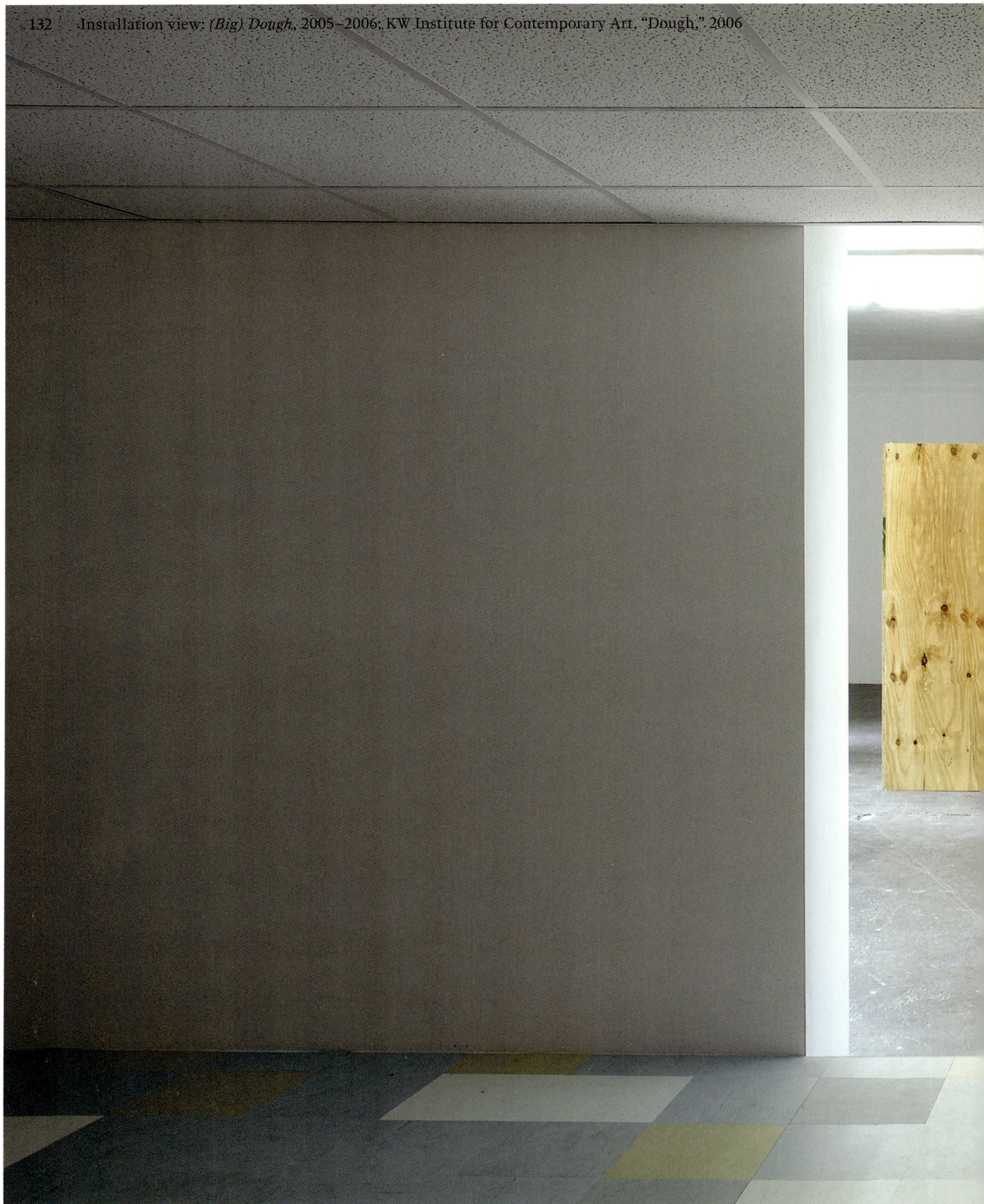

 Installation view: *(Big) Dough*, 2005–2006; KW Institute for Contemporary Art, "Dough," 2006

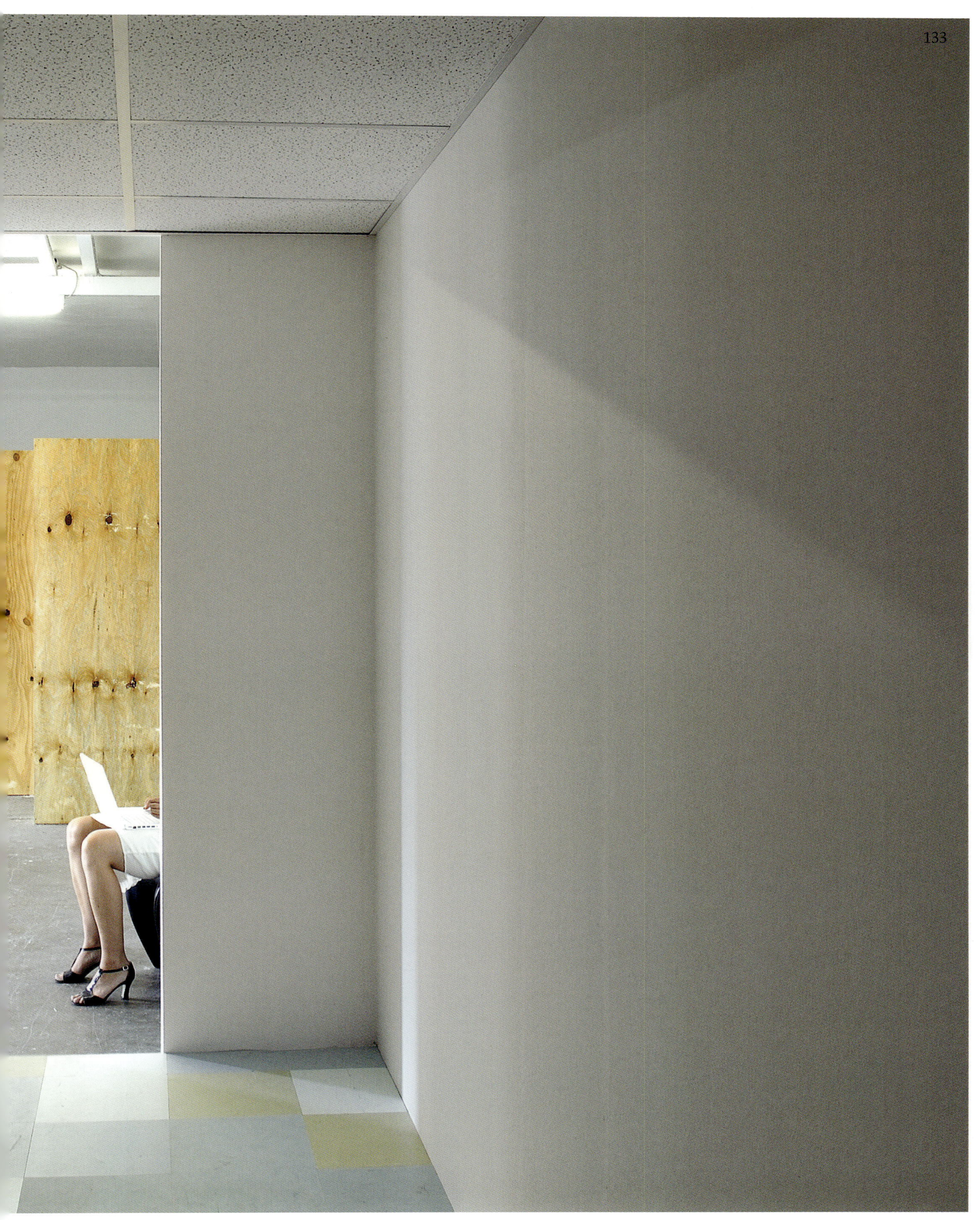

 Installation view: *(Big) Dough*, 2005–2006; KW Institute for Contemporary Art, "Dough," 2006

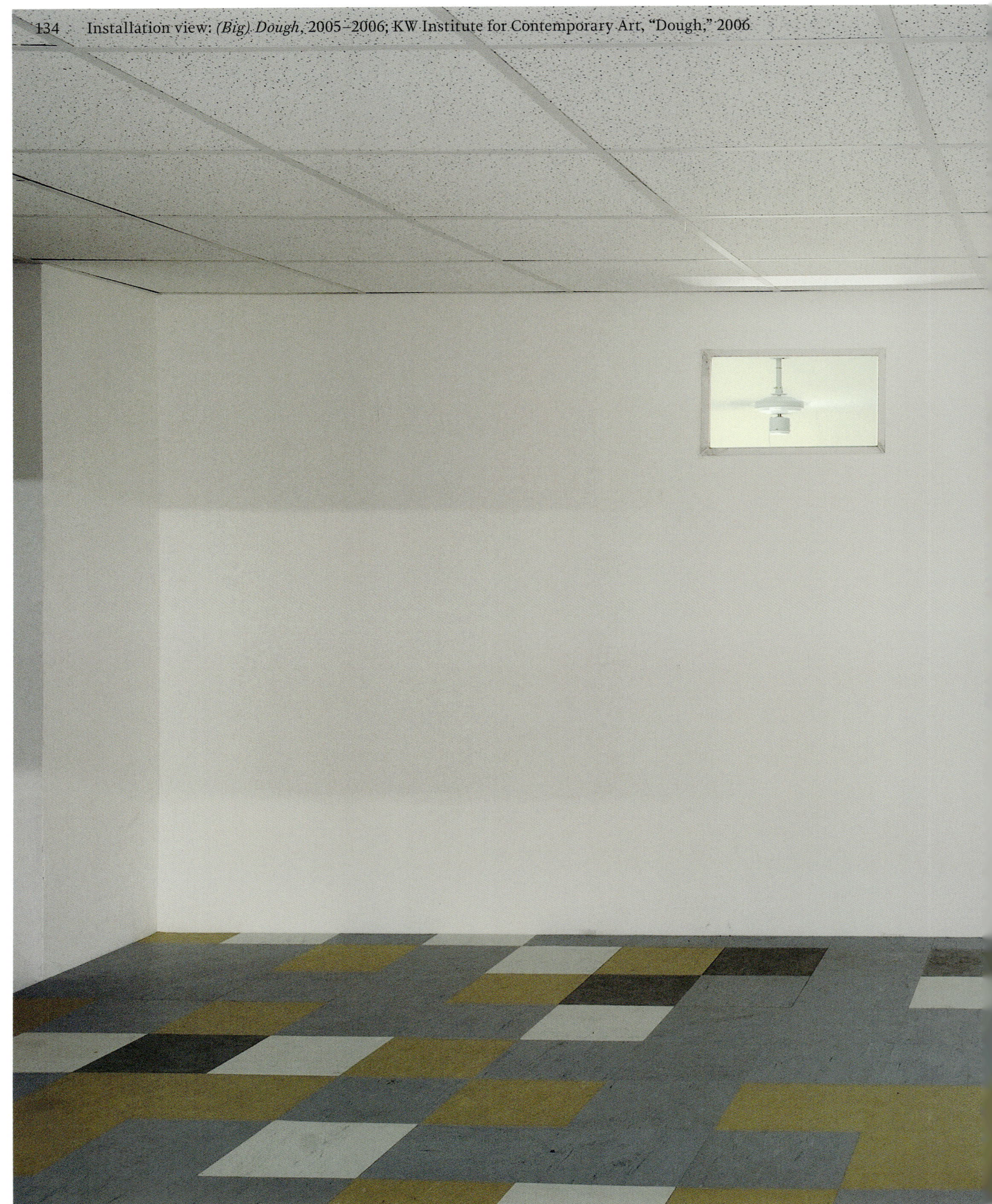

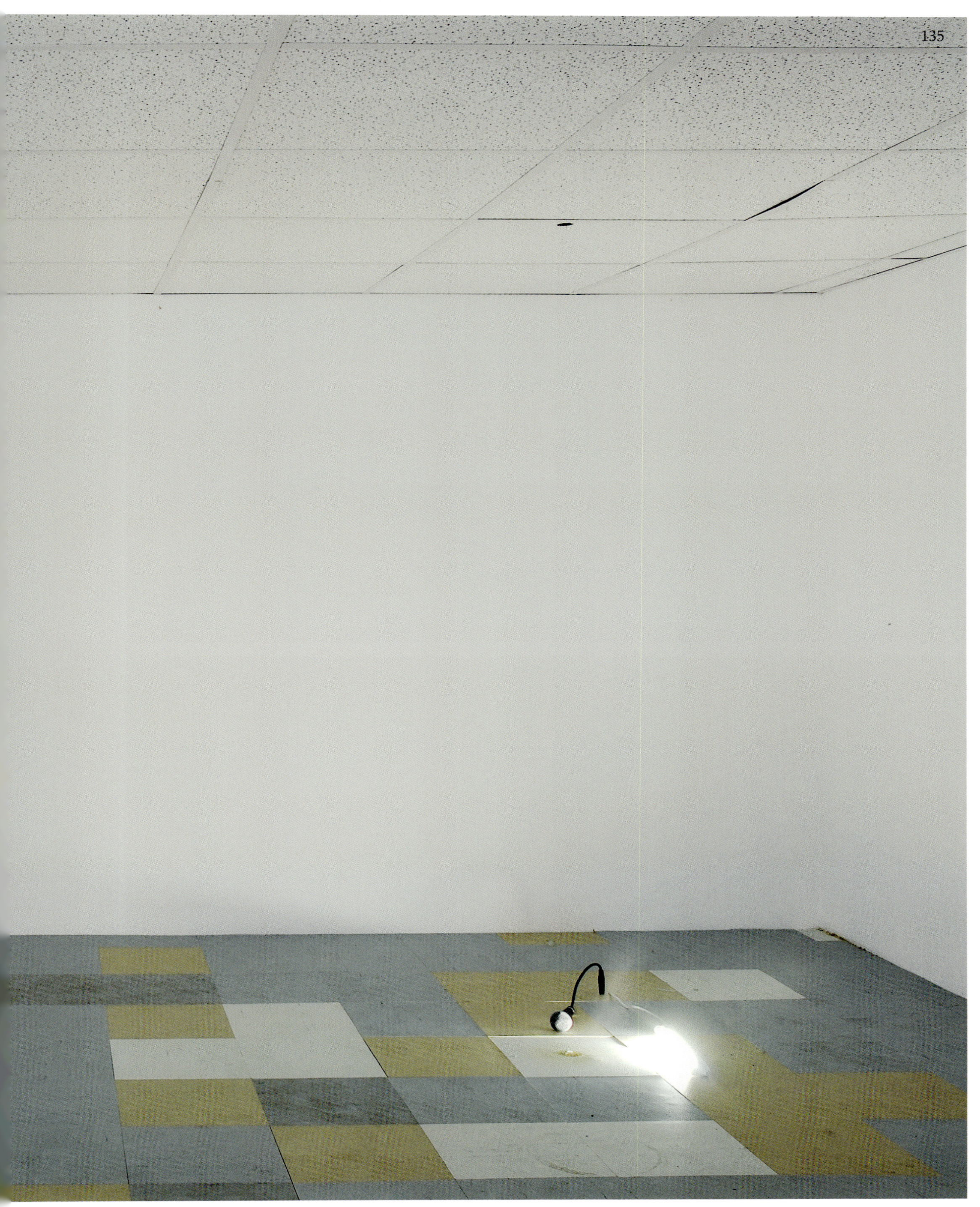

 Installation views: *(Big) Dough*, 2005–2006; KW Institute for Contemporary Art, "Dough," 2006

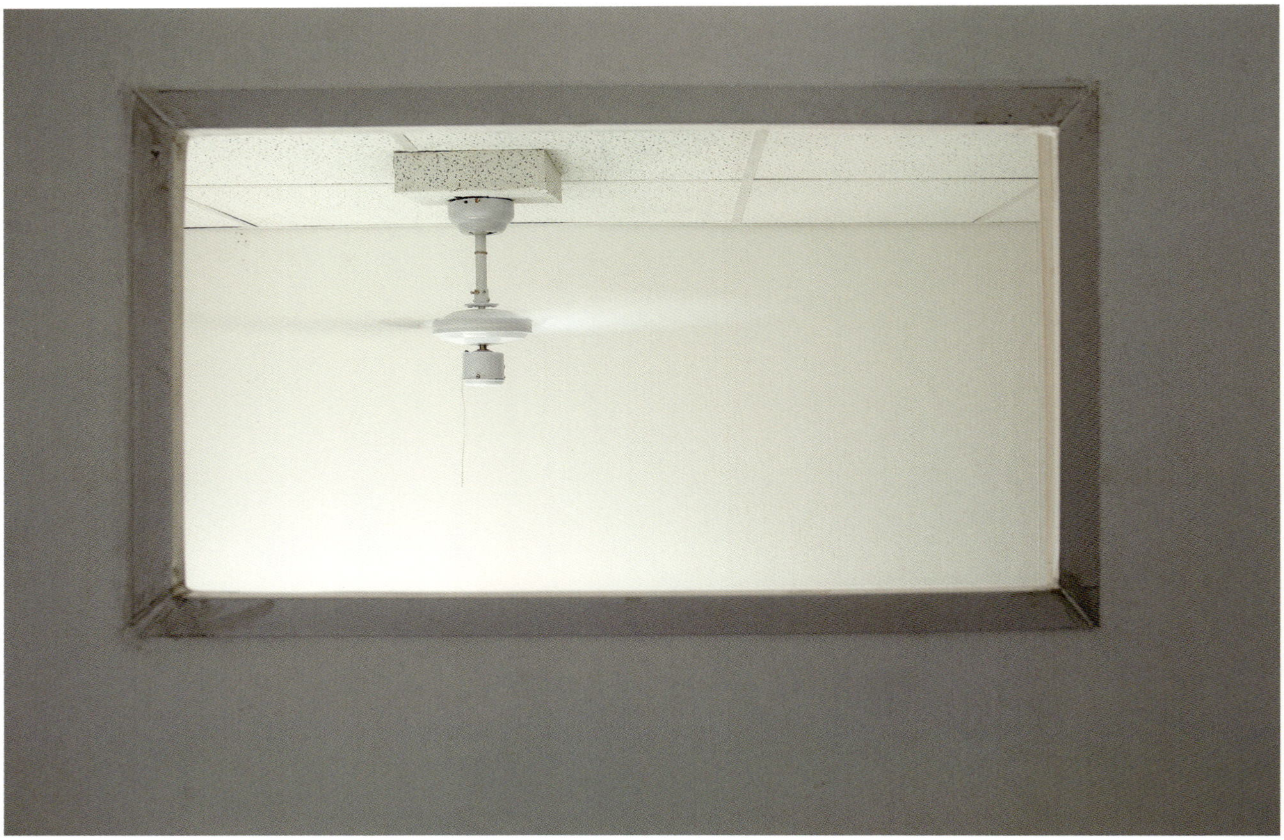

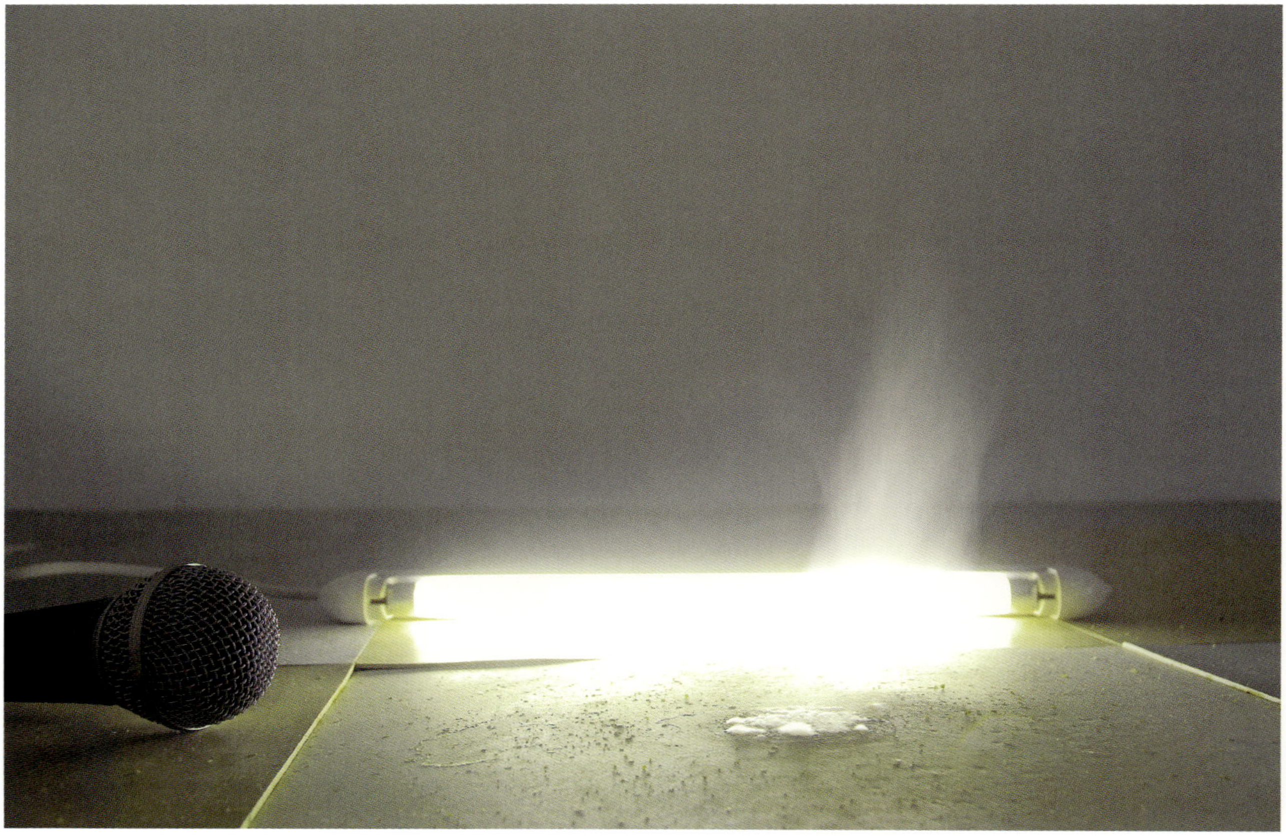

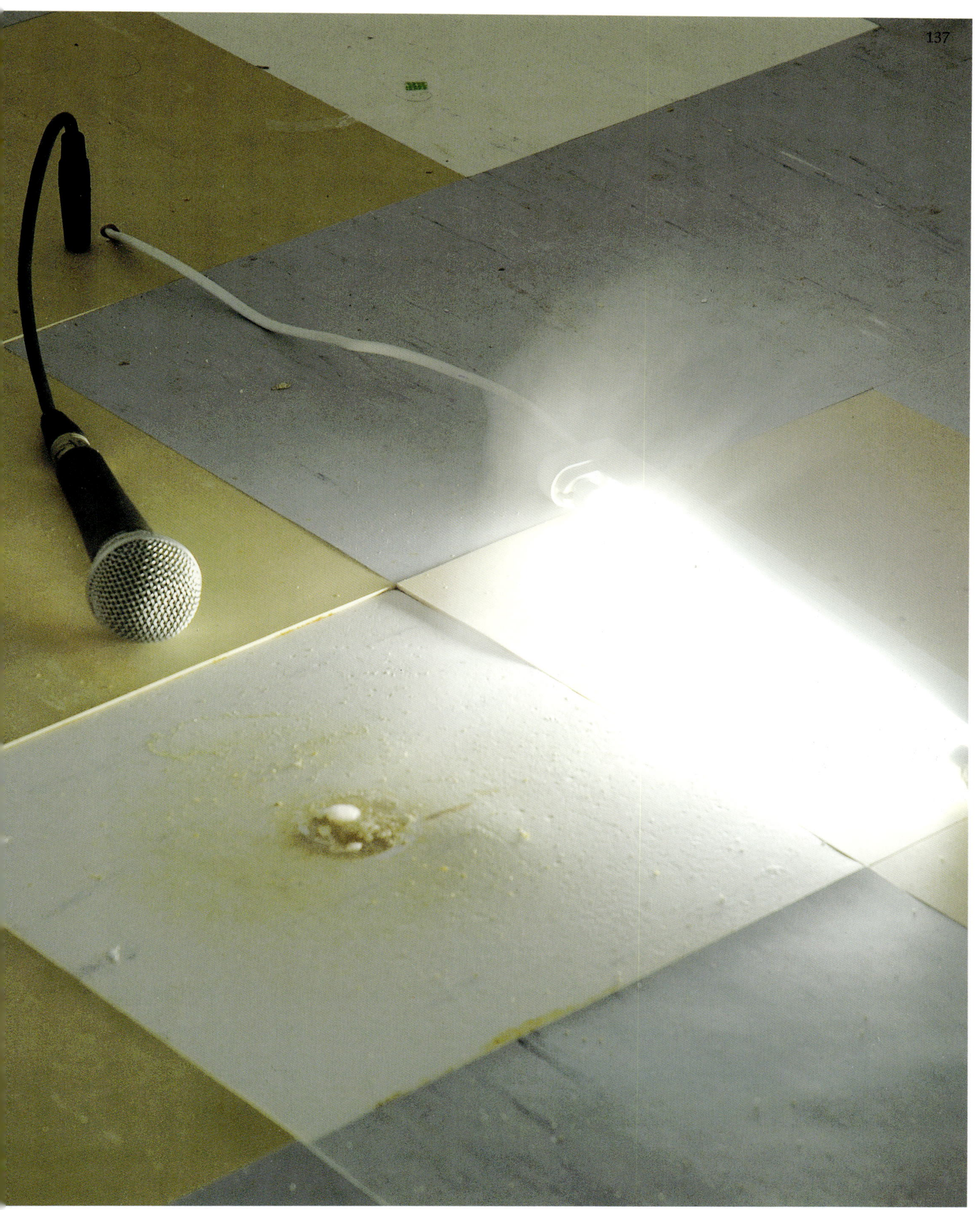

 Interior installation views: *(Big) Dough*, 2005–2006; La Maison Rouge, "Mika Rottenberg," 2009

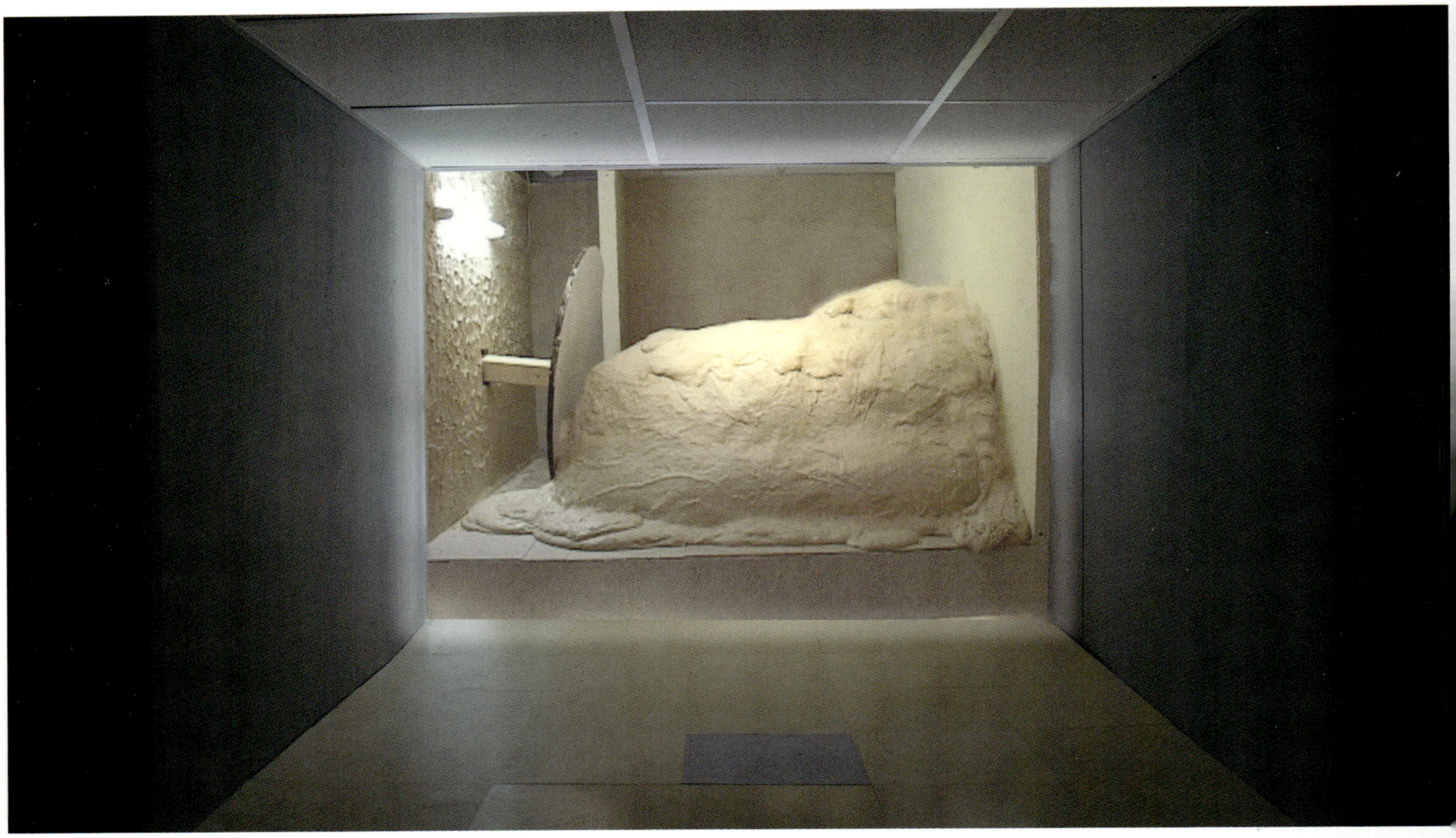

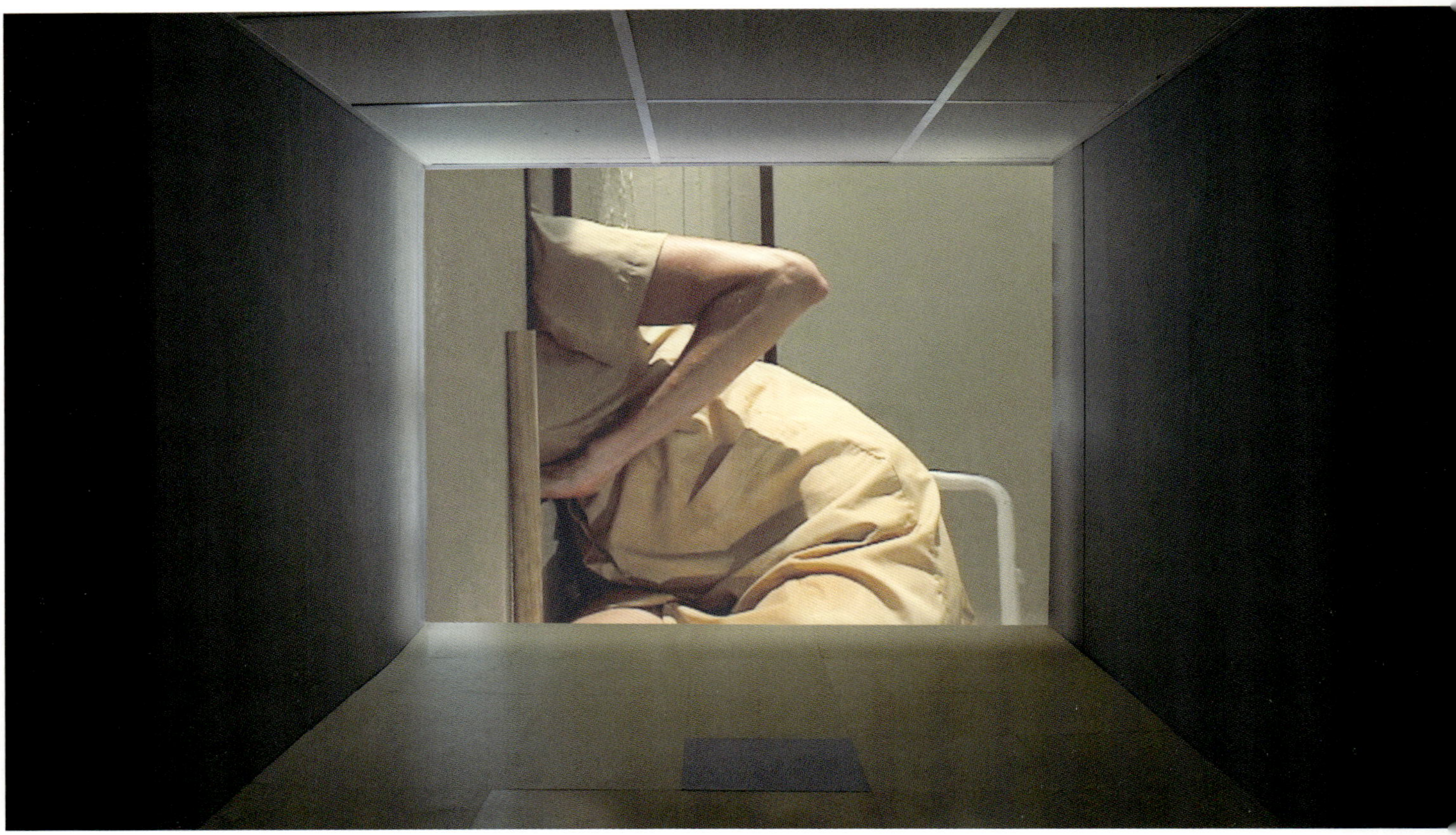

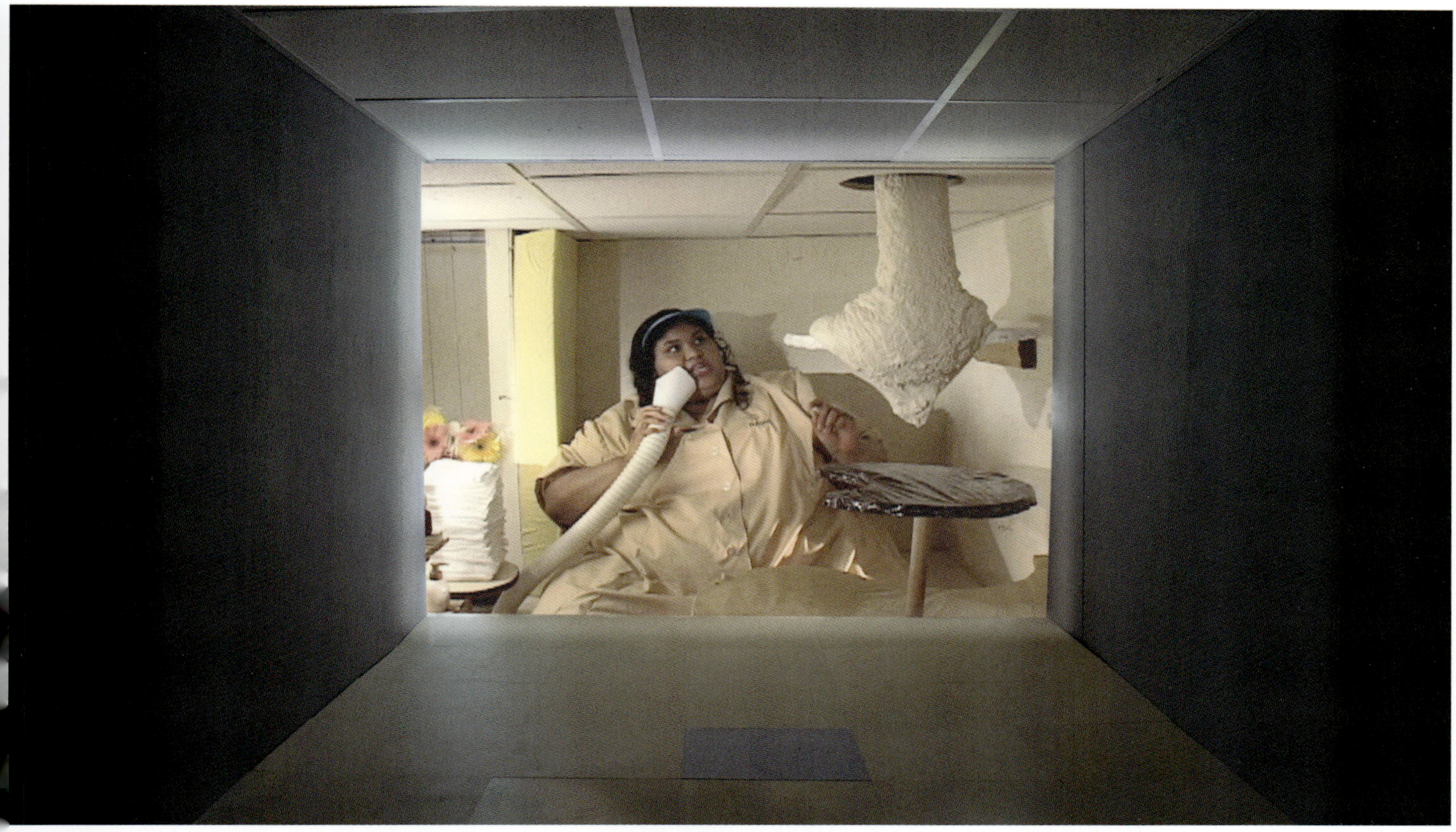

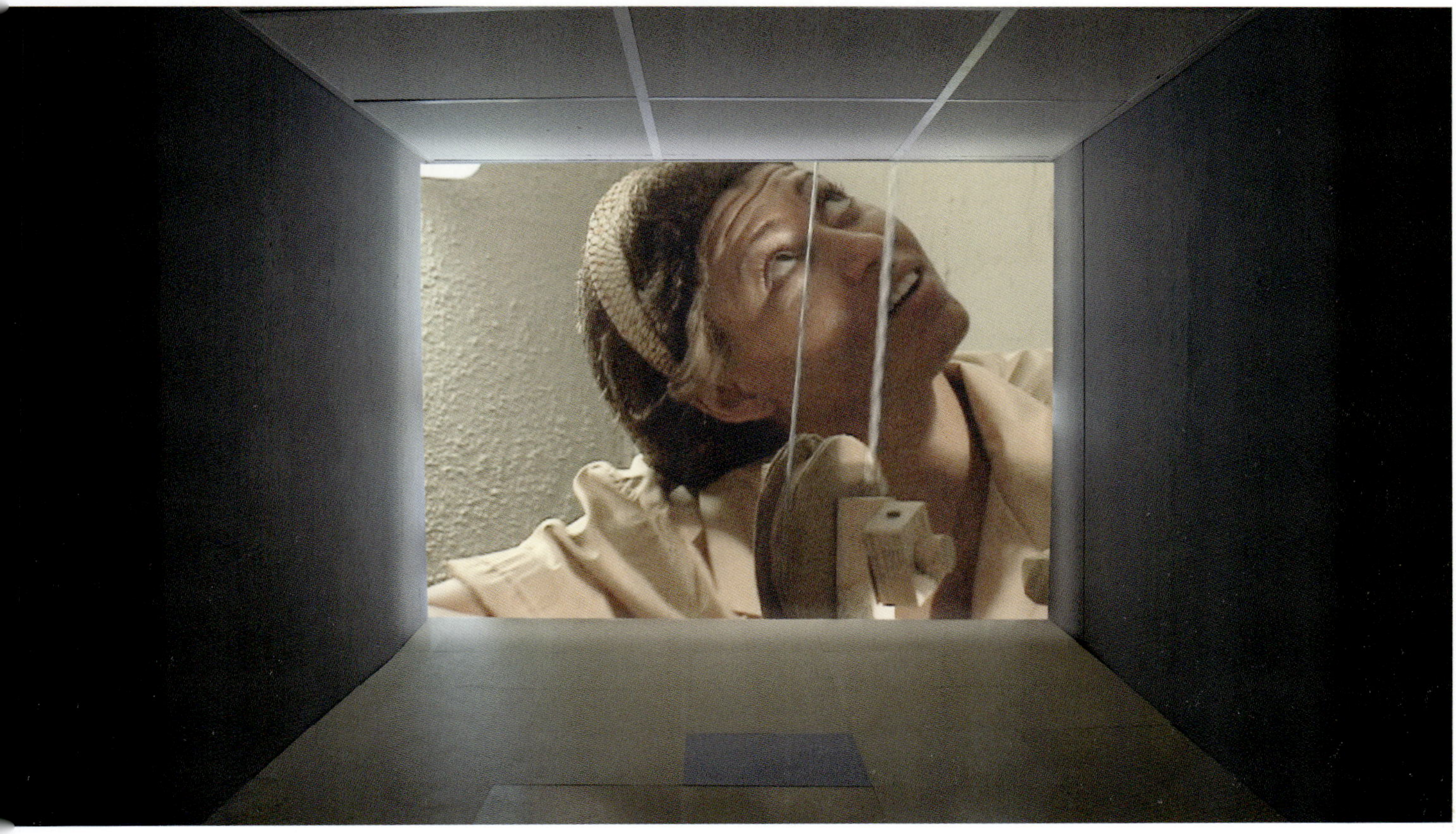

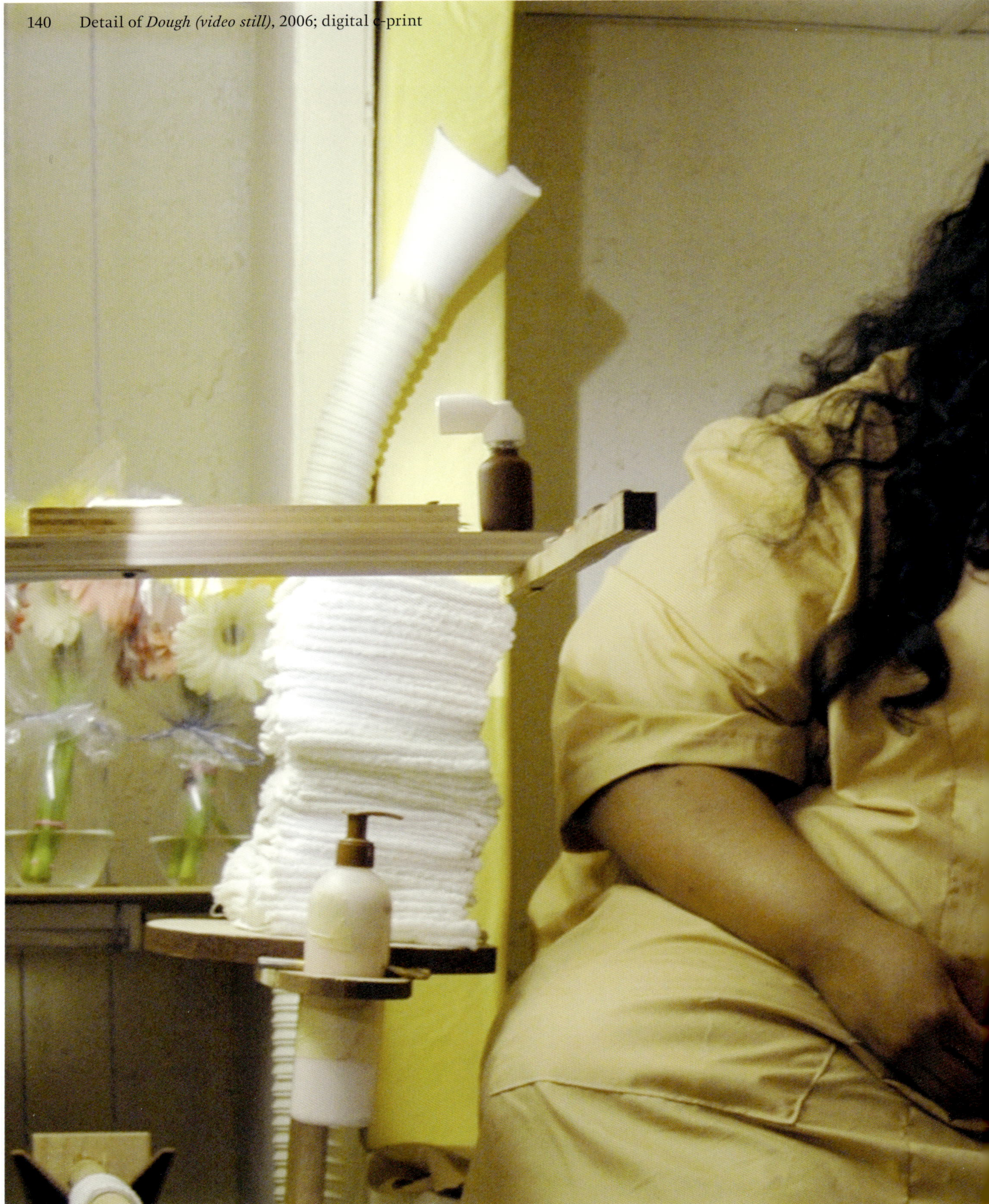

Detail of *Dough (video still)*, 2006; digital c-print

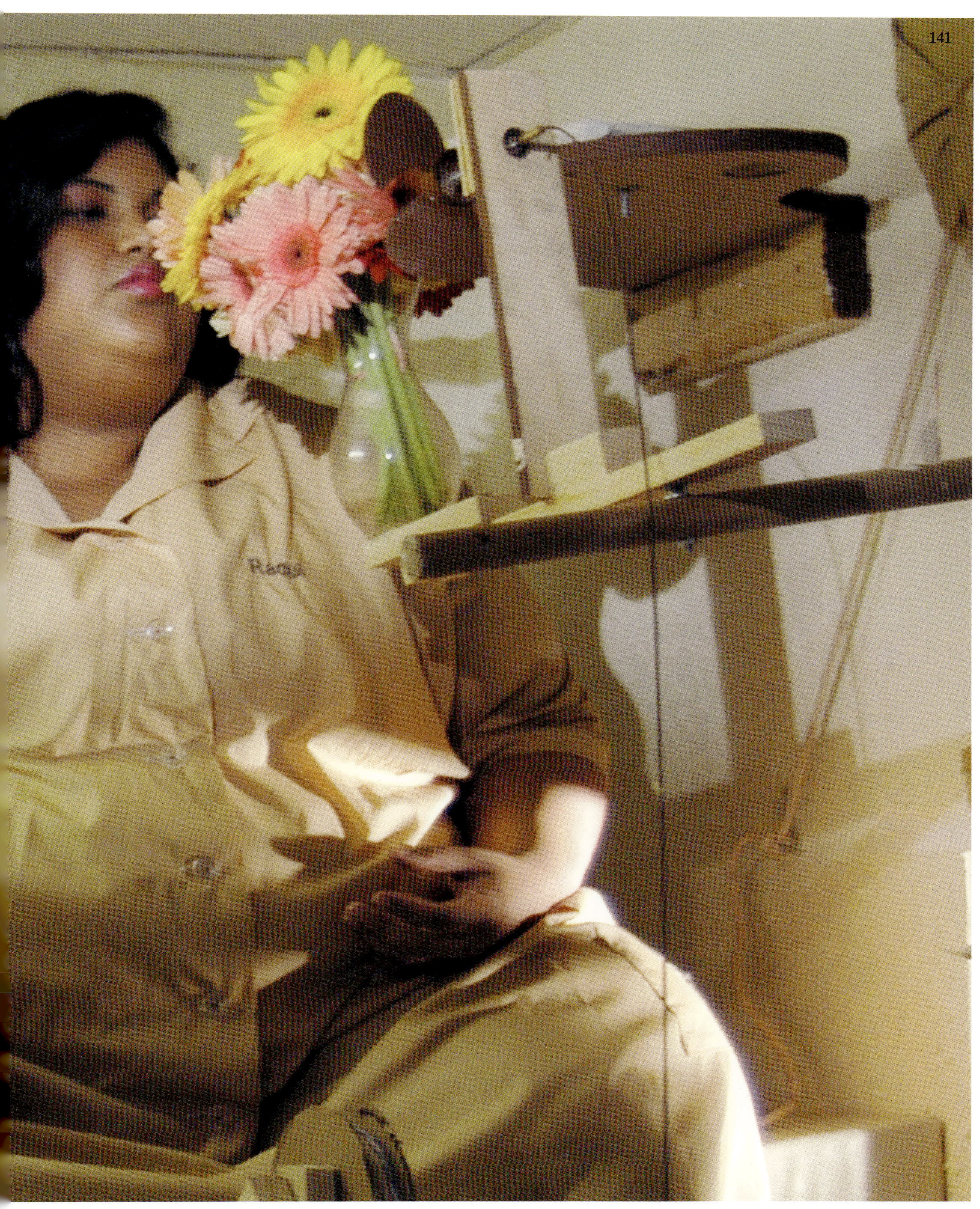

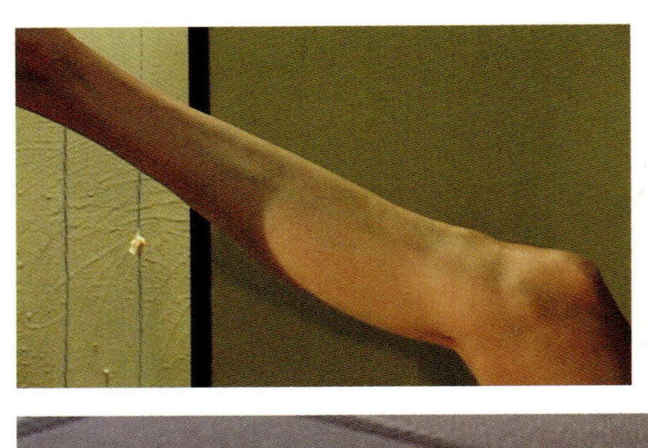
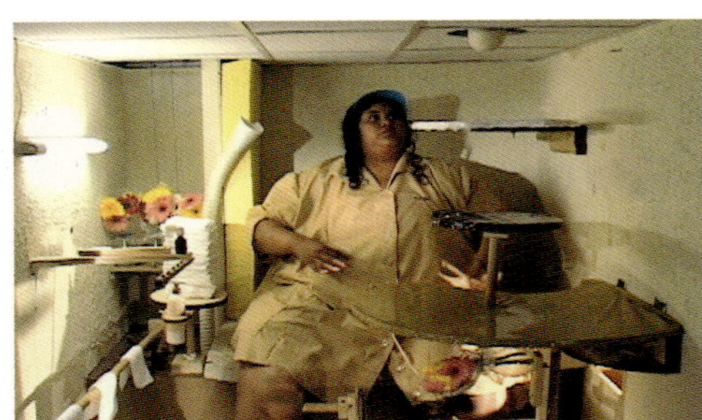
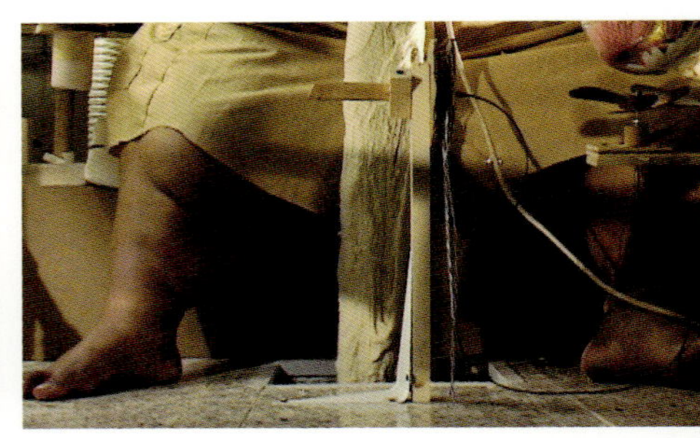
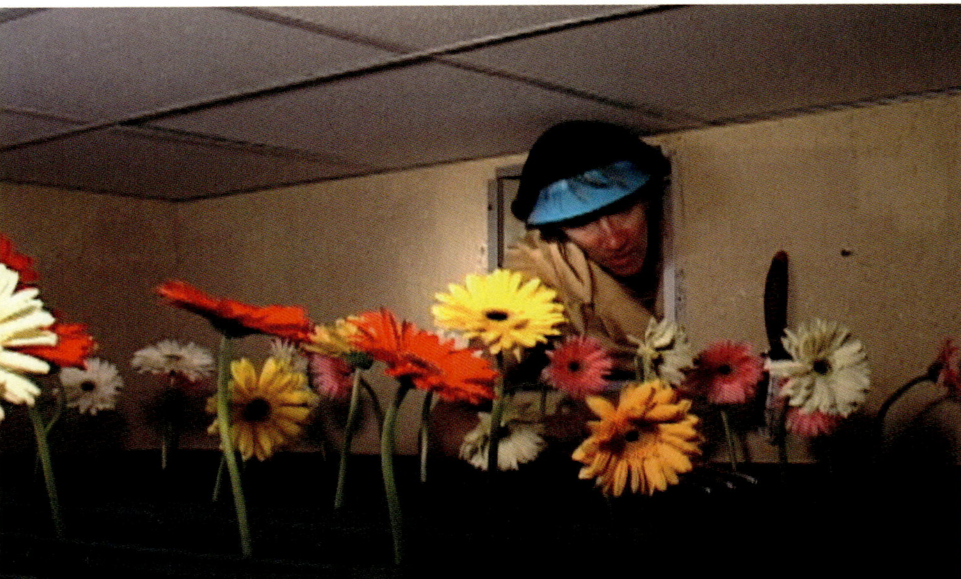
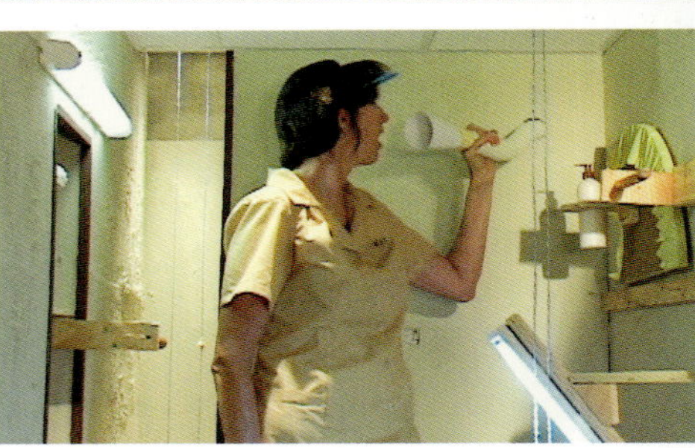
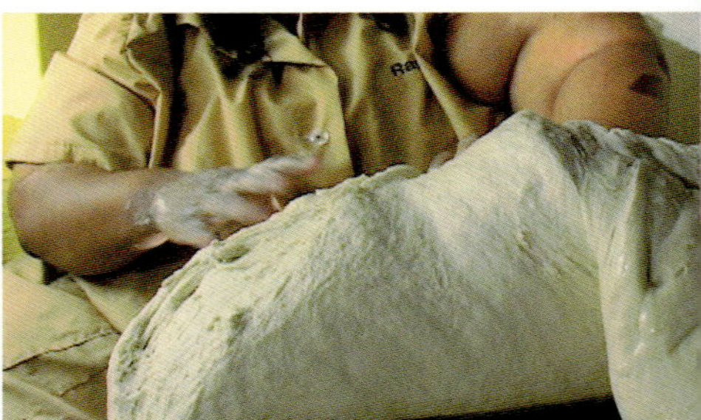
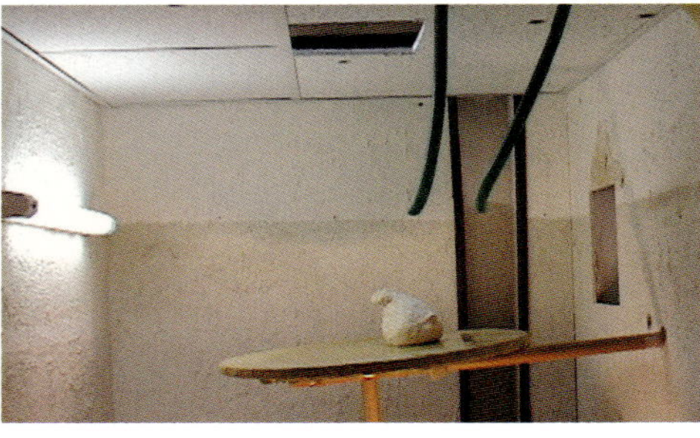
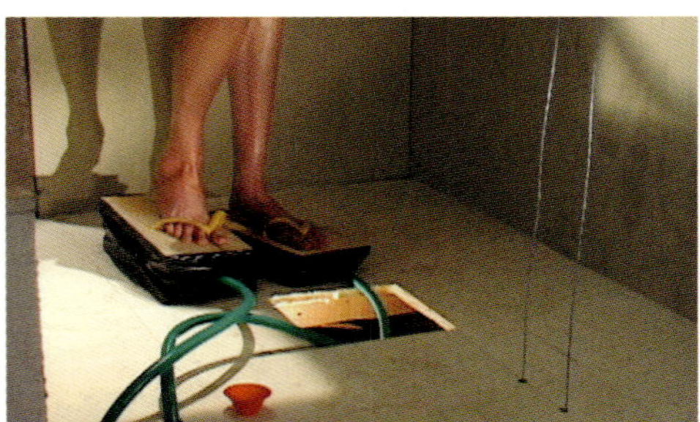
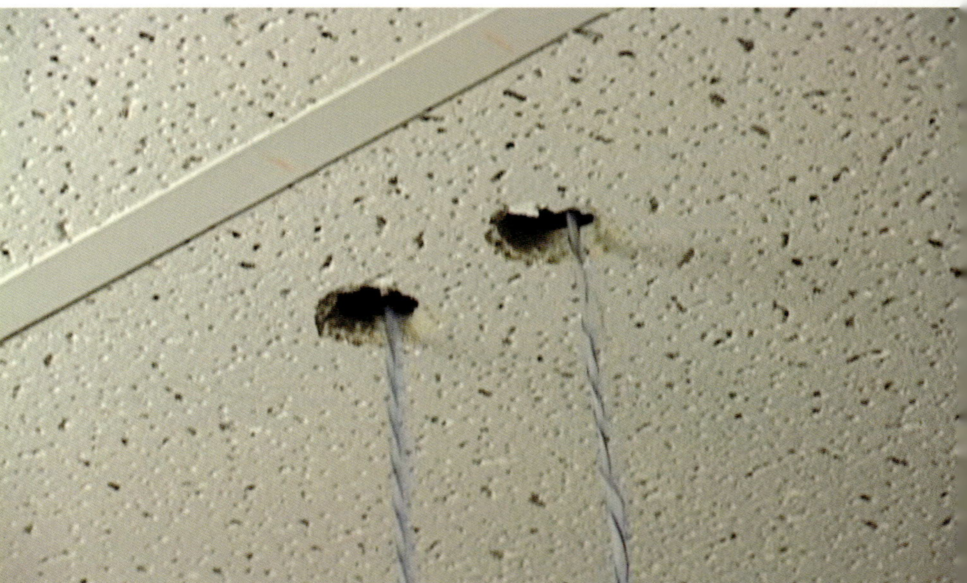

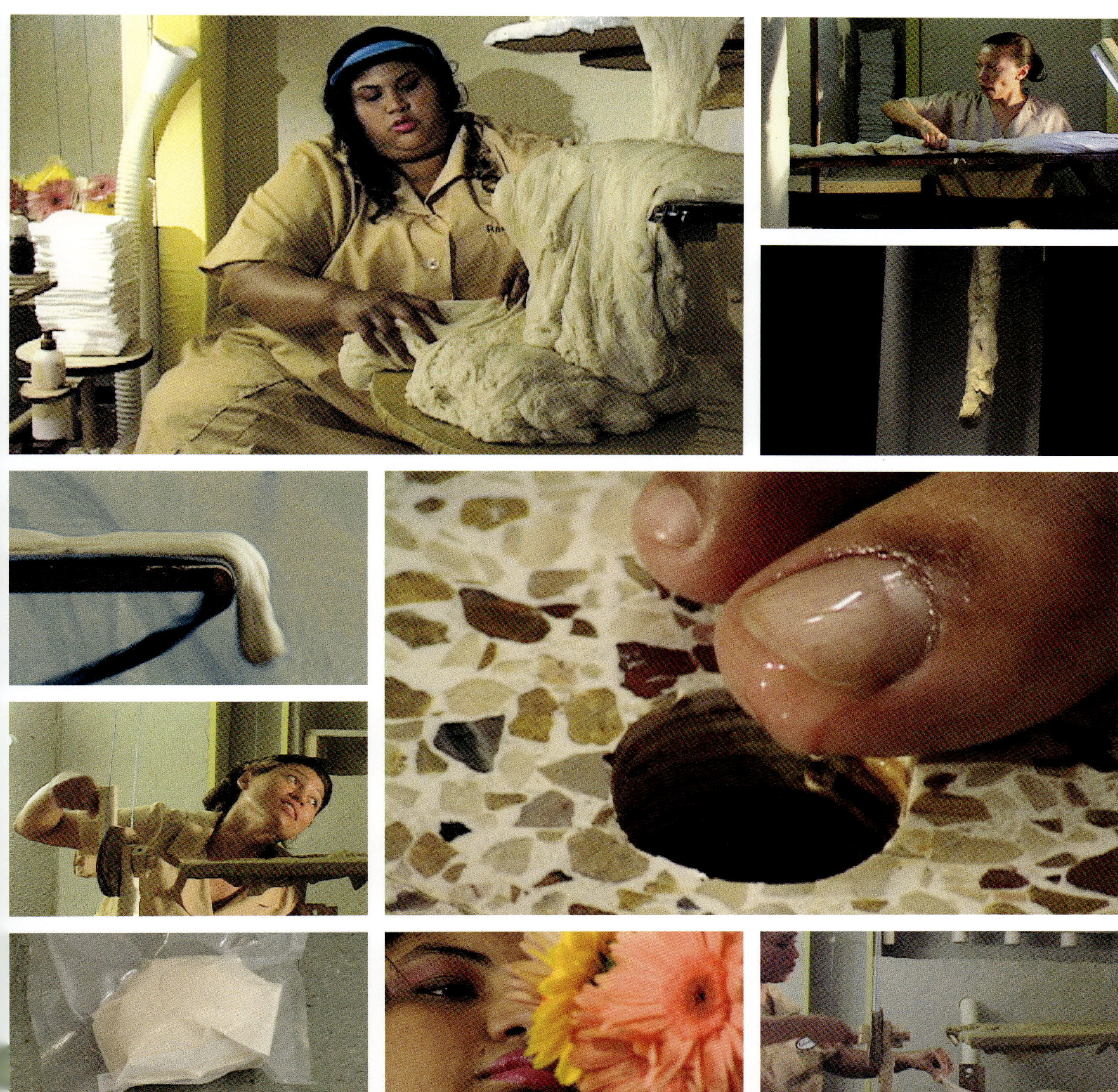

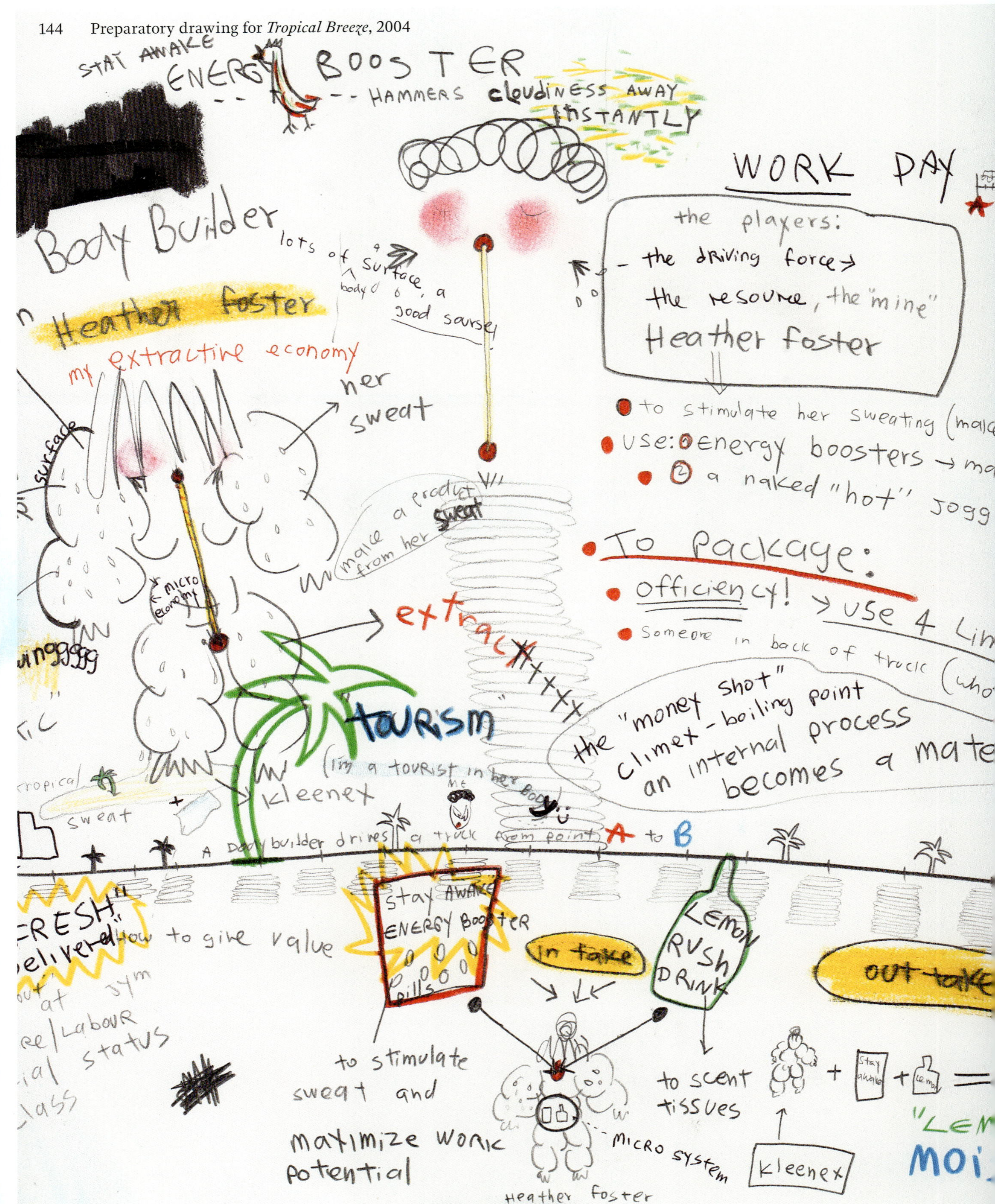

Preparatory drawing for *Tropical Breeze*, 2004

tropical breeze

CB: In the past, you have used rhyming titles to establish relationships between and among works, for instance, *Cheese*, *Squeeze*, *Sneeze*, and *Tropical Breeze*. Can you explain why you do this?

MR: It developed naturally. I suddenly noticed when considering titles for a show that many of these rhyme. It made a lot of sense because they are really born one out of the other. There is usually a minor, sometimes unplanned, detail in a piece that becomes the main idea in the next piece. In *Dough*, the woman farms flowers. In the next piece, *Cheese*, farming is a main element. When *Squeeze* came, I was so happy that the title felt natural to the piece—and rhymed!

 Installation view: Magasin 3 Stockholm Konsthall, “Sneeze to Squeeze,” 2013

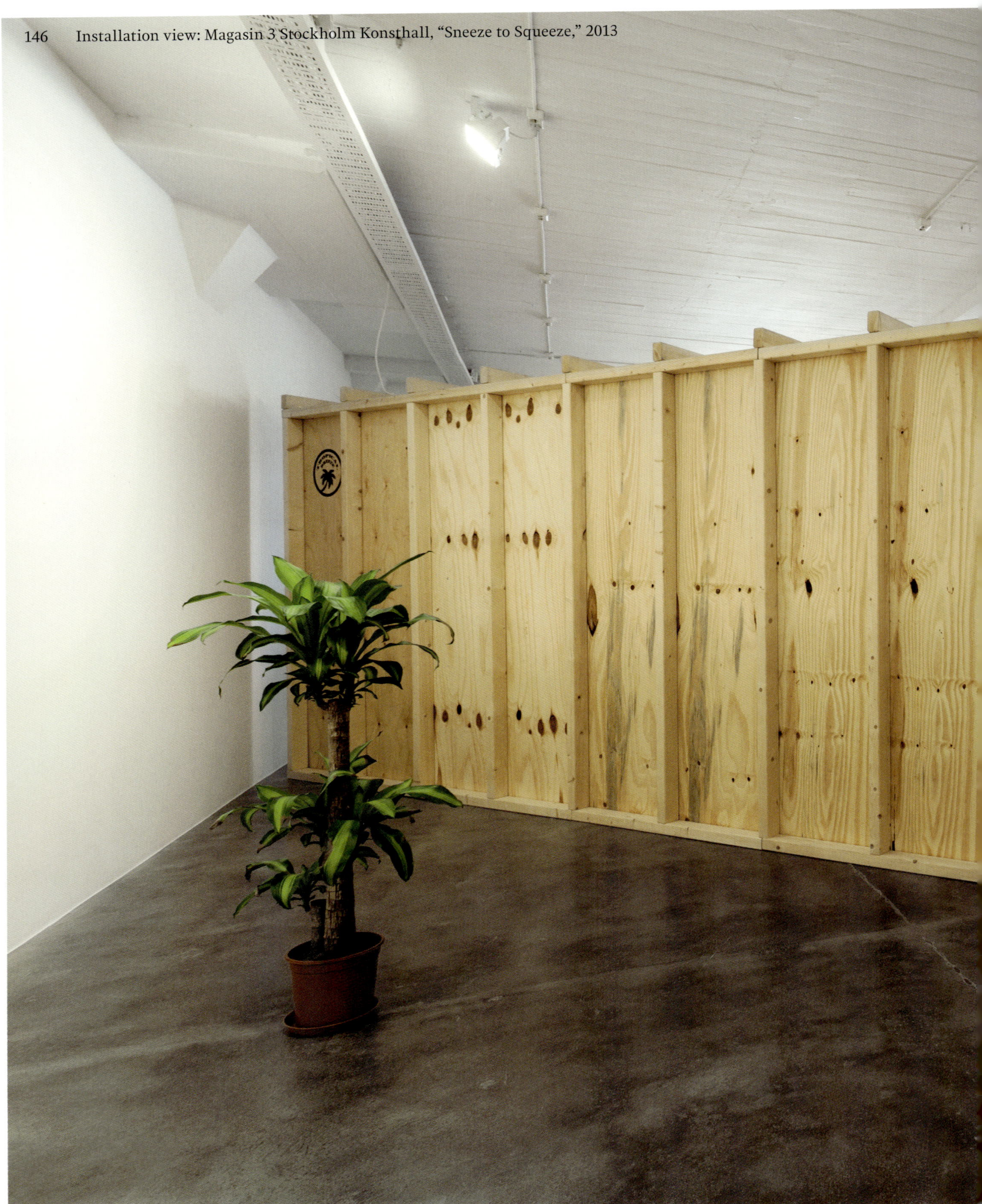

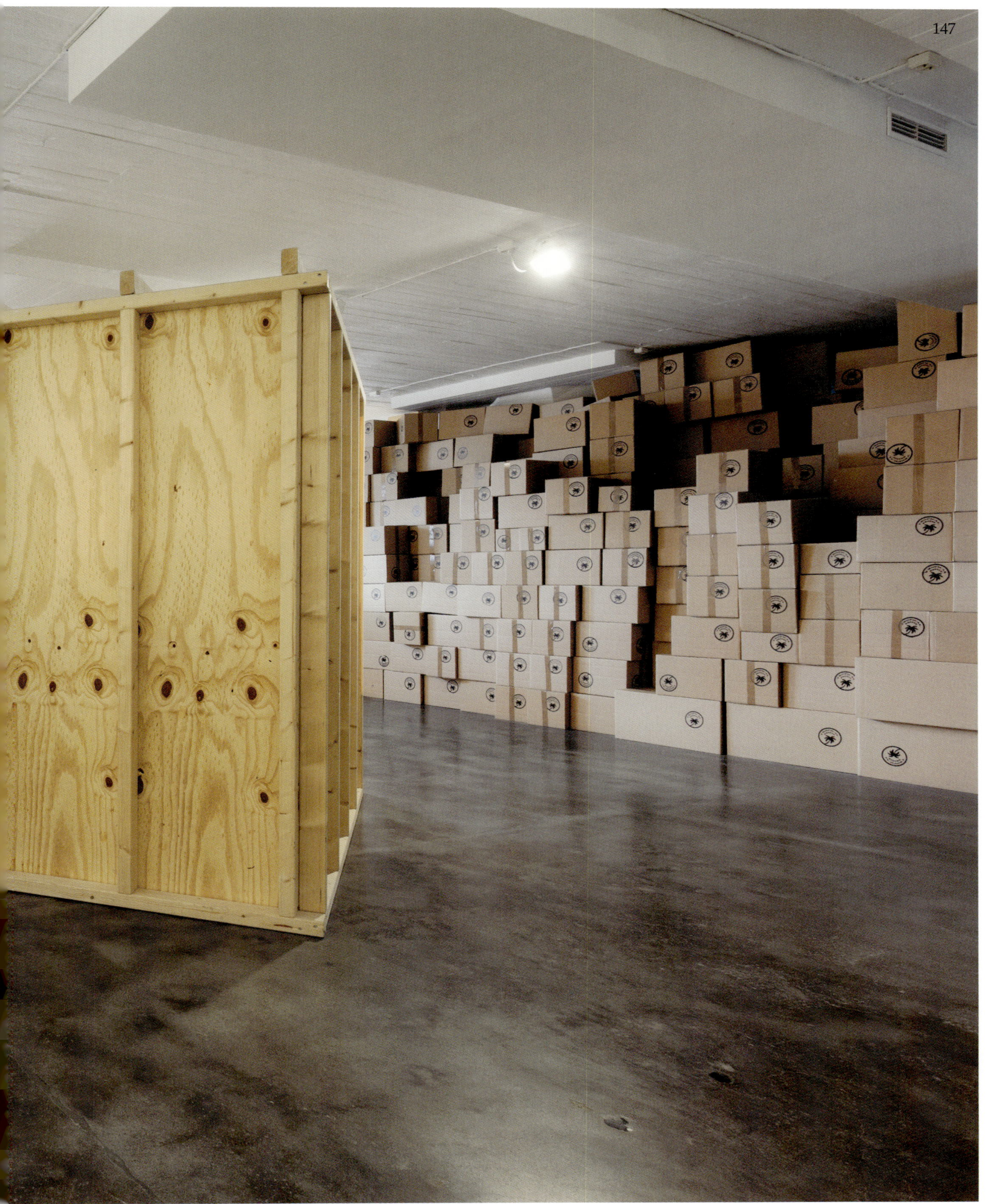

Installation view: Magasin 3 Stockholm Konsthall, “Sneeze to Squeeze,” 2013

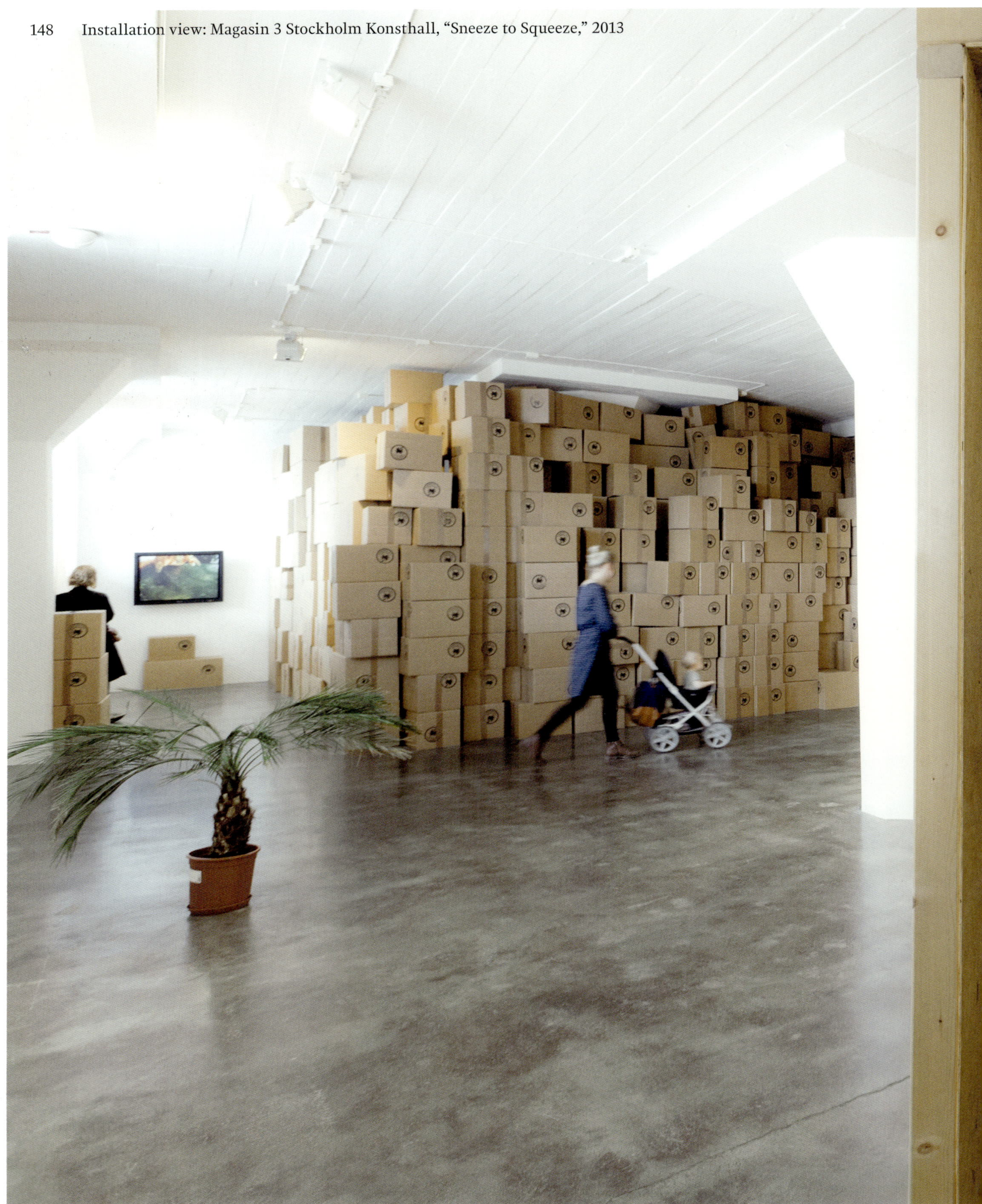

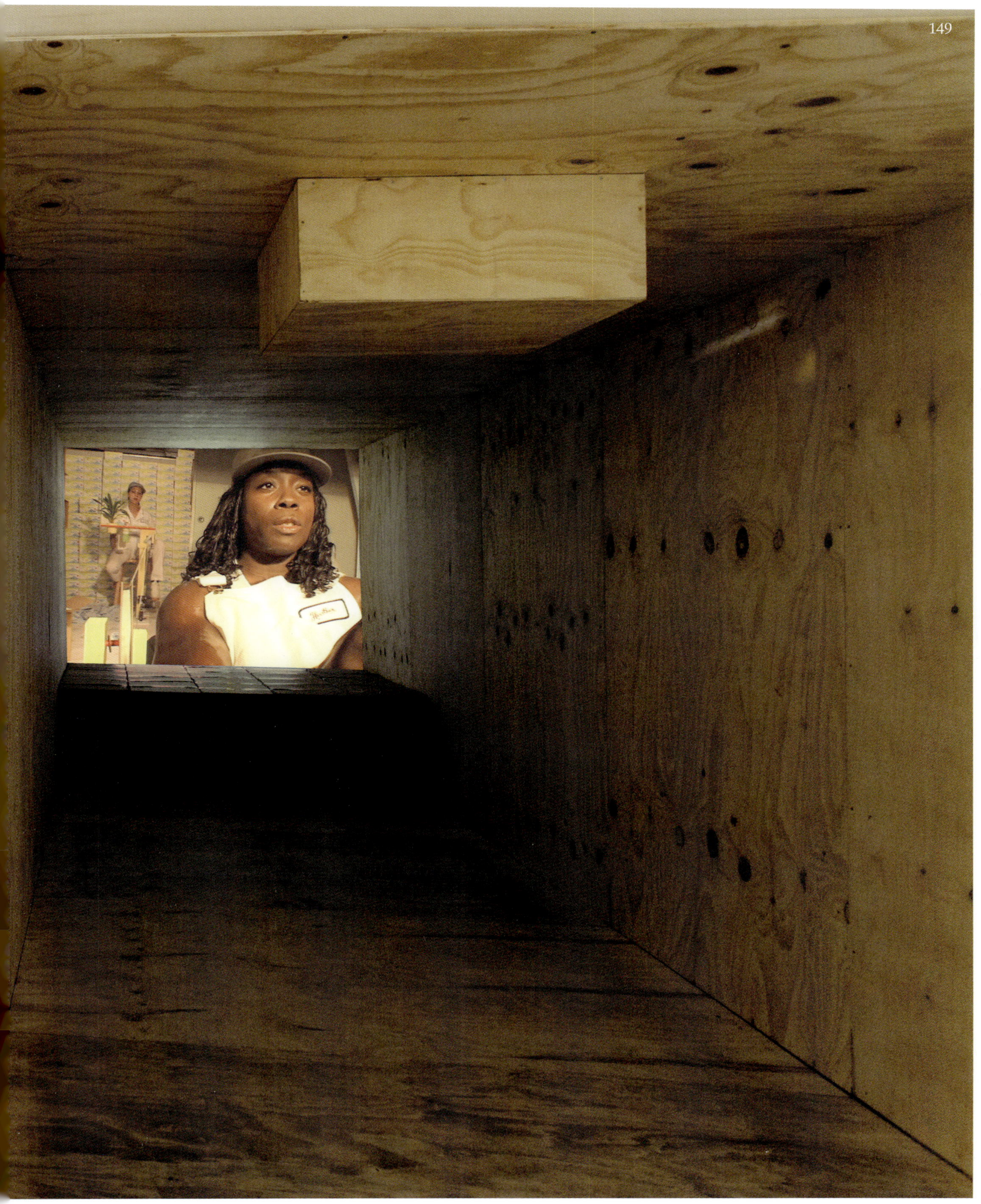

Interior installation views: La Maison Rouge, "Mika Rottenberg," 2009

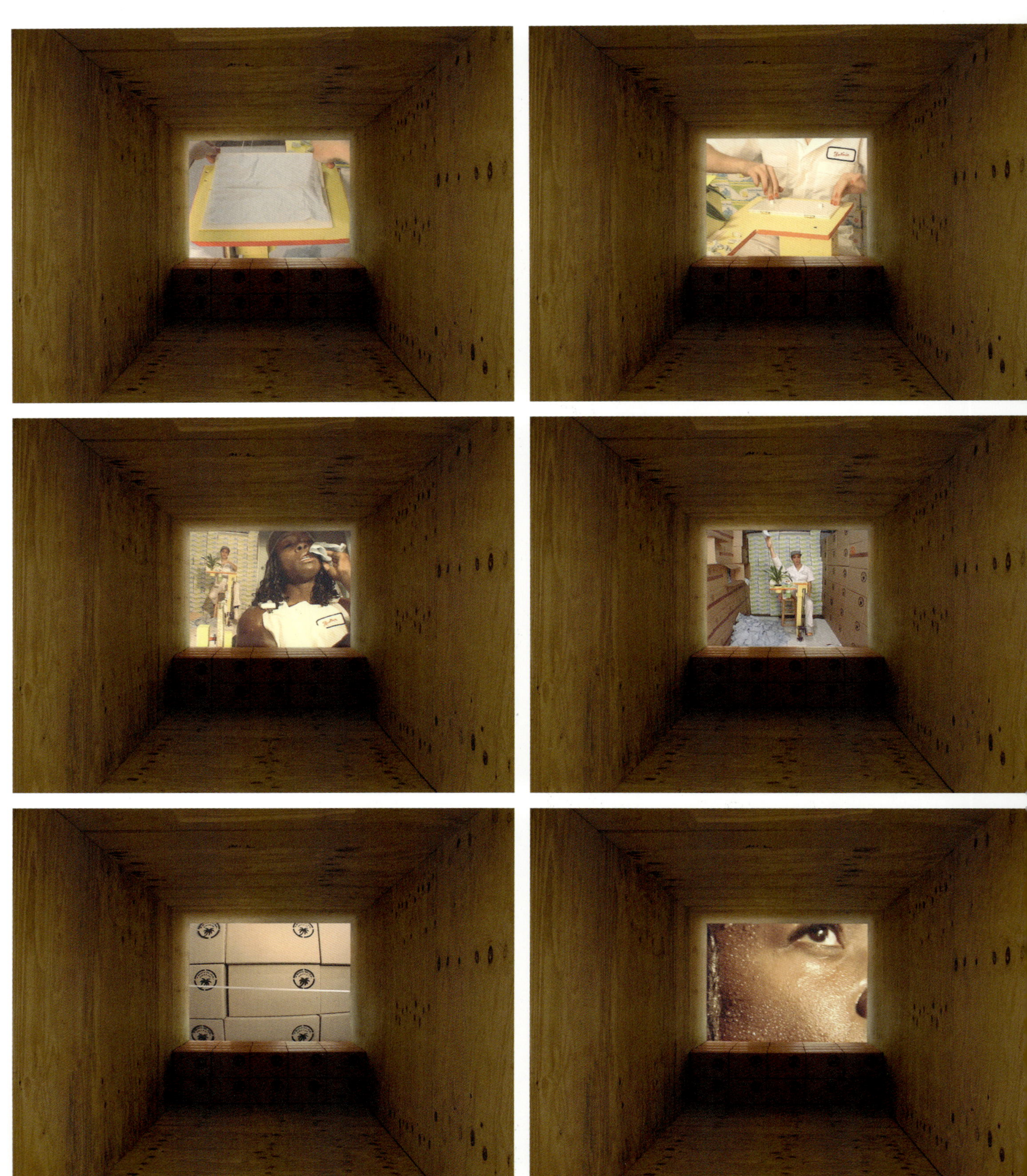

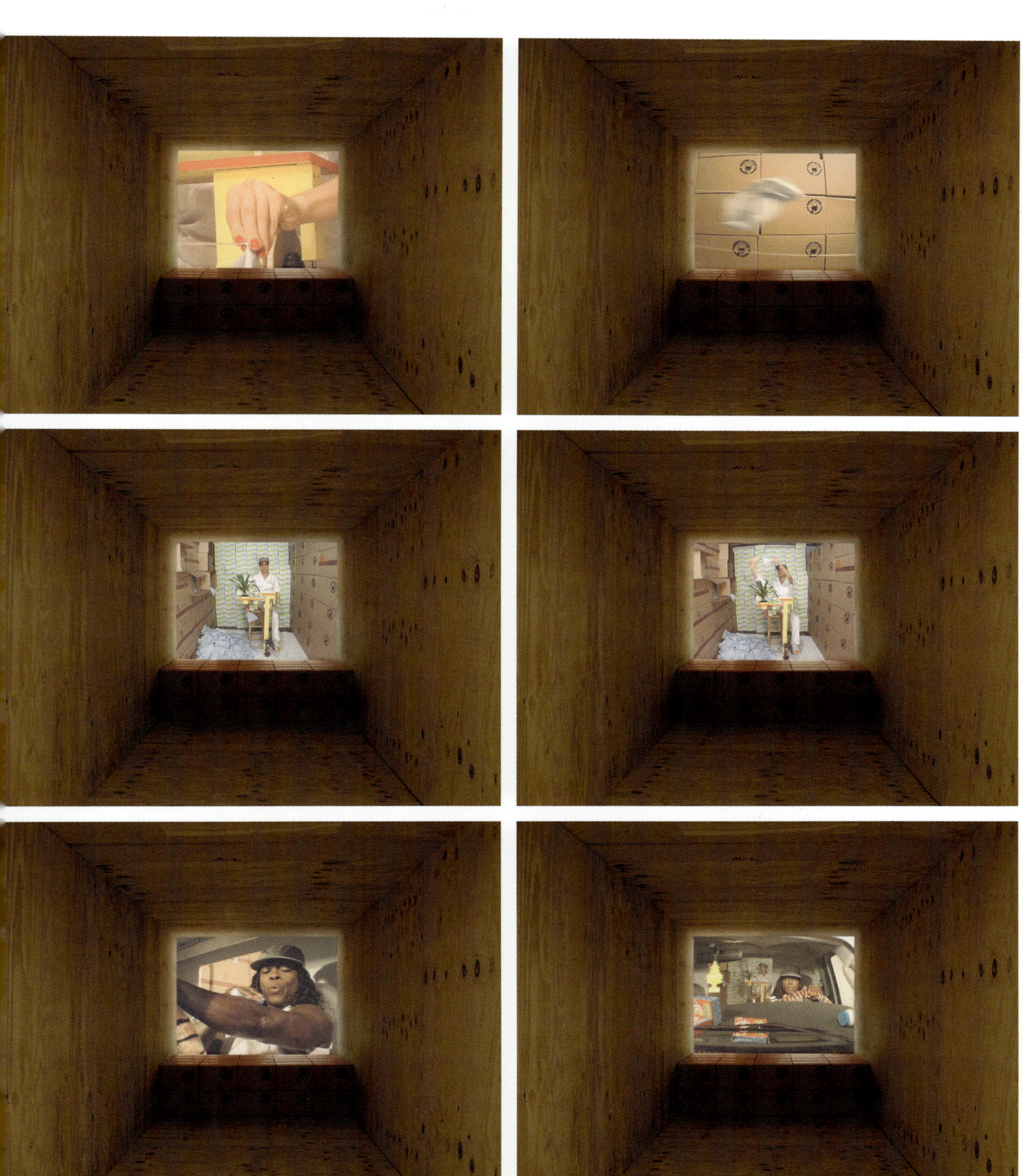

Installation views: de Appel arts centre, “Mika Rottenberg: Dough Cheese Squeeze and Tropical Breeze: Video Works 2003–2010,” 2011

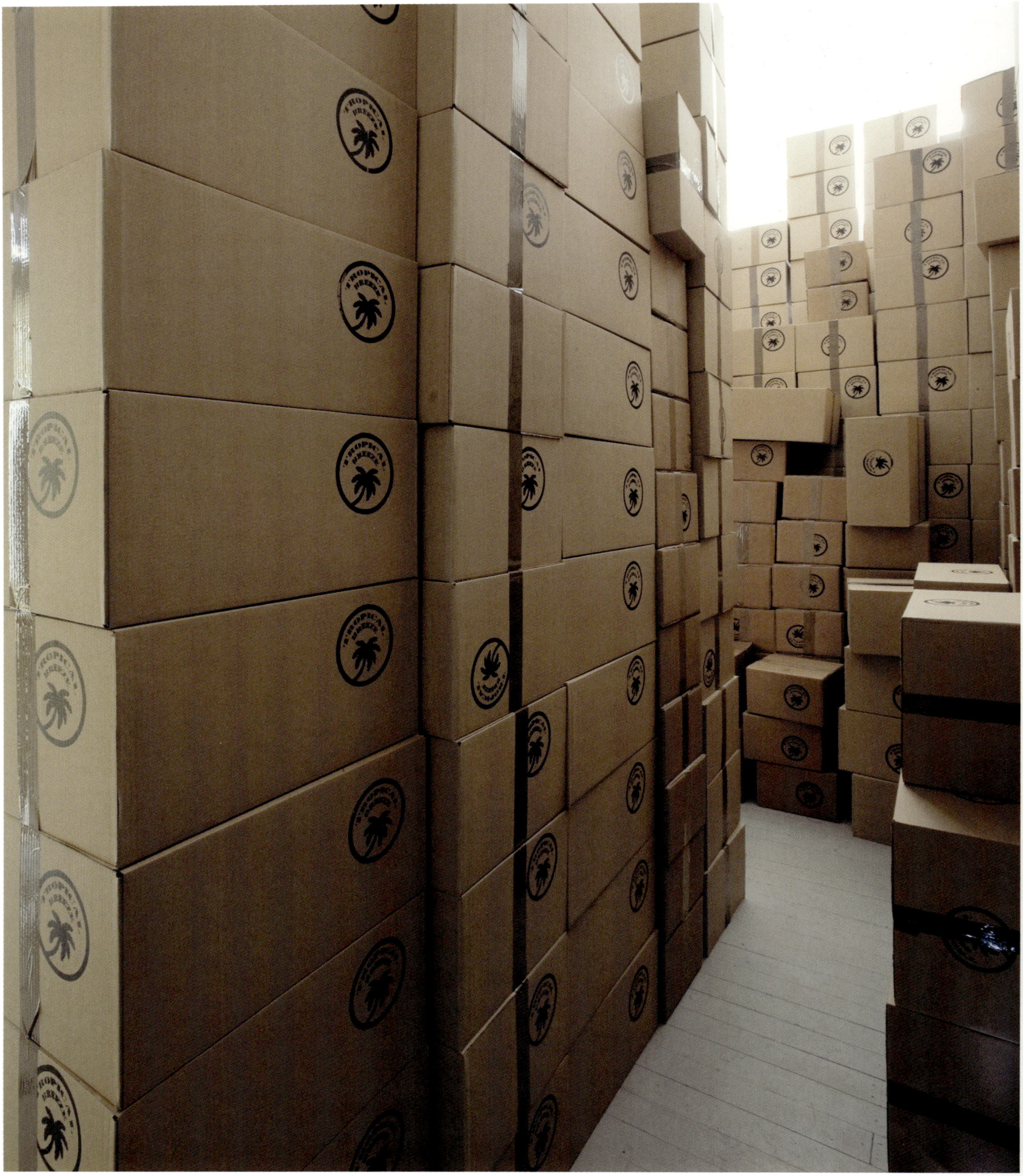

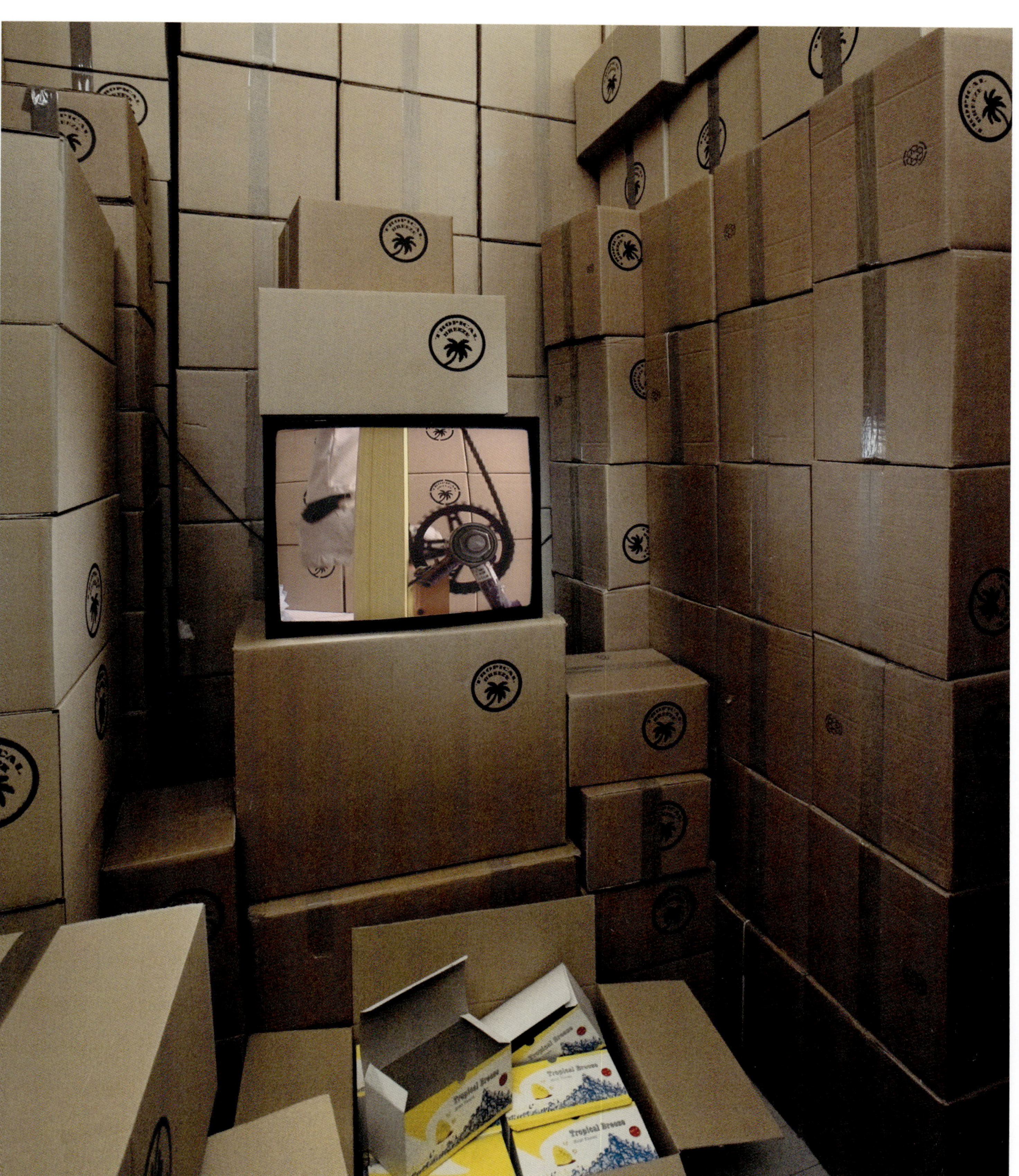
TROPICAL BREEZE
Tropical Breeze

Installation view (composite): Nottingham Contemporary, “Mika Rottenberg,” 2012

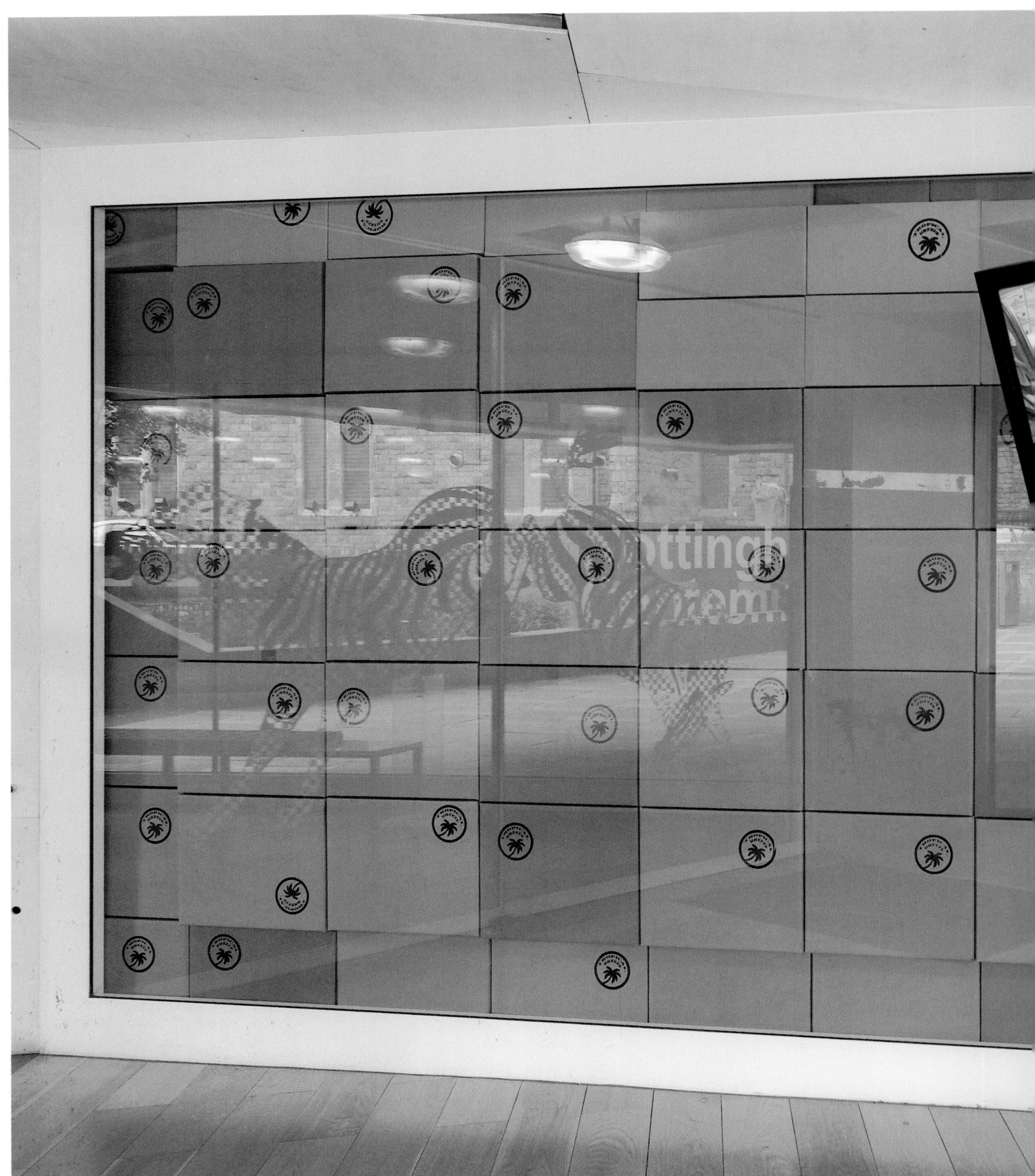

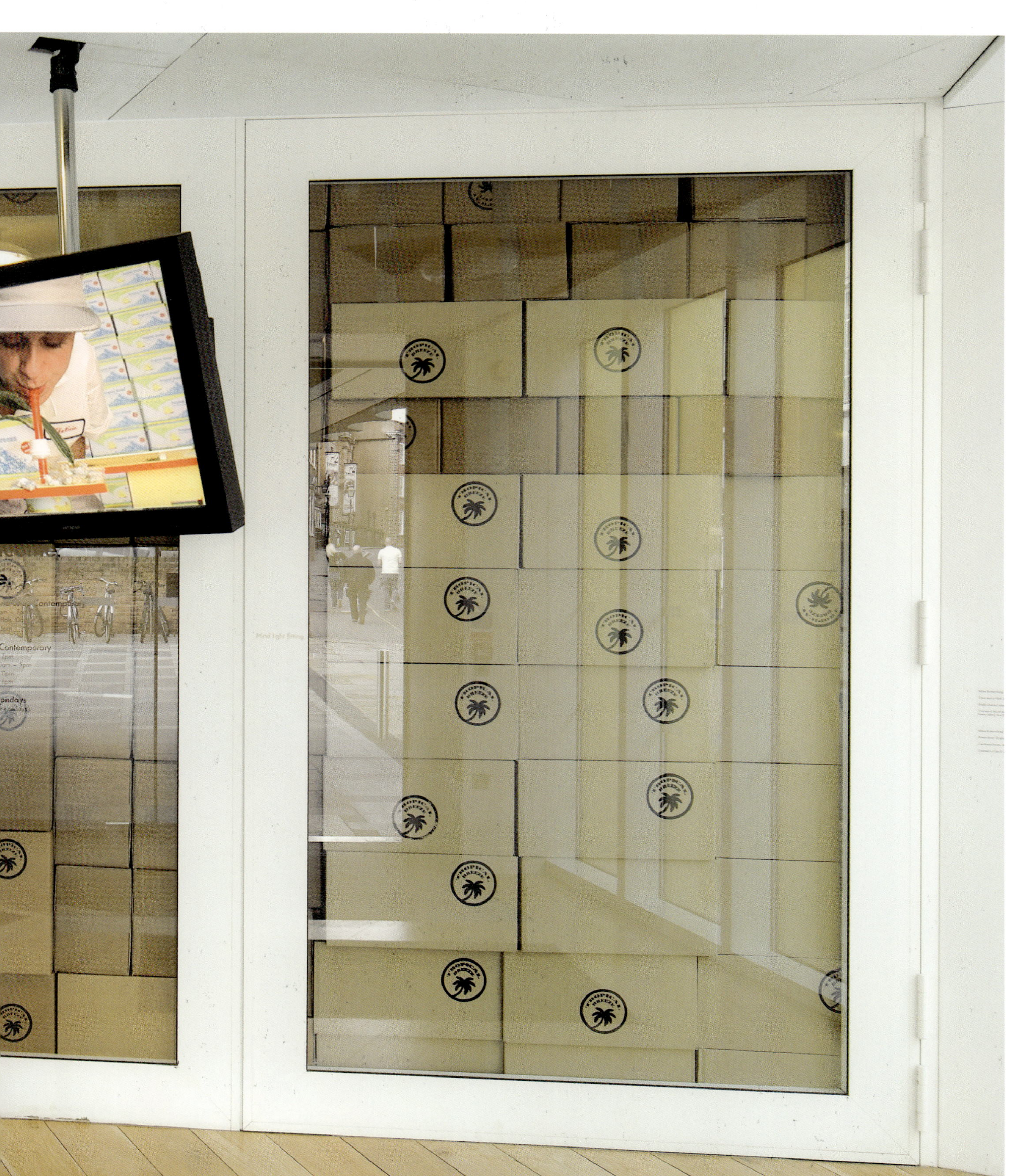

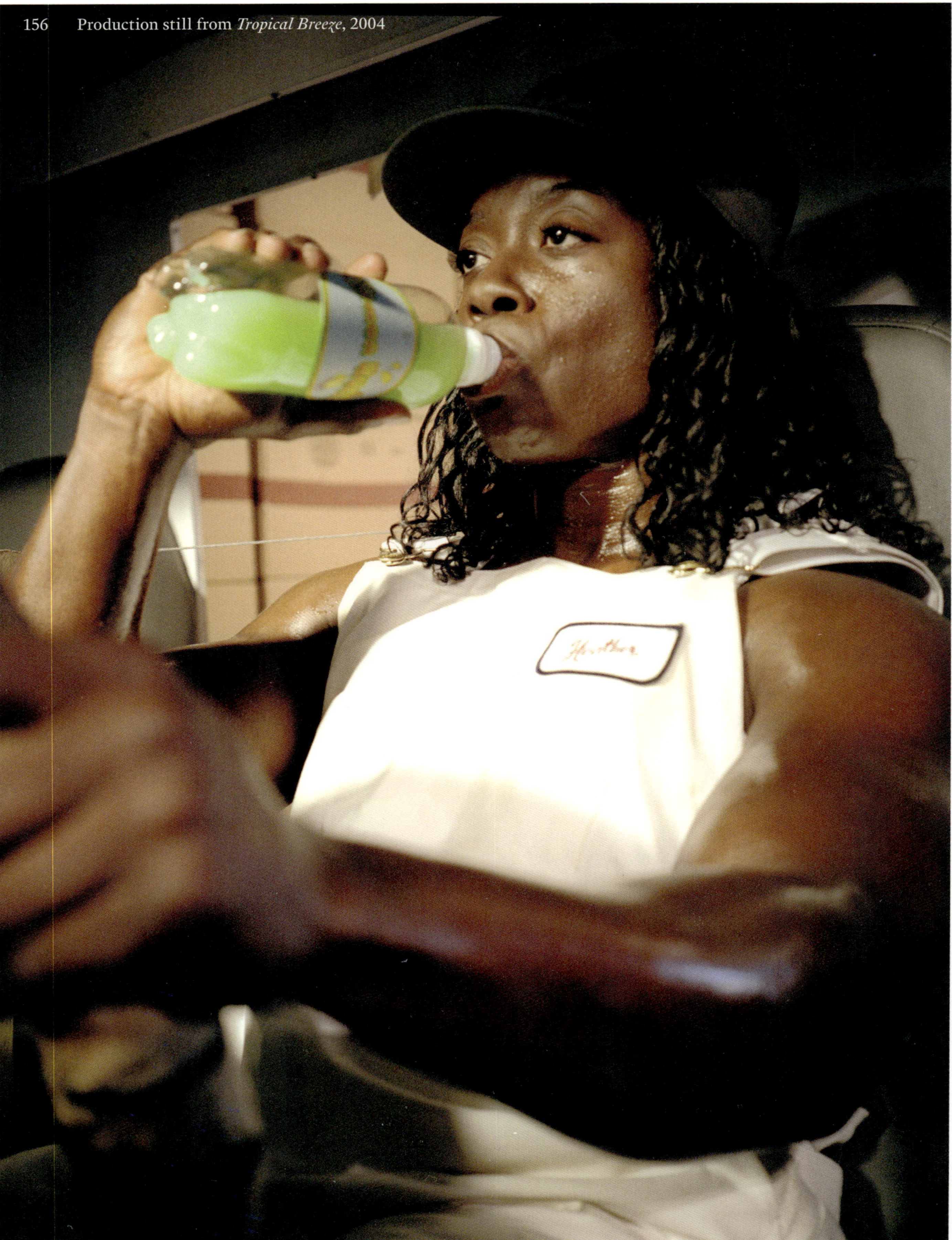

Production still from *Tropical Breeze*, 2004

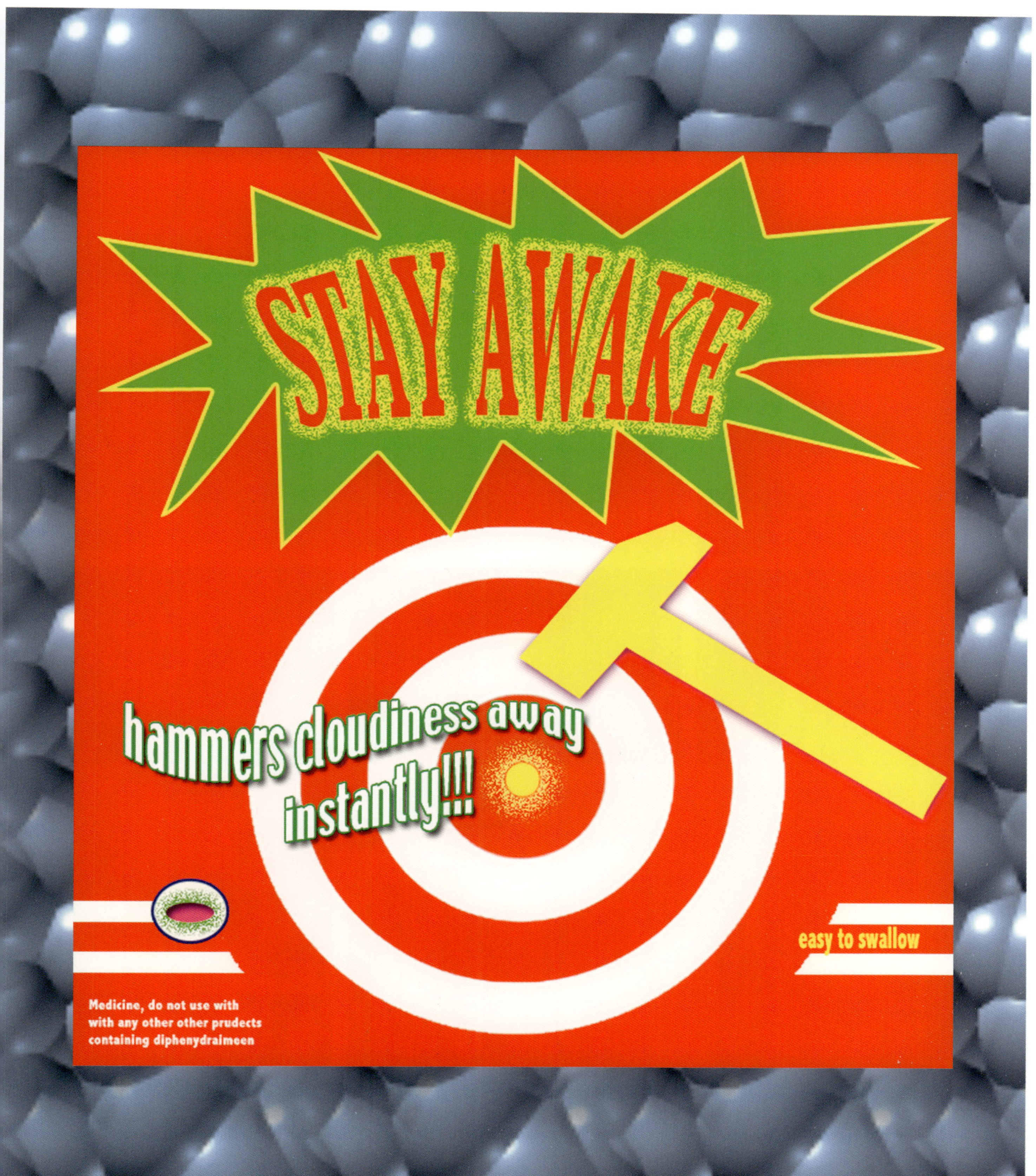
STAY AWAKE
hammers cloudiness away
instantly!!!
easy to swallow
Medicine, do not use with
with any other other prudects
containing diphenydraimeen

Stills from *Tropical Breeze*, 2004

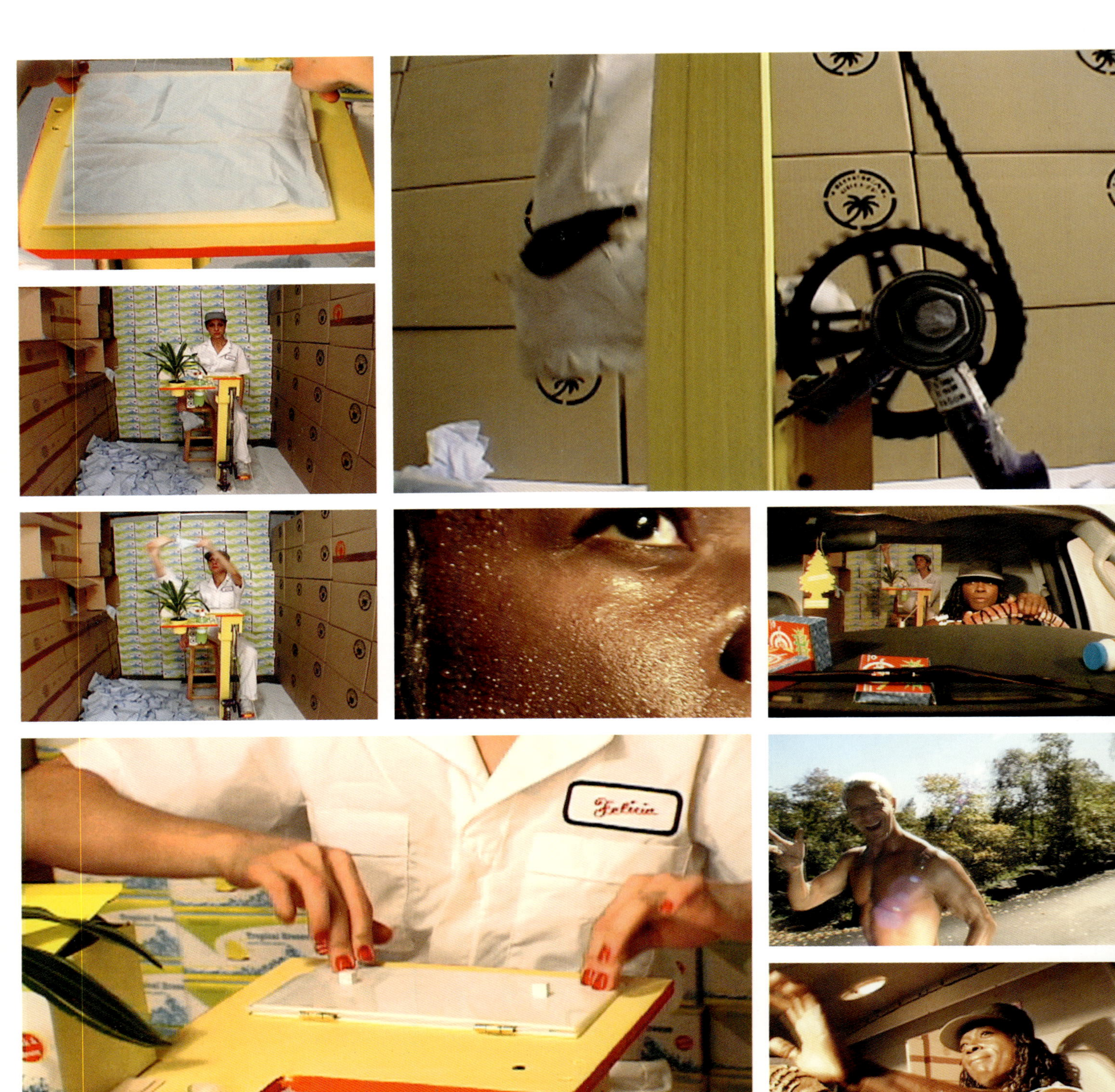

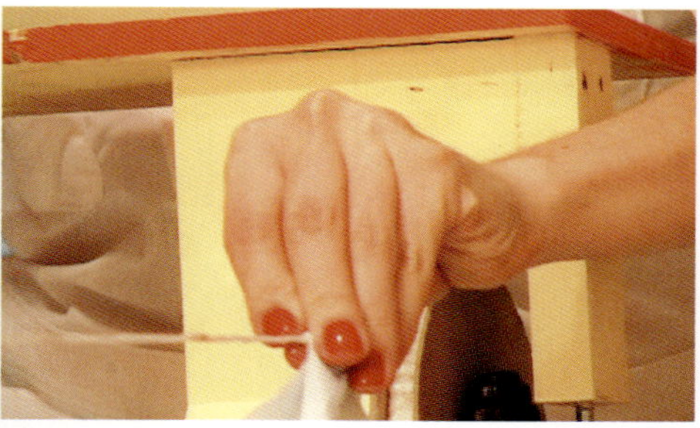

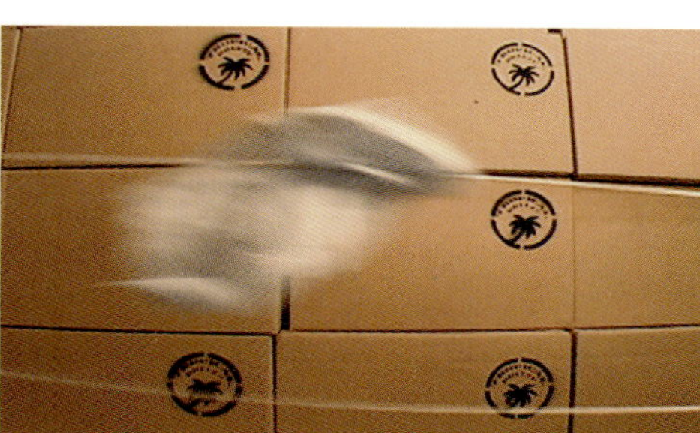

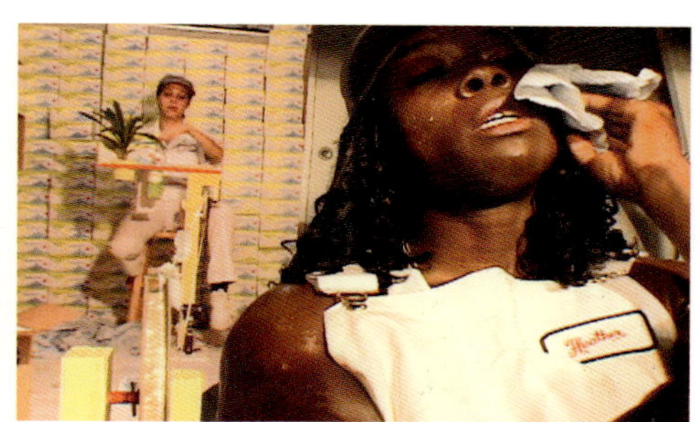

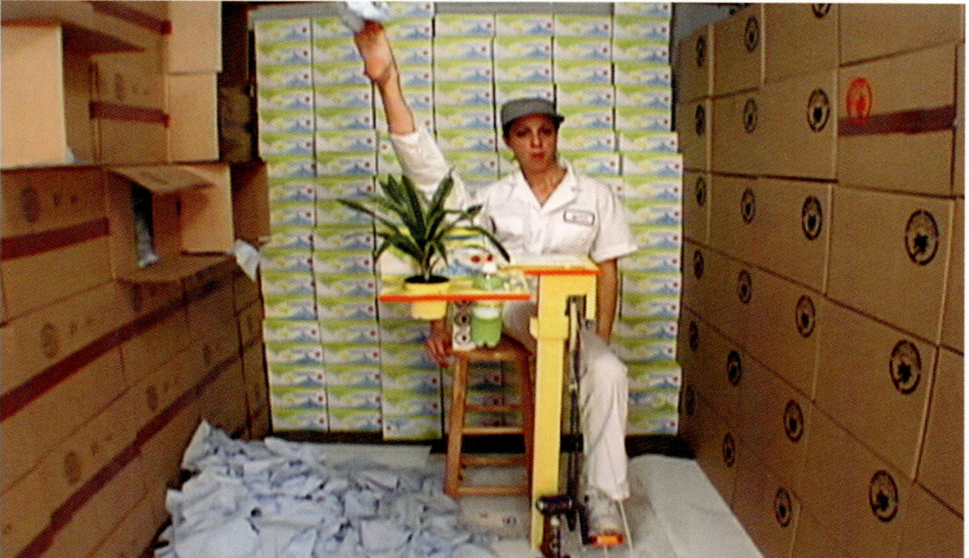

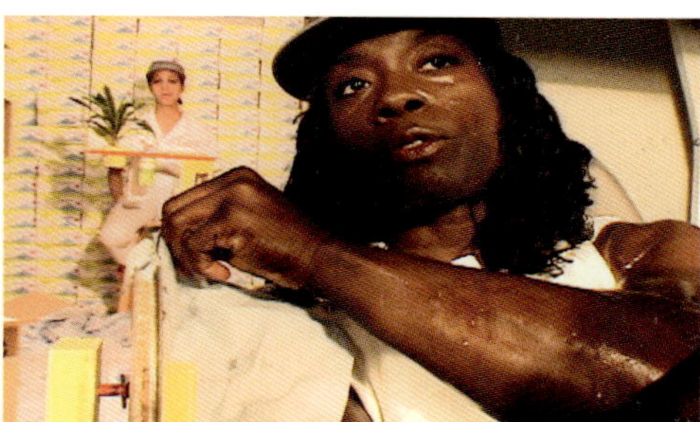

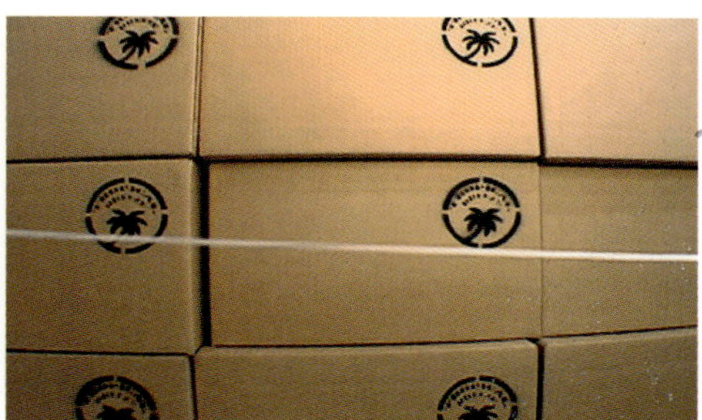

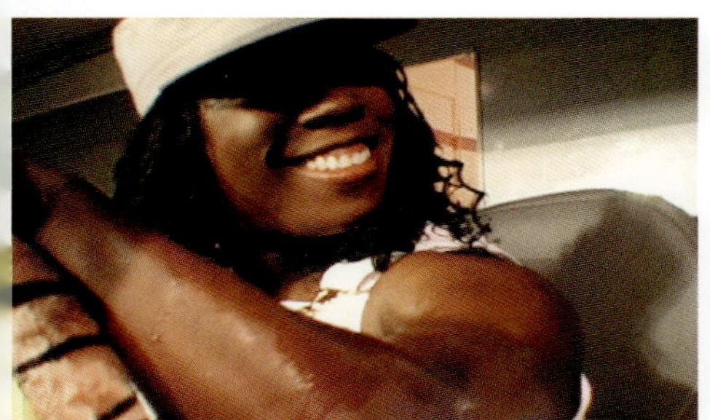

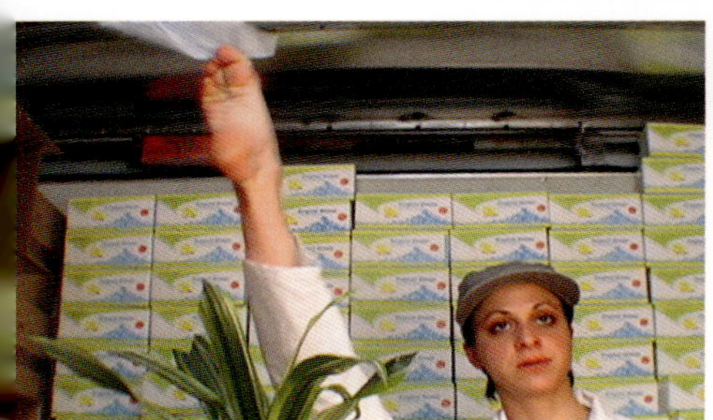

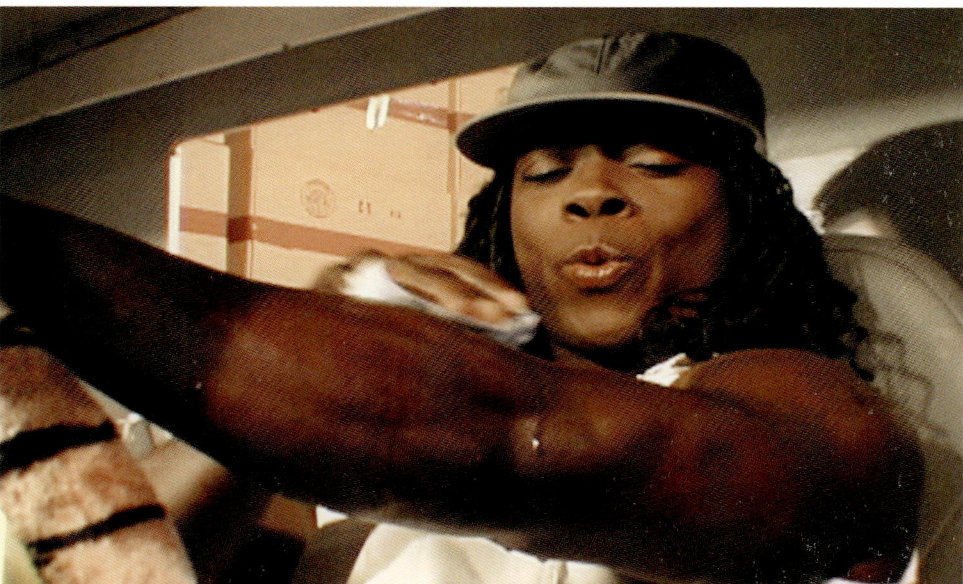

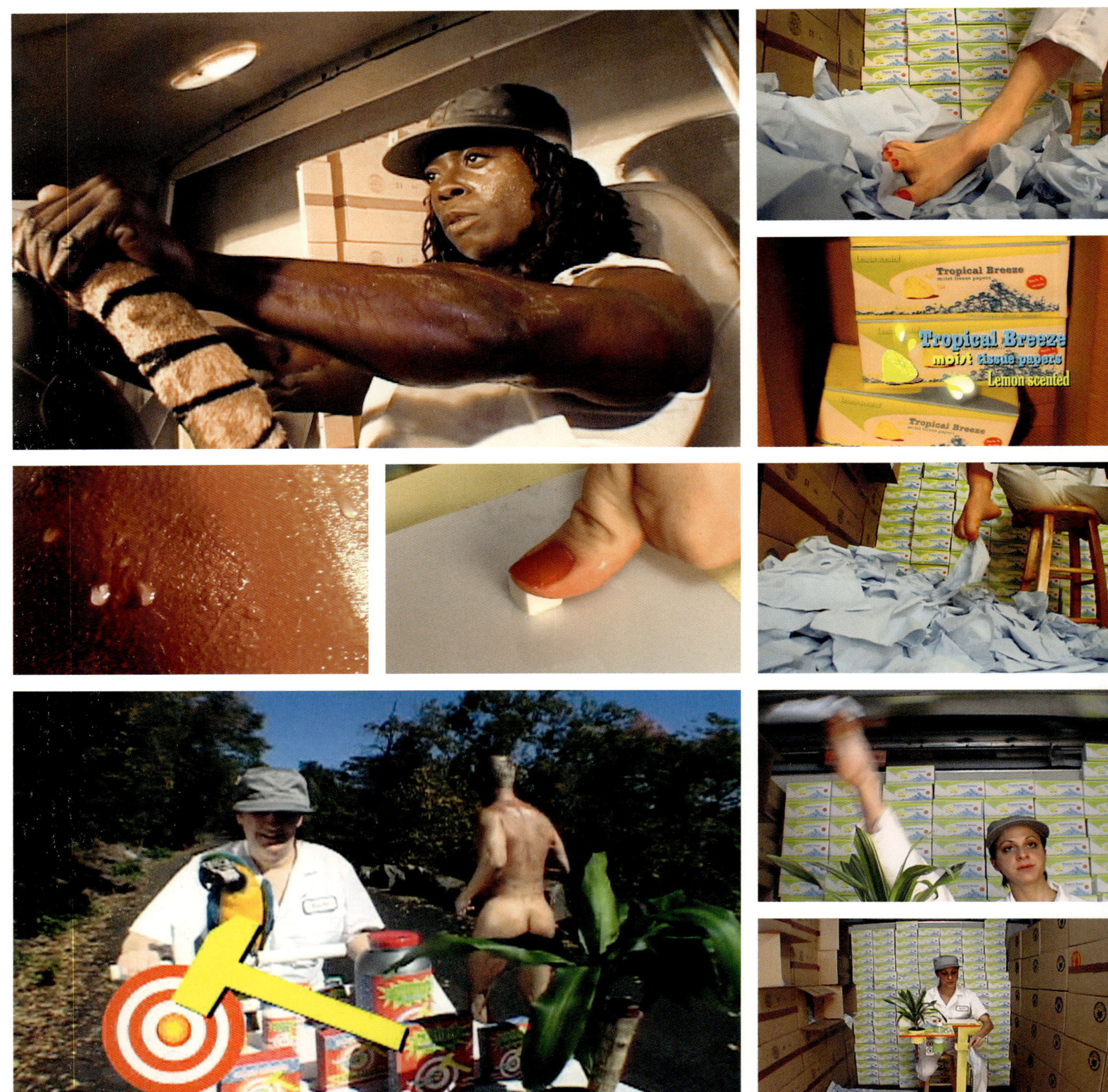
Tropical Breeze
moist tissue papers
Lemon scented

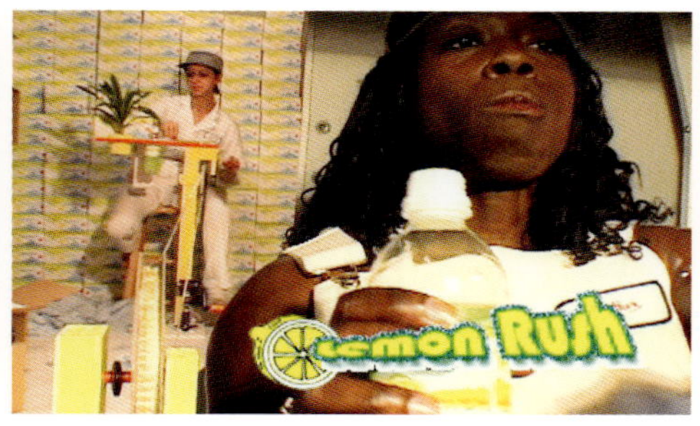
Lemon Rush

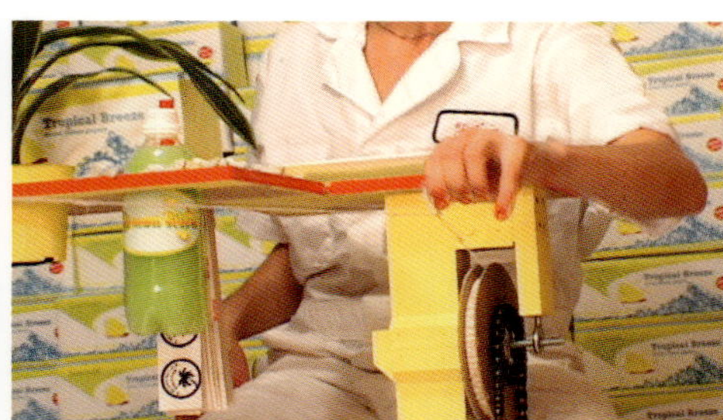

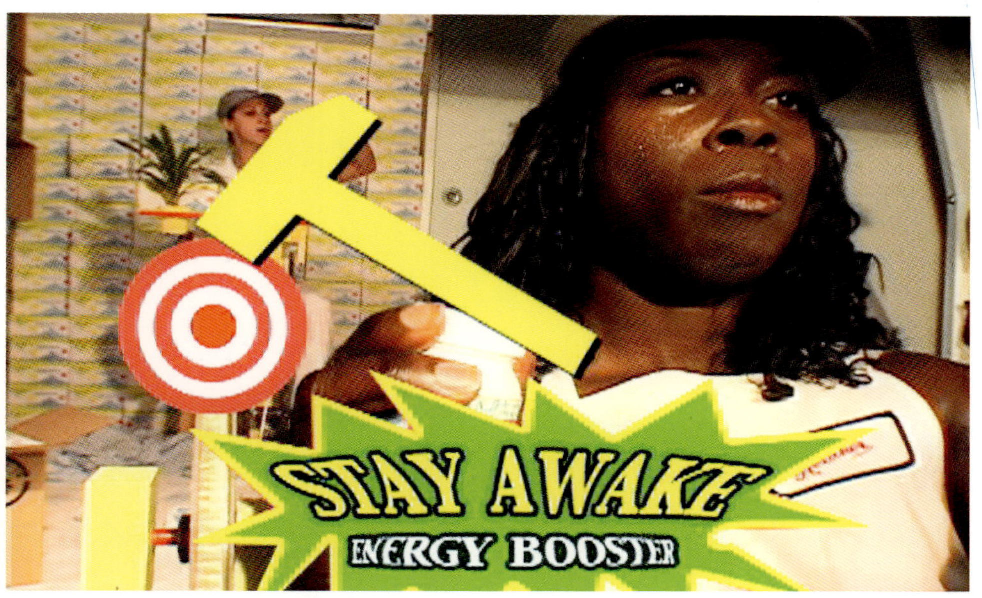
STAY AWAKE
ENERGY BOOSTER

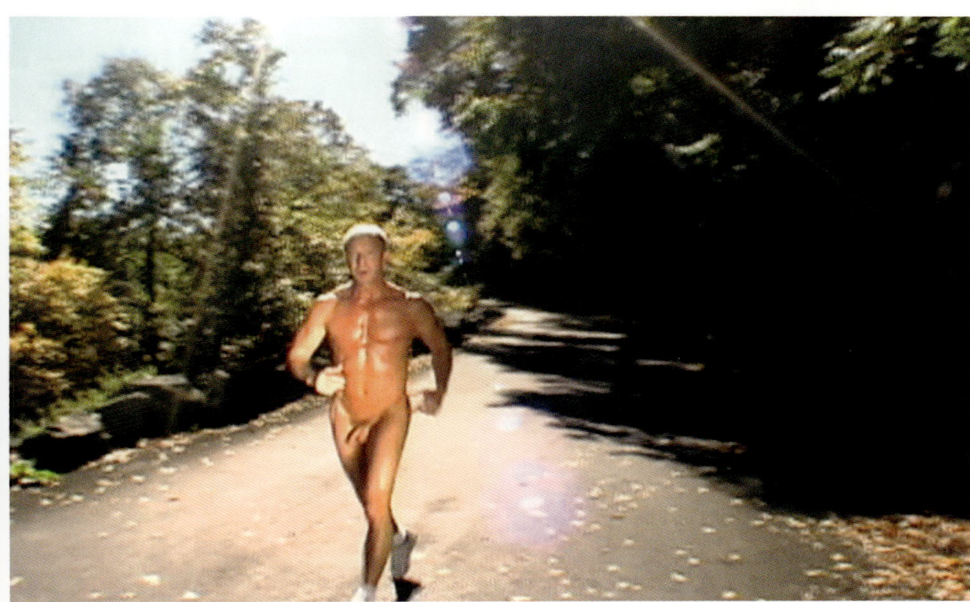

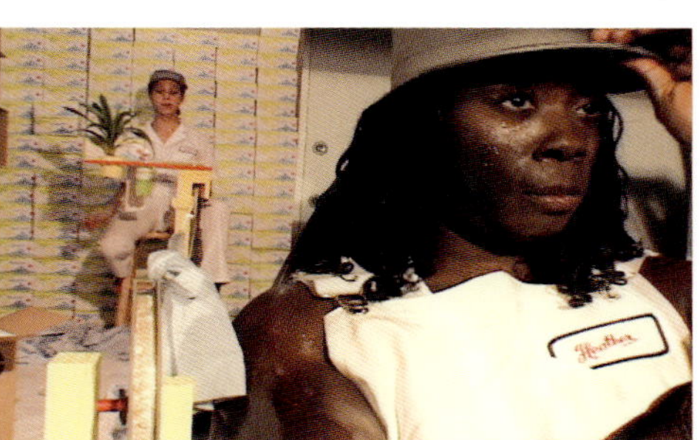

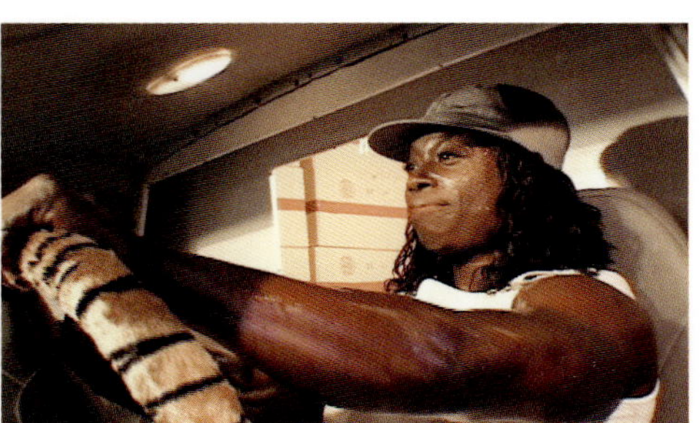

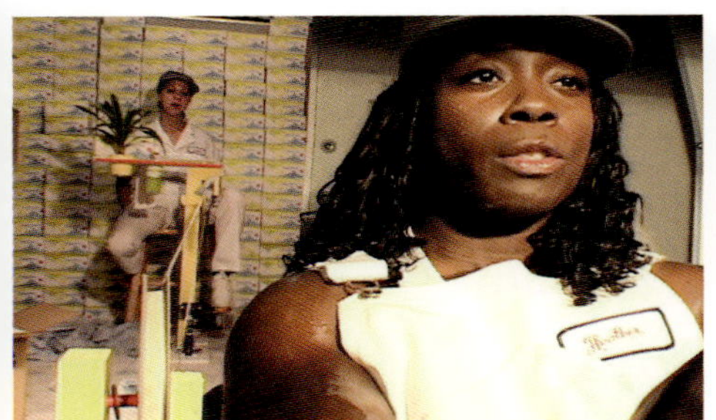

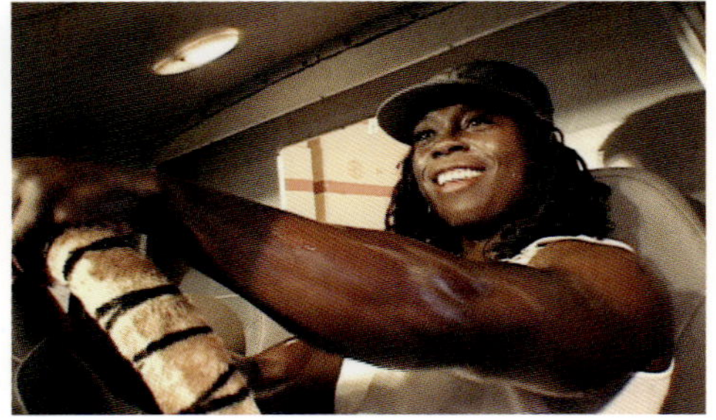

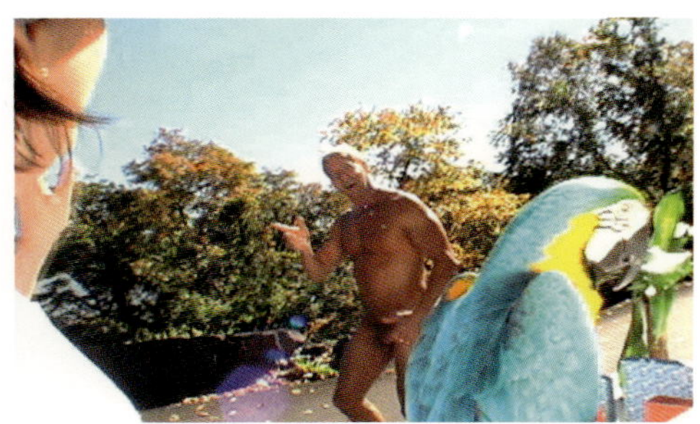

 Detail from *Tropical Breeze*, 2004

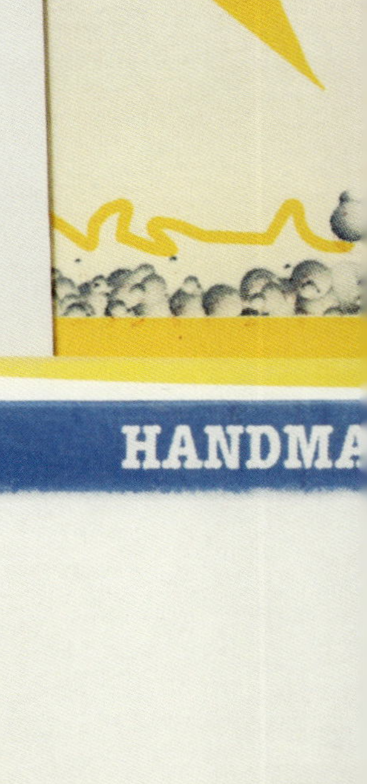

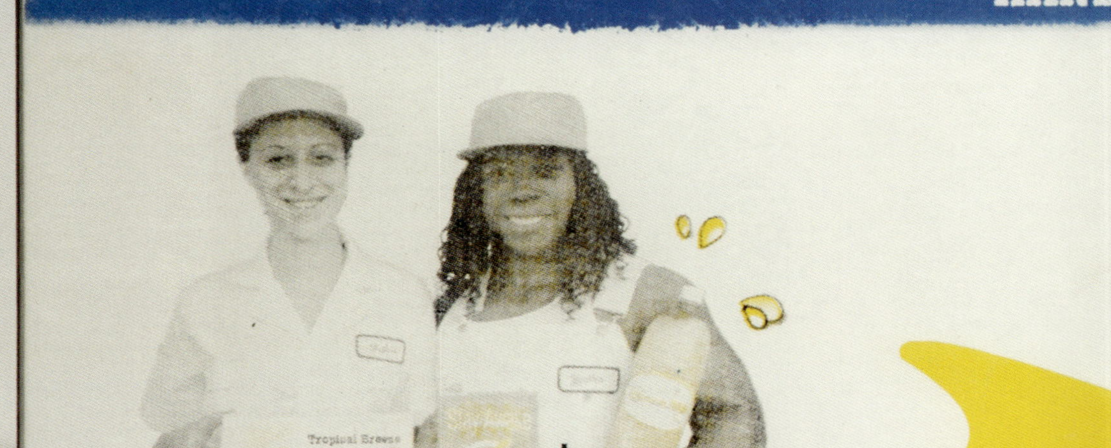

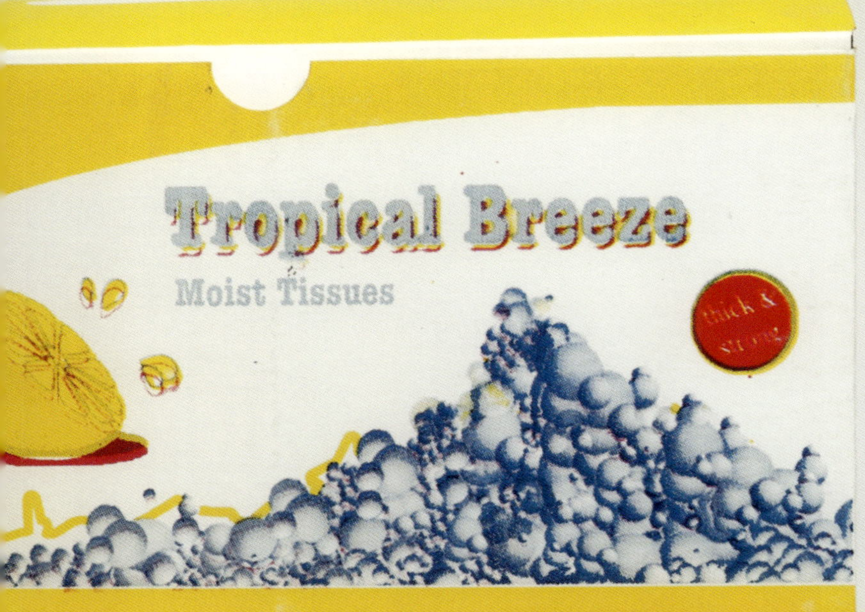
Tropical Breeze
Moist Tissues
thick & strong

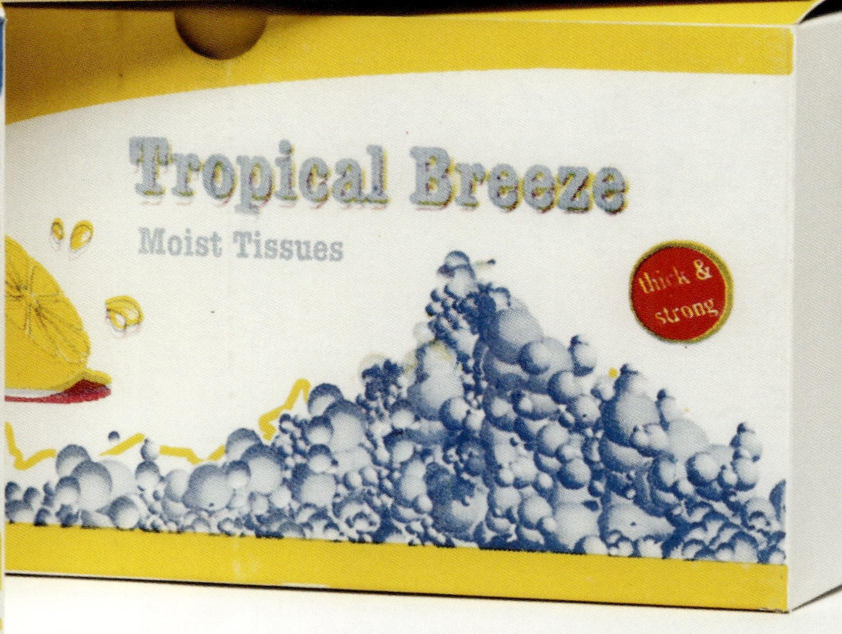
Tropical Breeze
Moist Tissues
thick & strong

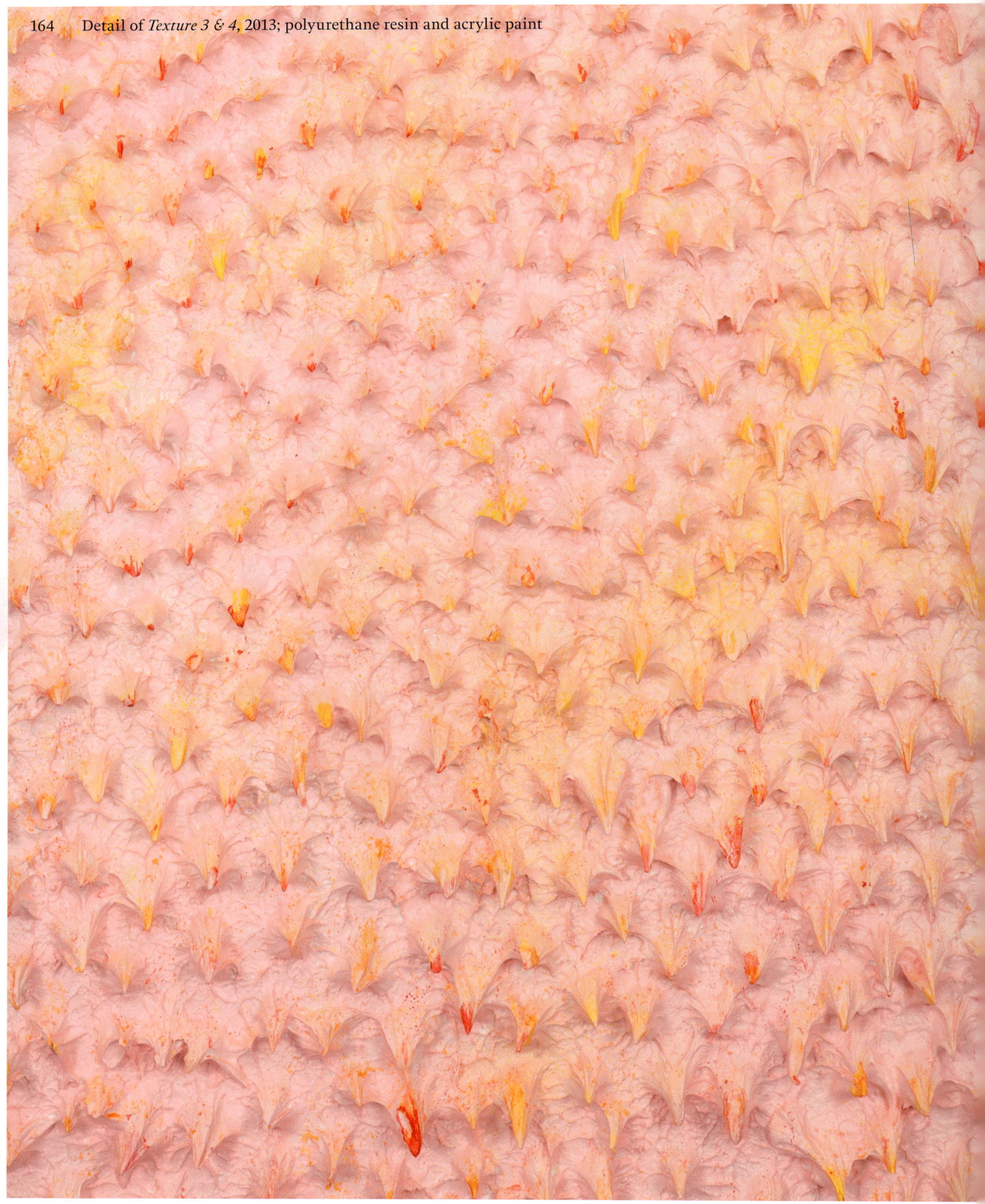

Detail of *Texture 3 & 4*, 2013; polyurethane resin and acrylic paint

mary's cherries

CB: Making the feel of things—textures—palpable for the viewer is something you strive for in much of your work. Do you want to connect the viewer to the physical process of making something?

MR: Texture is a way to address other senses besides the visual. Texture provides a way to get drawn in. It stimulates sensory perceptions. Maybe you can imagine how it would feel to touch a texture, to lick it, to smell it. Texture is also in sound; it is not just visual. Video can have a tendency to cancel textures and flatten reality if you don't actively manipulate the craft. I love the craft of video, because it can be a great tool to emphasize texture if you control it. Textures are traces or residues of an action; they leave the hand in. You can feel the person or physical phenomenon behind something, and that is important to me. For example, texture triggers and flirts with your retina and you can kind of feel that process working when the texture is perceived or represented effectively.

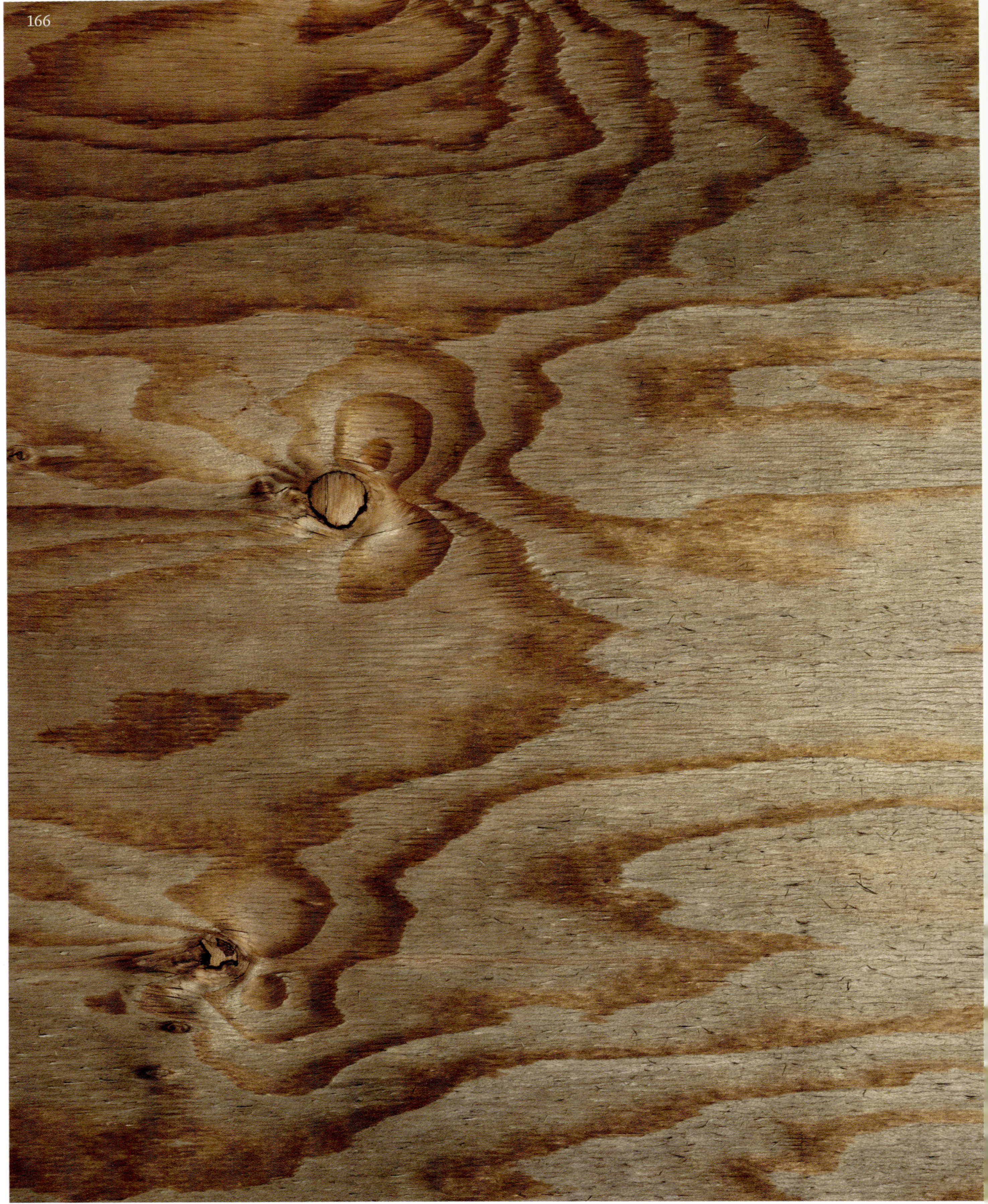

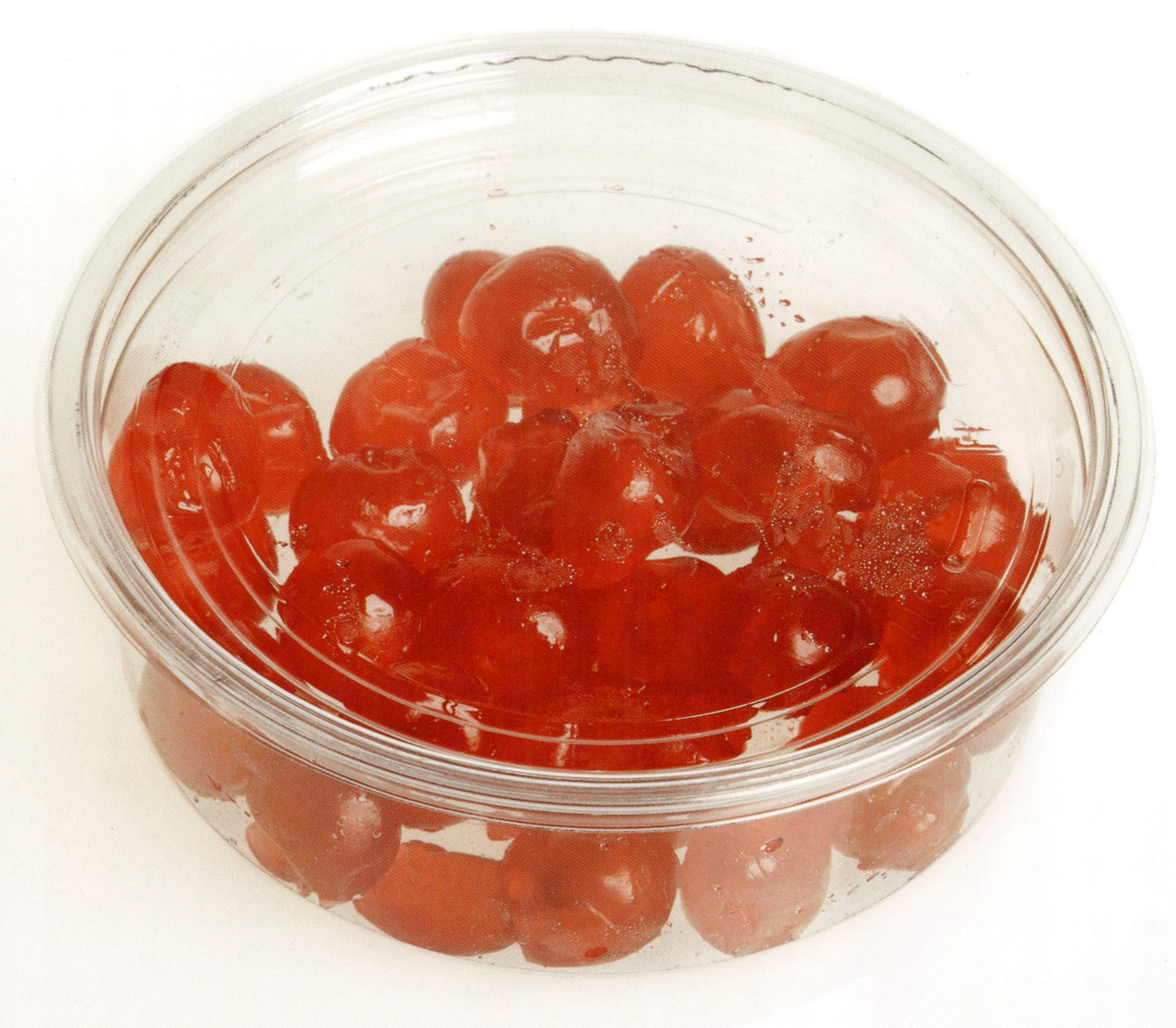

 Installation views: FRAC Languedoc-Roussillon, "Mary's Cherries," 2012

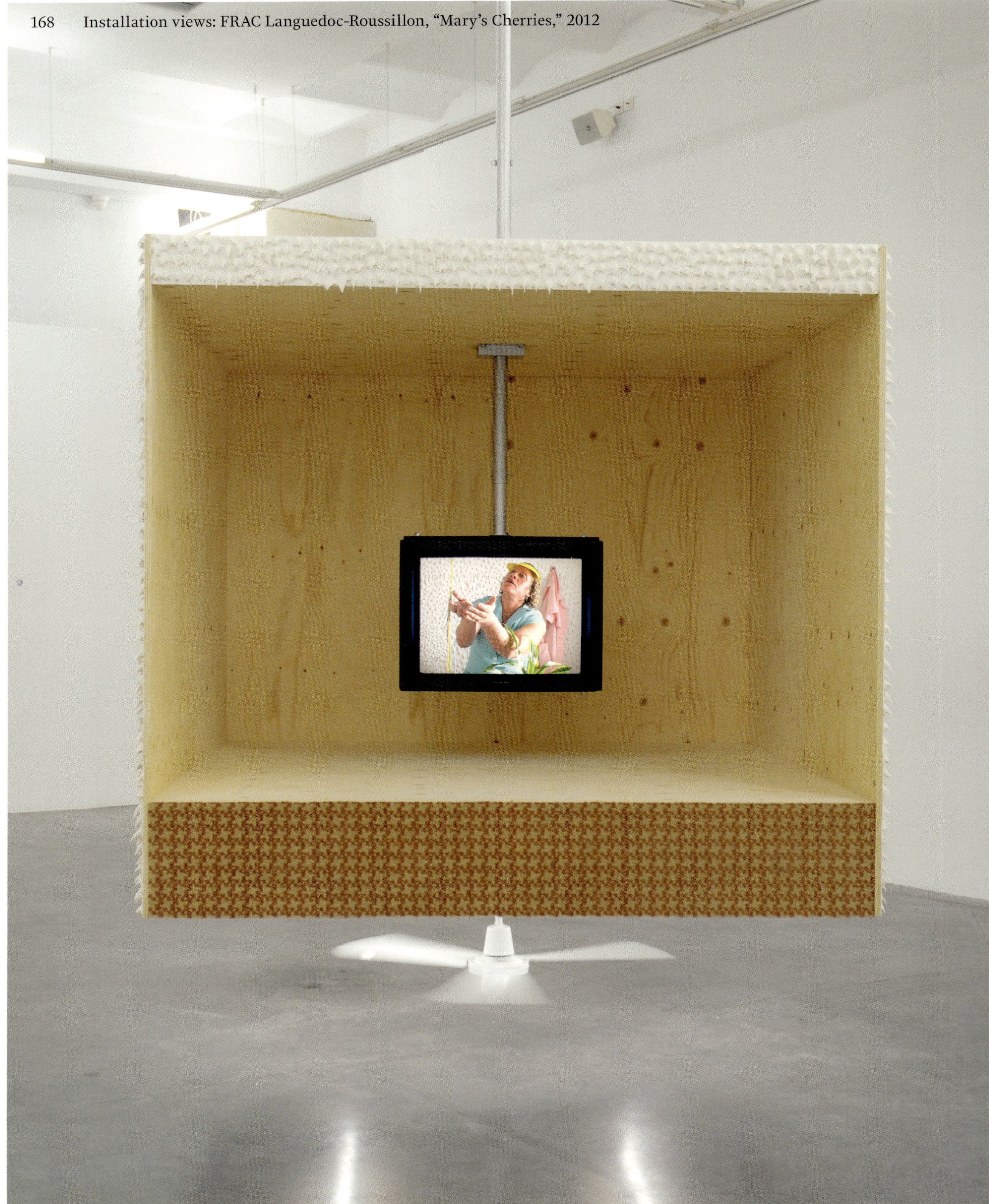

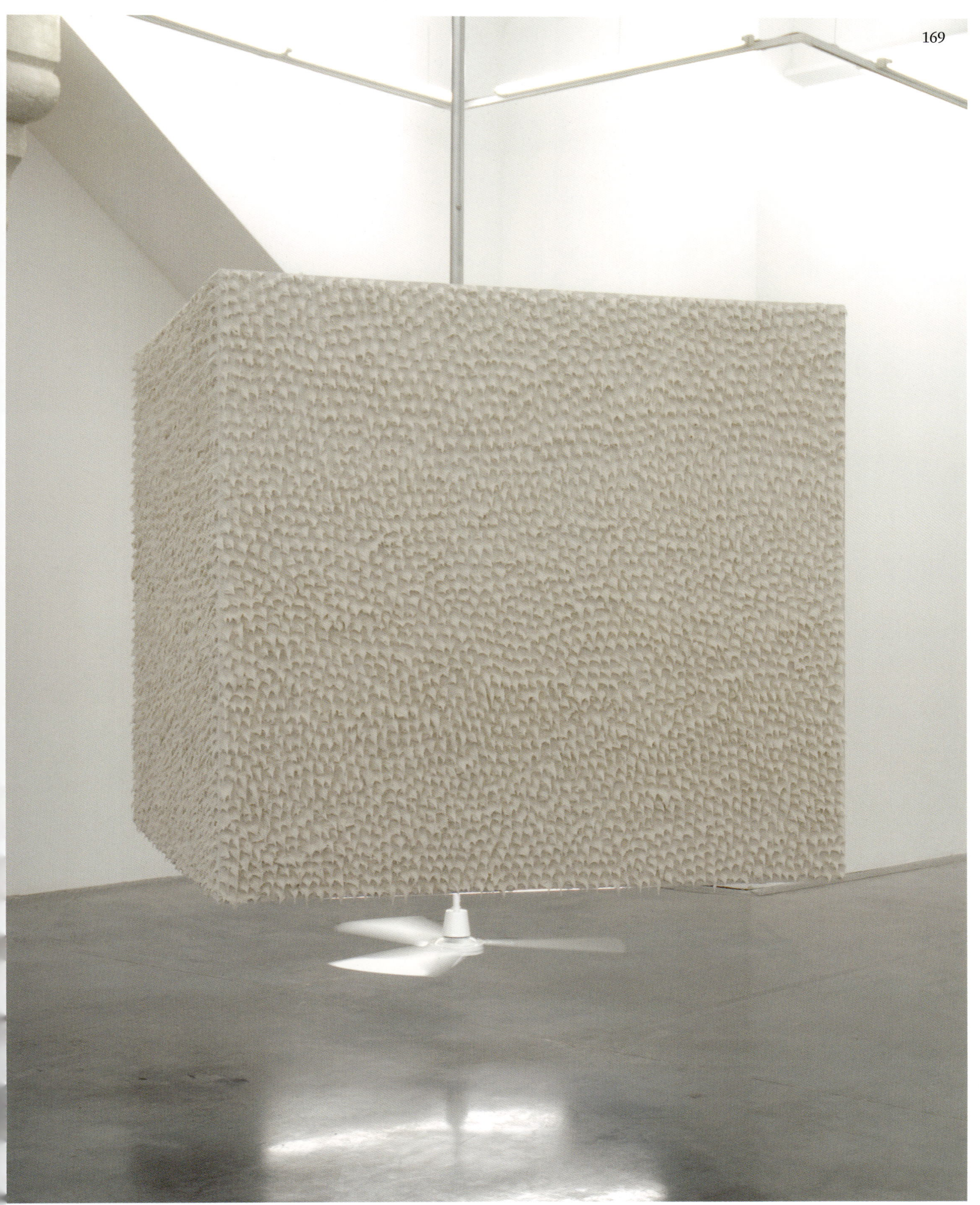

Interior installation view: Tate Modern, “The Irresistible Force,” 2007

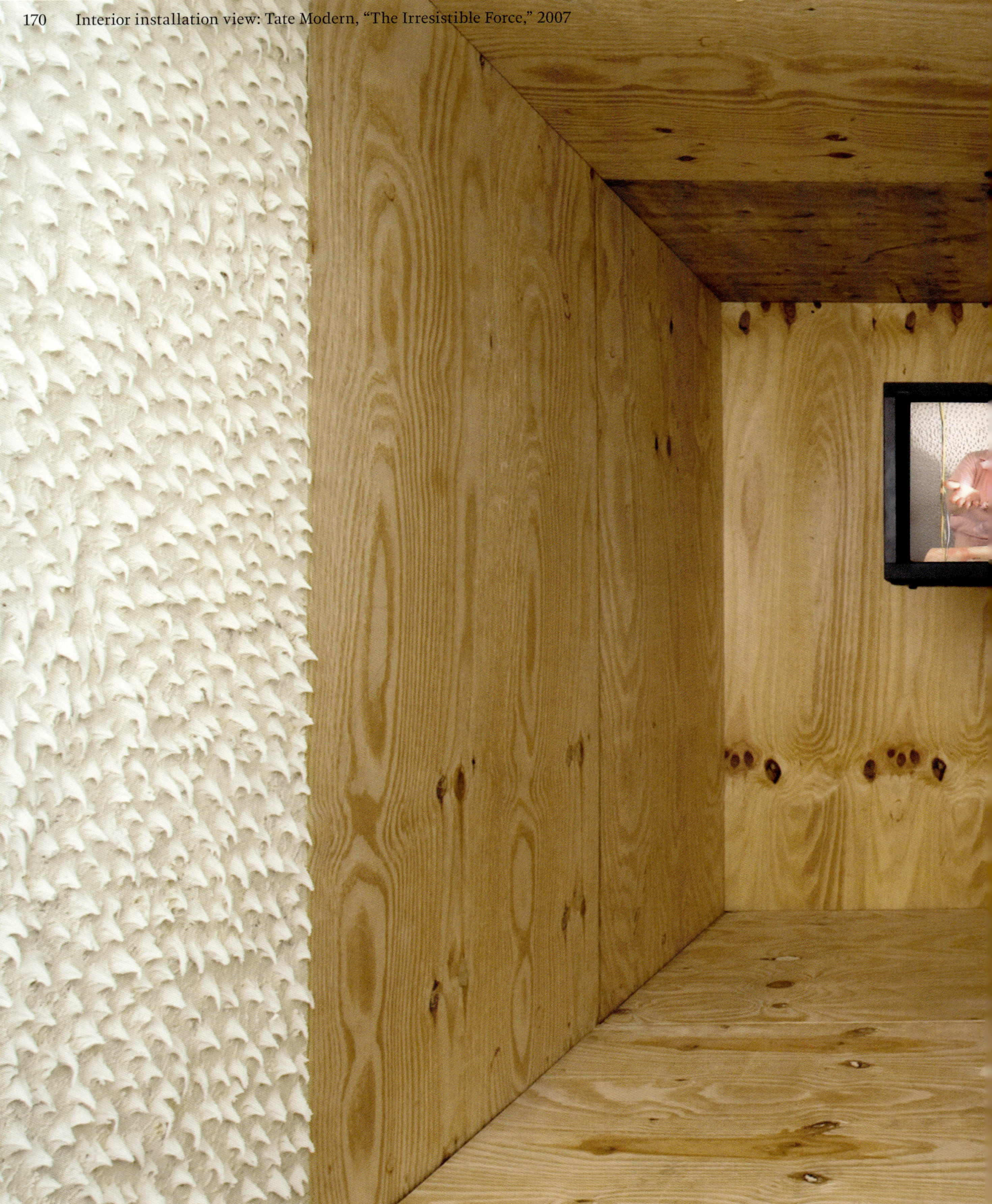

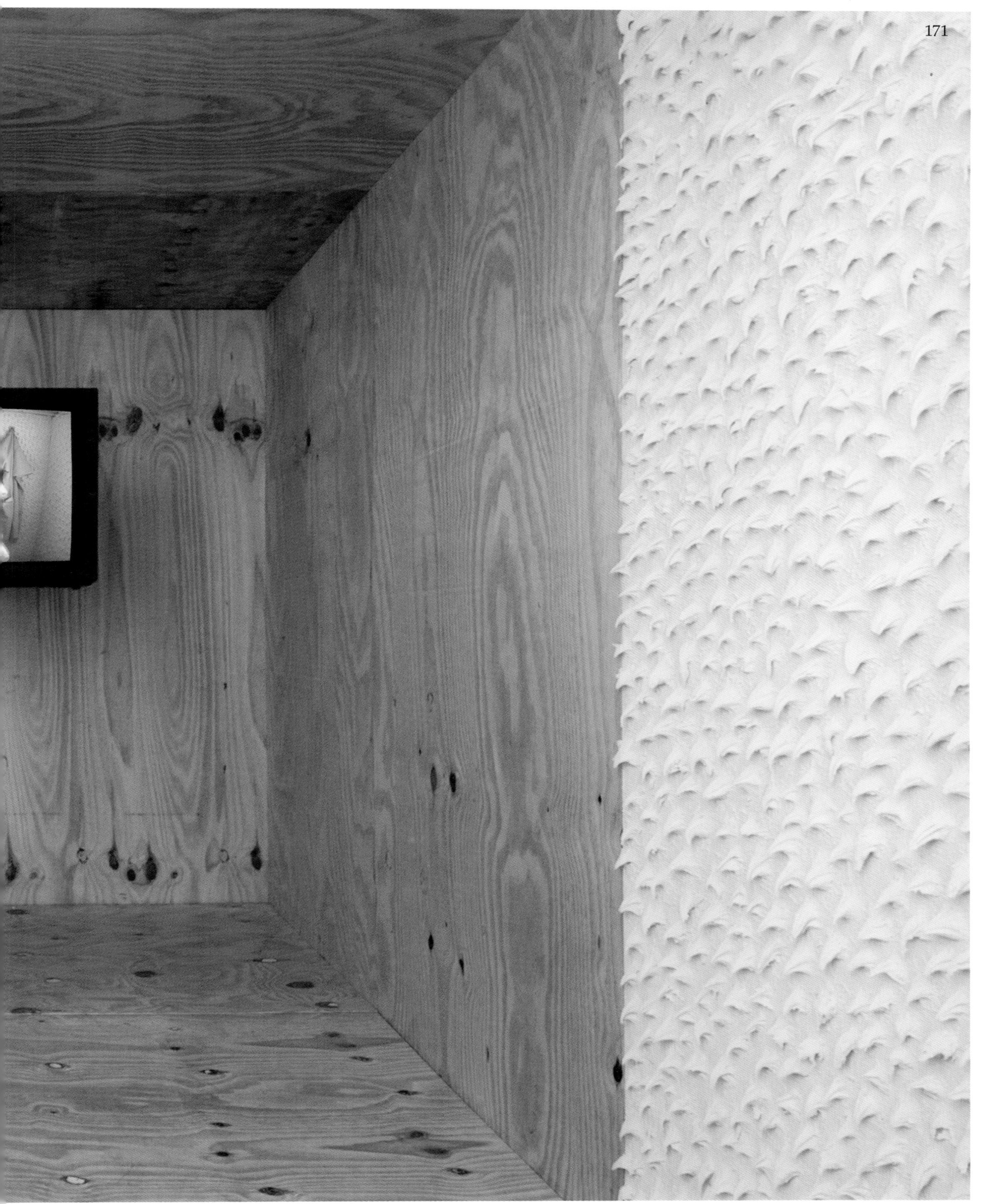

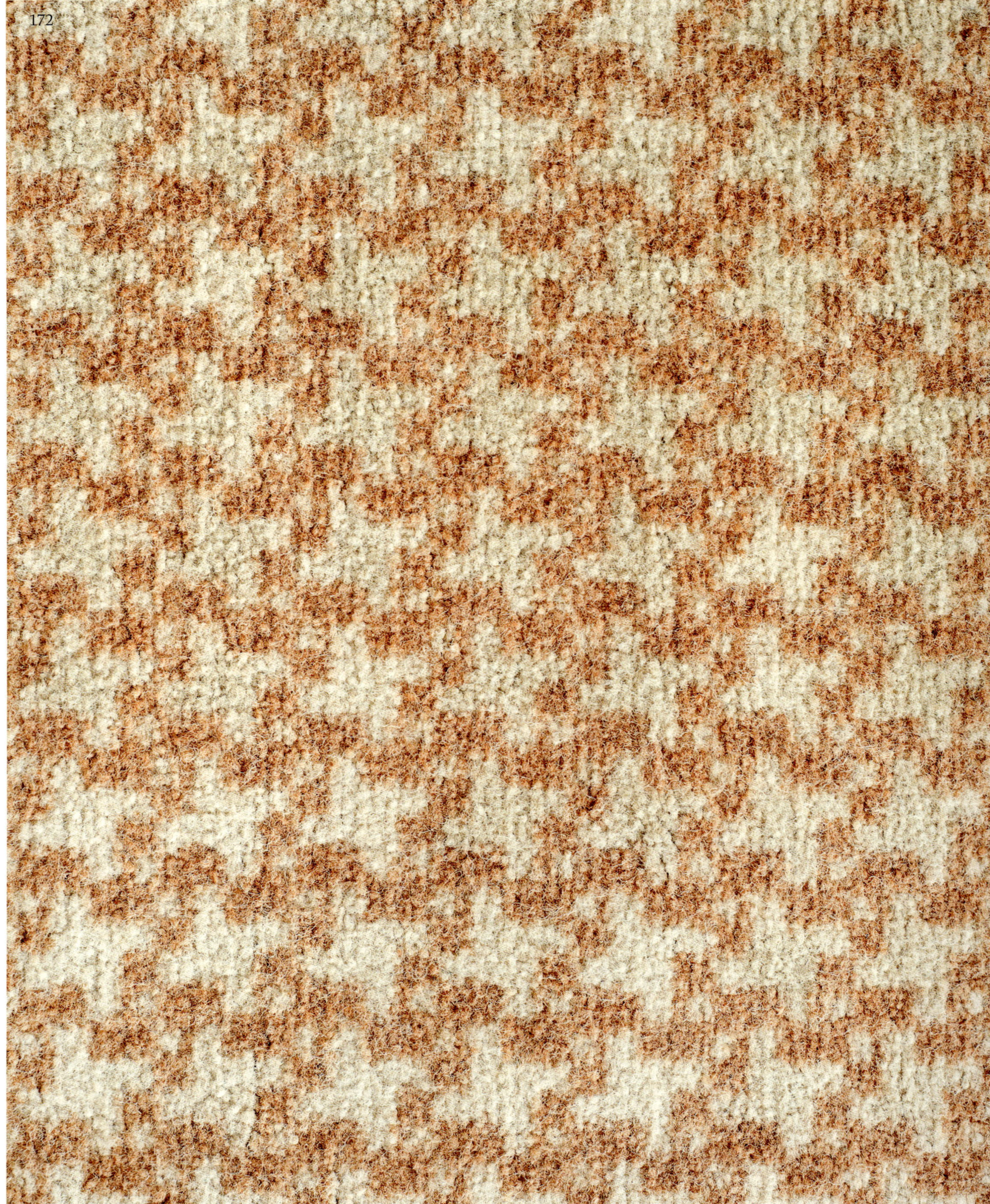

Installation view: Nottingham Contemporary, “Mika Rottenberg,” 2012

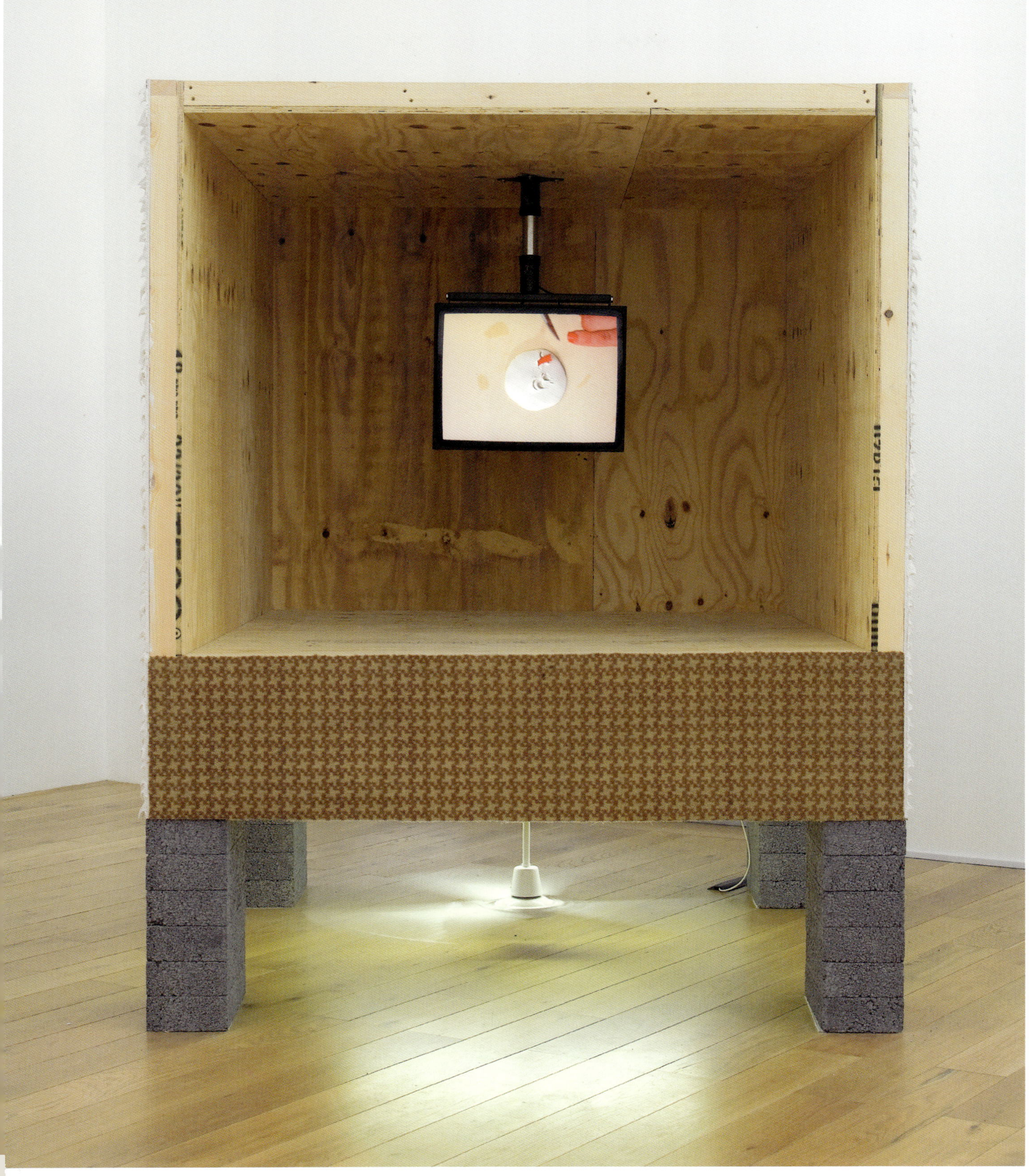

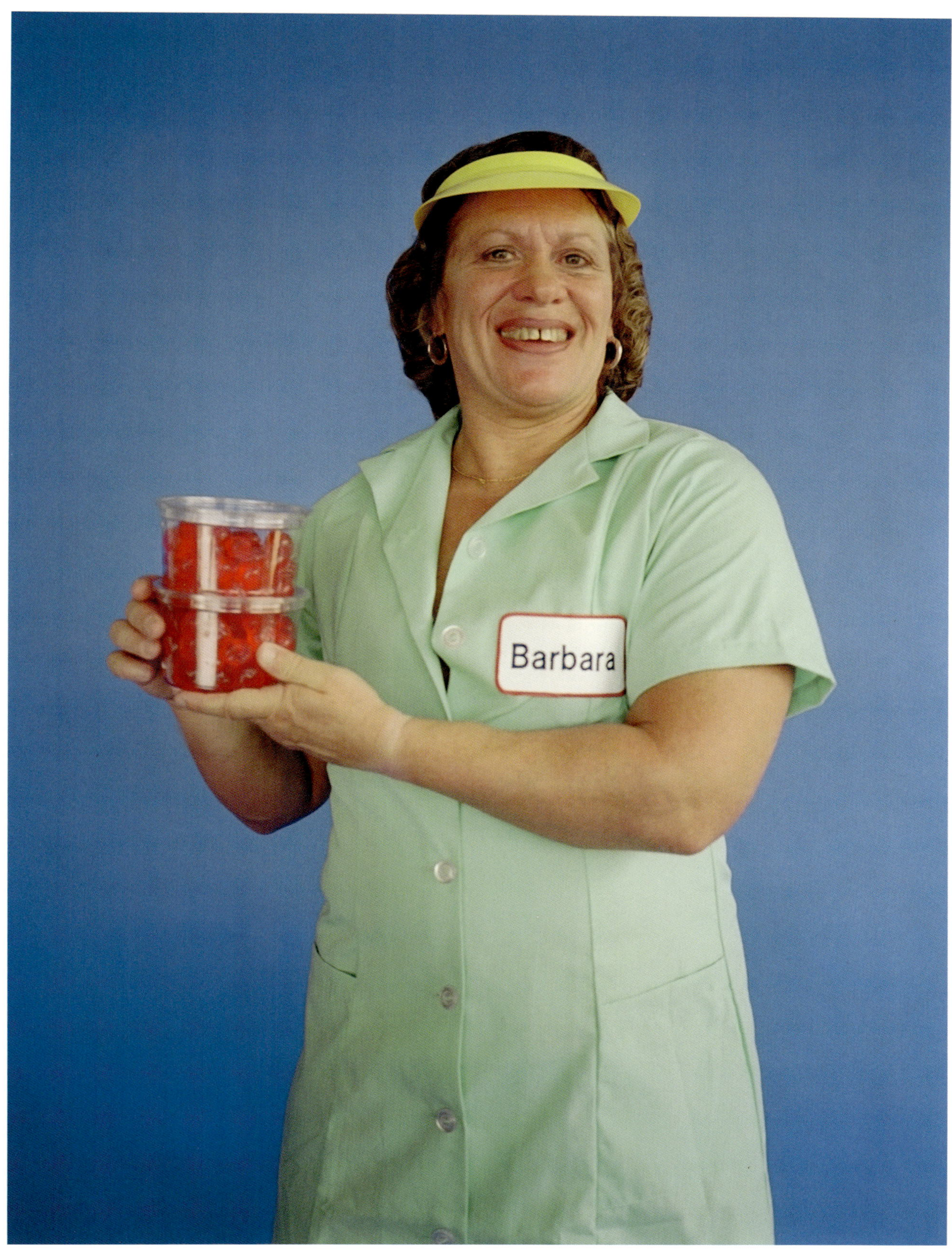
Barbara

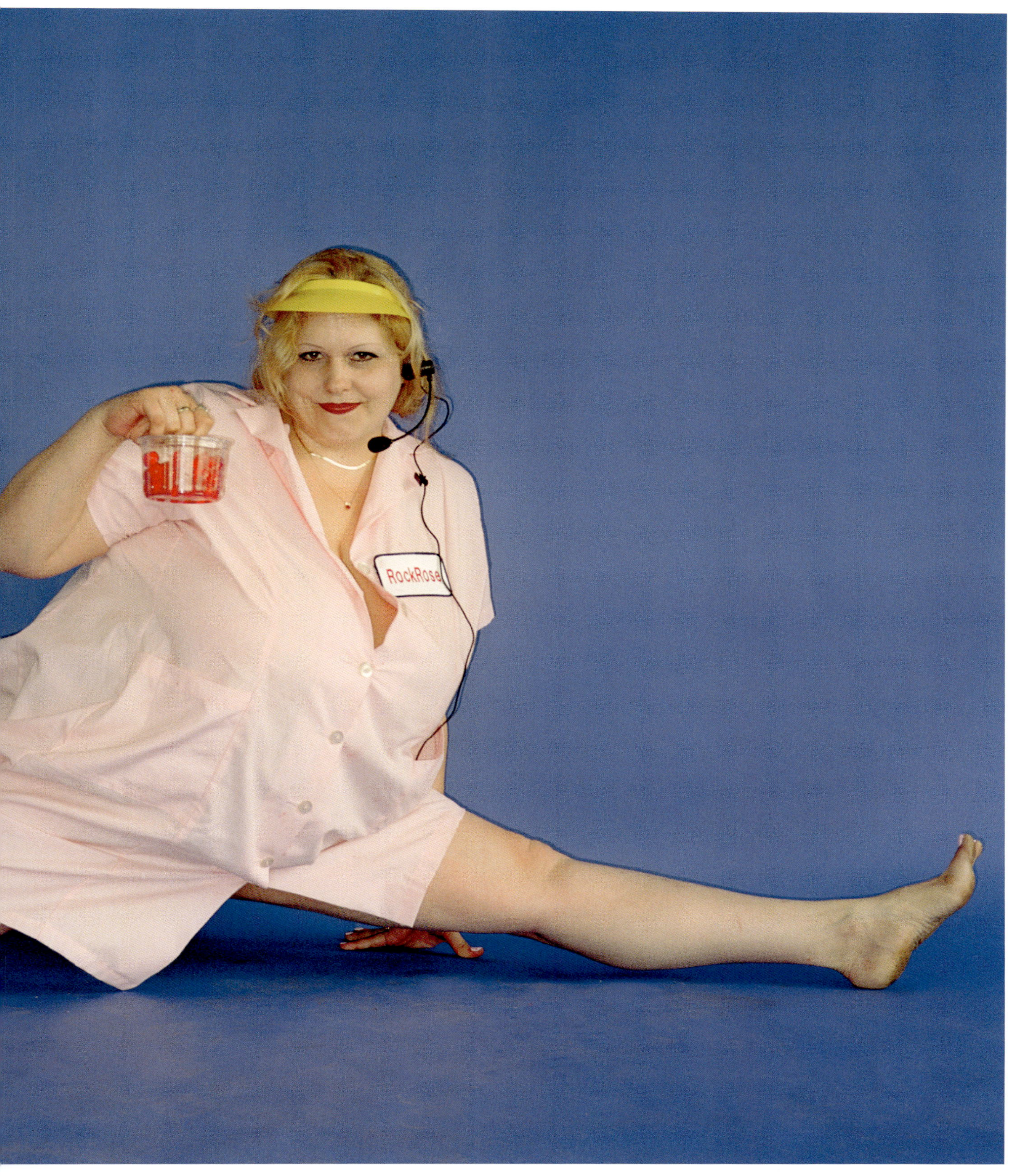
RockRose

 Stills from *Mary's Cherries*, 2004

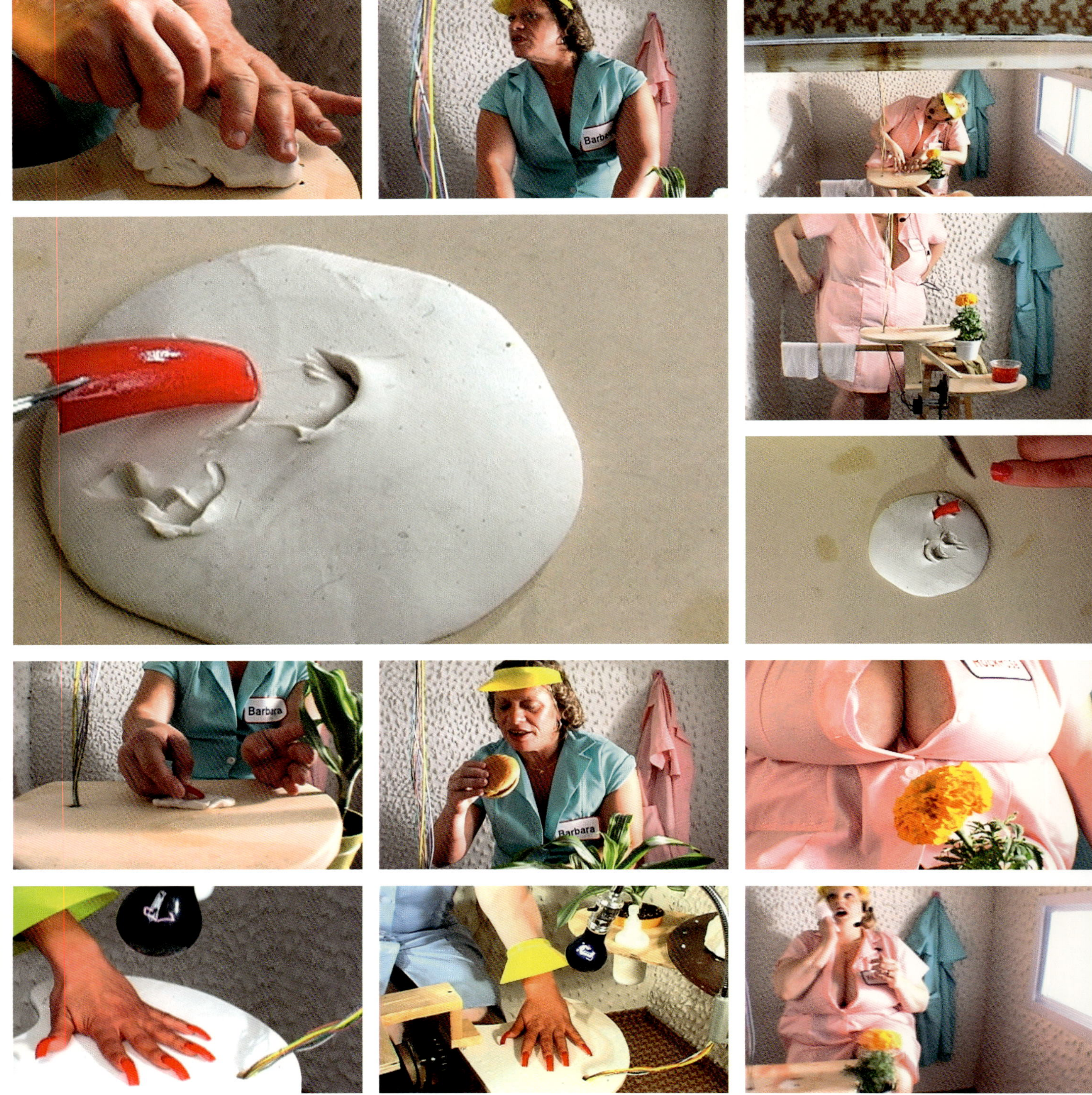

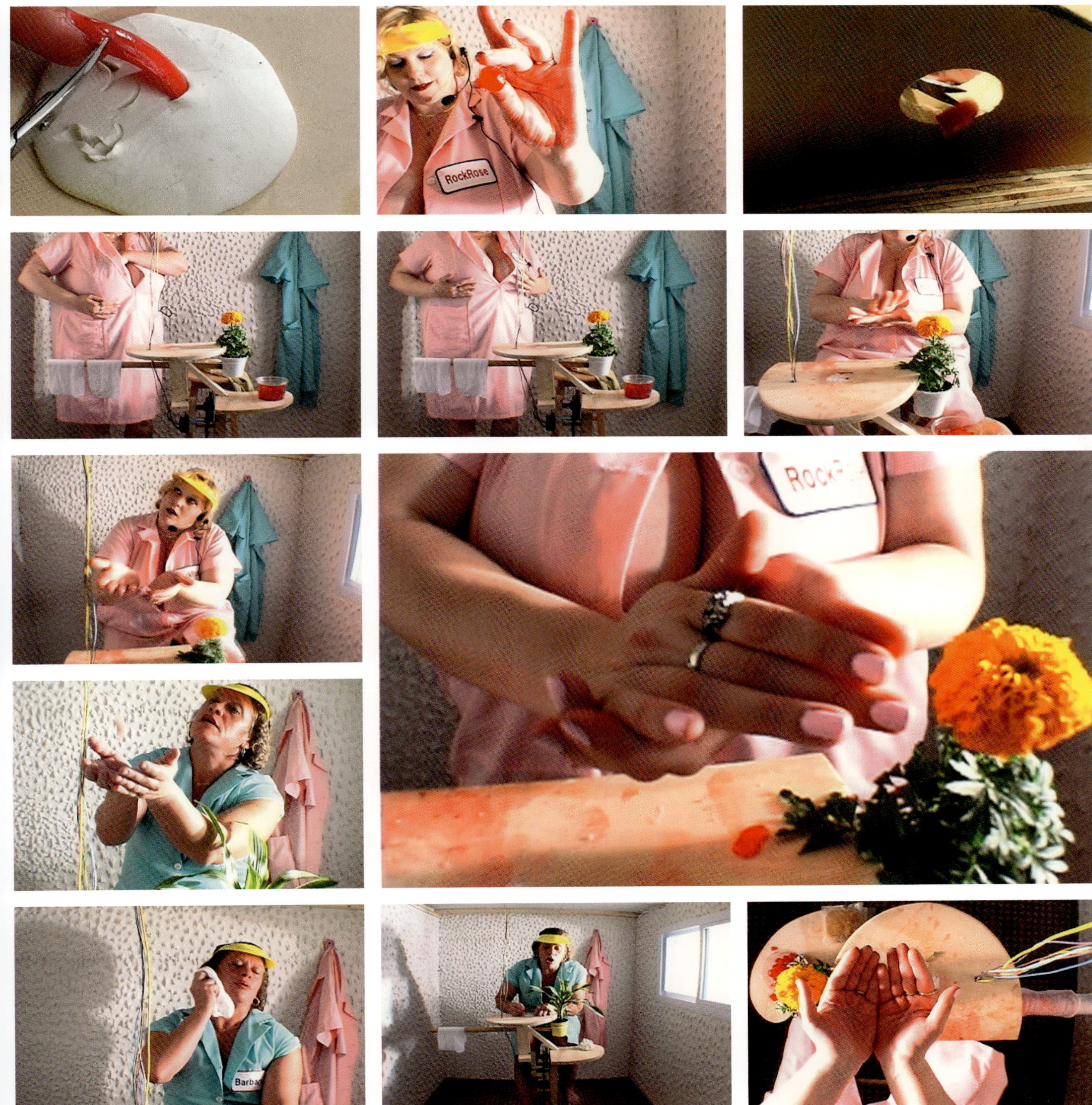
RockRose

 Detail of *Texture 3 & 4*, 2013; polyurethane resin and acrylic paint

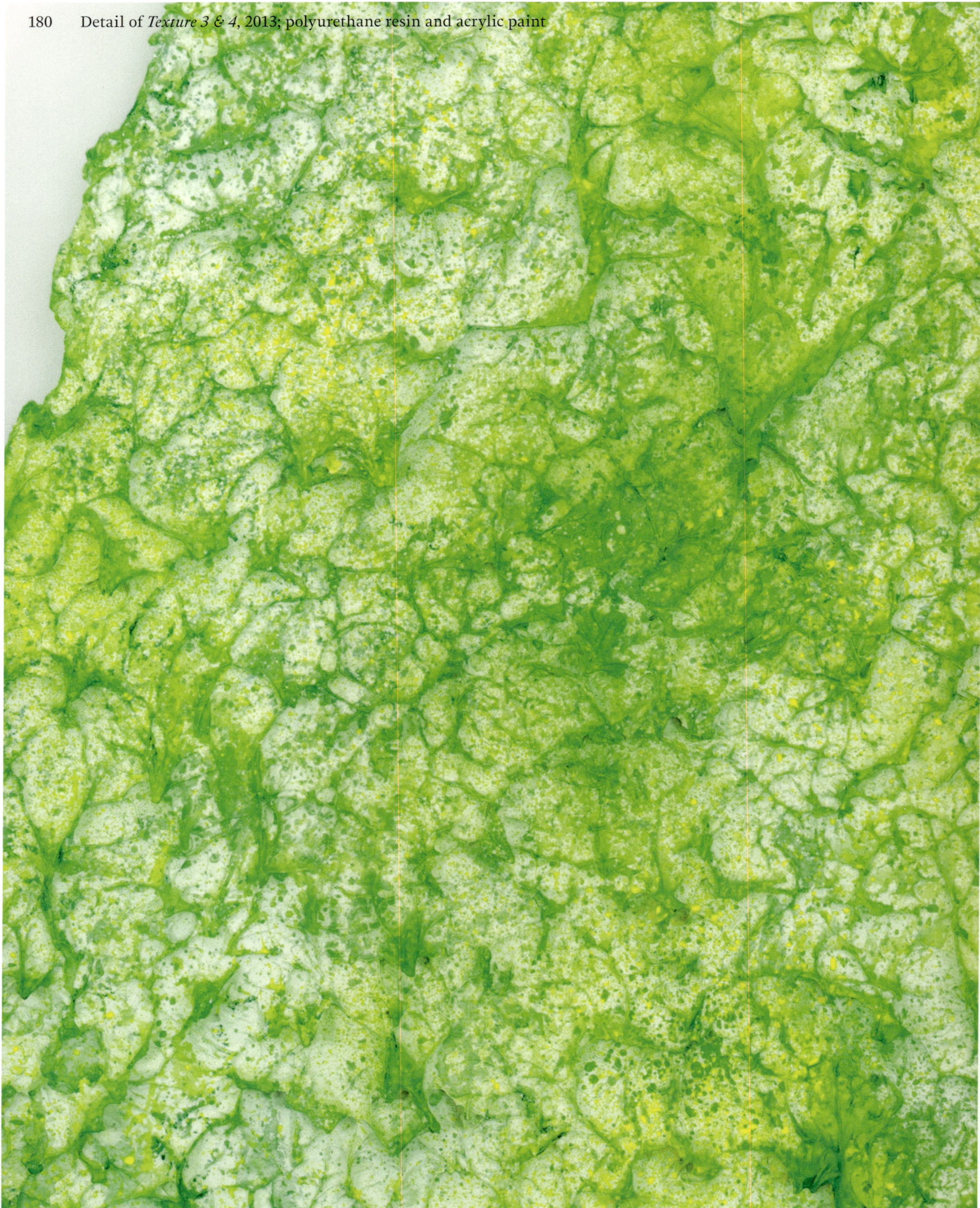

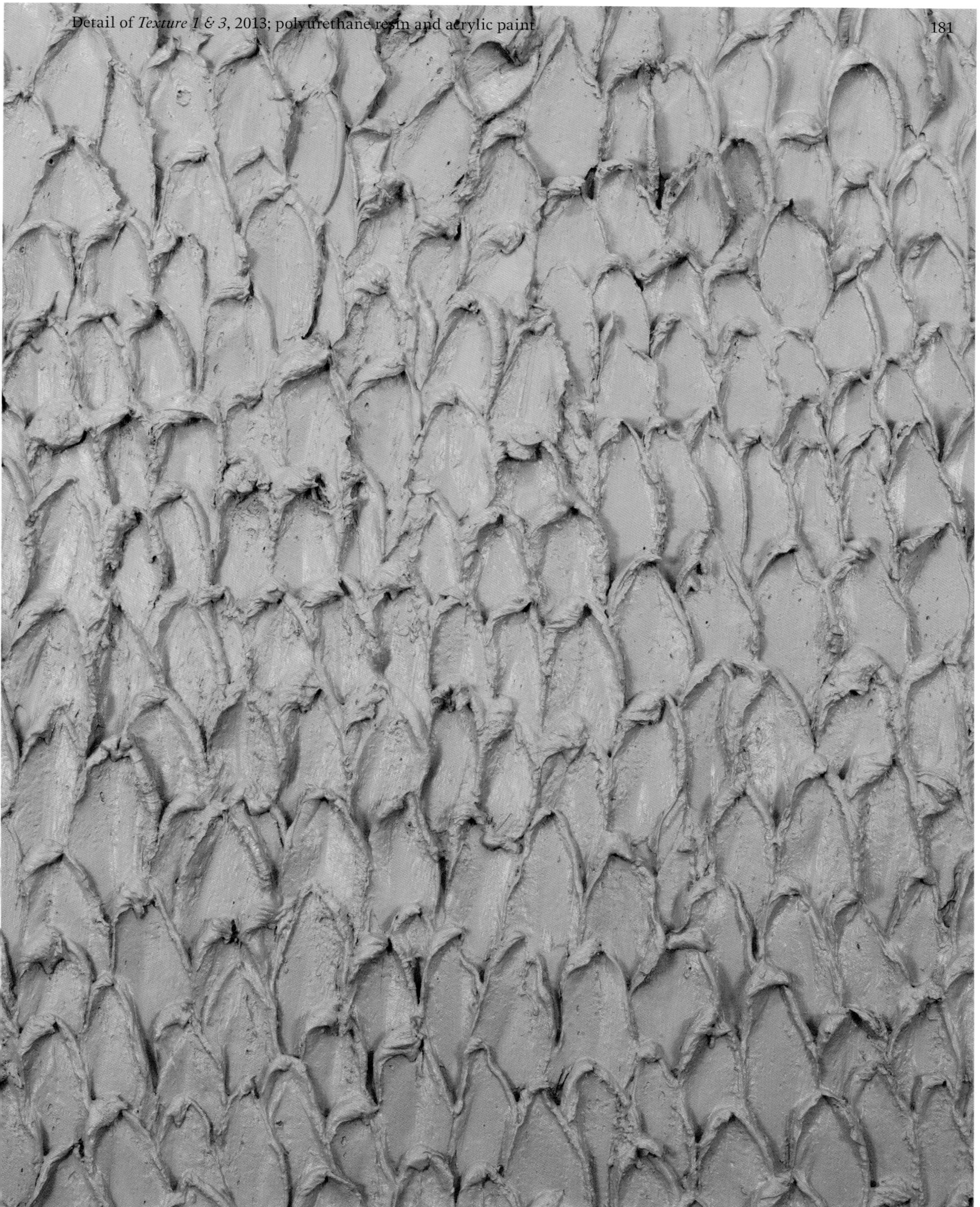

Detail of *Texture 1 & 3*, 2013; polyurethane resin and acrylic paint

 Detail of *Texture 6 & 5*, 2013; polyurethane resin and acrylic paint

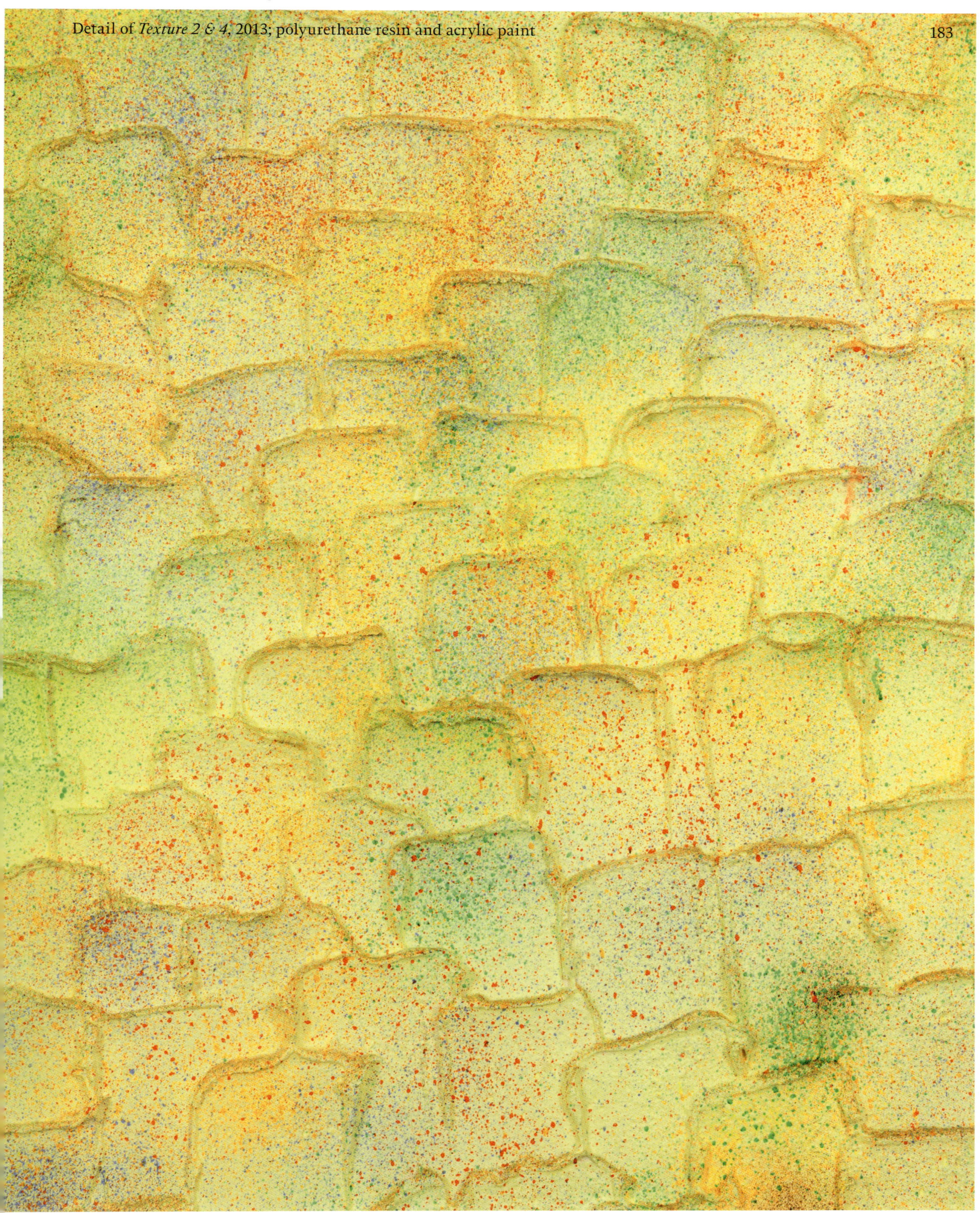
Detail of *Texture 2 & 4*, 2013; polyurethane resin and acrylic paint

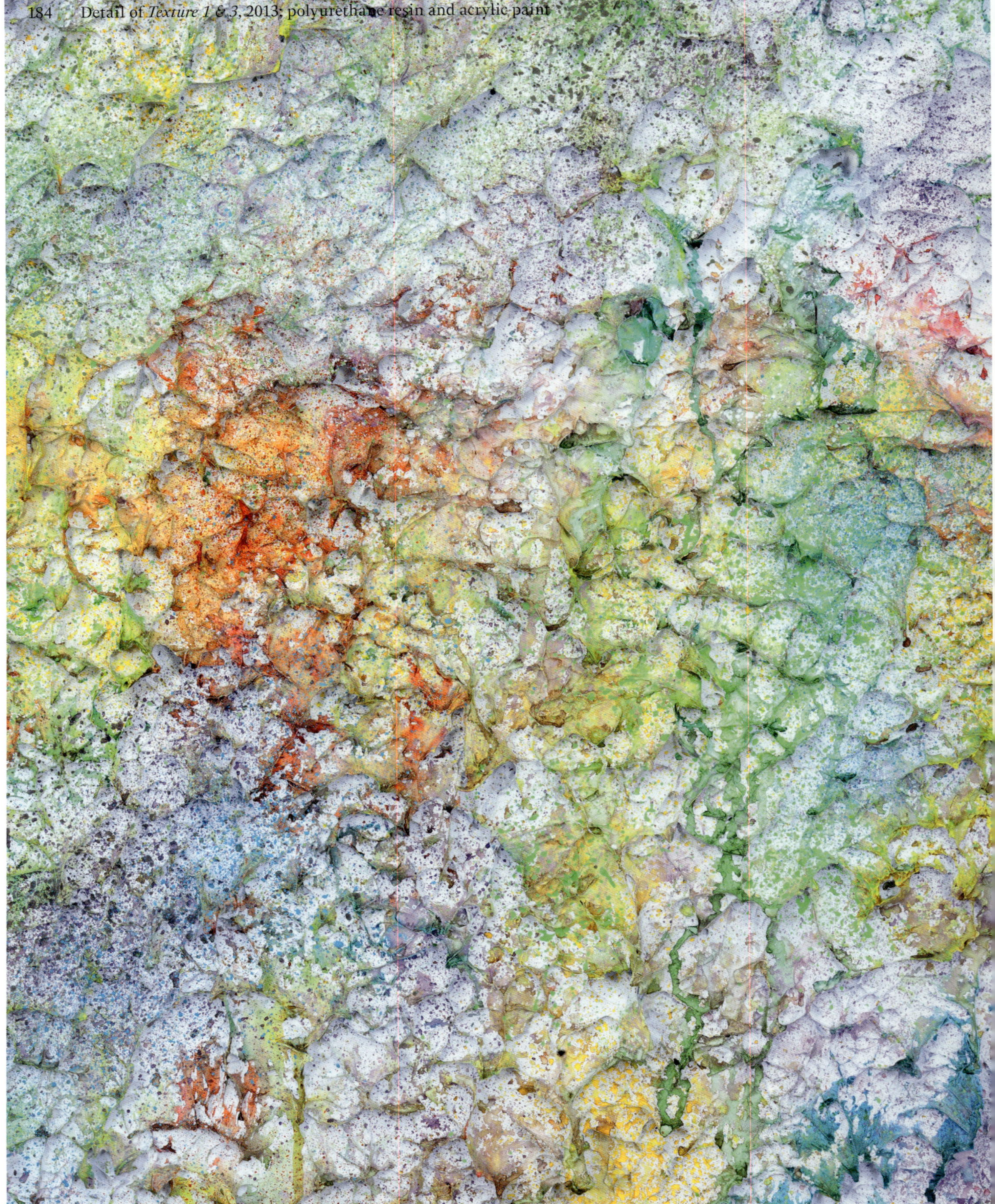

Detail of *Texture 1 & 3*, 2013; polyurethane resin and acrylic paint

Detail of *Texture 6 & 5*, 2013; polyurethane resin and acrylic paint

 Still from *Sneeze*, 2012

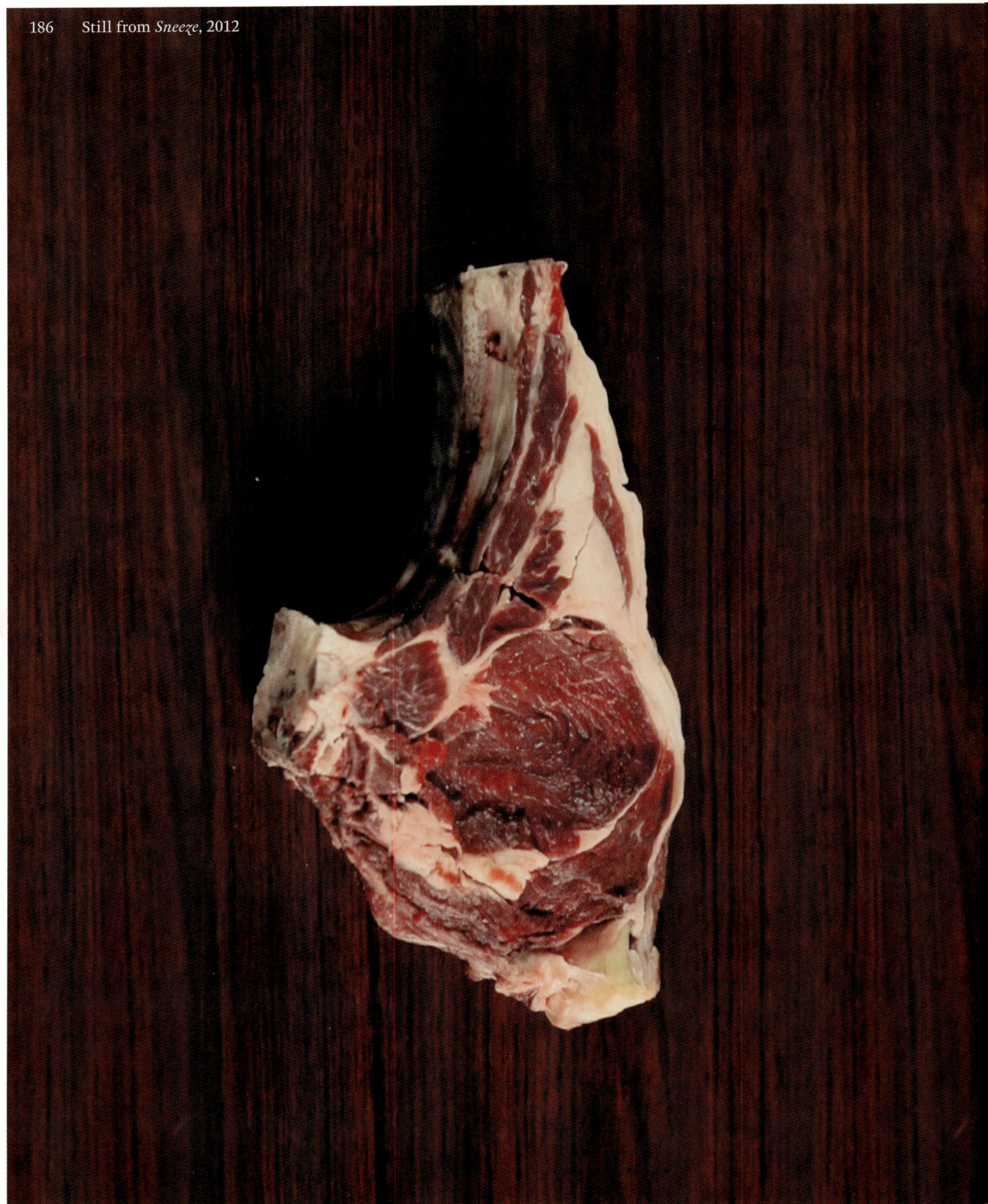

sneeze

CB: Objectifying bodily functions and using them as the starting point for complex narrative ideas are an ongoing emphasis in your work. Can you explain why?

MR: I like to think about a body as a tool, a thing that is there to serve you and which sometimes misbehaves. Video has a great power in that it can make visible otherwise abstract internal processes. Someone sneezing a light bulb is like someone who has the idea to create a light bulb and then goes through the process of actually making it. This process refers to the idea that every object you see is an extension of a person or a group of people. It's interesting to think about objects as extensions of mind rather than as autonomous things. *Sneeze* was inspired by the money shot in hardcore pornographic cinema and how it tries to represent pleasure. Pleasure is abstract, it does not have a shape; but the money shot gives it form. An internal process becomes an object.

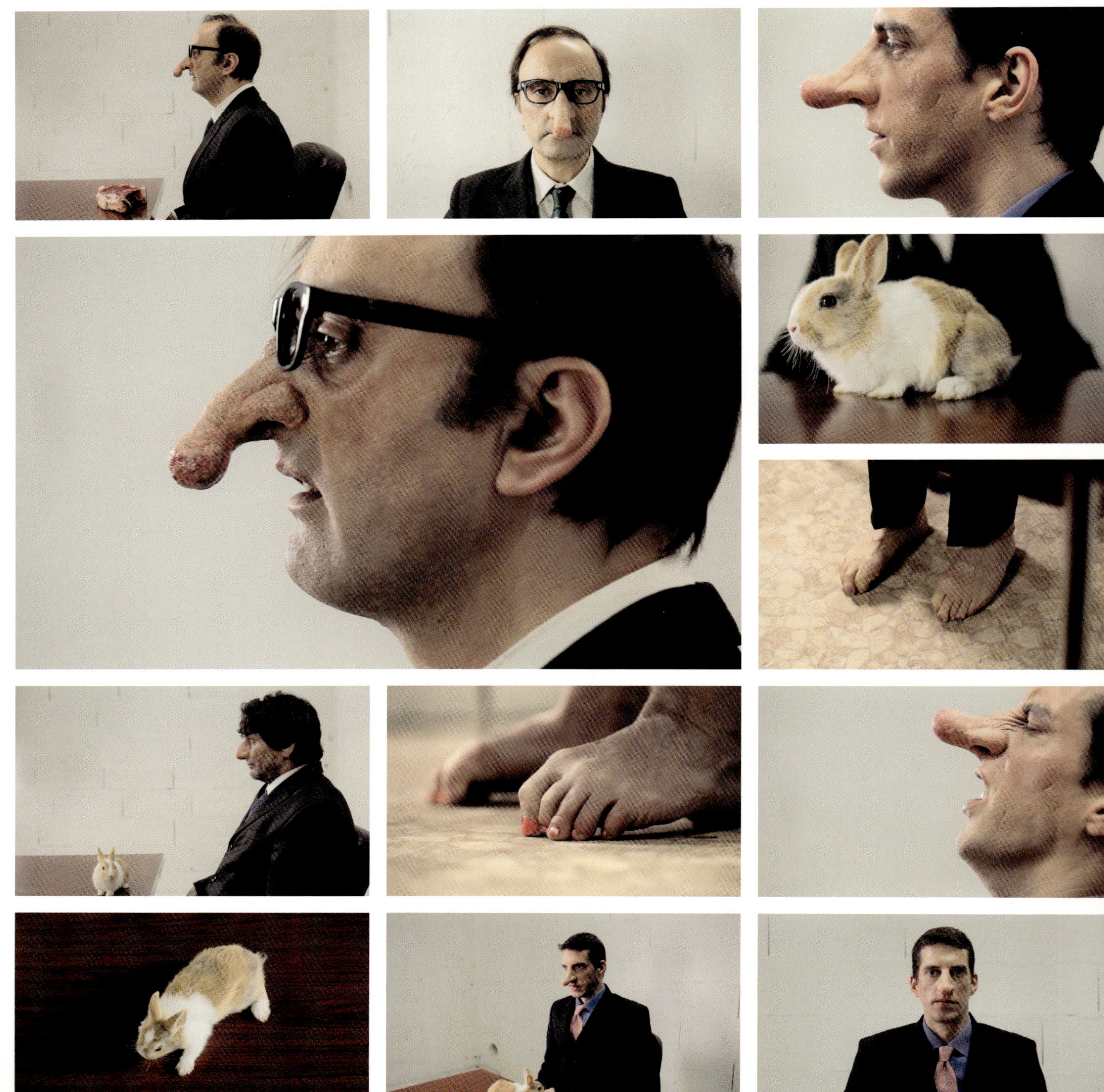

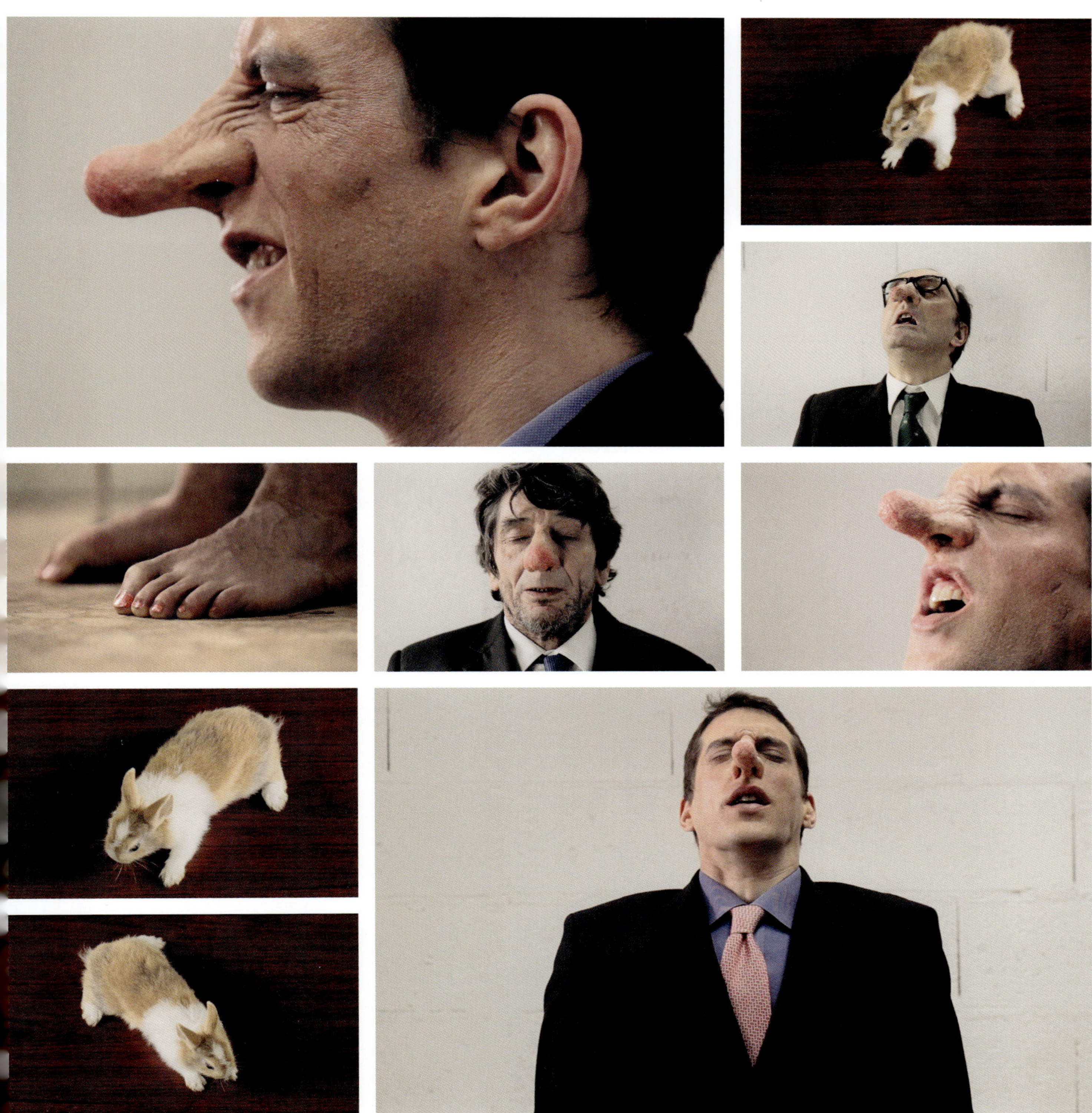

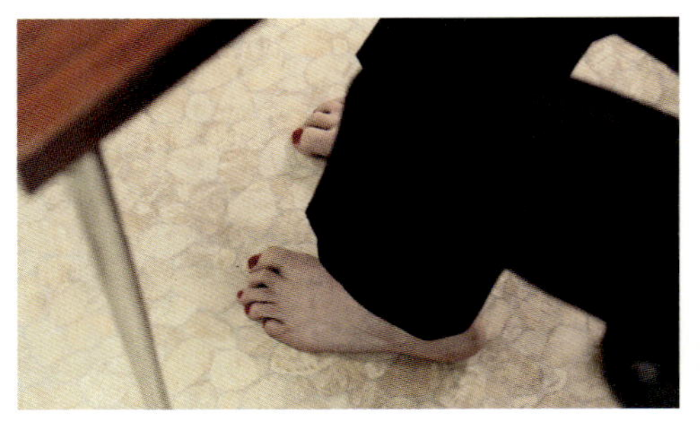
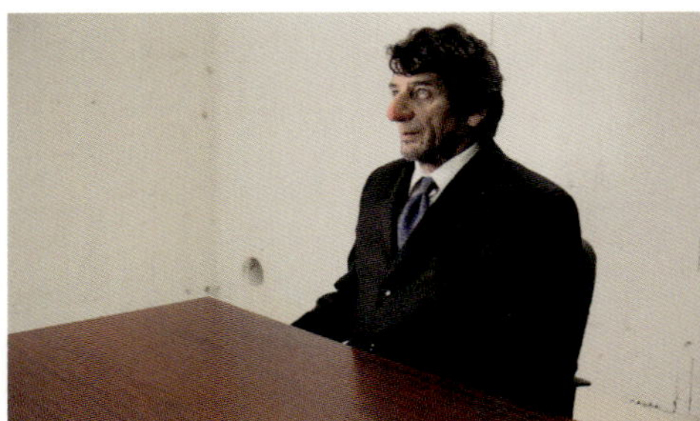
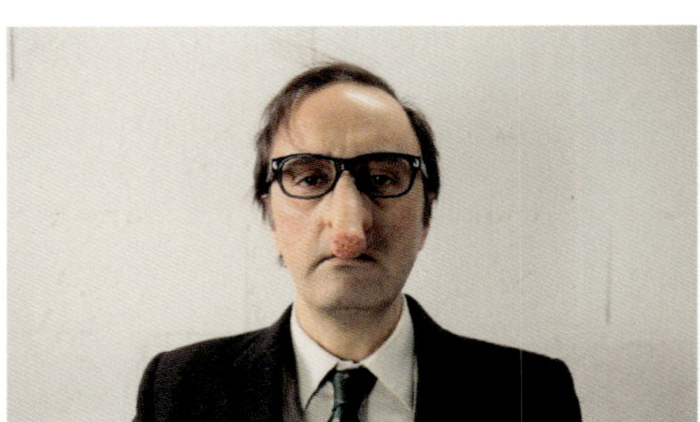
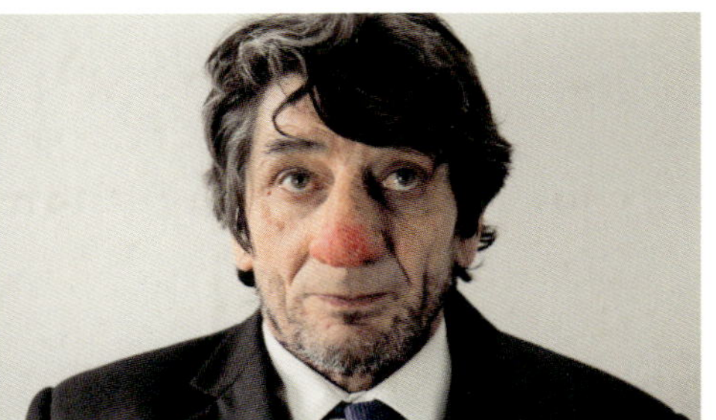
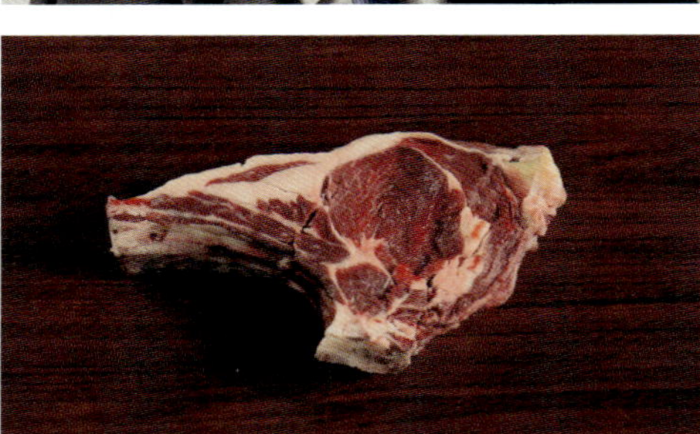
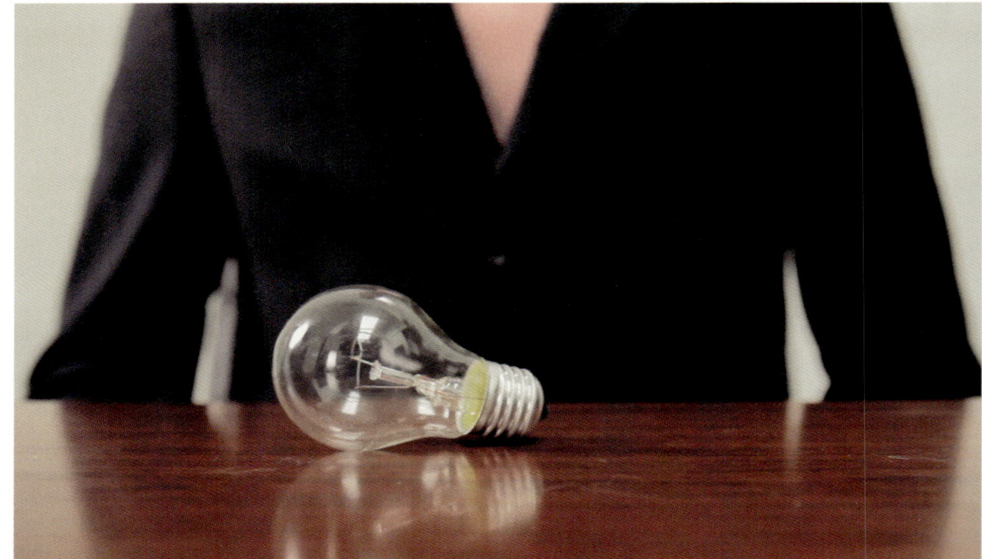
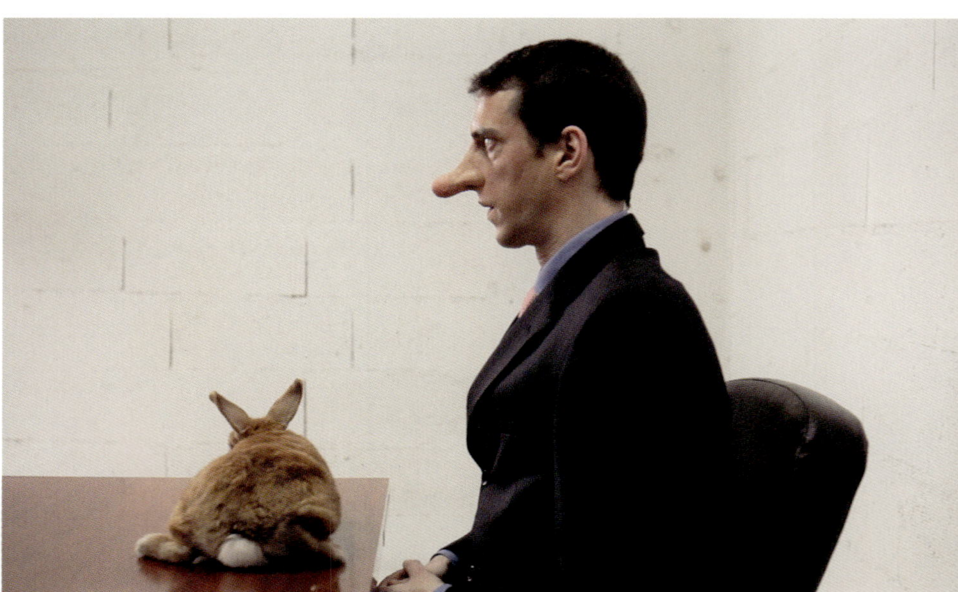
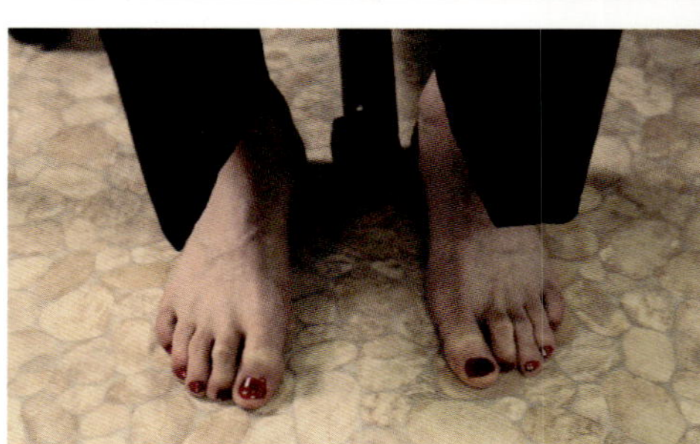
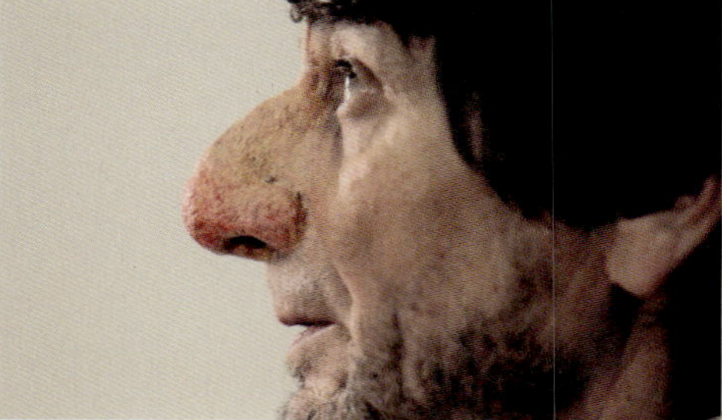

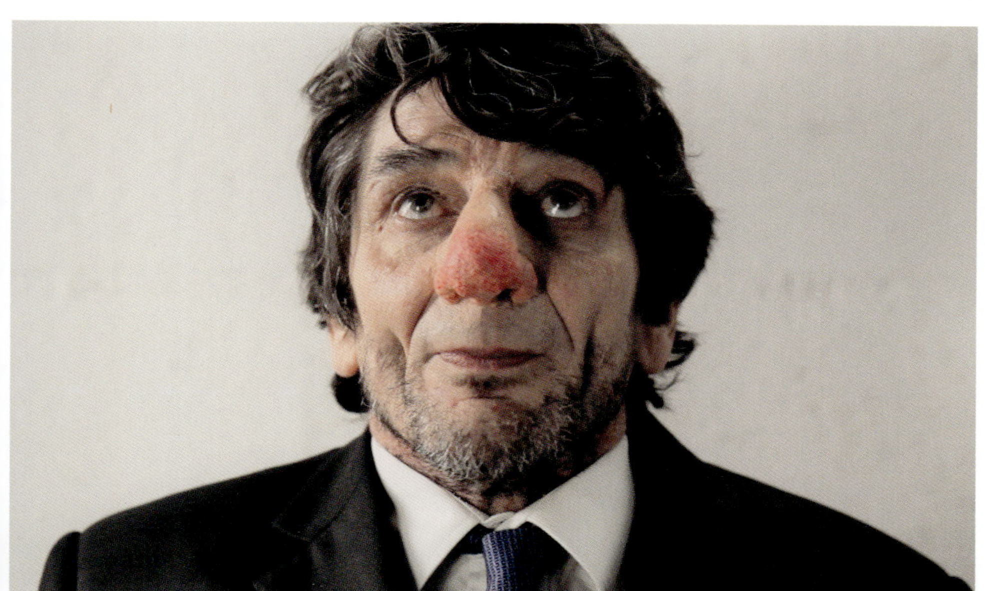
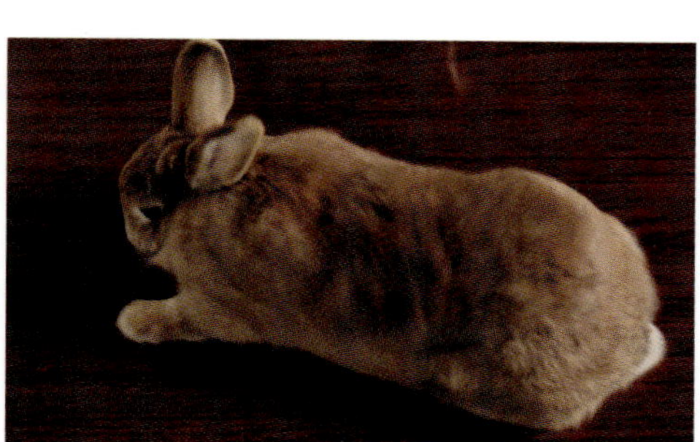
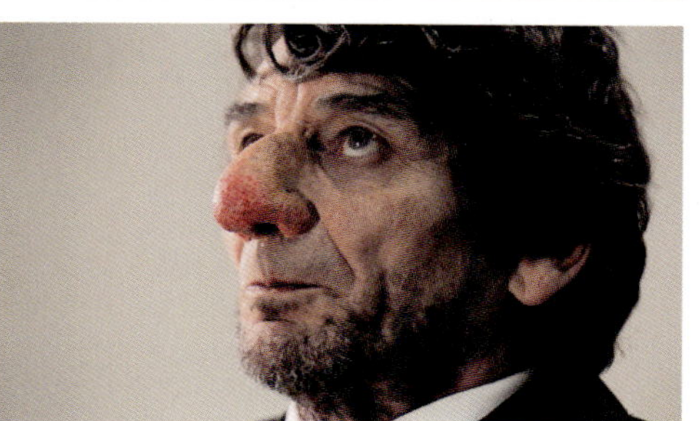
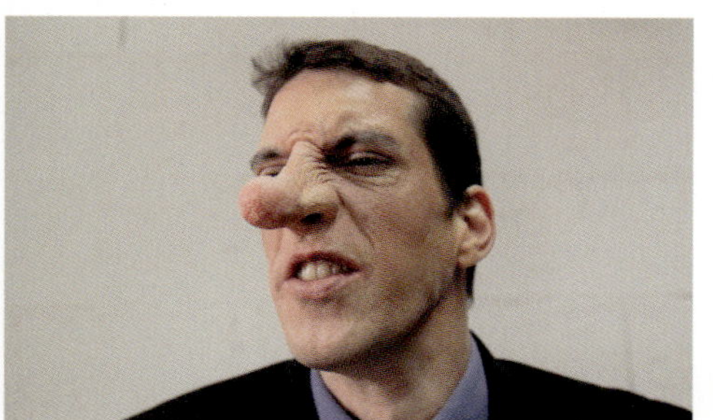
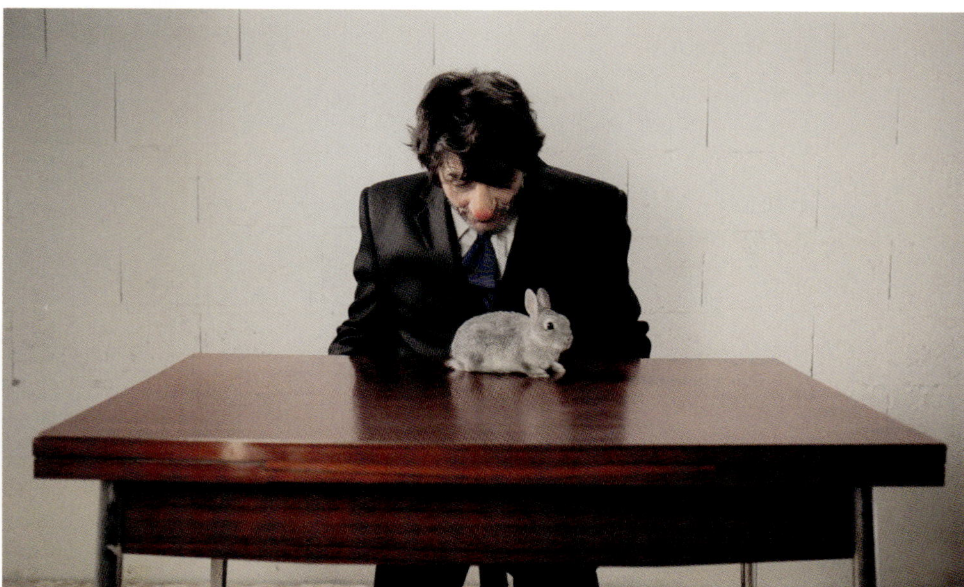
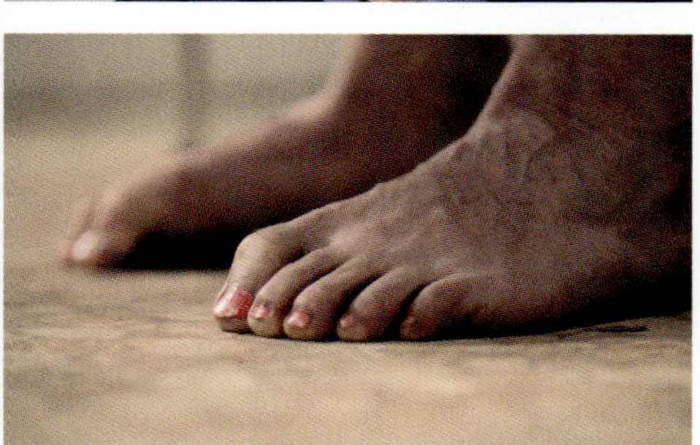
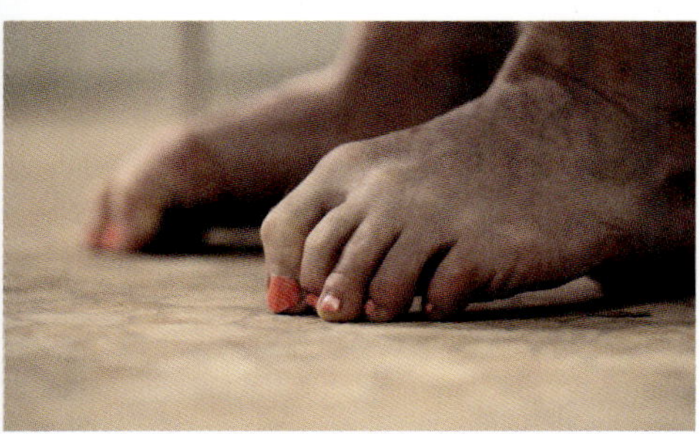
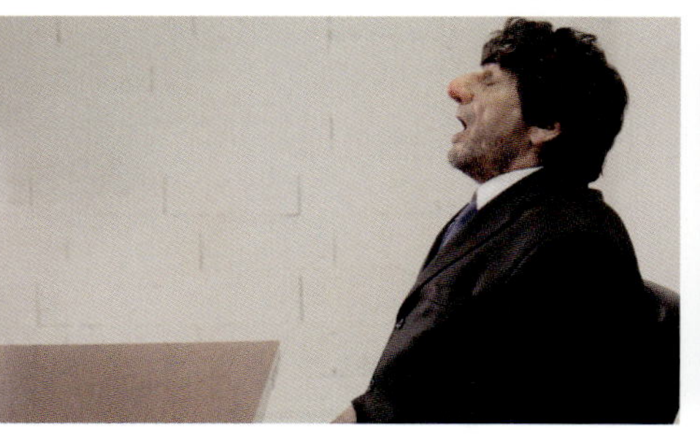
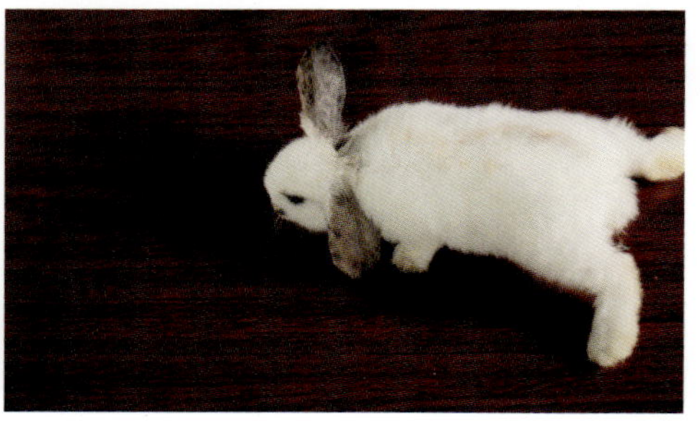

Installation view: de Appel arts centre, "Mika Rottenberg: Dough Cheese Squeeze and Tropical Breeze: Video Works 2003–2010," 2011

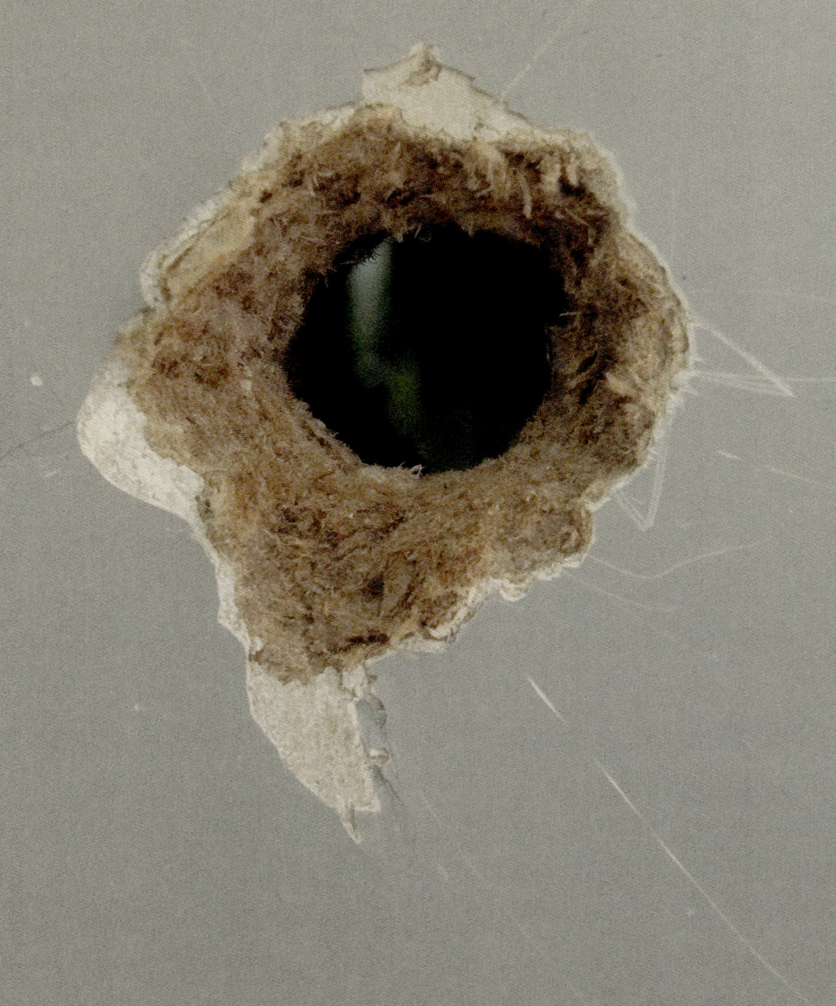

fried sweat

CB: The circumstances under which your videos are experienced by the viewer are rarely if ever neutral. In the case of *Fried Sweat*, we are asked to look through a crack in the wall. What is the intended effect?

MR: Voyeurism. Being aware of yourself watching. Being slightly uncomfortable like the people on the screen. Being aware of how architecture manipulates your behavior.

 Installation view: Nottingham Contemporary, “Mika Rottenberg,” 2012

 Installation view: Santa Barbara Museum of Art, "Labour and Wait," 2013

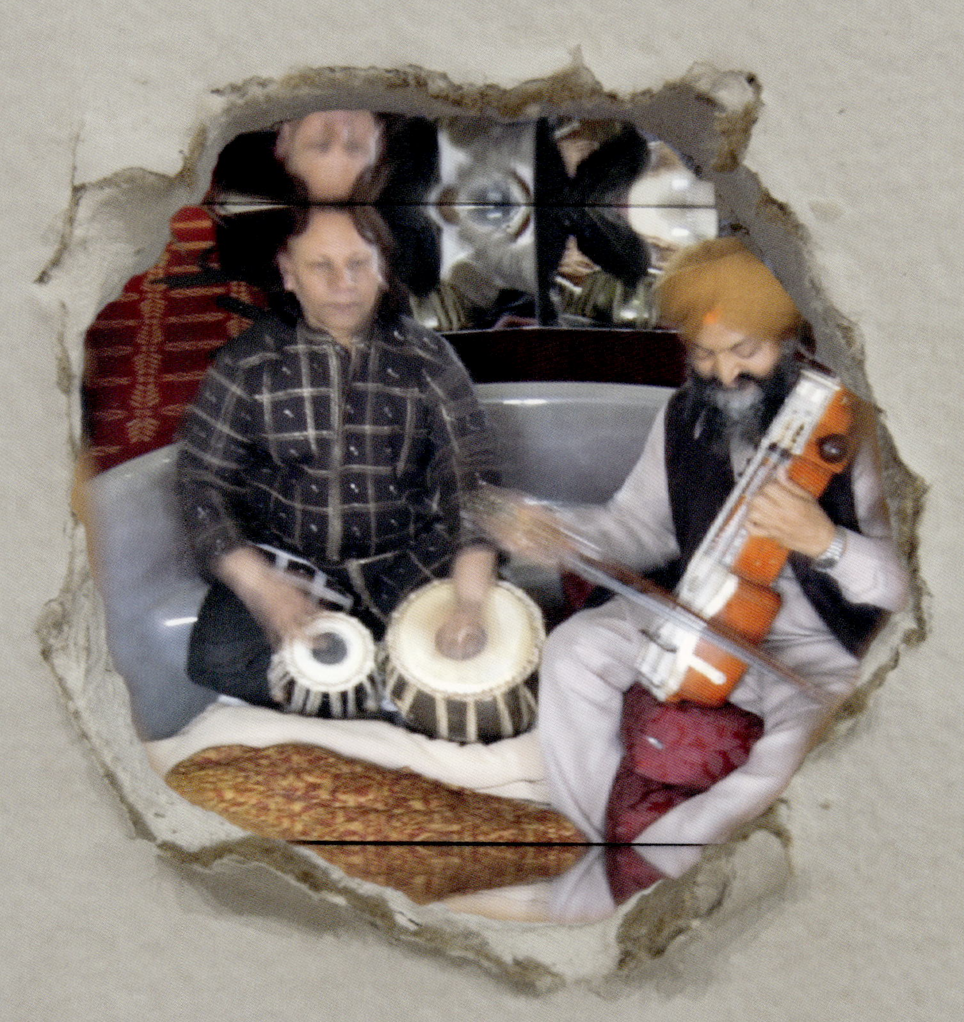

 Installation view: de Appel arts centre, “Mika Rottenberg: Dough Cheese Squeeze and Tropical Breeze: Video Works 2003–2010,” 2011

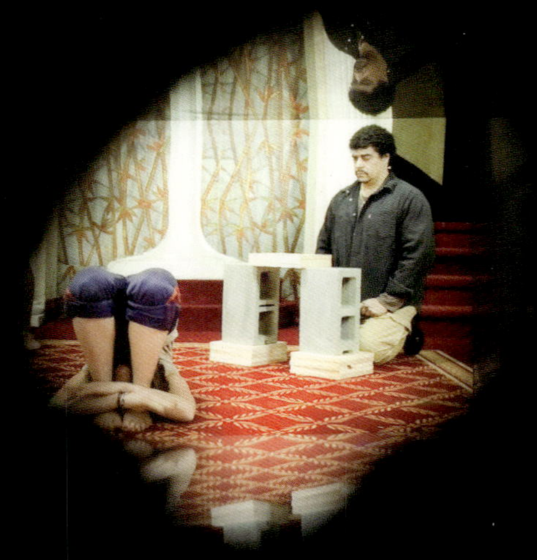

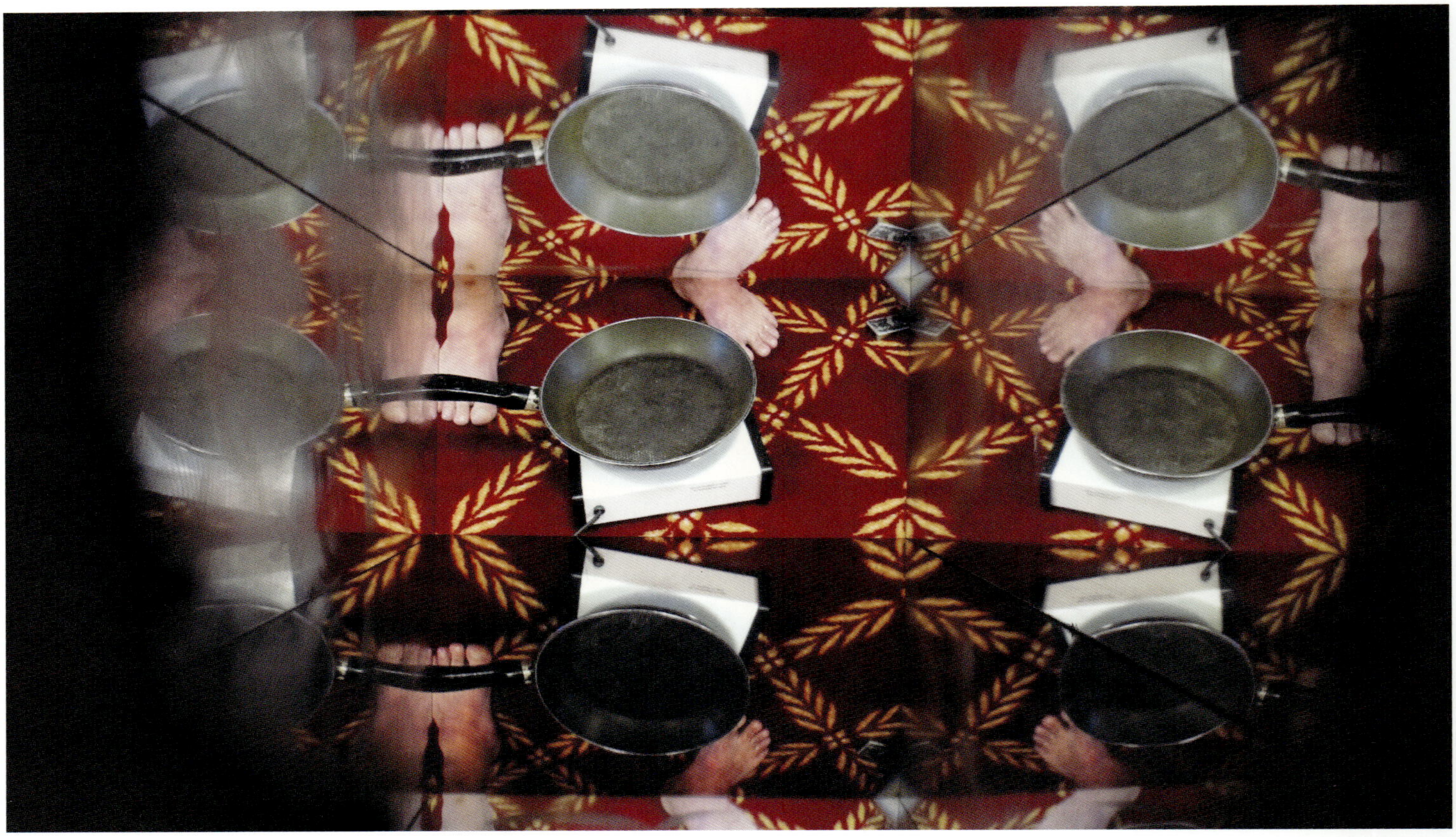

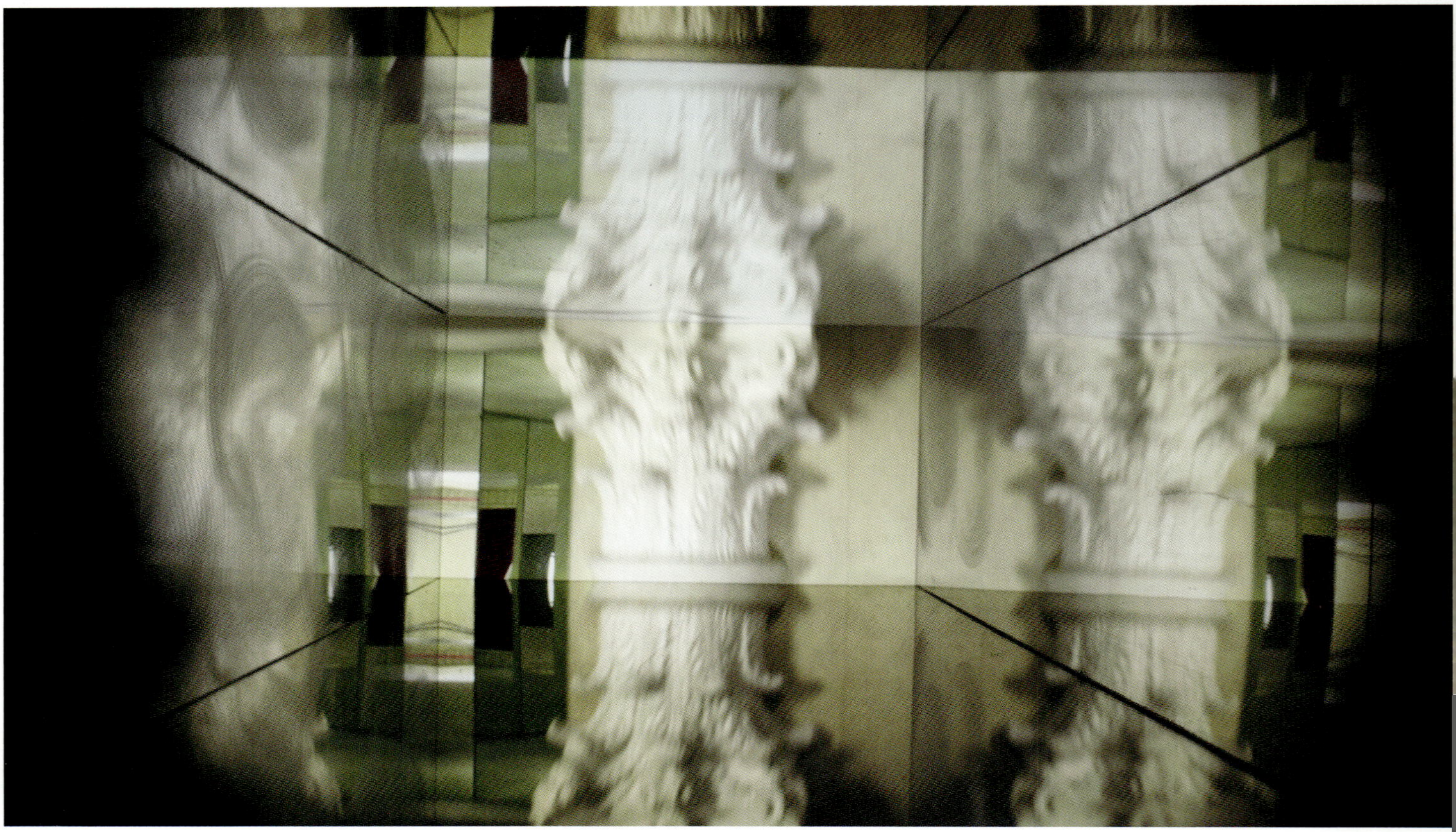

Installation views: de Appel arts centre, "Mika Rottenberg: Dough Cheese Squeeze and Tropical Breeze: Video Works 2003–2010," 2011; Magasin 3 Stockholm Konsthall, "Mika Rottenberg: Sneeze to Squeeze," 2013

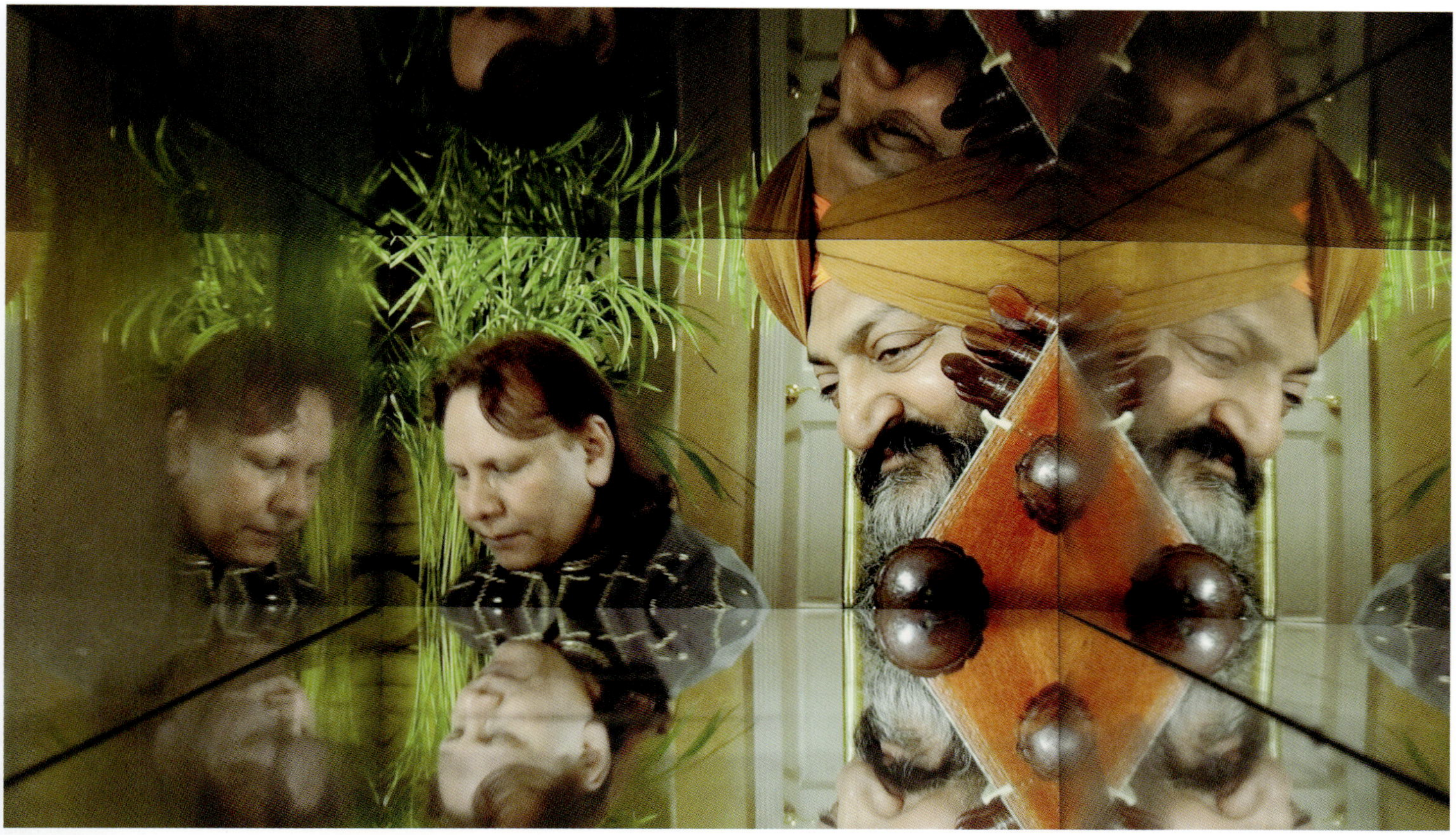

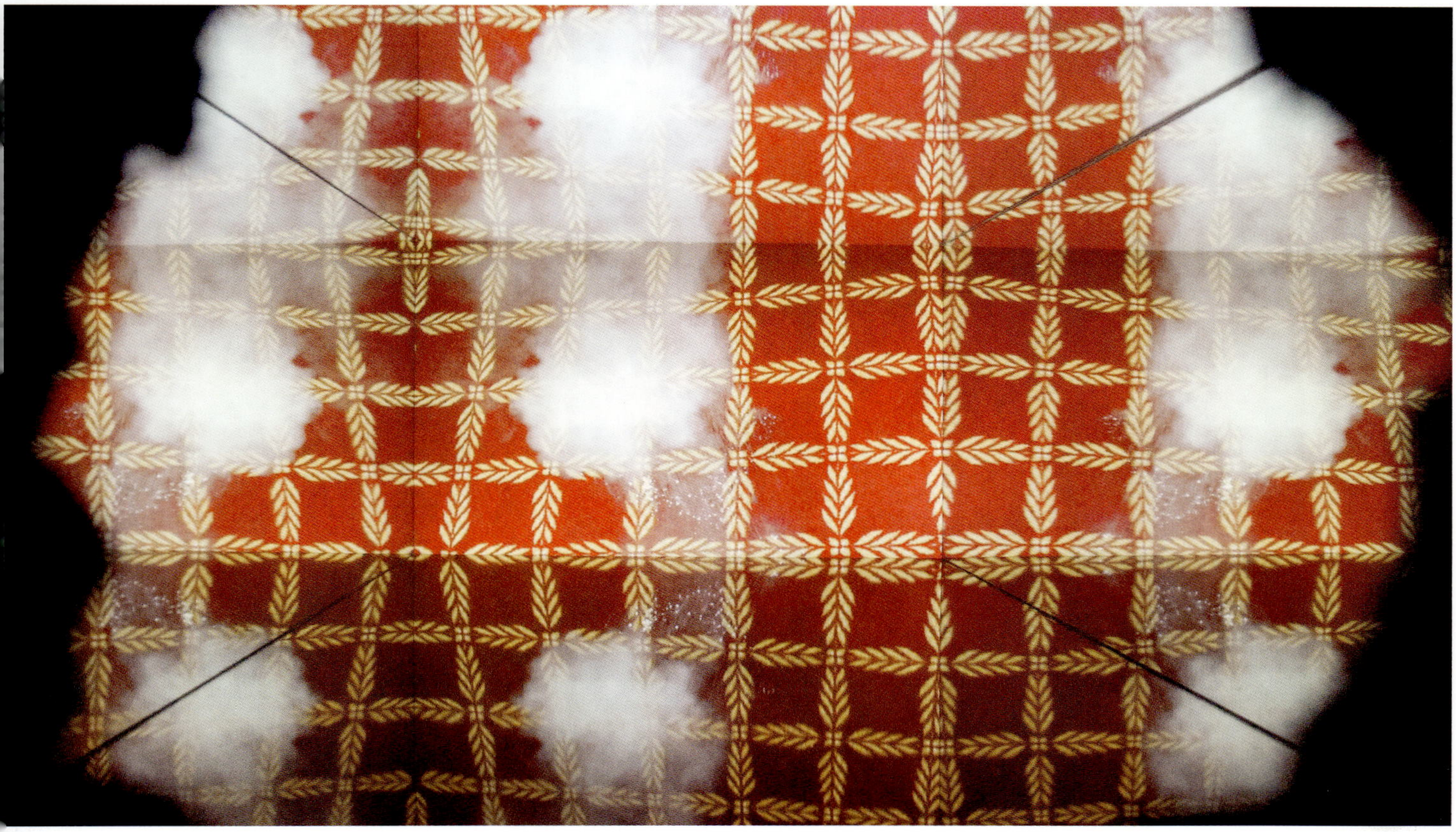

 Stills from *Fried Sweat*, 2008

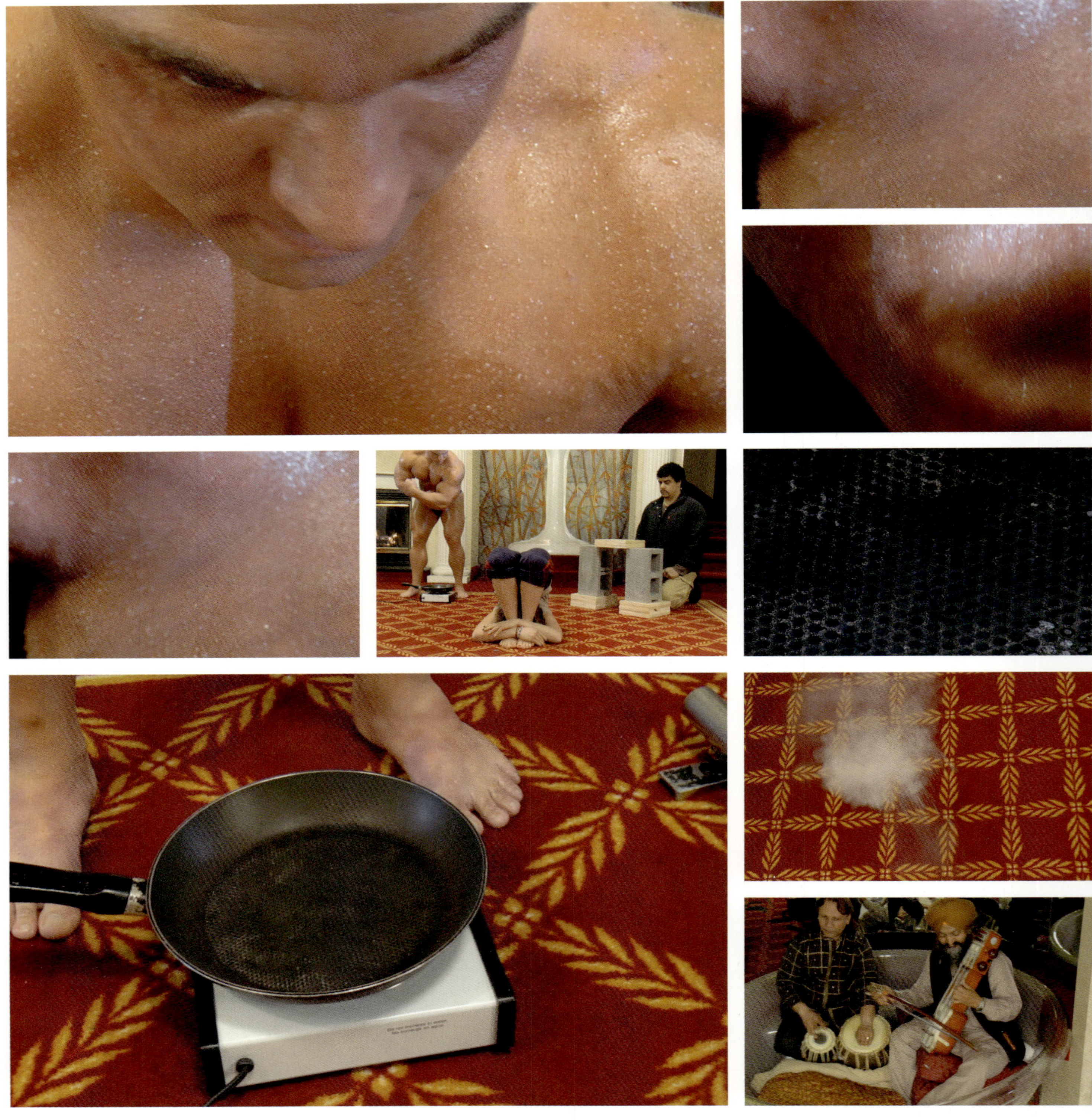

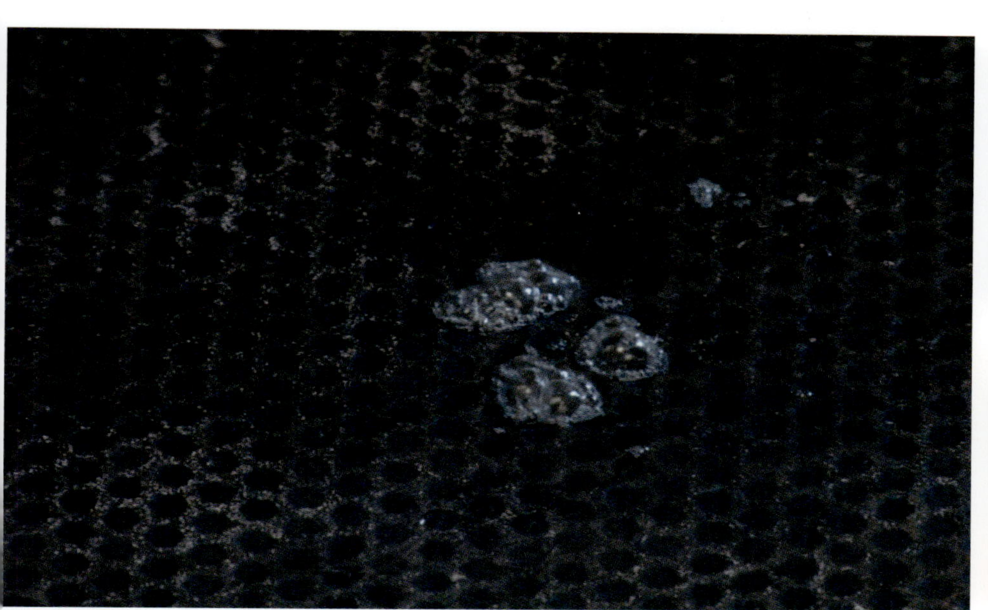

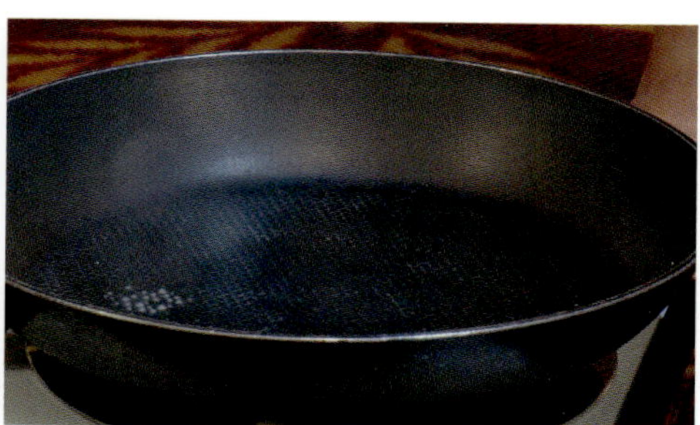

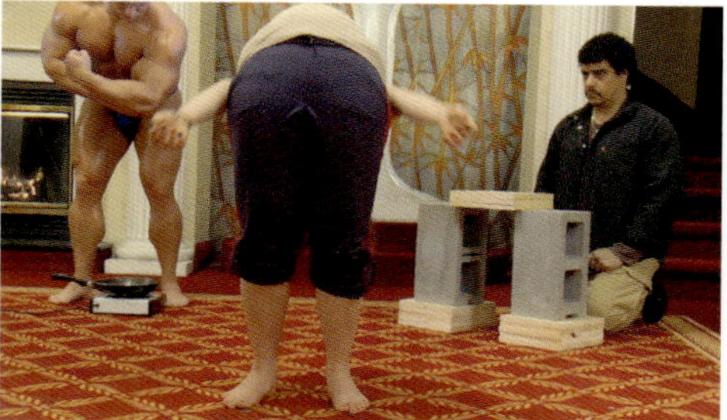

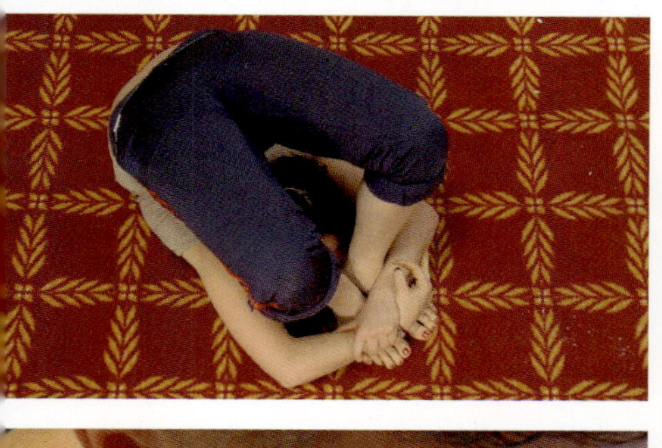

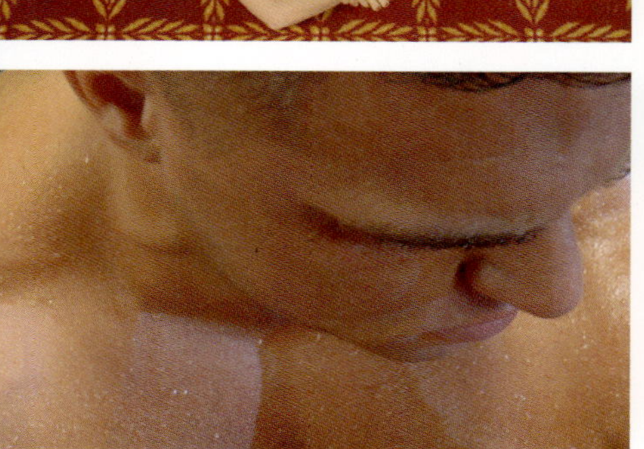

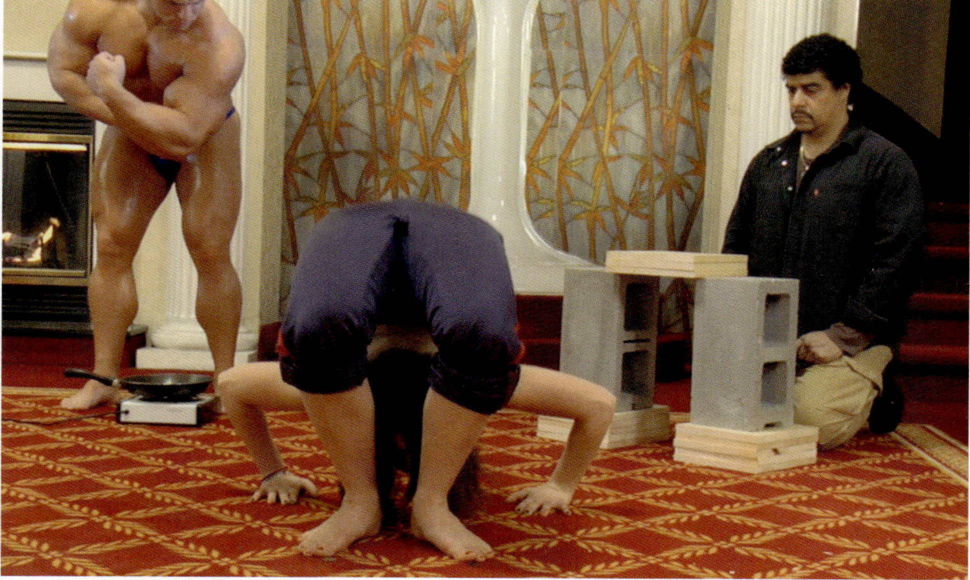

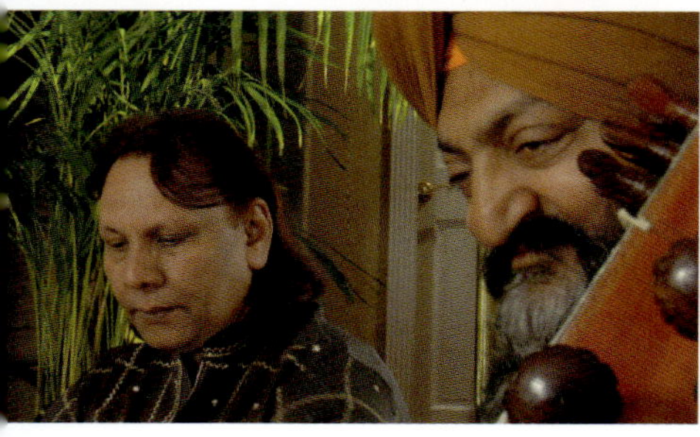

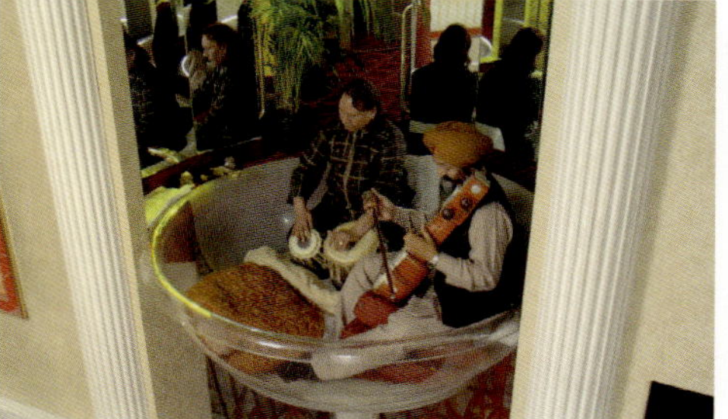

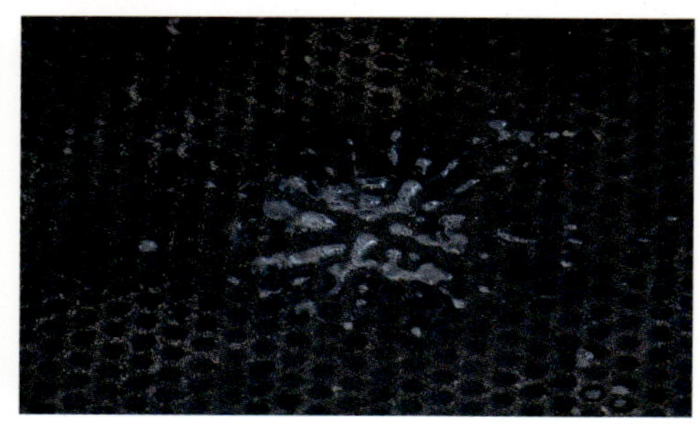

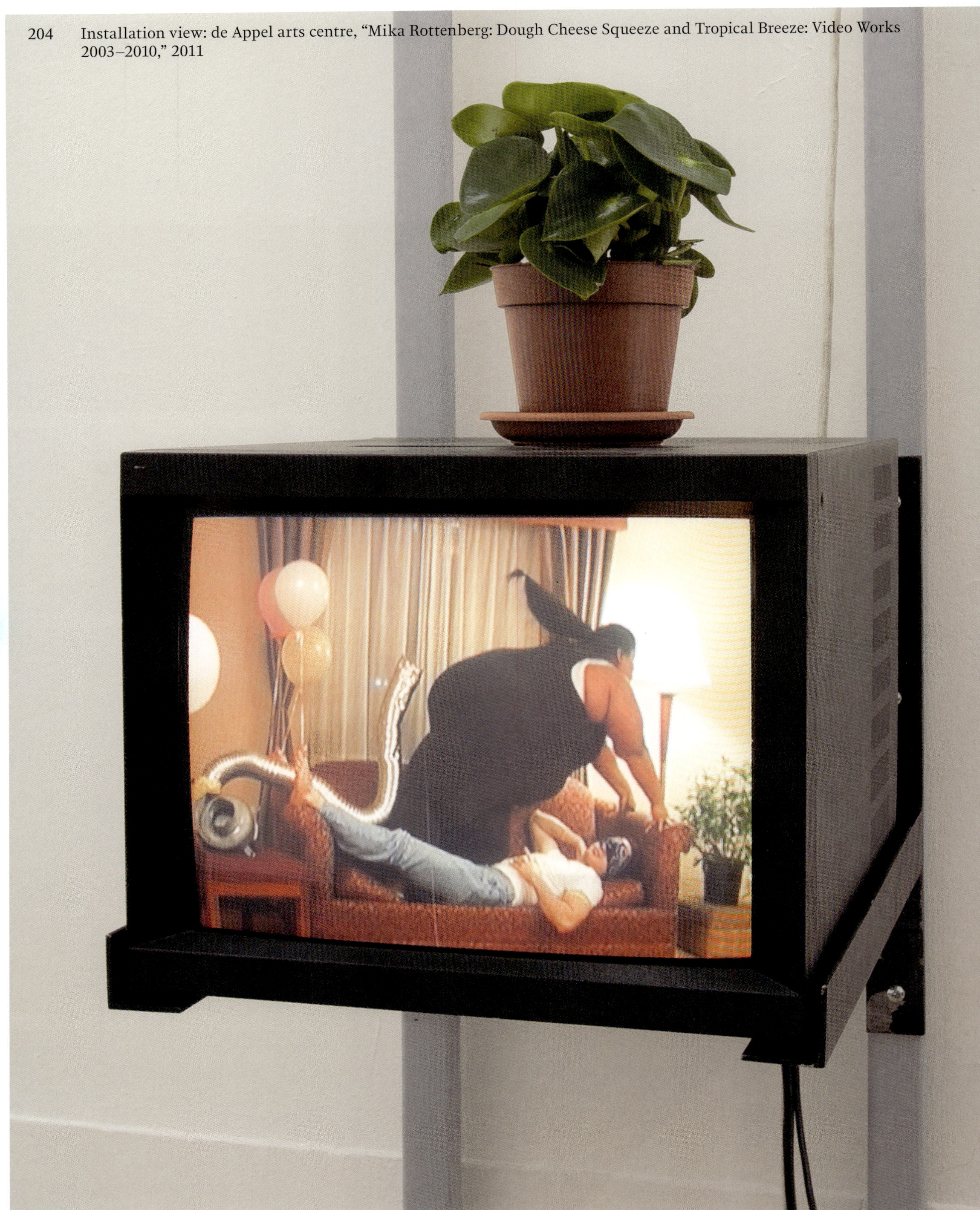

Installation view: de Appel arts centre, “Mika Rottenberg: Dough Cheese Squeeze and Tropical Breeze: Video Works 2003–2010,” 2011

5 second party

CB: Do you consider yourself a feminist? How, if at all, does your work intersect with and relate to feminist traditions in the visual arts?

MR: The dictionary definition of "feminism" includes the belief that men and women have equal rights. I think we all agree about that. Another part of the definition references an organized activity on behalf of women's rights. My work functions in that way because it gives space and a stage to women who don't always obey gender and conventional beauty expectations. It is satisfying for me to introduce and hopefully empower through my work an individual whom I find inspiring and who is usually marginalized, like a very large woman or a female body builder. But my intention is to make an interesting artwork, not to serve a political agenda. Sometimes these two forces collide. I can see a connection between my work and art traditions such as 1970s body works, working with soft formless substances, food as a recurring element, etc., but this is not a premeditated connection I am seeking in my work.

 Installation view: de Appel arts centre, “Mika Rottenberg: Dough Cheese Squeeze and Tropical Breeze: Video Works 2003–2010,” 2011

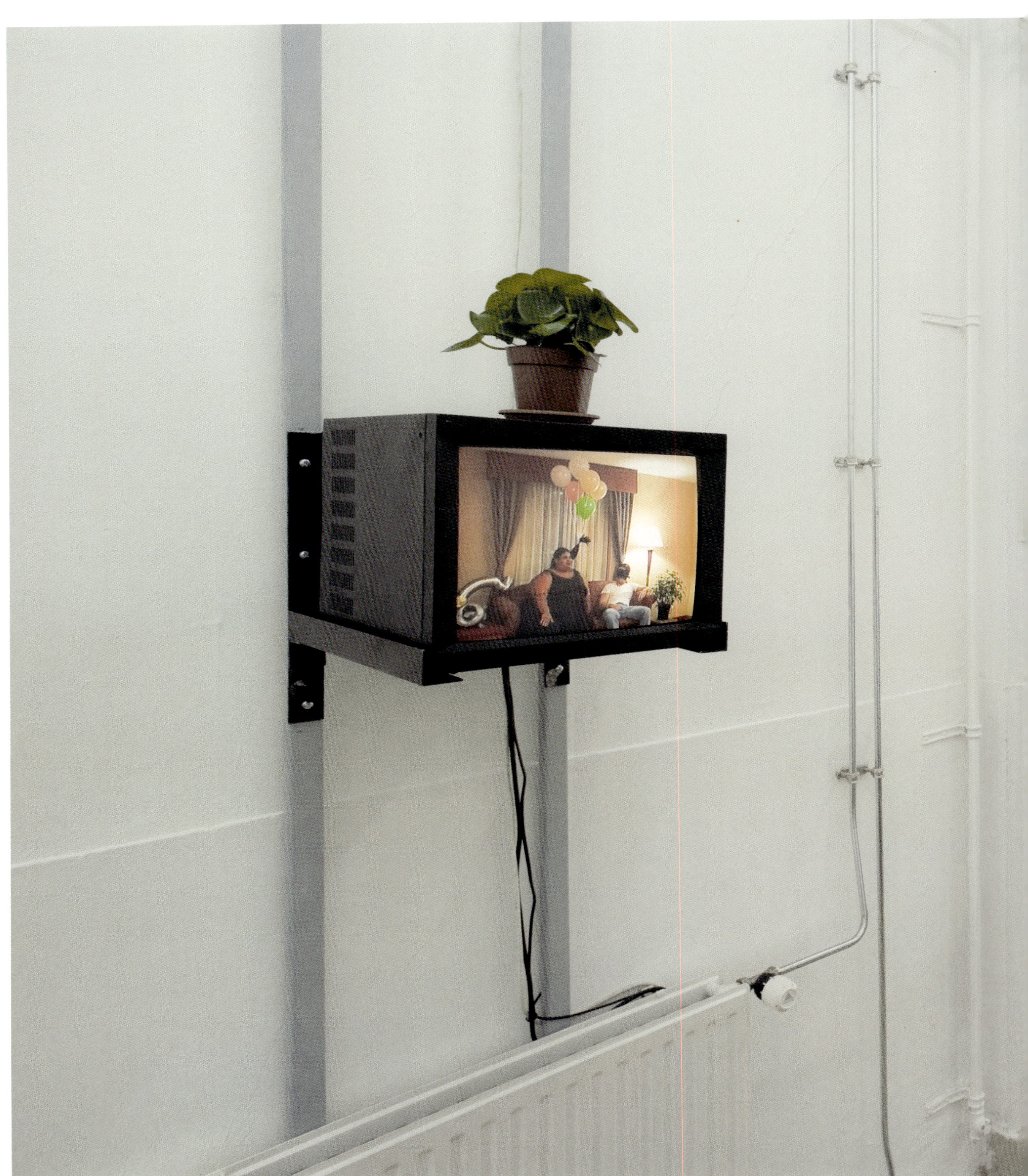

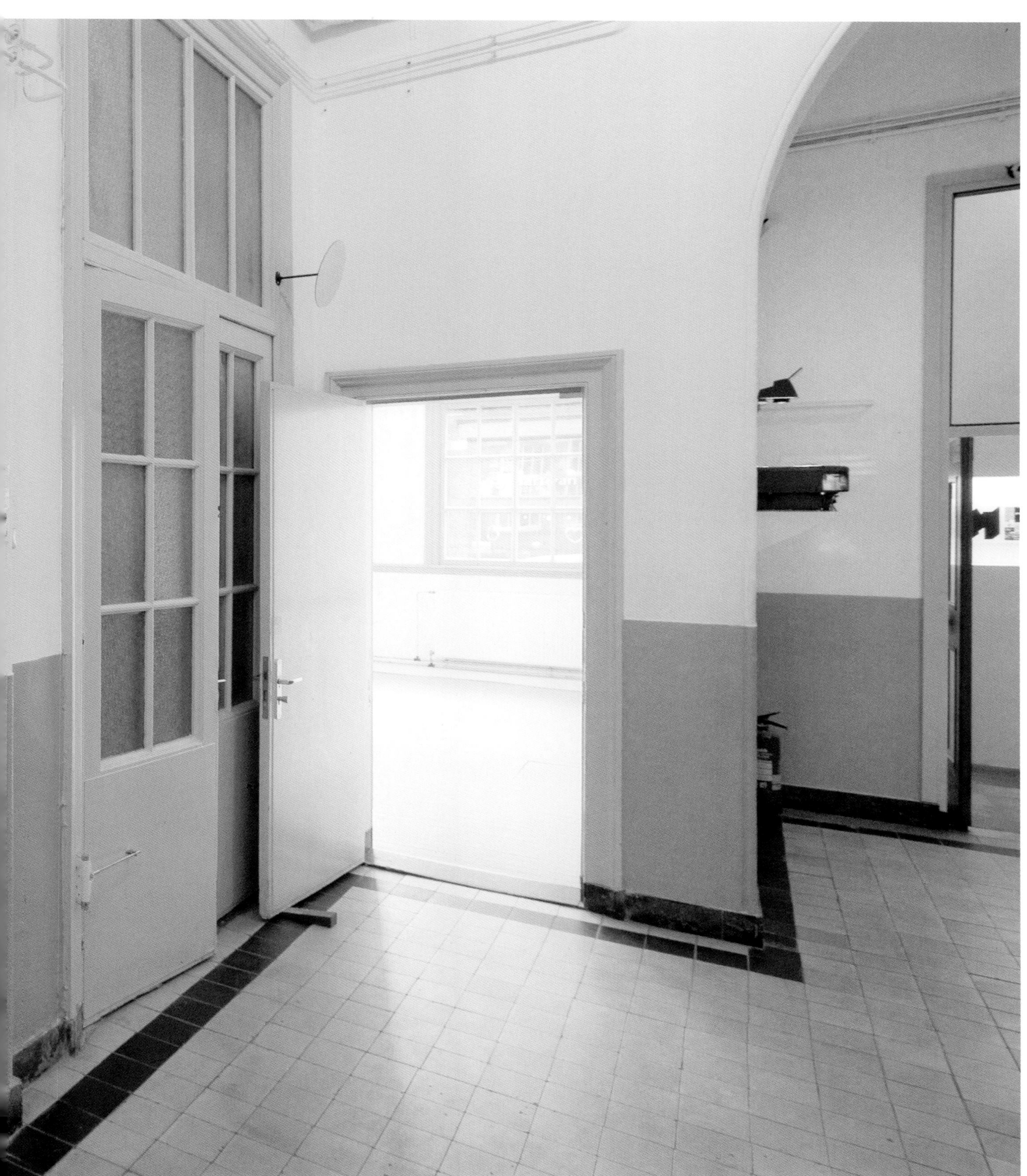

 5 Second Party, 2006; digital c-print

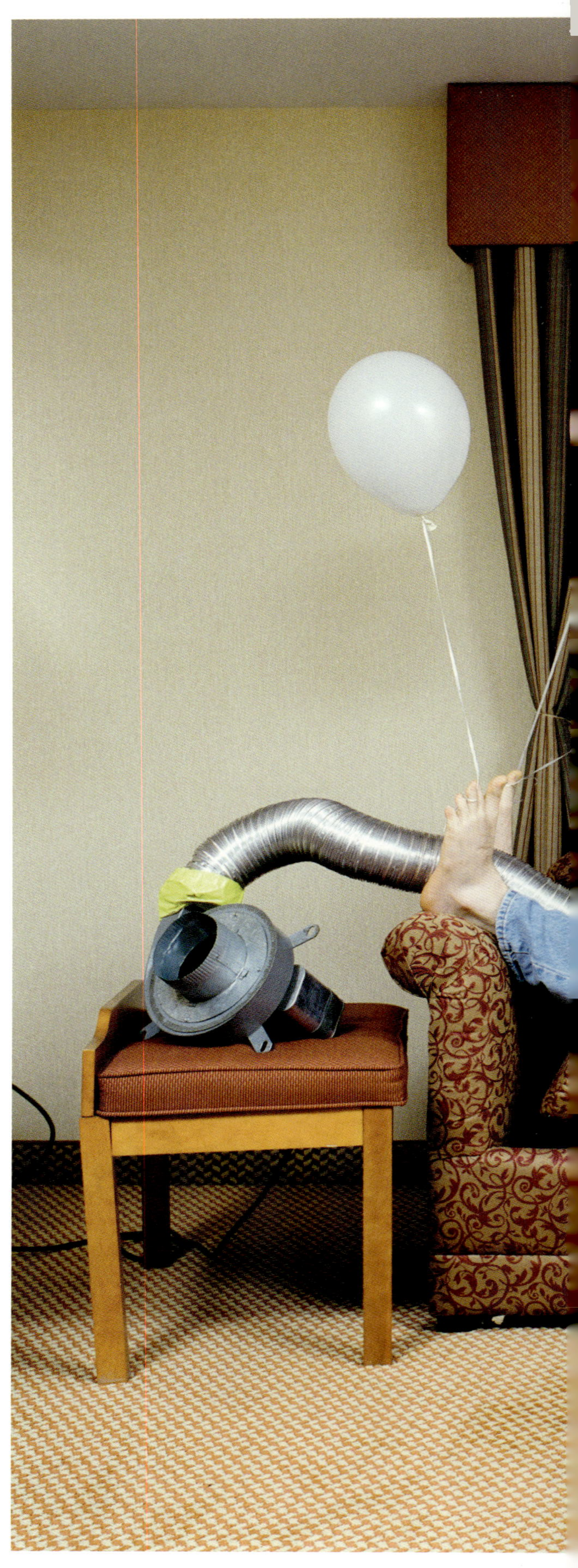

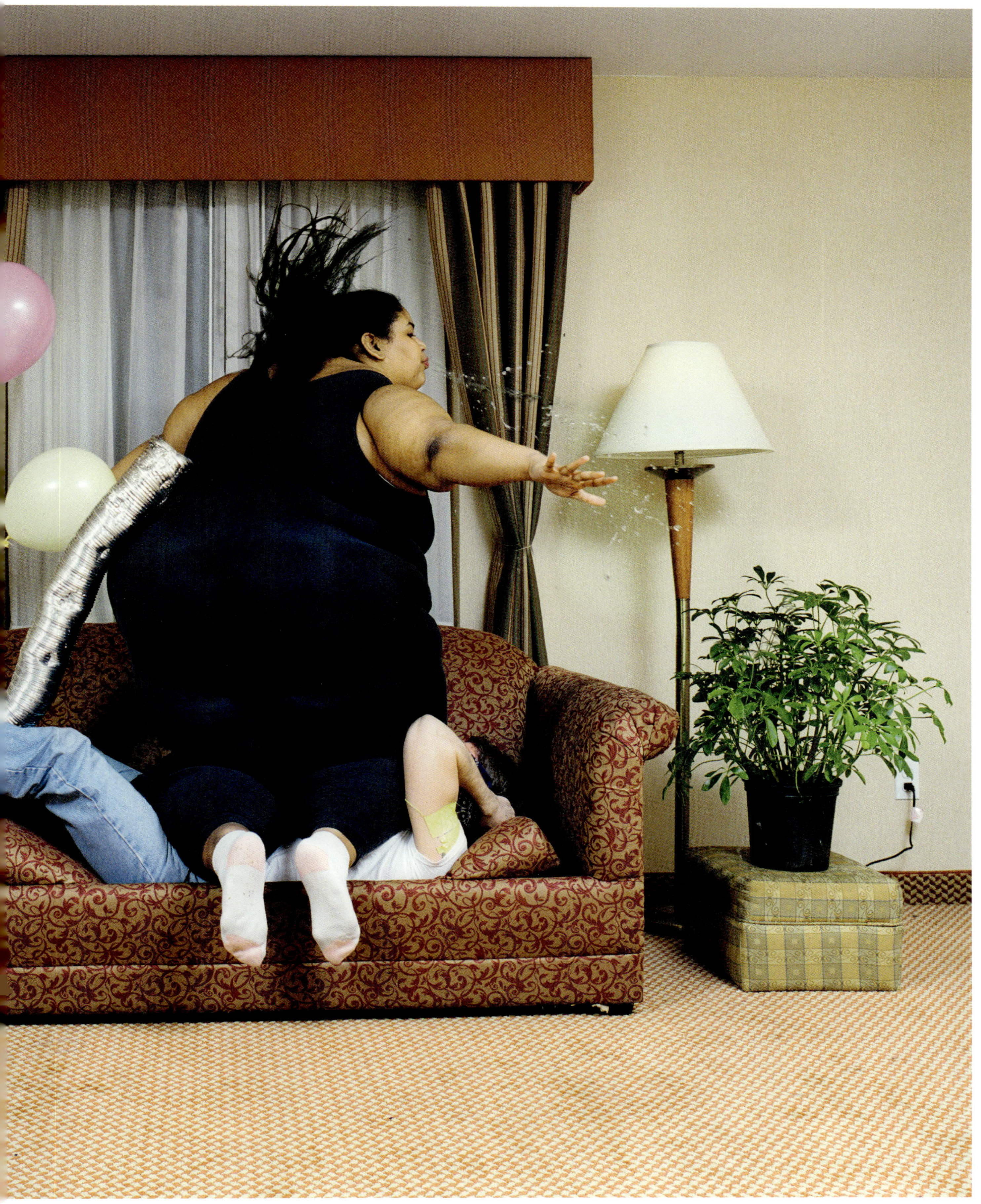

Stills from *5 Second Party*, 2006

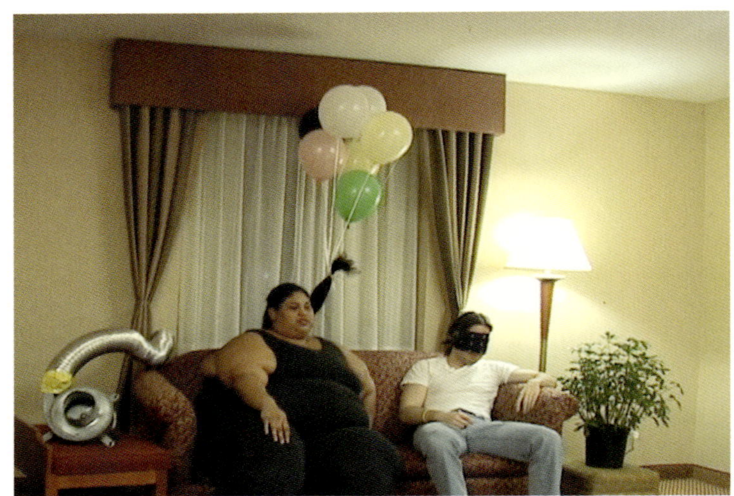

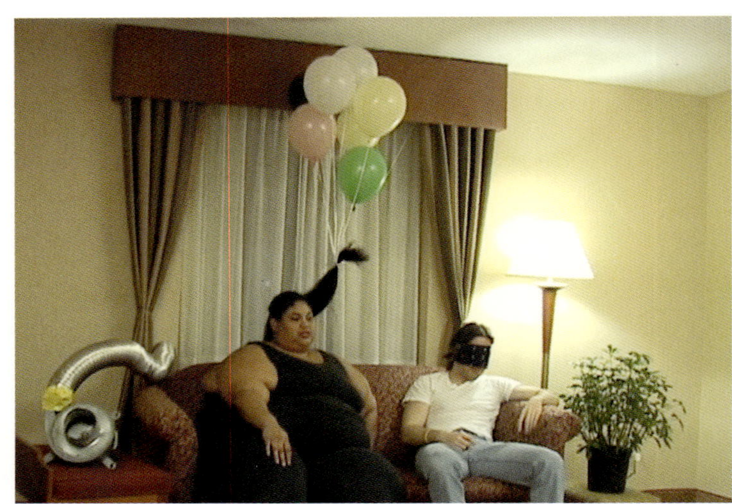

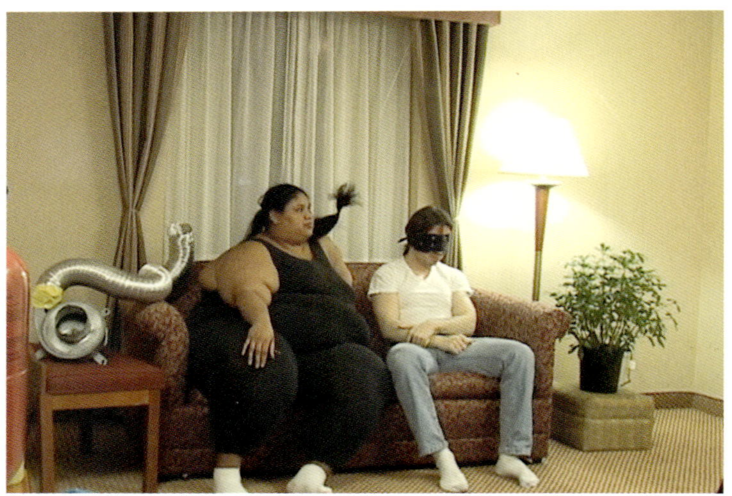

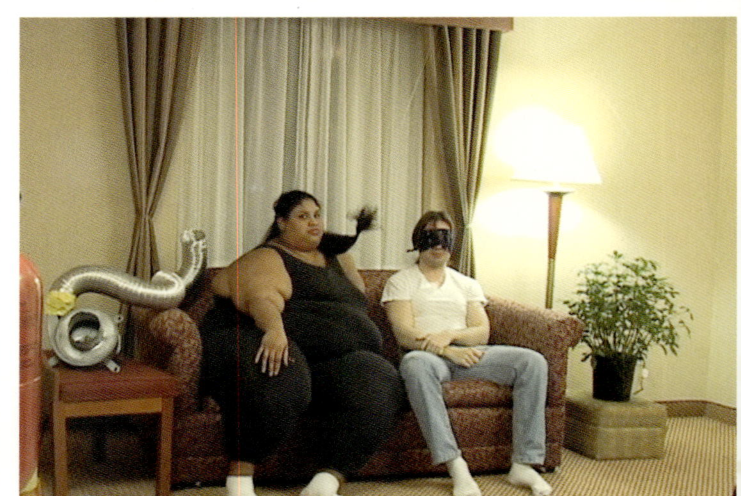

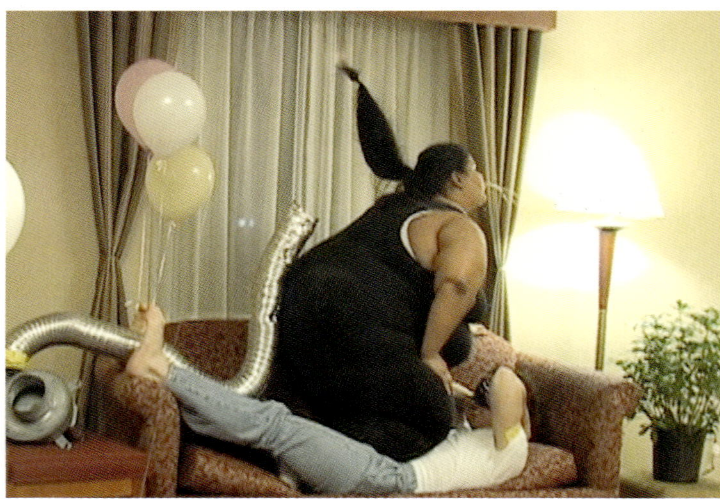

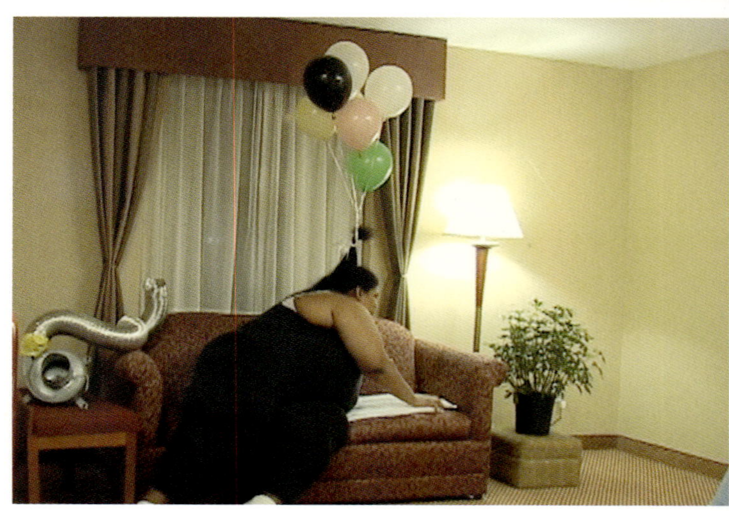

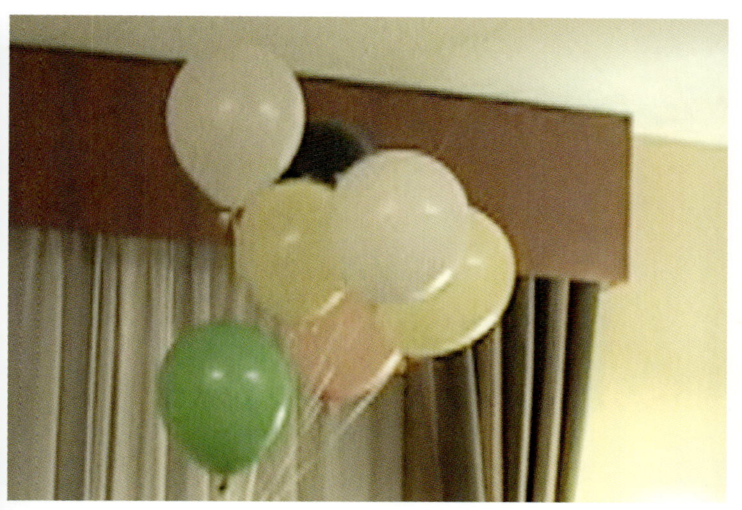

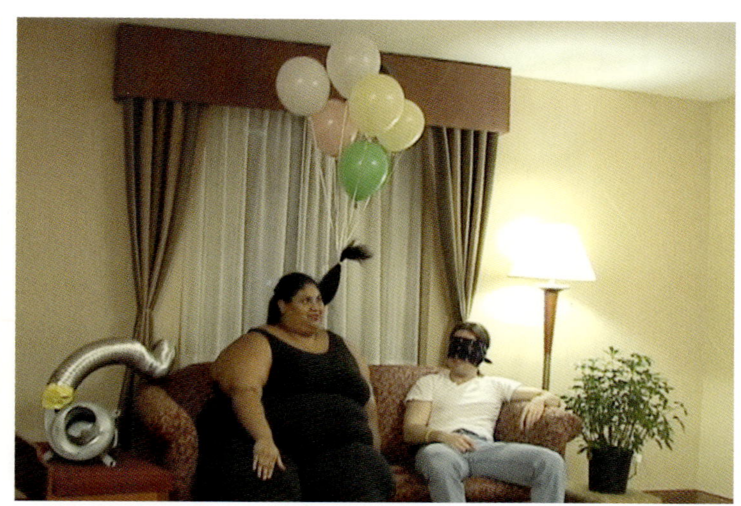

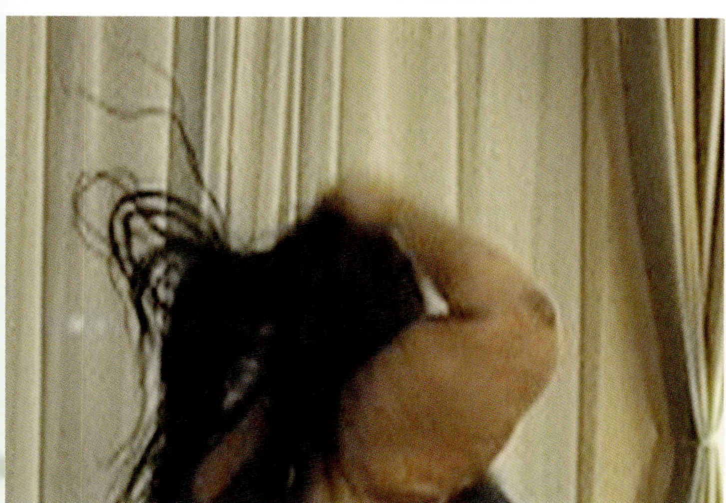

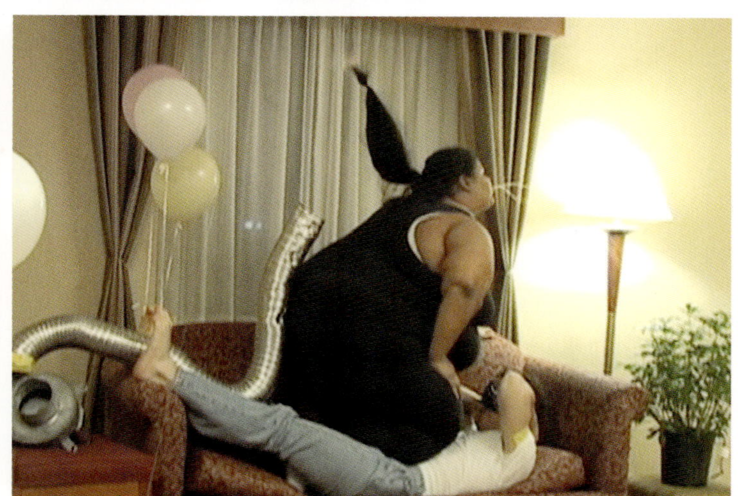

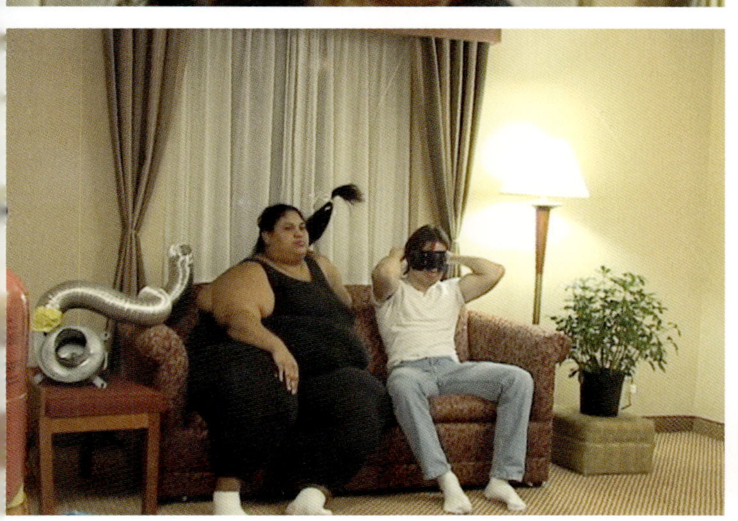

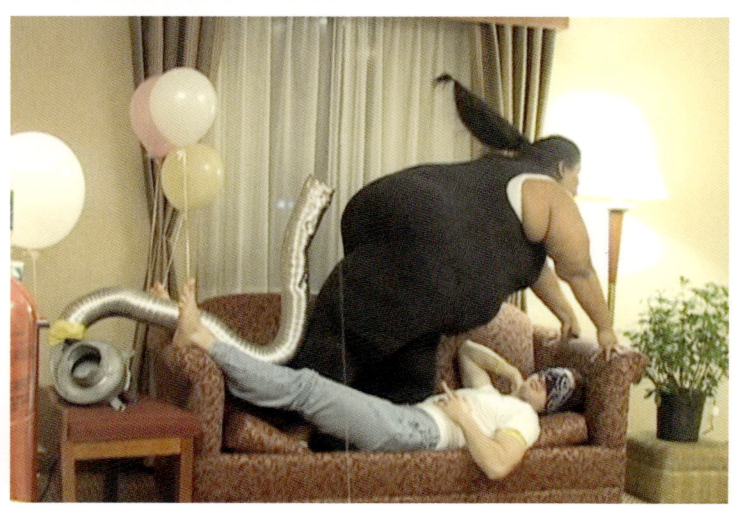

 Detail of *One Second Sculpture with Ahtoy*, 2003; digital c-print

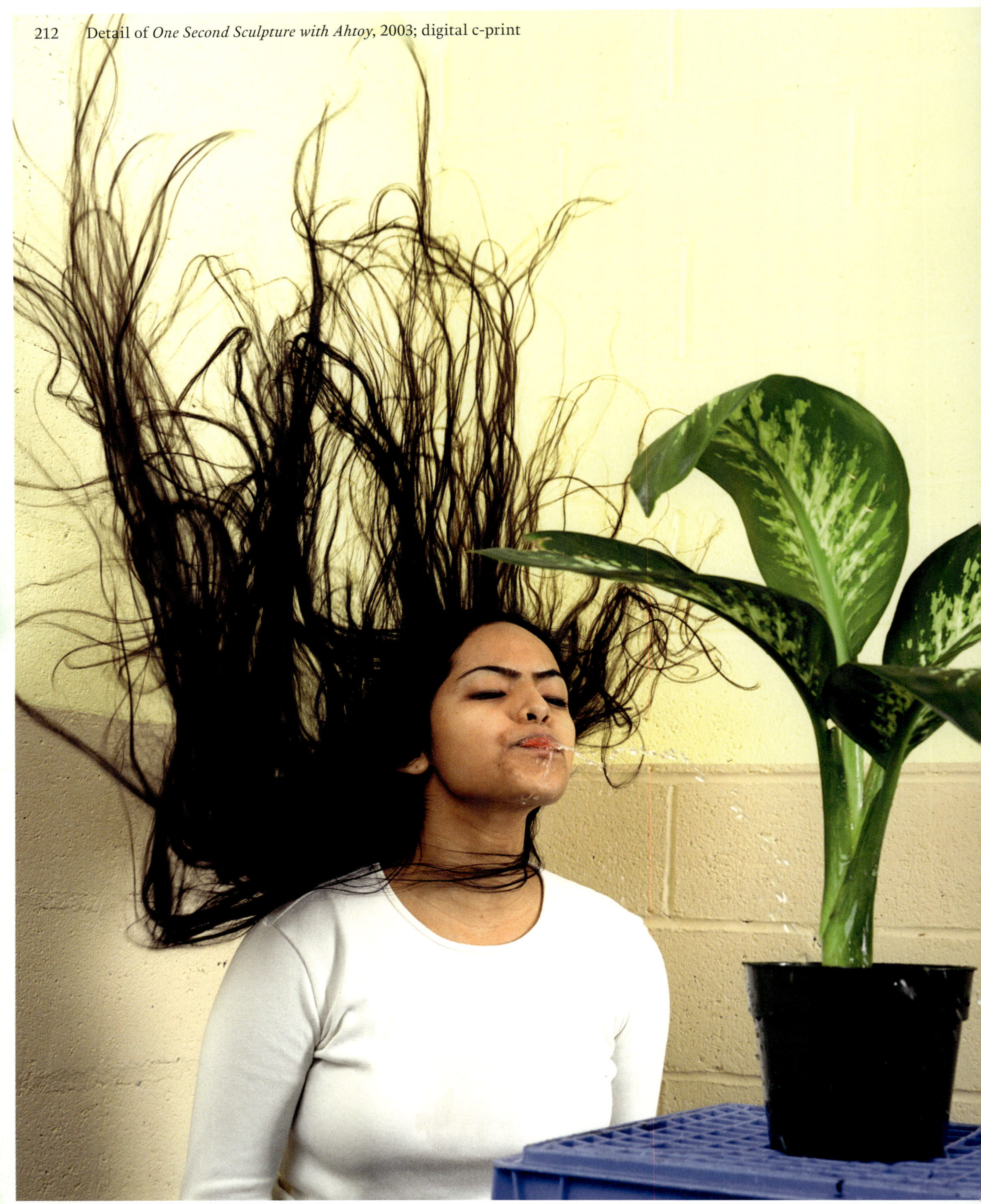

time and a half

CB: You rarely if ever use found footage in your video work. Rather, you prefer to film on location, and often this impulse takes you to far-flung and obscure locations. How does the location in *Time and a Half* function for you?

MR: This particular piece was shot in a Chinese take-out restaurant in the East Village. It's true that I never use found footage, but I love when I find a location that's a readymade. I've been fascinated by Chinese take-out restaurants for a long time—by how they all look very similar but they don't belong to any one entity. The décor is so self-referential: the formica, the pictures of the food, the murals … You feel transported into a location that doesn't really exist elsewhere. Direct architectural intervention became important in my later work; in *Time and a Half*, the intervention is in the space of the video. In this piece, it manifested in the decision to bring in more plants and to change the seating arrangement to push the restaurant even more into the realm of the fantastic.

 Installation view: The Israel Museum, "Squeeze: Video Works by Mika Rottenberg," 2013

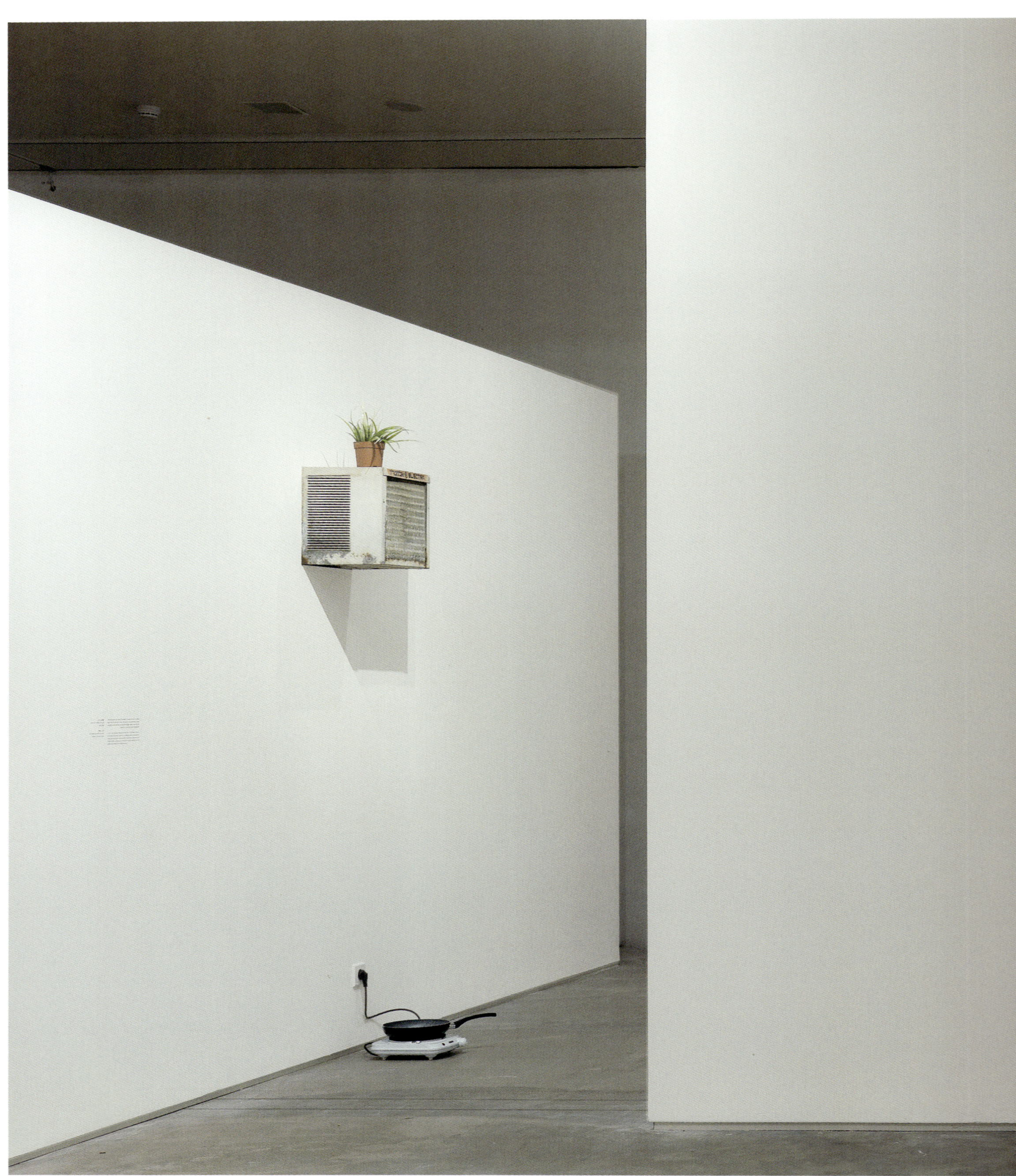

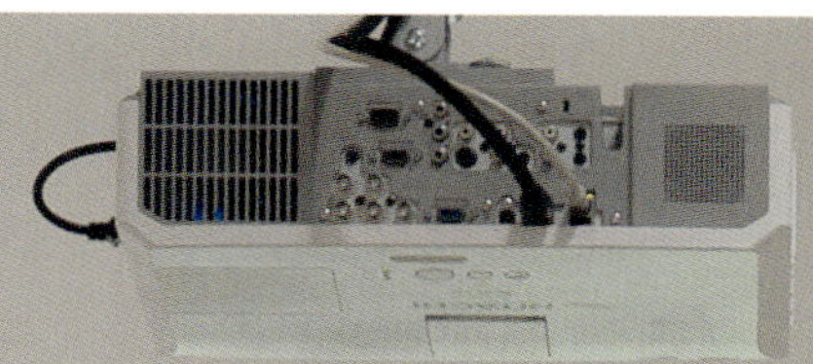

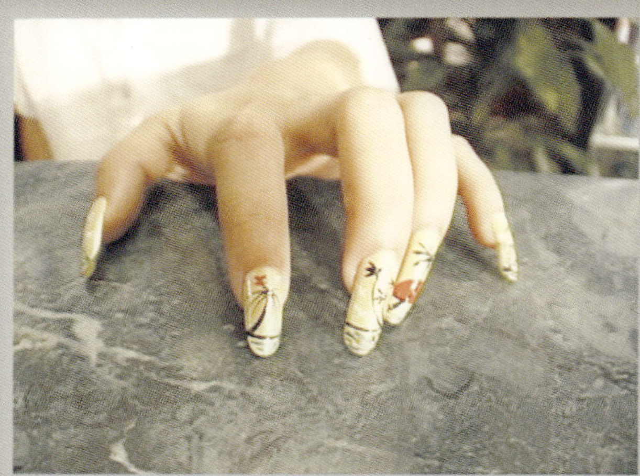

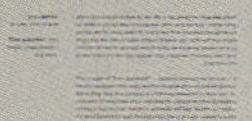

Installation view: de Appel arts centre, “Mika Rottenberg: Dough Cheese Squeeze and Tropical Breeze: Video Works 2003–2010,” 2011

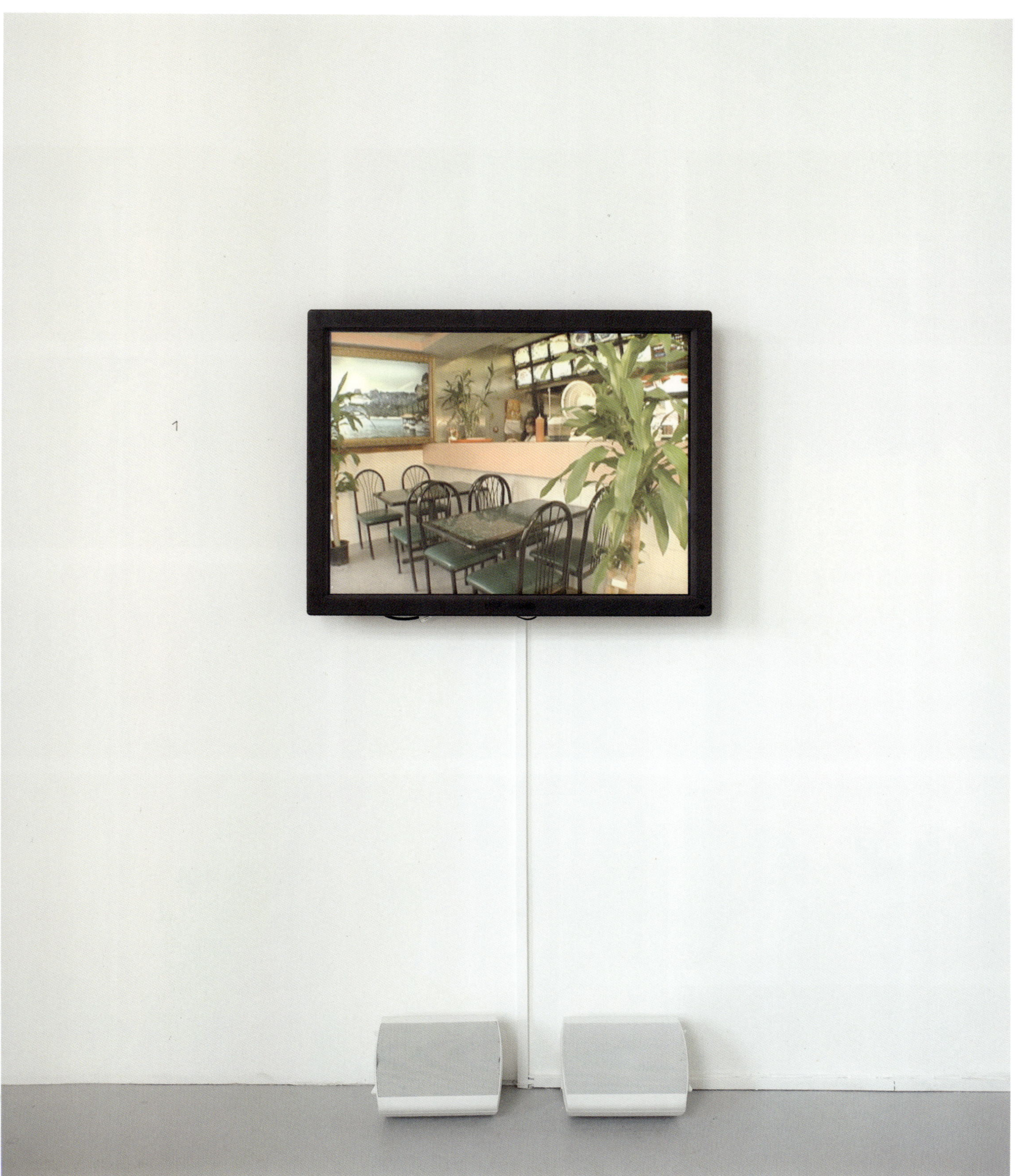

Stills from *Time and a Half*, 2003

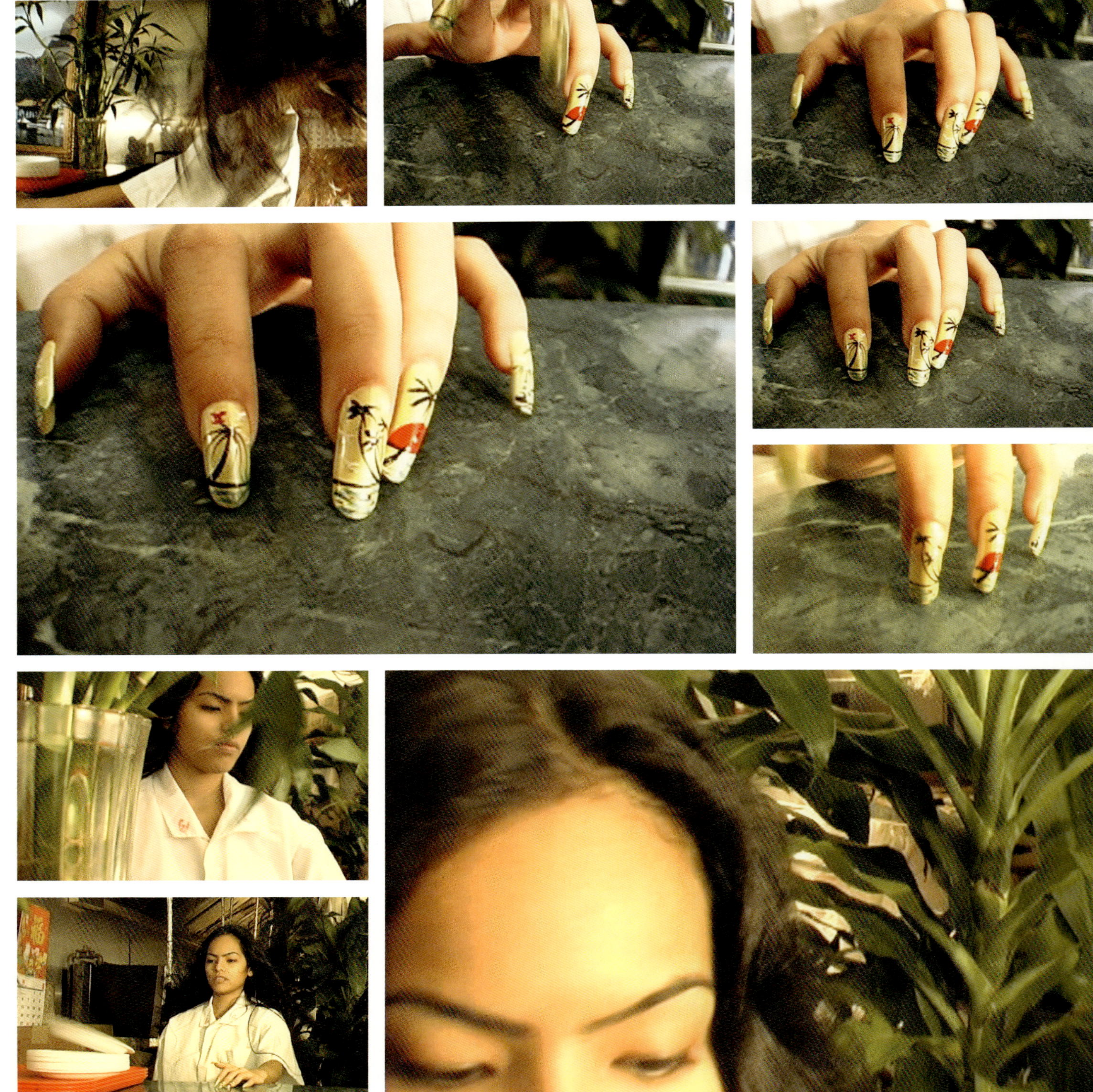

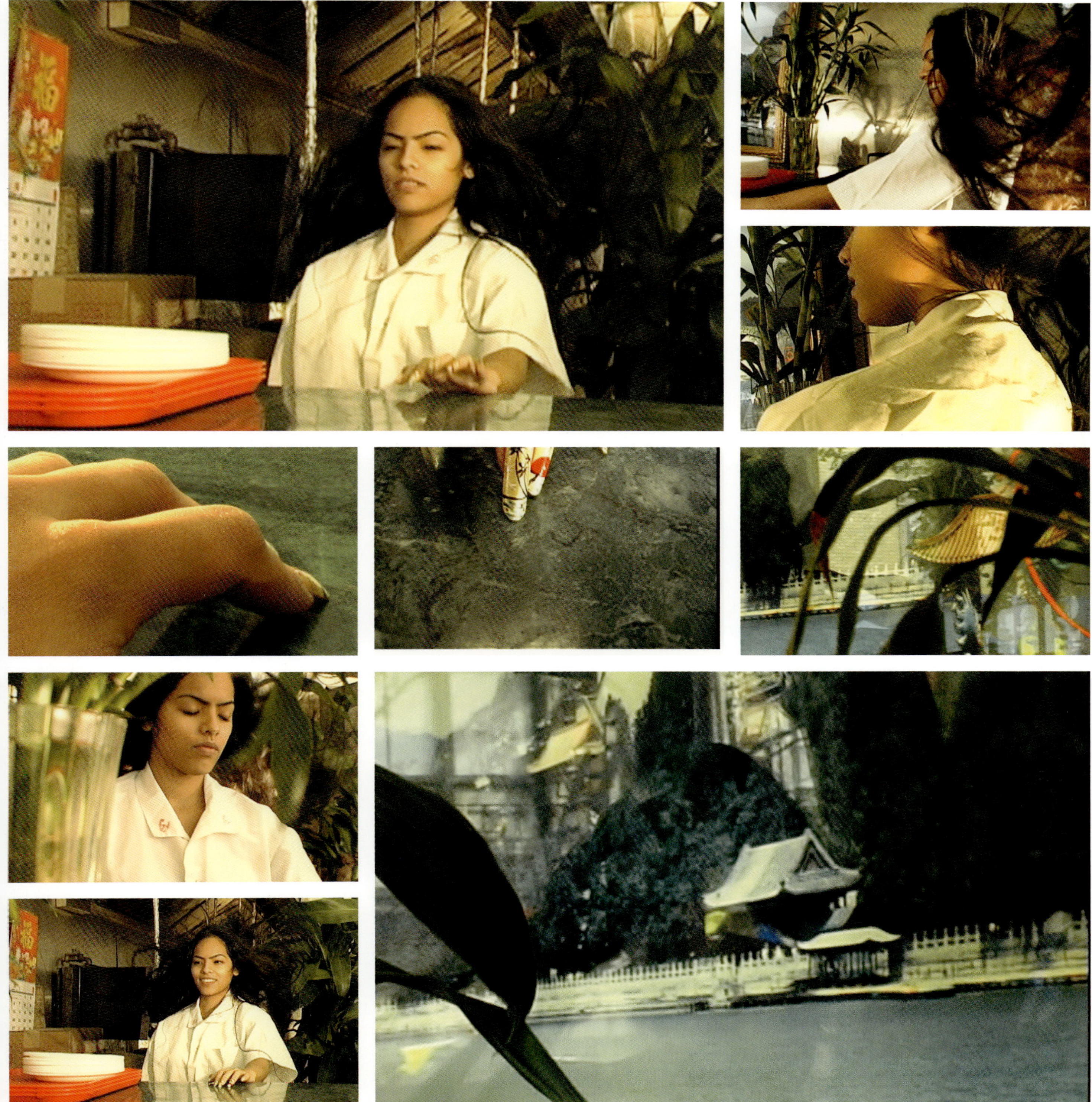

Installation view: de Appel arts centre, "Mika Rottenberg: Dough Cheese Squeeze and Tropical Breeze: Video Works 2003–2010," 2011

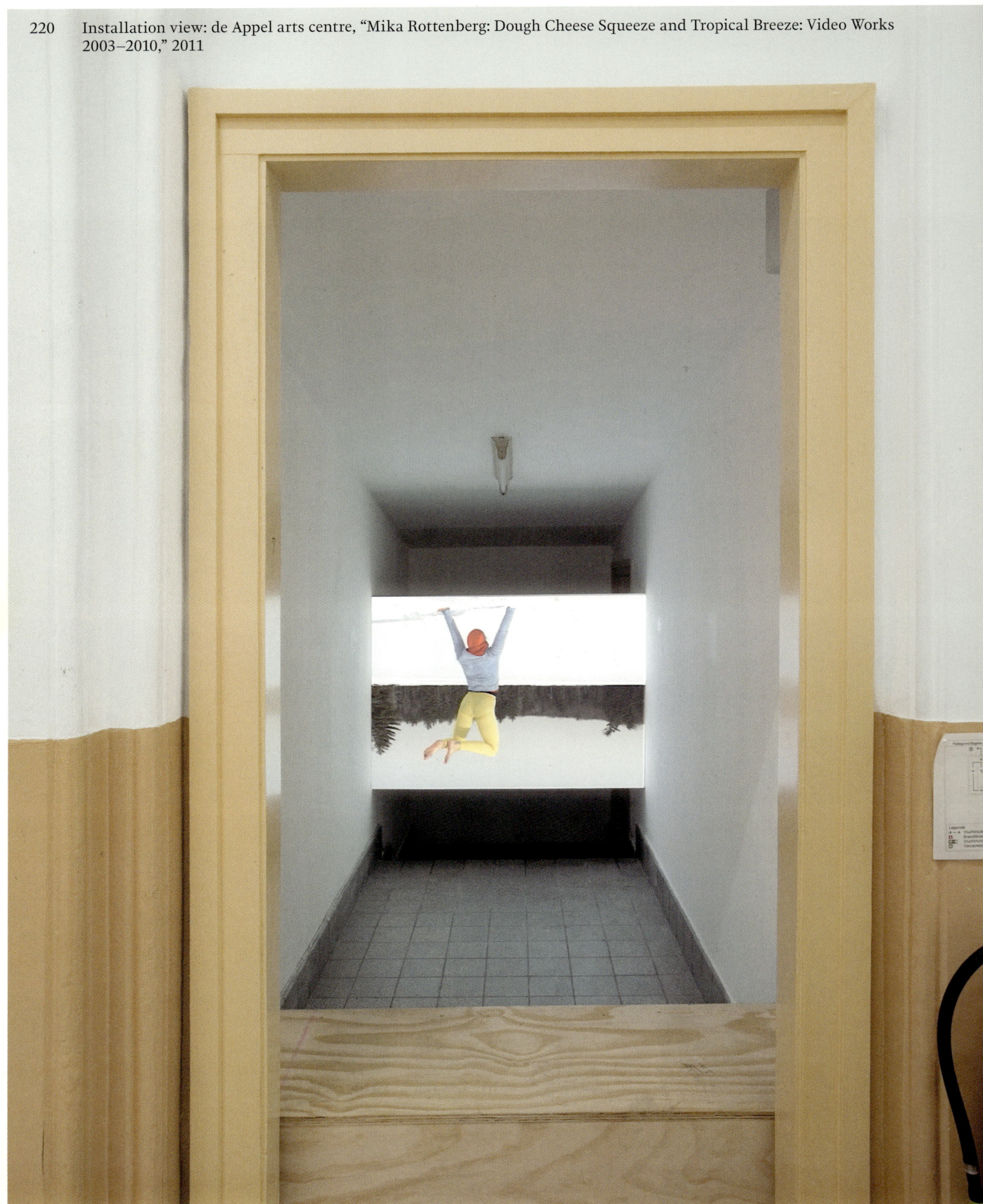

julie

CB: Rosalind Krauss wrote famously about what she called "sculpture in the expanded field." When I look at your work, I often think about the expanded field of video, a way of working that leaves behind the screen and the black box in favor of an integrated multimedia environment. Does this idea resonate for you or motivate the work you do?

MR: "Multimedia" is a funny term. I guess it is an accurate description of my work, but it feels kind of dated. Regardless, yes, I want to create physical relations between the viewer and the work. I hope to engage someone's body as well as his or her mind. I also want to take advantage of what presenting video in a gallery can allow, as opposed to TV or cinema. In a gallery, you can control the size and environment where a video is viewed. It is great that the presentation of a video can be so specific. In other mediums like sculpture or painting, it is obvious that a work has specific dimensions and light conditions; I think video should be treated in the same way. Actually, *Julie* is one of my only works with a straightforward projection without a surrounding, constructed environment. Maybe because of the upside down camera action, however, an environment is created between the viewer and the monitor.

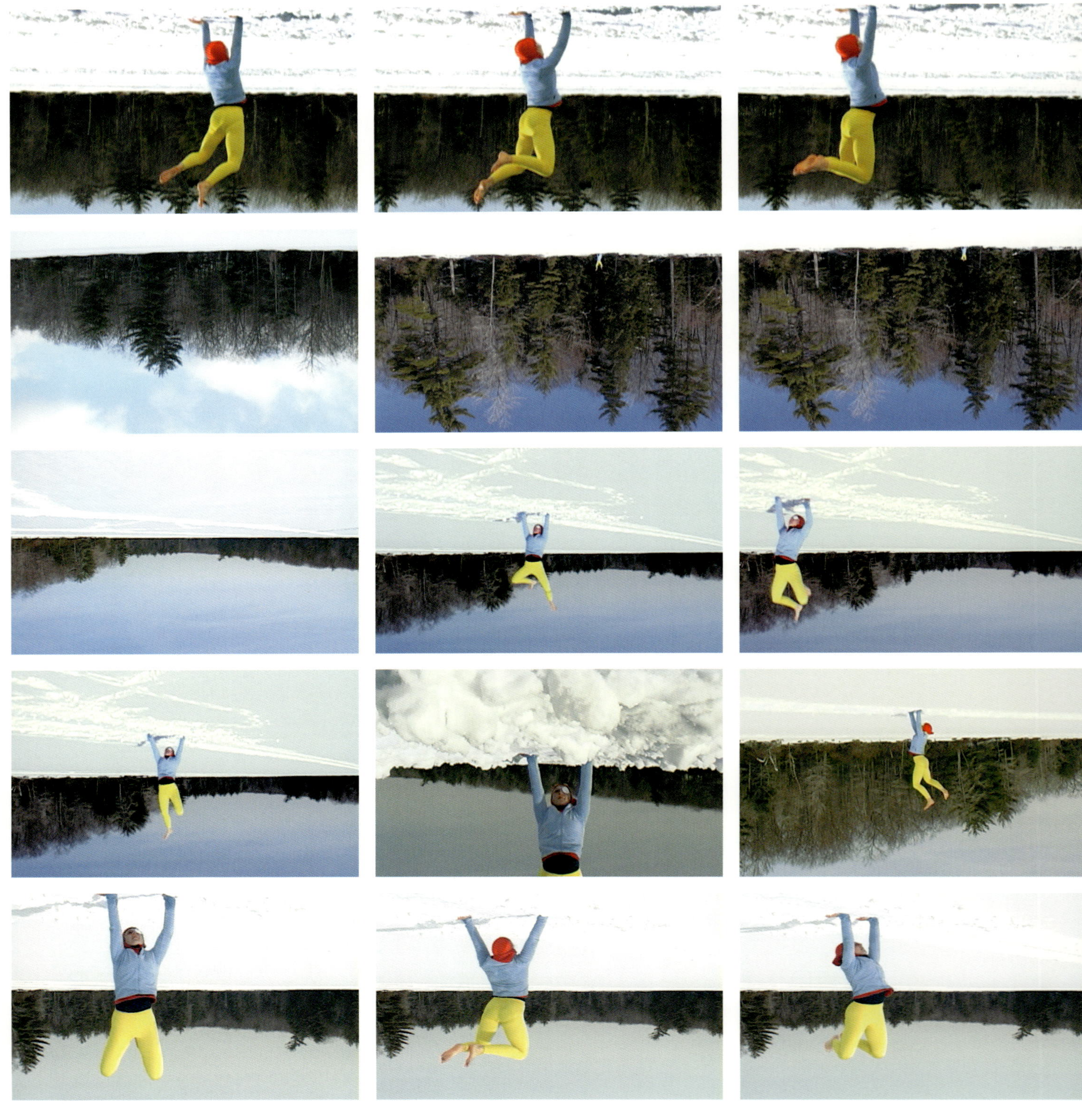

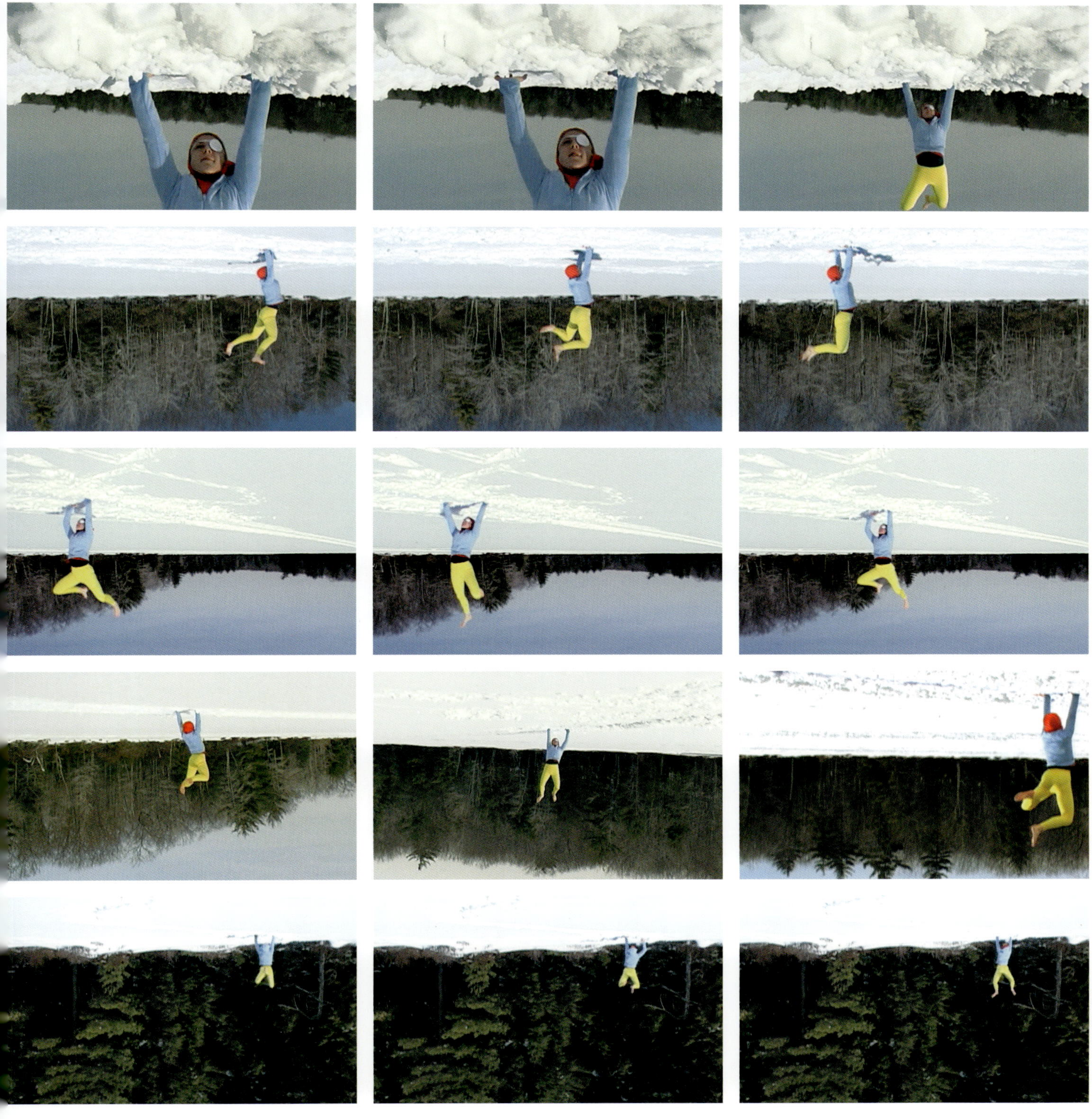

This Usefulness Does Not Dangle in Mid-Air

Wayne Koestenbaum

"The usefulness of a thing makes it a use-value. But this usefulness does not dangle in mid-air. It is conditioned by the physical properties of the commodity, and has no existence apart from the latter. It is therefore the physical body of the commodity itself, for instance, iron, corn, a diamond, which is the use-value or useful thing."

— Karl Marx, *Capital*

[*Mary's Cherries*]

1 I spent the darkest days of winter watching Mika Rottenberg's videos. From their laconic stream, I learned many useful things about pleasure and unpleasure—a dialectic that her work cheerfully sidesteps and overturns.

2 Unpleasure, a sine qua non for precise cognition, should not be repressed; notice and savor it, if only for the sake of eventually undermining its reign.* For instance, my own fingernails unnerve me; so do the fingernails of a woman who mutates them, by a mysterious process, into maraschino cherries. Rottenberg allows her viewers to enter the space of being-unnerved, but then to transmute that state into something pacific, at ease, curious, untrammeled by the punished dialectic of attraction/repulsion.

3 Endure and interrogate unpleasure; thereby understand economic systems.

---

* The word *unpleasure* I owe to Freud, who called it *Unlust.* In *Beyond the Pleasure Principle*, he writes: "On the other hand we would readily express our gratitude to any philosophical or psychological theory which was able to inform us of the meaning of the feelings of pleasure and unpleasure which act so imperatively upon us."

 Detail of *ST4*, 2010; graphite, acrylic, colored pencil on paper

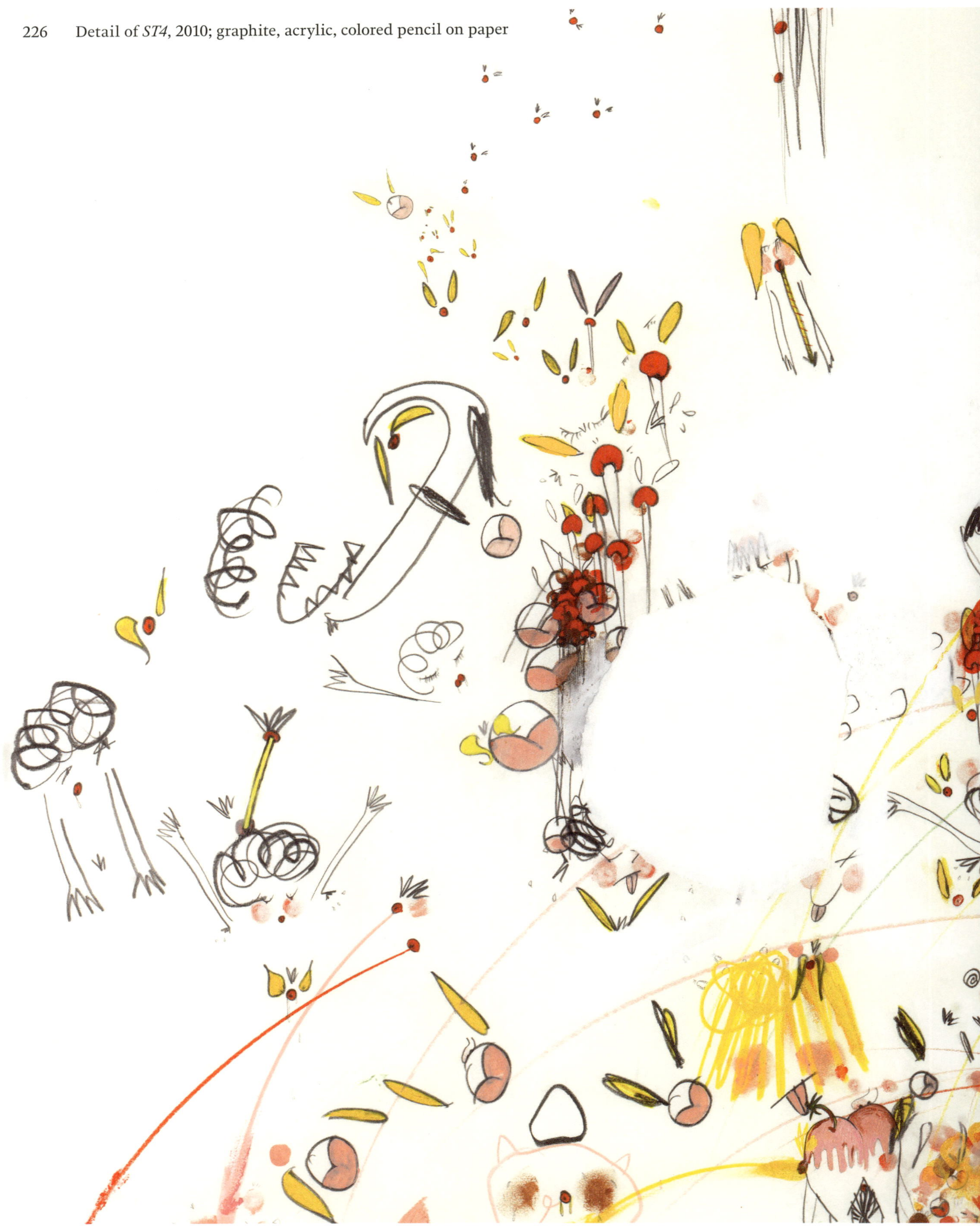

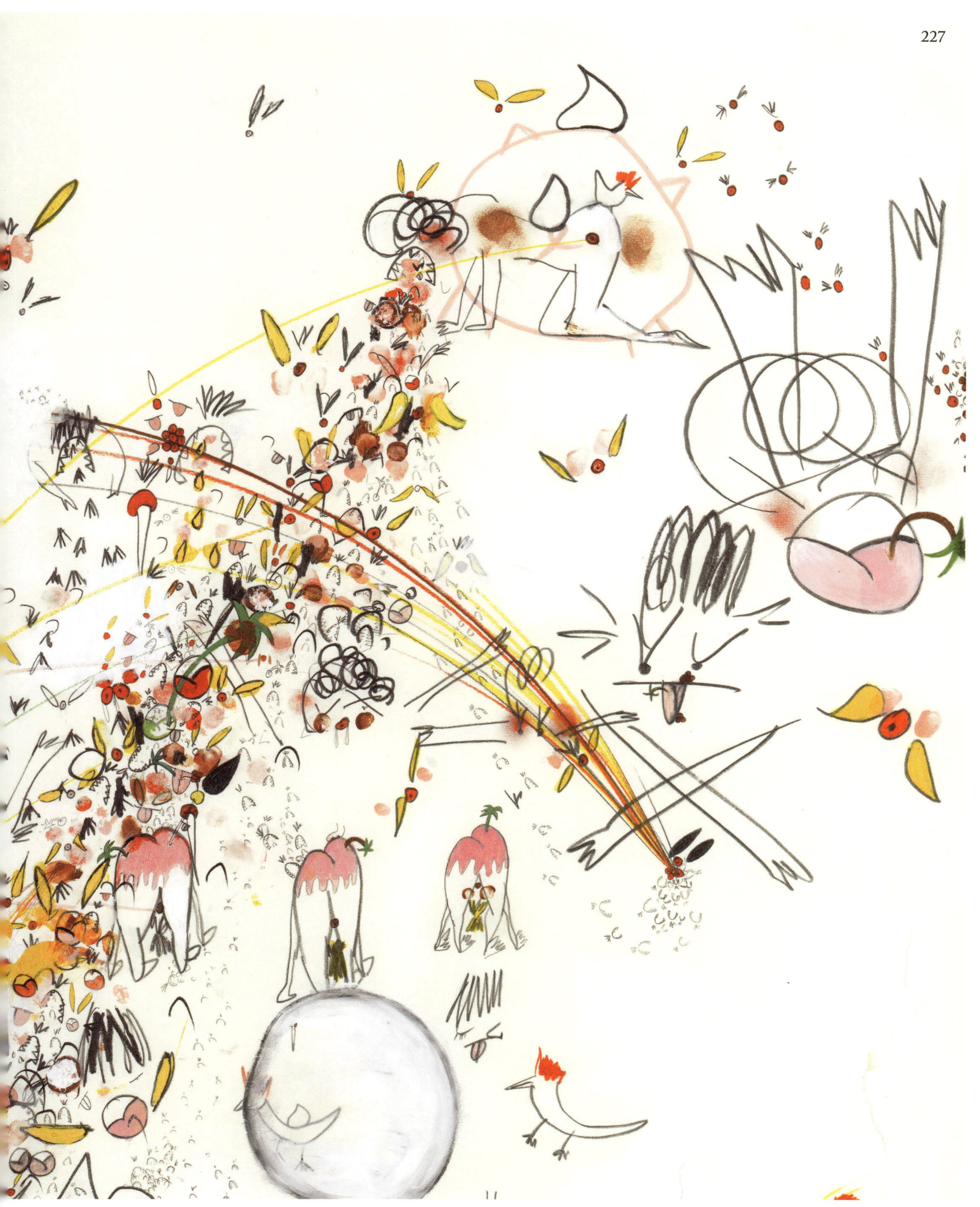

4 A movie camera's peregrinations indicate a presiding consciousness, and yet perhaps no thoughts inhabit a camera or direct its movements.

5 Often we request food—"burger, please"—without wanting it. I might request a burger because I am in the habit of asking for burgers. But a burger might not be what I want. "Burger" is a screen. I say "burger" because I don't know how to say what I really want.

6 Color—yellow, blue, pink—focuses attention. Find a nonjudgmentally chromatic way of looking at the world, a way that gives precedence to color rather than to identity. Rather than say "I want a burger," learn to say "I want redness."

[*Time and a Half*]

7 Fingernails, a musical instrument, make sounds. (Fingernails recur in Rottenberg's videos.) We can choose to develop our fetishism rather than to disavow it. We can decide, "I will make music out of my fingernails, and I will love their delicate percussiveness."

8 Actors in porn—even in self-created, amateur images—obey a distinct yet unwritten codebook of facial expressions. Porn delight—stylized—crosses a face. We, as viewers, understand this transport not as actual pleasure but as a variegated simulacrum—performance flecked and veined with reality.

9 Sounds obey laws of periodicity. Noises, mercurial, intensify and subside.

10 A movie camera's movements express will: the will to dominate, to scrutinize, to absorb, to contain, to be patient. Perhaps *readiness* is a more accurate description of a camera's desire—the readiness to dominate, to scrutinize, to absorb, to witness ...

11 Even a delicate sound has the power to unnerve a listener.

[*Tropical Breeze*]

12 Certain motions—squooshing, for example—produce pleasure, but the pleasure thereby obtained does not lead to the formation of a recognized subculture.

13 Much of a human life can be spent in pursuit of these uncatalogued pleasures, such as squooshing or being squooshed.

14 Assembly lines undergird capitalist production and exploitation but also provide a metaphor for sexual pleasure—i.e., my eroticism functions as an assembly line.

15 I might choose to simulate an assembly line within my own body, or I might choose to interpret my sexual desire as *assembly-line-esque*. For example, if we can say "The day is windy," we might say, "My hunger for your body is *assembly-line-esque*." Like arabesque, or romanesque.

[*Dough*]

16 A camera's movements needn't express horniness, restlessness, patience, or fatigue. Sometimes a camera has the power to seem unsure of which objects it seeks; such a camera we might call *unmoored*, and we might propose its flexible stance as a paradigm of undogmatic beholding.

17 We do not merely dwell within our bodies; we produce our bodies, whether actively or unconsciously. We might condemn the result as demonic, or we might praise it as paradisaical. In any case, we can't pretend indifference to the bodies that our actions—squooshing, kneading, dreaming—produce.

18 Mental health depends on understanding the difference between *bread dough* and *turd*. There might be certain people who don't understand this difference—people for whom *bread dough* is just another way of saying *turd*. Such people—turd-focused individuals—continue to make bread and to eat bread, but their understanding of bread is turd-inflected, as is their understanding of human intimacy.

19 The world is actually *two* worlds—an overworld and an underworld. The underworld has been variously described as the unconscious, Hell, unhappiness, wretchedness, destitution, illness. Dispense with any known way of describing overworld and underworld. Instead, note the proliferation of this polarity—over and under. Grow comfortable with reversing the dualism, and recognizing the underworld as an overworld in disguise.

20 Alienated laborers might be alienated from the products of their labor, but they are not necessarily alienated from each other. Laborers, in

Detail of *SQ1*, 2009; graphite, acrylic, colored pencil, industrial paint on paper

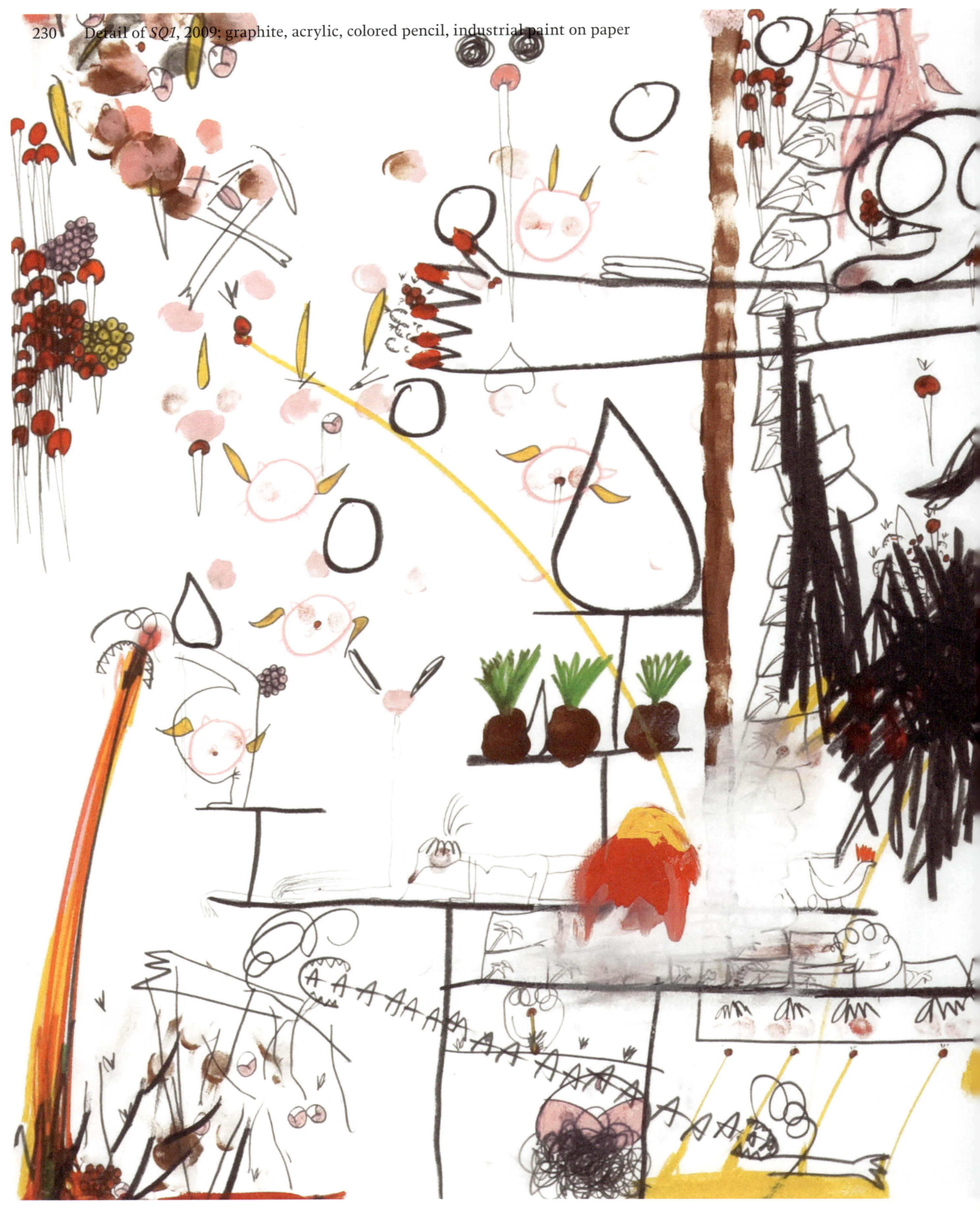

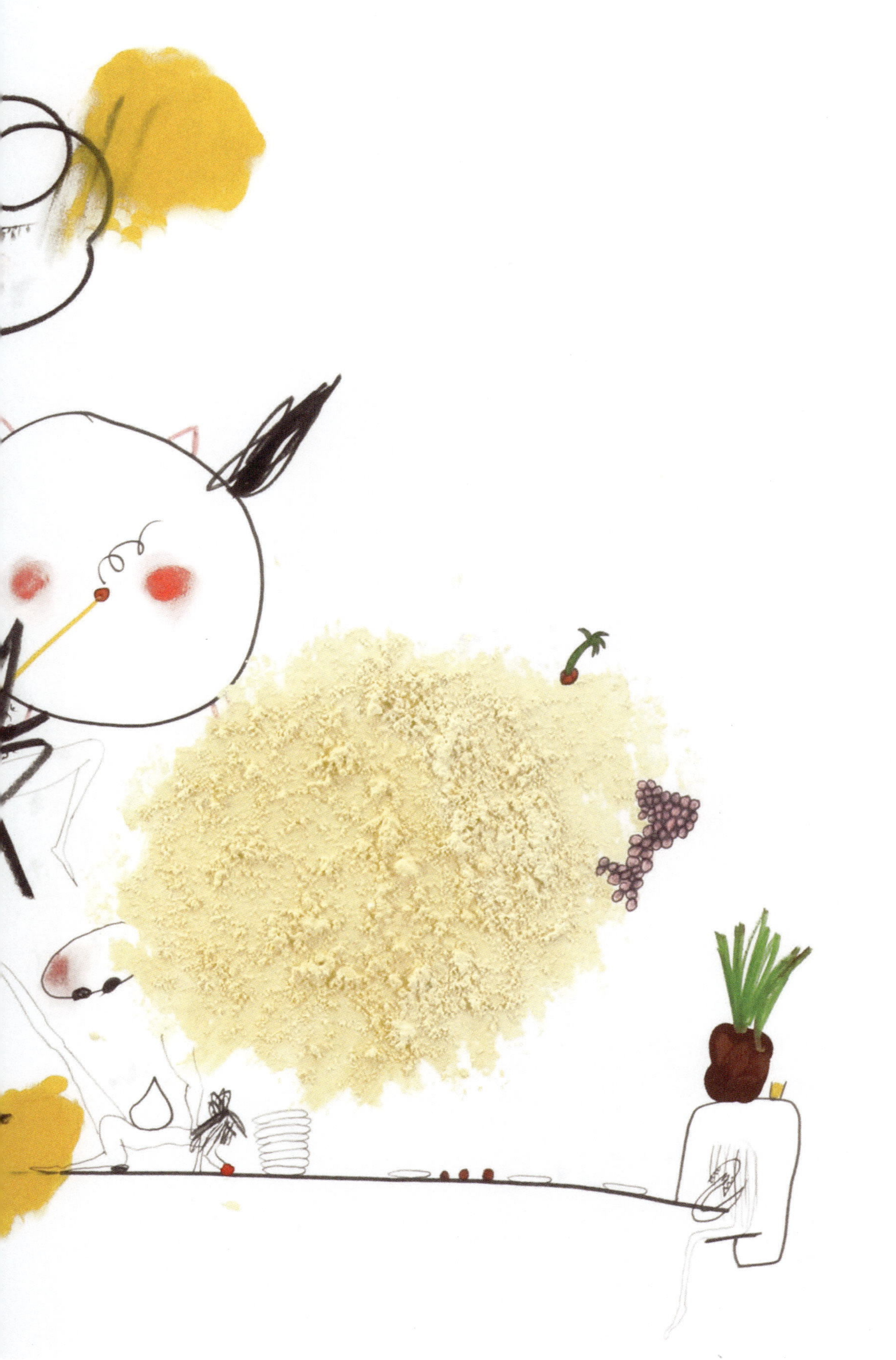

fact, might have a surplus of affection and solidarity with other laborers—a crowning excess of identification and curiosity. The communication might occur through secret channels, elaborately constructed—like glory holes, small moons carved out of dividing walls.

21 The last words of many millions of people are unknown. Not only Anne Frank's. Certainly her last spoken words are unrecorded, and we justly cling to "Anne Frank" as a sign for all we don't know of other people's martyrdoms.

[*Fried Sweat*]

22 We notice a similarity between plant fronds and human fingers; we seek analogies, in botany, for human limbs and capacities. We could accuse ourselves of anthropomorphism, a culpable bias toward humankind; or we could continue to imagine that a plant's leaves resemble human fingers, and see how our conduct changes as a result of this misperception.

23 Making art is hard work but doesn't necessarily induce the artist to sweat. Thinking, dreaming, and breathing don't officially produce smelly moisture, though the anxiety and excitement associated with these activities—including the least physically demanding forms of art-making—activate the sudoriferous glands. Now, writing with a Palamino Blackwing 602 pencil, I sense syntax's tense laws in my drenched palms.

[*Squeeze*]

24 The arm dimple, where flesh gathers at the elbow to create a crease or pucker, proves the body to be not merely *more of the same body we already know* but *a landscape of unheralded differentiations and novelties*.

25 Sensuality intensifies when forced through an aperture. Try not to demand that your sensuality arrive directly, without mediation. Ask, instead, that it come to you through an inhuman hole. Imagine that sensuality is always *in the next room*. To reach the realm of tactile satisfaction, you must find a way to tunnel into the next room. Easiest passageway might be obtained through sawing a hole in the wall or floor or ceiling.

26 Feminism contains glory holes. One glory hole leads into Marxism.

Another allows entrance into psychoanalysis. Imagine that political movements and intellectual discourses are rooms that "give" onto each other not through doorways but through illegitimately-carved holes. To travel easily between discourses, imagine yourself not as human but as animal, as an adaptable creature, capable of condensing your body to squeeze through a draconian opening.

27 Sight is a confinement, a harrowing, a labor. The alternative—blindness—has its own thorns, and we certainly prefer seeing, with its bewildering possibilities and exactions.

28 A relation exists between a guillotine and urination, though I don't have the power at this moment to explain the nebulous link.

29 Kafka's vision of a penal colony unwittingly responds to Sade's system; both writers describe situations of fascinated horror, and they also describe *the compulsion to describe*. We who film and we who describe are Sade's—and Kafka's—inheritors, creating boxes, condensing experience into willed, enumerated reenactments.

30 Myths irradiate a woman who performs a supposedly menial act; perhaps different myths—more or less noxious?—envelop a man executing the same task, an act that, like most human performances, menial or otherwise, stints on transcendence, doling it out a dram at a time, and then revoking it.

31 Andrea Dworkin long ago described the segmentation of women's bodies—through the beauty industries—into areas requiring treatment, upkeep, and ministration; fetishism multiples the bodily sites demanding laborious cosmetic attention. The beauty industries diversify our consciousness by splitting it into segments—lip, eyebrow, thigh, toenail—and into the many possible products (and brands) aimed at improving these microclimates. Marvel at the weary expense of spirit in service to compartmentalized flesh. We can't singlehandedly choose to "buck the system" and denude ourselves of segmented consciousness. We can, however, notice the flow of energies and supplies around the segments—assembly lines roping through manifold apertures. And we can regret this flow. We can wish ourselves immunity from its toxicities. Any flow is liable to be turned into capital. Water or air—these, too, succumb. Paradise, we surmise, is absolute stillness, without capitalizable flow. (Or is stillness itself a reified, marmoreal falseness? And do we now long again, with a recidivist's surrender, for promiscuous flow?)

 Detail of *u11*, 2010; graphite, acrylic, colored pencil on paper

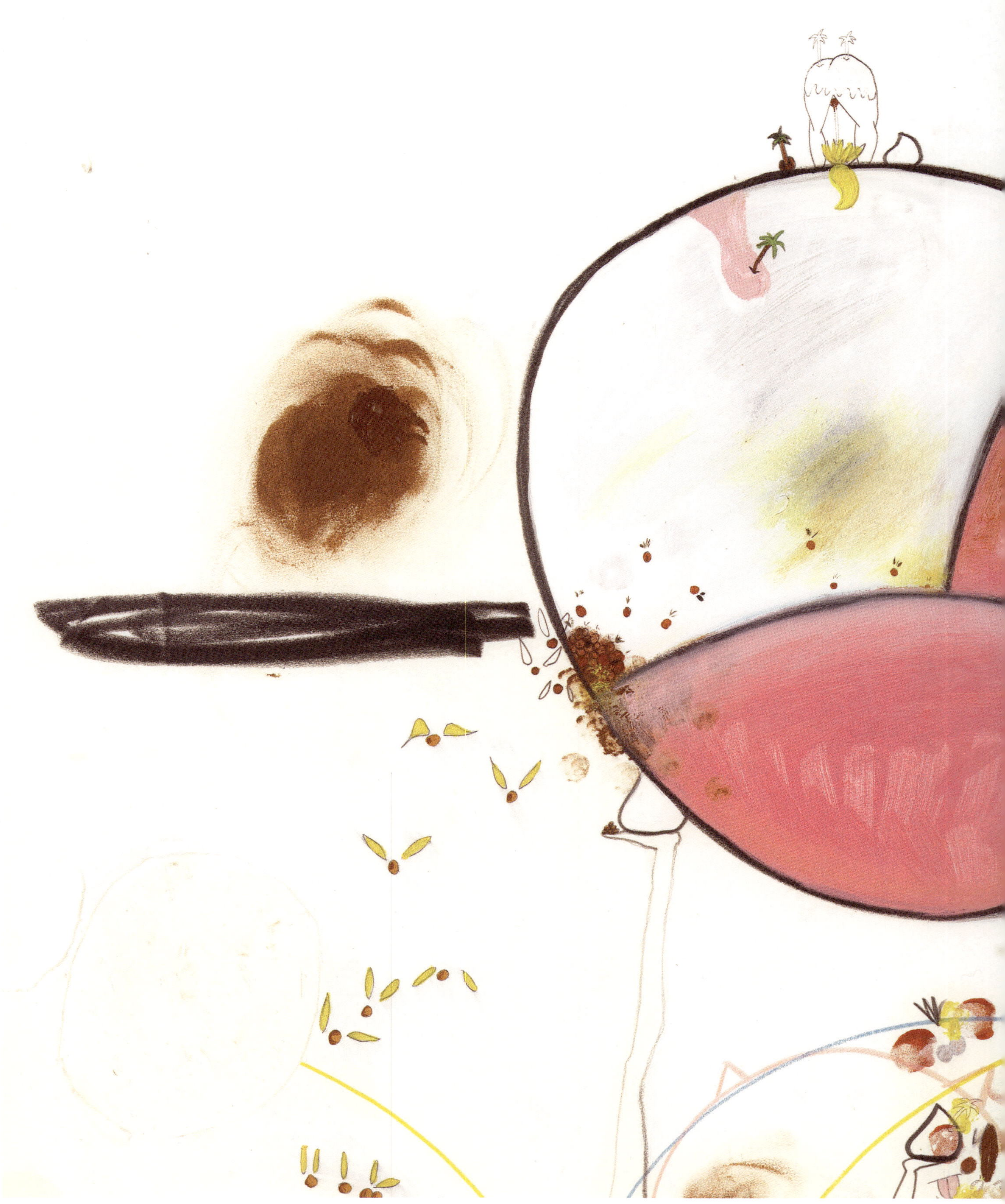

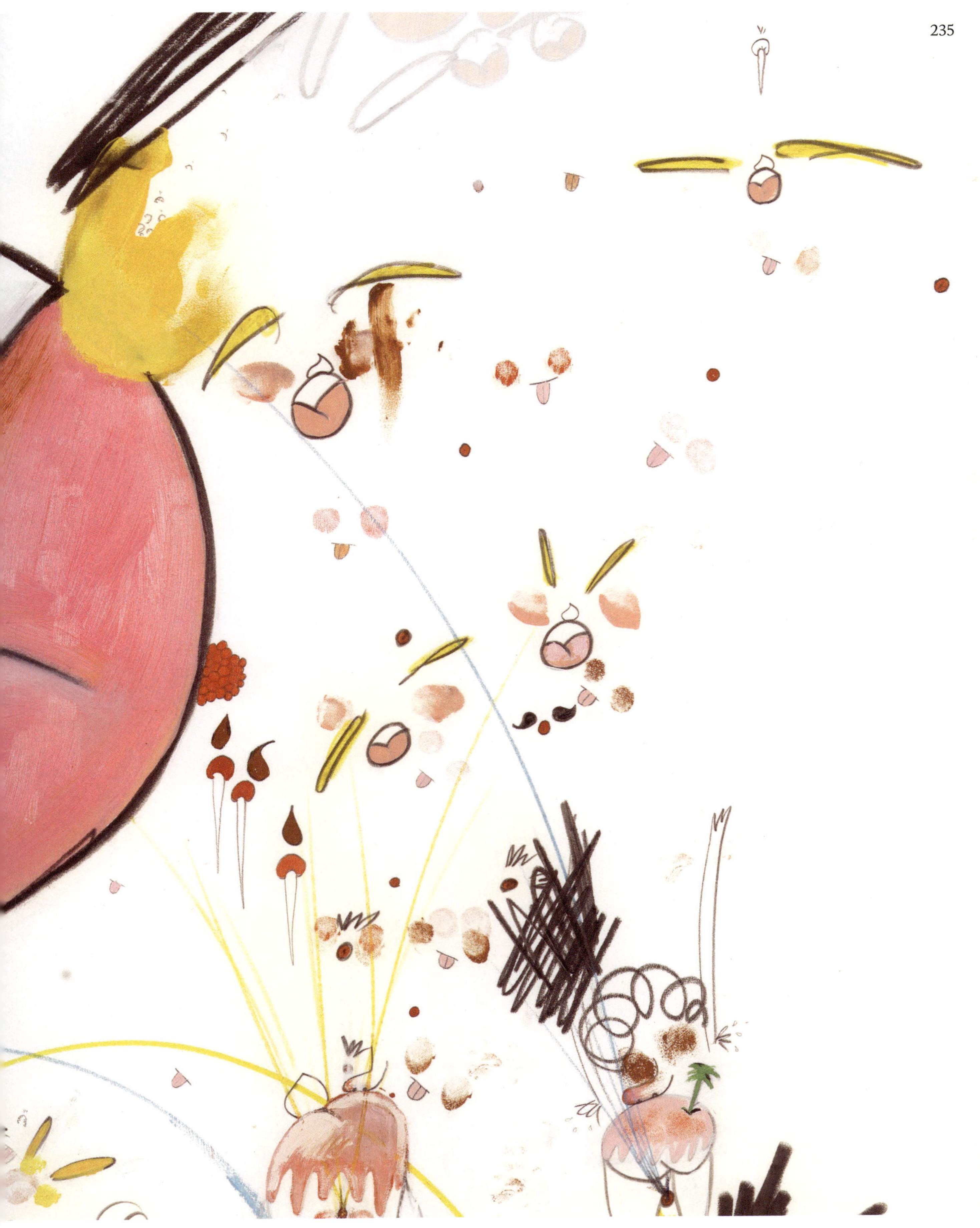

32 The tongue not only receives moisture but gives it. *Drool* is one unattractive term for what the tongue bestows. Can we interpret *spittle* as benedictory? Must *spittle* be derisive, a waste product?

33 I have a pair of buttocks. *My* buttocks. They are attached to my body. They are an outgrowth of my legs. But are these buttocks also not-mine? Are they not also a concept, a shared resource of which I am temporary caretaker?

34 In the middle of a noisy situation, quietness might suddenly emerge. During this surprising interlude, we might find ourselves listening to the earth—the sounds the ground makes when it doesn't know that we are eavesdropping.

35 Sweat and urine—two of the body's liquid byproducts—have no consciousness of themselves. Sweat emerges without a narrative (*I am sweat*). Available to us is the sentence *I am sweaty*, but sweat itself cannot narrate, in the first person, its own story. Same goes for urine. What stories urine could tell, if it were allowed to speak!

36 When water, or another kind of liquid, passes over sheets of clothing, paper, or any surface (whether sheer or dimpled), the water offers commentary on the surface. The water, setting up a relation to the surface, might berate: the water (if we could hear it speak) might be hectoring the surface over which it streams. It might be praising the surface, or forgiving it.

37 Human skin doesn't contain transcendence, singularity, or self-consciousness. Human skin—like any textile, leaf, or bark—is a clumsy vehicle, without intrinsic merit. Because we recognize its likeness to pulp or paper, we might devalue this wily membrane that protects our vascular system. Seen uncharitably, our own skin becomes a *second person* encasing us; we pity our skin, a site of the not-I. Our skin, we believe, is forlorn, because we have ejected it, exiled it from our inner ark, and deemed it a ratty coating rather than a numinous essence.

38 Production, an unsolvable labyrinth, never ends. Or else the assembly line of production—the movement of natural goods into unnatural products—culminates in a wilderness, a death-night, *Todnacht*, where human multiplicity gets condensed and concentrated. I don't want to use the term "concentration camp" metaphorically—we have been instructed

never to use it as mere figure of speech—but we inevitably notice analogical relations between incommensurate procedures. Inspired by the work of Giorgio Agamben, we beg the right to hypothesize—even if we dismiss the awful hunch after first glimpsing it—that the capitalist model of production (extracting product from natural beings) belongs to the same world as the anti-human logarithm of concentration camps, extinguishing under the guise of producing.

[*Sneeze*]

39 When I sneeze, pieces of me come out of my mouth.

40 My relation to the Internet is diseased: it's as if I've sneezed out all the particles that come streaming back to me through the web.

41 Out my mouth, when I sneeze, comes a light bulb, a steak, a rabbit, and then another rabbit. Out my mouth, when I sneeze, comes the Internet. The entire contents of Google come out my mouth, but they seem to be *out there*, on the screen, external to my inner matrix of motivations and urgencies, that ugly cluster we call my "I."

42 My nose gets bigger and bigger, every time I sneeze. I begin the episode as a young man, but by the time my sneezing attacks are finished, I've grown old.

43 Sneezing, unlike childbirth, produces no creature or flotsam capable of consciousness. (Is spittle conscious?)

44 The problem with the shattered or split self (what Melanie Klein once called the ego "in bits") is that its pieces seem to be *out there*, where scapegoating occurs—the land of the not-self, the externalized, the world. Consciousness is, like sneezing, a continual (and Sisyphean) project of externalizing self's sputum into diverse particles. The particles of information that adhere to the world's wall, like sputum clumps or like hits (sites?) on the Internet, are centripetally scattered objects that don't inspire love—only anger or envy. You can't love the sputum your "self" has thrust (with a sneeze) onto the wall; you can only wish that your spirit had the moist glamour and externality of the sneezed-out, rabbit-like crud on the wall.

 Detail of *s26*, 2008; graphite, acrylic, colored pencil on paper

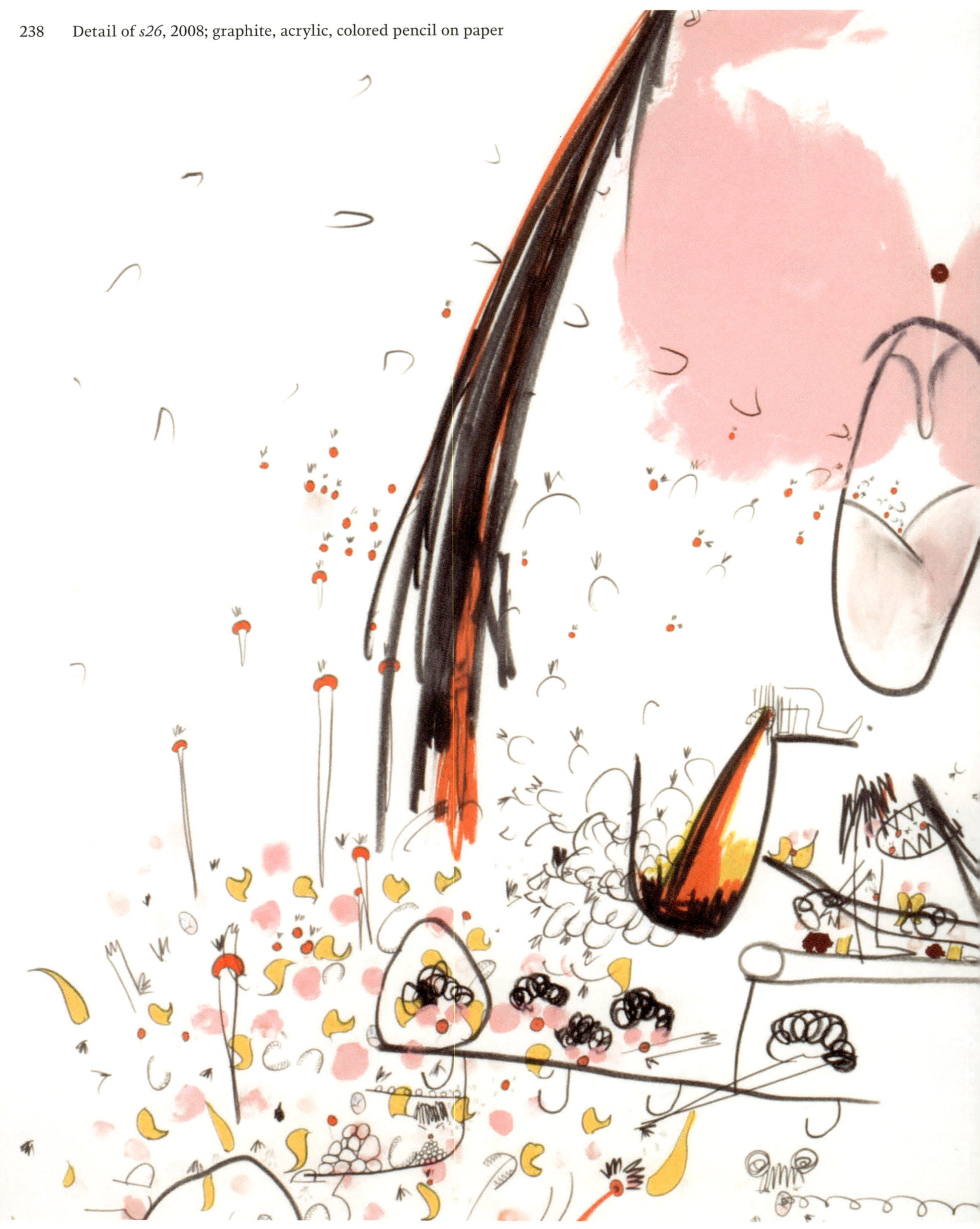

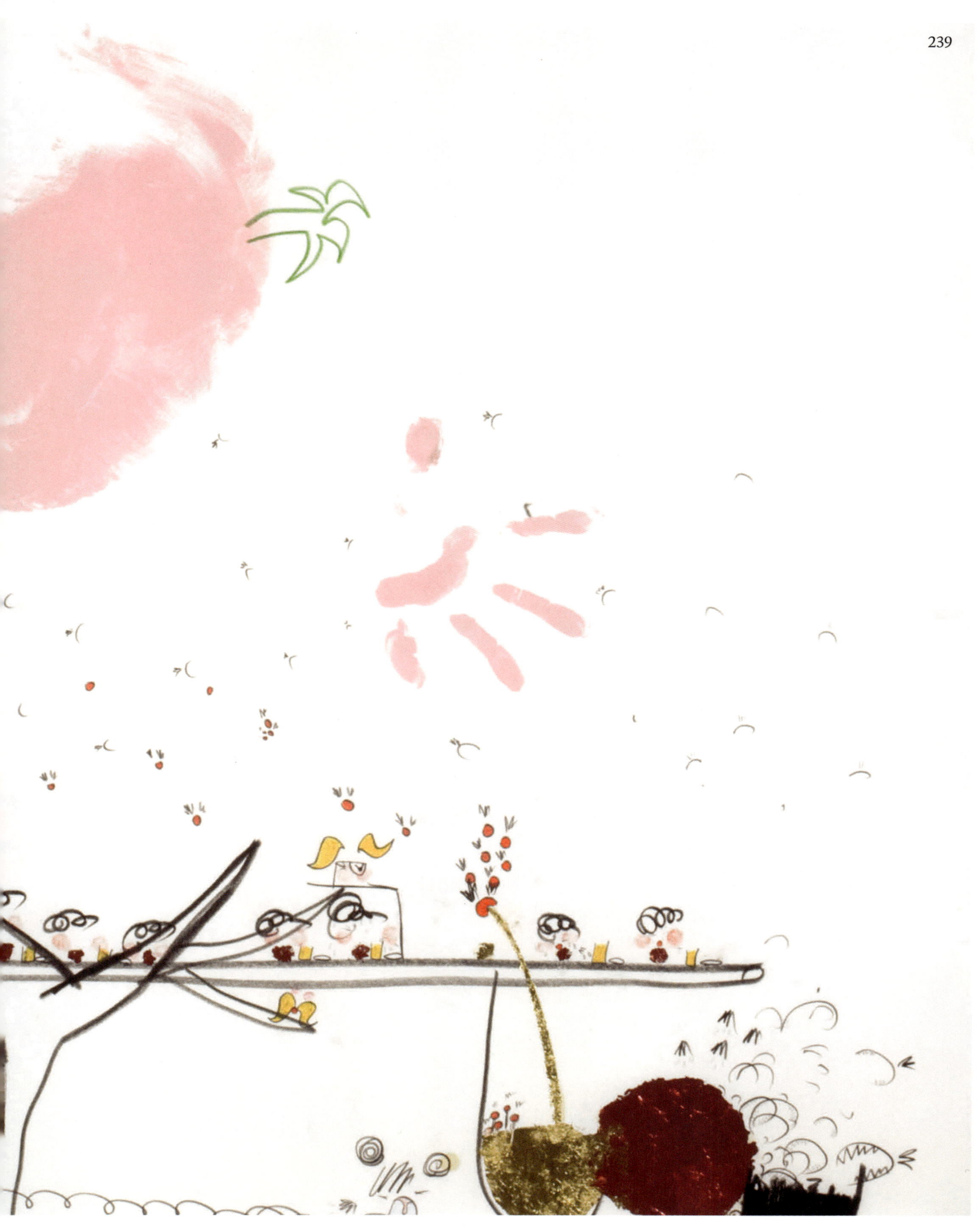

45 Realism, as an artistic technique, is good at helping us appreciate strange faces. (Every face, if seen properly, is strange.)

46 Exceptionally acute realistic art redefines strangeness by helping us see its canyons and runnels as picturesque. (I allude to acne.)

[*SEVEN*]

47 I'm jealous of people who flow. I'm jealous of people who walk quickly. I'm jealous of people who live far from the hype of commodity. I'm jealous of commodities—their shiny self-sufficiency, their immunity to my craving for them.

48 We are walking toward a sunrise; we don't know what narrative encases us in its bossy grip.

49 The sun is gradually rising, no thanks to us; our labor didn't help the sun rise, though we profit from its light.

50 We are drinking a hot beverage. Needn't explain why we're always drinking the same hot beverage. Because we desire immunity from *overstory* (concept, narrative, history), we seek refuge in art. Art frees us from explanation. Or it delays explanation's arrival. Synopsis, when it arrives, destroys our calm. Again and again, I make the mistake of generalizing about "art;" the work of art lures us into wondering why we love it and why we fear everything that is *not* art. We dread any impediment that distracts us from single-mindedly focusing on art's ability to make hibernation seem an ethical good. Even art that insists on human interconnectiveness might demonstrate a formal tropism toward the monastic cubicle; this tropism—toward the procedural, the sealed-off—seems cool on the surface but hides a hot interior.

51 Duration is itself an object of beauty; maybe Leibniz had duration in mind when he used the word *extension*. I might be wrong, but when I think of time's ability to stretch out—a moment becomes a minute, and then two minutes, and then five, and then an hour—I think of the word *extension*, and of Leibniz, and of monads placed one by one along a circumference or edge. When we take a long walk (on a desert plain, a sidewalk, a savannah, a mountain path) we put our footsteps together into a linear composition of extensiveness, and someone conceptualizing our journey, or someone watching it in a film, could call our journey a *duration*, a beautiful, observable thing.

52 Just because we wear a shirt that says *Adidas* doesn't mean we worship Adidas. Logos have a life separate from what they represent. Can we pinpoint the moment in history when logos began? And, if the logo has a scene of origin, could we imagine *the day before the first logo* as a radiant prelapsarian threshold? Start visualizing *the day before the first logo.*

53 Shakespeare described the human being as "a poor, bare, forked animal." Naked, houseless man is especially forked. In *King Lear*, the homeless king has lost the logo of Lear, though his language now wears the logo of the Shakespearean and thus affords him shelter. Cast inside a sentence, the outcast achieves housing. If you are a man with a beard, and if you pull on that beard, and if you compose a sentence that contains "beard," then you have obtained a meager foothold, one stop on the train past the hell of the bare and the forked.

54 To avoid the fate of the stunted tree, we need to find a way to labor. We don't want our products to be stolen from us; nor do we wish to forfeit the time we spend laboring. Time itself is our possession, and when we rent ourselves out so that our labor might be extracted from us, we lose our birthright. And yet, to avoid hunger and exposure, and to experience the satisfaction of process, we need to labor and we need to find a context for what we labor on.

55 I am struggling to describe the dignity of labor, the silence of labor, the stillness of labor, the genderlessness and freakishness of labor, the picturesqueness of labor, the wetness and dryness of labor, the compression and comedy and incomprehensibility of labor. ... If we have the privilege of watching a video of labor, we might imagine that the task unfolds for our benefit. But we must not assume an equivalence between labor as experienced by the laborer, and labor as witnessed by another person. *Labor* is a loose word, and I want to keep it loose, to accommodate all varieties of work, and to acknowledge travail's Biblical pedigree.

56 Imagine labor without boredom. Impossible? A tragic intensity of numbness arises from alienated action.

57 Cut through boredom by showing a man's underwear rising above the horizon of jeans. The man might be conscious of his own underwear as vista. He might conceptualize *underwear* as momentary liberation from labor's meaninglessness, its lack of context. Eroticism is the antidote to dull work.

 Detail of *s25*, 2008; graphite, acrylic, colored pencil on paper

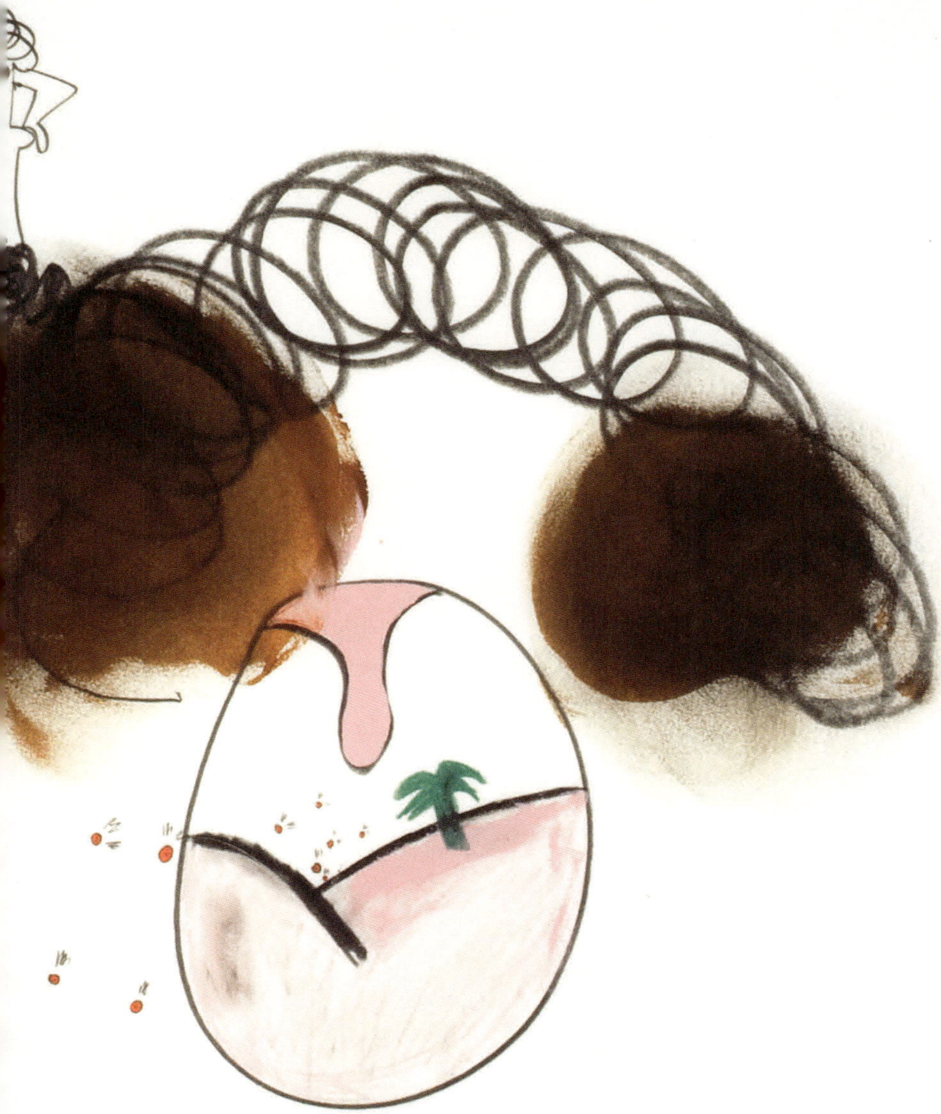

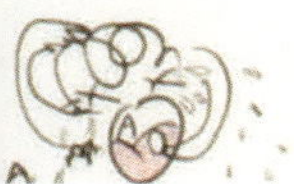

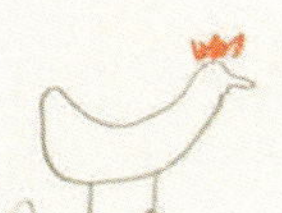

58 Observe a persistent flaw in my logic: *eroticism is the antidote.* I assume, here, that eroticism arrives, as rescuer, on an already existing scene; eroticism, I seem to assert, does not precede boredom but arises subsequently, like an alien visitor, to interrupt a dismal situation. But where did I get the idea that eroticism arrives, corrects, and interrupts? Perhaps, instead, eroticism waits, sleeps, festers, disintegrates. … Perhaps eroticism isn't a thing, a noun, a discernible form. Instead, eroticism is the movement of the equation itself, and a grim equation at that.

59 Feces are an apt analog to labor's products. Food travels through the body's factory and enjoys a process of compression and transformation. When the compressed substance leaves the body—with a squeeze, a bang, a flash, at some cost, at a protracted or fleet tempo—we can behold the result or we can turn our back on it and send it down the underground kingdom to an invisible destination. We don't purchase feces; we expel and repress them. No one watches the ceremony—except the fetishist, parent, or caretaker. We don't have a way of thinking feces, except by not thinking. Mayhap we're always thinking feces. Whatever Disneyland means or meant to you, whatever Disneyland symbolizes, is a near neighbor to feces—the movement of unregarded life, laboring to produce a phantasmagoria.

60 When we see a phenomenal spectacle (I'm thinking of Tinkerbell's fireworks at Disneyland, which I visited as a child), and we clap, we acknowledge that the spectacle is external to ourselves, that we are beholding an expelled, alien object, an object we further distance ourselves from by clapping it away. (Is expulsion the underside of applause?) Seeing a sublime spectacle, we stand at an alienated remove. Our position *outside the spectacle* accords us safety (we might be demolished if we were to enter the display and become one with it), but we are in a position of "bare, forked" homelessness, compared to the at-home plenitude of the witnessed fireworks.

61 Labor goes up, down, right, left; south, north, east, west; underground, aboveground; in circles. Into holes. Into undefined space. Even the treadmill is directional—the labor continues in time, and sends an arrow forward into the future. And what the treadmill produces—sweat, heat—can be quantified, and can be transformed, at least theoretically, into yet another form. And to the extent that labor must *travel*, that it must proceed along a trajectory, then it can't remain at rest within itself as a self-aware, self-nourished entity. Labor is thus impoverished—denuded—by its insistence on going somewhere, sending its products elsewhere. Labor, perpetually in the export business, denies its own body by always producing a supplement.

62 I'm not a philosopher, but I often pose as a philosopher—a pose for which I feel unremitting guilt.

63 Visual images can produce introspection, but they can't describe it. Watching someone engage in labor, we see only the labor, and not the inner narrative that accompanies it.

64 I'm wrong to expect exaltation from what I watch. And yet I keep expecting it. As if exaltation were the only reward, the only comfort. Perhaps I should seek equilibrium—tranquility-unto-paralysis—instead of jolts and spasms.

65 One touchstone for the cinema of watching women at work—in what seems like real time—is Chantal Akerman's *Jeanne Dielman, 23, quai du Commerce, 1080 Bruxelles*. From watching Delphine Seyrig making meatloaf we don't expect exaltation. And yet what if we receive it? How do we describe ourselves if we experience exaltation watching Delphine Seyrig make meatloaf?

66 A half-smile might appear on the face of the woman immersed in an apparently pointless process of making.

67 If we look at history by means of the objects it scatters on thought's horizon, then we have a dolmen-inflected relation to truth; we ask monuments (implicitly funerary) for navigational advice. We could call the dolmen-inflected relation to history a primarily *elegiac* intelligence—a mind that depends on the somber agency of afterimages. If, on the other hand, we can bear to look at history directly, without the dolmens it sets up as leftovers and symbolizations, then we might be said to have no intelligence at all, but to be a sourceless and untenanted irreducibility. Maybe when Deleuze and Guattari wrote about *lines of flight* they were hypothesizing the possibility of this emanation, a pure migration without a homeland to back it up.

68 We work very hard to produce very little and we are proud of the very little because it is what J. Halberstam has called "the queer art of failure," an art that celebrates how much work went into making so little.

69 We are not part of a factory assembly-line, as far as we can tell, but we are subject to the laws of factory consciousness; we operate within the commodity system. Even our cheerfulness and chattiness is part of the commodity, for, as Marx observed in chapter thirteen of *Capital*, "mere

 Detail of *J6*, 2011; graphite, acrylic, colored pencil on paper

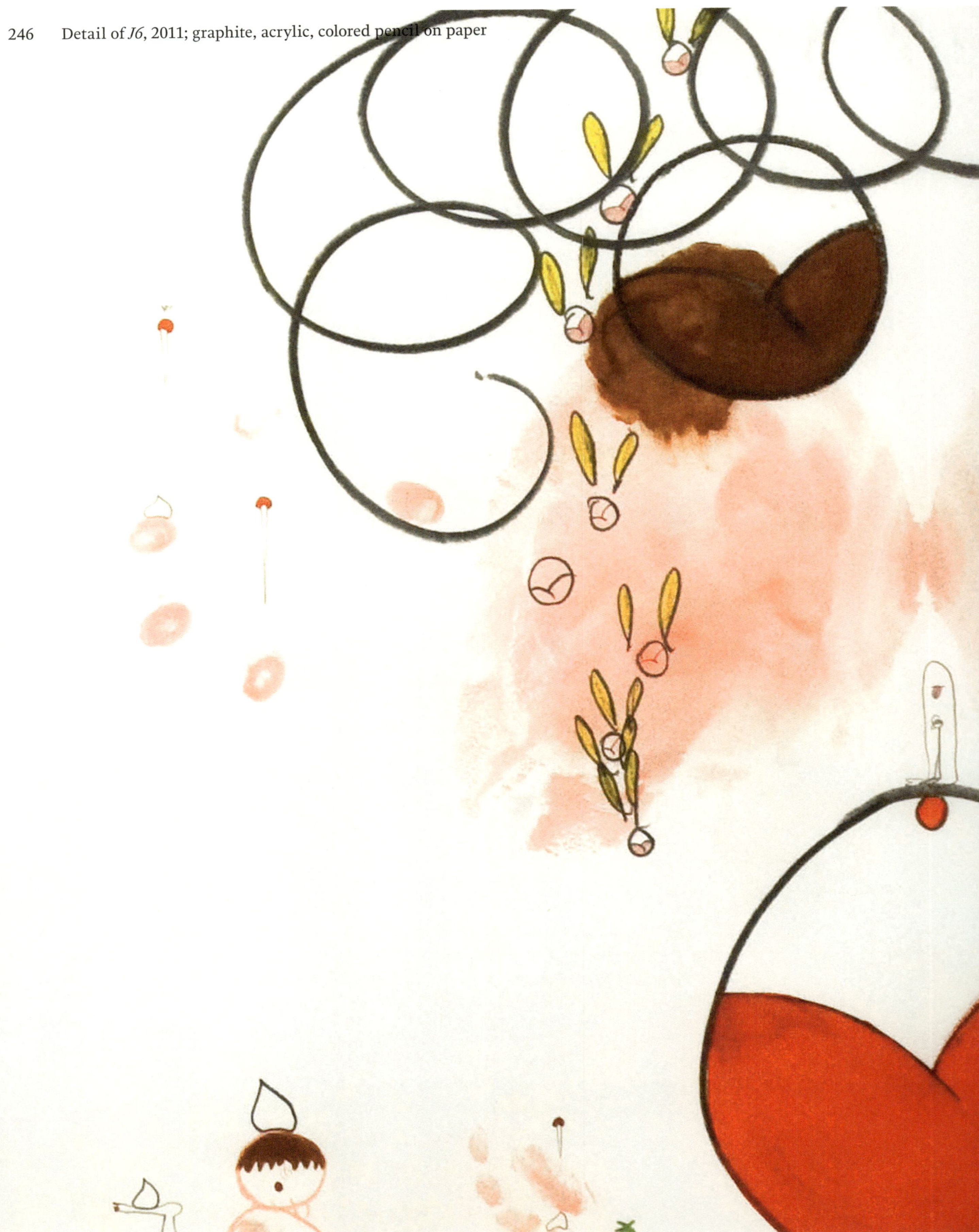

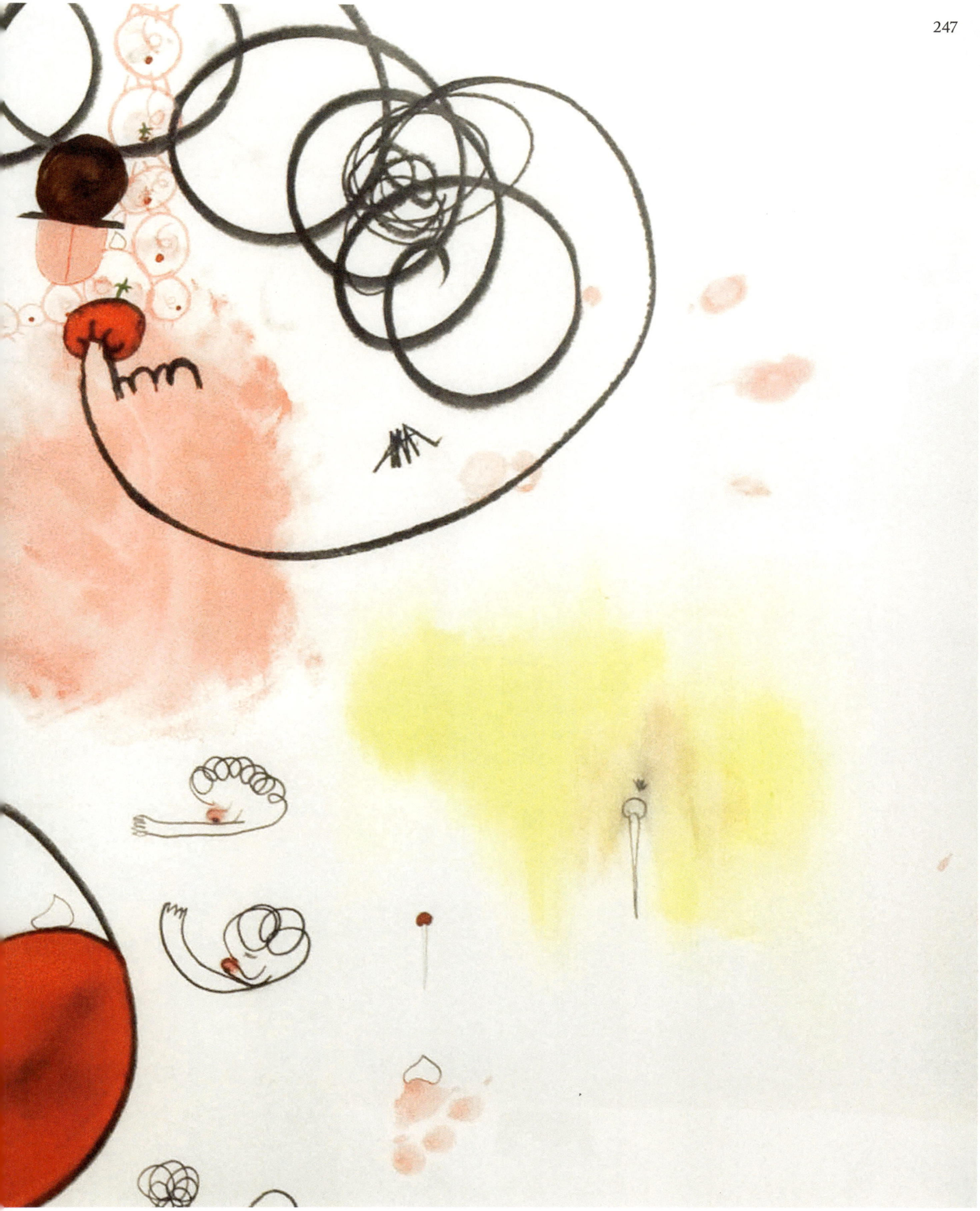

social contact begets in most industries a rivalry and a stimulation of the 'animal spirits,' which heightens the efficiency of each individual worker. This is why a dozen people working together will produce far more, in their collective working day of 144 hours[,] than twelve isolated men each working for 12 hours, and far more than one man who works 12 days in succession."

70 Can we be patient enough to sit still and to obey? (Questions besiege the dolmen-inflected intelligence, the kind of mind that Yeats called "gong-tormented.") Which forces should we obey and which should we rebel against? Should we rebel against the plurality of pockmarks on the earth's surface? Which bodies are privileged and which are not? Who is the scientist and who is the artist? What is the difference between intermediary steps and the final product? Is "final" a ruined word, given the shadow of *die Endlösung* (final solution)? Is awareness of genocidal logic, even when it emerges on the playground, a form of ridiculously hypersensitive vigilance? To stay attuned to the most frightening applications of the simplest procedures is a *gong-tormented* way of making art and of interpreting it.

71 The worker, not solitary, participates in the collaborative ecological project of bringing the goods to market. Is each worker equivalent, or is each worker (and each moment of work) different? If the rule of the monad dominates every artistic or ethical act, then every action, whether on the assembly line or in the artist's studio, is different from every other action, as Leibniz, who wrote the rulebook, declared, in *Monadology*: "Indeed, every monad must be different from every other. Because in nature there are never two beings that are perfectly alike, and between which it is not possible to discover some difference which is internal, or founded on an intrinsic denomination." Ethically attuned art registers differences even within sameness. Ethically attuned art, like a deli on the Lower East Side a century ago, is *appetizing*. Ethically attuned art (brand it *E.A.A.*?) animates and affirms appetite by observing each monad's textured distinctiveness, even if squeamish palates find its texture disturbing.

72 I have chosen not to speak directly of Mika Rottenberg's extraordinary work but to speak about it in reflection—to allow her work to cast a shadow on me, and then to record the shape of that shadow. My indirection is a lifetime's practice—of reticence, evasion, timidity. Call it an askesis. I enter a work of art to be disciplined by it; writing about the work, I describe the severe constraints it has put my body under. I need to mirror that bondage in the form my writing takes. And therefore the writing needs to obey certain limits. One of the first constraints is the injunction to *look away*

from the artwork while looking at it, to perform an act of double vision—looking toward, looking away. A second constraint is the injunction to relate to the work of art as if it were utterly separate from its maker, as if, in fact, it had no maker. (Often I disobey this rule.) In Rottenberg's case, I have chosen to mirror her work in my own words rather than to step outside her work and comment on it; perhaps I returned to this procedure because of the artist's name, which resembles the name of someone I once bottomlessly loved. The memory of the night he first made his body available to me is tenacious enough to bind me still, while I write about Mika Rottenberg, and to compel me into a situation of linguistic constraint, so that I can echo the effect of that love affair, a situation of looking toward and looking away.

[*Cheese*]

73 As always, when I write about art, I make the mistake of focusing on content and not on materials. A more straightforward reckoning of Rottenberg's video work would acknowledge the sculptural installations in which it is screened, and would address specificities of editing, lighting, sound, duration. My method, however, has always been to seek rigor through the back door, as if language must blindfold itself and pretend not to be handling the goods.

74 More questions assail the gong-tormented mind. What are the cultural meanings of long hair? What sounds do lambs and ducks and goats make? Can we always distinguish between urine and milk? Do we shake out our long hair to cleanse it of flies and muck? Do Rapunzel and Mélisande corner the market on mythic women with long hair?

75 I dreamt I was required to teach a high school math class, but I stopped showing up after the first couple of days. I asked the high school receptionist for a ledger book that listed class times; in it, I saw the word *DISAPPEARED* written by my name.

76 I disappear under my heavy mane of hair.

77 If we envy the freedom of barnyard animals, then we need to find specific ways to put that envy into practice, and to import freedom into our straitened lives. Additionally, we need to interrogate the notion of *animal* and the notion of *freedom*. Start by interrogating *animal*. Don't assume

 Detail of *m30*, 2011; graphite, acrylic, colored pencil on paper

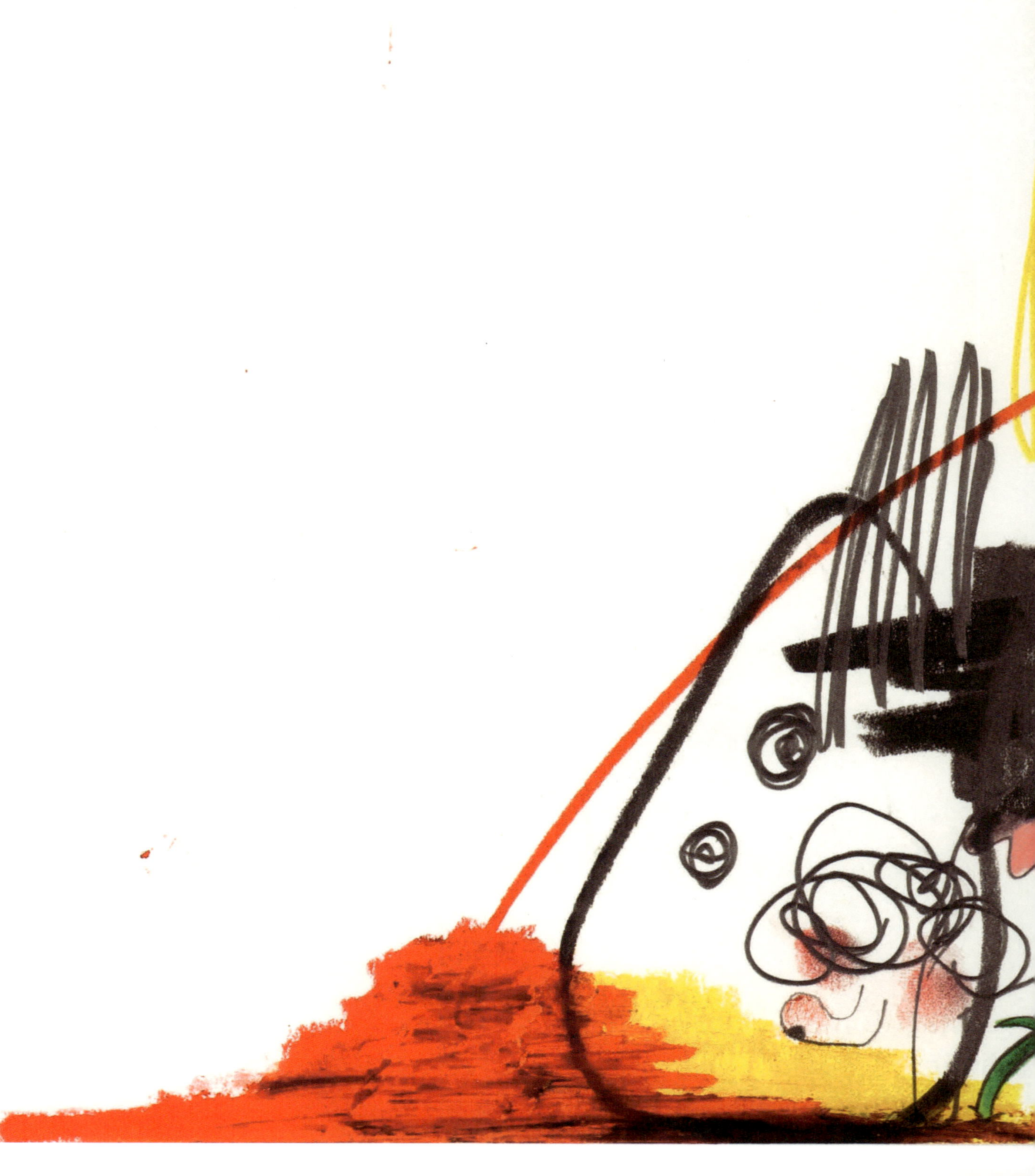

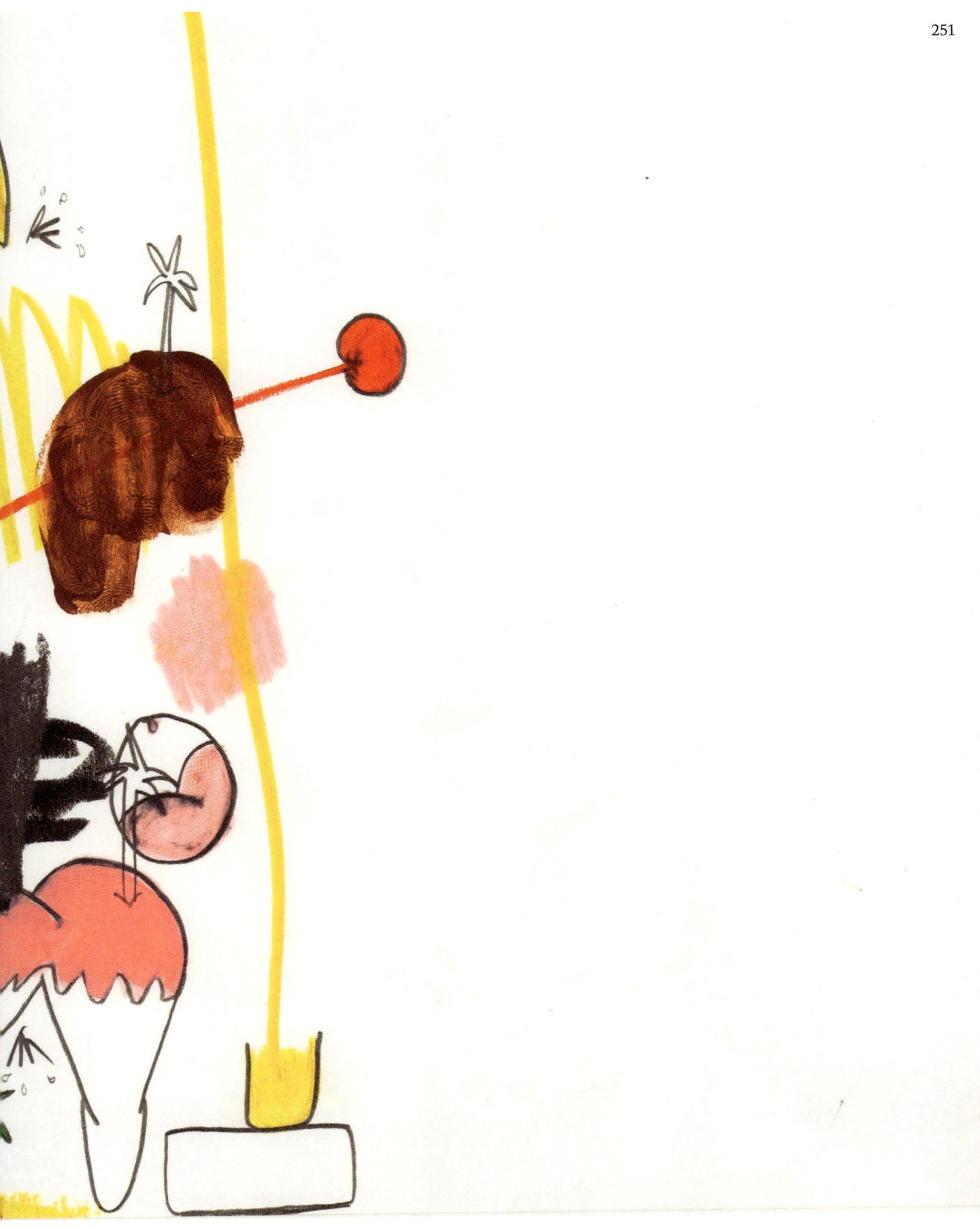

that we, as gong-tormented beings, aren't also and primarily animal. The concept *freedom* is the cheese we produce from our gong-tormented minds.

78 We make hair tonic from our hair; we make melancholy from our melancholy, elation from our elation. From the natural object itself we extract a commodity, a distillation. If hair produces hair tonic (within the fable that Rottenberg's video renovates), then melancholy produces the ability to become more melancholy, and consummation (complex ideas condensed into a discrete artifact, whether poem, video, or bouillon cube) produces a hunger for similarly consummated objects. In this condensation-driven world, where all differences are squeezed together into portable, comestible, market-ready cubes, every process seeks the Armageddon—the endpoint—that we call consummation, as if the answer to the conundrum of free will versus destiny were as simply obtained as bouillon, pickles, or cheese.

79 Aristotle compared cheese-making to human conception. (I learned this fact from social anthropologist Sandra Ott's article, "Aristotle Among the Basques: The 'Cheese Analogy' of Conception," published in a scholarly journal—oddly named *Man*—in December 1979.) Ott quotes from Aristotle's *De generatione animalium*: "When the material secreted by the female in the uterus has been fixed by the semen of the male (this acts in the same way as rennet acts upon milk, for rennet is a kind of milk containing vital heat, which brings into one mass and fixes the similar material. …)—when, I say, the more solid part comes together, the liquid is separated off from it …" The passage is long; Aristotle gets hung up on cheese, can't get his own sentence going. Cheese delays him. If long-haired women joined forces and made cheese collaboratively, maybe Aristotle could finish his sentence, or I could finish quoting it. You see how thinkers slow us down. You see how we're better off playing with our own long hair, whipping each other with our hair, washing it *ad infinitum*.

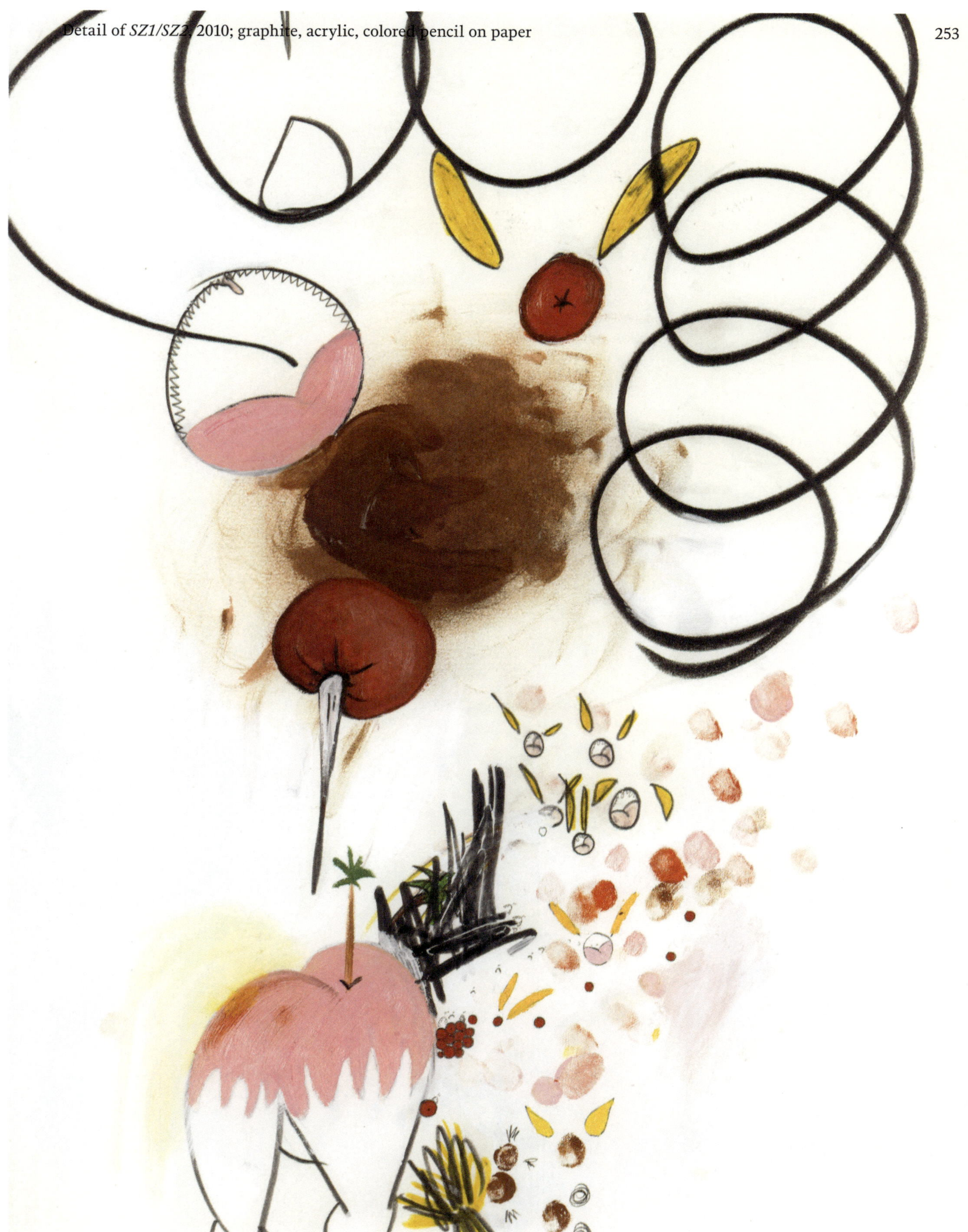

Detail of *SZ1/SZ2*, 2010; graphite, acrylic, colored pencil on paper

Biography

Mika Rottenberg

Born in Buenos Aires, Argentina, 1976
Lives and works in New York, NY

Education

1998 Hamidrasha, Bait Berl College of Arts, Israel

2000 Bachelor of Fine Arts, School of Visual Arts, New York, NY

2004 Master of Fine Arts, Columbia University, New York, NY

Solo Exhibitions

2014 *Bowls Balls Souls Holes*, Andrea Rosen Gallery, New York, NY, May 6–June 14

Mika Rottenberg: Bowls Balls Souls Holes, The Rose Art Museum, Brandeis University, Waltham, MA, February 2–June 8

2013 *Squeeze: Video Works by Mika Rottenberg*, The Israel Museum, Jerusalem, Israel, December 3–April 5

Sneeze to Squeeze, Magasin 3 Stockholm Konsthall, Sweden, February 8–June 2

2012 Galerie Laurent Godin, Paris, France, September 8–October 13

Mary's Cherries, FRAC Languedoc-Roussillon, Montpellier, France, June 7–September 29

Mika Rottenberg, Nottingham Contemporary, Nottingham, UK, May 5–June 1

Infinite #2 (collaboration with Alona Harpaz), Petach Tikva Museum of Art, Israel, February 9–July 22

2011 *Cheese, Squeeze, and Tropical Breeze: Video Works 2003–2010*, M–Museum Leuven, Leuven, Belgium, November 4–February 26, 2012

SEVEN (in collaboration with Jon Kessler), Performa 11 Commission at Nicole Klagsbrun Gallery, New York, NY, November 3–19

Fried Sweat, Tirana Art Center, Tirana, Albania, September 3

Take Ninagawa, Tokyo, Japan, May 14–June 25

Mika Rottenberg: Dough Cheese Squeeze and Tropical Breeze: Video Works 2003–2010, de Appel arts centre, Amsterdam, Netherlands, March 12–May 1

2010 *Squeeze*, Mary Boone Gallery in collaboration with Nicole Klagsbrun Gallery, New York, NY, October 30–December 18

New Work: Mika Rottenberg, San Francisco Museum of Modern Art, San Francisco, CA, July 9–October 3

2009 Galerie Laurent Godin, Paris, France, March 15–April 11

La Maison Rouge, Paris, France, February 18–May 3

Performance Stills, Nicole Klagsbrun Gallery, New York, NY, January 23–February 28

2008 *Drawings*, Nicole Klagsbrun Gallery, New York, NY, May 9–June 7

Infinite #1 (collaboration with Alona Harpaz), Nicole Klagsbrun Gallery, New York, NY, May 9–June 7

2006 *Dough*, KW Institute for Contemporary Art, Berlin, Germany, September 3–November 12

Dough, Nicole Klagsbrun Gallery, New York, January 27–February 25

2005 *Tropical Breeze*, Le Case D'Arte, Milan, Italy, May 5–September 2

2004 *Marta Dell'Angelo and Mika Rottenberg*, Le Case D'Arte, Milan, Italy, November 15–February 18, 2005

Mary's Cherries, Special Projects, P.S.1 Contemporary Art Center, Queens, NY, June 27–September 27

Group Exhibitions

2014 *Harvest*, Gallery of Modern Art, Brisbane, Australia, June 28–September 21

Des nouvelles de la kula, curated by Anne Giffon-Selle, Centre d'arts plastiques de Saint-Fons, Saint-Fons, France, February 21–April 26

2013 *Tell Me Her Story*, curated by Myung ji Bae, Coreana Museum of Art, Space*C, Seoul, Korea, October 17–December 14 (catalogue)

Mom, am I barbarian? 13th Istanbul Biennial, curated by Fulya Erdemci, Istanbul, Turkey, September 14–October 20 (catalogue)

Labor and Subjectivity, curated by Pilar Villela Mascaró, Casa del Lago, Universidad Nacional Autónoma de México (UNAM), Mexico City, Mexico, August 29–January 19, 2014

Labour and Wait, curated by Julie Joyce, Santa Barbara Museum of Art, Santa Barbara, CA, July 2–September 22 (catalogue)

Haim Steinbach: Once Again the World is Flat, CCS Bard Hessel Museum of Art, Annandale-on-Hudson, NY, June 22–December 20

Jew York, Untitled and Zach Feuer, New York, NY, June 20–July 26

The Distaff Side, The Granary, Melva Bucksbaum and Raymond Learsy Collection, Sharon, CT, April 21–present (catalogue)

Theatrical Gestures, Herzliya Museum of Contemporary Art, Herzliya, Israel, January 26–April 20

2012 *Number Three: From home to the factory. Works from the Centre national des arts plastiques*, La Virreina Centre de la Imatge, Barcelona, Spain, May 31–September 30

The Virgin Show, curated by Marilyn Minter, Family Business, New York, NY, February 16–February 25

Bending the Mirror, Columbus College of Art and Design, Columbus, OH, February 10–March 16

Campaign, curated by Amy Smith-Stewart, C24 Gallery, New York, NY, January 24–February 25

A Doll's House, curated by Fani Zguro, Isola Art Center, Milan, Italy, January 30–February 6

2011 *Show Me Your Hair*, Coreana Museum of Art, Seoul, South Korea, October 6–November 30

Daft, Shanghai Gallery of Art, Shanghai, China, September 7–October 1

Once Upon A Time, Deutsche Guggenheim, Berlin, Germany, July 8–October 9

Commercial Break, curated by Neville Wakefield, Garage Projects at the 54th Venice Biennale, Venice, Italy, June 1–November 24

On the Metaphor of Growth, cooperative exhibition of Kunstverein Hannover, Hannover, Germany, April 16–June 26; Kunsthaus Baselland, Muttenz, Switzerland, May 21–July 10; Frankfurter Kunstverein, Frankfurt, Germany, May 27–July 31 (catalogue)

Dark Waters, Station Project, c/o Platform Arts Gallery, Belfast, Northern Ireland, March 3–30

2010 *Christmas Show*, Galerie Laurent Godin, Paris, France, December 10–January 22, 2011

Re-dressing, Bortolami Gallery, New York, NY, September 15–November 6

Home and Origin, Bukowskis, Stockholm, Sweden, September 8–October 1

Foreign Studies, Andréhn-Schiptjenko, Stockholm, Sweden, August 26–October 3 (catalogue)

Sweat, curated by Marilyn Minter, Patricia Low Gallery, Gstaad, Switzerland, August 13–October 10

Workers Leaving the Workplace, curated by Joanna Skolowska, Muzeum Sztuki, Lodz, Poland, July 6–September 5

First group show of Contemporary Tel Aviv Art in the UK, JaffaCakes TLV, London, UK, April 16–May 15

I want to see how you see: Works from the Julia Stoschek Collection, Deichtorhallen, Hamburg, Germany, April 16–July 25 (catalogue)

Grotesque & Arabesque – ny amerikansk videokunst, Kunstnernes Hus, Oslo, Norway, January 30–March 7

Contemplating the Void: Interventions in the Guggenheim Museum, curated by Nancy Spector and David Van Der Leer, Solomon R. Guggenheim Museum, New York, NY, February 12–April 28

Odd Bodies: Selections from the Permanent Collection, Weatherspoon Art Museum at the University of North Carolina at Greensboro, Greensboro, NC, January 24–May 18

2009 *Eating the Universe. Vom Essen in der Kunst*, Kunsthalle Düsseldorf, Düsseldorf, Germany, November 28–February 28, 2010 (catalogue); traveled to Galerie im Taxispalais, Innsbruck, Austria, April 24–July 4, 2010; Kunstmuseum Stuttgart, Germany, September 18, 2010–January 9, 2011

October Show, Transmission Gallery, Glasgow, Scotland, October 10–November 7

A Tribute to Ron Warren, Mary Boone Gallery, New York, NY, September 12–October 24

Strange days and some flowers, Storey Gallery, Lancaster, UK, July 13–October 3

Work Now, Z33, Hasselt, Belgium, June 28–September 27 (catalogue)

Gallery Collection, Take Ninagawa, Tokyo, Japan, June 20–July 25

20 Years, Nicole Klagsbrun Gallery, New York, NY, June 17–July 25

Installations II: Video from the Guggenheim Collections, curated by Nat Trotman, Guggenheim Bilbao, Bilbao, Spain, March 3–January 17

Intemperie, 2. Bienal del Fin del Mundo, curated by Alfons Hug, Ushuaia, Argentina, April 24–May 25 (catalogue)

2008 *The Way Things Go*, Susan Inglett Gallery, New York, NY, November 20–December 20

Pilar Albarracín, Mika Rottenberg and Mickalene Thomas, Andréhn-Schiptjenko, Stockholm, Sweden, November 20–December 21

Creative Time Presents: Seeking Eden Through Illusion, 44 ½, New York, NY, November 15–December 31

Art TLV, curated by Andrew Renton, Tel Aviv, Israel, September 27–October 18

Number Two: Fragile, Julia Stoschek Collection, Düsseldorf, Germany, October 11–August 1 (catalogue)

Whatever's Whatever, curated by Dimitrios Antonitsis, Hydra School Project, Hydra, Greece, July 5–September 30 (catalogue)

Fried Sweat (with Marilyn Minter), Galerie Laurent Godin, Paris, France, March 24–July 26; traveled to Le Case D'Arte, Milan, Italy, March 10–25, 2009

Whitney Biennial 2008, Whitney Museum of American Art, New York, NY, March 6–June 22

Body Collective, Alogon Gallery, Chicago, IL, January 26–February 10

2007 *Americans in New York*, curated by Ami Barak, Galerie Michael Rein, Paris, France, November 24–January 12, 2008

The Rear, Herzliya Biennale, Herzliya Museum of Contemporary Art, Herzliya, Israel, September 23–December 15 (catalogue)

The Irresistible Force, curated by Ben Borthwick and Kerryn Greenberg, Tate Modern, London, UK, September 20–November 25

Welcome to My World, curated by Amy Davila and Matthew Day Jackson, Alexandre Pollazzon Ltd, London, UK, July 13–September 1

Foam of the Daze, Smith-Stewart Gallery, New York, NY, April 20–May 20

The Shapes of Space Part 2, Solomon R. Guggenheim Museum, New York, NY, April 14–September 5

Negatec, curated by Luis Camnitzer, Espacio Fundación Telefónica, Buenos Aires, Argentina, March 20–May 27

Second Moscow Biennale, curated by Nicholas Bourriaud, Moscow, Russia, March 1–April 1 (catalogue)

2006 *Intermittent*, curated by Paul O'Neill and Vaair Claffey, Gallery for One, Dublin, Ireland

New York, Interrupted, curated by Dan Cameron, pkm gallery, Beijing, China, November 18–February 20, 2007

Globalization: Indications, Side Effects, Warnings, Espacio 1414, Santurce, Puerto Rico, November 1–May 1, 2007

Everywhere, Busan Biennale, Busan Museum of Modern Art, Busan, South Korea, September 16–November 25

Remember Who You Are, curated by Amy Smith-Stewart, Mary Boone Gallery, New York, NY, September 7–30

25 Bold Moves, curated by Simon Watson and Craig Hensala, House of Campari, New York, NY, July 14–August 13 (catalogue)

Mid-Life Crisis, curated by Tara Subkoff and Ivana Salander, Salander-O'Reilly Galleries, New York, NY, June 2–23

*pa*per*ing*, Deutsche Bank Lobby Gallery in collaboration with Art in General, New York, NY, April 18–August 5

Survivor, curated by David Rimanelli, Bortolami Dayan, New York, NY, March 11–April 8

The Garden Party, Deitch Projects, New York, NY, March 9–May 20

2005 *Day Labor*, P.S.1 Contemporary Art Center, Queens, NY, October 23–January 9, 2006

KunstFilmBiennale, Cologne, Germany, October 19–24

Look at Me: The Perception of Video, Palazzo delle Papesse – Centro Arte Contemporanea, Siena, Italy, October 15–January 8, 2006

Uncertain States of America: American Art in the Third Millennium, curated by Daniel Birnbaum, Hans Ulrich Obrist, and Gunnar B. Kvaran, Astrup Fearnley Museum of Modern Art, Oslo, Norway, October 8–December 11 (catalogue); traveled to Bard College Center for Curatorial Studies, Annandale-on-Hudson, NY, June 24–September 10, 2006; Serpentine Gallery, London, UK, September 9–October 15, 2006; Reykjavik Art Museum, Reykjavik, Iceland, November 4, 2006–January 21, 2007; Centre for Contemporary Art Ujazdowski Castle, Warsaw, Poland, March 23–May 7, 2007; Le Musée de Sérignan, Montpellier, France; June 23–September 23, 2007

We Are the World, Museo Nacional Centro de Arte Reina Sofía, Madrid, Spain, September 14–18

New Work/New Acquisitions, The Museum of Modern Art, New York, NY, June 29–September 26

Greater New York, P.S.1 Contemporary Art Center, Queens, NY, March 13–September 26 (catalogue)

Art Review 25 Emerging Artists, Phillips de Pury & Company, New York, NY, March 10–24

Paper, Nicole Klagsbrun Gallery, New York, NY, January 29–February 26

Situational Prosthetics, curated by Nate Lowman, New Langton Arts, San Francisco, CA, January 19–February 19

2004 *Economies*, curated by Manuela Gandini, Art&Gallery, Milan, Italy, November 16–January 15, 2005

Always Already Passé, Gavin Brown's enterprise at Passerby, New York, NY, October 2–October 30

We Are the World, The Chelsea Art Museum, New York, NY, June 25–July 31

2003 *Miami Heat*, Placemaker Gallery, Miami, FL

My Sources Say Yes, Guild & Greyshkul Gallery, New York, NY

2002 *Tensionism*, Kenny Schachter's 132 Perry Street, New York, NY, February 8–March 22

2001 *Projects 2001*, Islip Museum, Central Islip, NY

2000 *Paladar*, Cuban Biennial 2000, Havana, Cuba, November 17–January 5, 2001

Short Cuts, The Luggage Store Gallery, San Francisco, CA, June 17–June 22

Short Films and Videos, Stanford University Gallery, Stanford, CA

A.V.A.F.S., *67 Gallery, Brooklyn, NY

1998 *Spring at the End of Summer*, curated by Ellen Ginton, Tel Aviv Museum of Art, Tel Aviv, Israel, August 21–October 17

Collections

Astrup Fearnley Museum of Modern Art, Oslo, Norway

Bard College Center for Curatorial Studies, Annandale-on-Hudson, NY

Fonds national d'art contemporain, Puteaux, France

Fonds régional d'art contemporain (FRAC) Languedoc-Roussillon, Montpellier, France

Fonds régional d'art contemporain (FRAC) Nord-Pas de Calais, Dunkirk, France

Fonds régional d'art contemporain (FRAC) Provence-Alpes-Cote d'Azur, Marseille, France

The Israel Museum, Jerusalem, Israel

Julia Stoschek Collection, Düsseldorf, Germany

La Maison Rouge, Paris, France

The Museum of Modern Art, New York, NY

San Francisco Museum of Modern Art, San Francisco, CA

The Solomon R. Guggenheim Museum, New York, NY

Weatherspoon Art Gallery at the University of North Carolina at Greensboro, Greensboro, NC

Whitney Museum of American Art, New York, NY

Awards

2014 Ruth Ann and Nathan Perlmutter Artist-in-Residence Award, The Rose Art Museum, Brandeis University

2011 Sommerakademie im Zentrum Paul Klee, Bern, curated by Pipilotti Rist Planete Doc Film Festival Selection, Warsaw

2010 The Flaherty International Film Seminar Fellow

New Vision Programme Selection, CPH: DOX Film Festival, Copenhagen

2009 5x5 Castello 09 Prize Finalist, Espai d'Art Contemporani de Castello, Spain

2006 The Cartier Award, in conjunction with the Frieze Art Fair

2004 The Rema Hort Mann Foundation

2002 The Dean Fellowship, Columbia University

2001 Projects 2001 Award, Islip Museum

Bibliography

Monograph

2011 Van Duyn, Edna, ed. *Mika Rottenberg* [Contributions by Ann Demeester, Hsuan L. Hsu, Efrat Mishori, and Linda Williams]. New York and Amsterdam: Gregory R. Miller & Co. and de Appel arts centre.

Exhibition Catalogues

2013 Amado, Liz Erçevik, ed. *13th Istanbul Biennial. Mom, am I a barbarian?* Istanbul: Istanbul Foundation for Culture and Arts, Yapi Kredi Publications.

Joyce, Julie, ed. *Labour & Wait*. Santa Barbara: Santa Barbara Museum of Art.

Make active choices. Kunst und ökologie: Wie Tun? Frieburg: Museum für Neue Kunst.

Mika Rottenberg: Sneeze to Squeeze. Stockholm: Magasin 3 Stockholm Konsthall.

Bae, Myung ji. *Tell Me Her Story*. Seoul: Coreana Museum of Art.

2010 Holzhey, Magdalena. *Eating the Universe. Vom Essen in der Kunst*. Cologne: DuMont Buchverlag.

2009 Bronfen, Elisabeth. *Julia Stoschek Collection. Number Two: Fragile*. Ostfildern: Hatje Cantz.

2008 Huldisch, Henriette, and Shamim M. Momin. *Whitney Biennial 2008*. New York: The Whitney Museum of American Art.

2007 Molok, Nikolai, ed. *2nd Moscow Biennale of Contemporary Art: Footnotes on Geopolitics, Market, and Amnesia*. Moscow: ArtChronika.

The Rear: The 1st Herzliya Biennial of Contemporary Art. Herzliya: The Department of Culture, Youth and Sports.

2006 *Uncertain States of America*. Oslo: Astrup Fearnley Museum of Modern Art.

Books

2013 Heartney, Eleanor, et al. *The Reckoning: Women Artists of the New Millennium*. New York: Prestel.

2012 Ilfeld, Etan Jonathan. *Beyond Contemporary Art*. London: Vivays.

2010 Wilson, Michael. “Subject to Change: Yoshitomo Nara and American Culture.” In *Yoshitomo Nara: Nobody’s Fool*, edited by Melissa Chiu and Miwako Tezuka. New York: Abrams, 229–239.

2007 Chong, Doryun, et al. *World’s Best New Art: Unreal Projects*. Nuremberg: Verlag Für Moderne Kunst Nürnberg.

Selected Articles, Interviews, and Reviews

2014 Smee, Sebastian. “The Rose’s gifts to us: Chutes, tongues, Erector sets.” *Boston Globe*, February 22.

2013 Rottenberg, Mika. Interview. *Artlover* 15: 22–25.

Rubin, Birgitta. “Absurda och hyllade videoverk.” *DN.se, Dagens Nyheter*, August.

Donelan, Charles. “Making and Meaning.” *The Independent*, July 18, p. 55.

Woodard, Josef. “Work Ethics, Revisited and Real-ized.” *Scene Magazine*, July 12–18: 47–48.

Jones, Ronald. “Mika Rottenberg.” *Artforum*, April: 277–278.

Ivanov, Alida. “Brutal Reality.” *Arterritory.com*, February 14.

Hurwitz, Laurie. “Mika Rottenberg.” *ARTnews*, January: 108.

2012 Griffin, Jonathan. “Rudely Transgressing the Boundaries Between the Elevated and the Profane.” *Tate Etc.*, Issue 26, Autumn.

Rottenberg, Mika. Interview. *The Believer*, October: 72–76.

Harbison, Isobel. “Image Games.” *Frieze*, October.

Rottenberg, Mika. “Paroles d’Artiste: Mika Rottenberg,” (interview). *Le Journal des Arts*, September.

Sherwin, Skye. “Artist of the week 191: Mika Rottenberg.” *The Guardian*, May 24.

Cumming, Laura. “Mika Rottenberg; James Gillray - review.” *The Observer*, May 6.

Rottenberg, Mika. Interview. *Monopol*, January 29.

2011 Rosenberg, Karen. “Sweating Chakras.” *Art in America*, November.

Smith, Roberta. “Art in Review: Mika Rottenberg and Jon Kessler, *SEVEN*.” *The New York Times*, November 10.

Boucher, Brian. “Performa Playbill: Mika Rottenberg and Jon Kessler.” *ArtinAmericaMagazine.com*, November 7.

Sutton, Benjamin. “Performa 11: Mika Rottenberg and Jon Kessler Harvest Bodily Fluids.” *The L Magazine*, November 7.

McGarry, Kevin. “Now Showing: Mika Rottenberg.” *Tmagazine.blogs.nytimes.com*, November 2.

Daly, Hannah. “Exercise Becomes Ritual.” *Artslant.com*, November 6.

Miller, Michael. “A Unique Art Opening Turns Sweat into Chakra at Nicole Klagsbrun Project Space.” *The New York Observer*, November 4.

Laster, Paul. “A+ Book Pick: Mika Rottenberg.” *Artspace.com*, September 7.

Levin, Kim. “Talking Trash.” *ARTNews*, June.

Vermij, George. “Mika Rottenberg.” *Kunstbeeld*, May 31.

Ruyters, Domeniek. “Fenomeen Mika.” *Metropolis M*, May 8.

Heartney, Eleanor. “Interview: Mika Rottenberg.” *artpress*, April.

Ter Borg, Lucette. “Mika Rottenberg maakt arbeit absurd.” *NRC Handelsblad BV*, March 26.

Mertens, Dieuwertje. “De mens als zwetende machine.” *Parool*, March 24.

De Vries, Marina. “Mika Rottenberg.” *Volkskrant*, March 22.

Enright, Robert, and Meeka Walsh. “Fetishizing the Visual: An Interview with Mika Rottenberg.” *Border Crossings*, No. 117, Spring.

Buhr, Elke. “Portrait: Mika Rottenberg.” *Monopol*, March.

Bodin, Claudia. “Schweiß, Salat, 7 Tränen.” *ART Germany*, March.

Kordoski, Kyra. “Mika Rottenberg @ San Francisco Museum of Modern Art.” *WhiteHotMagazine.com*, January 22.

Chen, Joanne. “Mika Rottenberg.” *Art.Investment* (China), January.

Frankel, David. “Mika Rottenberg, Mary Boone Gallery.” *Artforum*, January: 216.

2010 Saltz, Jerry. “Critic’s Pick: Mika Rottenberg, *Squeeze*.” *New York Magazine*, December 20–27.

Indrisek, Scott. “Mika Rottenberg: *Squeeze*.” *Artinfo.com*, December 16.

Herschthal, Eric. “Art and Israel: Some Sunny News.” *The Jewish Week*, December 8.

“Mika Rottenberg,” in “Goings on about Town: Art.” *The New Yorker*, December 6.

Smith, Roberta. “Mika Rottenberg: *Squeeze*.” *The New York Times*, November 25.

Laster, Paul. “Mika Rottenberg, *Squeeze*.” *Time Out New York*, November 25–December 1.

Yablonsky, Linda. “Artifacts: *Squeeze* Therapy.” *The New York Times Magazine*, November 24.

Heinrich, Will. “Autumn’s Real Ghouls.” *The New York Observer*, November 8.

Swenson, Kirsten. “Review: Mika Rottenberg, San Francisco Museum of Modern Art.” *Art in America*, October.

Hudson, Judith. “Mika Rottenberg,” *BOMB Magazine*, Fall: 26–33.

Hsu, Hsuan L. “Mika Rottenberg’s Productive Bodies.” *Camera Obscura: Feminism, Culture, and Media Studies*, No. 74, September: 40–73.

Silberg, Jon. “Small Camera Delivers Immersive Experience: Mika Rottenberg’s ‘Squeeze’ at SFMOMA.” *CreativePLANETnetwork.com*, August 31.

Spears, Dorothy. “Mika Rottenberg’s *Squeeze* at the San Francisco Museum of Modern Art.” *TheHuffingtonPost.com*, August 27.

Melendez, Franklin. “Mika Rottenberg’s Post-Feminist Wonka Factories.” *ARTslant.com*, August 23.

Mizota, Sharon. “It’s OK for serious art to be funny.” *Los Angeles Times*, August 15.

Curcio, Seth. “Mika Rottenberg at SFMOMA.” *DailysServing.com*, August 4.

Curiel, Jonathan. “Mika Rottenberg’s *Squeeze* uses real people to imagine unreal worlds.” *San Francisco Weekly*, July 21.

Peetz, John Arthur. “500 Words: Mika Rottenberg.” *Artforum.com*, July 20.

Rapold, Nicholas. “Work in Progress.” *Artforum.com*, July 6.

Dostert, Elisabeth. "Auseinandersetzung als innere Notwendigkeit." Interview with Julia Stoschek, *Süddeutsche Zeitung*, May 17.

Daly, Ian. "The New Kings of the Art World." *Details*, April.

2009 Burnichon, Marie-Cécile. "Mika Rottenberg." *artpress*, April.

"Mika Rottenberg." *Le Monde*, April 8.

Delos, Celine. "Le Guide Culturelle: Mika Rottenberg." *Elle* (France), March.

Launay, Aude. "Mika Rottenberg." *Zérodeux*, Spring.

Ayers, Robert. "Through the Eye of the Needle: Mika Rottenberg's Video Installations." *EIKON Magazin #65*, February–April.

"Mika Rottenberg: *Performance Stills*." *The New Yorker*, March 2.

2008 Vishmidt, Marina. "Situation Wanted: Something About Labour." *Afterall*, Issue 19, Autumn/Winter: 20–34.

"Mika Rottenberg." *Bil Bok International*, No. 28.

MacAdam, Barbara. "Mika Rottenberg." *ARTnews*, December (cover).

"The Art Issue." *W Magazine*, November.

"Diaries of a Young Artist." *Art on Paper*, July/August.

"Mika Rottenberg." *Studio Magazine*, May/June.

Saltz, Jerry. "When Cool Turns Cold." *NYmag.com*, March 13.

Camhi, Leslie. "Low Stakes and Open Rules Dominate: The 2008 Whitney Biennial." *The Village Voice*, March 11.

Cotter, Holland. "Art's Economic Indicator." *The New York Times*, March 7.

Peers, Alexandra. "Opening Night at the Whitney Biennial." *NYmag.com*, March 5.

Ayers, Robert. "The Best of the Biennial." *Artinfo.com*, March 5.

"Work in Progress." *V Magazine*, March.

2007 Ozuna, Tony. "Altered States." *The Prague Post*, December 1.

Wolff, Rachel. "Young Masters: A portrait gallery of ten of the most promising New York artists to have emerged from the boom." *New York Magazine*, October 15–21: 53.

Coomer, Martin. "Reviews: Welcome to My World." *ArtReview*, October: 154.

Sheffi, Smadar. "Rear Window." *Haaretz*, October 2.

Kerr, Merrily. "Mika Rottenberg: Long Hair Lover," (interview). *Flash Art*, Vol. XL, July–September: 112–114.

Wolin, Joseph R. "Structural Elements: Space is in the Building." *Time Out New York*, August 16–22.

Robinson, Walter. "Weekend Update." *Artnet.com*, July 30.

Smith, Roberta. "Space Exploration, Conducted on a Spiral." *The New York Times*, July 20, p. 9.

"The New Pop A-List: *Interview*'s 50 to Watch (Age 30 or Under)." *Interview*, June.

Iglesias, Claudio. "Perceptive Curatorship: Arte Y Corporaciones." *Exito*, May.

Battistozzi, Ana Maria. "Tecnología Para Qué." *Clarín*, May 12.

Morales, Mariana. "Mika Rottenberg." *Codigo 06140*, April/May.

Navarro, Santiago Garcia. "Negatec." *Los Inrockuptibles*, April.

Sanchez, Julio. "La otro cara de la tecnología." *La Nacion*, March 25.

Gutman, Yifat. "Interview: Mika Rottenberg." *The Marker: Women*, March: 26–34.

Liebs, Holger. "Selected Exhibitions 2006: Mika Rottenberg." *Art - das Kunstmagazin*, January: 46–81.

2006 Rottenberg, Mika. "The Artists' Artists: Anna Craycroft, The Agency of the Orphan." *Artforum*, December.

Stevens, Mark, and Karen Rosenberg. "The Year in Art." *New York Magazine*, December 18–24: 120.

Sischy, Ingrid. "The New New York School." *Vanity Fair*, December: 315.

Antonini, Marco. "Mika Rottenberg." *Around Photography*, November 9.

Needham, Alex. "Make it Big: Mika Rottenberg." *ArtReview*, October: 22.

Koerner von Gustorf, Oliver. "Baseball, Jazz, and the Anticipation of Happiness: *pa*per*ing* in the Lobby Gallery at Deutsche Bank New York." *db artmag*, Issue 1, October/November: 19.

Ward, Ossian. "The Body Factory: An Interview with Mika Rottenberg." *db artmag*, Issue 1, October/November: 3–4.

Kenning, Dean. "Uncertain States of America." *Art Monthly*, Vol. 300, October.

Wullschlager, Jackie. "Bright, brash, unmissable: the US legacy." *Financial Times*, September 15.

Searle, Adrian. "Rebels without a cause." *The Guardian*, September 12.

Dorment, Richard, "America's new age of anxiety." *The Daily Telegraph*, September 12.

Lovelace, Carey. "Mika Rottenberg at Nicole Klagsbrun." *Art in America*, September: 164–165.

Seidl, Claudius. "Die nackte Wahrheit über der Stadt." *Frankfurter Allgemeine Sonntagszeitung*, September 3, p. 18.

Smith, Roberta. "Endgame Art? It's Borrow, Sample, and Multiply in an Exhibition at Bard College." *The New York Times*, July 7.

Genocchio, Benjamin. "Art Review: How Young Europeans View America's 'Uncertain' State." *The New York Times*, July 9.

Sugiura, Kunie. "Review of Exhibition: *Dough* at P.S.1, by Mika Rottenberg." *BT: Monthly Art Magazine Bijutsu Techo 878*, Vol. 58: 158.

"Utmetnicka Scena: Borba autora u ponudi vizije." *Europa*, June 22.

Jelisavac, Lj. "Ekskluzivna izlozba video-radova." *Kultura*, June 20.

"Most za centar sveta utmtnosti." *Danas*, June.

Borchert, Gesine. "Die Monopol Watchlist: Fünf Künstler, die uns aufgefallen sind." *Monopol*, No. 6, June 1.

Sonnenborn, Katie Stone. "Survivor." *Frieze*, Issue 100, June–August.

Tamir, Chen. "Mika Rottenberg: Dough." *C Magazine*, Issue 90, Summer: 42–43.

Kley, Elisabeth. "Mika Rottenberg." *ARTnews*, Summer: 180–181.

Barliant, Claire. "Mika Rottenberg: Nicole Klagsbrun Gallery." *Artforum*, Vol. 44, No. 8, April.

Bellini, Andrea. "The Body and Weapons." *Flash Art*, March/April: 105.

Kerr, Merrily. "Mika Rottenberg: Dough." *Time Out New York*, February 23–March 1: 68.

Smith, Roberta. "Mika Rottenberg: Dough." *The New York Times*, February 17.

Harris, Edna V. www.*anonymousfemaleartist.blogspot.com*, February.

Gell, Aaron. "Factory Girl" in "Art Spotlight." *Elle*, February: 129.

2005 Rimanelli, David. "Greater New York 2005." *Artforum*, May: 239–240.

Saltz, Jerry. "Lesser New York." *The Village Voice*, March 22.

Kunitz, Daniel, and Joao Ribas. "The ArtReview 25: Emerging US Artists." *ArtReview*, Vol. 3, No. 3: 121.

Taylor, Robert. "What the Peeps is going on?" *The Sunday Times* (London), February 6.

2004 Smith, Roberta. "Art Review; Summertime at P.S.1: Where Opposites Like Hands On/Off Attract." *The New York Times*, July 16.

"A Look Ahead." *The New York Sun*, May.

Davis, Nicole. "Miami Heat." *Artnet.com*, February 9.

2003 Saltz, Jerry. "Babylon Rising." *The Village Voice*, September 9.

2000 Hamburger, Susan. "Artburger." *Waterfrontweek*, December.

Shout Magazine, December.

Nahshon, Ilan. "Paint." *Yedio Ahronot*, October.

Studio Art Magazine, September.

Online Video Features

Opening at La Maison Rouge, http://vernissage.tv/blog/2008/10/27/julia-stoschek-collection-number-two-fragile-interview-with-julia-stoschek-part-12/, 2009

W Magazine: Behind the scenes of the November 2008 "Art Issue," http://www.wmagazine.com/artdesign/video/2008/11/mika_rottenberg, 2008

Interview for Coolhunting.com feature on Whitney Biennial artists, http://www.coolhunting.com/archives/2008/03/mika_rottenberg.php, 2008

Artnet TV Interview by Nicole Davis, http://www.youtube.com/watch?v=pm3cLqdDUdc, 2008

Interview for "The Irresistible Force," Tate Modern exhibition, http://www.tate.org.uk/modern/exhibitions/theirresistibleforce/video.shtm, 2007

Index of Works

Pages 10, 28–31
Bowls Balls Souls Holes (Hotel), 2014, Video and sculpture installation, Video duration: 30 min, Variant of 6 with 1 artist proof

Installation view details: *Mika Rottenberg: Bowls Balls Souls Holes*, The Rose Art Museum, Brandeis University, Waltham, MA, February 14–June 8, 2014. Photo by Charles Mayer, Image courtesy the Rose Art Museum, Waltham, MA

Pages 12, 26–27, 32–41
Stills from *Bowls Balls Souls Holes (Hotel),* 2014, Video and sculpture installation, Video duration: 30min, Variant of 6 with 1 artist proof

Pages 14–25
Installation views: *Mika Rottenberg: Bowls Balls Souls Holes*, The Rose Art Museum, Brandeis University, Waltham, MA, February 14–June 8, 2014. Photo by Charles Mayer, Image courtesy the Rose Art Museum, Waltham, MA

Pages 42, 46–51
Performance view: *SEVEN,* 2011, in collaboration with Jon Kessler; Live performance for 9 performers; mixed media installation with video, 37 min, continuous loop, Dimensions variable, A Performa Commission at Nicole Klagsbrun Gallery. Photo by Paula Court, Image courtesy Performa, New York

Pages 44–45
Mika Rottenberg and Jon Kessler, *SEVEN (Sunita)*, 2012; Blue version (5 of 7 unique variants, with 2 artist proofs)

Mika Rottenberg and Jon Kessler, *SEVEN (Jason)*, 2012; Indigo version (6 of 7 unique color variants, with 2 artist proofs)

Mika Rottenberg and Jon Kessler, *SEVEN (Alex)*, 2012; Yellow version (3 of 7 unique color variants, with 2 artist proofs)

Mika Rottenberg and Jon Kessler, *SEVEN (Juan)*, 2012; Green version (4 of 7 unique color variants, with 2 artist proofs)

Mika Rottenberg and Jon Kessler, *SEVEN (Cecil)*, 2012; Red version (1 of 7 unique color variants, with 2 artist proofs)

Mika Rottenberg and Jon Kessler, *SEVEN (Marshall)*, 2012; Violet version (7 of 7 unique color variants, with 2 artist proofs)

Mika Rottenberg and Jon Kessler, *SEVEN (Chris)*, 2012; Orange version (2 of 7 unique color variants, with 2 artist proofs)

All variants: Mixed media with three-channel video, Video duration: 36:08 min, 36 3/4 x 45 1/2 x 20 in., 93.3 x 115.6 x 50.8 cm (closed), 36 3/4 x 91 x 10 in., 93.3 x 231.1 x 25.4 cm (open)

Pages 52–55
Stills from *SEVEN,* 2011, in collaboration with Jon Kessler; Live performance for 9 performers; mixed media installation with video, 37 minutes, continuous loop, Dimensions variable, Image courtesy Mika Rottenberg and Jon Kessler

Pages 56–57
Open view: Mika Rottenberg and Jon Kessler, *SEVEN (Chris)*, 2012; Orange version (2 of 7 unique color variants, with 2 artist proofs). Mixed media with three-channel video, Video duration: 36:08 min, 36 3/4 x 45 1/2 x 20 in., 93.3 x 115.6 x 50.8 cm (closed), 36 3/4 x 91 x 10 in., 93.3 x 231.1 x 25.4 cm (open). Photo by Jessica Eckert, Image courtesy Andrea Rosen Gallery, New York.

Pages 58–59
Closed view: Mika Rottenberg and Jon Kessler, *SEVEN (Chris)*, 2012; Orange version (2 of 7 unique color variants, with 2 artist proofs). Mixed media with three-channel video, Video duration: 36:08 min, 36 3/4 x 45 1/2 x 20 in., 93.3 x 115.6 x 50.8 cm (closed), 36 3/4 x 91 x 10 in., 93.3 x 231.1 x 25.4 cm (open). Photo by Jessica Eckert, Image courtesy Andrea Rosen Gallery, New York.

Pages 60–61
Preparatory drawing for *Squeeze*, 2010

Pages 62–65
Squeeze, 2010, Single-channel video installation, digital c-print, Video duration: 20 min, Overall dimensions variable, Edition of 6 with 2 artist proofs.

Installation view: *Squeeze*, Mary Boone Gallery, New York, in collaboration with Nicole Klagsbrun Gallery, New York, October 30–December 18, 2010. Photo by Adam Reich, Image courtesy Mary Boone Gallery, New York, and Nicole Klagsbrun Gallery, New York

Page 66
Tsss, 2013 (Exhibition Version), Air conditioner, plant, hotplate, frying pan, water, Dimensions variable, Edition of 3 with 1 artist proof.

Installation view detail: *Squeeze: Video Works by Mika Rottenberg*, The Israel Museum, Jerusalem, Israel, December 3–April 5, 2013. Photo by Elie Posner, Image courtesy The Israel Museum, Jerusalem

Page 67
Installation view: *Cheese, Squeeze, and Tropical Breeze: Video Works 2003–2010*, M–Museum Leuven, Belgium, November 4, 2011–February 26, 2012. Photo by Dirk Pauwels, Image courtesy M–Museum Leuven, Belgium

Pages 68–69
Installation view: *New Work: Mika Rottenberg*, San Francisco Museum of Modern Art, San Francisco, July 9–October 3, 2010. Photo by Ian Reeves Photography, Image courtesy San Francisco Museum of Modern Art, San Francisco

Page 70
Interior installation views: *Tell Me Her Story*, Coreana Museum of Art, Space*C, Seoul, Korea, October 17–December 14, 2013. Photo by Park Hyun-jin, Image courtesy Coreana Museum of Art, Space*C, Seoul

Page 71
Interior installation views: *Cheese, Squeeze, and Tropical Breeze: Video Works 2003–2010*, M–Museum Leuven, Belgium, November 4, 2011–February 26, 2012. Photo by Dirk Pauwels, Image courtesy M–Museum Leuven, Belgium

Pages 72–73
Production still from *Squeeze*, 2010

Pages 74–77
Squeeze production, 2010. Photo by Henry Prince

Page 78
(Detail of *Squeeze*, 2010) *Mary Boone with Cube*, 2010, Digital c-print, 64 x 36 in., 162.6 x 91.4 cm (image), 65 1/4 x 37 1/2 in., 165.7 x 95.3 cm (framed), Edition of 6. Image courtesy Mary Boone Gallery, New York, and Nicole Klagsbrun Gallery, New York

Page 79
(Detail of: *Squeeze*, 2010) Tropical Shipping Incoming Condition Report, Single-channel video installation, digital c-print, Video duration: 20 min, Overall dimensions variable, Edition of 6 with 2 artist proofs

Pages 80–81
Certificate of Authenticity for *Squeeze*, 2010

Pages 82–85
Stills from *Squeeze*, 2010, Single-channel video installation, digital c-print, Video duration: 20 min, Overall dimensions variable, Edition of 6 with 2 artist proofs

Page 86
Photo by Barney Kulok

Page 87 (detail)
Ponytail Girl, 2010, Digital c-print, 14 x 21 in., 35.6 x 53.3 cm, Edition of 5 with 1 artist proof

Page 88
Preparatory drawing for *Cheese*, 2008

Pages 90–92, 94–97
Cheese #3, 2008, Six-channel video installation, Dimensions variable.

Installation views: *Theatrical Gestures*, Herzliya Museum of Contemporary Art, Herzliya, Israel, January 26–April 20, 2013. Photo by Yigal Pardo, Image courtesy Herzliya Museum of Contemporary Art, Herzliya, Israel

Page 93
Cheese #2, 2008, Six-channel video installation, Dimensions variable.

Interior installation view: *Mika Rottenberg: Dough Cheese Squeeze and Tropical Breeze: Video Works 2003–2010*, de Appel arts centre, Amsterdam, March 12–May 8, 2011. Photo by Cassander Eeftinck Schattenkerk, Image courtesy de Appel arts centre, Amsterdam

Pages 98–99
Cheese, 2008, (La Maison Rouge Exhibition Version), Six-channel video installation, Dimensions variable.

Installation views: *Mika Rottenberg*, La Maison Rouge, Paris, February 18–May 3, 2009. Photo by Marc Domage, Image courtesy La Maison Rouge, Paris

Pages 100–101
Still from Cheese, 2007, Digital c-print, 16 x 24 in., 40.6 x 61 cm, (image), 17 x 25 in., 43.2 x 63.5 cm (framed), Edition of 7 with 1 artist proof

Pages 102–103
The Seven Sutherland Sisters, circa 1900, photographed with Fletcher Sutherland, Image courtesy Niagara County Historical Society, Lockport, NY

Pages 104–105
Original packaging and product: Seven Sutherland Sisters Hair Grower. Photo by Barney Kulok

Pages 106–107
Detail of original advertisement and product insert: Seven Sutherland Sisters' Hair Grower

Pages 108–111
Stills from *Cheese*, 2008, Six-channel video installation, Dimensions variable

Page 113
Fig 1. Still from *Dough*, 2005-2006, Single-channel video installation, Duration: 7 min., Dimensions variable, Edition of 3 with 1 artist proof

Fig 2. Still from *Mary's Cherries*, 2004, Single-channel video installation, Duration: 5:50 min, Dimensions variable, Edition of 5 with 1 artist proof

Fig 3. Still from *Squeeze*, 2010, Single-channel video installation and digital c-print, Video duration: 20 min, Overall dimensions variable, Edition of 6 with 2 artist proofs

Page 114
Fig 4. Still from *Squeeze*, 2010, Single-channel video installation and digital c-print, Video duration: 20 min, Overall dimensions variable, Edition of 6 with 2 artist proofs

Fig 5. *(Big) Dough*, 2005–2006, Single-channel video installation, Duration: 7 min., Dimensions variable, Edition of 2 with 1 artist proof

Installation view: *Dough*, KW Institute for Contemporary Art, Berlin, September 3–November 12, 2006. Photo by Uwe Walter, Image courtesy KW Institute for Contemporary Art, Berlin

Page 115
Fig 6. *Cheese #1*, 2008, Six-channel video installation

Installation view: *2008 Whitney Biennial*, Whitney Museum of American Art, New York, March 6–June 1, 2008. Photo by Christopher Burke Studio

Fig 7. *Tropical Breeze*, 2004, Single-channel video installation, Duration: 3:45 min, Dimensions variable, Edition of 5 with 1 artist proof

Installation view: *Greater New York 2005*, MOMA P.S.1, Queens, NY, March 13–September 26, 2005

Page 116
Fig 8. Mona Hatoum, *Corps étranger*, 1994, Video installation with cylindrical wooden structure, video projector, video player, amplifier and four speakers, 137 13/16 x 118 1/8 x 118 1/8 in. (350 x 300 x 300 cm). © Mona Hatoum, Photo by Philippe Migeat, Image courtesy Centre Pompidou, Paris

Fig 9. Gordon Matta-Clark, documentation of *Conical Intersect*, 1975. Image courtesy The Estate of Gordon Matta-Clark and David Zwirner, New York/ London; Gordon Matta-Clark: © 2014 Estate of Gordon Matta-Clark / Artists Rights Society (ARS), New York

Page 117
Fig 10. Still from *Mary's Cherries*, 2004, Single-channel video installation, Duration: 5:50 min, Dimensions variable, Edition of 5 with 1 artist proof

Fig 11. *Texture 1 & 3*, 2013, Polyurethane resin and acrylic paint, Installed dimensions variable, Comprised of two parts, Part A Caramel: 62 x 44 3/4 x 1 1/2 in., 157.5 x 113.7 x 3.8 cm, Part B Multi-color: 65 x 43 x 2 in., 165.1 x 109.2 x 5.1 cm. Photo by Pierre Le Hors, Image courtesy Andrea Rosen Gallery, New York

Fig 12. Lynda Benglis, *For Bob*, 1971, Purified pigmented beeswax and dammar resin on Masonite, 36 x 5 1/4 x 2 5/8 in., 91.44 x 13.34 x 6.67 cm, The Museum of Contemporary Art, Los Angeles, Partial and promised gift of Blake Byrne, Art © Lynda Benglis/Licensed by VAGA, New York, NY. Photo by Brian Forrest

Page 118
Fig 13. *Dough* production, 2005

Fig 14. *Squeeze* production, 2010

Fig 15. Still from *Tropical Breeze*, 2004, Single-channel video installation, Duration: 3.45 min, Dimensions variable, Edition of 5 with 1 artist proof

Page 119
Fig 16. Amie Siegel, still from *Provenance*, 2013, HD video, color, sound, 40' 30". Image courtesy the artist and Simon Preston, New York

Fig 17. Detail of *Squeeze*, 2010: *Mary Boone with Cube*, 2010, Digital c-print, 64 x 36 in., 162.6 x 91.4 cm (image), 65 1/4 x 37 1/2 in., 165.7 x 95.3 cm (framed), Edition of 6. Image courtesy Mary Boone Gallery, New York, and Nicole Klagsbrun Gallery, New York

Page 120
Fig 18. Still from *Cheese*, 2008, Six-channel video installation

Page 122
Figs 19–21. Stills from *Squeeze*, 2010, Single-channel video installation, digital c-print, Video duration: 20 min, Edition of 6 with 2 artist proofs

Page 123
Figs 22–24. Stills from *Bowls Balls Souls Holes (Hotel)*, 2014, Video and sculpture installation, Video duration: 27 min, Variant of 6 with 1 artist proof

Page 124
Photo by Barney Kulok

Pages 126–127
Preparatory drawing for *Dough*, 2005–2006

Pages 128–129
Dough, 2005-2006, Single-channel video installation, Duration: 7 min, Small version, dimensions variable, Edition of 3 with 1 artist proof

Installation view: *Number Two: Fragile*, Julia Stoschek Collection, Düsseldorf, October 11, 2008–August 1, 2009. Photo by Achim Kukulies, Image courtesy The Julia Stoschek Collection

Pages 130–131
Dough, 2005-2006, Single-channel video installation, Duration: 7 min, Dimensions variable, Edition of 3 with 1 artist proof

Installation view: *Mika Rottenberg: Dough Cheese Squeeze and Tropical Breeze: Video Works 2003-2010*, de Appel arts centre, Amsterdam, March 12–May 1, 2011. Photo by Cassander Eeftinck Schattenkerk, Image courtesy de Appel arts centre, Amsterdam

Pages 132–137
(Big) Dough, 2005–2006, Single- channel video installation, Duration: 7 min, Dimensions variable, Edition of 2 with 1 artist proof

Installation view: *Dough*, KW Institute for Contemporary Art, Berlin, September 3–November 12, 2006. Photo by Uwe Walter, Image courtesy KW Institute for Contemporary Art, Berlin

Pages 138–139
Interior views: *(Big) Dough*, 2005–2006, Single-channel video installation, Duration: 7 min, Dimensions variable, Edition of 2 with 1 artist proof

Installation views: *Mika Rottenberg*, La Maison Rouge, Paris, February 18–May 3, 2009. Photo by Marc Domage, Image courtesy La Maison Rouge, Paris

Pages 140–141 (detail)
Dough (video still), 2006, Digital c-print, 16 x 20 in., 40.6 x 50.8 cm, Edition of 7 with 2 artist proofs

Pages 142–143
Stills from *Dough*, 2005–2006, Single-channel video installation, Duration: 7 min, Dimensions variable, Edition of 3 with 1 artist proof

Page 144
Preparatory drawing for *Tropical Breeze*, 2004

Pages 146–149
Tropical Breeze, 2004, Single-channel video installation, Duration: 3:45 min, Dimesions variable, Edition of 5 with 1 artist proof

Installation view: *Mika Rottenberg, Sneeze to Squeeze*, Magasin 3 Stockholm Konsthall, Sweden, February 8–June 2, 2013. Photo by Christian Saltas, Image courtesy Magasin 3 Stockholm Konsthall, Sweden

Pages 150–151
Tropical Breeze, 2004, Single-channel video installation, Duration: 3:45 min, Dimensions variable, Edition of 5 with 1 artist proof

Interior installation views: *Mika Rottenberg*, La Maison Rouge, Paris, February 18–May 3, 2009. Photo by Marc Domage, Image courtesy La Maison Rouge, Paris

Pages 152–153
Installation views: *Mika Rottenberg: Dough Cheese Squeeze and Tropical Breeze: Video Works 2003–2010*, de Appel arts centre, Amsterdam, March 12–May 8, 2011. Photo by Cassander Eeftinck Schattenkerk, Image courtesy de Appel arts centre, Amsterdam

Pages 154–155
Installation view (composite): *Mika Rottenberg*, Nottingham Contemporary, Nottingham, UK, May 4–June 30, 2012. Photo by Andy Keate, Image courtesy Nottingham Contemporary, Nottingham, UK

Page 156
Production still from *Tropical Breeze*, 2004

Page 157
Graphics from *Tropical Breeze*, 2004

Pages 158–161
Stills from *Tropical Breeze*, 2004, Single-channel video installation, Duration: 3:45 min, Dimensions variable, Edition of 5 with 1 artist proof

Pages 162–163 (detail)
Tropical Breeze, 2004, Single-channel video installation, Duration: 3:45 min, Dimensions variable, Edition of 5 with 1 artist proof. Photo by Barney Kulok

Page 164 (detail)
Texture 3 & 4, 2013, Polyurethane resin, acrylic paint, Installed dimensions variable, Comprised of two parts, Part A Pink: 57 x 29 1/2 x 2 in., 144.8 x 74.9 x 5.1 cm, Part B Green: 65 1/4 x 44 x 1 3/4 in., 165.7 x 111.8 x 4.4 cm. Photo by Pierre LeHors, Image courtesy Andrea Rosen Gallery, New York

Pages 166–167
Photo by Barney Kulok

Pages 168–169
Mary's Cherries, 2004, Single-channel video installation, Duration: 5:50 min, Dimensions variable, Edition of 5 with 2 artist proofs

Installation views: *Mary's Cherries*, FRAC Languedoc -Roussillon, Montpellier, France, June 7–September 29, 2012. Photo by C. Pérez, Image courtesy FRAC Languedoc -Roussillon, Montpellier

Page 170
Interior installation view: *The Irresistible Force*, Tate Modern, London, September 20–November 25, 2007, Image courtesy Tate Modern, London

Page 172
Photo by Alejandra Ugarte Bedwell

Page 173
Mary's Cherries, 2004, Single-channel video installation, Duration: 5:50 min, Dimensions variable, Edition of 5 with 2 artist proofs

Installation view: *Mika Rottenberg*, Nottingham Contemporary, Nottingham, UK, May 4–June 30, 2012. Photo by Andy Keate, Image courtesy Nottingham Contemporary, Nottingham, UK

Page 175
Barbara from *Mary's Cherries*, 2004

Page 177
Rock Rose from *Mary's Cherries*, 2004

Page 178
Stills from *Mary's Cherries*, 2004, Single-channel video installation, Duration: 5:50 min, Dimensions variable, Edition of 5 with 2 artist proofs

Page 180 (detail)
Texture 3 & 4, 2013, Polyurethane resin, acrylic paint, Installed dimensions variable, Comprised of two parts, Part A Pink: 57 x 29 1/2 x 2 in., 144.8 x 74.9 x 5.1 cm, Part B Green: 65 1/4 x 44 x 1 3/4 in., 165.7 x 111.8 x 4.4 cm). Photo by Pierre Le Hors, Image courtesy Andrea Rosen Gallery, New York

Page 181 (detail)
Texture 1 & 3, 2013, Polyurethane resin, acrylic paint, Installed dimensions variable, Comprised of two parts, Part A Caramel: 62 x 44 3/4 x 1 1/2 in., 157.5 x 113.7 x 3.8 cm, Part B Multi-color: 65 x 43 x 2 in., 165.1 x 109.2 x 5.1 cm. Photo by Pierre Le Hors, Image courtesy Andrea Rosen Gallery, New York

Page 182 (detail)
Texture 6 & 5, 2013, Polyurethane resin, acrylic paint, Installed dimensions variable, Comprised of two parts, Part A Light-blue: 68 3/4 x 36 x 1 1/2 in., 174.6 x 91.4 x 3.8 cm, Part B Purple: 42 x 22 1/4 x 1 1/4 in., 106.7 x 56.5 x 3.2 cm. Photo by Pierre Le Hors, Image courtesy Andrea Rosen Gallery, New York

Page 183 (detail)
Texture 2 & 4, 2013, Polyurethane resin, acrylic paint, Installed dimensions variable, Comprised of two parts, Part A Speckled gold: 68 x 31 x 1 3/8 in., 172.7 x 78.7 x 3.5 cm, Part B Blue: 57 x 30 x 2 in., 144.8 x 76.2 x 5.1 cm. Photo by Pierre Le Hors, Image courtesy Andrea Rosen Gallery, New York

Page 184 (detail)
Texture 1 & 3, 2013, Polyurethane resin, acrylic paint, Installed dimensions variable, Comprised of two parts, Part A Caramel: 62 x 44 3/4 x 1 1/2 in., 157.5 x 113.7 x 3.8 cm, Part B Multi-color: 65 x 43 x 2 in., 165.1 x 109.2 x 5.1 cm. Photo by Pierre Le Hors, Image courtesy Andrea Rosen Gallery, New York

Page 185 (detail)
Texture 6 & 5, 2013, Polyurethane resin, acrylic paint, Installed dimensions variable, Comprised of two parts, Part A Light-blue: 68 3/4 x 36 x 1 1/2 in., 174.6 x 91.4 x 3.8 cm, Part B Purple: 42 x 22 1/4 x 1 1/4 in., 106.7 x 56.5 x 3.2 cm. Photo by Pierre Le Hors, Image courtesy Andrea Rosen Gallery, New York

Page 186
Still from *Sneeze*, 2012, Single-channel video, Duration: 3:02 min, Overall dimensions variable, Edition of 6 with 2 artist proofs

Pages 188–191
Stills from *Sneeze*, 2012, Single-channel video, Duration: 3:02 min, Overall dimensions variable, Edition of 6 with 2 artist proofs

Pages 192, 198, 201 top
Fried Sweat, 2008, Single-channel video installation, One component of two-part collaboration, Duration: 2 min, Dimensions variable, Edition of 5 with 2 artist proofs

Installation views: *Mika Rottenberg: Dough Cheese Squeeze and Tropical Breeze: Video Works 2003–2010*, March 12–May 8, 2011, de Appel arts centre, Amsterdam. Photo by Cassander Eeftinck Schattenkerk, Image courtesy de Appel arts centre, Amsterdam

Pages 194, 200
Installation views: *Mika Rottenberg*, Nottingham Contemporary, Nottingham, UK, May 4–June 30, 2012. Photo by Andy Keate, Image courtesy Nottingham Contemporary, Nottingham, UK

Page 196
Installation view: *Labour and Wait*, Santa Barbara Museum of Art, July 2–September 22, 2013. Photo by Brian Forrest, Image courtesy Santa Barbara Museum of Art, Santa Barbara

Pages 199, 201 bottom
Installation views: *Mika Rottenberg: Sneeze to Squeeze*, Magasin 3 Stockholm Konsthall, Sweden, February 8–June 2, 2013. Photo by Christian Saltas, Image courtesy Magasin 3 Stockholm Konsthall, Sweden

Pages 202–203
Stills from *Fried Sweat*, 2008, Single-channel video installation, One component of two-part collaboration, Duration: 2 min, Dimensions variable, Edition of 5 with 2 artist proofs

Pages 204, 206–207
5 Second Party, 2006, Video installation, Duration: 26 sec, Edition of 3 with 1 artist proof

Installation view: *Mika Rottenberg: Dough Cheese Squeeze and Tropical Breeze: Video Works 2003–2010*, March 12–May 8, 2011, de Appel arts centre, Amsterdam. Photo by Cassander Eeftinck Schattenkerk, Image courtesy de Appel arts centre, Amsterdam

Page 208
5 Second Party, 2006, Digital c-print, 50 x 60 in., 127 x 152.4 cm, Edition of 6 with 2 artist proofs

Pages 210–211
Stills from *5 Second Party*, 2006, Video installation, Duration: 26 sec, Edition of 3 with 1 artist proof

Page 212
One Second Sculpture with Ahtoy, 2003, Digital c-print, 40 x 35 in., 101.6 x 88.9 cm, Edition of 5 with 2 artist proofs

Page 214
Installation view: *Squeeze: Video Works by Mika Rottenberg*, The Israel Museum, Jerusalem, Israel, December 3–April 5, 2013. Photo by Elie Posner, Image courtesy The Israel Museum, Jerusalem

Page 217
Time and a Half, 2003, Single-channel video, Duration: 3:40 min, Edition of 5 with 2 artist proofs

Installation view: *Mika Rottenberg: Dough Cheese Squeeze and Tropical Breeze: Video Works 2003–2010*, March 12–May 8, 2011, de Appel arts centre, Amsterdam. Photo by Cassander Eeftinck Schattenkerk, Image courtesy de Appel arts centre, Amsterdam

Pages 218–219
Stills from *Time and a Half*, 2003, Single-channel video, Duration: 3:40 min, Edition of 5 with 2 artist proofs

Page 220
Julie, 2003, Single-channel video, Duration: 3:30 min, Edition of 5 with 1 artist proof

Installation view: *Mika Rottenberg: Dough Cheese Squeeze and Tropical Breeze: Video Works 2003–2010*, March 12–May 8, 2011, de Appel arts centre, Amsterdam. Photo by Casander Eeftinck Schattenkerk, Image courtesy de Appel arts centre, Amsterdam

Pages 222–223
Stills from *Julie*, 2003, Single-channel video, Duration: 3:30 min, Edition of 5 with 1 artist proof

Page 226
ST4, 2010, Graphite, acrylic, colored pencil on paper, 29 3/4 x 44 in., 75.6 x 111.8 cm, (image), 31 1/2 x 45 1/2 in., 80 x 115.6 cm (framed). Photo by Christopher Burke Studio, Image courtesy Nicole Klagsbrun Gallery, New York

Page 230
SQ1, 2009, Graphite, acrylic, colored pencil on paper, 36 1/2 x 38 in., 92.7 x 96.5 cm (image), 38 1/4 x 39 1/2 in., 97.2 x 100.3 cm (framed). Photo by Christopher Burke Studio, Image courtesy Nicole Klagsbrun Gallery, New York

Page 234
u11, 2010, Graphite, acrylic, colored pencil on paper, 23 x 30 in., 58.4 x 76.2 cm (image), 24 1/2 x 31 1/2 in., 62.2 x 80 cm (framed). Photo by Christopher Burke Studio, Image courtesy Nicole Klagsbrun Gallery, New York

Page 238
s26, 2008, Graphite, acrylic, colored pencil on paper, 30 x 40 in., 76.2 x 101.6 cm (image), 32 3/4 x 46 1/2 in., 83.2 x 118.1 cm (framed). Photo by Christopher Burke Studio, Image courtesy Nicole Klagsbrun Gallery, New York

Page 242
s25, 2008, Graphite, acrylic, colored pencil on paper, 30 x 40 in., 76.2 x 101.6 cm (image), 32 3/4 x 46 1/2 in., 83.2 x 118.1 cm (framed). Photo by Christopher Burke Studio, Image courtesy Nicole Klagsbrun Gallery, New York

Page 246
J6, 2011, Graphite, acrylic, colored pencil on paper, 30 1/4 x 33 3/4 in., 76.8 x 85.7 cm. Photo by Christopher Burke Studio, Image courtesy Nicole Klagsbrun Gallery, New York

Page 250
m30, 2011, Graphite, acrylic, colored pencil on paper, 11 x 14 in., 27.9 x 35.6 cm (image), 13 1/2 x 17 1/4 in., 34.3 x 43.8 cm (framed). Photo by Cary Whittier, Image courtesy Nicole Klagsbrun Gallery, New York

Page 253 (detail)
SZ1/SZ2, 2010, Graphite, acrylic, colored pencil on paper, Diptych, overall dimensions variable, Component one: 23 x 15 in., 58.4 x 38.1 cm (image), 24 3/4 x 17 in., 62.9 x 43.2 cm (framed), Component two: 21 7/8 x 14. 3/8 in., 55.6 x 36.6 cm (image), 24 1/2 x 15. 3/4 in., 62 x 40.1 cm (framed). Photo by Christopher Burke Studio, Image courtesy Nicole Klagsbrun Gallery, New York

Page 273
Image courtesy of Mr. Stretch

Pages 274–277
Image courtesy of Leona, www.longhairdivas.com

Page 278
Image courtesy of Rock Rose

Page 280
Image courtesy of Heather Foster

Page 281
Image courtesy of Heather Foster. Photo by Gene X Hwang / Orange Photography

Pages 282–285
Image courtesy of Raqui

Pages 286–287
Image courtesy of Tall Kat

Page 288
Image courtesy of Bunny Glamazon

Selected Production Credits

Tropical Breeze

Cast:
Heather, Felicia, Vincent, Dexter
Credits:
Cinematography: Aaron Young
Sound Design: Paul Ruest

Mary's Cherries

Cast:
Barbara, Rock Rose
Credits:
Cinematography: Aaron Young
Sound Design: Paul Ruest

Dough

Cast:
Raqui, Tall Kat, Audrey, Adonna
Credits:
Cinematography: Ann Rossetti
Sound Design: Paul Ruest
Prop Design and Special Effects: Katrin Altekamp

Cheese

Cast:
Dyq, Heidi, Jeanette, Kelsey, Lady Grace, Leona
Credits:
Cinematography: Mahyad Tousi
Sound Design: Tina Hardin, Pomann Sound
Special Effects and Installation: Katrin Altekamp, Edo Born, Deville Cohen
Special thanks to Robby Williams's Flying W Air Ranch Petting Zoo and Airport

Squeeze

Cast:
Trixxter Bombshell; Bunny Glamazon; Rock Rose; Cara Fogel; Tongue; Linda, VK, Sheley, Lx and Lin from Refined Sparkling Nails & Spa Inc., New York; Mary Boone; Kathleen Boddington; Mariangelica Cuervo; Dolores Lopresti; Julia Schell; Martha and the Pick'n Clean Crew from Church Brothers Produce, Yuma, Arizona; Mahesh Manohan and workers from Boise Estate, Kerala, India.
Credits:
Cinematography: Mahyad Tousi
Set Engineer: Quentin Conybeare
Prop Design and Special Effects: Katrin Altekamp
Sound Design: Ronen Nagel, Trim Postproduction
Production: Andrew Fierberg
Production Assistants: Paulina Bebecka, Henry Prince
Still Photography: Christopher Burke Studio
Acoustic Consultant: Steve Hamilton

Sneeze

Cast:
Édouard Achache, Gabriel de Pimodan, Gaetano Lucido
Credits:
Makeup Artist: Jérôme Jardin
Director of Photography: Mahdi Lepart
Gaffer: Olivier Régent
Assistant Director: Mitra Hekmat
Sound Designer: Nati Taub
Re-recording Mixer: Ronen Nagel
Sound Design: Sound Around Studios

Bowls Balls Souls Holes

Cast:
Enid Alicea, Sakeena Jordan, Garry Turner, and extras from West Side Bingo Hall
Credits:
Cinematographer: Eric van den Brulle
Second Camera: Therese McPherson, Mahyad Tousi
Assistant Camera: Igor Ibradzic
Art Department: Katrin Altekamp
Assistant Director: Mitra Hemkat
Line Producer: Natalie Campbell
Jib Operator: Ian McGrew
Lights: Alan Hostetter
PAs: Elizabeth Jaeger, Tanner Cornacchini
Hair and Makeup: Merria Dearman, Debbie Peiser
Set: Joshua Pelletier, Zach Rockhill
Steadicam: Aaron Brown
Sound Designer and Mixer: Ronen Nagel, Nati Taub
Additional Sound Recording: Paul Ruest, Argot Studios; Francisco LaTorre
Color Correction: Omri Peled
Special Effects: Eran Muskatel, EMU Visual Design
Media Manager: Jillian Iscaro
Intern: Chloe YinTzuHuang
Special thanks to Belle Fisch and the staff of West Side Bingo Hall

Acknowledgments

I would like to thank Andrea Rosen Gallery, Gregory R. Miller & Co., and the Rose Art Museum for making this book materialize. In particular, I would like to thank Andrea Rosen for her vision and support, and Chris Bedford for initiating the exhibition "Bowls Balls Souls Holes" as well as Kristin Parker for making it happen. Special thanks to Gregory Miller for his dedication, as well as to Cornelia Blatter and Marcel Hermans of COMA for such an inspired book design. I would also like to thank Teneille Haggard at Andrea Rosen Gallery for overseeing the production of this book and for all her input, commitment, and care, and Andrea Cashman, Amy Ontiveros, Nen Reyes and Isabel Venero for all of their hard work.

Special thanks to Nicole Klagsbrun for her support of many of my works throughout the years, and to Natalie Campbell for contributing in numerous ways to several of the projects in this publication. I also want to thank Julia Stoschek for her support of my work.

The works in this book could not have come to life without the spirit, sweat, and talent of the crews and performers. Special thanks to the cast for their inspiration—Queen Raqui, Tall Kat, Rock Rose, Heather Foster, Leona, Lady Grace, Bunny Glamazon, Trixxter Bombshell, and Gary Mr. Stretch; the owner, staff, and guests of West Side Bingo Hall in Harlem; the staff and residents of Gweta Lodge and village in Botswana; Alex Lamke for the animation of *SEVEN*; Mahyad Tousi for filming many of the works and for his ideas and commitment; Steve Hamilton for his input and spirit; Katrin Altekamp for finding solutions to everything; and to Ronen Nagel and Nati Taub for the sound and magic. Additional thanks to Sean Bluechel and Anna Craycroft for their honest critique and ideas, and to Galerie Laurent Godin, Paris.

— Mika Rottenberg

In both her videos and the sculptural environments that contain them, Mika Rottenberg takes the world we share apart and returns it to us in a form that is as strange and foreign as it is deeply felt and resonant. The Rose Art Museum is thrilled to be the site of Rottenberg's most recent transformation. For her first solo museum exhibition in the United States, Rottenberg has developed an exhibition that relates directly to the space of the Rose and its Lois Foster Gallery. Beautifully spare and bracing, the exhibition contains three works—*Squeeze* (2010), *Tsss* (2013), and *Bowls Balls Souls Holes* (2014), a major new work commissioned and funded in part by the museum.

In addition to presenting her most recent achievements, the exhibition offers a selective account of the thematic and formal interests that have structured Rottenberg's development to date. This presentation was in large part made possible by the continued support of the Ruth Ann and Nathan Perlmutter Award, given annually in recognition of an emerging artist's achievement. The award also supports extended artist engagement with the Brandeis academic community. We are grateful for the Perlmutters' commitment to the Rose, which allows the museum to present innovative exhibitions and to foster new work as well as related and interdisciplinary conversations.

As a university museum, the Rose is fortunate to benefit from the rich and varied resources of Brandeis University. We are thankful for the enthusiastic support of the Brandeis community and the collaboration of a number of university branches, including the Department of Fine Arts, the Office of the Provost, the Office of the Arts, and the Office of the President. We are grateful for President Frederick Lawrence's spirited leadership and we are extraordinarily glad to have him in our corner and on our board. To him, our entire Board of Advisors, and to our Board Chair, Lizbeth Krupp, I extend my heartfelt thanks.

The Rose itself is built on tremendous teamwork, and I am grateful for each person who played a role in making this project a success. For their commitment as well as camaraderie, thanks go to Kristin Parker, Nancy

Gunn, Roy Dawes, Joe Leduc, Caitlin Julia Rubin, Nicole Rosenberg, Hepzibah Rapoport, Betsy Nelson, and Jennifer Yee. Thanks also to the staff of Andrea Rosen Gallery, especially Andrea Rosen, Andrea Cashman, and Teneille Haggard. The Rose exhibition, as well as this book, was made possible through their support.

This publication extends the work of Rottenberg's exhibition at the Rose, providing a comprehensive account of the artist's conceptual interests and material sensibilities as they have grown over the course of her career. Like the exhibition it accompanies, the book is also a product of many. I am deeply appreciative of Julia Bryan-Wilson and Wayne Koestenbaum's contributions. Attending to the specific, visceral experience of Rottenberg's videos and viewing spaces, their essays contextualize and, in poetic and weird ruminations that mirror the fantastical twists of Rottenberg's own production lines, make the experience of reading about this work nearly as rich as the work itself. Cornelia Blatter and Marcel Hermans of COMA worked tirelessly to design and produce a volume that captures the originality of Rottenberg's works. Publisher Gregory Miller effectively supported and guided our team of collaborators throughout all phases of this book project, and to him we all owe a huge debt of thanks.

Primary thanks, of course, are owed to Mika Rottenberg: for her vision and collaboration. Mika's imagination allows her to tread new ground with each new work, and it has been the privilege of everyone associated with this project to join her on that journey.

— Christopher Bedford

Contributors

Prior to joining the Rose Art Museum as the Henry and Lois Foster Director in September 2012, **Christopher Bedford** was Chief Curator at the Wexner Center for the Arts at The Ohio State University in Columbus. In his almost four years at the Wexner Center, Bedford organized numerous exhibitions, including *Hard Targets*, a multimedia show exploring sports and masculinity; *Mark Bradford*, a major mid-career survey; a small Susan Philipsz show; an Alyson Shotz project; and monographic exhibitions of artists Katy Moran, Erwin Redl, Tobias Putrih, Pipilotti Rist, Nathalie Djurberg, Ernst Caramelle, Elliott Hundley, Paula Hayes, Sarah Morris, David Smith, Omer Fast, and Paul Sietsema. For the two years prior to joining the Wexner Center, Bedford was an assistant curator in the Department of Contemporary Art at the Los Angeles County Museum of Art (LACMA). Before joining LACMA, Bedford served as a curatorial assistant and then consulting curator in the Department of Sculpture and Decorative Arts at the Getty Museum. Along with co-curators Jennifer Wulffson and Kristina Newhouse, Bedford was the recipient of the 2008 Fellows of Contemporary Art Curators' Award for the exhibition *Superficiality and Superexcrescence*. Bedford has published essays, book reviews, editorials, and exhibition reviews in *The Burlington Magazine*, *Artforum*, *Artforum.com*, *Art in America*, *Tema Celeste*, *Sculpture Journal*, *Frieze*, *The Art Book*, *Afterall*, *October*, *Word & Image*, and *caa.reviews*, as well as numerous essays in anthologies and exhibition catalogues. He is currently working on edited volumes for Duke University Press, MIT Press, and *Sculpture Journal*, and is a contributing editor to the Los Angeles–based contemporary art journal *X-TRA*.

Julia Bryan-Wilson is Associate Professor of Modern and Contemporary Art in the History of Art Department at University of California, Berkeley. Her research interests include questions of artistic labor, feminism, queer theory, performance, photography, video, and textile handicraft. She is the author of *Art Workers: Radical Practice in the Vietnam War Era* (UC Press, 2009), and editor of *OCTOBER Files: Robert Morris*, which was published in 2013 by The MIT Press. A scholar and critic, Bryan-Wilson has written about artists such as Laylah Ali, Ida Applebroog, Lisa Anne Auerbach, the Cockettes, Sharon Hayes, Harmony Hammond, Ana Mendieta, Yoko Ono, Yvonne Rainer, and Anne Wilson, in publications that include *Art Bulletin, Artforum, The Craft Reader, The Textiles Reader, October, The Journal of Modern Craft,* and many exhibition catalogues. Her article "Invisible Products" received the 2013 *Art Journal* award. She has held grants from the Getty, the Clark Art Institute, the Henry Moore Institute, and the Center for Craft, Creativity & Design.

Wayne Koestenbaum is a poet, critic, and artist. He has published nine books of nonfiction on such subjects as hotels, Harpo Marx, humiliation, Jackie Onassis, opera, and Andy Warhol; his cult classic, *The Queen's Throat: Opera, Homosexuality, and the Mystery of Desire* (Poseidon, 1993), was nominated for a National Book Critics Circle Award. His latest book of prose is *My 1980s & Other Essays* (Farrar, Straus and Giroux, 2013). His six books of poetry include *Blue Stranger with Mosaic Background* (Turtle Point, 2012) and *Best-Selling Jewish Porn Films* (Turtle Point, 2006). He has also published a novel, *Moira Orfei in Aigues-Mortes* (Soft Skull, 2004). His first solo exhibition of paintings was at White Columns in New York in 2012. He is a Distinguished Professor of English at the CUNY Graduate Center.

COMA conceptualizes, art directs, designs, and produces work in a range of formats and media. COMA has received many awards and has been nominated for the Rotterdam Design Prize and the Swiss Design Prize. COMA's work is in the permanent design collections of the Museum of Modern Art, New York, and the Art Institute of Chicago. Cornelia Blatter and Marcel Hermans of COMA also curate and facilitate workshops for U.S. graduate students in Amsterdam and Berlin.

Published in 2014 by Gregory R. Miller & Co. in association with the Rose Art Museum on the occasion of the exhibition *Mika Rottenberg: Bowls Balls Souls Holes* (February 14 – June 8, 2014)

GREGORY R. MILLER & CO.

Gregory R. Miller & Co.
62 Cooper Square
New York, NY 10003
grmandco.com

THE ROSE

The Rose Art Museum
15 South Street
Waltham, MA 02453
brandeis.edu/rose

Generous support for this publication provided by:
Andrea Rosen Gallery, New York

Available through:
ARTBOOK | D.A.P.
155 Sixth Avenue
New York, NY 10013
artbook.com

Concept and Design:
COMA Amsterdam/New York

Copy editor: Amy Ontiveros

Printed and bound in Lithuania

Library of Congress Cataloging-in-Publication Data

Mika Rottenberg: The Production of Luck.
pages cm
"Published in 2014 by Gregory R. Miller & Co. in association with the Rose Art Museum on the occasion of the exhibition *Mika Rottenberg: Bowls Balls Souls Holes* (February 14-June 8, 2014)."
Includes bibliographical references.
ISBN 978-1-941366-00-4 (alk. paper)
1. Rottenberg, Mika, 1976--Exhibitions.
2. Video installations (Art)--Exhibitions.
I. Koestenbaum, Wayne, author. II. Bedford, Christopher, author. III. Bryan-Wilson, Julia, author. IV. Rottenberg, Mika, 1976- Works. Selections. V. Rose Art Museum.
N6639.R67A4 2014
709.2--dc23
2014008712

source

CB: Atypical bodily attributes—highly developed musculature, unusually long fingers, great height, elastic skin, to name a few—whether natural or cultivated, fascinate you. Can you explain why?

MR: I am fascinated by extremes in general. I love the *Guinness Book of World Records*. I like to think about the body as architecture, as something you inhabit. So I look at people who challenge a body's borders and limitations. Also, it's interesting to me to see how some people use their body as a way to generate income in an unexpected way, like the clothespin guy in *Bowls Balls Souls Holes*. He makes a living from a medical condition that allows him to stretch his skin in extreme ways, which got him the world record for putting the most clothespins on his face. That's a great day job! I also think about the psychological dimension of the body as architecture, particularly how you can feel trapped in the body. The skin as a membrane differentiates the self from the world and defines an internal-external divide. The body raises the question of what you can control and what is beyond you. I find that people who use their bodies unexpectedly really embody these questions.

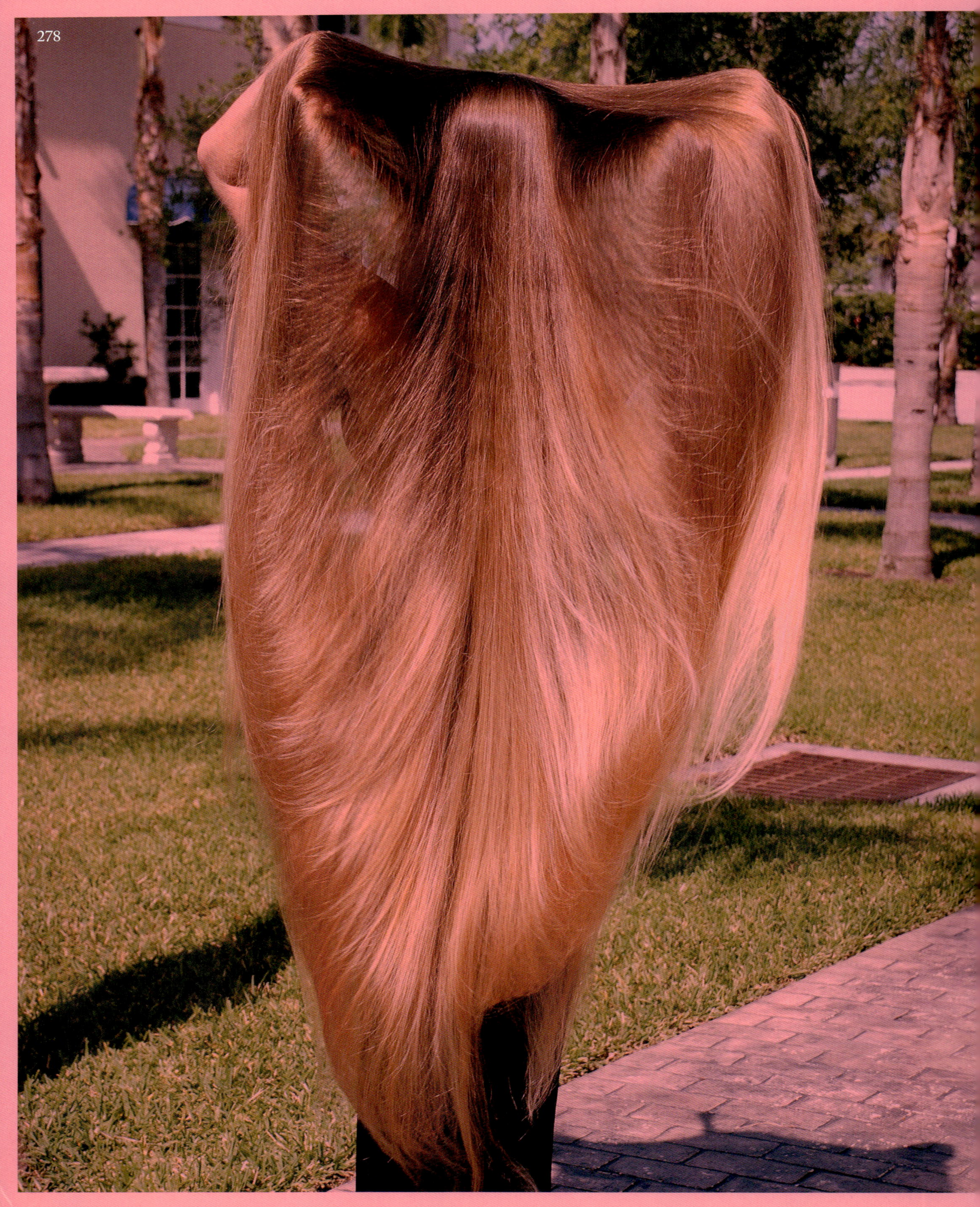

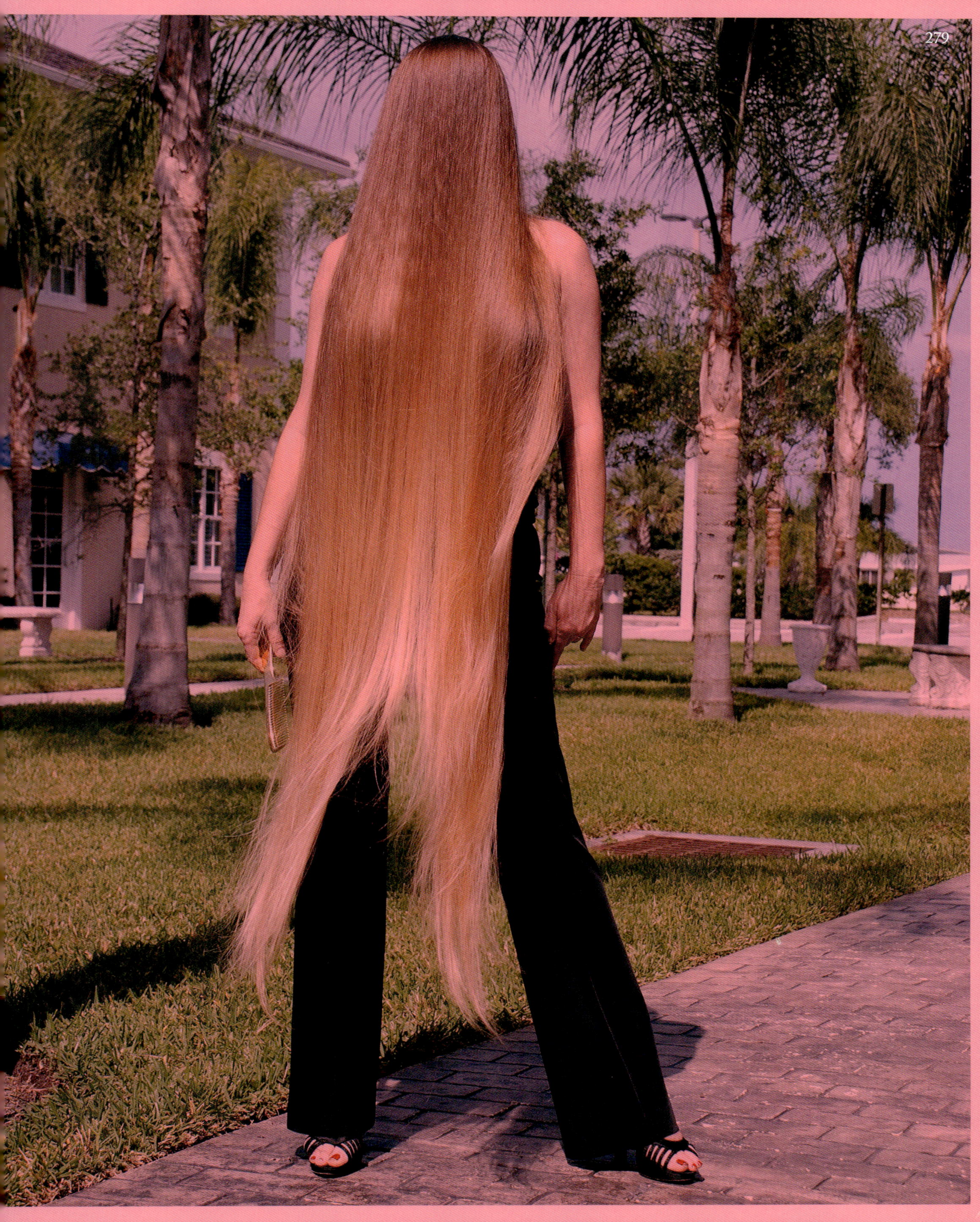

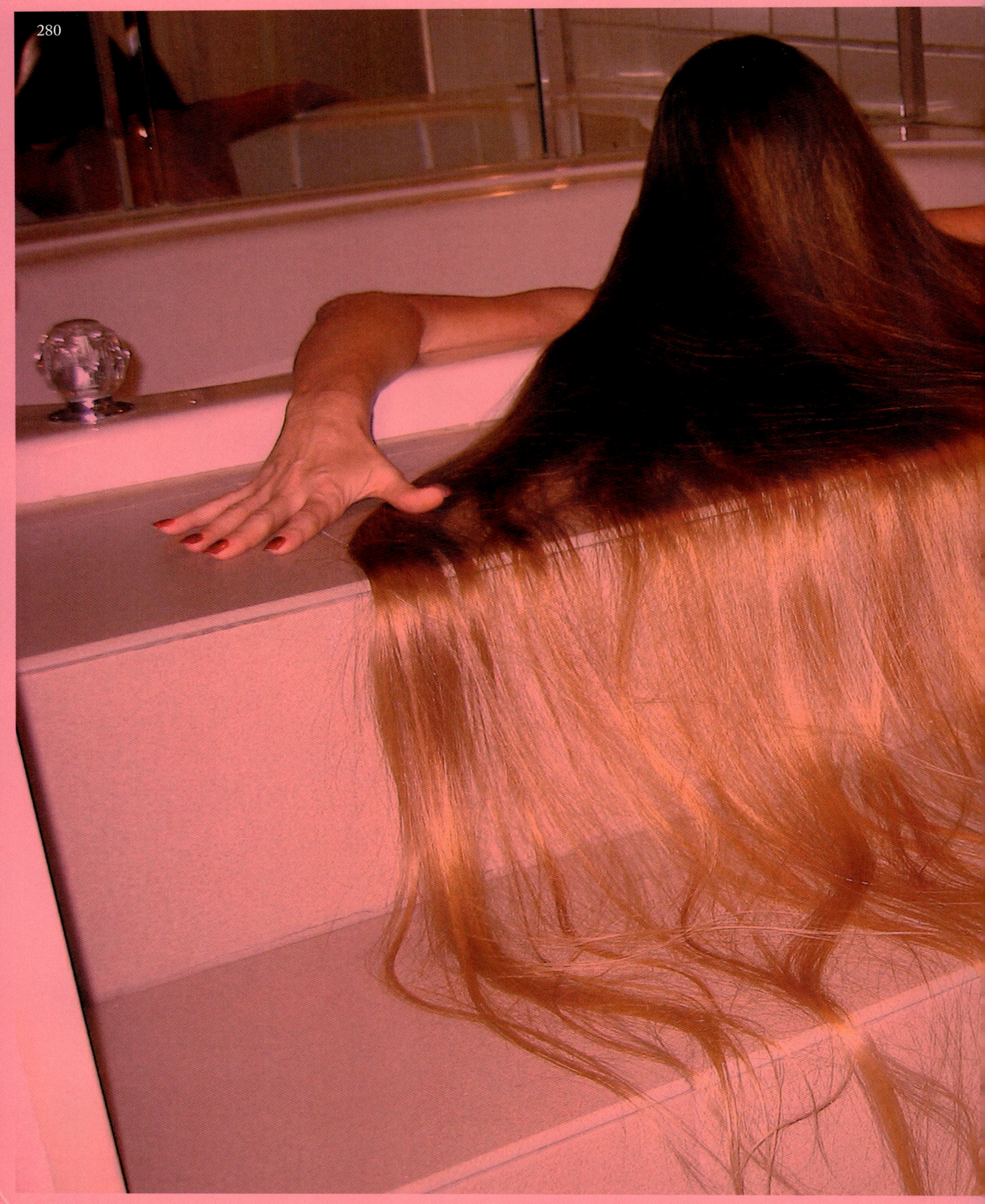

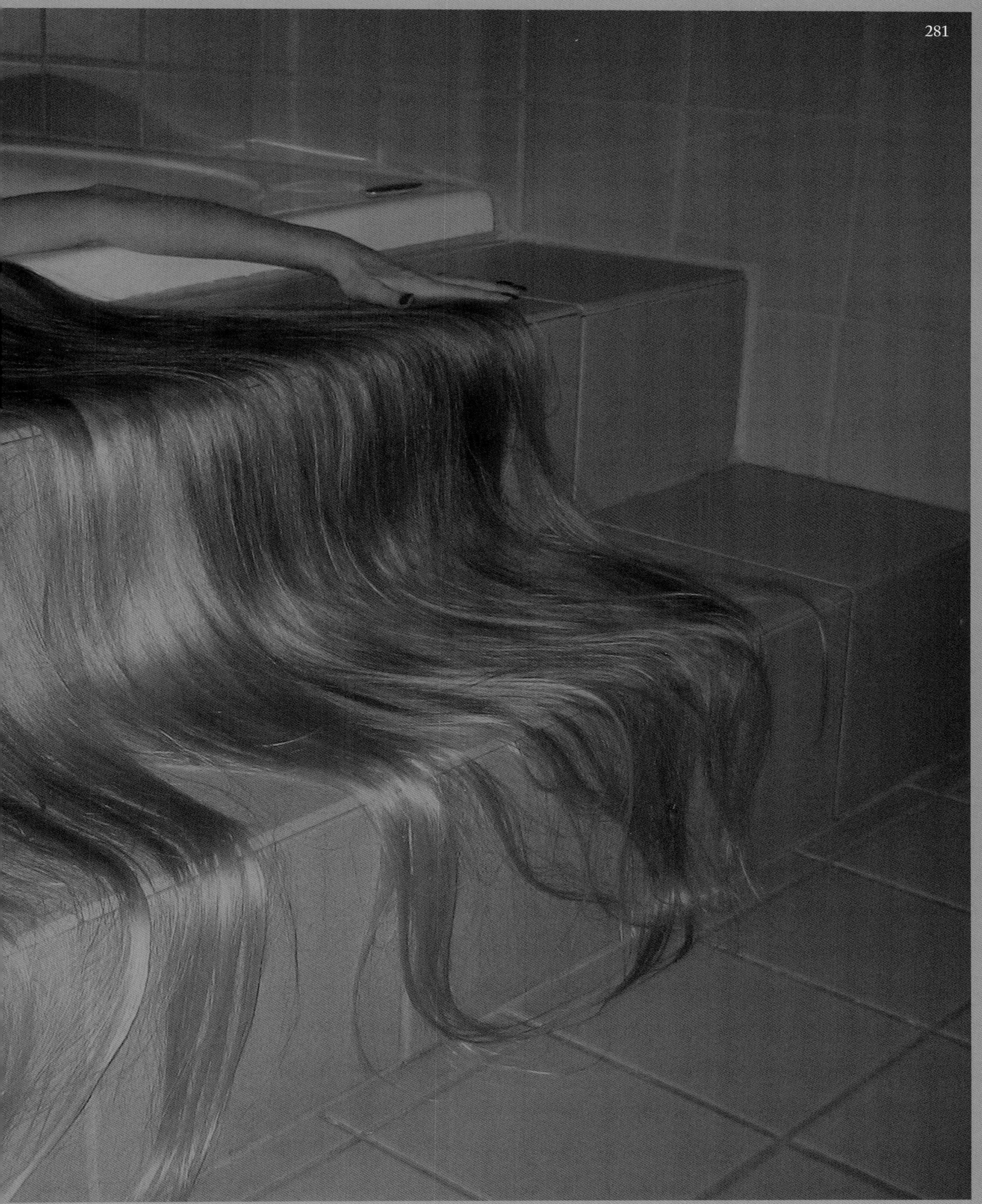

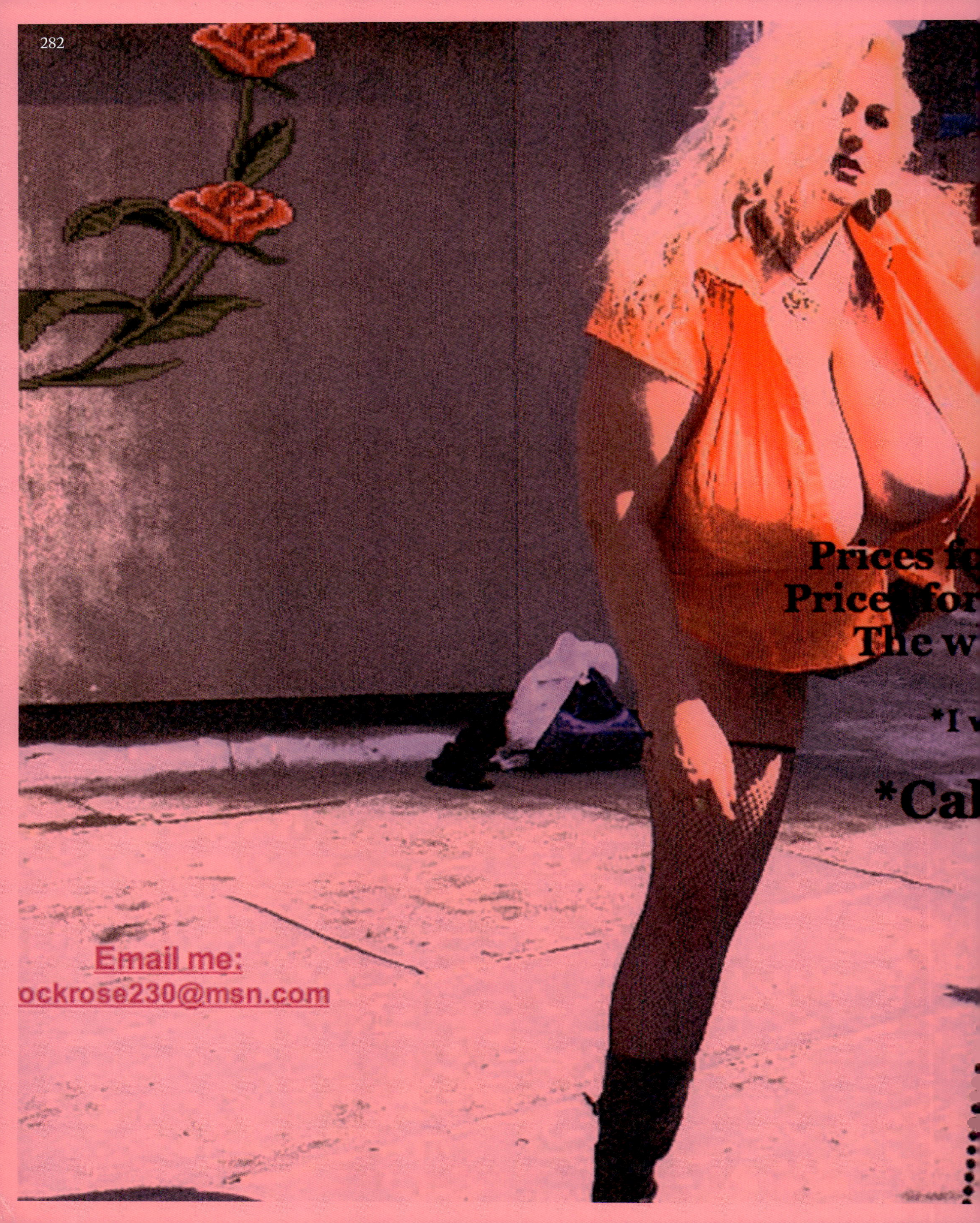
Email me:
ockrose230@msn.com

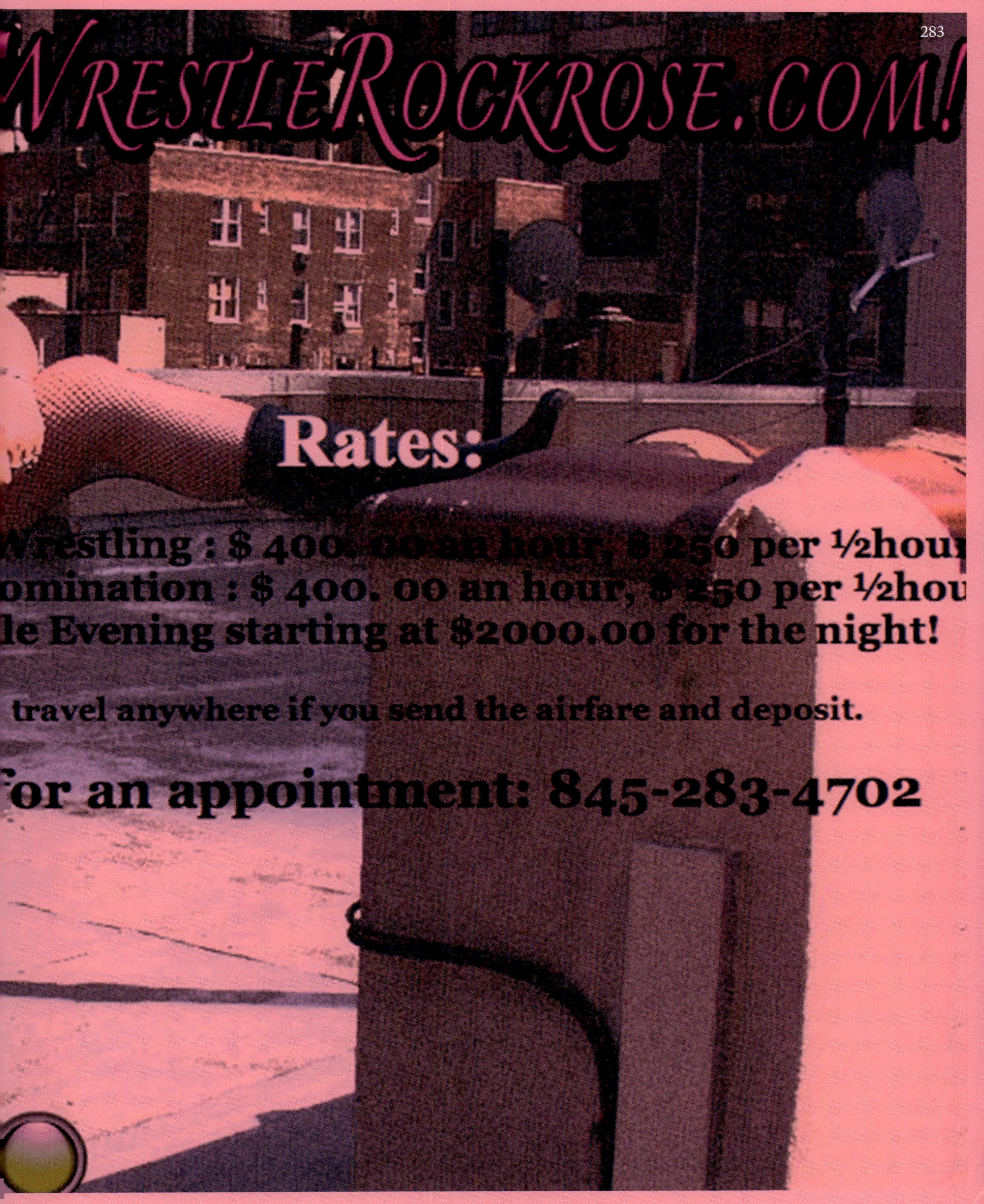

WrestleRockrose.com!
Rates:
Wrestling : $ 400. 00 an hour, $ 250 per ½hou
omination : $ 400. 00 an hour, $ 250 per ½hou
le Evening starting at $2000.00 for the night!
travel anywhere if you send the airfare and deposit.
for an appointment: 845-283-4702

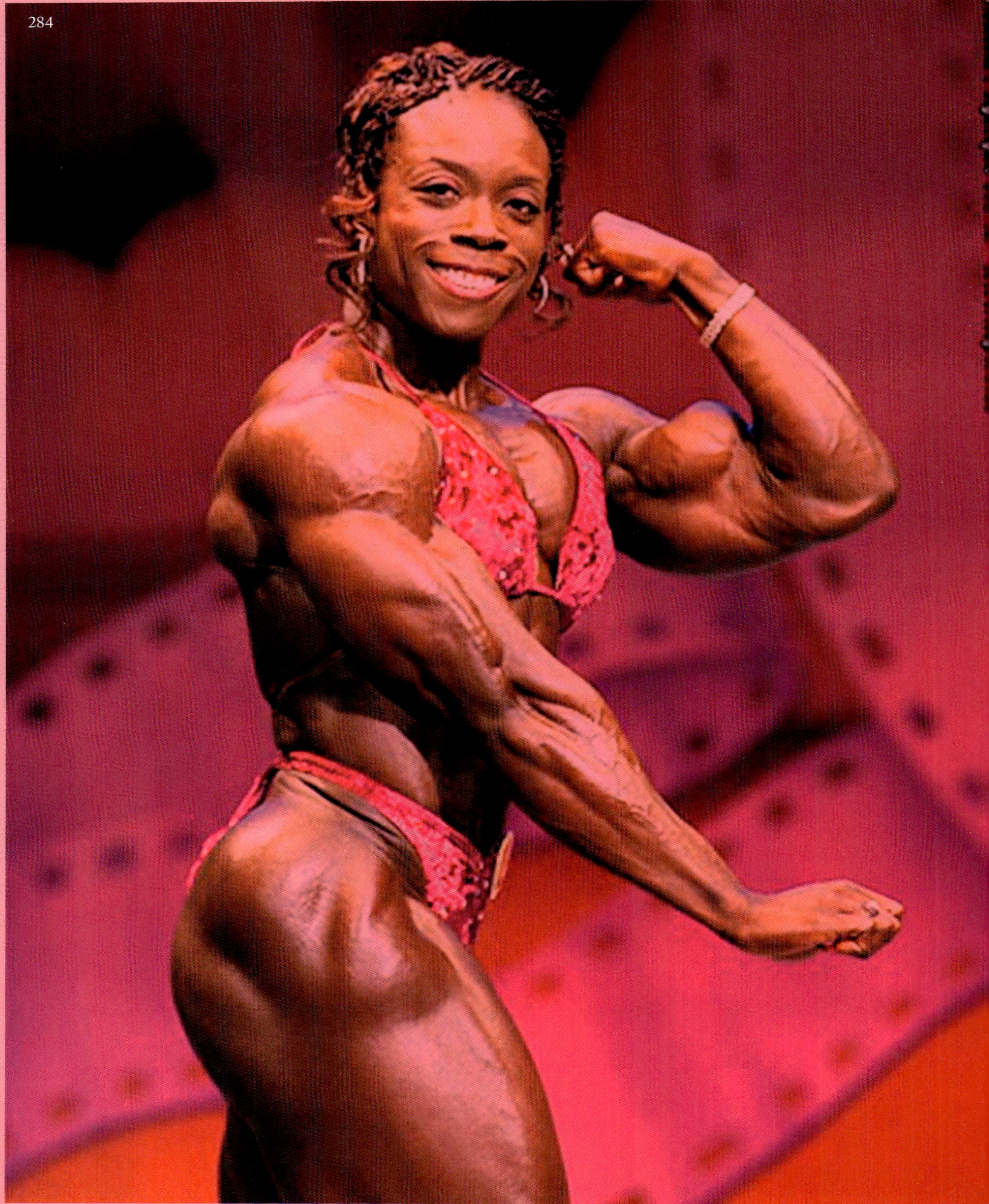

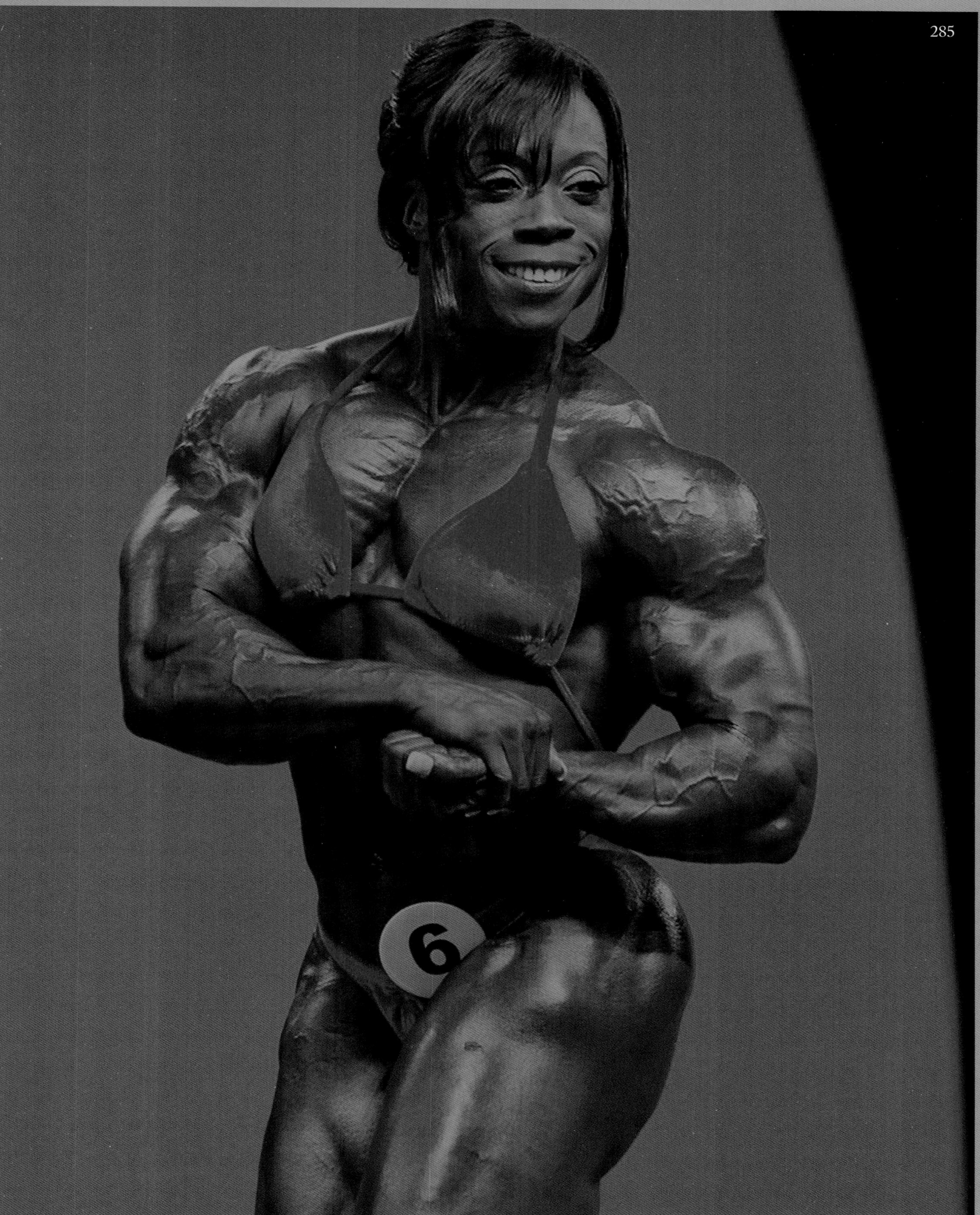
6

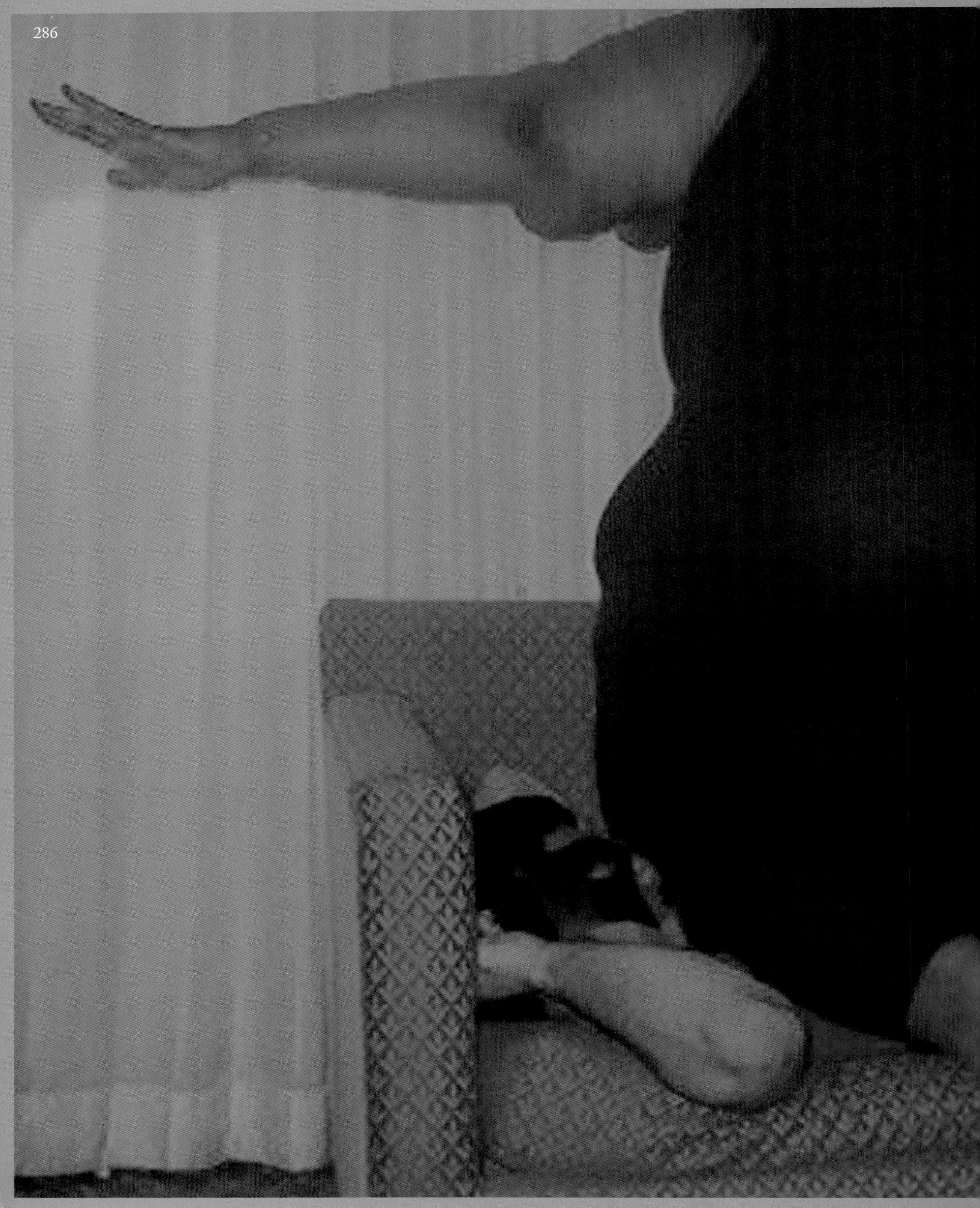

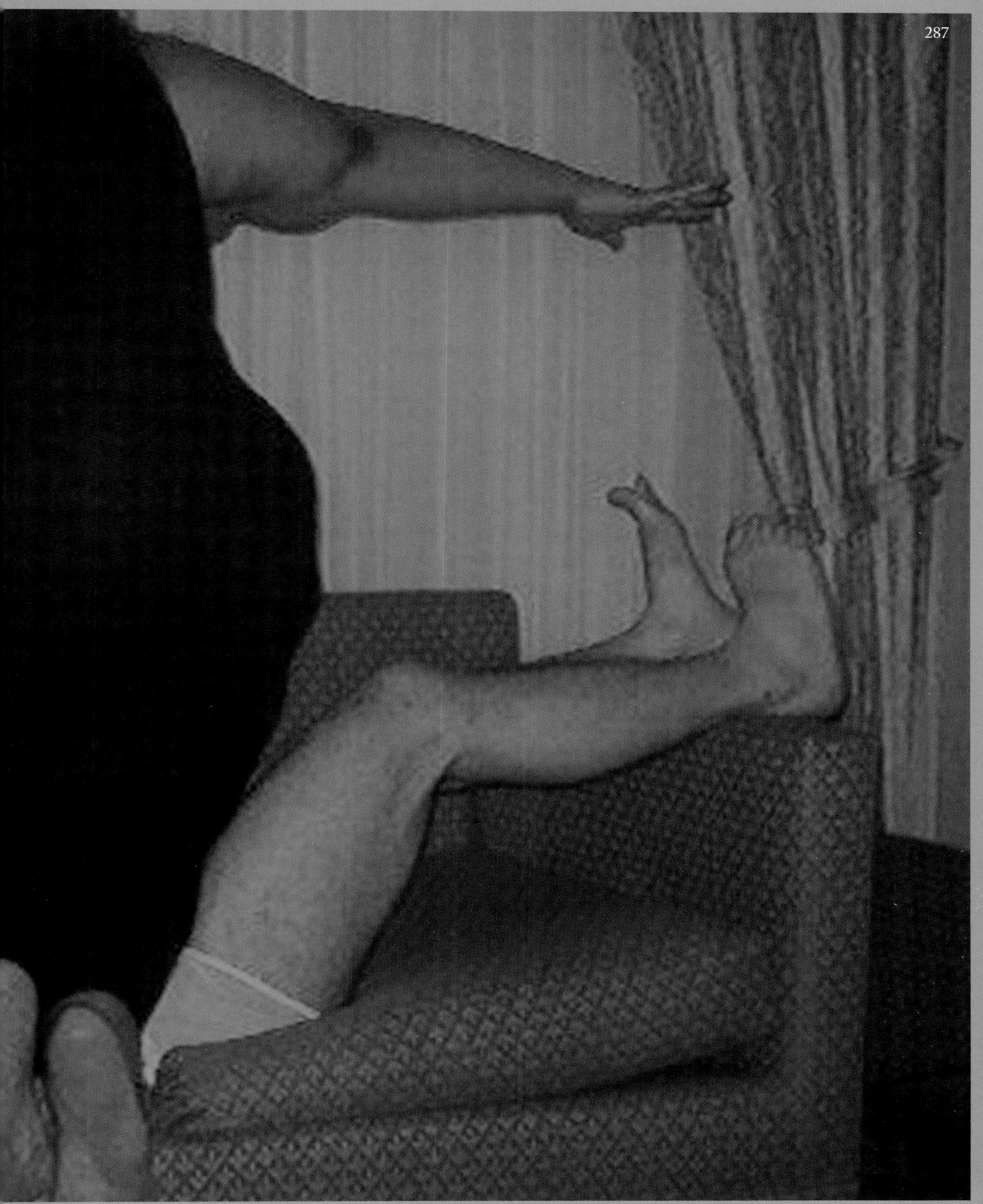

QueenRaqui.com is an Adult site, if you Love Amazon Women, Heavy weight squashers, Trampling extreme, Size comparisons, lifting stretching and carrying, beautiful Super Sized Models, YOU HAVE ARRIVED at the right site!

If you are under 18 leave immediately
To Enter QueenRaqui.com you MUST READ and AGREE to the Terms Below

QueenRaqui.com - Entrance Agreement

This is a site designed and intended SOLELY for ADULTS -- people who are at least 18 years old -- who are interested in and

You have READ and AGREED to the Terms Above.
You will be BOUND to the Terms and by Entering QueenRaqui.com,
You are showing your AGREEMENT and VERIFICATION of age.

Knowing this you to Choose to

ENTER QUEENRAQUI.COM

QueenRaqui.com believes in the rights of each Adult to view sites of his/her interest. We also strongly support parental controls on the Internet. The prevention of minors from viewing Adult sites, is the responsibility of the Adults in each environment. These web pages are not intended to be viewed by minors. If you are an Adult who wants to block sites of a Adult nature, please contact one of the following:
Cyber Sitter Cyber Patrol Net Nanny Surfwatch

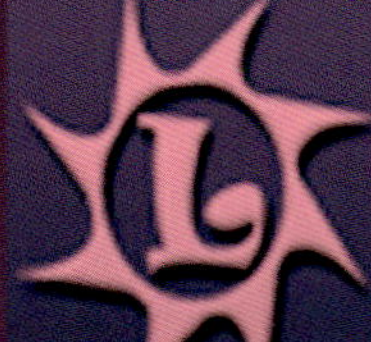

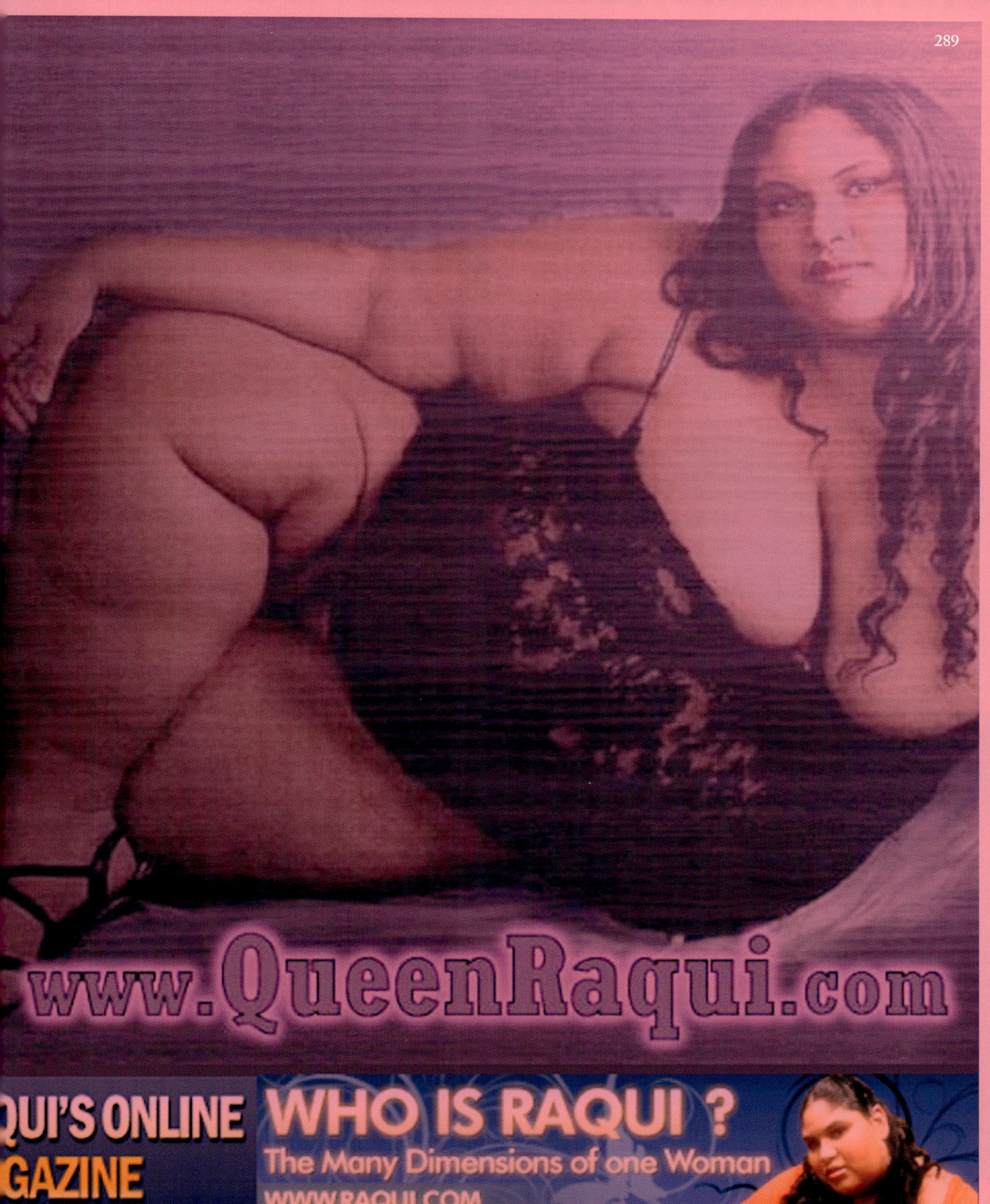
www.QueenRaqui.com
QUI'S ONLINE
GAZINE
WHO IS RAQUI ?
The Many Dimensions of one Woman
WWW.RAQUI.COM

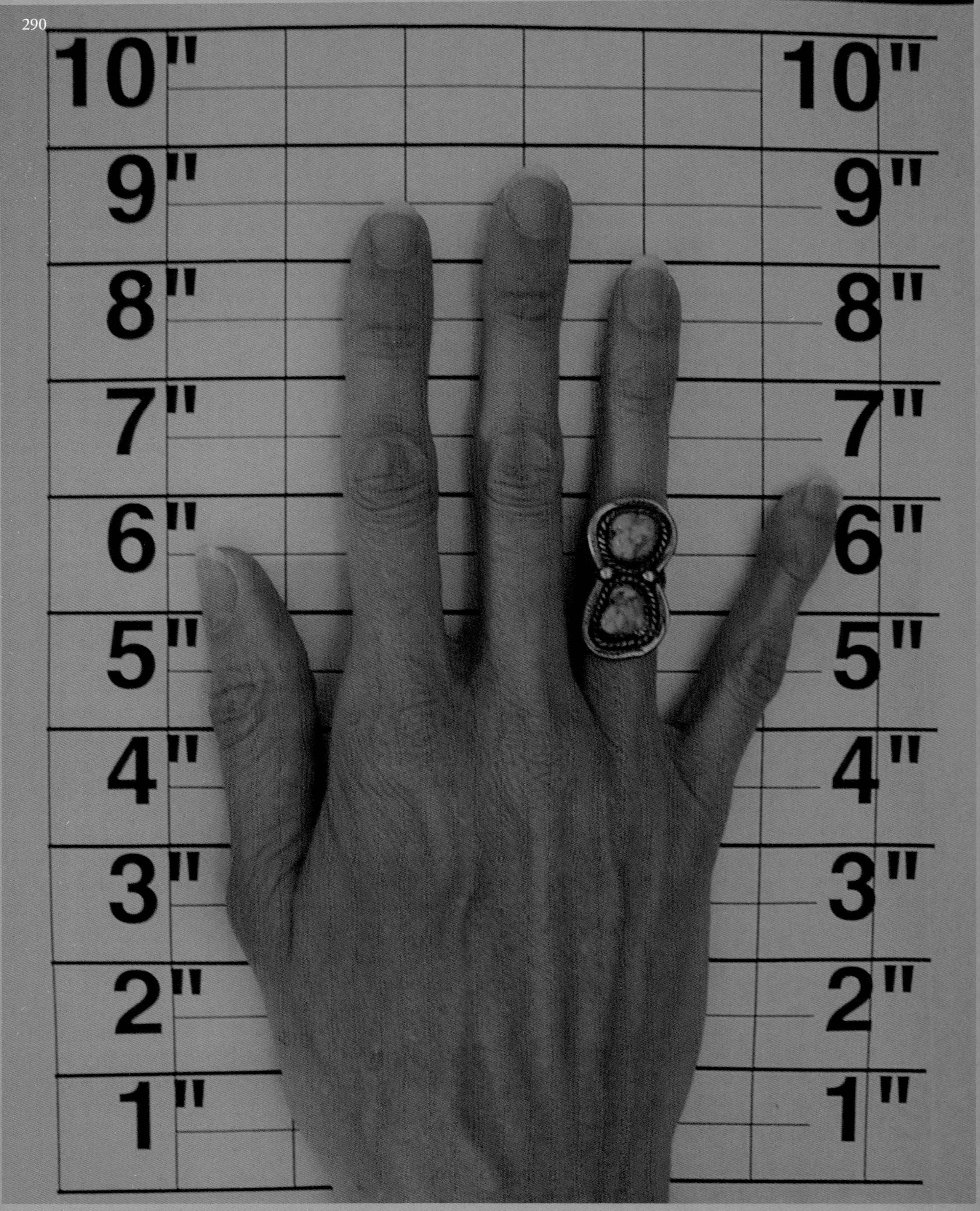

10" 10"
9" 9"
8" 8"
7" 7"
6" 6"
5" 5"
4" 4"
3" 3"
2" 2"
1" 1"

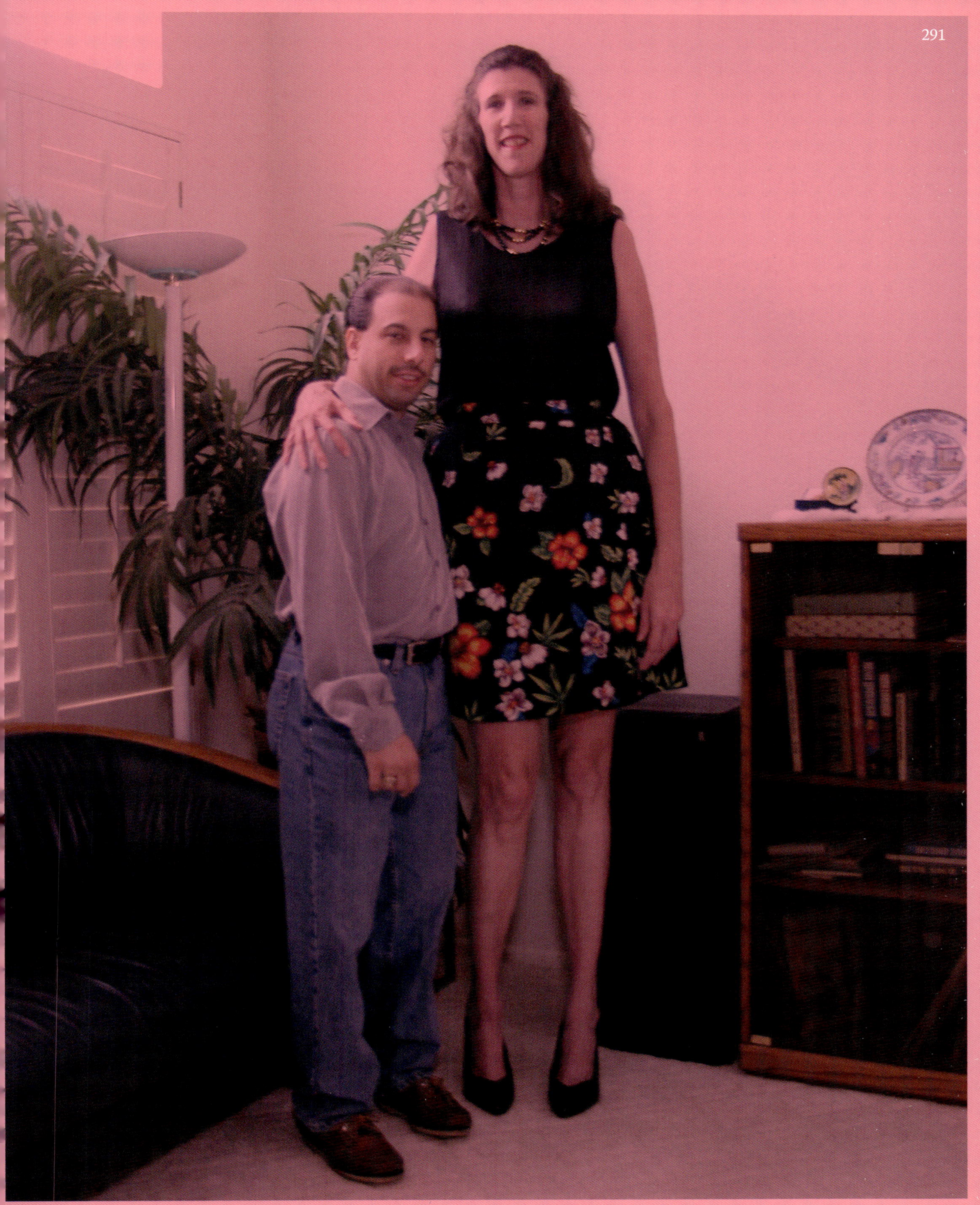

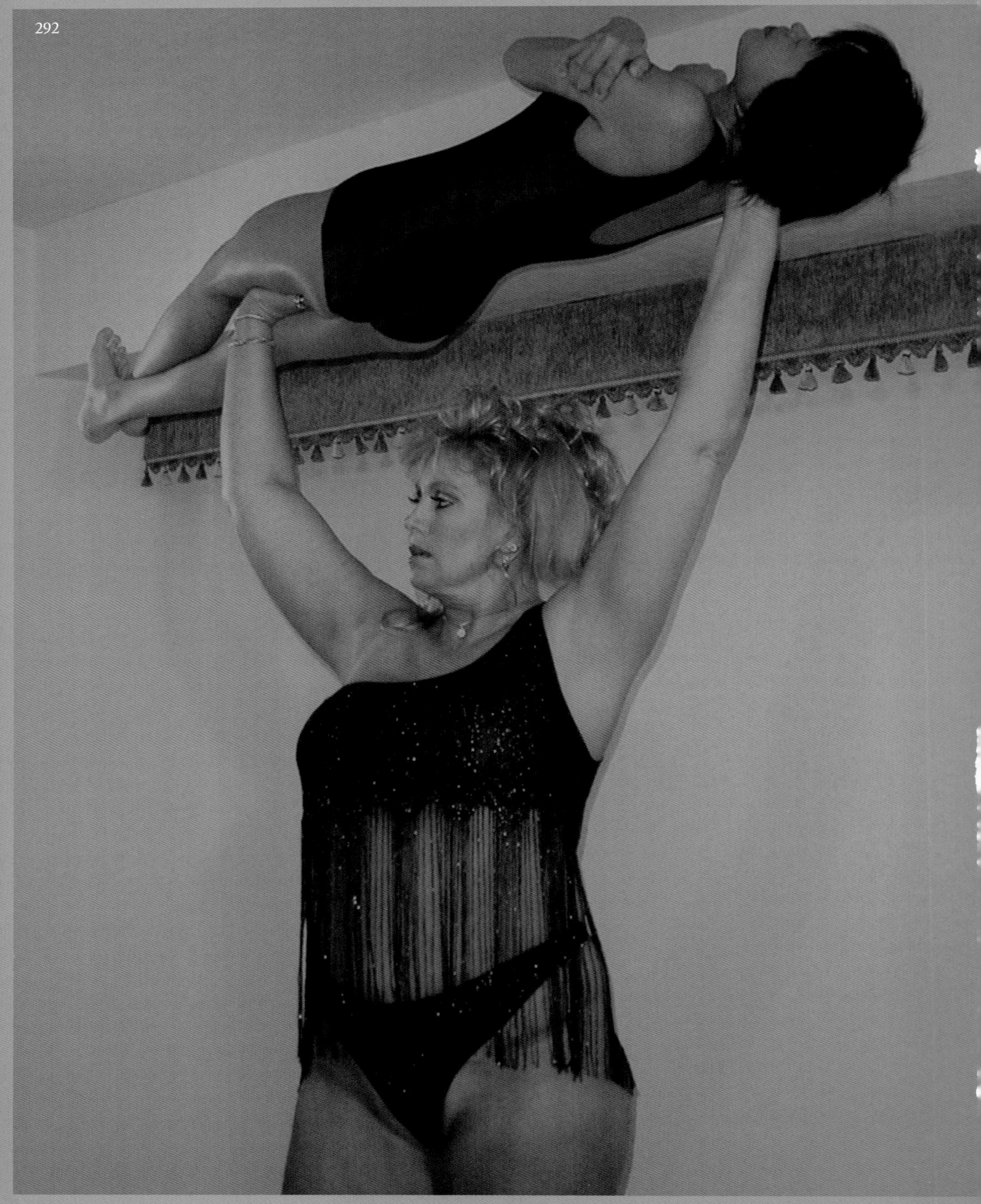